What readers

"I've depended on Damron [...] four years. Thank you [...]

"You guys really helped us enjoy our trip.... The Road Atlas we sometimes found better for navigation than AAA." —Gil D.

"It's a "must" on the budget every year." —David Mindrup, Pittsburgh, PA

"Excellent! I recommend it to anyone that wants to make the most out of any trip." — S. H., Hunstville, AL

*all quotes taken from readers' letters and survey responses received in 2000-2001

A note from the Editor

Why do you need *this* atlas? Do you really need a *lesbian & gay* map guide? Do you really need a *map guide* to the most popular cities and gay resorts in North America and Europe?

The honest truth—you don't. This book of maps is a travel accessory. Yes, you can travel without it. You can also travel without luggage. But why would you?

Why, then, *this* Damron travel guide instead of another guidebook? The reason to get this **Atlas** is on almost every page, in full color—*the maps*. Yes, you could easily find more detailed maps. But you'd have to wade through acres of crumpled fold-out maps, just to find the heart of a city's gay culture. Example: the *Thomas Brothers Guide* is a lifesaver for finding every hidden cul-de-sac in California. But their attention to detail is eye-blurring, mind-numbing. Using such an exhaustive map would take you hours upon hours, just to isolate the locations of the gay bars, accommodations, and stores we've mapped for you in this book, using easily spotted, brightly colored shapes (see the **Legend To Maps**, right there -->).

In a glance, you can see where most of the LGBT businesses are clustered. Usually, the majority of numbered dots will be shown on the **Detail Map**—your key to each city's gay heart. Nearby you'll find an **Overview Map** that allows you to see where all these hot spots are in relation to the rest of the city. Now, if you want to, you're ready to go back and pore over that Rand McNally map.

But don't take my word. Go ahead. Thumb through the pages. The maps speak for themselves. Plus they're light, easy-to-pack, and don't take up nearly the room that several continents' worth of maps might. Now that's the perfect travel accessory!

The Damron Company

Who We Are

In 1964, a businessman published a book of all the gay bars he knew from his constant travels across the United States. This book could fit comfortably in the palm of your hand. Despite its small size, it was an impressive accomplishment. Each one of the listings he had visited himself. Every last copy of that book he sold himself. The name of this pioneering businessman—**Bob Damron**.

Thirty-five years later, his little book, the **Damron Address Book**, is still a bestseller. And it has remained the model for the countless gay travel guides that have followed in its wake. Including our own ever-expanding fleet: The **Damron Women's Traveller** for lesbians, this **Damron Road Atlas**, **Damron Accommodations** B&B listings and photos, and the recently debuted **Damron City Series**—pocket-sized all-inclusive gay tourist guides.

How We Maintain the Accuracy of Our Listings

Our editors contact every single listing in our database annually, usually by phone, fax, or email. They also receive updated information directly from business owners and you, our readers. If you send in new, verifiably correct information, Damron will send you a **free copy** of the next edition as our way of saying a very sincere "thank you" for your help.

The Damron Road Atlas

produced by

Publisher	Damron Company
President & Editor-in-Chief	Gina M. Gatta
Managing Editor	Ian Philips
Design & Layout	Rebecca Davenport
Art Director	Kathleen Pratt
Editors	Erika O'Connor
	Chane Binderup
Cover Design	Rick Avila

Board of Directors

Edward Gatta, Jr., Mikal Shively
Louise Mock, Gina M. Gatta

How to Contact Us

phone	(415) 255-0404
mail	PO Box 422458, San Francisco, CA 94142-2458
email	info@damron.com
web	http://www.damron.com

Copyright © 2001 Damron Co. Inc. Printed in Hong Kong. All rights reserved. Reproduction of the **Damron Road Atlas** in whole or in part without written permission from the Damron Company is prohibited.

Damron Guides

The Damron Men's Travel Guide

Formerly the *Damron Address Book*. This is THE classic gay men's travel guide, published since 1964. Over 750 pages and over 10,000 listings cover North America, the Caribbean, and many major European cities like London, Paris, Berlin, Amsterdam, Rome, Barcelona, Madrid, and Vienna. Features an annual calendar of pride events, film fests, circuit parties, conferences, and more! **$18.95**

Damron Accommodations

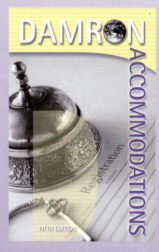

Hundreds of full-color photographs and meticulously detailed listings for over 1,800 gay-friendly accommodations worldwide make finding that "home away from home" easy. Whether you're looking for a quiet B&B, a mountain retreat, a luxurious hotel with all the amenities, or a resort getaway for you and your sweetheart, you'll find it in *Damron Accommodations*. **$22.95**

The Damron Women's Traveller

The most up-to-date and comprehensive travel guide by-and-for lesbians! Nearly 9,000 listings pinpoint where the girls are — throughout North America & major European cities. Special sections cover lesbian tours, women's festivals, events, and camping/RV spots. City overviews dish out the details on local lesbian spots, as well as basic tourist info, like how to get around town and what weather to expect. **$15.95**

To order, call **(800) 462-6654**
or write to **Damron Mail Order,
PO Box 422458
San Francisco, CA 94142-2458**

Cities Covered in the Damron

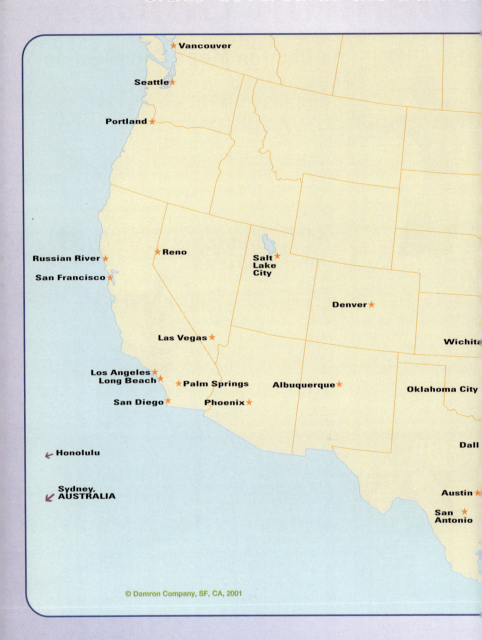

Road Atlas 9th Edition

Please note: If you don't see a city you're looking for, try another Damron guide. The Damron Men's Travel Guide and Damron Women's Traveller cover the entire US, Canada, Mexico, the Caribbean, Costa Rica, and the following cities: Vienna, London, Paris, Berlin, Rome, Amsterdam, Barcelona, Madrid, and Sitges. Damron Accommodations has more international listings than any other Damron guide, including South Africa and Australia. If you still can't find your destination, check out Damron Online (http://www.damron.com) to peruse our entire whopping database of over 20,000 listings.

Table of Contents

United States

Alabama
- Birmingham 8

Arizona
- Phoenix 10

Arkansas
- Little Rock 13

California
- Long Beach 15
- Los Angeles 17
- Palm Springs 31
- Russian River 38
- San Diego 42
- San Francisco 48

Colorado
- Denver 72

Connecticut
- Hartford 76

Delaware
- Rehoboth Beach 78

District of Columbia
- Washington 80

Florida
- Fort Lauderdale 86
- Key West 95
- Miami/South Beach 99
- Orlando 104
- St Petersburg 108
- Tampa 110

Georgia
- Atlanta 113

Hawaii
- Honolulu 119

Illinois
- Chicago 124

Indiana
- Indianapolis 134

Kansas
- Wichita 138

Kentucky
- Louisville 140

Louisiana
- New Orleans 142

Maryland
- Baltimore 148

Massachusetts
- Boston 152
- Provincetown 157

Michigan
- Detroit 162
- Saugatuck 164

Minnesota
- Minneapolis/St Paul 166

Missouri
- Kansas City 172
- St Louis 174

Nevada
- Las Vegas 179
- Reno 182

New Jersey
- Atlantic City 184

New Mexico
- Albuquerque 186

New York
- Fire Island 188
- Long Island 189
- New York City 190

North Carolina
- Charlotte 202
- Raleigh/Durham/Chapel Hill .. 204

Ohio
- Cincinnati 208
- Cleveland 210
- Columbus 213

Oklahoma
- Oklahoma City 217

Oregon
- Portland 220

Table of Contents

Pennsylvania
- Philadelphia 225
- Pittsburgh 228

Rhode Island
- Providence 230

Tennessee
- Memphis 232
- Nashville 234

Texas
- Austin 236
- Dallas 240
- Houston 244
- San Antonio 248

Utah
- Salt Lake City 251

Virginia
- Norfolk 254

Washington
- Seattle 256

Wisconsin
- Milwaukee 261

Canada

British Columbia
- Vancouver 265

Ontario
- Toronto 269

Province of Québec
- Montréal 274
- Québec 280

Caribbean

Puerto Rico
- San Juan 282

Europe

England
- London 285

France
- Paris 294

Germany
- Berlin 304

The Netherlands
- Amsterdam 312

Spain
- Madrid 320

Australia
- Sydney 325

ALABAMA • USA

Damron Road Atlas

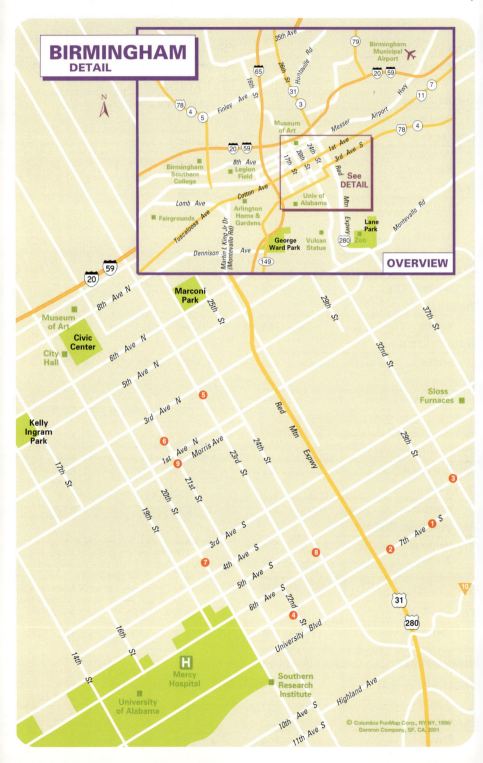

BIRMINGHAM

Between the Sloss Furnaces (205/324-1911) and the 55-ft.-tall iron statue of Vulcan atop Red Mountain (205/328-6198), there's no doubt about Birmingham's historical link to the steel industry. Visitors will also want to explore the Birmingham Civil Rights Institute (205/328-9696) and the surrounding historic district. Music fans will enjoy a trip to the Alabama Jazz Hall of Fame (205/254-2731).

Queer Resources

COMMUNITY INFO
Gay Info Line 205/326-8600. 7pm-10pm Mon-Fri. web: www.gaybham.com.

AIDS RESOURCES
AIDS Outreach 205/322-4197.

RECOVERY
AA 205/326-8600.

City Calendar

LGBT PRIDE
June.

ANNUAL EVENTS
April/May - Festival of the Arts.
June - City Stages.
Shakespeare Renaissance Fair 334/271-5353 or 800/841-2173.

Tourist Info

AIRPORT DIRECTIONS
Birmingham Int'l. From Airport Blvd take I-20 West to the 22nd St exit. 22nd runs one way south.

PUBLIC TRANSIT & TAXIS
ABC Taxi 205/833-6974.
Birmingham Transit Authority 205/521-0101.

TOURIST SPOTS & INFO
Alabama Jazz Hall of Fame 205/254-2731.
Birmingham Zoo & Botanical Gardens 205/879-0408.
Civil Rights Museum 205/328-9696.
Vulcan Statue at 20th St S & Valley Ave atop Red Mountain.
Visitor's Center: 205/458-8000, web: www.birminghamal.org.

WEATHER
Hot and humid in the 80°s and 90°s during the summer, mild in the 50°s to low 40°s during the winter.

BEST VIEWS
Overlook Park.

ALABAMA

Birmingham

ACCOMMODATIONS
The Tutwiler [GF,WC] 205/322-2100 ■ 2021 Park Pl N (at 21st St N) ■ upscale, also restaurant & lounge ■ www.wyndham.com

BARS
1 Club 729 [W,D,S,K,WC] 205/324-0997 ■ 2830 7th Ave S (at 29th St) ■ 3pm-close, patio
2 Kings Knight [M,D,CW,S] 205/326-3637 ■ 2627 7th Ave S (btwn 26th & 27th) ■ 24 hrs, drag shows, 2 outdoor patios ■ www.kings-knight.com
3 Misconceptions Tavern [MW,V,WC] 205/322-1210 ■ 600 32nd St S (at 6th Ave S) ■ noon-3am, patio
   Tool Box [M,NH,D,CW,WC] 205/595-5120 ■ 5120 5th Ave S (at 51st) ■ 2pm-close, till 2am Sat, more women Wed-Th for CW, home bar of 'Steel City Centurions' (L), patio

NIGHTCLUBS
4 22nd Street Jazz Cafe [GF,WC,MR,F,E] 205/252-0407 ■ 710 22nd St S (at 7th Ave S) ■ 5pm-close, clsd Sun-Tue, live music
5 Bill's Club [M,S,$,WC] 205/254-8634 ■ 208 N 23rd St (btwn 2nd & 3rd) ■ 6pm-close, clsd Mon-Wed, strippers ■ www.thenewbillsclub.com
6 Club 21 [★GF,D,MR-AF,S] 205/322-0469 ■ 117-1/2 21st St N (btwn 1st & 2nd Ave N) ■ 10pm-close Th-Sat
7 The Club Latroy [MW,D,MR,S,19+,WC,$] 205/322-8338 ■ 316 20th St S (btwn 3rd & 4th Ave S) ■ 11pm-close Fri-Sat, noon-9pm Sun, no cover Sun, also restaurant
8 The Quest Club [M,D,S,PC,WC] 205/251-4313 ■ 416 24th St S (at 5th Ave S) ■ 24hrs, 19+ Wed-Sun (nights only), patio ■ www.quest-club.com
9 The Station [★GF,D,WC,$] 205/254-3750, 888/453-3299 ■ 2025 Morris Ave (at 21st) ■ 10pm-6am Fri-Sat, patio

RESTAURANTS
Anthony's [WC] 205/324-1215 ■ 2131 7th Ave S (at 20th) ■ dinner, Sun brunch, clsd Mon, cont'l/ Italian, full bar
Bottega Cafe & Restaurant [WC] 205/939-1000 ■ 2240 Highland Ave (btwn 22nd & 23rd) ■ lunch & dinner, clsd Sun, full bar
Crestwood Grill [WC] 205/595-1995 ■ 5500 Crestwood Blvd ■ lunch & dinner, full bar
Highlands Bar & Grill [WC] 205/939-1400 ■ 2011 11th Ave S (at 20th) ■ 6pm-10pm, bar from 4pm, clsd Sun-Mon
John's [WC] 205/322-6014 ■ 112 21st St N (btwn 1st & 2nd Ave N) ■ 11am-10pm, clsd Sun, seafood & steak, full bar
PT's Sports Grill [WC] 205/879-8519 ■ 350 Hollywood Blvd (at Hwy 280 S) ■ 11am-close

ALABAMA/ ARIZONA • USA

Silvertron Cafe 205/591-3707 ■ 3813 Clairmont Ave S (at 39th St S) ■ 11am-10pm, till 9pm Sun, also full bar, more gay Mon

Entertainment & Recreation
Terrific New Theater 205/328-0868 ■ 2821 2nd Ave S (in Dr Pepper Design Complex)

Bookstores
10 Lodestar Books [F,WC] 205/328-0144 ■ 2827 Highland Ave (at 29th St S) ■ 10am-8pm, till 5pm Sun, feminist bookstore w/ lgbt section, also vegetarian cafe ■ www.lodestarbooks.com

Retail Shops
The Bad Seed [GO] 205/933-7333 ■ 2030 11th Ave S (btwn 20th & 21st) ■ noon-8pm, clsd Sun, music, videos & gifts

Erotica
Alabama Adult Books 205/322-7323 ■ 801 3rd Ave N (at 8th) ■ 24hrs
Birmingham Adult Books [★] 205/836-1580 ■ 7610 1st Ave N (at Oporto-Madrid Blvd) ■ 24hrs, booths
The Downtown Bookstore 205/328-5525 ■ 2731 8th Ave N (at 28th St) ■ video arcade, booths
Pleasure Books 205/836-7379 ■ 7606 1st Ave N (at 77th St) ■ video arcade, booths
Top Hat Cinema 205/833-8221 ■ 9221 Todd Dr ■ theater, booths

ARIZONA

Phoenix

Accommodations
1 ▶ Arizona Royal Villa Resort [MO,SW,N,NS] 602/266-6883, 888/266-6884 ■ 1110 E Turney Ave #8 ■ hot tub ■ www.RoyalVilla.com
2 Arizona Sunburst Inn [MO,SW,N,GO] 602/274-1474, 800/974-1474 ■ 6245 N 12th Pl (at Rose Ln) ■ hot tub ■ www.azsunburst.com
Arrowzona 'Private' Casitas [MW,SW] 623/561-1200 ■ condos, hot tub

Arizona Royal Villa Resort
Largest and most popular property in town. Walking distance to bars, bath, and restaurants. 19 units with private bath, TV, phone, fridge, AC.
Rooms from $65 single/ $75 double. Heated pool and jacuzzi. Day passes $10. Laundry on premises. Visa/MC/AMEX/DISC/Diners.
www.royalvilla.com, e-mail: AzRoyalVil@aol.com
Phone **(888) 266-6884**

3 Casa de mis Padres [MO,SW] 480/675-0247, 800/996-4108 ■ 5965 E Orange Blossom Ln ■ luxury multi-room suites, 5 minutes to Old Town Scottsdale ■ www.casadmp.com
4 Larry's B&B [MW,SW,N,NS,WC] 602/249-2974 ■ 502 W Claremont Ave (btwn Maryland & Bethany Home) ■ full brkfst, hot tub
6 Yum Yum Tree Guest House [GS,SW,GO] 602/265-2590 ■ 90 W Virginia Ave #1 (at 3rd Ave) ■ suites in historic neighborhood, courtyard ■ www.yytguesthouse.com

Bars
7 307 on Central [MW,NH,D,TG,F,S,WC] 602/252-0001 ■ 10am-4am
8 Ain't Nobody's Bizness [W,D,MR,E,K,WC] 602/224-9977 ■ 3031 E Indian School #7 (at 32nd St) ■ 4pm-1am, opens 2pm wknds, live music, karaoke Mon
9 Amsterdam [MW,E] 602/258-6122 ■ 718 N Central Ave (btwn Roosevelt & Fillmore) ■ 4pm-1am, upscale bar, live music Sun-Mon ■ www.amsterdambar.com
10 Apollo's [M,NH,K] 602/277-9373 ■ 5749 N 7th St (S of Bethany Home) ■ 10am-1am, diverse crowd ■ www.apollos.com
11 Boot Camp [M] 602/212-9888 ■ 3702 N 7th St (at Weldon) ■ 3pm-1am, from noon Sun, men's cruise bar, underwear night Fri ■ www.cruisemen.com
12 The Bunkhouse [M] 602/200-9154 ■ 4428 N 7th Ave (at Indian School) ■ noon-1am, patio
13 Cash Inn Country [W,D,CW,WC] 602/244-9943 ■ 2140 E McDowell Rd (at 22nd St) ■ 4pm-1am, clsd Mon
14 Charlie's [M,D,CW,WC] 602/265-0224 ■ 727 W Camelback Rd (at 7th Ave) ■ 2pm-1am, till 3am Fri-Sat, Sun bbq ■ www.charliesonline.com
15 The Crowbar [MW,D,S] 602/258-8343 ■ 702 N Central (N of Van Buren) ■ 9pm-3am Fri-Sun, women's night Tue ■ www.clubsoncentral.com/crowbar/
16 Cruisin' Central [M,OC,WC] 602/253-3776 ■ 1011 N Central Ave (at Roosevelt) ■ 6am-1am, from 10am Sun
17 Harley's 155 [M,D] 602/274-8505 ■ 155 W Camelback Rd (btwn 3rd & Central Aves) ■ noon-1am ■ www.harleysclub155.com
18 Incognito Lounge [MW,D,S,WC] 602/955-9805 ■ 2424 E Thomas Rd (at 24th St) ■ 3pm-1am, till 3am wknds, clsd Mon
19 JC's Fun One [M,D,S,WC] 623/939-0528 ■ 5542 N 43rd Ave (at Missouri), Glendale ■ noon-1am, from 11am wknds
20 Johnny Mc's [M,NH] 602/266-0875 ■ 138 W Camelback Rd (btwn 3rd & Central Aves) ■ 10am-1am
21 Marlys' [MW,NH] 602/867-2463 ■ 15615 N Cave Creek Rd (btwn Greenway Pkwy & Greenway Rd) ■ 3pm-1am
22 Misty's [W,D,MR,K,S,WC] 602/265-3233 ■ 4301 N 7th Ave (at Indian School Rd) ■ 4pm-close, 11am-1am wknds ■ droseclub2@webtv.net
23 Nasty's Sports Bar [W,NH,K] 602/231-9427 ■ 3108 E McDowell Rd (at 32nd St) ■ noon-1am
24 Nu Towne Saloon [M,NH,WC] 602/267-9959 ■ 5002 E Van Buren (at 48th St) ■ 10am-1am, popular Sun & Tue
25 Paco Paco's [M,D,MR-L,TG,S] 602/263-8424 ■ 3045 N 16th St (at Thomas) ■ 7pm-1am, clsd Mon
26 Padlock [M,D,L] 602/266-5640 ■ 998 E Indian School Rd (at 10th St) ■ 3pm-1am, special events ■ www.padlockaz.com
27 The Park [M,D,E,K,S] 602/957-6055 ■ 3002 N 24th St (at Thomas) ■ 1pm-1am, strippers

Arizona • USA

PHOENIX

Phoenix, the centerpiece of Arizona's Valley of the Sun, boasts over 300 sunny days a year. Summers can be brutal, though, so take advantage of the milder winter, spring, and fall weather to explore the area. The Heard Museum (602/252-8840) showcases traditional and contemporary Native American culture and art. Urban hikers will enjoy Papago Park, Squaw Peak, and Camelback Mountain's trails. There are over 200 golf courses in Arizona, with more than 100 right in the Valley. Call 'Golf Arizona' at 800/942-5444 for more information. Nearby Scottsdale offers Rawhide (480/502-5600), a charming, if touristy, re-created Old West town, and the Gallery District.

Queer Resources

COMMUNITY INFO
Valley of the Sun Gay/Lesbian Center 602/265-7283. Call for location.
Lesbian/Gay Community Switchboard 602/234-2752. 10am-10pm (volunteers permitting).

AIDS RESOURCES
Arizona AIDS Project 602/253-2437.

RECOVERY
602/264-1341(AA#). 2622 N 16th St, call for meeting times. Lambda Club.

City Calendar

LGBT PRIDE
April. 602/279-1771, web: www.azpride.org

ANNUAL EVENTS
October - AIDS Walk 602/253-2437.

Tourist Info

AIRPORT DIRECTIONS
Sky Harbor International (enter via 24th St or 44th St). Go north on 24th or 44th to McDowell Rd, then take a left. Turn right onto 7th Ave and go past Indian School Rd.

PUBLIC TRANSIT & TAXIS
Yellow Cab 602/252-5252.
Super Shuttle 602/244-9000.
Phoenix Transit 602/253-5000.

TOURIST SPOTS & INFO
Castles & Coasters Park on Black Canyon Fwy & Peoria 602/997-7577.
Heard Museum 602/252-8840.
Phoenix Zoo & Desert Botanical Garden in Papago Park.
Visitor's Center: 602/254-6500.
Arizona Office of Tourism 602/230-7733 or 800/842-8257, web: www.phxcenter.org; www.phoenixcenter.org.

WEATHER
Beautifully mild and comfortable (60°s-80°s) October through March or April. Hot (90°s-100°s) in summer. August brings the rainy season (severe monsoon storms) with flash flooding.

BEST VIEWS
South Mountain Park at sunset, watching the city lights come on.

---

28 **Pookie's Cafe** [MW,E,V,WC] 602/277-2121 ■ 4540 N 7th St (at Camelback) ■ 11am-midnight, kitchen till 11pm, Sun brunch ■ www.pookiescafe.com

29 **Pumphouse II** [M,NH] 602/275-3509 ■ 4132 E McDowell Rd (at 41st St) ■ noon-1am, sports bar

30 **Roscoe's on 7th** [M,F] 602/285-0833 ■ 4531 N 7th St (at Minnezona) ■ 3pm-1am, from 11am Sun, sports bar ■ www.roscoeson7.com

31 **The Waterhole** [MW,NH,K] 623/937-3139 ■ 8830 N 43rd Ave (at Dunlap) ■ 3pm-1am

32 **Winks** [★M,E,S] 602/265-9002 ■ 5707 N 7th St (btwn Bethany Home & Missouri) ■ 10am-1am, lunch Mon-Fri, Sun brunch, cabaret ■ peterwinks@aol.com

NIGHTCLUBS

33 **Boom** [★M,D,YC,WC] 602/254-0231 ■ 1724 E McDowell (at 16th St) ■ 4pm-1am, till 3am Fri, till 4am Sat, dancers Fri, circuit crowd Sat, retro Sun ■ www.boomnightclub.com

RESTAURANTS

Alexi's [WC] 602/279-0982 ■ 3550 N Central (in 'Valley Bank Bldg' at Osborn) ■ lunch & dinner, int'l, full bar, patio

Katz's Deli 602/277-8814 ■ 5144 N Central (at Camelback) ■ 6:30am-3pm, till 7pm Tue-Fri, from 8am Sun, kosher-style deli

Los Dos Molinos 602/243-9113 ■ 8646 S Central Ave ■ 11am-9pm, clsd Sun-Mon, homecooking

28 **Pookie's Cafe** [MW,E,V,WC] 602/277-2121 ■ 4540 N 7th St (at Camelback) ■ 11am-midnight, kitchen till 11pm, Sun brunch, also full bar ■ www.pookiescafe.com

Vincent Guerithault on Camelback [WC] 602/224-0225 ■ 3930 E Camelback Rd (at 40th St) ■ lunch Mon-Fri, dinner nightly, Southwestern, some veggie

Entertainment & Recreation

The Alternative 602/286-9330 ■ 2030 N 23rd Pl (at Monte Vista) ■ social group for gay & bi men 18-29, call for events ■ www.thealt.org

Friends of Ellen Brunch 602/307-9931 ■ 16th St & Camelback (at Einstein's Bagels) ■ 10:30am 1st & 3rd Sun ■ Abitcrazy4@home.com

Lather, Rinse, Repeat 602/279-5577 ■ 645 E Missouri, Ste 360 ■ KZZP 104.7FM 7pm-11pm Sun ■ www.kzzp.com

Lesbian Social Network 480/946-5570 ■ 4400 N Central Ave (at the Community Church of Hope) ■ 7:30pm-10pm Fri, popular informal social evenings of games, videos, and discussions ■ womenscenterinc@aol.com

Bookstores

34 **Obelisk the Bookstore** [WC] 602/266-2665 ■ 24 W Camelback #A (at Central) ■ 10am-10pm, noon-9pm Sun, lgbt ■ www.obeliskbooks.com

Retail Shops

35 **Unique on Central** [WC] 602/279-9691, 800/269-4840 (mail order) ■ 4700 N Central Ave #105 (at Highland) ■ 10am-9pm, till 6pm Sun, cards & gifts

Publications

Echo Magazine 602/266-0550 ■ bi-weekly lgbt newsmagazine ■ www.echomag.com

HeatStroke 602/264-3646 ■ bi-weekly lgbt newspaper ■ alkalphx@aol.com

Men's Clubs

Chute [MO,B,L] 602/234-1654 ■ 1440 E Indian School Rd ■ 24hrs

Flex Complex [SW,PC] 602/271-9011 ■ 1517 S Black Canyon Hwy (btwn 19th Ave & I-17) ■ 24hrs ■ www.flexbaths.com

Hideout 602/431-1010 ■ 4030 E Elwood Dr (at 40th St) ■ private shows 10am-1am, stage shows 7pm-1am

Erotica

Adult Shoppe 602/306-1130 ■ 111 S 24th St (at Jefferson) ■ also 5021 W Indian School Rd (at 51st Ave), 623/245-3008

Castle Megastore 602/266-3348 ■ 300 E Camelback (at Central) ■ also 5501 E Washington, 602/231-9837; 8802 N Black Canyon Fwy, 602/995-1641; 8315 E Apache Tr, 480/986-6114

International Bookstore 602/955-2000 ■ 3640 E Thomas Rd (at 36th St) ■ 8am-1am, from noon Sun

Pleasure World [V] 602/275-0015 ■ 4029 E Washington (at 40th St)

Tuff Stuff 602/254-9651 ■ 1716 E McDowell Rd (at 17th St) ■ clsd Sun-Mon, custom leather shop ■ www.tuffstuffleather.com

Little Rock

If you want a city with a pace of life all its own, a city whose history reflects the dramatic changes within the South, and a city surrounded by natural beauty, you've made the right choice to visit Little Rock. Here you can enjoy the summer days in the shade beside the slow-moving Arkansas River that winds through town. Or you can take off to the nearby lakes and national forests to camp, rock climb or water-ski. Stay in town and you can spend your days exploring the State Capitol, touring the historic homes of the Quapaw Quarter district, or browsing in Little Rock's many shops. Rumor even has it that Bill Clinton's boyhood home is owned by a friendly lesbian couple.

Queer Resources

Community Info
▼ Women's Project 501/372-5113. 2224 Main St, 10am-5pm Mon-Fri.

Recovery
AA Gay/Lesbian 501/224-6764. 8pm Wed & 6pm Sun.

City Calendar

LGBT Pride
June.

Annual Events
October - State Fair.

Tourist Info

Airport Directions
Little Rock National. Follow the signs to downtown, along 440 West, 30 East, then 630 West to Center St.

Public Transit & Taxis
Black & White Cab 501/374-0333.
Central Arkansas Transit 501/375-1163.

Tourist Spots & Info
Check out Bill & Hillary's old digs at 18th & Center Sts.
Decorative Arts Museum 501/372-4000.
Visitor's Center: Arkansas Dept of Tourism 800/628-8725.
What's Going on in Little Rock 502/244-8463, web: www.littlerock.com.

Weather
When it comes to natural precipitation, Arkansas is far from being a dry state. Be prepared for the occasional severe thunderstorm or ice storm. Summers are hot and humid (mid 90°s). Winters can be cold (30°s) with some snow and ice. Spring and fall are the best times to come and be awed by the colorful beauty of Mother Nature.

Best Views
Quapaw Quarter (in the heart of the city).

ARKANSAS • USA

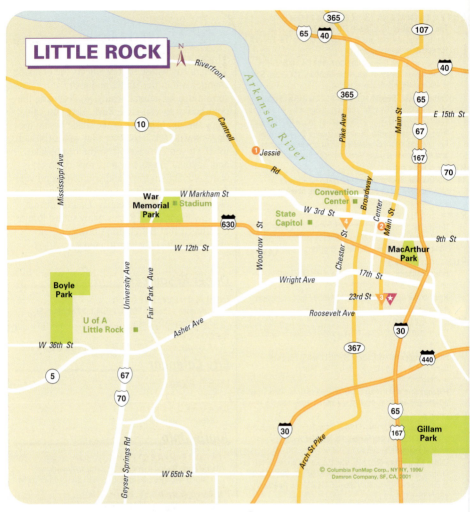

ARKANSAS

Little Rock

Bars
1 **Backstreet** [MW,D,CW,S,PC,WC] 501/664-2744 ■ 1021 Jessie Rd #Q (btwn Cantrell & Riverfront) ■ 9pm-5am ■ jblondehell@aol.com
2 **The Factory** [M,NH,D,F,E,K,WC,GO] 501/372-3070 ■ 412 S Louisiana St (btwn 4th & Center) ■ 5pm-2am, 7pm-1am Sat, clsd Sun ■ www.thefactorybar.com

Nightclubs
1 **Discovery: The Experience** [★GS,D,TG,S,PC,WC] 501/664-4784 ■ 1021 Jessie Rd (btwn Cantrell & Riverfront) ■ 9pm-5am Sat, largest club in area

Cafes
Beyond the Edge Cafe 501/372-0560 ■ 1009 W 7th St ■ 10am-2pm & 5pm-10pm, clsd Sun-Mon

Restaurants
Vino's Pizza [BW] 501/375-8466 ■ 923 W 7th St (at Chester) ■ 11am-midnight, till 10pm Tue-Wed

Entertainment & Recreation
The Weekend Theatre [BW,GO] 501/374-3761 ■ W 7th St (at Chester) ■ plays & musicals on wknds

Bookstores
3 **Women's Project** 501/372-5113, 501/372-6853 (TDD) ■ 2224 Main St (at 23rd) ■ 10am-5pm Mon-Fri, feminist resource, call for info ■ WProject@aol.com

Retail Shops
4 **A Twisted Gift Shop** 501/376-7723 ■ 1007 W 7th St (at Chester) ■ 11am-10pm, clsd Tue, gift shop; also 7201 Asher Ave, 501/568-4262 ■ twistedgifts@webtv.net
Wild Card 501/223-9071 ■ 400 N Bowman (at Maralynn) ■ 10am-8pm, noon-5pm Sun, novelties & gifts

CALIFORNIA

Long Beach

ACCOMMODATIONS
1 **Queen Mary** [GF,WC] 562/435-3511, 800/437-2934 ■ 1126 Queens Hwy ■ historic ocean liner ■ queenmary.com

BARS
2 **The Brit** [M,NH] 562/432-9742 ■ 1744 E Broadway (at Cherry) ■ 10am-2am
3 **The Broadway** [MW,NH,K,WC] 562/432-3646 ■ 1100 E Broadway (at Cerritos) ■ 10am-2am
4 **Club 5211** [MW,NH,WC] 562/428-5545 ■ 5211 N Atlantic St (at 52nd) ■ noon-10pm, 11am-3am wknds
5 **Club Broadway** [W,NH,V,WC] 562/438-7700 ■ 3348 E Broadway (at Redondo) ■ 11am-2am
6 **The Crest** [M,L] 562/423-6650 ■ 5935 Cherry Ave (at South) ■ 2pm-2am
7 **The Falcon** [M,NH,WC] 562/432-4146 ■ 1435 E Broadway (at Falcon) ■ 8am-2am
15 **Fire Island** [M,D,WC] 562/597-0014 ■ 3325 E Anaheim St (at Redondo) ■ 3pm-2am, from noon wknds, patio ■ www.clubfireisland.com
8 **Mineshaft** [★M,WC] 562/436-2433 ■ 1720 E Broadway (btwn Gaviota & Hermosa) ■ 10am-2am ■ www.mineshaftbar.com
9 **Pistons** [M,B,L] 562/422-1928 ■ 2020 E Artesia (at Cherry) ■ 6pm-2am, till 4am Fri-Sat, from 3pm Sun, patio ■ www.pistonsbar.com
10 **Que Será** [GS,D,A,E] 562/599-6170, 562/918-0529 ■ 1923 E 7th St (at Cherry) ■ 5pm-2am, from noon Sun

LONG BEACH

Though it's often overshadowed by Los Angeles, Long Beach is a large harbor city with plenty of entertainment. In the early 1900s, Long Beach was a seaside resort for silent film stars. With 5-1/2 miles of oceanfront, Long Beach still attracts visitors in search of sun and surf. The city itself is melded from overlapping suburbs and industrial areas. The cleaner air, mild weather, and reasonable traffic make it an obvious choice for those looking for a livable refuge from L.A. The antiquing along 4th St. is divine, and check out the world's largest mural, "Planet Ocean," at 300 E. Ocean Blvd. The Queen Mary (562/435-3511) is a must, housing restaurants and a full-service hotel.

Queer Resources

COMMUNITY INFO
▼ Lesbian/Gay Center & Switchboard 562/434-4455. web: www.centerlb.org. 2017 E 4th St (at Cherry), 9am-10pm, till 6pm Sat, 3pm-9pm Sun. South Bay Center 310/379-2850. 2009 Artesia Blvd #A (at Cherry), Redondo Beach, 7pm-10pm Wed.

RECOVERY
AA Gay/Lesbian (Atlantic Alano Club) 562/432-7476. At 441 E 1st St, call for mtg times. South Bay Gay/Lesbian AA 562/379-2850. At the South Bay Center, 8pm Th.

City Calendar

LGBT PRIDE
3rd wknd in May. 562/987-9191, web: www.longbeachpride.com.

ANNUAL EVENTS
April - AIDS Walk.
September - Pride Picnic.
November - The Gatsby Show at the Sheraton, benefitting the Center.

Tourist Info

AIRPORT DIRECTIONS
Long Beach Airport. From airport exit, turn right on Lakewood, then right on Spring St. Take a left on Redondo Ave. Some bars are on Redondo, while Broadway is a gay mecca. Bus 111 goes from the airport to Redondo and Broadway.

PUBLIC TRANSIT & TAXIS
Long Beach Taxi Co-op 562/435-6111.
Long Beach Transit & Runabout (free downtown shuttle) 562/591-8753.

TOURIST SPOTS & INFO
Belmont Shores area on 2nd St, south of Pacific Coast Highway — lots of restaurants & shopping, only blocks from the beach.
Long Beach Downtown Marketplace, 10am-4pm Fri.
The Queen Mary 562/435-3511.
Visitor's Center: 562/436-3645, web: www.golongbeach.org.

WEATHER
Quite temperate: highs in the mid-80°s July through September, and cooling down at night. In the winter, January to March, highs are in the upper 60°s, and lows in the upper 40°s.

BEST VIEWS
On the deck of the Queen Mary, docked overlooking most of Long Beach. Or Signal Hill, off 405. Take the Cherry exit.

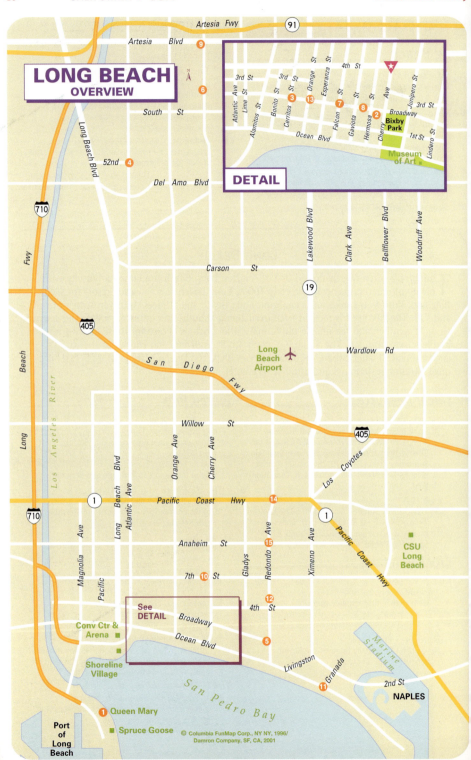

Los Angeles • CALIFORNIA

Los Angeles

Los Angeles is divided into 7 geographical areas:
LA—Overview
LA—West Hollywood
LA—Hollywood
LA—West LA & Santa Monica
LA—Silverlake
LA—Midtown
LA—Valley

LA—Overview

ACCOMMODATIONS
Elderbank House [M,GO] 213/840-1963 ■ 3920 Elderbank Dr (at Paige) ■ www.bcity.com/elderbankhouse

ENTERTAINMENT & RECREATION
The Celebration Theatre 323/957-1884 ■ 7051-B Santa Monica Blvd (at La Brea) ■ lgbt theater, call for more info

Gay Men's Chorus 323/650-0756, 800/636-7464 ■ www.gmcla.org

The Getty Center 310/440-7300 ■ 1200 Getty Center Dr, Brentwood ■ clsd Mon, LA's shining city on a hill & world-class museum; of course, it's still in LA so you'll need to make reservations for parking (!)

Highways 310/315-1459 (reservation line), 310/453-1755 (admin line) ■ 1651 18th St, Santa Monica ■ 'full-service performance center'

IMRU Gay Radio 818/985-2711 ■ KPFK LA 90.7 FM ■ 7pm Mon

Outfest 323/960-9200 ■ lgbt media arts foundation that sponsors the annual lgbt film festival each July ■ www.outfest.org

Sunwolf Farms 661/245-9653 ■ private ranch w/ customized day trips, lesbian-owned/ run ■ www.sunwolffarms.com

PUBLICATIONS
Fab! 323/655-5716 ■ 6363 Wilshire #350 ■ hip gay newspaper w/ club listings ■ www.gayfab.com

Female FYI 323/655-1266 ■ monthly coverage of LA & southern CA lesbian club scene

Frontiers 323/848-2222 ■ 8380 Santa Monica Blvd Suite 200 ■ huge lgbt newsmagazine w/ listings for everything ■ www.frontiersweb.com

GBF (Gay Black Female) 323/376-2157 ■ nat'l newsmagazine w/ some listings for LA ■ www.gayblackfemale.com

IN Los Angeles 323/848-2200 ■ gay news & entertainment magazine for LA ■ editor@inlamag.com

Lesbian News (LN) 310/787-8658, 800/458-9888 ■ nat'l w/ strong coverage of southern CA ■ www.LesbianNews.com

Nightlife 323/462-5400 ■ club listings ■ nlmagazine@aol.com

Odyssey Magazine 323/874-8788 ■ all the dish on LA's club scene

The Women's Yellow Pages 818/995-6646 ■ www.wypwrs.com

---

11 **Ripples** [★M,D,MR,F,E,S,K,V,YC] 562/433-0357 ■ 5101 E Ocean (at Granada) ■ noon-2am, patio, Latin night 2nd Sat, Asian night 3rd Sat ■ www.clubripples.com

12 **Silver Fox** [M,K,V,WC] 562/439-6343 ■ 411 Redondo (at 4th) ■ 4pm-2am, from noon wknds, popular happy hour ■ www.silverfoxlongbeach.com

13 **Sweetwater Saloon** [M,NH,WC] 562/432-7044 ■ 1201 E Broadway (at Orange) ■ 6am-2am, popular days, cruisy

NIGHTCLUBS
14 **Executive Suite** [★W,D,E] 562/597-3884 ■ 3428 E Pacific Coast Hwy (at Redondo) ■ 4pm-close, from 5pm wknds, Latin night Th, 2 levels

Pussycat Lounge [W,D] 562/901-3040 ■ monthly dance party, call for location and times

CAFES
Cafe Haven 562/437-3785 ■ 1708 E Broadway (at Gaviota) ■ 6am-midnight, till 1am Tue, till 3am Fri-Sat

RESTAURANTS
Cha Cha Cha [WC] 562/436-3900 ■ 762 8th (at Pacific Ave) ■ lunch & dinner

Egg Heaven 562/433-9277 ■ 4358 E 4th St ■ 7am-2pm, till 3pm wknds, some veggie

Hamburger Mary's [MW,V] 562/983-7001 ■ 740 E Broadway (at Alamitos)

House of Madame JoJo [★MW,BW,WC] 562/439-3672 ■ 2941 E Broadway (btwn Temple & Redondo) ■ 5:30pm-10pm, Mediterranean, some veggie

Omelette Inn [GO] 562/437-5625 ■ 108 W 3rd St (at Pine) ■ 7am-2:30pm

Original Park Pantry [MW,WC] 562/434-0451 ■ 2104 E Broadway (at Junipero) ■ lunch & dinner, int'l, some veggie

RETAIL SHOPS
Hot Stuff 562/433-0692 ■ 2121 E Broadway (at Cherry) ■ 11am-7pm, 10am-6pm wknds, cards, gifts & novelties ■ www.hotstuffgifts.com

Toto's Revenge [GO] 562/434-2777, 877/688-8686 ■ 2947 E Broadway Ave (at Orizaba) ■ 10am-9pm, unique cards & gifts, dog-friendly, also mail-order ■ www.totosrevenge.com

MEN'S CLUBS
1350 Club [PC] 310/830-4784 ■ 510 W Anaheim St (at Neptune), Wilmington ■ 24hrs ■ www.midtowne.com

EROTICA
The Crypt on Broadway 562/983-6560 ■ 1712 E Broadway (btwn Cherry & Falcon) ■ leather, toys

The Rubber Tree 562/434-0027 ■ 5018 E 2nd St (at Granada) ■ gifts for lovers, women-owned

CALIFORNIA • USA

Damron Road Atlas 9

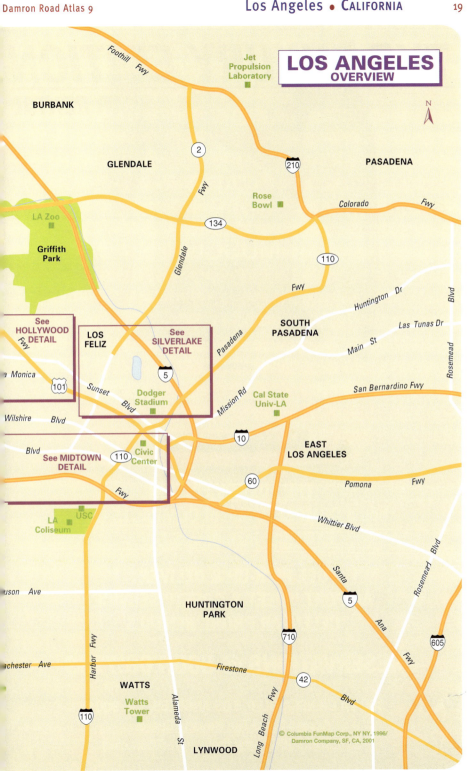

Los Angeles

There is no city more truly American than the city that is known simply as L.A. Here fantasy and reality have become inseparable. The mere mention of the 'City of Angels' conjures up images of palm-lined streets, sun-drenched beaches, and wealth beyond imagination, along with smog, over-crowded freeways, searing poverty, and urban violence. Most travellers come only for the fantasy. But if you take a moment to focus your gaze past the usual tourist traps, you'll see the unique—and often tense—diversity that L.A. offers as a city on the borders of Latin America, the Pacific Rim, Suburbia USA, and the rest of the world. You'll find museums, centers and theatres celebrating the cultures of the many peoples who live in this valley.

Queer Resources

COMMUNITY INFO
▼ Los Angeles Gay/Lesbian Community Center 323/993-7400, web: www.laglc.org. 1625 N Schrader Ave (1 blk W of Wilcox, see Hollywood map), 9am-9pm, till 2pm Sat, clsd Sun.
▼ The Village (Community Center Extension) 323/860-7302. 1125 McCadden Pl (at Santa Monica, see Hollywood map).

AIDS RESOURCES
AIDS Project LA 323/993-1600.

RECOVERY
Alcoholics Together Center 323/663-8882. 1773 Griffith Park Blvd, Silverlake, 7:30am-10:30pm.

City Calendar

LGBT PRIDE
June. 323/969-8302. Christopher St West.

ENTERTAINMENT
Gay Men's Chorus 323/650-0756, web: www.gmcla.org.

ANNUAL EVENTS
April - AIDS Walk-a-thon 323/466-9255.
May/June - California AIDS Ride 323/874-7474 or 800/825-1000. AIDS benefit bike ride from San Francisco to LA.
July - Outfest 323/960-9200. Los Angeles' lesbian/ gay film & video festival.
August - Sunset Junction Fair 323/661-7771. Carnival, arts & information fair on Sunset Blvd in Silverlake benefits Sunset Junction Youth Center.
October - Gay Night at Disneyland: gayland@aol.com.

Tourist Info

AIRPORT DIRECTIONS
Los Angeles International LAX near West LA, Burbank Airport in the Valley, John Wayne in Orange County. To get from LAX to West Hollywood, take the airport exit to the 405 Freeway North. Get off, going northeast onto Santa Monica. Take Santa Monica past Melrose.

PUBLIC TRANSIT & TAXIS
United Taxi 323/870-4664.
LA Express 800/427-7483.
Super Shuttle 310/782-6600.
Metro Transit Authority 213/626-4455.

TOURIST SPOTS & INFO
3rd St. outdoor mall in Santa Monica.
Chinatown, near downtown.
City Walk in Universal Studios.
Graveline Tours — tours of (in)famous deaths, violence & the supernatural 323/469-4149.
Mann's Chinese Theater on Hollywood Blvd 323/464-8111.
Melrose Ave, hip commercial district in West Hollywood.
Theme Parks: Disneyland, Knotts Berry Farm or Magic Mountain.
Watts Towers, not far from LAX 213/847-4646.
Westwood Village premiere movie theaters & restaurants.
Venice Beach.
Visitor's Center: 800/228-2452, web: www.lacvb.com.

WEATHER
Summers are hot, dry, and smoggy with temperatures in the 80°s-90°s. LA's weather is at its finest — sunny, blue skies and moderate temperatures (mid 70°s) — during the months of March, April and May.

BEST VIEWS
Drive up Mulholland Drive, in the hills between Hollywood and the Valley, for a panoramic view of the city, and the Hollywood sign.

LA—West Hollywood • CALIFORNIA

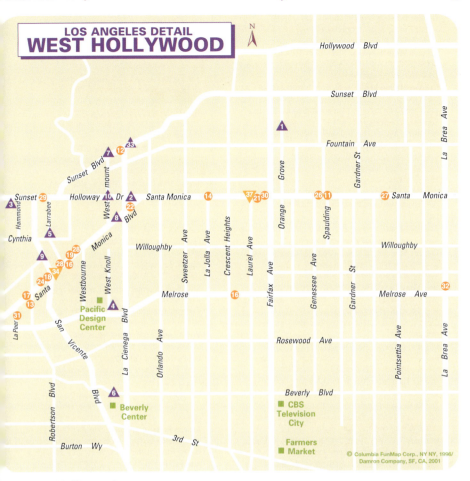

A—West Hollywood

ACCOMMODATIONS

The Grafton on Sunset [GF,SW,WC] 323/654-4600, 800/821-3660 ■ 8462 W Sunset Blvd (at La Cienega) ■ sundeck, panoramic views, located in heart of Sunset Strip ■ www.graftononsunset.com

The Grove Guesthouse [MW,SW,WC] 323/876-8887, 888/524-7683 ■ 1325 N Orange Grove Ave (at Sunset) ■ 1-bdrm villa, hot tub ■ www.groveguesthouse.com

Holloway Motel [GS] 323/654-2454, 888/654-6400 ■ 8465 Santa Monica Blvd (at La Cienega), West Hollywood ■ centrally located ■ www.hollowaymotel.com

Hyatt West Hollywood [GF,SW] 323/656-1234, 800/233-1234 ■ 8401 Sunset Blvd (at Kings Rd)

▶ Le Montrose Suite Hotel [★GF,SW,NS,WC] 310/855-1115, 800/776-0666 ■ 900 Hammond St (at Sunset) ■ rooftop patio & pool, gym, also full restaurant ■ www.lemontrose.com

Le Parc Suite Hotel [★GF,F,SW,WC] 310/855-8888, 800/578-4837 ■ 733 N West Knoll Dr (at Melrose) ■ tennis courts, also restaurant ■ www.leparcsuites.com

San Vicente Inn

Acknowledged as "one of the 10 best Gay Bed & Breakfasts in North America, and recipient of *Out and About* "Editor's Choice Award" for the past five years.

Come relax, meet new friends, and enjoy the only Gay clothing optional Tropical Paradise in the heart of the City. Located mere steps from WeHo's vibrant entertainment & shopping, gyms, restaurants, clubs, and more.

email: infodesk@sanvicenteinn.com
web: www.sanvicenteinn.com

PHONE **310/854-6915** FAX **310/289-5929**

CALIFORNIA • USA

5 **Le Rêve Hotel** [GF,SW,WC] 310/854-1114, 800/835-7997 ■ 8822 Cynthia St (at Larrabee), West Hollywood ■ all-suite hotel, hot tub ■ www.lerevehotel.com

8 **Ramada West Hollywood** [GF,F,SW,WC] 310/652-6400, 800/845-8585 ■ 8585 Santa Monica Blvd (at La Cienega) ■ art deco ■ www.ramada-wh.com

9 ▶**San Vicente Inn Resort** [M,SW,N,GO] 310/854-6915 ■ 845 N San Vicente Blvd (at Santa Monica), West Hollywood ■ hot tub ■ see ad on previous page ■ www.sanvicenteinn.com

Southern Comforts [M,SW,GO] 323/850-5623, 800/889-7359 ■ in the Hollywood Hills, garden patio ■ www.SouthernComforts.com

10 **Summerfield Suites by Wyndham** [GS,SW] 310/657-7400, 800/833-4353 ■ 1000 Westmount Dr (nr Holloway), West Hollywood ■ www.wyndham.com

10 **West Hollywood Suites** [M,SW,WC,GO] 310/652-9400 ■ full service hotel, hot tub ■ www.FriendsTravel.com

BARS

11 **7702 SM Club** [MW,NH,D] 323/654-3336 ■ 7702 Santa Monica Blvd (at Spaulding) ■ noon-2am

12 **Comedy Store** [GF] 323/650-6268 ■ 8433 Sunset Blvd (at La Cienega) ■ 8pm-2am, stand-up club ■ www.comedystore.com

14 **Gold Coast** [★M,NH,WC] 323/656-4879 ■ 8228 Santa Monica Blvd (at La Jolla) ■ 11am-2am, from 10am wknds

16 **Improvisation** [GF] 323/651-2583 ■ 8162 Melrose Ave (at Crescent Heights) ■ stand-up comedy, 'Hell's Kitchen' restaurant

17 **Micky's** [★M,D,F,V,YC,GO] 323/657-1176 ■ 8857 Santa Monica Blvd (at San Vicente) ■ noon-2am, after-hours wknds, lunch on patio Mon-Fri ■ www.mickys.com

18 **Mother Lode** [★M,NH,K,WC] 310/659-9700 ■ 8944 Santa Monica Blvd (at Robertson) ■ 2pm-2am

19 **The Normandie Room** [GS,NH,WC] 310/659-6204 ■ 8737 Santa Monica Blvd (at Westbourne) ■ 5pm-2am, great cosmopolitans

21 **Numbers** [★M,F,WC] 310/652-7700 ■ 8741 Santa Monica Blvd (at Hancock, 2nd flr) ■ 5pm-2am

22 **The Palms** [★W,NH,D,MR,K,WC] 310/652-6188 ■ 8572 Santa Monica Blvd (at La Cienega) ■ 4pm-2am, from 2pm wknds, BBQ Sun, theme nights

24 **Rage** [★M,D,F,S,V,YC,WC] 310/652-7055, 877/648-RAGE ■ 8911 Santa Monica Blvd (at San Vicente) ■ 11am-2am, lunch & dinner daily

24 **Revolver** [★M,A,V] 310/659-8851 ■ 8851 Santa Monica Blvd (at San Vicente) ■ 4pm-2am, from 2pm wknds

26 **Spike** [★M,D,WC] 323/656-9343 ■ 7746 Santa Monica Blvd (at Spaulding) ■ 3pm-5am, 24hrs Sat, clsd Mon-Tue, cruise bar, patio

27 **Tempest** [★GS,D,E] 323/850-5115 ■ 7323 Santa Monica Blvd (E of Fuller Ave) ■ 8:30pm-close

Tiki Bar at Tahiti [M] 323/651-1213 ■ 7910 W 3rd St (W of Fairfax) ■ 5pm-close, more gay Wed, also restaurant

28 **Trunks** [M,NH,YC] 310/652-1015 ■ 8809 Santa Monica Blvd (at Larrabee) ■ 1pm-2am, sports video bar

29 **Viper Room** [GF,D,S,$] 310/358-1880 ■ 8852 Sunset Blvd (btwn San Vicente & Larabie) ■ 9pm-2am ■ www.viperroom.com

NIGHTCLUBS

30 **7969** [GS,D,TG,S] 323/654-0280 ■ 7969 Santa Monica Blvd (at Fairfax) ■ 9pm-2am, drag Mon & Fri, also 'Michelle's XXX Review', strip show/ dance club for women, 9pm Tu ■ michellesxxx@usa.net

31 **The Factory** [M,D,A,S,V,YC] 310/659-4551 ■ 652 N La Peer Dr (at Santa Monica) ■ 9pm-2am Wed-Sun ■ www.factorynightclubLA.com

31 **Girl Bar** [W,D] 877/447-5252 ■ 652 N La Peer (at Santa Monica, at 'The Factory') ■ 9pm-3am Fri only, call hotline for events ■ www.girlbar.com

32 **La Plaza** [M,D,MR-L,S] 323/939-0703 ■ 739 N La Brea Ave (at Melrose) ■ 8pm-2am, clsd Tue, shows nightly at 10:15pm & midnight

13 **Ultra Suede** [GS,D,A,E] 310/659-4551 ■ 661 N Robertson Blvd (at Santa Monica) ■ 9pm-2am Wed-Sun, popular Asian night Th

CAFES

Eat-Well [★] 323/656-1383 ■ 8252 Santa Monica Blvd (at La Jolla) ■ 7am-3pm & 5:30pm-10pm, 8am-3pm wknds

Mani's Bakery [WC] 323/938-8800 ■ 519 S Fairfax Ave (at Maryland Dr) ■ 6:30am-midnight, coffee & dessert bar

Stonewall Gourmet Coffee Company [★MW,E,WC] 818/769-4517 ■ 8717 Santa Monica Blvd (nr La Cienega) ■ 7am-midnight, till 1am Fri-Sat, from 8am Sun ■ www.stonewallinc.com

WeHo Lounge 310/659-6180 ■ 8861 Santa Monica Blvd (at San Vicente) ■ 2pm-2am, desserts & light lunch fare

Who's On Third Cafe 323/651-2928 ■ 8369 W 3rd St (at Orlando) ■ 7:30am-3pm wkdays, from 8am wknds

RESTAURANTS

The Abbey [★MW,WC] 310/289-8410 ■ 692 N Robertson (at Santa Monica) ■ 7am-3am, American/ cont'l, full bar, patio

African Restaurant Row Fairfax btwn Olympic & Pico ■ many Ethiopian, Nigerian & other African restaurants to choose from on this block

Alto Palato 310/657-9271 ■ 755 N La Cienega Blvd (at Waring) ■ 5pm-10:30pm, bargain pasta & comfortable chairs, full bar ■ www.restaurantpages.com/pages/altopalato

Baja Bud's [WC] 310/659-1911 ■ 8575 Santa Monica Blvd (at La Cienega) ■ 7am-10pm, till 11pm Fri-Sat, healthy Mexican, patio

Benvenuto Cafe [WC] 310/659-8635 ■ 8512 Santa Monica Blvd (at La Cienega) ■ lunch Tue-Fri, dinner nightly, Italian, full bar, patio

Bossa Nova [BW,WC] 310/657-5070 ■ 685 N Robertson Blvd (at Santa Monica) ■ 11am-11pm, Brazilian, patio

Caffe Luna [WC] 323/655-9177 ■ 7463 Melrose Ave (btw Vista & Gardner) ■ 10:30am-midnight, till 4am wknds, popular after-hours, country Italian, some veggie

Canter's Deli [WC] 323/651-2030 ■ 419 N Fairfax (btwn Melrose & Beverly) ■ 24hrs, hip after-hours, Jewish/ American, some veggie

The Cobalt Cantina [WC] 310/659-8691 ■ 616 N Robertson Blvd (at Melrose) ■ noon-11pm, 10am-10pm Sun, bar open till 2am wknds, Cal-Mex, some veggie, patio

Il Pastaio 310/205-5444 ■ 400 N Cannon Dr (at Brighton Wy), Beverly Hills ■ lunch & dinner, homemade pasta & great colorful risotto

LA—West Hollywood/Hollywood • CALIFORNIA

Il Piccolino Trattoria [WC] 310/659-2220 ■ 350 N Robertson Blvd (btwn Melrose & Beverly) ■ lunch & dinner, clsd Sun, full bar, patio

Itana Bahia [WC] 310/657-6306 ■ 8711 Santa Monica Blvd (at Westbourne) ■ lunch & dinner Tue-Sat, reservations req'd for dinner, great Brazilian food, full bar, live music Wed-Fri

Koo Koo Roo [BW,WC] 310/657-3300 ■ 8520 Santa Monica Blvd (at La Cienega Blvd) ■ 11am-11pm, lots of healthy chicken dishes, plenty veggie

L'Orangerie 310/652-9770 ■ 903 N La Cienega Blvd (btwn Melrose & Santa Monica) ■ dinner, clsd Mon, haute French, patio ■ loranger@pacbell.net

Louise's Trattoria [BW] 323/651-3880 ■ 7505 Melrose Ave (at Gardner) ■ 11am-11pm, till midnight Fri-Sat, Italian, great foccacia bread

Lucques [WC] 323/655-6277 ■ 8474 Melrose Ave (at La Cienega) ■ lunch & dinner, clsd Mon, French, patio, full bar

Luna Park [E,WC] 310/652-0611 ■ 665 N Robertson (btwn Melrose & Santa Monica) ■ dinner, clsd Mon, progressive American, some veggie, cabaret, patio, 3 bars

Marco's Trattoria [WC] 323/650-2771 ■ 8136 Santa Monica (at Crescent Hts) ■ 11am-10pm, from 3pm Sun

Marix Tex Mex [MW,WC] 323/656-8800 ■ 1108 N Flores (btwn La Cienega & Fairfax) ■ 11:30am-11pm, great margaritas

Mark's Restaurant 310/652-5252 ■ 861 N La Cienega Blvd (at Santa Monica) ■ 6pm-10pm, till 11:30pm Fri-Sat, Sun brunch, full bar

North [★] 323/654-1313 ■ 8029 W Sunset (at Laurel Canyon, enter rear) ■ 6pm-2am, from 8pm Mon, 70s ski lodge decor, full bar

Real Food Daily [BW,WC] 310/289-9910 ■ 414 N La Cienega (btwn Beverly & Melrose) ■ 11:30am-11pm, organic vegetarian ■ www.realfood.com

Sante Libre 323/857-0412 ■ 345 N La Brea (btwn Melrose & Beverly) ■ 10am-10pm, pastas, salads & wraps, plenty veggie; also 13016 San Vicente (at 26th) in Venice, 310/451-1813

Skewers [BW] 310/271-0555 ■ 8939 Santa Monica Blvd (at Robertson) ■ Middle Eastern, lowfat grill

Tacos Tacos [WC] 310/657-4832 ■ 8948 Santa Monica Blvd (at N Robertson) ■ 11am-11pm, till 1am wknds, yummy, fresh, cheap Mexican, plenty veggie

Tango Grill [MW,BW,WC] 310/659-3663 ■ 8807 Santa Monica (at San Vicente) ■ 11:30am-11:30pm, Argentinian, some veggie

Tommy Tang's [★BW] 323/937-5733 ■ 7313 Melrose Ave (at Poinsettia) ■ noon-10pm, till 11pm wknds, drag night Tue

Trocadero [WC] 323/656-7161 ■ 8280 Sunset Blvd (at Sweetzer) ■ 6pm-2am, clsd Sun-Mon, eclectic American, patio, full bar

Yukon Mining Co [★BW,WC] 323/851-8833 ■ 7328 Santa Monica Blvd (at Fuller) ■ 24hrs, champagne brunch wknds

ENTERTAINMENT & RECREATION
Stonewall Dollar Bingo 818/769-4517 ■ 8717 Santa Monica Blvd (nr La Cienega) ■ 8pm Th, celebrity guest stars ■ info@stonewallinc.com

BOOKSTORES
37 A Different Light [★] 310/854-6601 ■ 8853 Santa Monica Blvd (btwn San Vicente & Larrabee) ■ 10am-10pm, till 11pm Fri-Sat, lgbt ■ www.adlbooks.com

Book Soup 310/659-3110 ■ 8818 W Sunset Blvd (at Larrabee) ■ 9am-midnight, lgbt section

RETAIL SHOPS
34 Dorothy's Surrender 323/650-4111 ■ 7985 Santa Monica Blvd #111 (at Laurel) ■ 10am-11:30pm, cards, periodicals, T-shirts, gifts

GayMartUSA 323/656-7732 ■ 8214 Santa Monica Blvd (at N LaJolla Ave) ■ 10am-10pm, clothes & gifts ■ www.gaymartusa.com

Perfect Beat 310/273-3337 ■ 8941 Santa Monica Blvd ■ 11am-midnight, till 2am Fri-Sun, club music ■ www.perfectbeat.com

Raving Rainbow 310/358-1935 ■ 8515 Santa Monica Blvd ■ 11am-7:30pm, clsd Sun, circuit toys, pride gear ■ www.ravingrainbow.com

Syren 323/936-6693, 800/667-9736 ■ 7225 Beverly Blvd ■ clsd Sun-Mon, leather & latex ■ www.syren.com

GYMS & HEALTH CLUBS
Easton's Gym [GF] 323/651-3636 ■ 8053 Beverly Blvd (at Crescent Hts)

MEN'S CLUBS
Melrose Spa [★PC] 323/937-2122 ■ 7269 Melrose Ave ■ 24hrs ■ www.midtowne.com

Slammer 213/388-8040 ■ 3688 Beverly Blvd (2 blks E of Vermont) ■ 9pm-4am, from 3pm Sun ■ www.slammerclub.com

EROTICA
Circus of Books 323/656-6533 ■ 8230 Santa Monica Blvd (at La Jolla) ■ 6am-2am, videos, erotica, toys

Drake's 310/289-8932 ■ 8932 Santa Monica Blvd (at San Vicente) ■ also 7566 Melrose Ave, 323/651-5600

Hustler Hollywood 310/860-9009 ■ 8920 Sunset Blvd (at San Vicente) ■ chic erotic department store, also cafe

Pleasure Chest 323/650-1022 ■ 7733 Santa Monica Blvd (at Genesee) ■ 10am-midnight, till 1am Fri-Sat ■ www.thepleasurechest.com

Unicorn Bookstore [WC] 310/652-6253 ■ 8940 Santa Monica (at Robertson) ■ 10am-2:30am

LA—Hollywood

ACCOMMODATIONS
2 Coral Sands Hotel [M,SW] 323/467-5141, 800/367-7263 ■ 1730 N Western Ave (at Hollywood Blvd) ■ hot tub, sauna, cruisy ■ www.coralsands-la.com

1 Holiday Inn Hollywood [GF,F,SW,WC] 323/850-5811 ■ 2005 N Highland (at Franklin) ■ exercise room

3 Hollywood Celebrity Hotel [GF] 323/850-6464, 800/222-7017 ■ 1775 Orchid Ave (btwn Hollywood & Franklin) ■ 1930s art deco hotel ■ www.hotelcelebrity.com

4 Hollywood Metropolitan Hotel [GF] 323/962-5800, 800/962-5800 ■ 5825 Sunset Blvd (btwn Bronson & Van Ness) ■ also restaurant ■ www.metropolitanhotel.com

5 Ramada Hotel Hollywood [GF,SW,WC] 323/660-1788, 800/272-6232 ■ 1160 N Vermont Ave (at Santa Monica) ■ www.ramadahollywood.com

BARS
6 Blacklite [MW,NH,TG] 323/469-0211 ■ 1159 N Western (at Santa Monica) ■ 6am-2am

CALIFORNIA • USA

Damron Road Atlas

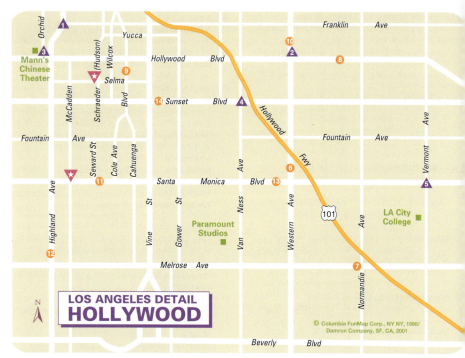

LOS ANGELES DETAIL HOLLYWOOD

7 **Faultline** [★M,D,B,L,V] 323/660-0889 ■ 4216 Melrose Ave (at Normandie) ■ 4pm-2am, 2pm-4am Fri-Sat, clsd Mon, patio, occasional women's events ■ www.faultlinebar.com

8 **Ming's Dynasty** [M,NH,MR-A,K,S,V] 323/462-2039 ■ 5221 Hollywood Blvd (nr Harvard) ■ 8pm-2am, clsd Mon

7 **Spit** [★M,D,L,A] 323/969-2530 ■ 4216 Melrose Ave (at 'Faultline') ■ 9pm-3am 3rd Sat ■ www.brainex.com/spit

9 **Spotlight** [M,NH,WC] 323/467-2425 ■ 1601 N Cahuenga (at Hollywood) ■ 6am-2am

10 **Study** [★M,NH,MR-AF] 323/464-9551 ■ 1723 N Western (at Hollywood) ■ 1pm-2am, from noon wknds

Nightclubs

14 **Beige at 360° Restaurant & Lounge** [★MW,D,F] 323/871-2995 ■ 6290 Sunset Blvd (at Vine) ■ Tue only

11 **The Circus** [★M,D,MR-L,S,V] 323/462-1291 ■ 6655 Santa Monica Blvd (at Seward) ■ 9pm-2am Tue & Fri-Sat, more gay Tue & Fri ■ www.circusdisco.com

12 **Icon** [★M,D,S,PC,$] 323/692-5657 ■ 836 N Highland Ave (btwn Santa Monica & Melrose) ■ after hours Sat & 6pm-midnight Sun

The Palace [M,D] 323/731-3848 ■ 1735 N Vine (at Hollywood) ■ after hours on wknds, check local paper for info

13 **Tempo** [M,D,MR-L,S] 323/466-1094 ■ 5520 Santa Monica Blvd (at Western) ■ 9pm-2pm, from 2pm Sun, till 3am Th-Sat

Restaurants

360° Restaurant & Lounge [★D,WC,GO] 323/871-2995 ■ 6290 Sunset Blvd (at Vine) ■ dinner, modern day supper club, amazing views, live jazz wknds, more gay Tue ■ www.360hollywood.com

Hollywood Canteen 323/465-0961 ■ 1006 N Seward St (at Santa Monica) ■ 11:30am-midnight, till 1am Fri-Sat, dinner only Sat, clsd Sun, classic, full bar

La Poubelle [WC] 323/465-0807 ■ 5907 Franklin Ave (at Bronson) ■ noon-2am, from 6pm Mon, French/ Italian, some veggie

Lucy's Cafe El Adobe [S] 323/462-9421 ■ 5536 Melrose Ave (nr Gower St) ■ lunch & dinner, clsd Sun, Mexican, patio

Musso & Frank Grill 323/467-7788 ■ 6667 Hollywood Blvd (nr Las Palmas) ■ 11am-11pm, clsd Sun-Mon, the grand-dame diner/ steakhouse of Hollywood, great pancakes, potpie & martinis!

Off Vine [BW] 323/962-1900 ■ 6263 Leland Wy (at Vine) ■ lunch & dinner, Sun brunch

Prado [WC] 323/467-3871 ■ 244 N Larchmont Blvd (at Beverly) ■ lunch & dinner, dinner only Sun, Caribbean, some veggie

Quality [WC] 323/658-5959 ■ 8030 W 3rd St (at Laurel) ■ 8am-3pm, homestyle brkfst, some veggie

Rosco's House of Chicken & Waffles 323/466-7453 ■ 1514 N Gower (at Sunset) ■ 8:30am-midnight

Retail Shops

Archaic Idiot/ Mondo Video-A-Go-Go 323/953-8896 ■ 1718 N Vermont (at Hollywood) ■ noon-10pm, vintage clothes, cult & lgbt videos ■ mondofamilyfilms@mailcity.com

Mr S Leather & Fetter USA 323/663-7765 ■ 4232 Melrose Ave (at New Hampshire) ■ noon-8pm, leather, erotica

Videoactive [WC] 323/669-8544 ■ 2522 Hyperion Ave (at Griffith Park Blvd) ■ 10am-11pm, till midnight wknds, lgbt section, adult videos

Gyms & Health Clubs

Gold's Gym [GF] 323/462-7012 ■ 1016 N Cole Ave (nr Santa Monica & Vine)

LA—Hollywood/ West LA • CALIFORNIA

MEN'S CLUBS
Flex Complex [SW] 323/663-7786 ■ 4424 Melrose Ave (btwn Normandie & Vermont) ■ 24hrs ■ www.flexbaths.com
Hollywood Spa [★PC] 323/463-5169 ■ 1650 N Ivar (nr Hollywood & Vine) ■ 24hrs ■ www.hollywoodspa.com
The Zone [PC] 323/464-8881 ■ 1037 N Sycamore Ave (at Santa Monica) ■ www.thezoneLA.com

EROTICA
Highland Books 323/463-0295 ■ 6775 Santa Monica Blvd (at Highland) ■ 24hrs
Le Sex Shoppe 323/464-9435 ■ 6315-1/2 Hollywood Blvd (at Vine) ■ www.goalie-usa.com

LA—West LA & Santa Monica

ACCOMMODATIONS
The Georgian Hotel [GF,F,WC] 310/395-9945, 800/538-8147 ■ 1415 Ocean Ave (btwn Santa Monica & Broadway), Santa Monica ■ great location ■ www.georgianhotel.com
The Inn at Venice Beach [GF,WC] 310/821-2557, 800/828-0688 ■ 327 Washington Blvd (at Via Dolce), Marina Del Ray ■ European-style inn ■ www.innatvenicebeach.com
Sea View Inn at the Beach [GF,SW] 310/545-1504 ■ 3400 Highland Ave (at Rosecranz), Manhattan Beach ■ 1 blk from beach ■ www.seaview-inn.com
W Hotel Los Angeles [GF,F,SW] 310/208-8765, 800/421-2317 ■ 930 Hilgard Ave (at Le Conte) ■ suites, gym, day spa ■ www.whotels.com/cities/los_angeles/

BARS
Annex [M,NH,D,MR-AF,K,WC] 310/671-7323 ■ 835 S La Brea (at Arbor Vitae), Inglewood ■ 2pm-2am, ladies night Sun
Dolphin [MW,NH,K,WC] 310/318-3339 ■ 1995 Artesia Blvd (at Aviation Blvd), Redondo Beach ■ noon-2am, patio ■ www.maxframe.com/dolphin
Friendship [MW,NH,K,WC] 310/454-6024 ■ 112 W Channel Rd (at Pacific Coast Hwy), Santa Monica ■ noon-2am, patio, on the beach, upstairs lounge ■ www.TheFriendship.com
Roosterfish [★M,NH] 310/392-2123 ■ 1302 Abbot Kinney Blvd (at Cadiz), Venice ■ 11am-2am, patio ■ surf.to/roosterfish

NIGHTCLUBS
Insomnia [M,D,$] 213/833-3300 ■ 3414 W Washington Blvd (4th Ave) ■ 11pm-dawn Sat, patio

CAFES
Anastasia's Asylum 310/394-7113 ■ 1028 Wilshire Blvd (at 11th St), Santa Monica ■ 8am-1am, plenty veggie, live music evenings

RESTAURANTS
12 Washington 310/822-5566 ■ 12 Washington Blvd (at Pacific), Venice ■ dinner from 6pm, cont'l
Border Grill 310/451-1655 ■ 1445 Fourth St, Santa Monica ■ lunch & dinner ■ www.bordergrill.com
▶**Cantalini's Salerno Beach Restaurant** [BW,E] 310/821-0018 ■ 193 Culver Blvd (at Vista del Mar), Playa del Rey ■ 4pm-10:30pm, clsd Mon, Italian, on the beach, lesbian-owned/ run, see ad next page

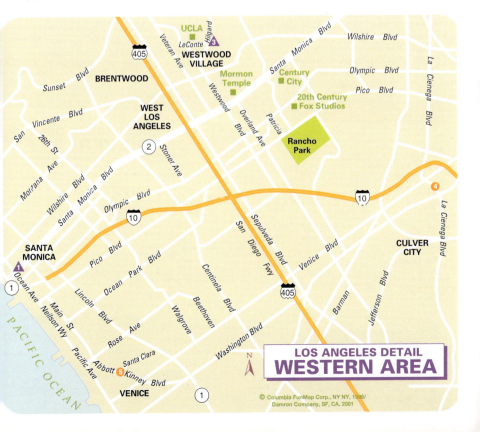

Cantalini's Salerno Beach Restaurant

The Best in Traditional Italian Cuisine. Tucked away in the cozy enclave of neighboring Playa del Rey and steps from the sand, is Cantalini's Salerno Beach Restaurant, a local landmark of forty years. Complete with homemade pastas, hand-tossed pizza, a full selection of fine wines and imported Italian beer, you will leave satisfied. Perfect for group gatherings, family events or intimate occasions, we pride ourselves on creating the feeling of warmth and comfort that comes with good food. You're family at Cantalini's! Open Tue-Sun 4pm–10:30pm.

PHONE **310/821-0018**

Drago [WC] 310/828-1585 ■ 2628 Wilshire Blvd (btwn 26th & Princeton), Santa Monica ■ lunch Mon-Fri, dinner nightly, Sicilian Italian

Golden Bull 310/230-0402 ■ 170 W Channel Rd (at Pacific Coast Hwy), Santa Monica ■ dinner only, Sun brunch (summers), American, full bar

The Local Yolk 310/546-4407 ■ 3414 Highlands Ave (at Rosecranz), Manhattan Beach ■ 6:30am-2:30pm

Real Food Daily [BW,WC] 310/451-7544 ■ 514 Santa Monica Blvd (btwn 5th & 6th) ■ 11:30am-10pm, organic vegetarian ■ www.realfood.com

Wolfgang Puck Cafe 310/393-0290 ■ 1323 Montana Ave (at 14th St), Santa Monica ■ lunch & dinner, colorful entrees à la Puck (fast-food versions)

RETAIL SHOPS
David Aden Gallery 310/396-2949 ■ 350 Sunset Ave, Studio #4 (at 4th), Venice Beach ■ 11am-5pm, fine art photography, large collection of male imagery ■ www.davidaden.com

MEN'S CLUBS
Centaur [MO,V,PC,GO] 310/836-8800 ■ 3341 La Cienega Pl (at Jefferson) ■ 8pm-late Wed-Sun ■ www.clubcentaur.com

Roman Holiday 310/391-0200 ■ 12814 Venice Blvd (at Beethoven), Mar Vista ■ 24hrs

LA—Silverlake

ACCOMMODATIONS
1 **Sanborn GuestHouse** [GS,GO] 323/666-3947, 800/663-7262 ■ 1005 1/2 Sanborn Ave (nr Sunset) ■ private unit w/ kitchen ■ www.sanbornhouse.com

BARS
3 **AKBar** [★GS,NH,D,WC] 323/665-6810 ■ 4356 W Sunset Blvd (at Fountain) ■ 6pm-2am

3 **Cuffs** [★M,L,WC] 323/660-2649 ■ 1941 Hyperion Ave (nr Fountain) ■ 4pm-2am, 2pm-4am wknds, leather/ levi cruise bar

4 **Detour** [M,L,V] 323/664-1189 ■ 4100 Sunset Blvd ■ 3pm-2am, from 2pm wknds, cruise bar

5 **Gauntlet II** [★M,L,WC] 323/669-9472 ■ 4219 Santa Monica Blvd (at Hoover) ■ 4pm-2am, from 2pm Sat, uniform bar, cruisy ■ www.gauntletii.com

6 **Hyperion** [★M,NH,D,MR,S,WC] 323/660-1503 ■ 2810 Hyperion Ave (at Rowena) ■ 1pm-2am, till 4am Sat, Latin night Sat

8 **Little Joy** [GS,NH,MR-L] 213/250-3417 ■ 1477 W Sunset Blvd (at Portia) ■ 4pm-2am, from 1pm wknds

9 **The Other Side** [M,NH,E,OC] 323/661-4233 ■ 2538 Hyperion Ave (at Griffith Park) ■ noon-2am, piano bar

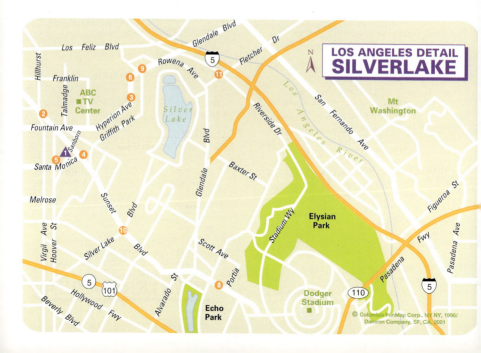

LA—Midtown/Valley • CALIFORNIA

0   Silverlake Lounge [M,NH,MR-L,S] 323/663-9636 ■ 2906 Sunset Blvd (at Silver Lake Blvd) ■ 3pm-2am

NIGHTCLUBS
1   Dragstrip 66 [★GS,D,A,S,$] 323/969-2596 ■ 2500 Riverside Dr (at Fletcher, in 'Rudolpho's') ■ 9pm-4am 2nd Sat, trashy pansexual rock 'n' roll club ■ www.dragstrip66.com

1   Rudolpho's [MW,D,E] 323/669-1226 ■ 2500 Riverside Dr (at Fletcher) ■ 8pm-2am, more gay Sat, theme nights, salsa music & dancing lessons, patio

CAFES
The Coffee Table 323/644-8111 ■ 2930 Rowena Ave ■ 7am-11pm, till midnight wknds, patio, fab mosaic magic

RESTAURANTS
Casita Del Campo [★] 323/662-4255 ■ 1920 Hyperion Ave ■ 11am-10pm, till 11:30pm Fri-Sat, Mexican, patio, also 'The Plush Life' cabaret Sat, call 323/ 969-2596 for details ■ www.plushlife.com

Cha Cha Cha [MW,WC] 323/664-7723 ■ 656 N Virgil (at Melrose) ■ 8am-10pm, till 11pm Fri-Sat, Caribbean, plenty veggie

The Cobalt Cantina [★MW,WC] 323/953-9991 ■ 4326 Sunset Blvd (at Fountain) ■ lunch & dinner, Cal-Mex, some veggie, patio, full bar

The Crest Restaurant 323/660-3645 ■ 3725 Sunset Blvd (at Lucille) ■ 6am-10pm, diner/ Greek

Da Giannino [BW] 323/664-7979 ■ 2630 Hyperion Ave (at Griffith Park Blvd) ■ dinner Tue-Sun, clsd Mon, patio

El Conquistador [BW] 323/666-5136 ■ 3701 W Sunset Blvd (at Lucille) ■ dinner from 4pm, lunch and dinner wknds, Mexican, patio

Lunch to Latenite Kitchen [GO] 323/664-3663 ■ 4348 Fountain Ave (at Sunset Blvd) ■ noon-1am, 10am-3am Fri-Sat, from veggie entrees to chicken & dumplings

Vida 323/660-4446 ■ 1930 Hillhurst Ave (at Franklin, in Los Feliz) ■ 6pm-11pm, hip w/ Asian accent

Zen Restaurant [K] 323/665-2929, 323/665-2930 ■ 2609 Hyperion Ave (at Griffith Park) ■ open late, Japanese, full bar

RETAIL SHOPS
Rough Trade 323/660-7956 ■ 3915 Sunset Blvd ■ noon-10pm, clsd Mon, toys, leather, gifts

GYMS & HEALTH CLUBS
Body Builders [GF] 323/668-0802 ■ 2516 Hyperion Ave (at Griffith Park Blvd)

EROTICA
Circus of Books 323/666-1304 ■ 4001 Sunset Blvd (at Sanborn) ■ 24hrs wknds

LA—Midtown

BARS
The Redhead Bar (Redz) [W,NH,MR-L] 323/263-2995 ■ 2218 E 1st St (btwn Soto & Chicago, Boyle Hts) ■ 2pm-midnight, till 2am wknds

1   Score [MW,NH,D,MR-L,S] 213/625-7382 ■ 107 W 4th St (at Main) ■ 2pm-2am Mon-Th, from 11:30am Fri-Sun, 'Sweatbox' Fri

NIGHTCLUBS
2   Jewel's Catch One Disco [★MW,D,A,MR-AF,K,WC] 323/734-8849 ■ 4067 W Pico Blvd (at Crenshaw) ■ noon-2am, till 5am Fri-Sat, clsd Mon-Tue, women dancers Th & Sat

RESTAURANTS
Atlas [D,E,WC] 213/380-8400 ■ 3760 Wilshire Blvd (at Western) ■ 11am-2am, clsd Sun, global, plenty veggie, full bar ■ www.clubatlas.com

Cassell's 213/480-8668 ■ 3266 W 6th St (at Vermont) ■ 10:30am-4pm, clsd Sun, great burgers

Du-Par's 323/933-8446 ■ 6333 W 3rd St (at the Farmer's Market) ■ 6am-10pm, plush diner schmoozing

MEN'S CLUBS
Midtowne Spa [SW,PC] 213/680-1838 ■ 615 S Kohler (at Central) ■ 24hrs ■ www.midtowne.com

LA—Valley
includes San Fernando & San Gabriel Valleys

BARS
1   Apache Territory [★M,D,K,WC] 818/506-0404 ■ 11608 Ventura Blvd (at Laurel Canyon), Studio City ■ 3pm-2am, from noon wknds

2   Bananas [★M,NH,D,K,S,WC] 818/996-2976 ■ 7026 Reseda Blvd (at Hart), Reseda ■ 3pm-2am, patio, Latin Wed ■ www.bananasbar.com

3   The Bullet [M,L,WC] 818/762-8890 ■ 10522 Burbank Blvd (at Cahuenga), North Hollywood ■ noon-2am, till 4am Fri-Sat, patio ■ www.bulletbar.com

4   Escapades [★MW,NH,D,K,S,WC] 818/508-7008 ■ 10437 Burbank Blvd (at Cahuenga), North Hollywood ■ 1pm-2am

5   Gold 9 [M,NH,K,WC] 818/986-0285 ■ 13625 Moorpark St (at Woodman), Sherman Oaks ■ 11am-2am

California • USA

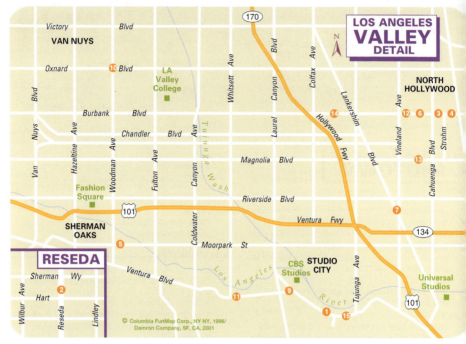

6   **Jox** [M,NH,K] 818/760-9031 ■ 10721 Burbank Blvd (btwn Cahuenga & Vineland), North Hollywood ■ 4pm-2am, from noon wknds

7   **The Lodge** [★M,D,MR-L,MR-AF,S,WC] 818/769-7722 ■ 4923 Lankershim Blvd (at Vineland), North Hollywood ■ 2pm-2am, till 4am wknds, theme nights ■ www.ClubL.net

9   **Oasis** [MW,NH] 818/980-4811 ■ 11916 Ventura Blvd (btwn Laurel Canyon & Colfax), Studio City ■ 2pm-2am, piano bar, patio

10 **Oxwood Inn** [W,NH,D,K] 818/997-9666 (pay phone) ■ 13713 Oxnard (at Woodman), Van Nuys ■ 3pm-2am, from 2pm wknds

12 **Rawhide** [M,D,CW,K,S,WC] 818/760-9798 ■ 10937 Burbank Blvd (nr Vineland), North Hollywood ■ 1pm-2am ■ www.rawhidebar.com

13 **Rumours** [W,NH,D,K] 818/506-9651 ■ 10622 Magnolia Blvd (at Cahuenga), North Hollywood ■ 6pm-2am, from 3pm Fri

14 **Silver Rail** [MW,NH] 818/980-8310 ■ 11518 Burbank Blvd (btwn Colfax & Lankershim) ■ 4pm-2am, from noon wknds

    Sugar Shack [MW,NH,WC] 626/448-5679 ■ 4101 Arden Dr (at Valley Blvd), El Monte ■ 5pm-close, clsd Mon, DJ wknds

Nightclubs

    La Victoria [GS,D,MR-L,F,S] 818/998-8364 ■ 19655 Sherman Way (at Corbin Ave), Reseda ■ 9pm-2am, more gay Wed-Th, dinner served 7:30pm-11pm

15 **Oil Can Harry's** [M,D,CW,S] 818/760-9749 ■ 11502 Ventura Blvd (at Tujunga & Colfax), Studio City ■ 8pm-2am, from 7:30pm Tue & Th, clsd Sun, dance lessons Tue & Th

11 **Queen Mary** [★GF,D,K,S] 818/506-5619 ■ 12449 Ventura Blvd (at Whitsett), Studio City ■ 7pm-2am, from 5pm Fri-Sun, clsd Mon, shows wknds
    ■ www.queenmarynightclub.com

Cafes

    Coffee Junction [E] 818/342-3405 ■ 19221 Ventura Blvd Tarzana ■ 7am-7pm, till 11pm Fri-Sat, 9am-5pm Sun

Restaurants

    Venture Inn [★MW,WC] 818/769-5400 ■ 11938 Ventura Blvd (at Laurel Canyon), Studio City ■ lunch & dinner, champagne brunch wknds, cont'l, full bar

Gyms & Health Clubs

    Gold's Gym 818/506-4600 ■ 6233 N Laurel Canyon Blvd (at Oxnard), North Hollywood

Men's Clubs

    The North Hollywood Spa [V] 818/760-6969 ■ 5636 Vineland (at Burbank) ■ 24hrs, no membership req'd

    Roman Holiday [SW] 818/780-1320 ■ 14435 Victory Blvd (at Van Nuys), Van Nuys ■ 24hrs

Erotica

    Le Sex Shoppe 818/760-9352 ■ 12323 Ventura Blvd (at Laurel Canyon), Studio City ■ 24hrs

    Le Sex Shoppe 818/992-9801 ■ 21625 Sherman Wy (at Nelson), Canoga Park

    Le Sex Shoppe 818/501-9609 ■ 4539 Van Nuys Blvd (at Ventura), Sherman Oaks ■ 24hrs

    Le Sex Shoppe 818/760-9529 ■ 4877 Lankershim Blvd (at Houston), North Hollywood ■ 24hrs

    Stan's Video 818/352-8735 ■ 7505 Foothill Blvd (at Fernglen Blvd), Tujunga ■ till 2am

    Video & Stuff 818/761-3162 ■ 11612 Ventura Blvd (at Colfax), Studio City

Palm Springs

Accommodations

The 550 [★MO,B,V,SW,N] 760/320-7144, 800/669-0550 ■ 550 Warm Sands Dr (at Ramon) ■ hot tub, kitchens, bears welcome ■ www.the550.com

Alexander's Barely Inn [★MO,B,SW,N] 760/327-6911, 800/448-6197 ■ 598 Grenfall Rd (btwn Ramon & Sunny Dunes) ■ hot tub, very bear-friendly ■ www.alexanderpalmsprings.com

All Worlds Resort [MO,SW,N] 760/323-7505, 800/798-8781 ■ 526 Warm Sands Dr (at Ramon) ■ hot tub, intimate & secluded resort, kitchens, spa ■ www.gaytraveling.com/InnTrigue

The Atrium [★MO,SW,N,GO] 760/322-2404, 800/669-1069 ■ 981 Camino Parocela (at Warm Sands) ■ steam & spa ■ www.mirage4men.com

1. Avalon [MO,SW,N,GO] 760/322-2404, 800/669-1069 ■ 568 Warm Sands (at Ramon) ■ spa & steam, porn channels ■ www.mirage4men.com

4. Bacchanal [★MO,SW] 760/323-0760, 800/806-9059 ■ 589 Grenfall Rd (at Parocela) ■ kitchens, hot tub, private patios, mist system ■ www.bacchanal.net

5. Ballantine's [GF,SW] 760/320-1178 ■ 1420 N Indian Canyon Dr (at Vista Chino) ■ '50s chic ■ palmsprings.com/frames/ballantines.html

6. Bee Charmer Inn [WO,SW,NS] 760/778-5883, 888/321-5699 ■ 1600 E Palm Canyon Dr (btwn Calle Marcus & Sunrise) ■ lesbian-owned/ run ■ www.beecharmer.com

7. Camp Palm Springs [★MO,SW,N] 760/322-2267, 800/793-0063 ■ 1466 N Palm Canyon Dr (at Monte Vista) ■ kitchens, sauna ■ www.camp-palm-springs.com

---

Palm Springs

Palm Springs has a well-deserved reputation as one of the top resort destinations for lesbian and gay travelers. The hot desert sun—which shines over 325 days a year—will take even the deepest winter chill out of your bones. Palm Springs boasts a bumper crop of gay men's accommodations, as well as three exclusively for women. Annual events like the White Party and the Nabisco Golf Tournament (aka 'Dinah Shore', which turns Palm Springs into a lesbian paradise) bring visitors from all over the country. For a little danger and an amazing view, catch a ride on the Aerial Tram that goes from the desert floor to the top of Mount San Jacinto. When you come back to earth, it's time to lie back and treat yourself to some sun and outdoor fun.

Queer Resources

AIDS Resources
AIDS Project 760/323-2118.

Recovery
760/324-4880 (AA#).

City Calendar

LGBT Pride
November.

Annual Events
Spring - Nabisco Dinah Shore Golf Tournament 760/324-4546 & 888/443-4624, one of the biggest gatherings of lesbians on the continent. White Party, popular circuit party/fundraiser, web: www.jeffreysanker.com.
December - Out on Film 760/778-4100, lesbian/gay film & cultural festival.

Tourist Info

Airport Directions
Palm Springs Airport. Tahquitz Canyon Dr runs from the airport to the main drag—Palm Canyon Dr. This curves to become E Palm Canyon.

Public Transit & Taxis
Airport Taxi 760/321-4470.
Rainbow Cab 760/325-2868.
Desert Valley Shuttle 760/329-3334 or 800/413-3999.
Sun Line Transit Agency 760/343-3451.

Tourist Spots & Info
Palm Springs Aerial Tramway to the top of Mt San Jacinto, on Tramway Rd.
Visitor's Center: Palm Springs Visitors Bureau 760/778-8418, web: www.palm-springs.org.
Desert Gay Tourism Guild 888/200-4469.

Weather
Palm Springs is sunny and warm in the winter, with temperatures in the 70°s. Summers are scorching (100°+).

Best Views
Top of Mt San Jacinto. Driving through the surrounding desert, you can see great views of the mountains. Be careful in the summer-always carry water in your vehicle, and be sure to check all fluids in your car before you leave and frequently during your trip.

CALIFORNIA • USA

8 ► **Canyon Boys Club** [★MO,SW,N] 760/322-4367, 800/295-2582 ■ 960 N Palm Canyon Dr (btwn Tachevah & El Alameda) ■ kitchens, hot tub & patios ■ www.CanyonBoysClub.com

9 **Casitas Laquita** [WO,SW,NS,WC,GO] 760/416-9999, 877/203-3410 ■ 450 E Palm Canyon Dr (nr Camino Real) ■ resort ■ www.casitaslaquita.com

10 **CCBC Resort Hotel** [★MO,SW,N,WC,GO] 760/324-1350, 800/472-0836 ■ 68-369 Sunair Rd (btwn Melrose & Palo Verde), Cathedral City ■ hot tub, steam ■ www.ccbc-gay-resort.com

11 ► **Chestnutz** [MO,SW,N] 760/325-5269, 800/621-6973 ■ 641 San Lorenzo Rd (at Random) ■ full brkfst, hot tub, private patios ■ www.chestnutz.com

12 ► **The Citadel** [MO,SW,N,GO] 760/325-2686, 877/644-4111 ■ 1491 Via Soledad (at Sonora & S Palm Canyon) ■ full brkfst, jacuzzi, O&A rated '4 palms' ■ www.citadelps.com

13 **Cobalt** [MO,SW,N,GO] 760/416-0168, 888/289-9555 ■ 526 S Camino Real (at Ramon Rd) ■ neo-industrial decor, suites, jacuzzi ■ www.cobaltpsp.com

14 **Columns Resort** [★MO,SW,N,GO] 760/325-0655, 800/798-0655 ■ 537 Grenfall Rd (at Ramon) ■ studios, hot tub ■ www.pscolumns.com

15 **The Desert Bear** [MO,SW,N,GO] 760/325-6767, 877/464-7695 ■ 530 Mel Ave ■ hot tub ■ www.thedesertbear.com

16 **Desert Palms Inn** [M,SW,GO] 760/324-3000, 800/801-8696 ■ 67-580 E Palm Canyon Dr (at Gene Autry Tr), Cathedral City ■ courtyard, bar & restaurant

17 ► **Desert Paradise Resort Hotel** [★MO,SW,N] 760/320-5650, 800/342-7635 ■ 615 Warm Sands Dr (at Parocela) ■ jacuzzi, firepit, outdoor shower ■ www.desertparadise.com

18 ► **The East Canyon Hotel & Spa** [★MO,SW,GO] 760/320-1928, 877/324-6835 ■ 288 E Camino Monte Vista ■ Palm Springs premiere boutique luxury hotel for men, day spa on site, 5-palm award winner by Out & About ■ www.eastcanyonhotel.com

19 **El Mirasol Villas** [★MO,SW,N,GO] 760/327-5913, 800/327-2985 ■ 525 Warm Sands Dr (at Ramon) ■ newly renovated bungalows, eucalyptus steam room & outdoor fireplace ■ www.elmirasol.com

Escape 2 Palm Springs Condo Rentals [GS,SW,GO] 760/323-4848 ■ weekly rates

Canyon Boys Club

Canyon Boys Club

Palm Spring's Largest Gay Resort Since 1993

Quiet, friendly and relaxed clothing optional resort: 32 rooms, 50 ft. pool, 16-man spa, steam room, dry sauna, full gym, in-room video and refrigerators. Kitchens and patios available. New penthouse studios overlook entire pool/courtyard. Walk to downtown shops and restaurants. Convenient to nightlife. www.canyon-boysclub.com

PHONE **800/295-2582** or **760/322-4367**

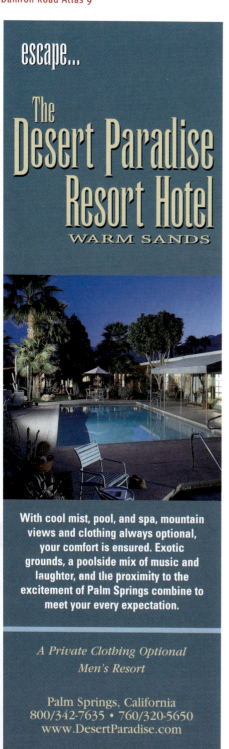
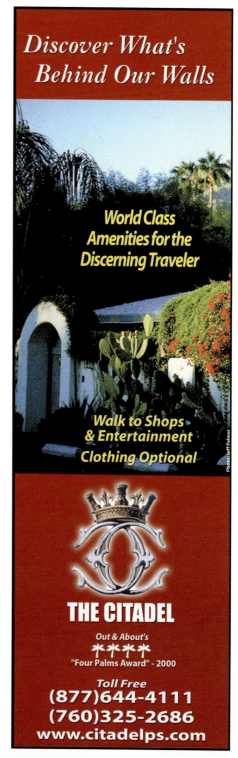

CALIFORNIA • USA

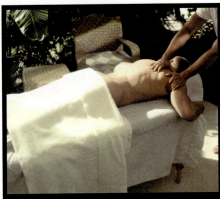

East Canyon Hotel & Spa

A Luxury Men's Resort
Day Spa on Site Offering
Complete Facial
& Body Treatments

"Stunning new 5 Palm Property, think Four Seasons comforts and amenities, but even more attentive service…"
Out and About 2000

877.324.6843
760.320.1928
288 E. Camino Monte Vista
Palm Springs, CA 92262
www.eastcanyonhotel.com

---

20 **Estrella Inn & Villas** [GF,SW] 760/320-4117, 800/237-3687 ■ 415 S Belardo Rd (at Ramon) ■ jacuzzi ■ www.estrella.com

21 **Five Palms Guest House** [M,SW] 760/778-6178 ■ 3755 Calle de Ricardo ■ 2 furnished studios in quiet setting, kitchenettes ■ www.fivepalmsps.com

22 ▶ **The Hacienda at Warm Sands** [★MO,V,SW,N,WC,GO] 760/327-8111, 800/359-2007 ■ 586 Warm Sands Dr (at Parocela) ■ 2 pools & hot tub ■ www.thehacienda.com

23 **Harlow Club Hotel** [MO,SW] 760/323-3977, 888/547-7881 ■ 175 E El Alameda (at Palm Canyon) ■ lunch buffet, hot tub, gym ■ www.harlowhotel.com

24 **Indianola Tiki Guest House** [MO,SW] 760/323-3203, 877/337-0393 ■ 354 E Stevens Rd (at Indian Canyon) ■ B&B decorated in hip '50s 'Polynesian Pop' style, full kitchens ■ www.indianola-tiki.com

25 **Ingleside Inn** [GF,F,SW,NS,WC] 760/325-0046, 800/772-6655 ■ 200 W Ramon Rd (at Palm Canyon Dr) ■ jacuzzi, also restaurant, cont'l ■ www.inglesideinn.com

26 ▶ **Inn Exile** [★MO,F,SW,N] 760/327-6413, 800/962-0186 ■ 545 Warm Sands Dr (at Ramon) ■ resort, hot tub, gym ■ www.innexile.com

27 ▶ **INNdulge Palm Springs** [★MO,SW,N] 760/327-1408, 800/833-5675 ■ 601 Grenfall Rd (at Parocela) ■ hot tub ■ www.inndulge.com

28 **Inntimate** [MO,SW,N,WC,GO] 760/778-8334, 800/695-3846 ■ 556 Warms Sands Dr (at Ramon) ■ theinntimate.com

30 **La Posada** [★MO,SW,N] 760/323-1402, 888/411-4949 ■ 120 W Vereda Sur (at N Palm Canyon) ■ jacuzzi, private garden ■ www.laposada.com

31 **Mirage** [MO,SW,N,GO] 760/322-2404, 800/669-1069 ■ 555 Grenfall Rd (at Ramon) ■ private resort, kitchens, waterfall, spa & steam ■ www.mirage4men.com

32 **Mountain View Villa** [GS,SW,NS,GO] 305/294-1525 (FL#) ■ vacation rental at Mesquite Country Club ■ www.vacationdepot.com

33 **Pink Coyote Resort** [M,SW] 760/318-0519, 877/845-5200 ■ 370 W Arenas Rd ■ spa, 180° view of mtns ■ www.PinkCoyotePS.com

---

Inn Exile

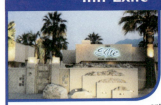

Close your eyes and fantasize about a place where being gay is a way of life and clothing is always optional. Inn Exile is walled, gated, and located on 2 1/2 acres. With 4 pools and 2 jacuzzis, there is a place to splash around everywhere you look. Also featured are a steam room, complete gymnasium, billiard room, and an outdoor fireplace lit at sunset. The atmosphere couldn't be more inviting.

545 Warm Sands Dr., Palm Springs, CA 92264
www.innexile.com

PHONE 800/962-0186 or 760/327-6413

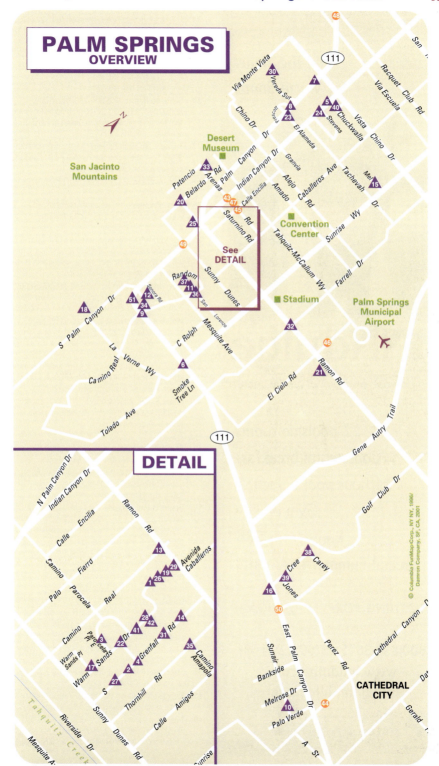

CALIFORNIA • USA

In the Heart of Warm Sands

INNdulge
PALM SPRINGS
"to pamper, pleasure, or gratify oneself"

22 poolside rooms
Continental breakfast
24 hour pool & Jacuzzi
Gym on site
Rates from $85
Special Summer Discounts

CLOTHING FOREVER OPTIONAL

(800)833-5675 ▼ (760)327-1408
www.inndulge.com
info@inndulge.com
Fax (760)327-7273

601 Grenfall Road, at Parocela
Palm Springs, CA 92264

IGLTA

---

34 **Queen of Hearts Resort** [WO,SW] 760/322-5793, 888/275-9903 ■ 435 E Avenida Olancha ■ full kitchens ■ www.queenofheartsps.com

35 **Sago Palms Resort** [MO,SW,N,NS] 760/323-0224, 800/626-7246 ■ 595 Thornhill Rd (btwn Sunny Dunes & Ramon) ■ hot tub, kitchens, fireplaces, patios ■ www.webworksps.com/sago/

36 **Santiago Resort** [MO,SW,N] 760/322-1300, 800/710-7729 ■ 650 San Lorenzo Rd (at Mesquite) ■ hot tub, sauna & shower garden, brkfst & lunch included ■ www.santiagoresort.com

37 **Triangle Inn Palm Springs** [★MO,SW,N] 760/322-7993, 800/732-7555 ■ 555 San Lorenzo Rd (at Random Rd) ■ hot tub ■ www.triangle-inn.com

51 **Vagabond Inn** [GS,SW,NS,GO] 760/325-7211 ■ 1699 S Palm Canyon

39 **Villa Mykonos** [MW,SW] 760/321-2898, 800/471-4753 ■ 67-590 Jones Rd (at Cree), Cathedral City ■ www.villamykonos.com

38 **The Villa—Palm Springs** [★GS,F,SW] 760/328-7211, 800/845-5265 ■ 67-670 Carey Rd (at Cree), Cathedral City ■ bungalows, swimming, also 2 restaurants & bars ■ www.thevilla.com

40 **Ville Orleans Resort** [M,SW,N,GO] 760/864-6201, 800/700-8075 ■ 269 Chuckwalla Rd ■ rms, studios & courtyard villas, also sports spa ■ www.villeorleans.com

Viola's Resort [MW,SW,N,GO] 760/318-8400, 800/843-6908 ■ 1200 S Palm Canyon Dr ■ 'hotel w/ B&B feel for gays & lesbians, their families & their friends' ■ violasresort.com

41 **Vista Grande Villa** [★MO,SW,N,GO] 760/322-2404, 800/669-1069 ■ 574 Warm Sands Dr (at Ramon) ■ private resort, kitchens ■ www.mirage4men.com

42 **Warm Sands Villas** [MO,SW,N] 760/323-3005, 800/357-5695 ■ 555 Warm Sands Dr (at Ramon) ■ hot tub ■ warmsandsvillas.com

BARS

43 **Badlands** [M,NH] 760/778-4264 ■ 200 S Indian Canyon Dr (at Arenas) ■ 8am-2am, from 6am wknds

38 **Dates** [M] 760/328-7211 ■ 67-670 Carey Rd (at 'The Villa' resort), Cathedral City ■ 11am-midnight, poolside bar, patio, also cafe w/ brkfst, lunch & dinner

16 **Desert Palms' Poolside Bar** [★M,F,E] 760/324-3000, 800/801-8696 ■ 67-580 E Palm Canyon Dr (at the 'Desert Palms Inn'), Cathedral City ■ 10am-close, from 9am wknds

44 **Ground Zero** [MW,D,K] 760/321-0031 ■ 36-737 Cathedral Canyon Dr (at Commercial), Cathedral City ■ 2pm-2am, country/ western Sat

45 **Hunter's** [★M,D,V] 760/323-0700 ■ 302 E Arenas Rd (at Calle Encilia) ■ 10am-2am, video bar

46 **Oscar's** [MW,NH] 760/325-7072 ■ 440 El Cielo Rd (off Ramon) ■ 11am-midnight, bar & grill (food till 10pm)

Skip's Cabana Club [M,F] 760/341-7547 ■ 71-380 Hwy 111 (at Bob Hope), Rancho Mirage ■ 11:30am-midnight, till 1am wknds, also restaurant, lunch, dinner & Sun brunch, patio ■ SkipsClub@aol.com

47 **Streetbar** [★M,NH,WC] 760/320-1266 ■ 224 E Arenas Rd (at Indian) ■ 10am-2am

48 **Sweetwater Saloon** [MW,NH,F,E] 760/320-8878 ■ 2420 N Palm Canyon (at Racquet Club Dr) ■ 11am-2am

49 **Tool Shed** [M,NH,L] 760/320-3299 ■ 600 E Sunny Dunes Rd (at Palm Canyon) ■ 8am-2am, 6am-4am wknds, call for events, also leather shop ■ www.toolshed-ps.com

Palm Springs • CALIFORNIA

The Wolf's Den [M,D,B,L] 760/321-9688 ■ 67-625 E Palm Canyon (at Canyon Plaza), Cathedral City ■ 2pm-2am, 'a man's bar', patio, cruisy ■ www.wolfsdenbar.com

RESTAURANTS

Billy Reed's 760/325-1946 ■ 1800 N Palm Canyon Rd (at Vista Chino) ■ some veggie, bakery, full bar

Coffee Dot Com [★] 760/322-5280 ■ 241 Tahquitz Canyon Wy ■ 7am-9pm, Internet access, full bar

El Gallito Mexican Restaurant [BW] 760/328-7794 ■ 68820 Grove St (at Palm Canyon), Cathedral City

Las Casuelas 760/325-3213 ■ 368 N Palm Canyon Dr (btwn Amado & Alejo) ■ 10am-11pm, traditional Mexican, some veggie

Le Peep 760/416-1444 ■ 2665 E Palm Canyon Dr ■ brkfst & lunch only

The Left Bank 760/320-6116 ■ 150 E Vista Chino (at Indian Canyon) ■ dinner only, French, full bar

Maria's Italian Cuisine [BW] 760/328-4378 ■ 67-778 Hwy 111 (at Perez), Cathedral City ■ 5:30pm-9:30pm, clsd Mon, plenty veggie

Muriel's Supper Club 760/325-8839 ■ 210 S Palm Canyon Dr ■ clsd Mon-Tue, super swanky ($$$) & fun ■ www.muriels.com

Rainbow Cactus Cafe [E] 760/325-3868 ■ 212 S Indian Canyon (at Arenas) ■ lunch & dinner, Sun brunch only, authentic Mexican, full bar

Red Tomato [BW,WC] 760/328-7518 ■ 68-784 E Palm Canyon (btwn Date Palm & Cathedral Canyon), Cathedral City ■ 5pm-10pm, Italian

Shame on the Moon [WC] 760/324-5515 ■ 69-950 Frank Sinatra Dr (at Hwy 111), Rancho Mirage ■ 6pm-10:30pm, cont'l, some veggie, patio, full bar

Simba's [E] 760/778-7630 ■ 190 N Sunrise ■ lunch & dinner, clsd Mon-Tue, ribs

SweetHeat Palm Springs [BW,GO] 760/323-5691 ■ 448 S Indian Canyon Dr (at Ramon) ■ dinner only, clsd Mon ■ www.sweetheat.net

Tomboyz Cafe [BW] 760/322-9915 ■ 214 E Arenas Rd (at Indian) ■ 7am-11pm

Triangles 760/321-9555 ■ 68-805 Hwy 111, Cathedral City ■ 5pm-10pm, till midnight Fri-Sat

The Wilde Goose [E] 760/328-5775 ■ 67-938 Hwy 111 (at Perez), Cathedral City ■ 5pm-close, cont'l/ wild game, some veggie, full bar

ENTERTAINMENT & RECREATION

Ruddy's 1930s General Store Museum 760/327-2156 ■ 221 S Palm Canyon Dr ■ 10am-4pm Th-Sun, 'the most you can spend is 50¢'

RETAIL SHOPS

Blink 760/323-1667 ■ 319 E Arenas Rd (at Indian Canyon) ■ noon-10pm, books, queer gifts & clothing

Bravo for Men 760/322-3077 ■ 328 N Palm Canyon Dr (at Amado)

GayMartUSA 760/416-6474 ■ 305 E Arenas Rd (at Indian Canyon) ■ www.gaymartusa.com

PUBLICATIONS

The Bottom Line 760/323-0552 ■ lgbt bar guide & classifieds ■ www.psbottomline.com

Desert Daily Guide 760/320-3237 ■ lgbt weekly ■ www.desertdailyguide.com

Gay/ Lesbian Times 760/320-5676 ■ lgbt newsmagazine for the Desert ■ editorps@uptownpub.com

GYMS & HEALTH CLUBS

Basic Gym [GF] 760/320-1009 ■ 1584 S Palm Canyon Dr ■ 6am-8pm, 8am-2pm wknds, day passes available

Gold's Gym [GF] 760/322-4653 ■ 40-70 Airport Center Dr (at Ramon)

Muscle Club [GF] 760/325-8898 ■ 441 S Calle Encilia #5 ■ 6am-8pm, 8am-6pm wknds, day passes available

EROTICA

Black Moon Leather 760/322-5924 ■ 531 Industrial Pl ■ noon-9pm, till 2am Fri-Sat, clsd Mon-Tue; also 'Tool Shed' bar location

Hidden Joy Book Shop 760/328-1694 ■ 68-424 Commercial (at Cathedral Canyon), Cathedral City ■ 24hrs

World Wide Book Store 760/321-1313 ■ 68-300 Ramon Rd (at Cathedral Canyon), Cathedral City

RUSSIAN RIVER

The Russian River resort area is hidden in the redwood forests of northern California, an hour and a half north of the San Francisco Bay Area. If you're in the mood for soothing and sensual delights, you're in luck. Life at 'the River' is laid back. You can take a canoe ride, hike under the redwoods, or just lie on the river bank and soak up the sun. 'The River' is in the heart of the famous California Wine Country. Plan a tour to the many wineries, or see some of the world's most beautiful coastline as you cruise the car along the Pacific Coast Highway—only fifteen minutes away!

Queer Resources

COMMUNITY INFO
Gay/Lesbian Business Association (GLBA) 707/869-9000 (24hr touchtone), web: www.gayrussianriver.com.

AIDS RESOURCES
Face To Face 707/869-7390.

RECOVERY
Santa Rosa AA 707/544-1300.

City Calendar

ANNUAL EVENTS
May & September - Women's Weekend 707/869-9000.
September - Jazz Festival.

Tourist Info

AIRPORT DIRECTIONS
The closest airport is the Sonoma County Airport in Santa Rosa, or San Francisco International, 2 hours south.

PUBLIC TRANSIT & TAXIS
Bill's Taxi Service 707/869-2177.
The area is easiest to reach by car.

TOURIST SPOTS & INFO
Armstrong Redwood State Park.
Bodega Bay.
Mudbaths of Calistoga.
Wineries of Napa and Sonoma counties.
Visitor's Center: Russian River Visitors Info 800/253-8800.

WEATHER
Summer days are sunny and warm (80°s-90°s) but usually begin with a dense fog. Winter days have the same pattern but are a lot cooler and wetter. Winter nights can be very damp and chilly (low 40°s).

BEST VIEWS
Anywhere in Armstrong Woods, the Napa Wine Country and on the ride along the coast on Highway 1.

Russian River

ACCOMMODATIONS

1 **Applewood** [GF,F,SW,NS] 707/869-9093, 800/555-8509 ■ 13555 Hwy 116 (at Mays Canyon), Guerneville ■ 21+, full brkfst ■ www.applewoodinn.com

2 **Avalon Inn** [GF,SW] 707/869-9566 ■ 16484 4th St (at Brookside Ln), Guerneville

   Eagle's Peak [M,GO] 707/887-9218 ■ 11644 Our Peak Rd (at McPeak Rd), Forestville ■ vacation house w/ deck & spa on 26 acres ■ eaglespeak.net

3 **Faerie Ring Campground** [GF,GO] 707/869-2746 ■ 16747 Armstrong Woods Rd, Guerneville ■ on 14 acres, camping & RV ■ marvel@sonic.net

   Fern Falls [★MW,NS,GO] 707/632-6108 ■ beautiful hideaway beside waterfall, hot tub, weight room ■ www.fernfalls.com

4 **Fife's Resort** [MW,F,SW,WC] 707/869-9500, 800/734-3371 ■ 16467 River Rd (at Brookside Ln), Guerneville ■ cabins & campsites, also full bar (M,D) & restaurant ■ www.fifes.com

5 ▶ **Highlands Resort** [MW,SW,N] 707/869-0333 ■ 14000 Woodland Dr, Guerneville ■ country retreat on 4 wooded acres, hot tub ■ www.HighlandsResort.com

6 **Huckleberry Springs Country Inn & Spa** [GF,V,SW,NS] 707/865-2683, 800/822-2683 ■ 8105 Old Beedle, Monte Rio ■ full brkfst, private cottages, Japanese spa, massage therapy ■ www.huckleberrysprings.com

   Jacques' Cottage at Russian River [MW,SW,N] 707/575-1033 ■ 6471 Old Trenton Rd, Forestville ■ hot tub ■ www.wco.com/~jacques

   Redwood Properties [GS,NS] 707/869-7368 ■ rental homes, some w/ pools & hot tubs ■ www.russianriverrental.com

7 ▶ **Retreat Resort & Spa** [GS,SW,NS,GO] 707/869-2706, 866/737-3529 ■ 14711 Armstrong Woods Rd, Guerneville ■ newly renovated 4-acre resort w/ full-service spa, jacuzzi ■ www.retreatresort.com

8 **Rio Villa Beach Resort** [GF] 707/865-1143 ■ 20292 Hwy 116 (at Bohemian Hwy), Monte Rio ■ cabins on the river ■ www.riovilla.com

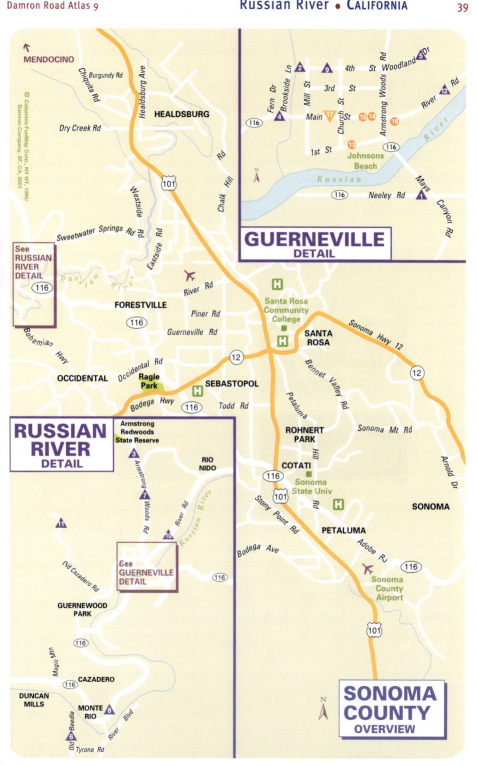

CALIFORNIA • USA

retreat
RESORT + SPA

experience the new russian river

Photos by Robert Bengtson

4 acres
day spa
pool
jacuzzi
deluxe rooms
sumptuous robes
thick towels
fireplaces
cable tv + dvd
cd players
complimentary breakfast
sundecks
kitchenettes
wine tasting
bicycle rentals
hiking trails
ample parking

your hosts . gus . scott . lou

Russian River • CALIFORNIA

retreat@retreatresort.com
www.retreatresort.com

luxury . service . total rejuvenation

reservations | 866.73.RELAX
office | 707.869.2706

14711 ARMSTRONG WOODS ROAD . GUERNEVILLE . CA 95446

CALIFORNIA • USA

River Village Resort & Spa [GS,SW] 707/869-8139, 800/529-3376 ■ 14880 River Rd, Guerneville ■ cottages, hot tub ■ www.rivervillageresort.com

9 **Russian River Resort/ Triple 'R' Resort** [MW,E,V,SW,N,WC] 707/869-0691, 800/417-2763 ■ 16390 4th St (at Mill), Guerneville ■ hot tub, also bar & restaurant, some veggie ■ www.RussianRiverResort.com

Russian River View Retreat [GF,SW] 707/869-3040 ■ vacation home w/ deck, hot tub, private dock & boat ■ RussianRiverView.com

10 **Schoolhouse Canyon Park** [GF,SW] 707/869-2311 ■ 12600 River Rd (at Oddfellows Park Rd), Guerneville ■ open May-Sept, private beach, camping & RV

Tim & Tony's Treehouse [GS,SW,N,NS,GO] 707/887-9531, 888/887-9531 ■ studio cottage, hot tub, sauna

11 **Wildwood Resort Retreat** [GF,SW] 707/632-5321 ■ Old Cazadero Rd (off River Rd), Guerneville ■ facilities are for groups of 20 or more ■ www.wildwoodretreat.com

12 **The Willows** [MW,NS] 707/869-2824, 800/953-2828 ■ 15905 River Rd (at Hwy 116), Guerneville ■ old-fashioned lodge & campground ■ www.willowsrussianriver.com

BARS

13 **Mc T's Bullpen** [GS,NH,WC] 707/869-3377 ■ 16246 1st St (at Church), Guerneville ■ 8am-2am, sports bar, patio

14 **Rainbow Cattle Co** [M,NH] 707/869-0206 ■ 16220 Main St (at Armstrong Woods Rd), Guerneville ■ 6am-2am

15 **The Russian River Eagle** [MW,NH,A,B,L,WC] 707/869-3400 ■ 16225 Main St (at Armstrong Woods Rd), Guerneville ■ noon-2am, Bruce the Barber spins on wknds ■ www.russianrivereagle.com

NIGHTCLUBS

16 **Club Fab** [★,M,D,S] 707/869-5708 ■ 16135 River Rd (at Armstrong Woods Rd), Guerneville ■ 9pm-2am, 4pm-close Sun, clsd Mon-Wed, 4 levels ■ www.fabpresents.com

CAFES

Coffee Bazaar 707/869-9706 ■ 14045 Armstrong Woods Rd (at River Rd), Guerneville ■ 6am-8pm, soups, salads & pastries

RESTAURANTS

Big Bertha's Burgers [BW] 707/869-2239 ■ 16357 Main St, Guerneville ■ 11am-9pm

Highlands Resort

At the Russian River

Adult resort on three beautifully landscaped acres with mature Redwood trees. Stay in cottages with fireplaces, some with wet bars or kitchenettes. Single rooms are available with private or shared bath. Enjoy the rustic atmosphere (no TV's or phones). Clothing optional pool & hot tub. Enjoy a complimentary continental breakfast. Camping during the summer. Day use. A short walk to town. Rates from $45-125.

PHONE **707/869-0333**

Burdon's [MW,WC] 707/869-2615 ■ 15405 River Rd (at Orchard Rd), Guerneville ■ dinner Wed-Sat, cont'l/ pasta, plenty veggie, full bar

Cape Fear Cafe 707/865-9246 ■ 25191 Main St, Duncans Mills ■ 9am-9pm, clsd 3pm-5pm

Cat's Place at George's Hideaway 707/869-3634 ■ 18100 Hwy 116 (at Old Cazadero Rd) ■ 4pm-9pm, till 10pm wknds, clsd Mon-Tue, homecooking, full bar

Flavors Unlimited 707/869-0425 ■ 16450 Main St/ River Rd, Guerneville ■ hrs vary, custom-blended ice cream

Mill St Grill [MW,WC] 707/869-0691 ■ 16390 4th St (at 'Triple 'R' Resort'), Guerneville ■ some veggie, full bar, patio

River Inn Restaurant [WC] 707/869-0481 ■ 16141 Main St, Guerneville ■ seasonal, local favorite

Sweet's River Grill [★] 707/869-3383 ■ 16251 Main St (at Armstrong Woods Rd), Guerneville ■ 11am-9pm, full bar

BOOKSTORES

17 **River Reader** [WC] 707/869-2240 ■ 16355 Main St (at Mill), Guerneville ■ 10am-6pm, extended hrs in summer

RETAIL SHOPS

Up the River 707/869-3167 ■ 16212 Main St (at Armstrong Woods Rd), Guerneville ■ cards, gifts, T-shirts

San Diego

ACCOMMODATIONS

1 **Balboa Park Inn** [GF] 619/298-0823, 800/938-8181 ■ 3402 Park Blvd (at Upas) ■ charming guest house in the heart of San Diego ■ www.balboaparkinn.com

5 **Beach Area B&B/ Elsbree House** [GF,NS] 619/226-4133 ■ 5054 Narragansett Ave (at Sunset Cliffs Blvd) ■ 3-bdrm condo ■ www.oceanbeach-online.com/b&b

2 **The Beach Place** [MW,N] 619/225-0746 ■ 2158 Sunset Cliffs Blvd (at Muir) ■ apts, hot tub, nr beach ■ www.beach.place.cc

3 **The Blom House B&B on Kensington** [GF,NS] 858/467-0890, 800/797-2566 ■ 1372 Minden Dr (nr Friars & Ulric) ■ 1948 cottage-style home, also condo, full brkfst ■ www.bbhost.com/blomhousekensington

4 **Dmitri's Guesthouse** [MW,SW,N,NS,WC] 619/238-5547 ■ 931 21st St (at Broadway) ■ overlooks downtown, hot tub ■ dmitrisbb@aol.com

6 **The Gallery B&B** [W] 619/692-0041, 888/355-6439 ■ 1404 Meade Ave (at Maryland St) ■ 1907 home, spa ■ www.gallerybandb.com

7 **Harbor House Resort** [MO] 619/338-9966, 888/338-9966 ■ 642 W Hawthorn (btwn Columbia & State) ■ outdoor jacuzzis, also 'Moby Dick's' bar ■ www.HarborHouseResort.com

8 **Hillcrest Inn Hotel** [MW,WC] 619/293-7078, 800/258-2280 ■ 3754 5th Ave (btwn Robinson & Pennsylvania) ■ int'l hotel in the heart of Hillcrest, hot tub ■ hillcrestinn@juno.com

9 **Inn Suites Hotel** [GF,F,SW,WC] 619/296-2101 ■ 2223 El Cajon Blvd (btwn Louisiana & Mississippi) ■ also restaurant ■ www.innsuites.com

10 **Keating House** [GF,NS,GO] 619/239-8585, 800/995-8644 ■ 2331 2nd Ave (at Juniper) ■ 150-yr-old Victorian on Bankers Hill, full brkfst ■ www.keatinghouse.com

11 **Park Manor Suites** [GF] 619/291-0999, 800/874-2649 ■ 525 Spruce St (btwn 5th & 6th) ■ 1926 hotel ■ www.parkmanorsuites.com

San Diego • California

San Diego

San Diego is a west coast paradise. This city sprawls from the bays and beaches of the Pacific to the foothills of the desert mountains. In addition to the world-famous San Diego Zoo, visitors will find the beautiful weather perfect for outdoor activities, including the country's largest gay rodeo event every September. The Hillcrest area is home to San Diego's gay and lesbian community.

Queer Resources

Community Info
▼ Lesbian/Gay Community Center 619/692-2077. 3909 Centre St, 9am-10pm, till 7pm Sat, till 5pm Sun.

AIDS Resources
800/590-2437.

Recovery
Live & Let Live Alano Club 619/298-8008. 3867 Monroe St, 10:30am-10pm, from 8:30am wknds.

City Calendar

LGBT Pride
July. 619/297-7683, web: www.sdpride.org.

Tourist Info

Airport Directions
San Diego International – Take Harbor Dr east, then left on Laurel. For the women's bars, go left toward India. To get to Hillcrest area, take a left on 5th up to University.

Public Transit & Taxis
Orange Cab 619/234-6161.
San Diego Cab 619/232-6566.
Silver Cab/Co-op 619/280-5555.
Cloud Nine Shuttle 800/974-8885.
San Diego Transit System 619/233-3004. San Diego Trolley (through downtown or to Tijuana).

Tourist Spots & Info
Globe Theatre 619/231-1941.
San Diego Wild Animal Park 760/747-8702.
San Diego Zoo 619/234-3153.
Sea World 619/226-3915.
Visitor's Center: San Diego Visitors Bureau 619/232-3101, web: www.sandiego.com.

Weather
San Diego is sunny and warm (upper 60°s-70°s) year-round, with higher humidity in the summer.

Best Views
Cabrillo National Monument on Point Loma or from a harbor cruise.

Drink Specials

Smoke Friendly Patio

Patio Giant Screen TV • Pool Table • Video Games • Pinballs

The Place To Be.... Noon - 2am

#1 Fifth Ave.
3845 FIFTH AVE SAN DIEGO CA.
(619) 299-1911

photo: Brad Eriksen

CALIFORNIA • USA

12 **Villa Serena B&B** [GF,SW] 619/224-1451, 888/416-7415 ■ 2164 Rosecrans St (btwn Udall & Voltaire) ■ Italian villa in residential neighborhood ■ www.villaserena.org

BARS

13 **Bourbon Street** [★M,E] 619/291-0310 ■ 4612 Park Blvd (at Adams) ■ 2pm-2am, from 11am wknds, piano & jazz ■ tomox@aol.com

14 **The Brass Rail** [MW,D,WC] 619/298-2233 ■ 3796 5th Ave (at Robinson) ■ noon-2am

15 **The Caliph** [M,P,E,K,OC] 619/298-9495 ■ 3100 5th Ave (at Redwood) ■ 11am-2am, piano bar

16 **Chee Chee Club** [M,NH] 619/234-4404 ■ 929 Broadway (at 9th Ave) ■ 6am-2am, hustlers

17 **Cheers** [M,NH,F] 619/298-3269 ■ 1839 Adams Ave (at Park) ■ 10am-2am, from 9am wknds, brunch Sun

18 **Club Bombay** [★W,D,F,E,WC] 619/296-6789 ■ 3175 India St (enter on Spruce St) ■ 4pm-2am, from 2pm wknds, Sun BBQ ■ clubbombay@home.com

19 **The Flame** [★W,D] 619/295-4163 ■ 3780 Park Blvd (at University) ■ 5pm-2am, from 4pm Fri

20 **Flick's** [★M,V,YC] 619/297-2056 ■ 1017 University Ave (at 10th Ave) ■ 2pm-2am ■ www.sdflicks.com

21 **The Hole** [M,D,LS] 619/226-9019 ■ 2820 Lytton St (at Rosecrans) ■ 2pm-2am, from noon Sat-Mon ■ www.theholesandiego.com

22 **Kickers** [★M,D,CW,WC] 619/491-0400 ■ 308 University Ave (at 3rd Ave) ■ 7pm-2am (lessons 7pm Wed-Sat), T-dance Sun

23 **The Loft** [M,NH,WC] 619/296-6407 ■ 3610 5th Ave (at Brookes) ■ 11am-2am

7 **Moby Dick's** [M] 619/338-9942 ■ 642 W Hawthorn (at Harbor House Resort) ■ noon-10pm ■ www.HarborHouseResort.com

24▶ **No 1 Fifth Ave (no sign)** [M,P,V] 619/299-1911 ■ 3845 5th Ave (at University) ■ noon-2am, patio

25 **Numbers** [★M,D,V,WC] 619/294-9005 ■ 3811 Park Blvd (at University) ■ noon-2am, patio

26 **Pecs** [M,L,WC] 619/296-0889 ■ 2046 University Ave (at Alabama) ■ noon-2am

27 **Redwing Bar & Grill** [M] 619/281-8700 ■ 4012 30th St (at Lincoln) ■ 10am-midnight, till 2am Fri-Sat, cocktail lounge, patio

28 **Shooterz/ Club Odyssey** [M,NH,D] 619/574-0744 ■ 3815 30th St (at University) ■ noon-2am, sports & cruise bar ■ shooterzbar@juno.com

29 **SRO Lounge** [M,NH,P,OC] 619/232-1886 ■ 1807 5th Ave (at Elm) ■ 10am-2am

30 **Wolf's** [M,L,BW] 619/291-3730 ■ 3404 30th St (at Upas) ■ 8pm-4am, leather shop in back

31 **Zone** [M,NH,L,WC] 619/295-8072 ■ 3040 North Park Wy (at 30th) ■ 4pm-2am, from 2pm wknds ■ www.zonesd.com

NIGHTCLUBS

32 **Club Montage** [★M,D,F,E,V,WC] 619/294-9590 ■ 2028 Hancock St (at Washington Ave) ■ 8pm-2am, till 4am Fri-Sat ■ www.clubmontage.com

33 **Rich's** [★M,D,V,YC] 619/295-2195, 619/497-4588 (club line) ■ 1051 University Ave (at Vermont) ■ open Th-Sun ■ www.richs-sandiego.com

CAFES

The Big Kitchen [WC] 619/234-5789 ■ 3003 Grape St (at 30th) ■ 8am-2pm, 7am-3pm wknds, some veggie

Cafe Roma 858/450-2141 ■ UCSD Price Center #76 (at Voight), La Jolla ■ 7am-midnight

David's Place [MW,E,WC] 619/296-4173 ■ 3766 5th Ave (at Robinson) ■ 7am-midnight, till 1am wknds, coffeehouse for positive people & their friends, patio

Extraordinary Desserts 619/294-7001 ■ 2929 5th Ave ■ 8:30am-11pm, till midnight Fri-Sat, the name says it all

RESTAURANTS

Adams Avenue Grill [BW,WC,GO] 619/298-8440 ■ 2201 Adams Ave (at Mississippi) ■ lunch, dinner & Sun brunch, bistro

Bayou Bar & Grill [WC] 619/696-8783 ■ 329 Market St (btwn 3rd & 4th) ■ lunch & dinner, Sun brunch, Creole/ Cajun

Cafe Eleven [WC] 619/260-8023 ■ 1440 University Ave (at Normal) ■ dinner, clsd Mon, country French, some veggie

California Cuisine [WC] 619/543-0790 ■ 1027 University Ave (at 10th Ave) ■ 11am-10pm, clsd Mon, French/ Italian, some veggie

City Deli [BW] 619/295-2747 ■ 535 University Ave (at 6th Ave) ■ 7am-midnight, till 2am Fri-Sat, NY deli, plenty veggie

The Cottage 858/454-8409 ■ 7702 Fay (at Klein), La Jolla ■ 7:30am-3pm, fresh-baked items

Crest Cafe [WC] 619/295-2510 ■ 425 Robinson (btwn 4th & 5th) ■ 7am-midnight, some veggie

Hamburger Mary's [WC] 619/491-0400 ■ 308 University Ave (at 3rd) ■ 9am-11pm, till midnight wknds, some veggie, full bar, patio ■ www.hamburgermarys.com

Liaison [WC] 619/234-5540 ■ 2202 4th Ave (at Ivy) ■ dinner only, clsd Mon, French country, prix fixe dinner

Lips 619/295-7900 ■ 2770 5th Ave (at Olive) ■ clsd Mon, 'the ultimate in drag dining', 'Bitchy Bingo' Wed, DJ wknds ■ www.lipsrestaurant.com

The Mission [MW,GO] 858/488-9060 ■ 3795 Mission Blvd (at San Jose), Mission Beach ■ brkfst & lunch

Mixx [MW,E,GO] 619/299-6499 ■ 3671 5th Ave ■ dinner only

Vegetarian Zone 619/298-7302 ■ 2949 5th Ave (at Quince) ■ 10am-9pm, deli & restaurant

ENTERTAINMENT & RECREATION

Aztec Bowl 619/283-3135 ■ 4356 30th St, North Park ■ gay Th night

Diversionary Theatre 619/220-6830, 619/220-0097 (box office #) ■ 4545 Park Blvd #101 (at Madison) ■ lgbt theater ■ www.diversionary.org

BOOKSTORES

Groundworks Books [WC] 858/452-9625 ■ UCSD Student Center 0323 (at Gilman Dr), La Jolla ■ 9am-7pm, 10am-6pm Fri-Sat, clsd Sun, alternative, lgbt section

34 **Obelisk the Bookstore** [WC] 619/297-4171 ■ 1029 University Ave (at 10th) ■ 10am-11pm, till 9pm Sun, lgbt ■ www.obeliskbooks.com

RETAIL SHOPS

Auntie Helen's [WC] 619/584-8728 ■ 4028 30th St (at Lincoln) ■ 10am-5pm, clsd Sun-Mon, thrift shop benefits PWAs

Flesh Skin Grafix 619/424-8983 ■ 1155 Palm Ave, Imperial Beach ■ tattoos & piercing

GayMartUSA 619/543-1221 ■ 550 University Ave (at 6th Ave) ■ 10am-10pm ■ www.gaymartusa.com

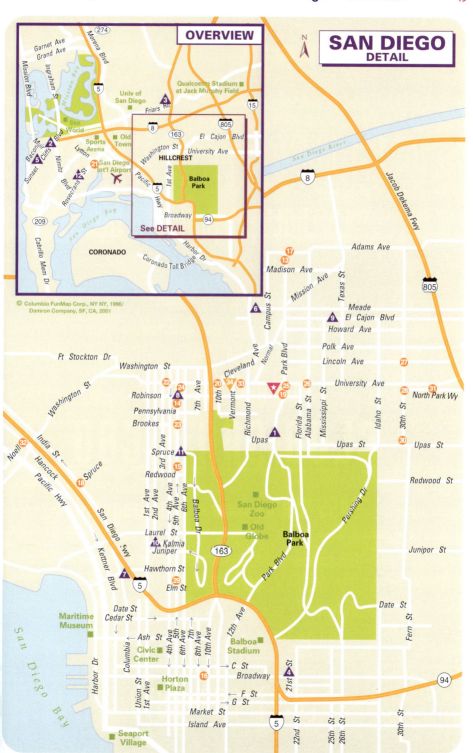

open 24 hours
CLUB SAN DIEGO

3955 4th avenue ○ San Diego CA

VIP suites and jr suites • 52 private rooms
26 TV rooms • 300 lockers • 2 video lounges
steam room • sauna Jacuzzi • smoking lounge
snack room • 12 hour time limits
One night memberships

(619) ○ 295 ○ 0850

Mastodon 858/272-1188, 800/743-8743 ■ 4638 Mission Blvd (at Emerald), Pacific Beach ■ body piercing
Rainbow Road 619/296-8222 ■ 141 University Ave (at 3rd) ■ 10am-10pm, gay gifts, videos

PUBLICATIONS
Gay/ Lesbian Times 619/299-6397, 800/438-8786 ■ 3911 Normal St ■ lgbt newsmagazine ■ www.gaylesbiantimes.com
Update 619/299-4104 ■ www.sandiegogaynews.com

GYMS & HEALTH CLUBS
Frog's Athletic Club 619/291-3500 ■ 901 Hotel Circle South (at Washington), Mission Valley

MEN'S CLUBS
▶**Club San Diego** [PC] 619/295-0850 ■ 3955 4th Ave (btwn Washington & University) ■ 24hrs ■ csdboy@home.com
Mustang Spa [SW,PC] 619/297-1661 ■ 2200 University Ave (at Mississippi) ■ 24hrs
▶**Vulcan Steam & Sauna** [PC] 619/238-1980 ■ 805 W Cedar St (at Pacific Coast Hwy) ■ 24hrs

EROTICA
Condoms Plus [WC] 619/291-7400 ■ 1220 University Ave (at Vermont) ■ safer sex gifts for men & women
The Crypt 619/692-9499 ■ 3841 Park Blvd (at University) ■ also 30th St location, 619/ 284-4724
The Crypt 619/284-4724 ■ 4094 30th St (at University) ■ 24hrs
F St Bookstore 619/298-2644 ■ 2004 University Ave (at Florida) ■ 24hrs
F St Bookstore 619/221-0075 ■ 3112 Midway Dr (at Rosecrans) ■ 24hrs
F St Bookstore 858/581-0400 ■ 4626 Albuquerque ■ 24hrs
F St Bookstore 619/236-0841 ■ 751 4th Ave (at 'F' St) ■ 24hrs
F St Bookstore 858/292-8083 ■ 7865 Balboa Ave (at Mercury), Kearny Mesa ■ 24hrs
F St Bookstore 858/549-8014 ■ 7998 Miramar Rd (at Dowdy) ■ 24hrs
F St Bookstore [WC] 619/585-3214 ■ 1141 3rd Ave (btwn Naples & Oxford), Chula Vista ■ 24hrs
F St Bookstore 619/447-0381 ■ 158 E Main (at Magnolia), El Cajon ■ 24hrs
F St Bookstore 760/480-6031 ■ 237 E Grand Ave (at Broadway), Escondido ■ 24hrs
F St Bookstore 619/690-2070 ■ 4650 Border Village (at San Ysidro Blvd), San Ysidro ■ 24hrs
Gemini Adult Books [WC] 619/287-1402 ■ 5265 University Ave (at 52nd)
Midnight Books 619/299-7186 ■ 1407 University Ave (at Richmond) ■ 24hrs
Midnight Books 619/222-9973 ■ 3606 Midway Dr (at Kemper) ■ 24hrs
Midnight Videos 619/582-1997 ■ 4790 El Cajon Blvd (at 48th) ■ 24hrs
Pleasureland 619/237-9056 ■ 836 5th Ave (btwn E & F Sts) ■ 24hrs
Trademark 619/296-1700 ■ pro & amateur videos, skin care, by appt only

San Francisco

San Francisco is divided into 7 geographical areas:
SF—Overview
SF—Castro & Noe Valley
SF—South of Market
SF—Polk Street Area
SF—Downtown & North Beach
SF—Mission District
SF—Haight, Fillmore, Hayes Valley

SF—Overview

ACCOMMODATIONS
Dockside Boat & Bed [GF,NS] 510/444-5858, 800/436-2574 ■ 489 Water St, Oakland ■ private yachts, charters available ■ www.boatandbed.com
Mi Casa Su Casa [MW] 510/531-4511, 800/215-2272 ■ int'l home exchange network ■ www.well.com/user/homeswap

ENTERTAINMENT & RECREATION
Beach Blanket Babylon [★GF] 415/421-4222 ■ 678 Green St (at Powell, in 'Club Fugazi') ■ the USA's longest running musical revue & wigs that must be seen to be believed, also restaurant, full bar
Black Sand Beach first exit (Alexander) past GG Bridge (go left under Fwy, right on Outlook Rd, look for dirt parking lot), Golden Gate Nat'l Rec Area ■ popular nude beach, look for trail
Brava! [WC] 415/641-7657 ■ 2781 24th St (btwn York & Hampshire) ■ culturally diverse performances by women ■ www.brava.org
Castro Theatre 415/621-6120 ■ 429 Castro (at Market) ■ art house cinema, many lgbt & cult classics, live organ evenings
Cruisin' the Castro 415/550-8110 ■ 5-star walking tour of the Castro, brunch included ■ www.webcastro.com/castrotour
Frameline 415/703-8650, 800/869-1996 (outside CA) ■ lgbt media arts foundation that sponsors the annual SF Int'l Lesbian/ Gay Film Festival each June ■ www.frameline.org
Hanarchy Now Productions 415/550-1902 ■ queer & alternative events in & around San Francisco ■ www.hanarchy.com
Luna Sea 415/863-2989 ■ 2940 16th St Rm 216-C (btwn Capp & S Van Ness) ■ lesbian performance space
The Marsh 415/641-0235 ■ 1062 Valencia (at 22nd St) ■ queer-positive theater ■ www.themarsh.org
National AIDS Memorial Grove [WC] 415/750-8345, 888/294-7683 ■ Golden Gate Park ■ guided tours available ■ www.aidsmemorial.org
The New Conservatory Theatre Center 415/861-8972 ■ 25 Van Ness Ave, Lower Lobby (at Market) ■ gay theater in historic Masonic Bldg ■ www.nctcsf.org
SF GayTours.com 415/648-7758, 877/734-2986 ■ SF Queer history tour, Tales of the City tour, commitment ceremonies ■ www.SFGayTours.com
Sistah Boom 510/595-4693 ■ women's percussion ensemble ■ www.sistahboom.homestead.com
Theatre Rhinoceros 415/861-5079 ■ 2926 16th St (at S Van Ness) ■ lgbt theater
Victorian Home Walks [GO] 415/252-9485 ■ custom-tailored walking tours w/ San Francisco resident ■ www.victorianwalk.com

Get out of the city. Get into the country.
Wine Country, that is.

Sonoma County Itinerary: 3 nights, 4 days

Day 1
Leisurely drive over the Golden Gate Bridge to Victorian riverfront town of Petaluma. Antiques! Old Adobe! Visit the California Welcome Center in Rohnert Park. Try a master chef's eclectic regional cuisine. Then Cotati's famous musical nightlife. Unwind in an area 4-star hotel tonight.

Day 2
Travel backroads, stopping at farms and wineries in Forestville, Graton, Occidental, and Freestone. Explore charming Sebastopol - shops, art galleries, and try local ciders and microbrews. Enjoy a spa treatment before an early meal of wine country cuisine.

Day 3
To the beach! Through the village town of Valley Ford to Bodega Bay. Visit an artist studio. Horseback ride down the beach with a picnic of local breads, cheeses, fresh organic fruit, and wine. In picturesque Jenner, enjoy a sunset fresh-catch seafood dinner. Fall asleep in your vacation rental to the sounds of the ocean.

Day 4
On to Windsor to experience a breathtaking hot air balloon ride and winery brunch. Enjoy Santa Rosa's urban blend of art and culture. Meander into the wine-centric Valley of the Moon (Kenwood, Glen Ellen, and Sonoma). Perhaps a spa treatment before a candlelight dinner.

SONOMA™ COUNTY
The Wine Country Experience

Stay in Sonoma County and experience more of what the Wine Country can offer.
For more itineraries visit **www.sonomacounty.com**.
Call 1-800-576-6662 to request a free Visitor's Guide.

specialty rentals

Whatever the reason —

business trip, special occasion, vacation journey or to "test drive" prior to making a purchase, we probably have the perfect vehicle for you.

Specialty Rentals has provided a winning combination of outstanding cars and personal service for over a decade and we look forward to serving you soon.

Check us out online to view our selection.
Or call us at 1-800-400-8412.
Our knowledgeable staff will be happy to assist you.

Serving San Francisco and West Los Angeles.

We offer a variety of sports cars, convertibles, luxury sedans and SUVs including

Porsche Boxster

❖

Jaguar XK8

❖

Mercedes E320

❖

Lexus RX300

www.specialtyrentals.com

San Francisco

San Francisco may be a top tourist destination because of its cable cars, colorful Victorian homes, and the Haight-Ashbury district, but for many, a bigger draw is its large, visible gay and lesbian community. The Castro is a must for shopping and bar-hopping, while South of Market (SoMa) is home to the city's dance clubs and infamous leather scene. Women will enjoy the cafe scene and progressive performance spaces of the Mission district. Literary fans (and aficionados of Italian cuisine) will want to visit North Beach, with its charming continental-style cafes, world-famous restaurants, and beatnik landmarks (City Lights Books, 415/362-8193). San Francisco's Chinatown is a colorful medley of food markets, restaurants, and tourist boutiques. You can visit the National AIDS Memorial Grove (888/294-7683), designated a National Memorial in 1996, in the vast urban oasis of Golden Gate Park (wheelchair access, guided tours available). Contact at: www.aidsmemorial.org.

Queer Resources

COMMUNITY INFO
▼ The Center 415/437-2257, web: www.sfgaycenter.org. Market & Octavia Sts (see Castro map). Scheduled to open fall 2001.
Lesbian/Gay Info/Pacific Center for Human Growth 510/548-8283, web: www.pacificcenter.org. 2712 Telegraph Ave, Berkeley. 10am-10pm Mon-Sat.

AIDS RESOURCES
Hotline 415/863-2437.

RECOVERY
AA Gay/Lesbian 415/621-1326.

City Calendar

LGBT PRIDE
June. 415/864-3733.

ENTERTAINMENT
Theatre Rhinoceros 415/861-5079, 2926 16th St.

ANNUAL EVENTS
June - San Francisco Int'l Lesbian/Gay Film Festival 415/703-8650.
July - Up Your Alley Fair 415/861-3247. Local SM/leather street fair held in Dore Alley, South-of-Market.
September - Folsom Street Fair 415/861-3247. Huge SM/leather street fair, topping a week of kinky events.
Festival of Babes 510/452 392-9255. Annual women's soccer tournament.
October - Castro Street Fair 415/467-3354. Arts and community groups street fair.

Tourist Info

AIRPORT DIRECTIONS
San Francisco International. To get to the Castro District take 101 North. Follow signs to Golden Gate Bridge. Take Mission/Van Ness exit. Continue up Duboce St (13th St) for 3 blocks to Market St. Take a left, go 5 blocks, and begin to pray to 'Asphalta,' the goddess of parking. (Or, better yet, hitch a ride on one of the reasonably priced shuttles.)
Oakland International is easily accessible via BART.

PUBLIC TRANSIT & TAXIS
Yellow Cab 415/626-2345.
Luxor Cab 415/282-4141.
Quake City Shuttle 415/255-4899.
Muni 415/673-6864.
Bay Area Rapid Transit (BART) 650/992-2278, subway.

TOURIST SPOTS & INFO
Alcatraz.
Chinatown.
Coit Tower.
De Young Museum 415/750-3600.
Exploratorium 415/561-0360.
Fisherman's Warf.
Golden Gate Park.
Haight & Ashbury Sts.
Japantown.
Mission San Francisco de Assisi.
North Beach.
SF Museum of Modern Art 415/357-4035.
Twin Peaks.
Visitor's Center: San Francisco Convention & Visitors Bureau 415/391-2000, web: www.sfvisitor.org

WEATHER
A beautiful summer comes at the end of September and lasts through October. Much of the city is cold and fogged-in June through September, though the Castro and Mission are usually sunny. The cold in winter is damp, so bring lots of layers. When there isn't a drought, it also rains in the winter months of November through February.

BEST VIEWS
After a great Italian meal in North Beach, go to the top floor of the North Beach parking garage on Vallejo near Stockton, next to the police station. If you're in the Castro or the Mission, head for Dolores Park, at Dolores and 20th St. Other good views: Golden Gate Bridge, Kirby Cove (a park area to the left just past the Golden Gate Bridge in Marin), Coit Tower, Twin Peaks.

CALIFORNIA • USA

PUBLICATIONS

BAR (Bay Area Reporter) 415/861-5019 ■ the weekly lgbt newspaper ■ www.ebar.com

Odyssey Magazine 415/621-6514 ■ all the dish on SF's club scene

Q San Francisco 800/999-9718 (subscriptions) ■ glossy w/ extensive arts, club & restaurant listings for the City ■ www.qsfmagazine.com

San Francisco Bay Times [★] 415/626-0260 ■ bi-weekly, a 'must read' for Bay Area resources & personals ■ sfbaytimes@aol.com

San Francisco Frontiers 415/487-6000 ■ lgbt newsmagazine ■ www.frontiersweb.com

SF—Castro & Noe Valley

ACCOMMODATIONS

1 **18th Inn Castro** [MW] 415/252-7192 ■ Victorian guesthouse in the Castro ■ www.18thinncastro.com

2 **24 Henry & Village House** [M,NS] 415/864-5686, 800/900-5686 ■ 24 Henry St & 4080 18th St (btwn Sanchez & Noe) ■ 1-bdrm apt also available ■ www.24Henry.com

3 **Albion House Inn** [GF,NS] 415/621-0896, 800/625-2466 ■ 135 Gough St (at Fell) ■ full brkfst ■ www.subtleties.com

4 **Beck's Motor Lodge** [GF] 415/621-8212 ■ 2222 Market St (at Sanchez) ■ in the heart of the Castro

Belvedere House [★MW] 415/731-6654, 877/226-3273 ■ 598 Belvedere St (at 17th) ■ wall-to-wall books, art & style, just up the hill from the heart of the Castro, French & German spoken ■ Belvederehouse@mindspring.com

Casa Buena Vista [GF] 916/974-7409 ■ near Market & Castro ■ www.vacationspot.com/casabuenavista.htm

5 **Castillo Inn** 415/864-5111, 800/865-5112 ■ 48 Henry St

6 **Castro Suites** [M,NS,GO] 415/437-1783 ■ 927 14th St (at Noe) ■ furnished apts ■ www.castrosuites.com

7 **Castro Vacation Rental** [MW,NS,GO] 415/626-7126, 888/626-7126 ■ 72 Eureka St (at Market) ■ apt 3 blks from the Castro, weekly ■ www.castrorental.com

38 **Castro Victorian Vacation Rental** [GS,GO] 415/621-3580 ■ 4069 19th St (at Castro) ■ furnished apt in the Castro

8 **Church Street B&B** [GS,NS] 415/621-7600 ■ 325 Church St (at 15th) ■ restored 1905 Edwardian ■ www.churchstbb.com

9 **Dolores Park Inn** [GF,NS] 415/621-0482 ■ 3641 17th St (btwn Church & Dolores) ■ hot tub, kitchens, fireplaces

10 **Edwardian San Francisco** [GF,NS] 415/864-1271, 888/864-8070 ■ 1668 Market St (btwn Franklin & Gough) ■ some shared baths ■ www.edwardiansfhotel.com

Ethel's Garden in the Castro [WO] 415/864-6171 ■ hot tub, kitchenette, private entrance, nr everything ■ ethelsgarden@aol.com

Friends [MW,GO] 415/826-5972 ■ B&B in private home, nr Castro ■ home.pacbell.net/donoharm/friends.htm

House O' Chicks Guesthouse [WO] 415/861-9849

11 **Inn on Castro** [MW,NS,GO] 415/861-0321 ■ 321 Castro St (btwn 16th & 17th) ■ full brkfst ■ www.inncastro2.com

Just Off Castro [M,GO] 415/552-3312 ■ 4408 18th St ■ Victorian, some shared baths ■ www.slip.net/~peteg

12 **Le Grenier** [MW] 415/864-4748 ■ 347 Noe St (at 16th St) ■ suite

Lemon Tree Homestay [M,NS] 415/861-4045 ■ PO Box 460424 ■ European-style B&B ■ LemontreeSF@aol.com

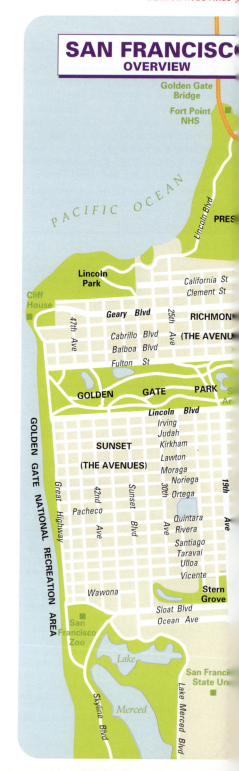

SF—Castro & Noe Valley • CALIFORNIA

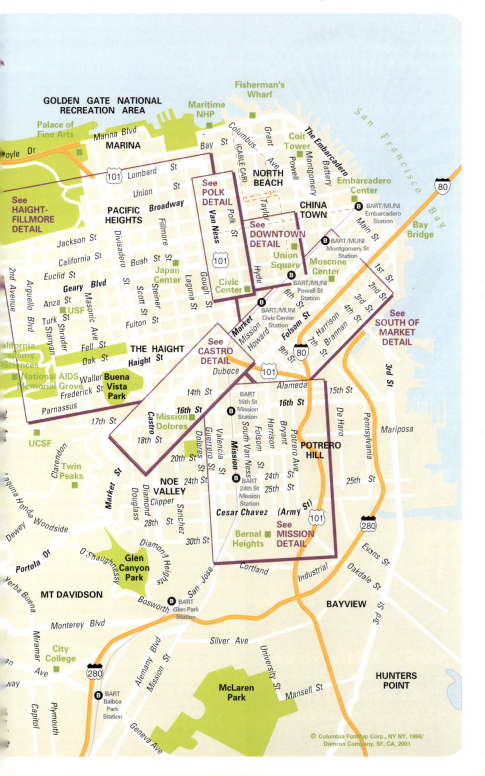

CALIFORNIA • USA

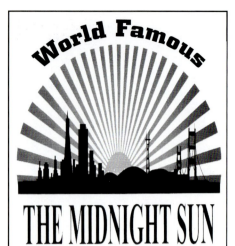

The Midnight Sun
4067 18th Street
San Francisco, CA 94114
415-861-4186
San Francisco's Premier Video Bar
Open Daily at 2pm

Nancy's Bed [WO,NS] 415/239-5692 ■ kitchen ■ nancysbed@aol.com

Noe's Nest B&B [GF,NS] 415/821-0751 ■ 3973 23rd St (at Noe) ■ full brkfst, kitchens, fireplace ■ www.noesnest.com

13 The Parker House Guest House [★M,NS,GO] 415/621-3222, 888/520-7275 ■ 520 Church St (at 17th) ■ Edwardian guesthouse w/ gardens, steam spa ■ www.parkerguesthouse.com

Ruth's House [WO,NS,GO] 415/641-8898 ■ shared bath, 2-day minimum, lesbian-owned/ run

Terrace Place [MW] 415/241-0425 ■ guest suite ■ www.terraceplace.com

14 Tom's Place [M,L] 415/861-0516 ■ 4510 18th St (at Douglass) ■ slinged play area ■ www.gaysf.com/sites/hotels/toms/

15 Travelodge Central [GF] 415/621-6775, 800/578-7878 ■ 1707 Market St (at Valencia) ■ smokefree rms available

16 The Willows Inn [MW,NS,GO] 415/431-4770 ■ 710 14th St (at Church) ■ www.WillowsSF.com

Bars

18 The Bar on Castro [★M,NH,WC] 415/626-7220 ■ 456 Castro St ■ 3pm-2am, from noon wknds, a little bit of NYC's Chelsea District swank in SF

19 The Cafe [★MW,D,YC] 415/861-3846 ■ 2367 Market St ■ 2pm-2am, deck overlooking Castro & Market

20 Cafe du Nord [GF,A,F,E] 415/861-5016 ■ 2170 Market St (at Sanchez) ■ 4pm-2am, live music, various theme nights ■ www.cafedunord.com

21 Daddy's [M,NH,L] 415/621-8732 ■ 440 Castro St ■ 9am-2am, from 8am wknds, very cruisy, 'Red Hanky Beer Bust' Tue

22 The Detour [★M,NH,A] 415/861-6053 ■ 2348 Market St (at Castro) ■ 2pm-2am, go-go boys Sat, hip cruise bar

23 The Edge [★M,NH,L] 415/863-4027 ■ 4149 18th St ■ noon-2am, classic cruise bar

24 ▶ Harvey's [★MW,NH,E,WC] 415/431-4278 ■ 500 Castro St ■ 11am-2am, from 9am wknds, also restaurant ■ www.harveysbar.com

25 Martuni's [★GS,NH,P] 415/241-0205 ■ 4 Valencia St (at Market) ■ 4pm-2am, piano bar & lounge, great martinis

26 Men's Room [M,NH] 415/861-1310 ■ 3988 18th St ■ noon-2am

27 The Metro [M,K,YC] 415/703-9750 ■ 3600 16th St (at Noe) ■ 4pm-2am, from 1pm wknds, deck overlooking Market St, also Chinese restaurant

28 ▶ Midnight Sun [★M,V] 415/861-4186 ■ 4067 18th St ■ noon-2am ■ www.midnightsunsf.com

29 The Mint [MW,K,V] 415/626-4726 ■ 1942 Market St (at Buchanan) ■ 11am-2am, popular karaoke bar nights, also restaurant ■ www.themint.net

30 Moby Dick's [M,NH,V] 4049 18th St

31 Pendulum [★M,MR-AF] 415/863-4441 ■ 4146 18th St ■ 6am-2am

32 Pilsner Inn [★M,NH,YC] 415/621-7058 ■ 225 Church St (at Market) ■ 9am-2am, great patio

17 SF Badlands [★M,NH,D,WC] 415/626-9320 ■ 4121 18th St (at Castro) ■ 2pm-2am, wknd beer busts

33 The Transfer [M,NH] 415/861-7499 ■ 198 Church St (at Market) ■ 11am-2am, from 6am wknds

34 Twin Peaks [M,OC,WC] 415/864-9470 ■ 401 Castro St ■ noon-2am

35 Uncle Bert's Place [M,NH] 415/431-8616 ■ 4086 18th St ■ 9am-2am, from 6am wknds, heated patio, wknd bbq

SF—Castro & Noe Valley • CALIFORNIA

CAFES

Cafe Flore [★MW,F,BW] 415/621-8579 ■ 2298 Market St ■ 7am-11pm, some veggie, great patio to see & be seen, come early for a seat

CHAT Cafe [GO] 415/626-4700 ■ 498 Sanchez (at 18th) ■ 7am-8pm, free Internet access w/ food or drink purchase ■ www.sfchatcafe.com

Jumpin' Java 415/431-5282 ■ 139 Noe St (at 14th St) ■ 6am-10pm, from 7am wknds

Just Desserts [MW] 415/626-5774 ■ 248 Church St ■ 7am-11pm, delicious cakes, quiet patio

Orbit Room Cafe [F] 415/252-9525 ■ 1900 Market St (at Laguna) ■ 8am-1am, till 2am Fri-Sat, till midnight Sun, great view of Market St, also bar

Starbucks [B] 415/626-6263 ■ 4094 18th St ■ 5:30am-11pm, till midnight wknds, formerly 'Pasqua Beach', always a bear jamboree

Sweet Inspiration 415/621-8664 ■ 2239 Market St ■ 7am-11pm, popular wknd nights, fabulous desserts

RESTAURANTS

2223 Market [★WC] 415/431-0692 ■ 2223 Market St ■ dinner, brunch Sun, contemporary American, full bar

Alfred Schilling 415/431-8447 ■ 1695 Market St (at Valencia) ■ lunch & dinner, gourmet fare, also outdoor cafe & chocolatier

Anchor Oyster Bar [MW,BW] 415/431-3990 ■ 579 Castro St (at 19th) ■ seafood, some veggie

Bagdad Cafe [MW] 415/621-4434 ■ 2295 Market St ■ 24hrs, diner, some veggie, great for people watching

Blue [★BW] 415/863-2583 ■ 2337 Market St (btwn Castro & Noe) ■ 11:30am-11pm, wknd brunch, homecooking served w/ style

Cafe Cuvee [GO] 415/621-7488 ■ 2073 Market St (at 14th St) ■ dinner Tue-Sat, brunch wknds, clsd Mon

Caffe Luna Piena [MW] 415/621-2566 ■ 558 Castro St ■ lunch & dinner, clsd Mon, patio

Carta [GO] 415/863-3516 ■ 1760 Market St (nr Gough) ■ lunch & dinner, Sun brunch

China Court [BW] 415/626-5358 ■ 599 Castro ■ lunch Mon-Fri, dinner nightly, some veggie

Chloe's [★] 415/648-4116 ■ 1399 Church St, Noe Valley (at 26th St) ■ 8am-3pm, come early for the excellent wknd brunch

Chow [★] 415/552-2469 ■ 215 Church St ■ 11am-11pm, till midnight Th-Sat, eclectic & affordable

Cove Cafe [MW,WC] 415/626-0462 ■ 434 Castro St ■ 7am-10pm, some veggie

Delfina 415/552-4055 ■ 3621 18th St (at Dolores) ■ 5:30pm-10pm, excellent Tuscan cuisine

Eric's Chinese Restaurant [★] 415/282-0919 ■ 1500 Church St, Noe Valley (at 27th St) ■ 11am-9pm

Hot 'N Hunky [MW] 415/621-6365 ■ 4039 18th St ■ 11am-midnight, burgers, some veggie

It's Tops 415/431-6395 ■ 1801 Market St (at Octavia) ■ 8am-3pm, till 3am Wed-Sat, classic diner, great hotcakes

Johnfrank [M] 415/503-0333 ■ 2100 Market St (at Church) ■ dinner, upscale American

M&L Market (May's) 415/431-7044 ■ 691 14th St (at Market) ■ clsd Sun, great huge sandwiches

Ma Tante Sumi [MW] 415/552-6663 ■ 4243 18th St (at Diamond) ■ 5:30pm-10pm, cont'l/ Japanese

Damron Codes

- ➤ advertiser
- ★ popular
- **MO** men only
- **GF** gay-friendly (mostly straight)
- **GS** gay/straight (evenly mixed)
- **MW** lesbians/gay men
- **M** mostly men
- **W** mostly women (listing names in this color)
- **WO** women only (listing names in this color)
- **NH** neighborhood bar
- **D** live DJ & dancing
- **A** alternative (grunge babes, goths)
- **CW** country western (music, dancing and/or dress)
- **B** bears
- **L** leather, fetish (often a dress code)
- **P** professional crowd
- **MRC** multiracial clientele
- **MR-AF** African-American clientele
- **MR-A** Asian clientele
- **MR-L** Latino/a clientele
- **TG** transgender-friendly
- **F** hot food served
- **E** live entertainment (piano, bands, comedy)
- **K** karaoke
- **S** shows (drag, strip, or cabaret)
- **V** videos
- **18+** 18 & older
- **YC** young crowd (mostly 20-somethings)
- **OC** older/more mature crowd (mostly over 40)
- **BW** beer and/or wine
- **BYOB** bring your own bottle (often "private" clubs)
- **SW** swimming onsite (usually a pool)
- **N** public nudity okay
- **NS** no smoking (anywhere inside business)
- **PC** private club (membership open to out-of-towners; often BYOB)
- **WC** wheelchair access (includes bathrooms)
- **GO** gay-owned/operated
- **AYOR** at your own risk (beware of bashers or cops)

Mecca [★WC] 415/621-7000 ■ 2029 Market St (at Dolores) ■ dinner from 5:30pm, Mediterranean, also swanky bar, valet parking

Orphan Andy's [GO] 415/864-9795 ■ 3991 17th St ■ 24hrs, diner

Pasta Pomodoro [★MW] 415/558-8123 ■ 2304 Market St ■ open till midnight, Italian; also 24th & Noe location

Patio Cafe [MW] 415/621-4640 ■ 531 Castro St ■ California cuisine, enclosed patio, popular brunch

Piaf's 415/864-3700 ■ 1686 Market St (at Gough) ■ 5pm-close, oyster & seafood bar, also cabaret, 'Queer Comedy' 8pm Mon ■ www.piafs.com

The Sausage Factory [MW,BW] 415/626-1250 ■ 517 Castro St ■ noon-1am, pizza & pasta, some veggie

Sparky's 415/626-8666 ■ 242 Church St ■ 24hrs, diner, some veggie, popular after-hours

Tin-Pan Asian Bistro [★] 415/565-0733 ■ 2251 Market St ■ 11am-11pm, wknd brunch, sake cocktails

Tita's Hale'aine [★WC] 415/626-2477 ■ 3870 17th St (btwn Sanchez & Noe) ■ 11am-10pm, from 9am Sat, till 3pm Sun, traditional Hawaiian, plenty veggie ■ www.citysearch.com/sfo/titas

Valentine's Cafe 415/285-2257 ■ 1793 Church St, Noe Valley (at 30th St) ■ dinner & wknd brunch, clsd Mon-Tue, vegetarian

Welcome Home [★MW,BW] 415/626-3600 ■ 464 Castro St ■ 8am-11pm, homestyle, some veggie

Zuni Cafe [★] 415/552-2522 ■ 1658 Market St (at Haight) ■ clsd Mon, upscale cont'l/ Mediterranean, full bar

ENTERTAINMENT & RECREATION

36 **Castro Country Club** [MW] 415/552-6102 ■ 4058 18th St ■ 2pm-11pm, 10am-11pm Sat, noon-8pm Sun, clsd Mon-Tue, alcohol & drug-free club

BOOKSTORES

37 **A Different Light** [★] 415/431-0891 ■ 489 Castro St ■ 10am-10pm, lgbt bookstore & queer info clearinghouse ■ www.adlbooks.com

Aardvark Books 415/552-6733 ■ 227 Church St ■ 10:30am-10:30pm, used, good lgbt section

Get Lost 415/437-0529 ■ 1825 Market St (at Guerrero) ■ 10am-7pm, till 6pm Sat, 11am-5pm Sun, travel books, lgbt section

RETAIL SHOPS

A Taste of Leather 415/552-4500, 800/367-0786 ■ 2370 Market (near Castro) ■ noon-8pm, 10am-10pm wknds ■ www.atasteofleather.com

Does Your Father Know? 415/241-9865 ■ 548 Castro St ■ 9:30am-10pm, till 11pm Fri-Sat, 10am-9pm Sun, lgbt gifts & videos

Does Your Mother Know? 415/864-3160 ■ 4079 18th St ■ 9:30am-10pm, cards & T-shirts

Don't Panic 415/553-8989 ■ 541 Castro St ■ 10am-10pm, till 11pm Fri-Sat, 11am-9pm Sun, T-shirts, gifts & more

Image Leather 415/621-7551 ■ 2199 Market St (at Sanchez) ■ 9am-10pm, 11am-7pm Sun, custom leather clothing, accessories & toys

Just for Fun [WC] 415/285-4068 ■ 3982 24th St, Noe Valley (at Noe) ■ 9am-9pm, till 8pm Sat, 10am-6pm Sun, gift shop

La Sirena Botanica 415/285-0612 ■ 1509 Church St (at 27th St) ■ noon-6pm, Afro-Caribbean religious articles

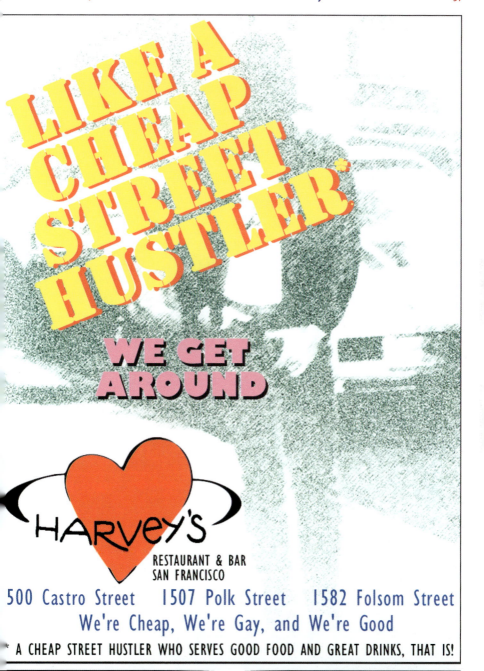

MODERN CLOTHING

ROLO®
san francisco

for men and women

REPLAY

DIESEL

STÜSSY

KIEHL'S SKIN CARE

PAUL SMITH

HELMUT LANG

LUCKY BRAND

CALVIN KLEIN UNDERWEAR

PAUL FRANK

2(x)ist

ROLO ON MARKET
2351 MARKET STREET
SAN FRANCISCO CA 94114
415.431.4545

ROLO DOWNTOWN
25 STOCKTON STREET
SAN FRANCISCO CA 94108
415.989.7656

ROLO GARAGE
1301 HOWARD STREET
SAN FRANCISCO CA 94103
415.864.0505

ROLO 450
450 CASTRO STREET
SAN FRANCISCO CA 94114
415.626.7171

UNDER COVER
535 CASTRO STREET
SAN FRANCISCO CA 94103
415.861.1999

SF—Castro / South of Market • CALIFORNIA

Leather Zone of San Francisco 415/255-8585 ■ 2352 Market St ■ 11am-7pm, noon-6pm Sun, open later in summer

► **Rolo** 415/431-4545 ■ 2351 Market St ■ 10am-8pm, till 7pm Sun, designer labels; also 450 Castro location, 415/626-7171

Stormy Leather 415/671-1295 ■ 582C Castro (upstairs) ■ noon-8pm, till 8pm Fri, leather, latex, toys & magazines, women owned/ run ■ www.stormyleather.com

Uncle Mame 415/626-1953 ■ 2241 Market St (btwn Sanchez & Noe) ■ noon-7pm, till 5pm Sun, kitsch lover's wonderland ■ www.unclemame.com

Under One Roof [WC] 415/252-9290 ■ 549 Castro ■ 11am-7pm, 100% donated to AIDS relief

GYMS & HEALTH CLUBS

Gold's Gym Castro [★MW] 415/626-4488 ■ 2301 Market St ■ day passes available

Muscle System [★MO] 415/863-4700 ■ 2275 Market St ■ day passes available

MEN'S CLUBS

Eros 415/864-3767 ■ 2051 Market St (btwn Church & Dolores) ■ safer sex club, various theme nights ■ www.erossf.com

EROTICA

Auto-Erotica 415/861-5787 ■ 4077-A 18th St, 2nd flr

Jaguar 415/863-4777 ■ 4057 18th St ■ info@jaguarbooks.com

Le Salon 415/552-4213 ■ 4126 18th St

The MMO (Mercury Mail Order) 415/621-1188 ■ 4084 18th St ■ leather, toys & more

Romantasy Exquisite Corsetry 415/585-0760 ■ call for appt, corsets & fetish clothing ■ www.romantasy.com

SF—South of Market

ACCOMMODATIONS

Ramada Market St [GF,WC] 415/626-8000, 800/227-4747 ■ 1231 Market St (btwn 8th & 9th)

Victorian Hotel [GF] 415/986-4400, 800/227-3804 ■ 54 4th St (btwn Market & Mission) ■ 1913 landmark, also restaurant & full bar ■ www.victorianhotel.com

BARS

3 **The Eagle Tavern** [★M,L,E] 415/626-0880 ■ 398 12th St (at Harrison) ■ noon-2am, great 'beer bust' Sun, patio ■ www.sfeagle.com

5 **Hole in the Wall Saloon** [★M,NH,L] 415/431-4695 ■ 289 8th St (at Folsom) ■ noon-2am, from 6am Fri-Mon, 'a nasty little biker bar'

6 **Loading Dock** [M,L] 415/864-1525 ■ 1525 Mission (btwn 11th & S Van Ness) ■ 7pm-2am, uniform bar w/ strict dress code ■ www.loadingdocksf.com

7 **Lone Star** [★M,B,L] 415/863-9999 ■ 1354 Harrison St (btwn 9th & 10th) ■ noon-2am, from 9am wknds, patio, bear bar, 'beer bust' wknds ■ lonestar-saloon.com

8 **My Place** [M,NH,L] 415/863-2329 ■ 1225 Folsom St (btwn 8th & 9th) ■ noon-2am, very cruisy

9 ► **Powerhouse** [M,NH,L] 415/552-8689 ■ 1347 Folsom St (at Dore Alley) ■ 4pm-2am, 'Ink & Metal' Tue, popular wknds w/ DJ Fri-Sat, patio, cruisy ■ www.powerhouse-sf.com

10 **Rawhide II** [M,D,CW] 415/621-1197 ■ 280 7th St (btwn Howard & Folsom) ■ 8pm-2am, clsd Mon

NIGHTCLUBS

11 **1015 Folsom** [★GS,D,$] 415/431-1200 ■ 1015 Folsom St (at 6th) ■ 10pm-4:30am, call for events ■ www.1015.com

12 **Asia SF** [★GS,D,MR-A,S,$] 415/255-2742 ■ 201 9th St (at Howard) ■ 10:30pm-close Wed-Sat, theme nights, go-go boys, also Cal-Asian restaurant w/ en-drag service 5pm-10pm ■ asiasf.com

12 **Azucar** [★M,D,MR-L,S] 415/255-2742 ■ 201 9th St (at 'Asia SF') ■ 10pm-3am 1st Sat, go-go boys & girls ■ www.papipresents.com

Club Asia [★M,D,MR-A,S,$] 415/285-2742 ■ 174 King St (in 'King St Garage') ■ 10pm-close 2nd & 4th Fri

13 **Club Q** [★W,D,$] 415/647-8258 (hit 2#) ■ 177 Townsend (btwn 2nd & 3rd) ■ 9pm-3am 1st Fri only

15 **Club Red** [WO,D,MR,S,WC] 415/339-8310 ■ 399 9th St (at 'The Stud') ■ 10pm-3am 3rd Fri ■ backstreetssf@hotmail.com

13 **Club Universe** [★M,D,$] 415/974-6020, 415/289-6650 ■ 177 Townsend (at 3rd St) ■ 9:30pm-7am Sat

14 **Endup** [M,D,MR] 415/357-0827 ■ 401 6th St (at Harrison) ■ clsd Tue, theme nights, popular Sun mornings

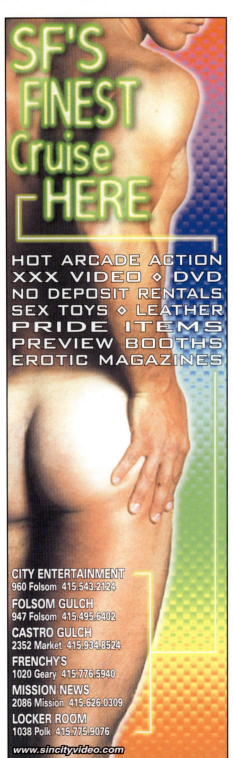

CALIFORNIA • USA

Fag Fridays [★M,D,YC,$] 415/263-4850 ■ 401 6th St (at 'The Endup') ■ 10pm-5:30am Fri ■ www.fagfridays.com

Futura [★M,D,MR-L,S,$] 415/665-6715 ■ 174 King St (in 'King St Garage') ■ 10pm-3am 2nd & 4th Sat, hot (¡muy caliente!) dancers ■ www.futurasf.com

Kandy Bar [W,D,$] 415/337-4962 (Endup#) ■ 401 6th St (at the 'Endup') ■ 9pm-close Sat only ■ www.clubskirts.com

Mass [M,D,$] 415/646-0890, 415/431-1200 (1015 Folsom #) ■ 1015 Folsom St (at 6th St) ■ 6pm-midnight 1st Sun ■ www.guspresents.com

Pleasuredome [M,D,$] 415/289-6699, 415/974-6020 ■ 177 Townsend (at 3rd St) ■ 9pm-3am Sun

Shaft [★M,D,MR-AF,YC] 415/252-7883 (Stud #) ■ 399 9th St (at 'The Stud') ■ 9am-2am Mon

The Stud [★MW,D,YC] 415/252-7883 (info line), 415/863-6623 ■ 399 9th St (at Harrison) ■ 5pm-2am, every night a popular theme night: 'Shaft' Mon, 'Trannyshack' Tue, disco/ oldies night Wed, 'Sugar' Sat, more women Fri (MR) ■ members.aol.com/thestudbar/site.html

Sugar [★M,D,A,YC] 415/252-7883 (Stud #) ■ 399 9th St (at 'The Stud') ■ 9pm-5am Sat, great music & wall-to-wall alternababes

Sundance Saloon [M,D,CW] 415/699-5764 ■ 174 King St ■ 6pm-11pm Sun, lessons at 6pm, DJ from 7:30pm ■ sundance.freehosting.net

Trannyshack [★M,D,TG,GO] 415/863-6623 ■ 399 9th St (at the Stud) ■ 10pm-3am Tue, weekly party for trannies & their friends & admirers ■ www.heklina.com

CAFES

Brain Wash [★E,BW] 415/861-3663, 415/431-9274 ■ 1122 Folsom St (at 7th St) ■ 7am-11pm, laundromat & cafe

RESTAURANTS

Ananda Fuara 415/621-1994 ■ 1298 Market St (at 9th) ■ 8am-8pm, till 3pm Wed, clsd Sun, vegetarian

Boulevard [★] 415/543-6084 ■ 1 Mission St (at Steuart) ■ lunch Mon-Fri & dinner daily, one of SF's finest

Butter 415/863-5964 ■ 354 11th St ■ 5pm-2am Tue-Sat ■ 'white trash bistro,' also bar, theme nights ■ www.smoothasbutter.com

Fringale [WC] 415/543-0573 ■ 570 4th St (btwn Bryant & Brannan) ■ lunch & dinner, clsd Sun, French bistro

Hamburger Mary's [WC] 415/626-5767, 415/626-1985 ■ 1582 Folsom St (at 12th St) ■ 11:30am-10:30pm, till 2am Fri-Sat, clsd Mon, some veggie, full bar

Hawthorne Lane 415/777-9779 ■ 22 Hawthorne St (btwn 2nd & 3rd off Howard) ■ dinner nightly, lunch Mon-Fri

Le Charm 415/546-6128 ■ 315 5th St (at Folsom) ■ lunch & dinner, dinner only Sat, clsd Sun

Lulu [★WC] 415/495-5775 ■ 816 Folsom St (at 4th St) ■ lunch & dinner, upscale Mediterranean, some veggie, full bar

Manora's Thai Cuisine 415/861-6224 ■ 1600 Folsom (at 12th) ■ lunch & dinner

Tu Lan 415/626-0927 ■ 8 6th St (at Market) ■ lunch & dinner, Vietnamese, some veggie, dicey neighborhood but delicious (& cheap) food

Wa-Ha-Ka! [BW] 415/861-1410 ■ 1489 Folsom (at 11th St) ■ Mexican, plenty veggie

Woodward's Garden [WC] 415/621-7122 ■ 1700 Mission St (at Duboce) ■ dinner seating at 6pm & 8pm, clsd Mon

SF—South of Market/Polk St • CALIFORNIA

RETAIL SHOPS
A Taste of Leather 415/252-9166, 800/367-0786 ■ 1339 Folsom (btwn 9th & 10th) ■ noon-8pm, till midnight Fri-Sat ■ www.atasteofleather.com

The Bear Store/ Brush Creek Media 415/552-1506 ■ 367 9th St (at Harrison) ■ toys, T-shirts, magazines & more for bears ■ www.brushcreek.com

Dandelion [GO] 415/436-9500, 888/548-1968 ■ 55 Potrero Ave (at Alameda St) ■ 10am-6pm, clsd Sun-Mon, gifts, books, erotica & more ■ steve@tampopo.com

Leather Etc 415/864-7558 ■ 1201 Folsom St (at 8th St) ■ 10:30am-7pm, 11am-6pm Sat, noon-5pm Sun

Mr S Leather 415/863-7764 ■ 310 7th St (at Folsom) ■ 11am-7pm, noon-6pm Sun, erotic goods, custom leather & latex

Stompers 415/255-6422 ■ 323 10th St (at Folsom) ■ noon-8pm, till 6pm Sun, boots, cigars & gloves

Stormy Leather 415/626-1672 ■ 1158 Howard St (btwn 7th & 8th) ■ noon-7pm, leather, latex, toys & magazines, women-owned/ run ■ www.stormyleather.com

GYMS & HEALTH CLUBS
Gold's Gym San Francisco [★GS] 415/552-4653 ■ 9th & Brannan ■ day passes available

MEN'S CLUBS
Blow Buddies [★PC] 415/863-4323 ■ 933 Harrison (btwn 5th & 6th) ■ open late Th-Sun ■ www.blowbuddies.com

Mack Folsom Prison [L,PC] 415/844-3959, 415/252-1221 (info line) ■ 1285 Folsom (at 9th) ■ open nightly, 24hrs wknds, fetish parties

Power Exchange Mainstation [18+,$] 415/487-9944 ■ 74 Otis St (btwn S Van Ness & Gough) ■ 9pm-4am, till 6am wknds, 4 flrs ■ www.powerexchange.com

SEX CLUBS
Power Exchange Substation I 415/487-9944 ■ 86 Otis St (btwn S Van Ness & Gough) ■ call for hrs, playspace for female, transgendered, bi & straight couples ■ www.powerexchange.com

EROTICA
▶ **City Entertainment** 415/543-2124 ■ 960 Folsom St ■ 24hrs wknds ■ www.sincityvideo.com

▶ **Folsom Gulch** 415/495-6402 ■ 947 Folsom (btwn 5th & 6th) ■ 24hrs wknds ■ www.sincityvideo.com

Golden Gate Video #4 415/495-5573 ■ 99 6th St (at Mission)

SF—Polk Street Area

ACCOMMODATIONS
▶ **Atherton Hotel** [GF,F] 415/474-5720, 800/474-5720 ■ 685 Ellis St (at Larkin) ■ full bar ■ www.hotelatherton.com

The Monarch Hotel [GF] 415/673-5232, 800/777-3210 ■ 1015 Geary St (at Polk) ■ completely renovated ■ www.themonarchhotel.com

▶ **The Phoenix Hotel** [★GF,SW] 415/776-1380, 800/248-9466 ■ 601 Eddy St (at Larkin) ■ 1950s style motor lodge, also fabulous 'Back Flip' bar ■ www.sftrips.com/hotels/phoenix.html

BARS
▶ **Back Flip** [★GF,D,F] 415/771-3547 ■ 601 Eddy St (at 'The Phoenix Hotel') ■ 7pm-2am, clsd Sun-Mon, cocktails w/ class, dinner nightly ■ www.sftrips.com/restaurants/backflip.html

The Cinch [M,NH,WC] 415/776-4162 ■ 1723 Polk St (at Clay) ■ 6am-2am, patio, lots of pool tables & no attitude

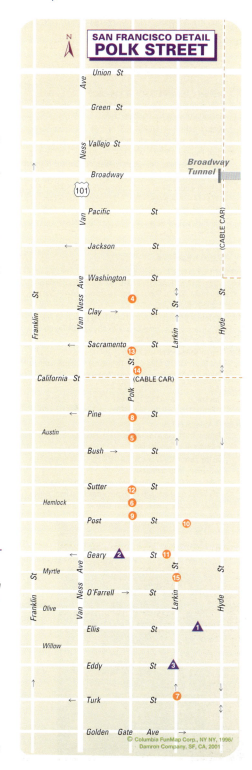

© Columbia FunMap Corp., NY NY, 1996/ Damron Company, SF, CA, 2001

CALIFORNIA • USA

5 **Club Rendez-Vous** [M,S] 415/673-7934 ■ 1312 Polk St (at Bush) ■ 9am-2am, strippers
15 **Gangway** [M,NH] 415/776-6828 ■ 841 Larkin St (btwn Geary & O'Farrell) ■ 10am-2am
6 **Giraffe Lounge** [M,NH,V,WC] 415/474-1702 ■ 1131 Polk St (at Post) ■ 8am-2am
7 **Jezebel's Joint** [GS,TG,S] 415/345-9832 ■ 510 Larkin (at Turk) ■ 6pm-2am Th-Sun, cocktail lounge, 'Devil's Den' downstairs ■ www.jezebelsjoint.com
8 **Kimo's** [M,NH,S] 415/885-4535 ■ 1351 Polk St (at Pine) ■ 8am-2am, live bands upstairs (GS,A,YC)
9 **Lush Lounge** [GS,NH,E,WC] 415/771-2022 ■ 1092 Post (at Polk) ■ 4pm-2am, from 3pm Fri-Sat, martini bar & piano lounge
10 **Mother Lode/ Divas** [M,NH,D,TG,S] 415/928-6006, 415/474-DIVA ■ 1081 Post St (at Larkin) ■ 6am-2am, TS/TVs & their admirers
11 **Old Rick's Gold Room** [M,NH] 415/928-4046 ■ 939 Geary St (at Polk) ■ 6am-2am
12 **Reflections** [M,NH] 415/776-6262 ■ 1160 Polk St (nr Sutter) ■ 6am-2am

NIGHTCLUBS
14 **dBar** [★,W,D,MR-A] 415/775-0442 ■ 1550 California St, 2nd flr (at Polk, at 'Tango Tango') ■ 9pm-2am 4th Sat only ■ dbary2@aol.com
13 **N' Touch** [M,NH,D,MR-A,S] 415/441-8413 ■ 1548 Polk St (at Sacramento) ■ 3pm-2am, also 'Club NRG' Th, go-go boys Th-Sat ■ www.ntouchsf.com
14 **Tango Tango** [GS,D,K,S] 415/775-0442 ■ 1550 California, 2nd flr (at Polk) ■ 5pm-2am, theme nights, popular drag shows Fri-Sat ■ www.clubtangotango.com

CAFES
Quetzal [E,V,BW] 415/673-4181 ■ 1234 Polk St (at Sutter) ■ 6am-11pm, roasts own coffee, also Internet access

RESTAURANTS
Antica Trattoria 415/928-5797 ■ 2400 Polk St (at Union) ■ dinner Tue-Sun, Italian
Bistro Zare 415/775-4304 ■ 1507 Polk St ■ dinner, clsd Sun-Mon, Mediterranean
California Culinary Academy [★] 415/771-3500 ■ 625 Polk St (at Turk) ■ lunch & dinner, cooking school where future top chefs serve up what they've learned

Edinburgh Castle [GF,NH,E] 415/885-4074 ■ 950 Geary St (at Polk) ■ 5pm-2am, mostly straight but rockin' Scottish pub w/ single malts, beer, darts & authentic fish & chips, live bands
El Super Burrito 415/771-9700 ■ 1200 Polk St (at Sutter) ■ 9am-11pm
Grubstake II [MW,BW] 415/673-8268 ■ 1525 Pine St (at Polk) ■ 5pm-4am, from 10am wknds, diner
Johnny Wok 415/928-6888 ■ 1237 Polk St (at Bush) ■ lunch & dinner, clsd Sun, Chinese
Tai Chi [★] 415/441-6758 ■ 2031 Polk St (at Pacific) ■ lunch Mon-Fri, dinner nightly, Chinese

BOOKSTORES
A Clean Well Lighted Place For Books 415/441-6670 ■ 601 Van Ness Ave (at Turk) ■ 10am-11pm, till 9pm Sun, general, lgbt section ■ www.bookstore.com
Aaben Books 415/563-3525 ■ 1546 California St (btwn Polk & Larkin) ■ 10am-10pm, till 11pm Fri-Sat, independent, new & used ■ www.aabenbooks.com

EROTICA
▶ **Frenchy's** 415/776-5940 ■ 1020 Geary St (at Polk) ■ 24hrs, videos, magazines, toys ■ www.sincityvideo.com
Le Salon Book Store 415/673-4492 ■ 1118 Polk St (at Sutter)
The Locker Room Bookstore 415/775-9076 ■ 1038 Polk St (at Post) ■ www.sincityvideo.com
The Magazine 415/441-7737 ■ 920 Larkin St (at Geary)

SF—Downtown & North Beach

ACCOMMODATIONS
1 ▶ **Allison Hotel** [GF] 415/986-8737, 800/628-6456 ■ 417 Stockton St (at Sutter) ■ some shared baths ■ www.allisonhotel.com
2 **Amsterdam Hotel** [GF] 415/673-3277, 800/637-3444 ■ 749 Taylor St (at Sutter) ■ European-style ■ www.amsterdamhotel.com
3 **Andrews** [GF] 415/563-6877, 800/926-3739 ■ 624 Post St (at Taylor) ■ Victorian hotel, also Italian restaurant ■ www.andrewshotel.com
4 ▶ **Canterbury Hotel** [GF] 415/474-6464, 800/227-4788 ■ 750 Sutter St (at Taylor) ■ also 'Murray's Glasshouse' restaurant & bar ■ www.canterburyhotel.com

The Hotel Atherton

A beautifully restored boutique hotel offering satelite TV with premium movies, data port phones, valet parking, complimentary morning coffee and newspapers.
1 block to Polk Street, 10 minutes to Castro.
Abbey Room Bar, Atherton Grill
AAA Approved $89-$149

685 Ellis Street, San Francisco, CA 94109
Tel. 415-474-5720, Fax 415-474-8256
Toll-Free 800-474-5720
www.hotelatherton.com
email: reservations@hotelatherton.com

Proudly Serving Our Community For 20 Years

SF—Downtown & North Beach • CALIFORNIA

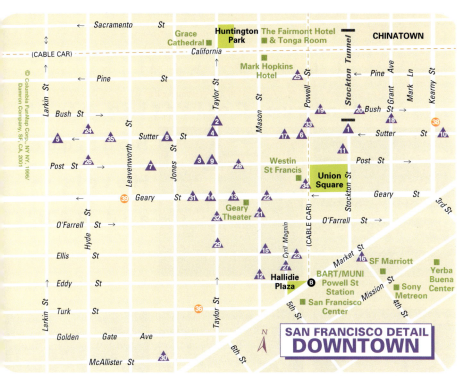

SAN FRANCISCO DETAIL DOWNTOWN

Carlton Hotel [GF] 415/673-0242, 800/922-7586 ■ 1075 Sutter (at Larkin) ■ www.carltonhotel.com

Cartwright Hotel [GF] 415/421-2865, 800/794-7661 ■ 524 Sutter St (at Powell) ■ free gym passes, afternoon tea, wine hour ■ www.cartwrighthotel.com

Clarion Bedford Hotel [GF] 415/673-6040, 800/252-7466 ■ 761 Post St (at Jones) ■ European-style, comp wine hour daily ■ www.hotelbedford.com

▶**The Commodore International Hotel** [GF] 415/923-6800, 800/338-6848 ■ 825 Sutter St (at Jones) ■ also the 'Titanic Cafe' diner & popular 'Red Room' lounge ■ www.sftrips.com/hotels/commodore.html

Dakota Hotel [GF] 415/931-7475 ■ 606 Post St (at Taylor) ■ nr Union Square ■ www.hotelsanfrancisco.com

Galleria Park Hotel [GF] 415/781-3060, 800/792-9639 ■ 191 Sutter St (at Kearny) ■ live jazz Wed-Sun ■ www.galleriapark.com

Grand Hyatt San Francisco [GF] 415/398-1234, 800/233-1234 ■ 345 Stockton St (at Sutter) ■ restaurant & lounge, gym ■ www.hyatt.com

Harbor Court Hotel [GF] 415/882-1300, 800/346-0555 ■ 165 Steuart St (btwn Howard & Mission) ■ in the heart of the Financial District, gym ■ www.harborcourthotel.com

2▶**Hotel Bijou** [GS,NS,WC] 415/771-1200, 800/771-1022 ■ 111 Mason St (at Eddy) ■ www.hotelbijou.com

3 **Hotel Diva** [GF] 415/885-0200, 800/553-1900 ■ 440 Geary (at Mason) ■ also Italian restaurant, gym ■ www.hoteldiva.com

Hotel Griffon [GF,WC] 415/495-2100, 800/321-2201 ■ 155 Steuart St (at Mission) ■ gym, also restaurant, bistro/ cont'l ■ www.hotelgriffon.com

14 **Hotel Monaco** [GF] 415/292-8132, 888/852-3551 ■ 501 Geary St (at Taylor) ■ also bar ■ www.hotelmonaco.com

15▶**Hotel Nikko San Francisco** [GS,SW,WC] 415/394-1111, 800/645-5687 ■ 222 Mason St ■ health club & spa, also ANZU restaurant ■ www.nikkohotels.com

16 **Hotel Palomar** [GF] 415/348-1111, 877/294-4711 ■ 12 4th St (at Market) ■ boutique hotel ■ www.hotelpalomar.com

17▶**The Hotel Rex** [GF,WC] 415/433-4434, 800/433-4434 ■ 562 Sutter St (at Powell) ■ also full bar ■ www.thehotelrex.com

Canterbury Hotel

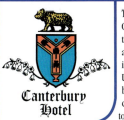

The newly renovated Canterbury is located in the chic Union Square area. Our cool location is just 3 blocks from Union Square stores, 2 blocks from the cable cars and moments away to everywhere else.

Our fabulous Murray's Glasshouse restaurant & bar features a year-round garden in full bloom and killer food. Gay and gay-friendly staff, plus we offer special rates for Damron readers. Call today for reservations!

PHONE **415/474-6464** or **800/528-1234**

SAN FRANCISCO'S
Unique Collection of Boutique Hotels and B&B's

Comfort Collection
- Phoenix Hotel

Deluxe Collection
- Maxwell Hotel

Luxury Collection
- Mill Valley Inn

Luxury Collection
- Archbishop's Mansion

Escapes Collection
- Costanoa

SAN FRANCISCO HOTELS

Archbishop's Mansion *
Hotel Bijou
Commodore Hotel
Hotel Del Sol
Jackson Court
Laurel Inn *
Maxwell Hotel
Phoenix Hotel *

MARIN HOTELS

Mill Valley Inn *
Acqua Hotel *

CALIFORNIA COAST

Costanoa Coastal Lodge & Camp *

800.SF.TRIPS
800.738.7477

Central Reservations
for all Joie de Vivre Hotels

Joie de Vivre
HOSPITALITY

www.sftrips.com

Some Locations Include
*Free Parking and Continental Breakfast

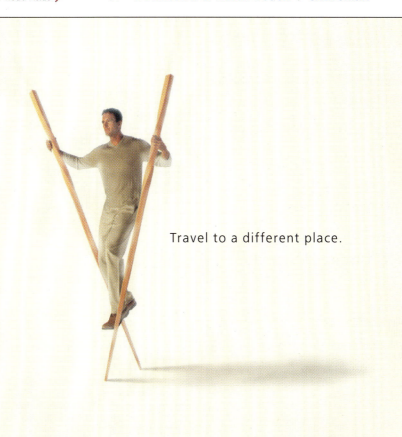

Allison Hotel
ON UNION SQUARE

**Unbeatable Location
Very Affordable Rates**

**Just 1 block from
Union Square
Cable cars
Chinatown, Shopping
& Theater Districts**

- *European Style*
- *Recently Renovated*
- *Private & Shared Baths*
- *Complimentary Continental Breakfast*
- *Color TV/Cable*
- *Close To Popular Attractions*

(415) 986-8737
Toll Free: 1-800-628-6456
Fax: (415) 392-0850
web: www.alisonhotel.com
email: info@allisonhotel.com
**417 Stockton, San Francisco
(Across From Grand Hyatt)**

---

18 **Hotel Triton** [GF,WC] 415/394-0500, 800/800-1299 ■ 342 Grant Ave (at Bush) ■ designer theme rooms ■ www.hotel-tritonsf.com

19 **Hotel Vintage Court** [GF,NS,WC] 415/392-4666, 800/654-1100 ■ 650 Bush St (at Powell) ■ also world-famous 5-star 'Masa's' restaurant, French ■ www.vintagecourt.com
Hyatt Regency San Francisco [GF] 415/788-1234, 800/233-1234 ■ 5 Embarcadero Center (at California) ■ luxury waterfront hotel ■ www.hyatt.com

20 **Juliana Hotel** [GF] 415/392-2540, 800/328-3880 ■ 590 Bush St (at Stockton) ■ featured on 'Lifestyles of the Rich & Famous' as one of SF's finest hotels ■ www.julianahotel.com

21 **King George Hotel** [GF,F,WC] 415/781-5050, 800/288-6005 ■ 334 Mason St (at O'Farrell) ■ also 'The Bread & Honey Tearoom' ■ www.kinggeorge.com

22▶ **Maxwell Hotel** [GF,WC] 415/986-2000, 888/734-6299 ■ 386 Geary St (at Mason) ■ 1908 art deco masterpiece, full brkfst ■ www.maxwellhotel.com

23 **Monticello Inn** [GF,F] 415/392-8800, 888/788-0231 ■ 127 Ellis St (at Powell) ■ boutique hotel, restaurant & bar ■ www.monticelloinn.com

24 **Nob Hill Hotel** [GF,NS] 415/885-2987, 877/662-4455 ■ 835 Hyde St (btwn Bush & Sutter) ■ European-style hotel ■ www.nobhillhotel.com

25▶ **Nob Hill Lambourne** [GF] 415/433-2287, 800/274-8466 ■ 725 Pine St (at Powell) ■ luxurious 'business accommodation', kitchens ■ www.nobhilllambourne.com

26 **Pensione International Hotel** [GS,NS] 415/775-3344, 800/358-8123 ■ 875 Post St (at Hyde) ■ Victorian-styled B&B hotel

27 **The Powell Hotel** [GS] 415/398-3200, 800/368-0700 ■ 28 Cyril Magnin St ■ www.thepowellhotel.com

28 **Prescott Hotel** [GF] 415/563-0303, 800/283-7322 ■ 545 Post St (btwn Taylor & Mason) ■ small luxury hotel ■ www.prescotthotel.com

29 **Ramada Union Square** [GF,WC] 415/673-2332, 800/228-2828 ■ 345 Taylor St (at Ellis) ■ also restaurant, full bar ■ ramadaunionsquare.com

30 **Renoir Hotel** [GS,WC] 415/626-5200, 800/576-3388 ■ 45 McAllister St (at Market St) ■ boutique-style, bar & Brazilian restaurant ■ www.renoirhotel.com
San Remo Hotel [GS] 415/776-8688, 800/352-7366 ■ 2237 Mason St (at Chestnut) ■ www.sanremohotel.com

31 **Savoy Hotel** [GF] 415/441-2700, 800/227-4223 ■ 580 Geary St (at Jones) ■ also popular restaurant & bar ■ www.savoyhotel.net

32 **Serrano Hotel** [GF,WC] 415/885-2500, 877/294-9709 ■ 405 Taylor St (at O'Farrell) ■ www.serranohotel.com

33 **Sir Francis Drake Hotel** [GF] 415/392-7755, 800/795-7129 ■ 450 Powell St (at Sutter) ■ also restaurant & 'Starlight Room' ■ www.sirfrancisdrake.com
Suites at Fisherman's Wharf [GF] 415/771-0200, 800/227-3608 ■ sundeck
Tuscan Inn [GF,WC] 415/561-1100, 888/206-7718 ■ 425 North Point St (at Taylor) ■ www.tuscaninn.com

34 **Villa Florence Hotel** [GF] 415/397-7700, 800/553-4411 ■ 225 Powell St (at Geary) ■ also restaurant ■ www.villaflorence.com

35 **The York Hotel** [GF] 415/885-6800, 800/808-9675 ■ 940 Sutter St (at Leavenworth) ■ boutique hotel, also cabaret ■ www.yorkhotel.com

SF—Downtown/Mission District • CALIFORNIA

BARS

36 **Aunt Charlie's Lounge** [M,NH] 415/441-2922 ■ 133 Turk St (at Taylor) ■ 6am-2am, drag shows Sat, 'Skid Marx' 2nd Fri (D,A,YC)

38 **Ginger's Trois** [M,NH,P] 415/989-0282 ■ 246 Kearny St (at Sutter) ■ 10am-10pm, from 2pm Sat, clsd Sun ■ www.gaysf.com

39 **Hob Nob** [M,NH] 415/771-9846 ■ 700 Geary St (at Leavenworth) ■ 6am-2am

CAFES

Caffe Trieste [★] 415/392-6739 ■ 601 Vallejo St ■ get a taste of the real North Beach (past & present) and a great cappuccino

RESTAURANTS

Cafe Claude [E,BW] 415/392-3505 ■ 7 Claude (nr Bush & Kearny) ■ 11:30am-close, clsd Sun, live jazz Th-Sat, as close to Paris as you can get in SF

Dottie's True Blue Cafe [GO] 415/885-2767 ■ 522 Jones St (at Geary) ■ 7:30am-3pm, clsd Wed, great brkfst

Mario's Bohemian Cigar Store Cafe [BW] 415/362-0536 ■ 566 Columbus Ave (at Union) ■ great foccacia sandwiches, some veggie

Masa's [★WC] 415/989-7154 ■ 650 Bush St (at 'Hotel Vintage Court') ■ world-famous 5-star French restaurant

Max's on the Square [★] 415/646-8600 ■ 398 Geary St (at Mason) ■ lunch & dinner, seafood, full bar

Millennium 415/487-9800 ■ 246 McAllister St (at Hyde, at the Abigail Hotel) ■ dinner only, Euro-Mediterranean, upscale vegetarian

Moose's [★] 415/989-7800 ■ 1652 Stockton (btwn Filbert & Union) ■ upscale bistro menu

Original Joe's 415/775-4877 ■ 144 Taylor (btwn Turk & Eddy) ■ lunch & dinner, Italian, since 1937, also art deco cocktail lounge

BOOKSTORES

City Lights Bookstore 415/362-8193 ■ 261 Columbus Ave, North Beach (at Pacific) ■ 10am-midnight, historic beatnik bookstore, many progressive titles, whole flr dedicated to poetry ■ www.citylights.com

RETAIL SHOPS

Billy Blue 415/781-2111, 800/772-BLUE ■ 54 Geary (at Grant) ■ 10am-6pm, clsd Sun, men's clothing, tailored for women

EROTICA

Circle J Video 415/474-6995 ■ 369 Ellis St (at Jones)

▶ **New Meat Campus Theater** [GO] 415/673-3384 ■ 220 Jones St (at Turk) ■ 11am-midnight, till 2am Fri-Sat, male dancers, Asian night Sun ■ www.newmeattheater.com

Nob Hill Theater 415/781-9468 ■ 729 Bush St (at Powell) ■ 24hrs, dancers, buddy booths, shower shows ■ www.nobhilltheatre.com

SF—Mission District

ACCOMMODATIONS

1 **Andora Inn** [MW,NS] 415/282-0337, 800/967-9219 ■ 2438 Mission (btwn 20th & 21st) ■ also restaurant, nr Castro ■ www.andorainn.citysearch.com

Clebia's Place [GS] 415/648-0135 ■ apt w/ great view, lesbian-owned/ run ■ www.clebiasplace.com

Elaine's Hidden Haven [GS,GO] 415/647-2726, 800/446-9050 ■ 4005 Folsom St ■ private garden apt, kitchen ■ www.sfhiddenhaven.com

2 **The Inn San Francisco** [GF,NS] 415/641-0188, 800/359-0913 ■ 943 S Van Ness Ave (btwn 20th & 21st) ■ Victorian mansion, hot tub, full brkfst ■ www.innsf.com

BARS

4 **El Rio** [GS,NH,MR-L,E] 415/282-3325 ■ 3158-A Mission St (at Cesar Chavez) ■ 3pm-2am, till midnight Mon, patio

5 **Joy** [★GS,NH,D] 415/431-8889 ■ 2925 16th St (btwn Mission & S Van Ness, at 'Liquid') ■ 9pm-2am Mon, eclectic mix of young & hip

6 **Lexington Club** [★W,NH,GO] 415/863-2052 ■ 3464 19th St (at Lexington) ■ 3pm-2am, hip younger crowd

7 **Phone Booth** [MW,NH] 415/648-4683 ■ 1398 S Van Ness Ave (at 25th) ■ 11am-2am

8 **Sadie's Flying Elephant** [GS,NH] 415/551-7988 ■ 491 Potrero (at Mariposa) ■ 3pm-2am, 9pm 1st Sun 'K'vetsh' queer open mike ■ www.flyingelephant.com

9 **Wild Side West** [GS,WC] 415/647-3099 ■ 424 Cortland, Bernal Heights (at Bennington) ■ 1pm-2am, patio, magic garden

CALIFORNIA • USA

SAN FRANCISCO DETAIL — MISSION

NIGHTCLUBS

10 **26 Mix** [GS,D,YC] 415/826-7378, 415/248-1319 ■ 3024 Mission St (btwn 26th & Cesar Chavez) ■ 5pm-2am, intimate dance club, some women's events ■ www.26mix.com

Backstreet [★WO,D,MR,S,$] 415/339-8310 ■ 550 Barneveld (2 blks off Bayshore) ■ 10pm-3am 2nd Sat, 3 dance floors ■ backstreetssf@hotmail.com

11 **Esta Noche** [M,D,MR-L,TG,S] 415/861-5757 ■ 3079 16th St (at Mission) ■ 1pm-2am, salsa & disco in a classic Tijuana dive

4 **Mango** [WO,D,MR,F] 415/339-8310 ■ 3158 Mission St (at 'El Rio') ■ 3pm-7:30pm 4th Sat April-Nov ■ backstreetssf@hotmail.com

10 **Sushi Sundays** [★W,D] 415/820-9611 ■ 3024 Mission St (at '26 Mix') ■ 7pm-midnight Sun only

CAFES

Cafe Commons [WC] 415/282-2928 ■ 3161 Mission St (btwn Cesar Chavez & Valencia) ■ 7am-9pm, 8am-10pm wknds, sandwiches, plenty veggie, patio

Farleys 415/648-1545 ■ 1315 18th St (at Texas St, Potrero Hill) ■ 7am-10pm, from 8am wknds

Red Dora's Bearded Lady [★W,TG,GO] 415/626-2805 ■ 485 14th St (at Guerrero) ■ 7am-7pm, from 9am wknds, funky brunch & sandwiches, also gallery, special events

RESTAURANTS

42 Degrees 415/777-5558 ■ 499 Illinois St, China Basin (nr 16th St) ■ Wed-Sun only, jazz supper club, full bar

The Barking Basset Cafe 415/648-2146 ■ 803 Cortland Ave (at Ellsworth) ■ 8am-3pm, clsd Tue, dinner Th-Sat only

Cafe Istanbul [WC] 415/863-8854 ■ 525 Valencia St ■ noon-11pm, till midnight Fri-Sat, Mediterranean, some veggie, authentic Turkish coffee, bellydancers Sat

Charanga [★BW,WC] 415/282-1813 ■ 2351 Mission St (at 20th St) ■ 5:30pm-10pm, till 11pm Th-Sat, clsd Sun-Mon, tapas

El Farolito [★] 415/824-7877 ■ 2777 Mission St (at 24th) ■ 11am-1am, till 3am Fri-Sat, delicious, cheap burritos

Firecracker [★] 415/642-3470 ■ 1007 1/2 Valencia St (at 21st) ■ Chinese, some veggie

Herbivore [BW] 415/826-5657 ■ 983 Valencia (nr 21st St) ■ 11am-10pm, till 11pm wknds, moderately priced vegan food in upscale setting

Just For You [★MW] 415/647-3033 ■ 1453 18th St, Potrero Hill (btwn Missouri & Connecticut) ■ 7am-2pm, 8:30am-3pm wknds, Southern brkfst, some veggie

Klein's Delicatessen [W,BW] 415/821-9149 ■ 501 Connecticut St (at 20th St, Potrero Hill) ■ 7am-7pm, 8am-5pm Sun, sandwiches & salads, some veggie, patio

Pancho Villa [BW,WC] 415/864-8840 ■ 3071 16th St (btwn Mission & Valencia) ■ 10am-midnight, some veggie, also 'El Toro' at 18th & Valencia

Pauline's Pizza Pie [★MW,BW] 415/552-2050 ■ 260 Valencia St (btwn 14th & Duboce) ■ 5pm-10pm, clsd Sun-Mon, gourmet pizza

Picaro [BW,WC] 415/431-4089 ■ 3120 16th St (at Valencia) ■ dinner only, Spanish tapas bar

The Slanted Door [★] 415/861-8032 ■ 584 Valencia St (at 17th) ■ lunch & dinner, clsd Mon, Vietnamese, reservations advised

Ti-Couz [BW,WC] 415/252-7373 ■ 3108 16th St (at Valencia) ■ 11am-11pm, from 10am wknds, dinner & dessert crepes, plenty veggie

Yamo Thai Kitchen 415/553-8911 ■ 3406 18th St (at Mission) ■ 11am-9:30pm, clsd Sun, small, no frills outfit w/ great cheap food

ENTERTAINMENT & RECREATION

Brendita's Latin Tour 415/921-0625 ■ walking tours of the Mission ■ www.imageoz.com/brendita

12 **Metronome Ballroom** [GS,$] 415/252-9000 ■ 1830 17th St (at De Haro) ■ dance lessons, salsa to swing, dance parties wknds, call for events ■ metronomeballroom.com

Women's Building 415/431-1180 ■ 3543 18th St (btwn Valencia & Guerrero) ■ check out some of the most beautiful murals in the Mission District

BOOKSTORES

13 **Bernal Books** 415/550-0293 ■ 401 Cortland Ave, Bernal Hts (at Bennington) ■ 10am-7pm, till 5pm Sat, till 4pm Sun, clsd Mon, community bookstore for Bernal Heights & beyond, lgbt section

14 **Dog Eared Books** [WC] 415/282-1901 ■ 900 Valencia St (at 20th) ■ 10am-10pm, till 8pm Sun, new & used, good lgbt section

SF—Mission/Haight • CALIFORNIA

15 **Modern Times Bookstore** [WC] 415/282-9246 ■ 888 Valencia St ■ 10am-9pm, till 10pm Fri-Sat, 11am-6pm Sun, progressive, lgbt section, readings

RETAIL SHOPS
Black & Blue Tattoo [W] 415/626-0770 ■ 483 14th St (nr Guerrero) ■ women-owned/ run
Body Manipulations 415/621-0408 ■ 3234 16th St (btwn Guerrero & Dolores) ■ noon-7pm, body piercing & jewelry

GYMS & HEALTH CLUBS
Osento [WO] 415/282-6333 ■ 955 Valencia St ■ 1pm-midnight, baths, hot tub, massage

EROTICA
Good Vibrations [W] 415/550-7399 ■ 1210 Valencia St (at 23rd) ■ 11am-7pm, till 8pm Fri-Sat, clean, well-lighted sex toy store, also mail order

▶ **Mission St News** 415/626-0309 ■ 2086 Mission St (at 17th) ■ 24hrs ■ www.sincityvideo.com

SF—Haight, Fillmore, Hayes Valley

ACCOMMODATIONS
1 **Alamo Square Inn** [GF,NS] 415/922-2055, 800/345-9888 ■ 719 Scott St (at Grove) ■ 1895 Queen Anne & 1896 Tudor Revival Victorian mansions, full brkfst ■ www.alamoinn.com
2 ▶ **The Archbishop's Mansion** [GF,NS,GO] 415/563-7872, 800/543-5820 ■ 1000 Fulton St (at Steiner) ■ one of San Francisco's grandest homes ■ www.archbishopsmansion.com
3 **Baby Bear's House** [GS,NS,GO] 415/255-9777 ■ 1424 Page St (btwn Central & Masonic) ■ 1892 Victorian, nr the Castro, gay families esp welcome ■ www.babybearshouse.com
4 **Bock's B&B** [GF,NS,GO] 415/664-6842 ■ 1448 Willard St (at Parnassus) ■ 1906 Edwardian
5 **Casa Loma Hotel** [GF] 415/552-7100 ■ 610 Fillmore St (at Fell) ■ shared bath
6 **The Chateau Tivoli** [GF,NS] 415/776-5462, 800/228-1647 ■ 1057 Steiner St (at Golden Gate) ■ historic SF B&B ■ www.chateautivoli.com
7 ▶ **Hayes Valley Inn** [GS] 415/863-9131, 800/930-7999 ■ 417 Gough St (at Hayes) ■ European-style pension ■ www.hayesvalleyinn.com
8 ▶ **Hotel Del Sol** [★GS,NS,SW] 415/921-5520, 877/433-5765 ■ 3100 Webster St (at Greenwich) ■ bright & fun California decor ■ www.thehoteldelsol.com
9 **Hotel Majestic** [GF,WC] 415/441-1100, 800/869-8966 ■ 1500 Sutter St (at Gough) ■ one of SF's earliest grand hotels, also restaurant, some veggie, full bar
10 **Inn 1890** [GS,NS,GO] 415/386-0486, 888/INN-1890 ■ 1890 Page St (nr Stanyan) ■ kitchens, fireplaces, apt available ■ www.inn1890.com
11 **Inn at the Opera** [GF] 415/863-8400, 800/325-2708 ■ 333 Fulton St (at Franklin) ■ also French restaurant ■ www.shellvacationsonline.com
12 ▶ **Jackson Court** [GF,NS] 415/929-7670 ■ 2198 Jackson St (at Buchanan) ■ 19th-century brownstone mansion ■ www.sftrips.com/hotels/jackson_ct.html
13 **Lombard Plaza Motel** [GF] 415/921-2444 ■ 2026 Lombard St (at Webster)
14 **Metro Hotel** [GF,F] 415/861-5364 ■ 319 Divisadero St (at Haight)
15 **The Queen Anne Hotel** [★GF,WC,GO] 415/441-2828, 800/227-3970 ■ 1590 Sutter St (at Octavia) ■ beautifully restored 1890 landmark, fireplaces ■ www.queenanne.com

16 **Radisson Miyako Hotel** [GF,WC] 415/922-3200, 800/533-4567 ■ 1625 Post St (at Laguna) ■ in Japantown
17 **Shannon-Kavanaugh Guest House** [GF,WC,GO] 415/563-2727 ■ 722 Steiner St (at Hayes) ■ 1-bdrm garden apt ■ www.shannon-kavanaugh.com
   Southern Comforts [M,NS,WC,GO] 323/850-5623, 800/889-7359 ■ 1800s Victorian mansion ■ www.SouthernComforts.com
18 **Stanyan Park Hotel** [GF,WC] 415/751-1000 ■ 750 Stanyan St (at Waller) ■ historic Victorian hotel, evening snacks ■ www.stanyanpark.com

BARS
19 **An Bodhran** [GF,NH,E] 415/431-4724 ■ 668 Haight St ■ 4pm-2am, from 6pm Sat, traditional Irish pub w/ live bands Wed & Sun
20 **Hayes & Vine** [GS] 415/626-5301 ■ 377 Hayes St (at Gough) ■ 5pm-midnight, till 1am wknds, 4pm-10pm Sun, wine bar ■ www.hayesandvine.com
21 **The Lion Pub** [M,P] 415/567-6565 ■ 2062 Divisadero St (at Sacramento) ■ 3pm-2am
22 **Marlena's** [M,NH,S,WC] 415/864-6672 ■ 488 Hayes St (at Octavia) ■ noon-2am, from 10am wknds, drag shows wknds, piano bar
23 **Noc Noc** [GF,BW] 415/861-5811 ■ 557 Haight St (at Fillmore) ■ 5pm-2am
24 **Traxx** [M,NH] 415/864-4213 ■ 1437 Haight St (at Masonic) ■ noon-2am

NIGHTCLUBS
25 **The Top** [GF,D,A] 415/864-7386 ■ 424 Haight St (at Webster) ■ theme nights, call for details ■ thetopdjbar.com

CAFES
Fillmore Grind 415/775-5680 ■ 711 Fillmore (at Hayes) ■ 6:30am-7pm

RESTAURANTS
Alamo Square Seafood 415/440-2828 ■ 803 Fillmore (at Grove) ■ dinner only
Blue Muse [WC] 415/626-7505 ■ 409 Gough St (at Fell) ■ 8am-10pm, wknd brunch, cont'l, some veggie, full bar
Cafe Delle Stelle [★BW] 415/252-1110 ■ 395 Hayes (at Gough) ■ Italian
Cha Cha Cha 415/386-7670 ■ 1801 Haight St (at Shrader) ■ Cuban/ Cajun, excellent sangria, worth the wait!

Hayes Valley Inn

Hayes Valley Inn

www.hayesvalleyinn.com

An inexpensive, gay-friendly hotel, Hayes Valley Inn is nestled in the heart of San Francisco's charming Hayes Valley, a neighborhood known for its fine restaurants, boutique shops, and art galleries. It is just two short blocks away from Davies Symphony Hall, War Memorial Opera House, Bill Graham Civic Auditorium, and San Francisco's sparkling City Hall. A small, pet-friendly bed and breakfast, it offers cozy accommodations at affordable prices ($58-$99).

PHONE **415/431-9131** RES **800/930-7999**

SF—Haight, Fillmore, Hayes Valley • CALIFORNIA

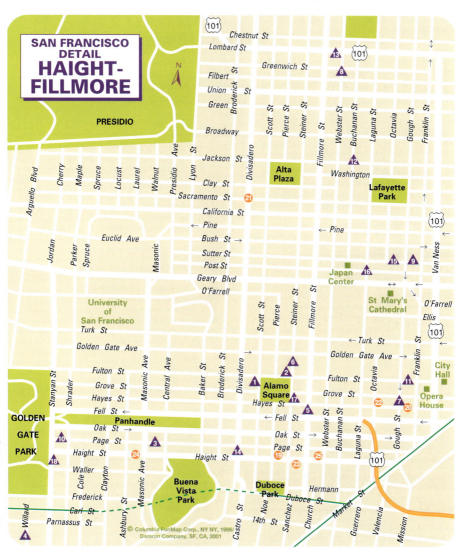

Doidge's [WC] 415/921-2149 ■ 2217 Union St (at Fillmore) ■ 8am-1:45pm, till 2:45pm wknds, great brkfst

Eliza's [★] 415/621-4819 ■ 2877 California (at Broderick) ■ dinner, excellent Chinese food & stylish decor

Ella's 415/441-5669 ■ 500 Presidio Ave (at California) ■ brkfst, lunch (Mon-Fri) & dinner, popular wknd brunch

Garibaldi's [WC,GO] 415/563-8841 ■ 347 Presidio (at Sacramento) ■ lunch & dinner, Mediterranean, full bar

Greens 415/771-6222 ■ Fort Mason, Bldg 'A' (nr Van Ness & Bay) ■ lunch Tue-Sun, dinner nightly, Sun brunch, gourmet vegetarian

Jardinière [★] 415/861-5555 ■ 300 Grove St ■ 5pm-midnight, till 10:30pm Sun-Mon, oh-so-chic Californian-French cuisine, full bar

Joubert's [★BW,GO] 415/753-5448 ■ 4115 Judah St (at 46th Ave) ■ dinner only, clsd Mon-Tue, excellent South African vegetarian (reservations a must Sat) ■ www.jouberts.com

Kan Zaman [BW] 415/751-9656 ■ 1793 Haight (at Shrader) ■ 5pm-midnight, noon-2am wknds, Mediterranean, some veggie, hookahs & tobacco available

Suppenküche [GO] 415/252-9289 ■ 525 Laguna St (at Fell) ■ German cuisine served at communal tables

Thep-Phanom [★BW] 415/431-2526 ■ 400 Waller St (at Fillmore) ■ 5:30pm-10pm, excellent Thai, worth the wait!

Retail Shops

La Riga 415/552-1525 ■ 1391 Haight St (at Masonic) ■ 11am-7pm, leather

Mainline Gifts 415/563-4438 ■ 1928 Fillmore St (at Bush)

Nomad 415/563-7771 ■ 575 Haight (at Steiner) ■ noon-7pm, piercing (walk-in), jewelry

Denver

Once home to the high plains Native Americans, Denver still boasts a diverse population. Visitors enjoy the Mile-High City's many attractions—from the 16th Street Mall's cafes and street performers to the Denver Art Museum's more than 40,000 works of art. Historic Lower Downtown (LoDo) houses many antique stores, galleries, and nightclubs.

Queer Resources

COMMUNITY INFO
▼ Gay/Lesbian/Bisexual Community Services Center of Colorado 303/733-7743 & 303/837-1598 (TDD). 234 Broadway, 10am-6pm Mon-Fri.

AIDS RESOURCES
Colorado AIDS Project 303/837-1501.

RECOVERY
303/322-4440.

City Calendar

LGBT PRIDE
June. 303/733-7743 ext 23.

ENTERTAINMENT
Denver Women's Chorus 303/274-4177.

ANNUAL EVENTS
February - Mtn States Gay & Lesbian Film Festival.
October - Annual Halloween Cheshire Ball.

Tourist Info

AIRPORT DIRECTIONS
Denver International. Take Trenton to 40 West which will take you through town, then look for desired exit.

PUBLIC TRANSIT & TAXIS
Yellow Cab 303/777-7777.
Metro Taxi 303/333-3333.
Super Shuttle 303/370-1300.
RTD 303/628-9000 or 303/299-6000 (infoline).

TOURIST SPOTS & INFO
16th Street Mall.
Black American West Museum 303/292-2566.
Denver Art Museum 720/865-5000.
Elitch Gardens 303/595-4386.
LoDo (Lower Downtown).
Molly Brown House 303/832-4092.
Visitor's Center: 303/892-1112,
   web: www.denverco.org.

WEATHER
Summer temperatures average in the 90°s and winter ones in the 40°s. The sun shines an average of 300 days a year with humidity in the single digits.

BEST VIEWS
Lookout Mountain (at night especially) or the top of the Capitol rotunda.

COLORADO

Denver

ACCOMMODATIONS

Bobby's B&B [MO,SW,NS] 303/831-8266, 800/513-7827 ■ jacuzzi & sauna ■ BobbysBnB123@aol.com

1 **Elyria's Western Guest House** [M,NS] 303/291-0915 ■ 1655 E 47th Ave (nr I-70 & Brighton) ■ hot tub ■ bestinns.net/usa/co/rdewgh.html

2 **The Gregory Inn, LoDo** [GF,GO] 303/295-6570, 800/925-6570 ■ 2500 Arapahoe St (at 25th St) ■ jacuzzis ■ www.gregoryinn.com

3 **Hotel Monaco** [GF] 303/296-1717, 800/397-5380 ■ 1717 Champa St (at 17th) ■ gym, spa, also Italian restaurant ■ www.monaco-denver.com

4 **Lumber Baron Inn** [GF] 303/477-8205 ■ 2555 W 37th Ave (at Bryant) ■ Victorian mansion, full brkfst, hot tub ■ www.lumberbaron.com

5 **Radisson Hotel Denver Stapleton Plaza** [GF,SW,WC] 303/321-3500, 800/333-3333 ■ 3333 Quebec St (at 35th) ■ also restaurant ■ www.radisson.com

6 **Victoria Oaks Inn** [GS,GO] 303/355-1818 ■ 1575 Race St (at 16th) ■ fireplaces ■ www.victoriaoaks.com

BARS

7 **BJ's Carousel** [★GS,NH,TG,F,K,S,WC,GO] 303/777-9880 ■ 1380 S Broadway (at Arkansas) ■ noon-2am, from 10am wknds, also restaurant ■ www.bjsdenver.com

8 **Brick's** [M,NH,WC] 303/377-5400 ■ 1600 E 17th Ave (at Franklin) ■ 10am-2am, lunch Mon-Fri, brunch wknds

9 **The Brig** [M,NH,S] 303/777-9378 ■ 117 Broadway (btwn 1st & 2nd Aves) ■ noon-2am, male dancers

10 **C's** [W,D] 303/322-4436 ■ 7900 E Colfax Ave (at Trenton) ■ 5pm-midnight, till 2am Fri-Sat

11 **Cafe Cero** [GS,NH,F] 303/282-1446 ■ 1446 S Broadway (btwn Arkansas & Florida) ■ 4pm-1:30am Tue-Sat, also restaurant

12 **Charlie's** [★M,D,CW,WC] 303/839-8890 ■ 900 E Colfax Ave (at Emerson) ■ 11am-4am, also restaurant ■ www.charliesonline.com

13 **Club Stud** [M,NH] 303/733-9398 ■ 255 S Broadway (at Byers) ■ 7am-2am

14 **The Compound** [M,NH,D,A] 303/722-5977 ■ 145 Broadway (at 2nd Ave) ■ 7am-2am, from 8am Sun

15 **The Den** [MW,NH,WC] 303/623-7998 ■ 5110 W Colfax Ave (at Sheridan) ■ 11am-2am, from 10am wknds, also restaurant, dinner nightly, brunch Sun

Denver • COLORADO

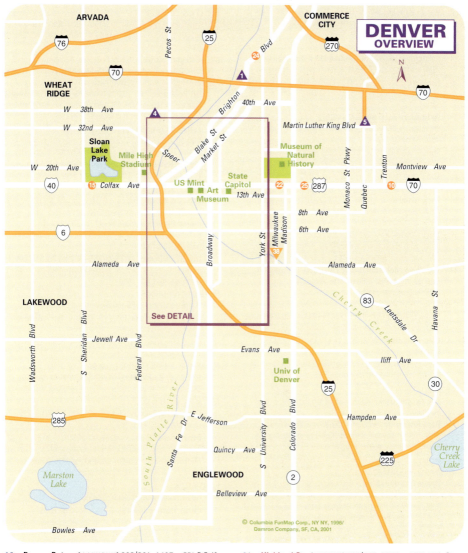

16 **Denver Detour** [★MW,E,WC] 303/861-1497 ■ 551 E Colfax Ave (at Pearl, use back entrance) ■ 11am-2am, lunch & dinner daily

17 **The Denver Wrangler** [M,B,WC] 303/837-1075 ■ 1700 Logan Ave (at 17th Ave) ■ 11am-2am, levi/ bear cruise bar ■ www.denverwrangler.com

18 **Down Under** [MW,NH,F,V] 303/777-4377 ■ 266 S Downing (at Alameda, enter on alley) ■ 3pm-2am, from noon wknds ■ www.downunder.com

19 **Fox Hole** [MW] 303/298-7391 ■ 2936 Fox St (at 20th St) ■ 9pm-2am, from 1pm Sun ■ members.aol.com/foxholebar/home.hmtl

20 **The Grand** [M,E,WC] 303/839-5390 ■ 538 E 17th Ave (at Pearl) ■ 3pm-2am, from 6pm wknds, upscale piano bar ■ www.thegrand.citysearch.com

21 **Highland Bar** [W,NH,WC] 303/455-9978 ■ 2532 15th St (at Boulder) ■ 2pm-2am

22 **The Longhorn** [MW,NH,S,WC] 303/321-6627 ■ 3014 E Colfax Ave (at St Paul) ■ 7am-2am

23 **Mr Bill's** [M,NH] 303/534-1759 ■ 1027 Broadway (at 11th Ave) ■ 10am-2am

24 **The Old Tequila Rose** [M,NH,MR-L] 303/295-2819 ■ 5190 Brighton Blvd ■ 11:30am-2am

25 **R&R Denver** [MW,NH] 303/320-9337 ■ 4958 E Colfax Ave (at Elm) ■ 1pm-2am, from 11am wknds

26 **Safari Bar** [MW,D] 303/298-7959 ■ 500 Denargo St (at 31st) ■ noon-2am, more women Th-Sat

27 **The Triangle** [M,L] 303/293-9009 ■ 2036 Broadway (at 20th Ave) ■ 3pm-2am, till 4am wknds, from 11am Sun ■ www.triangledenver.com

COLORADO • USA

28 The Zu [MW,D,K,S,WC] 303/777-0313 ■ 60 S Broadway (at Bayaud) ■ 2pm-2am, women-owned/ run ■ zubar@dimensional.com

NIGHTCLUBS

29 Amsterdam [★GS,D] 303/405-4458 ■ 2901 Walnut (at 29th) ■ after hours Fri-Sat

30 Bent [★MW,D,V,WC] 303/813-1159 ■ 1669 Clarkson (at E 17th) ■ 9pm-2am, from 5pm Fri & Sun, theme nights, patio

31 La Rumba [GF,D,E] 303/572-8006 ■ 99 W 9th Ave (at Broadway) ■ 9pm-2am, clsd Mon-Wed, salsa dance club/ lessons

32 Pure [GS,D] 303/298-7873 ■ 2637 Welton (btwn 26th & 27th) ■ 9pm-close, clsd Mon-Tue

33 The Raven [MR] 2217 Welton St (at 22nd) ■ no phone, unconfirmed

34 Rock Island [GF,D,A,YC,WC] 303/572-7625 ■ 1614 15th St (at Wazee) ■ 9pm-2am, call for events ■ www.rockislandclub.com

35 Tracks 2000 [★M,D,WC] 303/292-6600 ■ 2975 Fox St (btwn 20th & Chestnut) ■ 8pm-2am, from 5:30pm Fri, clsd Sun-Tue, women's night Fri ■ www.tracks2000.com

39 The Wave Nightclub [MW,D,S] 303/299-9283 ■ 2101 Champa St (at 21st) ■ 8pm-close Wed-Sat ■ www.thewavenightclub.com

CAFES

Bump & Grind Cafe [F] 303/861-3841 ■ 439 E 17th Ave (at Pennsylvania) ■ 7am-5:30pm, wknd brunch, clsd Mon

Diedrich Coffee [★] 303/837-1275 ■ 1201 E 9th (at Downing)

Java Creek [WC] 303/377-8902 ■ 287 Columbine St (at 3rd Ave) ■ 7am-6pm, 9am-4pm Sun

RESTAURANTS

The Avenue Grill 303/861-2820 ■ 630 E 17th Ave (at Washington)

Basil Ristorante [★BW,WC] 303/832-8009 ■ 846 Broadway (at Bayaud) ■ lunch Mon-Fri, dinner nightly, nouvelle Italian, plenty veggie

Benny's 303/894-0788 ■ 301 E 7th Ave (at Grand St) ■ 8am-11pm, Mexican

Dazzle 303/839-5100 ■ 930 Lincoln St (at 9th) ■ lunch & dinner, clsd Mon, also lounge

Janleone [E,WC] 303/863-8433 ■ 1509 Marion (at Colfax) ■ dinner, also Sun brunch, clsd Mon, patio

Las Margaritas [★WC] 303/777-0194 ■ 1066 Old S Gaylord St ■ 11am-close, bar till 2am, Mexican, some veggie

McCole 303/744-1940 ■ 1469 S Pearl (btwn Florida & Arkansas) ■ 6pm-10pm, from 5pm Fri-Sat, clsd Sun-Mon, some veggie, full bar

Painted Bench 303/863-7473 ■ 400 E 20th Ave (at Logan) ■ lunch & dinner, clsd Sun

Paris on the Platte 303/455-2451 ■ 1553 Platte (at 15th) ■ 7am-1am, till 3am wknds, popular after hrs

Racine's 303/595-0418 ■ 850 Bannock St (btwn 8th & 9th) ■ brkfst, lunch & dinner, plenty veggie, full bar

Wazee Supper Club [BW] 303/623-9518 ■ 1600 15th St (at Wazee) ■ 11am-2am, noon-midnight Sun

Zaidy's Deli 303/333-5336 ■ 121 Adams (at First) ■ 7am-4pm Mon-Tue, till 8pm Wed-Fri, 8am-4pm wknds

ENTERTAINMENT & RECREATION

Denver Women's Chorus 303/274-3177

BOOKSTORES

36 The Book Garden [WC] 303/399-2004, 800/279-2426 ■ 2625 E 12th Ave (at Elizabeth) ■ 10am-6pm, till 8pm Th, feminist ■ www.thebookgarden.com

37 Category Six [WC] 303/777-0766 ■ 42 S Broadway (at Ellsworth) ■ 10am-6pm, 11am-5pm Sun, exclusively gay men's titles ■ www.categorysixbooks.com

Isis Bookstore [WC] 303/321-0867 ■ 5701 E Colfax Ave (at Ivanhoe) ■ 10am-7pm, till 6pm Fri-Sat, noon-5pm Sun, new age, metaphysical ■ www.isisbooks.com

38 Tattered Cover Book Store [WC] 303/322-7727, 800/833-9327 ■ 2955 E 1st Ave (at Milwaukee) ■ 9am-11pm, 10am-6pm Sun; also 1536 Wynkoop St, 4 flrs

Vicious Rumors [★WC] 303/777-6060 ■ 630 E 6th Ave (at Washington) ■ 7am-10pm, till 3pm Sun

RETAIL SHOPS

Arco Iris Design 303/765-5116 ■ 19 East Bayaud ■ pride jewelry & design ■ www.a-iris.net

Bound By Design 303/830-7272, 303/832-TAT2 ■ 1336 E Colfax (at Humboldt) ■ 11am-11pm, noon-10pm Sun, piercing & tattoos

Unique of Denver [WC] 303/355-0689 ■ 2626 E 12th (btwn Elizabeth & Clayton) ■ 10am-6pm, till 7pm summers, lgbt gift shop

PUBLICATIONS

H Ink 303/722-5965 ■ www.denvergay.com

Out Front Colorado 303/778-7900 ■ statewide lgbt newspaper ■ www.outfrontcolorado.com

Pride Magazine 773/769-6328 ■ also publish Denver Pink Pages ■ pridemag@aol.com

GYMS & HEALTH CLUBS

Broadway Bodyworks [MW,WC] 303/722-4342 ■ 160 S Broadway (at Maple)

MEN'S CLUBS

Community Country Club [PC] 303/297-2601 ■ 2151 Lawrence St ■ 24hrs

Denver Swim Club [★V,YC,SW,PC] 303/321-9399 ■ 6923 E Colfax Ave (at Olive) ■ 24hrs ■ members.aol.com/dsc80220

Midtowne Spa [PC] 303/458-8902 ■ 2935 Zuni St (at 29th) ■ 24hrs ■ www.midtowne.com

EROTICA

Adult Book & Video 303/288-9529 ■ 4810 Pontiac St

Circus Theater 303/455-3144 ■ 5580 N Federal

The Crypt 303/733-3112 ■ 131 Broadway (btwn 1st & 2nd) ■ leather & more

Crypt Adult Entertainment 303/778-6584 ■ 139 Broadway (btwn 1st & 2nd) ■ all-male theaters & arcades

Dove Theater 303/893-0037 ■ 3480 W Colfax

Galaxy Theater 303/831-8319 ■ 633 E Colfax Ave (at Washington)

Heaven Sent Me [WC] 303/733-9000 ■ 116 S Broadway (btwn Alameda & Virginia)

Las Vegas Adult Palace 303/698-9119 ■ 550 W Mississippi Ave (at Santa Fe)

Pandora's Toy Box 303/778-8828 ■ 528 S Broadway

Pleasure Entertainment Center 303/722-5852 ■ 127 S Broadway (at Bayaud) ■ open 23hrs; also 3250 W Alameda, 303/ 934-2373 & 3490 W Colfax, 303/ 825-6505

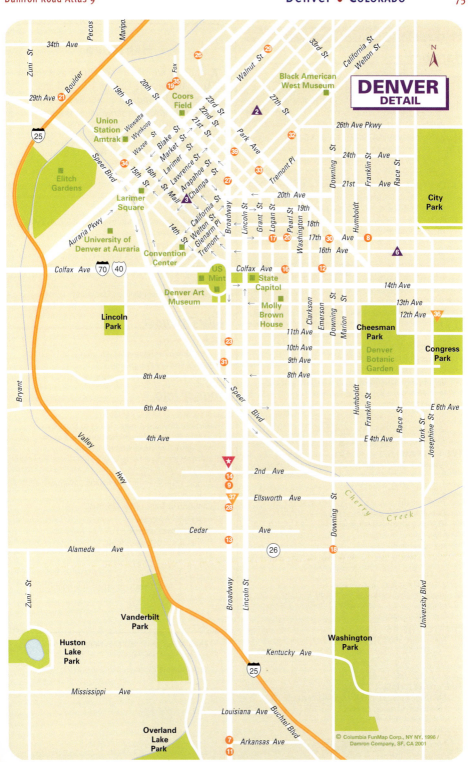

CONNECTICUT

Hartford

ACCOMMODATIONS
Butternut Farm [GS] 860/633-7189 ■ 1654 Main St, Glastonbury ■ 18th century house furnished with antiques, full brkfst ■ www.butternutfarmbandb.com

1 **Holiday Inn East Hartford** [GF,SW,WC] 860/528-9611 ■ 363 Roberts St, East Hartford ■ also restaurant

BARS
Bar One [W,D] 860/282-6106 ■ 1306 Main St, East Hartford ■ Sun only

2 **Chez Est** [★MW,D,E,S] 860/525-3243 ■ 458 Wethersfield Ave (at Main St) ■ 3pm-1am, till 2am wknds, 'Bushfire' women's night 2nd Sat, 4th Sat 'Hartford Eagle' (M,L) ■ members.aol.com/ChezEstBar

3 **The Polo Club** [MW,E] 860/278-3333 ■ 678 Maple Ave (btwn Preston & Mapleton) ■ 7pm-1am Th-Sat, till 2am wknds

1 **Women After Hours** [WO,D,OC] 860/895-1934 ■ 363 Roberts St (at the Holiday Inn), East Hartford ■ dance party 4th Sat ■ www.wahdance.com

NIGHTCLUBS
4 **Nick's Cafe** [MW,D,B,E,S] 860/956-1573 ■ 1943 Broad St (at Mapleton) ■ 4pm-1am, till 2am wknds, clsd Mon-Tue, women's night 2nd Fri, Latin & bear night Sat ■ www.nickscafe.info

9 **System** [M,D,18+] 860/524-9005 ■ 191 Ann St ■ 11pm-close Fri-Sat only

5 **Velvet** [GS,D,E,S] 860/278-6333 ■ 50 Union Pl ■ clsd Mon-Wed, gay night Sun w/ 'Universe' ■ www.velvetnightclub.com

6 **Webster Theatre** [GS,D,E] 860/246-8001 ■ 31 Webster St (at Whitmore) ■ 9pm-2am, goth/ fetish party 1st Sat, 'Club Lucy' (WO) 3rd Sat ■ www.webstertheatre.com

RESTAURANTS
Arugula 860/561-4888 ■ 953 Farmington Ave, West Hartford ■ lunch & dinner, clsd Sun-Mon, Mediterranean

Peppercorn's 860/547-1714 ■ 357 Main St ■ lunch & dinner, Italian

Pond House Cafe 860/231-8823 ■ 155 Asylum Rd, West Hartford ■ 11am-2:30pm & 5pm-9pm, Sun brunch, clsd Mon, patio

The Union 860/633-0880 ■ 2935 Main St, Glastonbury ■ lunch, dinner & Sun brunch, full bar till 1am, till 2am wknds, patio ■ www.theunionrestaurant.com

BOOKSTORES
7 **Reader's Feast Bookstore Cafe** 860/232-3710 ■ 529 Farmington Ave (at Sisson Ave) ■ 11am-6pm, 10am-2pm Sun, lgbt bookstore

RETAIL SHOPS
8 **MetroStore** 860/231-8845 ■ 493 Farmington Ave (at Sisson Ave) ■ 8:30am-8pm, till 5:30pm Tue, Wed & Sat, clsd Sun, magazines, travel guides, leather & more ■ metrostore@earthlink.net

PUBLICATIONS
Metroline 860/233-8334 ■ regional newspaper & entertainment guide, covers CT, RI & MA ■ www.metroline-online.com

EROTICA
Aircraft Book & News 860/569-2324 ■ 349 Main St (at Pratt), East Hartford

HARTFORD

Although not often thought of as a tourist destination, the Greater Hartford area boasts a wide range of museums, award-winning theatre companies, and numerous historic homes, including Mark Twain's whimsical mansion (860/247-0998). Stylish eateries, coffee bars, and night spots line Trumbull St.

Queer Resources

COMMUNITY INFO
▼ Gay/Lesbian Community Center 860/724-5542. 1841 Broad St, hours vary.

AIDS RESOURCES
Hartford Gay & Lesbian Health Collective 860/278-4163.

RECOVERY
7:30pm & 8:15pm daily at Community Center 860/724-5542.

City Calendar

LGBT PRIDE
June. 860/524-8114, email: et_pride@hotmail.com.

ANNUAL EVENTS
June - Lesbian/Gay Film Festival.

Tourist Info

AIRPORT DIRECTIONS
Hartford Brainard Airport. To get to State Capitol, take 91 North toward Hartford and exit on Capitol Ave. Head west on Capitol Ave.

PUBLIC TRANSIT & TAXIS
Yellow Cab 860/666-6666.
Airport Connection 860/627-3400 (downtown hotels only).
Connecticut Transit 860/525-9181.

TOURIST SPOTS & INFO
Bushnell Park Carousel.
Harriet Beecher Stowe House.
Mark Twain House 860/247-0998.
Real Art Ways 860/232-1006.
Wadsworth Atheneum 860/278-2670.
Visitor's Center: Greater Hartford Tourism District 800/793-4480.

Erotic Video [AYOR] 860/549-1896 ■ 35 W Service Rd (at Hwy 91 N) ■ 24hrs, hustlers

Very Intimate Pleasures 860/246-1875 ■ 100 Brainard Ave (exit 27 off I-91) ■ 9am-midnight, till 2am wknds ■ www.viphartford.com

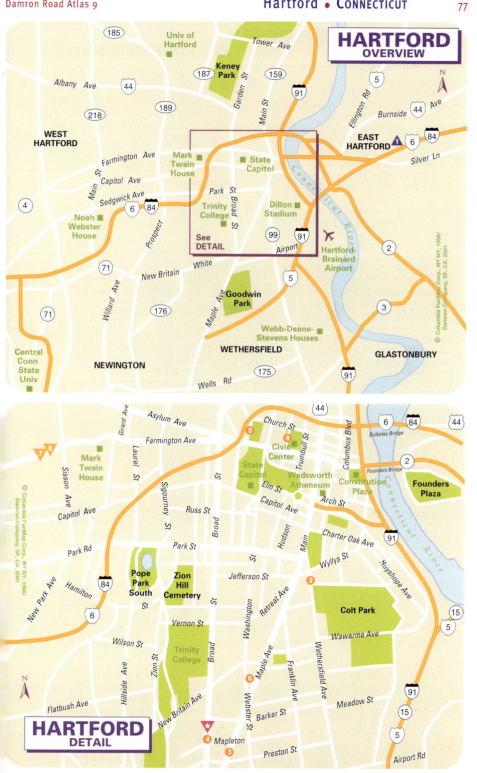

DELAWARE

Rehoboth Beach

ACCOMMODATIONS
An Inn by the Bay [GS,NS,GO] 302/644-8878, 866/833-2565 ■ 205 Savannah Rd, Lewes ■ www.geocities.com/aninnbythebay

1 **At Melissa's B&B** [GF] 302/227-7504, 800/396-8090 ■ 36 Delaware Ave (btwn 1st & 2nd) ■ women-owned/ run, 1 blk from beach ■ www.atmelissas.com

2 **Beach House B&B** [MW,SW,WC] 302/227-7074, 800/283-4667 ■ near boardwalk & beach ■ members.aol.com/thebchse/TheBeachHouse.htm

3 **Cabana Gardens B&B** [MW,SW,NS] 302/227-5429 ■ 20 Lake Ave (at 3rd St) ■ rooftop deck ■ www.cabanagardens.com

4 **Chesapeake Landing B&B** [GF,SW,NS,GO] 302/227-2973 ■ 101 Chesapeake St (at King Charles) ■ full brkfst ■ www.chesapeakelanding.com

5 **The Delaware Inn B&B** [GF,SW,GO] 302/227-6031, 800/246-5244 ■ 55 Delaware Ave ■ country inn atmosphere, near beach ■ www.delawareinn.com

The Hidden Treasure B&B [GS] 302/945-9356 ■ full brkfst, hot tub, 8 miles out of town ■ www.TheHiddenTreasure.com

5 **The Lighthouse Inn B&B** [GS] 302/226-0407, 800/600-9092 ■ 20 Delaware Ave ■ seasonal, B&B, also apt, 1 blk from beach ■ www.lighthouseinn.thebeaches.com

6 **Lord Hamilton Seaside B&B Inn** [MW,GO] 302/227-6960, 877/227-6960 ■ 20 Brooklyn Ave (at 1st) ■ Victorian home, 1/2 blk to beach & boardwalk ■ www.lordhamilton.com

7 **The Pelican Loft** [W,NS] 302/226-5080, 800/550-9551 ■ 45 Baltimore Ave ■ some shared baths, close to beach & boardwalk, lesbian-owned/ run ■ www.pelicanloft.com

The Ram's Head Inn [MO,SW,NS] 302/226-9171 ■ RD 2 Box 509 ■ hot tub, gym, sauna, open bar ■ www.theramshead.com

8 **Rehoboth Guest House** [MW] 302/227-4117, 800/564-0493 ■ 40 Maryland Ave (at King Charles) ■ seasonal, Victorian beach house, near boardwalk & beach ■ www.guesthse.com

9 **Renegade Restaurant & Lounge/ Motel** [★MW,D,F,K,SW,WC] 302/227-4713, 302/227-1222 ■ 4274 Hwy 1 (nr Rehoboth Ave) ■ 10-acre resort, restaurant (dinner only), full bar ■ www.therenegade.com

10 **Shore Inn at Rehoboth** [M,SW,GO] 302/227-8487, 800/597-8899 ■ 703 Rehoboth Ave (nr Church) ■ hot tub, sundeck ■ www.shoreinn.com

11 **Silver Lake Guest House** [MW] 302/226-2115, 800/842-2115 ■ 133 Silver Lake Dr ■ near Poodle Beach ■ www.silverlakeguesthouse.com

12 **Summer Place Hotel** [GS] 302/226-0766, 800/815-3925 ■ 30 Olive Ave (at 1st) ■ also apts, near beach ■ www.rehobothsummerplace.com

13 **The Sussex House B&B** [GS,NS,GO] 302/227-7860, 877/787-7392 ■ 601 Bayard Ave (at New Castle Ave) ■ 2 blks to beach, some shared baths ■ www.thesussexhouse.com

BARS
14 **The Blue Moon** [★MW] 302/227-6515 ■ 35 Baltimore Ave (btwn 1st & 2nd) ■ 4pm-2am, clsd Jan, popular happy hour & T-dance, also restaurant, dinner, Sun brunch, plenty veggie

REHOBOTH BEACH

A popular seaside resort, Rehoboth Beach attracts vacationers from Washington, DC, and the surrounding areas each summer. The charming mixture of eateries, shops (no sales tax!), and beaches makes for a relaxing atmosphere.

Queer Resources

COMMUNITY INFO
Camp Rehoboth 302/227-5620, web: www.camprehoboth.com.

RECOVERY
302/856-6452.

City Calendar

ANNUAL EVENTS
November - Rehoboth Beach Independent Film Festival 302/645-9095, web: www.rehobothfilm.com.
July - Fireworks 302/227-2772.

Tourist Info

AIRPORT DIRECTIONS
Rehoboth Beach is within 1 1/2 hours of several airports: Baltimore-Washington International, Greater Wilmington, Ronald Reagan Washington National, Philadelphia International.

PUBLIC TRANSIT & TAXIS
Seaport Taxi 302/645-6800.
Jolly Trolley 302/227-1197 (seasonal tour & shuttle).

TOURIST SPOTS & INFO
Main Street 302/227-2772.
North Shores beach.
Visitor's Center: Rehoboth Beach-Dewey Beach Chamber of Commerce 302/227-2233 & 800/441-1329.
Rehoboth Convention Center 800/282-8667 (in-state) and 800/441-8846 (out-of-state).

---

15 **Double L Bar** [M,L] 302/227-0818 ■ 622 Rehoboth Ave ■ 3pm-2am, clsd Sun ■ www.doublelbar.com

16 **Frogg Pond** [GF,NH,F] 302/227-2234 ■ 3 S 1st St (at Rehoboth Ave) ■ 10am-1am, popular happy hour

9 **The Renegade** [★MW,D,F,K,SW,WC] 302/227-4713 ■ at Renegade Motel ■ hosts very popular women's T-dance summers (check www.partygirl.net for more info) ■ www.therenegade.com

NIGHTCLUBS
17 **The Beach House Restaurant & Bar** [W,D,E,WC] 302/227-4227 ■ 316 Rehoboth Ave ■ seasonal, dinner & dance club

18 **Purple Parrot Grill** [GS,D,WC] 302/226-1139 ■ 247 Rehoboth Ave ■ call for hrs, also restaurant

CAFES
Java Beach 302/227-8418 ■ 167 Rehoboth Ave ■ 7am-6pm, open later in summer, patio

Rehoboth Beach • Delaware

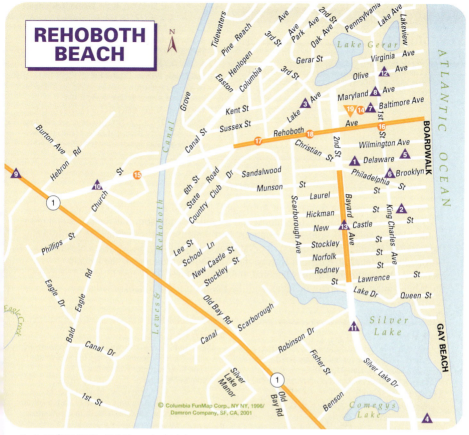

Lori's 302/226-3066 ■ 39 Baltimore Ave (at 1st) ■ seasonal, also sandwiches

Restaurants
Back Porch Cafe [WC] 302/227-3674 ■ 59 Rehoboth Ave ■ lunch & dinner, Sun brunch

Celsius [WC] 302/227-5767 ■ 50-C Wilmington Ave ■ dinner only Th-Sun, French-Mediterranean

Cloud Nine [★D,WC] 302/226-1999 ■ 234 Rehoboth Ave (at 2nd) ■ 4pm-2am, fusion bistro, full bar, dancing wknds ■ www.Cloud9restaurant.com

The Cultured Pearl 302/227-8493 ■ 19 Wilmington Ave A (off 1st St) ■ 5pm-10pm Th-Sat, sushi bar, cocktail lounge

Dream Cafe 302/226-2233 ■ 26 Baltimore Ave ■ 7am-5pm

La La Land 302/227-3887 ■ 22 Wilmington Ave ■ 6pm-1am (seasonal), seafood & more, full bar, patio ■ www.lalalandrestaurant.com

Sydney's Side Street Restaurant & Blues Place [E] 302/227-1339 ■ 25 Christian St (at 2nd St) ■ 4pm-1am (seasonal), patio, full bar

Tijuana Taxi [WC] 302/227-1986 ■ 207 Rehoboth Ave (at 2nd St) ■ 5pm-10pm, from noon wknds

Yum-Yum Pan Asian Bistro [★] 302/226-0400 ■ 37 Wilmington Ave ■ name says it all, patio, T-dance Sun

Entertainment & Recreation
Carpenter's Beach below S end of Boardwalk at foot of Queen St

North Shores S end of Cape Henlopen State Park (at jetty S of watch person) ■ popular women's beach, 20 min walk from boardwalk

Poodle Beach S of boardwalk ■ popular gay beach

Bookstores
19 Lambda Rising [WC] 302/227-6969 ■ 39 Baltimore Ave (btwn 1st & 2nd) ■ 10am-midnight, till 8pm in winter, lgbt

Publications
Letters from Camp Rehoboth 302/227-5620 ■ newsmagazine w/ events & entertainment listings ■ www.camprehoboth.com

Gyms & Health Clubs
Body Shop [MW] 302/226-0920 ■ 401 N Boardwalk (at Virginia)

The Firm Fitness Center 302/227-8363 ■ 6 Camelot Shopping Ctr / Rt 1 ■ 7am-9pm ■ pault@dmv.com

District of Columbia • USA

Washington

Accommodations

1. **1836 California** [GS] 202/462-6502 ■ 1836 California St NW (btwn 18th & 19th) ■ 1900s house w/ period furnishings & sundeck, some shared baths ■ members.aol.com/calif1836/

16▶ **The Bed and Breakfast at the William Lewis House** [★M,GO] 202/462-7574, 800/465-7574 ■ 1309 'R' St NW (at 13th) ■ 2 turn-of-the-century buildings, full brkfst wknds, hot tub ■ www.wlewishous.com

2. **The Brenton B&B** [M] 202/332-5550, 800/673-9042 ■ 1708 16th St NW (at 'R' St)

3. **Bull Moose B&B on Capitol Hill** [GS,NS] 202/547-1050, 800/261-2768 ■ 101 5th St NE (at 'A' St) ■ Victorian rowhouse ■ www.bullmoose-b-and-b.com

4. **The Carlyle Suites Hotel** [GS,F,WC] 202/234-3200, 800/964-5375 ■ 1731 New Hampshire Ave NW (btwn 'R' & 'S' Sts) ■ art deco hotel, gym, also restaurant & bar, popular gay Sun brunch ■ www.carlylesuites.com

Washington

Known worldwide as a showcase of American culture and as a command center of global politics, Washington is often overlooked as a tourist destination. But the US capital gives visitors almost unlimited sight-seeing options, both uplifting and sobering: the Smithsonian, the National Air and Space Museum, the National Gallery of Art, the Museum of Natural History, the Museum of American History, the Washington Monument, the Lincoln Memorial, the Vietnam Veterans Memorial, the United States Holocaust Memorial Museum, the White House, the Capitol building, and the Washington National Cathedral.

Queer Resources

Community Info
Gay/Lesbian Hotline 202/833-3234, 7pm-11pm.
Hola Gay (hotline for Spanish speakers) 202/332-2192, 7pm-11pm Th.
Washington Blade, web: www.washblade.com.

AIDS Resources
Whitman-Walker Clinic 202/797-3500, web: www.wwc.org.

Recovery
Triangle Club 202/659-8641. 2030 'P' St NW.

City Calendar

LGBT Pride
June. 202/986-1119.

Entertainment
Gay Men's Chorus 202/338-7464.

Annual Events
October - Reel Affirmations Film Festival 202/986-1119.
March - Women's History Month at various Smithsonian Museums 202/357-2700.

Tourist Info

Airport Directions
Washington Dulles International. To get downtown, take Dulles Airport Access and Toll Rd to I-66 and head east into Washington.
Baltimore/Washington International. To get downtown, follow 46 out of airport to the Baltimore/Washington Expressway. Take a left on the Expressway and head south to Washington.

Public Transit & Taxis
Yellow Cab 202/544-1212.
Washington Flier 703/661-8230 & 703/685-1400 (from Dulles or National).
Super Shuttle 800/809-7080.
Metro Transit Authority 202/637-7000.

Tourist Spots & Info
Ford's Theatre 202/347-4833.
Jefferson Memorial.
JFK Center for the Performing Arts.
Lincoln Memorial.
National Gallery 202/737-4215.
National Museum of Women in the Arts 202/783-5000.
National Zoo 202/673-4717.
Smithsonian 202/357-1300.
Vietnam Veteran's Memorial.
Visitor's Center: DC Visitors Assoc. 202/789-7000, web: www.washington.org.

Weather
Summers are hot (90°s) and MUGGY (the city was built on marshes). In the winter, temperatures drop to the 30°s and 40°s with rain. Spring is the time of cherry blossoms.

Best Views
From the top of the Washington Monument.

Washington • District of Columbia

Creekside B&B [W,SW,GO] 301/261-9438 ■ private home on the shore of the Chesapeake (40 minutes from DC), full brkfst ■ bcsellen@juno.com

5 **Dupont at the Circle** [GS] 202/332-5251, 888/412-0100 ■ 1604 19th St NW (at 'Q' St) ■ www.dupontatthecircle.com

6 **The Embassy Inn** [GF] 202/234-7800, 800/423-9111 ■ 1627 16th St NW ■ small hotel w/ B&B atmosphere
Embassy Suites Alexandria [GS,SW] 703/684-5900 ■ 1900 Diagonal Rd, Alexandria, VA ■ full brkfst ■ www.embassysuites.com
Embassy Suites–Chevy Chase Pavilion [GF,SW,WC] 202/362-9300, 800/362-2779 ■ 4300 Military Rd NW ■ www.embassysuites.com

7 **Kalorama Guest House at Kalorama Park** [GS] 202/667-6369 ■ 1854 Mintwood Pl NW (at Columbia Rd) ■ Victorian townhouse nr Dupont Circle, restaurants ■ www.washingtonpost.com/yp/kgh

8 **Kalorama Guest House at Woodley Park** [GS,NS] 202/328-0860 ■ 2700 Cathedral Ave NW (off Connecticut Ave) ■ nr National Zoo & Washington Cathedral ■ www.washingtonpost.com/yp/kgh

9 **Morrison-Clark Historic Inn & Restaurant** [GF] 202/898-1200 ■ Massachusetts Ave NW (at 11th St NW) ■ www.morrisonclark.com

10 **One Washington Circle Hotel** [GF,SW] 202/872-1680, 800/424-9671 ■ One Washington Cir NW ■ suites w/ kitchens, also restaurant & piano bar ■ www.onewashcirclehotel.com

11 **Radisson Barcelo Hotel Washington** [GF,F,SW] 202/293-3100, 800/333-3333 ■ 2121 'P' St NW (at 21st St) ■ www.radisson.com

12 **The River Inn** [GF,WC] 202/337-7600, 800/424-2741 ■ 924 25th St NW (at 'K' St) ■ suites w/ kitchen, gym, also 'Foggy Bottom Cafe' ■ www.theriverinn.com

13 **Savoy Suites Hotel** [GF,WC] 202/337-9700, 800/944-5377 ■ 2505 Wisconsin Ave NW (at Calvert, in Georgetown) ■ also Italian restaurant

14 **Swann House Historic B&B** [GS,SW] 202/265-4414 ■ 1808 New Hampshire Ave NW (at Swann St) ■ 1883 Victorian mansion in Dupont Circle, roof deck, fireplaces ■ www.swannhouse.com

15 **Washington Plaza** [GF] 202/842-1300, 800/424-1140 ■ 10 Thomas Cir NW (at 14th & Massachusetts) ■ full-service hotel, also restaurant ■ www.washingtonplazahotel.com

17 **The Windsor Inn** [GF] 202/667-0300, 800/423-9111 ■ 1842 16th St NW ■ small hotel w/ B&B atmosphere

Bars

18 **Back Door Pub** [M,D,MR-AF,F,S,WC] 202/546-5979 ■ 1104 8th St SE (at 'L' St) ■ 4pm-2am, till 3am Fri-Sat

19 **Badlands** [M,D,K,S,V,YC,WC] 202/296-0505 ■ 1415 22nd St NW (btwn 'P' & 'Q' Sts) ■ 9pm-2am, till 5am Fri-Sat, clsd Sun-Mon & Wed, also 'Annex' upstairs (M,K,S,V) ■ www.badlandsdc.com

20 **Club Chaos** [MW,D,MR,F,S,WC] 202/232-4141 ■ 1603 17th St NW (at 'Q' St) ■ 5pm-2am, women's night Wed, Latin Th, also restaurant ■ www.chaosdc.com

21 **DC Eagle** [★M,L,WC] 202/347-6025 ■ 639 New York Ave NW (btwn 6th & 7th) ■ 4pm-2am Sun-Th, till 3am Fri-Sat ■ www.dcpride.org/DCEagle

22 **The Fireplace** [M,NH,MR,V,WC] 202/293-1293 ■ 2161 'P' St NW (at 22nd St) ■ 1pm-2am, wknds till 3am

23 **JR's Bar** [★M,NH,V,YC] 202/328-0090 ■ 1519 17th St NW (at Church) ■ 11:30am-2am, till 3am Fri-Sat, cruisy, hot cocktail hour ■ jrseric@aol.com

24 **Larry's Lounge** [MW,NH,F,WC] 202/483-1483 ■ 1840 18th St NW (at 'T' St) ■ 5pm-2am, till 3am Fri-Sat ■ www.larryslounge.com

4 **The Lillies** [M,F,WC] 202/518-5011 ■ 1731 New Hampshire (at 18th & 'R' Sts, in the 'Carlyle Suites') ■ 5pm-2am, also restaurant, 7am-10:30pm

25 **Mr Henry's Capitol Hill** [★GF,MR,E] 202/546-8412 ■ 601 Pennsylvania Ave SE (at 6th St) ■ 11:30am-midnight, till 1am wknds, live jazz, also restaurant

22 **Mr P's** [M,MR,S,V] 202/293-1064 ■ 2147 'P' St NW (at 22nd) ■ 2pm-2am, till 3am wknds, patio, very cruisy, also piercing store

26 **Nob Hill** [MW,NH,D,MR-AF,S] 202/797-1101 ■ 1101 Kenyon NW (at 11th St) ■ 6pm-2am, till 3am wknds, clsd Mon-Tue, dancers

22 **Omega** [★M,MR,K,S,V] 202/223-4917 ■ 2122 'P' St NW (enter rear) ■ 4pm-2am, 8pm-3am Sat ■ www.omegadc.com

You are *always* welcome at the

WILLIAM LEWIS HOUSE

Washington's Finest Bed & Breakfast

(202) 462-7574
(800) 465-7574

Warm, Cozy, Convenient • Close to 17th St. and Dupont Circle
Minutes from the Mall Close to Metro
Great Restaurants Nearby
Perfect for Business
Great for Sightseeing
Friendly, First Class Accommodations
Visa, Master Card, American Express and Discover Accepted
Smoking Permitted in the Garden
Fax: (202)462-1608   E-mail: Info@WLewisHous.com
http://www.WLewisHous.com

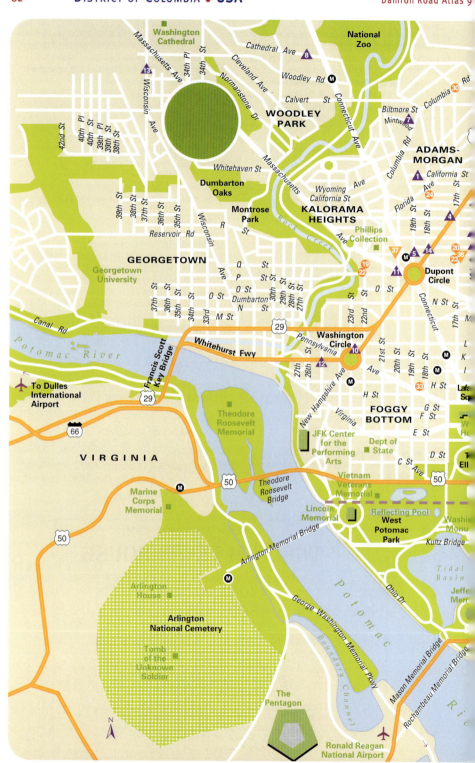

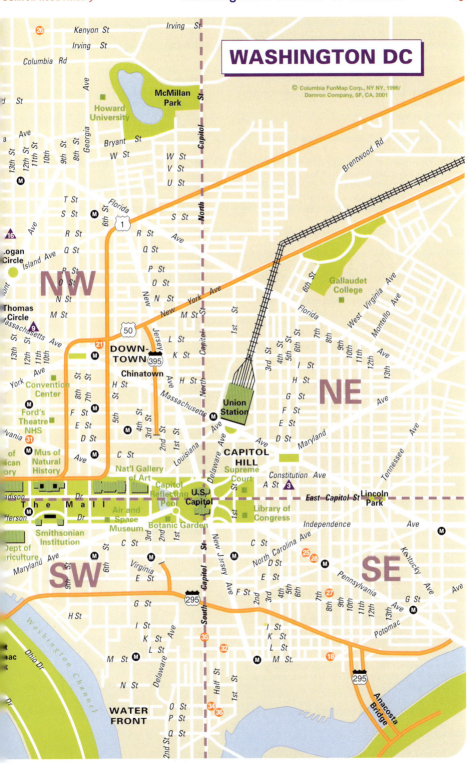

District of Columbia • USA

27 **Phase One** [W,NH,D,MR,E,WC] 202/544-6831 ■ 525 8th St SE (btwn 'E' & 'G' Sts) ■ 7pm-2am, till 3am Fri-Sat (clsd Mon-Tue winter), leather last Fri

28 **Remington's** [★M,D,CW,K,S,V] 202/543-3113 ■ 639 Pennsylvania Ave SE (btwn 6th & 7th) ■ 4pm-2am, till 3am Fri-Sat, dance lessons Mon, Wed-Th ■ www.remingtonsdc.com

20 **Windows** [M,D,E,K,OC] 202/328-0100 ■ 1635 17th St NW ■ piano bar/ cabaret

Nightclubs

29 **Atlas** [M,D] 202/331-4422 ■ 1520 14th St NW (at "The Saint") ■ dance parties, locations vary, call for info ■ www.atlasevents.com

18 **Bachelors Mill** [★M,D,MR-AF,S,WC] 202/544-1931 ■ 1104 8th St SE (downstairs at 'Back Door Pub') ■ 10pm-close, clsd Mon, more women Wed

30 **Chief Ike's Mambo Room** [GF,D,WC] 202/332-2211 ■ 1725 Columbia Rd NW (at Ontario) ■ 6pm-2am, 4pm-3am wknds, also restaurant, Cajun

29 **Club Diversité** [M,D,MR,F,S] 202/234-5740 ■ 1526 14th St NW (btwn 'P' & 'Q' Sts) ■ 11:30am-2am, till 3am wknds, restaurant till 10pm, Latin music Fri-Sat, mostly African-American clientele Sun

31 **Club One** [MW,D,MR,S] 202/544-6406 ■ 1129 Pennsylvania Ave SE (at 12th) ■ open Th-Sat, women's night Th, Latin Fri-Sat, also piano bar, open mic & special events

32 **The Edge** [M,D,MR,F,V,18+,WC] 202/488-1200 ■ 56 'L' St SE (at Half St) ■ 10pm-close, 11pm-5am Fri-Sat, clsd Sun, women's night Wed (MR), 'Boys Club' (MR-AF) Fri, also 'Wet' (M,F,V,WC), nude go-go boys in showers, women's party 3pm-7pm last Sat ■ www.edgewet.com

33 **Hung Jury** [★W,D,F,S,WC] 202/785-8181 ■ 1819 'H' St NW (at 18th) ■ 10pm-3am Fri, 9pm-4am Sat

34 **La Cage** [★M,S,V] 202/554-3615 ■ 18 'O' St SE (at S Capitol) ■ 8pm-2am, till 3am Fri-Sat, from 6pm Sun, clsd Mon, nude go-go boys ■ LACAGE.com

29 **Lizard Lounge** [★M,D,F] 202/331-4422 ■ 1520 14th St NW (at 'The Saint') ■ 8pm-2am Sun, call for info, also restaurant

35 **Velvet** [★M,D,S,YC,$] 202/554-1500 ■ at S Capitol & 'K' Sts SE (at 'Nation') ■ 10pm Sat ■ www.velvetnation.com

36 **Ziegfield's** [MW,D,A,MR,WC] 202/554-5141 ■ 1345 Half St SE (at 'O' St) ■ 8pm-3am, till 2am Th & Sun, clsd Mon-Wed

Cafes

Cafe Luna [★MW] 202/387-4005 ■ 1633 'P' St NW (at 17th) ■ 8am-11pm, from 10am wknds, till 1:30am Fri-Sat, plenty veggie

Franklyn's Coffee House [★BW] 202/319-1800 ■ 2000 18th St NW (at 'U' St) ■ 8am-8pm, patio

Jolt n' Bolt [★F] 202/232-0077 ■ 1918 18th St NW (at Florida) ■ 6am-12:30am, till 1:30am wknds, patio

Soho Tea & Coffee [WC] 202/463-7646 ■ 2150 'P' St NW ■ 6am-4am, till 5am Fri-Sat, cybercafe & more, patio

Stompin' Grounds [WC] 202/546-5228 ■ 666 Pennsylvania Ave SE (at 7th) ■ 7am-8pm, lesbian hangout, patio, outdoor music wknds, also poetry readings & events

Xando [★] 202/332-6364 ■ 1647 20th St ■ 6:30am-midnight, till 2am wknds, full bar from 4pm, make your own s'mores

Restaurants

17th Street Bar & Grill [★] 202/872-1126 ■ 1516 Rhode Island Ave NW (at 17th) ■ brkfst, lunch & dinner, popular Sun brunch, patio

Annie's Paramount Steak House [★] 202/232-0395 ■ 1609 17th St NW (at Corcoran) ■ 11am-4am, 24hrs Fri-Sat, full bar

Armand's Chicago Pizza 202/686-9450 ■ 4231 Wisconsin Ave NW (at Veazey) ■ 11:30am-10pm, full bar; also 226 Massachusetts Ave NE, Capitol Hill, 202/547-6600

Banana Cafe & Piano Bar [GO] 202/543-5906 ■ 500 8th St SE (at 'E' St) ■ lunch & dinner, Puerto Rican/ Cuban, some veggie, famous margaritas

Cafe Berlin [WC] 202/543-7656 ■ 322 Massachusetts Ave NE (btwn 3rd & 4th) ■ lunch Mon-Sat & dinner nightly, German

Cafe Japoné [★MR-A,K] 202/223-1573 ■ 2032 'P' St NW (at 21st) ■ 6pm-2am, Japanese, full bar, live jazz Wed-Th

Dupont Italian Kitchen & Bar 202/328-3222, 202/328-0100 ■ 1637 17th St NW (at 'R' St) ■ 11am-midnight, bar from 4pm, some veggie

Fio's 202/667-3040 ■ 3636 16th St NW (at the 'Woodner') ■ clsd Mon, dinner, Italian

Food For Thought 202/797-1095 ■ 1831 14th St NW (at the 'Black Cat') ■ 7pm-11pm Mon-Sat, plenty veggie, indie/ punk music shows

Gabriel [WC] 202/956-6690 ■ 2121 'P' St NW (at 21st) ■ 10:30am-10pm, Mediterranean/ Latin, full bar

Guapo's [WC] 202/686-3588 ■ 4515 Wisconsin Ave NW (at Albemale) ■ lunch & dinner, Mexican, full bar

Il Radicchio [★] 202/986-2627 ■ 1509 17th St NW (btwn 'P' & 'Q') ■ lunch & dinner, Italian

The Islander 202/234-4955 ■ 1201 'U' St (at 12th) ■ lunch & dinner, Caribbean, full bar

Jaleo [WC] 202/628-7949 ■ 480 7th St NW (at 'E' St) ■ lunch & dinner, tapas, full bar

La Frontera Cantina 202/232-0437 ■ 1633 17th St NW (btwn 'R' & 'Q') ■ 11am-11pm, till 1am Fri-Sat, Tex-Mex

Lauriol Plaza 202/387-0035 ■ 1835 18th St NW (at 'S') ■ lunch & dinner, Latin American

Mediterranean Blue [MW] 202/483-2583 ■ 1910 18th St NW (at 'T') ■ dinner, wknd brunch, upscale Middle Eastern

Mercury Grill [GO] 202/667-5937 ■ 1602 17th St NW ■ dinner, Sun brunch, full bar, patio

Occidental Grill 202/783-1475 ■ 1475 Pennsylvania Ave NW (btwn 14th & 15th) ■ lunch & dinner, political player hangout

Pearl [GO] 202/328-0846 ■ 2228 18th St NW (at Kalorama) ■ dinner only, upstairs lounge open wknds

Pepper's [★WC] 202/328-8193 ■ 1527 17th St NW (btwn 'P' & 'Q') ■ 11:30am-2am, wknds brunch, global American, full bar, patio, great people watching

Perry's 202/234-6218 ■ 1811 Columbia Rd NW (at 18th) ■ 5:30pm-11:30pm, fusion, popular drag brunch Sun, full bar, roof deck

Red Sea 202/483-5000 ■ 2463 18th St NW ■ lunch & dinner, Ethiopian, plenty veggie

Rocklands 202/333-2558 ■ 2418 Wisconsin Ave NW (at Calvert) ■ lunch & dinner, bbq & take-out

Roxanne 202/462-8330 ■ 2319 18th St NW (at Belmont) ■ lunch wknds, dinner nightly, Tex/ Mex, full bar, also 'Peyote Cafe'

Sala Thai 202/872-1144 ■ 2016 'P' St NW (at 21st) ■ lunch & dinner, some veggie

Washington • District of Columbia

Sheridan's [MW,D,CW,P,S,GO] 202/546-6955 ■ 713 8th St SE ■ dinner only, clsd Mon-Tue, steakhouse, saloon, and dance hall ■ www.sheridans1874.com

Skewers [★] 202/387-7400 ■ 1633 'P' St NW (at 17th) ■ 11:30am-11pm, Middle Eastern, full bar

Soul Vegetarian 202/328-7685 ■ 2606 Georgia Ave NW ■ 11am-9pm, till 3pm Sun (brunch), all-vegan menu

Trio 202/232-6305 ■ 1537 17th St NW ■ 7:30am-midnight, American, full bar

Trocadero Cafe [WC] 202/797-2000 ■ 1914 Connecticut Ave (in 'Hotel Sofitel') ■ lunch & dinner, intimate French restaurant

Two Quail [★GO] 202/543-8030 ■ 320 Massachusetts Ave NE ■ lunch Mon-Fri, dinner nightly, Sun brunch, full bar ■ twoquail@aol.com

Entertainment & Recreation

Anecdotal History Tours 301/294-9514 ■ variety of guided tours ■ dcsightseeing.com

Gay Men's Chorus 202/338-7464

Phillips Collection 202/387-0961 ■ 1612 21st St NW (at 'Q' St) ■ clsd Mon, America's oldest museum of modern art, nr Dupont Circle

Women in the Life [MR] 202/483-9818, 202/483-9818 ■ 1611 Connecticut Ave NW #2B ■ party 1st Fri, social events, sports teams, open mics ■ www.womeninthelife.com

Bookstores

ADC Map & Travel Center 202/628-2608, 800/544-2659 ■ 1636 'I' St NW (at 17th St) ■ 9am-5:30pm, till 6:30pm Wed-Th, 10am-4pm Sat, clsd Sun, extensive maps & travel guides

Kramer Books & Afterwords [WC] 202/387-1400 ■ 1517 Connecticut Ave NW (at 'Q') ■ 7:30am-1am, 24hrs wknds, also cafe

Lambda Rising [WC] 202/462-6969 ■ 1625 Connecticut Ave NW (btwn 'Q' & 'R' Sts) ■ 9am-10pm Mon-Th, till midnight Fri-Sun, lgbt

Sisterspace & Books 202/332-3433 ■ 1515 'U' St NW (at 15th St) ■ 10am-7pm, clsd Sun, specialize in books by & about African-American women, workshops & seminars ■ www.sisterspace.com

Retail Shops

Outlook [WC] 202/745-1469 ■ 1706 Connecticut Ave NW (btwn 'R' & 'S' Sts) ■ 10am-10pm, till 11pm Fri-Sat, cards, gifts, etc

Universal Gear 202/319-1157 ■ 1601 17th St NW (at 'Q') ■ 11am-10pm Sun-Th, till midnight Fri-Sat, casual, club, athletic & designer clothing ■ see ad on page 128 (in Chicago) ■ www.universalgear.com

Publications

MW (Metro Arts & Entertainment) 202/638-6830 ■ extensive club listings ■ mweekly1@aol.com

Washington Blade 202/797-7000 ■ huge lgbt newspaper w/ extensive resource listings ■ www.washblade.com

Woman's Monthly 202/965-5239 ■ articles & calendar of community/ arts events for greater DC/ Baltimore area ■ www.womo.com

Women in the Life 202/483-9818 ■ www.womeninthelife.com

Gyms & Health Clubs

Results—The Gym [GF] 202/518-0001 ■ 1612 'U' St NW (at 17th St) ■ also women-only fitness area; also 'Aurora Basics Health Cafe', 9am-10pm, 202/234-6822

Washington Sports Club [GF] 202/332-0100 ■ 1835 Connecticut Ave NW (at Columbia & Florida) ■ clsd Sun

Men's Clubs

Club Washington [PC,AYOR] 202/488-7317 ■ 20 'O' St SE (at S Capitol, upstairs) ■ 24hrs

Crew Club 202/319-1333 ■ 1321 14th St NW (at Rhode Island) ■ 24hrs

GHC (The Gloryhole) 202/863-2770 ■ 24 'O' St SE (at S Capitol & Half, downstairs) ■ 24hrs

Erotica

B&K Newsstand Video Arcade 202/628-7212 ■ 1340 'G' St NW (at 13th)

Leather Rack 202/797-7401 ■ 1723 Connecticut Ave NW (btwn 'R' & 'S' Sts)

Pleasure Place [WC] 202/483-3297 ■ 1710 Connecticut Ave NW (btwn 'R' & 'S' Sts) ■ 10am-midnight, till 10pm Mon-Tue, noon-7pm Sun, leather, latex, shoes & more ■ pleasureplace.com

Pleasure Place [WC] 202/333-8570 ■ 1063 Wisconsin Ave NW, Georgetown (at 'M' St) ■ 10am-midnight, till 10pm Mon-Tue, noon-7pm Sun, leather, latex, shoes & more ■ pleasureplace.com

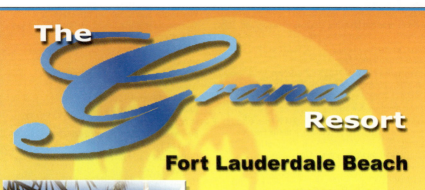

The Grand Resort
Fort Lauderdale Beach

Our Ocean View Sundeck, Heated Pool, Spa, Club and Fitness Rooms Are Just A Few Of The Amenities That Await The Most Discerning Gay Traveler.

800.818.1211
539 N. Birch Road, Ft. Lauderdale

WWW.GRANDRESORT.NET

Fort Lauderdale • Florida

FLORIDA

Fort Lauderdale

ACCOMMODATIONS

Bahama Hotel [GF,SW,WC] 954/467-7315, 800/622-9995 ■ 401 N Atlantic Blvd (at Bayshore) ■ full gym, pool, also restaurant & bar ■ www.bahamahotel.com

The Blue Dolphin [★MO,V,SW,WC,GO] 954/565-8437, 800/893-2583 ■ 725 N Birch Rd (at Vistamar) ■ rms & apts, nr beach ■ www.bluedolphinhotel.com

Brigantine for Men [MO,SW,N] 954/565-6911, 877/565-6911 ■ 2831 Vistamar St (at Bayshore) ■ newly redecorated rooms & apts, next to wildlife preserve & ocean ■ www.brigantinehotel.com

The Cabanas at Wilton Manors [M,SW,NS,GO] 954/564-7764, 866/564-7764 ■ 2209 NE 26th St ■ www.TheCabanasGuesthouse.com

California Dream Inn [GF,GO] 954/923-2100 ■ 300-315 Walnut St, Hollywood ■ located directly on oceanfront ■ www.californiadreaminn.com

4 **Comfort Suites Fort Lauderdale** [GS,SW] 954/767-8700, 800/760-0000 ■ 1800 S Federal Hwy (at 17th St) ■ www.comfortsuites.com/hotel/FL250

5 **Coral Reef Guesthouse** [MO,SW,N] 954/568-0292, 888/365-6948 ■ 2609 NE 13th Ct (off Sunrise Blvd) ■ 12-man jacuzzi, very secluded ■ www.coralreefguesthouse.com

49 **Deauville Inn** [GS,SW,WC] 954/568-5000 ■ 2916 N Ocean Blvd (Oakland Park Blvd & A-1-A) ■ in the heart of Fort Lauderdale Beach, lesbian-owned ■ ★www.ftlaud-deauville.com

6 **Edun House** [MO,SW,N,NS,GO] 954/565-7775, 800/479-1767 ■ 2733 Middle River Dr (nr Oakland Park Blvd) ■ patio ■ members.aol.com/edunhouse

7 **Eighteenth Street Inn** [GS,SW,GO] 954/467-7841, 888/828-4466 ■ 712 SE 18th St ■ www.eighteenthstinn.com

8 **Embassy Suites Hotel** [GF,SW,WC] 954/527-2700, 800/362-2779 ■ 1100 SE 17th St ■ full brkfst, hot tub, tropical outdoor pool ■ www.embassysuitesftl.com

9 **Eternal Sun Resort** [MO,SW,N,GO] 954/462-6035 ■ 1909 SW 2nd St ■ jacuzzi ■ www.EternalSunResort.com

FORT LAUDERDALE

Snowbirds from points north come to Fort Lauderdale every winter to soak up the sun on the city's beautiful beaches. The 'Venice of America'—so called for its canals— has recently benefited from developers who've spruced up the city, making it a world-class vacation spot. The tropical surroundings are also home to a spectacular range of flora and fauna, from Butterfly World (954/977-4400) to Flamingo Gardens (954/473-2955).

Queer Resources

COMMUNITY INFO
▼ Gay/Lesbian Community Center 954/563-9500, web: www.glccftl.org. 1717 N Andrews Ave, 9am-10pm, till 5pm wknds.
Gay Lauderdale, web: www.gaylauderdale.com.

AIDS RESOURCES
Broward House 954/522-4749.

RECOVERY
Lambda South 954/761-9072.

City Calendar

LGBT PRIDE
February. 954/561-2020, web: www.pridesouthflorida.org.

ANNUAL EVENTS
June - Film Fest.
December - AIDS Walk 954/563-9500.

Tourist Info

AIRPORT DIRECTIONS
Fort Lauderdale/Hollywood International Airport. Take Federal Hwy 1 north. This crosses Las Olas Blvd, Broward Blvd, and Sunrise Blvd, three of Fort Lauderdale's major avenues.

PUBLIC TRANSIT & TAXIS
Yellow Cab 954/565-5400.
Super Shuttle 954/764-1700.
Broward County Transit 954/357-8400.

TOURIST SPOTS & INFO
Broward Center for the Performing Arts 954/522-5334.
Butterfly World 954/977-4400.
Everglades.
Flamingo Gardens 954/473-2955.
Museum of Art 954/525-5500.
Museum of Discovery & Science 954/467-6637.
Sawgrass Mills, world's largest outlet mall 954/846-2350.
Six Flags Atlantis: The Water Kingdom.
Visitor's Center: 954/765-4466 or 800/227-8669, web: www.sunny.org.

WEATHER
The average year-round temperature in this sub-tropical climate is 75-90°.

Luxury

Charm

Magic

FORT LAUDERDALE'S ULTIMATE TROPICAL OASIS

**2901 Terramar St.,
Fort Lauderdale, FL 33304**

Call 800-237-PALM
Local 954-564-6444 Fax 954-564-6443
E-Mail: ryalpalms@aol.com • http://www.royalpalms.com

*Out & About 2001 "Editor's Choice Award"
and "5 Palm" Rating.
"A Magical Oasis, Rated One of the Very Best
Gay Accommodations in the USA."
1997 City of Fort Lauderdale Award for Excellence*

IGLTA

uxurious Rooms • Private Tropical Paradise • Clothing Optional • 10 Man Spa • Steps To Beach

New Zealand House

Join us for a New Zealand style tropical getaway! A moderately priced, cozy, 8-room guest house. All rooms include private bath, telephone, cable TV, VCR, A/C, refrigerator, and microwave. Clothing-optional pool. Convenient to all gay bars and restaurants.

Contact Ric & Warren
(888) 234-KIWI (5494)
Web: newzealandhouse.com
Email: imakiwi@worldnet.att.net

908 N.E. 15th Avenue
Ft. Lauderdale, FL 33304
954-523-7829 Fax: 954-523-7051

Proud member of

10 **Flamingo Resort** [M,SW,GO] 954/561-4658, 800/283-4786 ■ 2727 Terramar St (nr Birch) ■ efficiencies, art deco rooms & suites ■ www.theflamingoresort.com
Gemini House [MO,SW,N,NS,GO] 954/568-9791 ■ naturist B&B, full brkfst, hot tub, gym, shared baths ■ www.geminihse.com

11 **Gigi's Resort by the Beach** [M,N,GO] 954/463-4827, 800/910-2357 ■ 3005 Alhambra St (at Birch) ■ on the beach, hot tub ■ www.gigisresort.com

12 ▶ **The Grand Resort** [M,SW] 954/630-3000, 800/818-1211 ■ 539 N Birch Rd (at Windamar) ■ sundeck, spa, gym, ocean views ■ www.grandresort.net

13 **Inn Leather Guesthouse** [MO,L,SW,GO] 954/467-1444, 877/532-7749 ■ 610 SE 19th St (at SW 1st Ave) ■ sling in each rm, dungeon, hot tub ■ www.innleather.com

14 **JP's Beach Villas** [M,SW,GO] 954/772-3672, 888/992-3224 ■ 4621 N Ocean Dr (btwn Commercial & A1A), Lauderdale-by-the-Sea ■ all-suite hotel ■ www.jpsbeachvillas.com

15 **King Henry Arms Motel** [M,SW,GO] 954/561-0039, 800/205-5464 ■ 543 Breakers Ave (nr Bayshore) ■ just steps to the ocean ■ www.kinghenryarms.com
Liberty Apartment & Garden Suites [MW,SW,WC,GO] 954/927-0090, 877/927-0090 ■ 1501 SW 2nd Ave (at Sheridan), Dania Beach ■ furnished apts, nr beach, weekly rates ■ www.libertysuites.com

16 **The Mangrove Villas** [M,SW,N,WC] 954/527-5250, 800/238-3538 ■ 1100 N Victoria Park Rd (at 11th St) ■ self-contained houses, sundeck ■ www.mangrovevillas.com

17 ▶ **The New Zealand House B&B** [M,SW,N,WC,GO] 954/523-7829, 888/234-5494 ■ 908 NE 15th Ave (at Sunrise) ■ Key West-style guesthouse ■ www.newzealandhouse.com

18 ▶ **Orton Terrace** [MO,SW,N,GO] 954/566-5068, 800/323-1142 ■ 606 Orton Ave (at Terramar) ■ rms & apts ■ www.ortonterrace.com

19 **Palm Plaza Resort** [GS,SW,GO] 954/260-6568, 800/962-5517 x11 ■ 2801 Rio Mar St (at Birch) ■ hot tub, tropical gardens, steps to beach ■ www.palmplazaresort.com
Paradiso Tropical Guest Cottages [M,SW,N,NS,WC,GO] 954/764-8182, 800/644-7977 ■ 1115 Tequesta St (at Palm Ave) ■ full brkfst, hot tub ■ www.Paradiso-FTL.com

21 **Pineapple Point Guesthouse** [M,SW,WC,GO] 954/527-0094, 888/844-7295 ■ 315 NE 16th Terr (at NE 3rd Ct) ■ luxury guesthouse, spa, complimentary beer/ wine, nr gay bars & restaurants, nudity ok at pool ■ www.pineapplepoint.com

22 **Richard's Inn** [MO,SW,N,GO] 954/563-1111, 800/516-1111 ■ 1025 NE 18th Ave (at Sunrise) ■ richardsinn.com

10 ▶ **The Royal Palms Resort** [★M,SW,GO] 954/564-6444, 800/237-7256 ■ 2901 Terramar St (at Birch) ■ sundeck, jacuzzi, rated one of the very best gay accommodations in the USA by Out & About ■ royalpalms.com

23 **Saint Sebastian Guest House** [MO,SW,GO] 954/568-6161, 800/425-8105 ■ 2835 Terramar St (at Orton) ■ charming Bahamian-style villa ■ www.saintsebastianhotel.com

24 **Sea Grape House Inn** [M,SW,N,GO] 954/525-6586, 800/447-3074 (code: 44) ■ 1109 NE 16th Pl (at Dixie Hwy) ■ 2 clothing-optional pools, 7-man spa ■ www.seagrape.com

25 **Sun n' Splash** [MO,SW,N] 954/467-2669, 888/842-9352 ■ 1135 N Victoria Park Rd (at 13th) ■ studios & suites, gym, hot tub ■ www.GAY-FLA.com

12 **Venice Beach Guest Quarters** [M,SW,GO] 954/564-9601, 800/533-4744 ■ 552 N Birch Rd (at Terramar) ■ suites & studios, sundeck, nr beach ■ www.veniceqtrs.com

Fort Lauderdale • FLORIDA

8 **Villa Venice Resort** [M,SW,GO] 954/564-7855, 877/284-5522 ■ 2900 Terramar St (at Orton) ■ 2 blks to beach ■ www.villavenice.com

6 **Wilton Court** [M,SW,GO] 954/630-9155 ■ 2208-2212 NE 5th Ave (at NE 23rd St), Wilton Manors ■ furnished apts, seasonal

2▶ **The Worthington Guest House** [MO,SW,NS,GO] 954/563-6819, 800/445-7036 ■ 543 N Birch Rd (at Terramar) ■ resort ■ www.worthguesthouse.com

BARS

7 **Bill's Filling Station** [★M,NH] 954/525-9403 ■ 1243 NE 11th Ave (at 13th St) ■ 11am-2am, till 3am wknds, from noon Sun, patio, more women for bbq Sun

8 **Boots** [M,CW,L,WC] 954/792-9177 ■ 901 SW 27th Ave (at SW 9th St) ■ noon-2am, till 3am wknds, from 9am Sat

9 **The Bushes** [★M,NH,WC] 954/561-1724 ■ 3038 N Federal Hwy (at Oakland Park Blvd) ■ 9am-2am, till 3am wknds

0 **Cathode Ray Club** [★M,D,E,S,V] 954/462-8611 ■ 1307 E Las Olas Blvd (at 13th Ave) ■ 2pm-2am, till 3am wknds, sports & piano bars, also 'Bar Amici' restaurant next door ■ www.cathoderayclubflorida.com

Orton Terrace Guest House

Guest rooms and 1 & 2 bedroom apartments. All appointed with refrigerator, microwave, cable TV, VCR, videos. Property features: clothing-optional heated pool, barbecue grill, continental breakfast. Located just steps to the beach. Call about our affordable rates.

web: www.ortonterrace.com
email: orton@ortonterrace.com

PHONE **800/323-1142** or **954/566-5068**

Fort Lauderdale's Favorite All Male Resort
Stay at the beach!
The Worthington Guest House

- Clothing optional
- Fun Atmosphere
- Sunny Courtyard
- 400 feet to the beach
- All Male Resort
- Heated Pool
- Latest Music Releases
- Near Gay Beaches

Escape the ordinary, and come experience the extraordinary!

543 N Birch Rd., Fort Lauderdale, FL 33304
Toll-Free Phone: 1-800-445-7036 • Local Phone: 954-563-681
Fax: 954-563-4313

E-mail: info@worthguesthouse.com
Web: www.worthguesthouse.com

Fort Lauderdale • Florida

31 **Chainz** [M,D,L,WC] 954/462-9165 ■ 1931 S Federal Hwy (at 19th St) ■ 1pm-2am, till 3am wknds

32 **Chaps at the Corral** [M,L,WC] 954/767-0027 ■ 1727 N Andrews Wy (at 16th St) ■ 2pm-2am, till 3am wknds

33 **Cubby Hole** [M,NH,L,F,WC] 954/728-9001 ■ 823 N Federal Hwy (at 8th St) ■ noon-2am, till 3am Fri-Sat, Internet access ■ www.thecubbyhole.com

34 **Eagle** [★M,L,WC] 954/462-7224 ■ 1951 Powerline Rd/ NW 9th Ave (at NW 19th St) ■ 3pm-2am, till 3am wknds ■ www.eaglebar.net

35 **Georgie's Alibi** [★MW,F,V,WC] 954/565-2526 ■ 2266 Wilton Dr (at NE 6th Ave) ■ 11am-2am, till 3am Sat, sports bar

36 **Hideaway** [M,V] 954/566-8622 ■ 2022 NE 18th St (at Federal Hwy) ■ 2pm-2am, till 3am wknds, cruise bar

37 **J's Bar** [★W,D,E] 954/581-8400 ■ 2780 W Davie Blvd (at SW 28th Ave) ■ 3pm-2am, till 3am wknds, packed Wed & Fri

38 **Johnny's** [M,NH,F,S,WC] 954/522-5931 ■ 1116 W Broward Blvd (at 11th Ave) ■ 10am-2am, till 3am wknds, from noon Sun, male dancers nightly

39 **Kicks Sports Bar** [MW,NH] 954/564-8480 ■ 2008 Wilton Dr (at NE 20th St), Wilton Manors ■ 4pm-2am, from noon wknds ■ www.gayborhood.com/kicks

40 **Mona's** [M,NH] 954/525-6662 ■ 502 E Sunrise Blvd (at 6th Ave) ■ noon-2am, till 3am wknds

41 **Ramrod** [★M,D,B,L] 954/763-8219 ■ 1508 NE 4th Ave (at 16th St) ■ 3pm-2am, till 3am wknds, bbq Sun, cruise bar, patio, also 'Dungeon Bear Leather' store ■ www.ramrodbar.com

NIGHTCLUBS

42 **Coliseum** [M,D,S,E,18+] 954/832-0100 ■ 2520 S Miami Rd (at US1 & State Rd 84) ■ 18+ Tue & Fri ■ www.coliseumnightclub.com

FLORIDA • USA

43 **Copa** [M,D,MR,E,F,S,YC] 954/463-1507 ■ 2800 S Federal Hwy (N of airport) ■ 10pm-6am, also outside bars, oldest gay bar in FL ■ copaftlaud@aol.com

44 **Lord's Nightclub** [M,K,S] 954/563-4205 ■ 4200 N Federal Hwy (N of Oakland Park & Commercial Pkwy) ■ 4pm-2am, till 3am Fri-Sat, cabaret, karaoke Tue, bingo Sun, male dancers nightly

45 **The Saint** [MW,D] 954/525-7883 ■ 1000 State Rd 84 (at I-95) ■ 9pm-2am, till 3am wknds, clsd Mon, theme nights, more women wknds ■ thesaintnightclub.com

46 **The Sea Monster** [MW,D,TG,WC,GO] 954/463-4691 ■ 2 S New River Dr W (under the Andrews Drawbridge, across from Las Olas shopping ctr) ■ 8pm-2am, till 3am Fri-Sat, from 6pm Sun, clsd Mon-Tue, more women Sat, theme nights

47 **The Voodoo Lounge** [M,D,S] 954/522-0733 ■ 111 SW 2nd Ave (at Moffat St) ■ gay Sun only for drag show

CAFES

The Storks [WC] 954/567-3220 ■ 2505 NE 15th Ave (at NE 26th St) ■ 7am-midnight, patio

RESTAURANTS

Baraka Restaurant/ Hamsa Cafe 954/567-2515 ■ 3025 N Ocean Blvd (S of Oakland Park Blvd) ■ 10am-2am, clsd 4pm Fri, Middle Eastern, plenty veggie

Chardee's [MW,D,P,E,WC] 954/563-1800 ■ 2209 Wilton Dr (at NE 6th Ave) ■ dinner from 6pm, also bar, open 4:30pm-2am

Costello's [E] 954/563-7752 ■ 2345 Wilton Dr, Wilton Manors ■ dinner nightly, also bar

The Deck [WC] 954/467-7215 ■ 401 N Atlantic Blvd (at the 'Bahama Hotel') ■ also bar

Grandma's French Cafe 954/564-3671 ■ 3354 N Ocean Blvd (N of Oakland Park Blvd) ■ lunch & dinner, also ice cream parlor

Hi-Life Cafe 954/563-1395 ■ 3000 N Federal Hwy #12 (at Oakland Park Blvd, in the 'Plaza 3000') ■ dinner Tue-Sun, bistro, some veggie ■ www.gaylauderdale.com/hi-life

Lester's Diner [★] 954/525-5641 ■ 250 State Rd 84 ■ 24hrs, more gay late nights

Mustards Bar & Grill [WC,GO] 954/564-5116 ■ 2256 Wilton Dr (btwn 4th & 6th) ■ 5pm-10pm, till 11pm Fri-Sat, Mediterranean/ California cuisine

Simply Delish Cafe 954/565-8646 ■ 2287 Wilton Dr, Wilton Manors ■ 7am-3pm daily, 5pm-9pm Tue-Sun

Sukothai [★] 954/764-0148 ■ 1930 E Sunrise Blvd ■ lunch Mon-Fri, dinner nightly, Thai

Tropics Cabaret & Restaurant [MW,S,WC] 954/537-6000 ■ 2004 Wilton Dr (at 20th) ■ dinner from 6pm, new American, also piano bar 4pm-2am, till 3am Sat

Victoria Park [★BW] 954/764-6868 ■ 900 NE 20th Ave ■ dinner only, call for reservations

ENTERTAINMENT & RECREATION

Gold Coast Roller Rink 954/523-6783 ■ 2604 S Federal Hwy ■ 8pm-midnight Tue, gay skate

John U Lloyd State Park-Dania Beach Dania ■ popular gay beach, first parking lot over the bridge, off Dania Beach Blvd, walk right

BOOKSTORES

48 **Pride Factory & CyberCafe** 954/463-6600 ■ 845 N Federal Hwy (at Sunrise) ■ 9am-11pm Mon-Sat, 11am-7pm Sun, books, gifts & coffee ■ www.pridefactory.com

RETAIL SHOPS

Audace 954/522-7503 ■ 813 E Las Olas Blvd (at 8th St) ■ 10am-11pm, till midnight wknds, from 11am Sun, men's underwear & sportswear ■ www.audace.com

Catalog X Retail & Clothing Outlet 954/524-5050 ■ 850 NE 13th St ■ 9am-10pm, 10am-9pm Sat, 11am-7pm Sun

Clothes Encounters 954/522-2228 ■ 1952 E Sunrise Blv (at US 1) ■ 10am-7pm, till 10pm Fri-Sat, noon-6pm Sun clubwear, gifts & more ■ ncounters@aol.com

GayMartUSA 954/630-0360 ■ 2240 Wilton Dr (at NE 6th Ave) ■ 10am-10pm, clothes & gifts ■ www.gaymartusa.com

The Girl Next Door 954/786-8077 ■ 231 S Federal Hwy (of Atlantic Blvd) ■ clubwear, accessories & more

Pridestuff 954/764-0394, 877/442-9383 ■ 1735 N Andrews Ave Extn ■ noon-midnight, till 2am wknds ■ www.pridestuff.com

PUBLICATIONS

Hot Spots 954/928-1862, 800/522-8775 ■ Florida's weekly bar guide ■ www.hotspotsmagazine.com

She 954/474-0183 ■ Florida's hippest & hottest lesbian magazine, monthly ■ www.shemag.com

A Traveler's Dream...

THE CLUB Ft. Lauderdale
www.the-clubs.com

One Day Memberships · Free Parking
Private Dressing Rooms · In/Out Privileges
Centrally Located to Nightclubs
Steam · Sauna · Whirlpool
Outdoor Pool & Patio · Fully Equipped Gym
Weekend Bar-B-Ques

110 NW 5th Avenue
Ft. Lauderdale, Florida 33311
954-525-3344

Key West • FLORIDA

GYMS & HEALTH CLUBS

Better Bodies [GO] 954/561-7977 ■ 2270 Wilton Dr, Wilton Manors ■ 5am-11pm, 8am-9pm Sat, 9am-7pm Sun

Firm Fitness 954/767-6277 ■ 928 N Federal Hwy (at Sunrise) ■ 5am-11pm, 8am-8pm wknds

MEN'S CLUBS

▶ **Club Fort Lauderdale** [SW,PC] 954/525-3344 ■ 110 NW 5th Ave ■ 24hrs ■ www.the-clubs.com

Clubhouse II [V,PC] 954/566-6750 ■ 2650 E Oakland Park Blvd ■ 24hrs, full gym

Thinkers 954/564-0907 ■ 2929 NE 6th Ave (at Oakland Park Blvd) ■ 6pm-3am, till 5am Fri-Sat

EROTICA

Fetish Factory 954/462-0032 ■ 821 N Federal Hwy (at Sunrise)

Romantix 954/568-1220 ■ 3520 N Federal Hwy (at Oakland)

Secrets 954/748-5855 ■ 4509 N Pine Island Rd (btwn Oakland Park & Commercial), Sunrise

Tropixxx Video 954/522-5988 ■ 1514 NE 4th Ave (at 16th St), Wilton Manors

Wicked Leather 954/564-7529 ■ 2422 Wilton Dr, Wilton Manors ■ clsd Mon

Key West

ACCOMMODATIONS

1 **Alexander Palms Court** [GF,SW] 305/296-6413, 800/858-1943 ■ 715 South St (at Vernon) ■ hot tub ■ www.alexanderpalms.com

2 **Alexander's Guest House** [MW,SW,N,WC,GO] 305/294-9919, 800/654-9919 ■ 1118 Fleming St (at Frances) ■ sundeck, hot tub, private patios ■ www.alexghouse.com

3 **Ambrosia House Tropical Lodging** [GF,SW] 305/296-9838, 800/535-9838 ■ 615 & 618-622 Fleming St (at Simonton) ■ sea captain's house, lagoon pool ■ www.keywest.com/ambrosia.html

4 **Andrew's Inn** [GF,SW,NS] 305/294-7730, 888/263-7393 ■ Zero Whalton Ln (at Duval) ■ www.andrewsinn.com

5 **The Artist House** [GF,SW,NS] 305/296-3977, 800/582-7882 ■ 534 Eaton St (at Duval) ■ Victorian guesthouse, jacuzzi ■ www.artisthousekeywest.com

6 **Atlantic Shores Resort** [★MW,F,SW,N,WC] 305/296-2491, 877/778-7711 ■ 510 South St (at Duval) ■ complete resort w/ pool, pier, bars, restaurant, rooms & T-dance Sun, home of WomenFest ■ www.atlanticshoresresort.com

KEY WEST

Key West is truly an island paradise. With its perfect weather and laid-back attitude, Key West offers visitors a healthy dose of rest and relaxation.

Queer Resources

COMMUNITY INFO

▼ Gay/Lesbian Community Center 305/292-3223, web: www.glcckeywest.org. 1075 Duval St.
Key West Business Guild 305/294-4603, 800/535-7797, web: www.gaykeywestfl.com.

RECOVERY

305/296-8654.
Anchor's Aweigh Clubhouse, 305/296-7888, 404 Virginia St, 8am.

City Calendar

LGBT PRIDE

June. 305/293-9348, web: keywestpridealliance.org

ANNUAL EVENTS

February - Kelly McGillis Classic Women's & Girls' Flag Football Tournament 305/293-9315, web: www.iwffa.com.
September - WomenFest 800/535-7797, web: www.womenfest.net.
October - Fantasy Fest 305/296-1817. Week-long Halloween celebration with parties, masquerade balls & parades.
December - International Gay Arts Fest 800/535-7797. Cultural festival of film, theatre, art, concerts, seminars, parties & a parade.

Tourist Info

AIRPORT DIRECTIONS

Key West International Airport. To get to Duval St, turn left on S Roosevelt. After traffic signal, S Roosevelt becomes N Roosevelt. Follow Truman Ave to Duval St.

PUBLIC TRANSIT & TAXIS

Yellow Cab 305/294-2227.
Key West Transit Authority 305/292-8161.

TOURIST SPOTS & INFO

Audubon House and Gardens 305/294-2116.
Dolphin Research Center.
Glass-bottom boats.
Hemingway House 305/294-1575.
Mallory Market.
Red Barn Theatre 305/296-9911.
Southernmost Point USA.
Visitor's Center: Key West Business Guild 305/294-4603.

WEATHER

The average temperature year-round is 78°, and the sun shines nearly every day. Any time is the right time for a visit.

BEST VIEWS

Old Town Trolley Tour (1/2 hour).

FLORIDA • USA

7 **Author's Key West** [GS,SW,GO] 305/294-7381, 800/898-6909 ■ 725 White St (entrance on Petronia) ■ private fine arts gallery on premise, by appt only ■ www.authors-keywest.com

8 **Avalon B&B** [GF] 305/294-8233, 800/848-1317 ■ 1317 Duval St (at United) ■ restored Victorian, sundeck, hot tub ■ www.avalonbnb.com

9 **Bananas Foster B&B** [GF,SW,GO] 305/294-9061, 800/653-4888 ■ 537 Caroline St (at Simonton St) ■ hot tub, spa ■ bananasfoster.com

Beach Bungalow & Beach Guest Suite [GS,GO] 305/294-1525 ■ Box 165 ■ vacation rental, 3-day minimum stay ■ www.vacationdepot.com

10 **Big Ruby's Guesthouse** [M,SW,N,WC,GO] 305/296-2323, 800/477-7829 ■ 409 Appelrouth Ln (at Duval & Whitehead) ■ full brkfst, evening wine, sundeck ■ www.bigrubys.com

11 **Blue Parrot Inn** [GF,SW,N,WC,GO] 305/296-0033, 800/231-2473 ■ 916 Elizabeth St (at Olivia) ■ historic Bahamian home, sundeck ■ www.blueparrotinn.com

13 **Chelsea House** [MW,SW,N,WC,GO] 305/296-2211, 800/845-8859 ■ 707 Truman Ave (at Elizabeth) ■ www.chelseahousekeywest.com

14 **Coconut Grove Guesthouse for Men** [MO,SW,N] 305/296-5107, 800/262-6055 ■ 815 Fleming St (at William St) ■ 3 historic homes, sundeck, gym ■ coconutgrovekeywest.com

15 **Coral Tree Inn/ Oasis Guest House** [★MO,SW,N,GO] 305/296-2131, 800/362-7477 ■ 822 & 823 Fleming St (at William) ■ upscale suites, sundeck ■ www.keywest-allmale.com

16 **The Courtyard of Key West** [GF] 305/296-1148, 800/296-1148 ■ 910 Simonton St (at Truman) ■ apt suites ■ www.courtyardkeywest.com

17 **Cuban Club Suites** [GF] 305/296-0465, 800/432-4849 ■ 1102-1108 Duval St (at Virginia) ■ award-winning historic hotel, suites w/ kitchens ■ www.keywestcubanclub.com

18 **Curry House** [MO,SW,N,GO] 305/294-6777, 800/633-7439 ■ 806 Fleming St (at William) ■ full brkfst, hot tub, sundeck ■ www.gaytraveling.com/curryhouse

19 **Cypress House** [GF,SW] 305/294-6969, 800/525-2488 ■ 601 Caroline (at Simonton) ■ sundeck ■ www.cypresshousekw.com

20 **Deja Vu Resort** [GS,SW,N] 305/292-9339, 800/724-5351 ■ 611 Truman Ave (at Simonton) ■ hot tub ■ www.dejavukeys.com

21 **Duval House** [GF,SW,GO] 305/292-9491, 800/223-8825 ■ 815 Duval St (at Petronia) ■ Victorians w/ gardens, sundeck ■ www.duvalhouse.com

22 **Eaton Lodge** [GF,SW] 305/292-2170, 800/294-2170 ■ 511 Eaton St (at Duval) ■ 1886 mansion & conch house w/ gardens, hot tub ■ www.eatonlodge.com

23 **Equator Guest House** [MO,SW,N,NS,WC,GO] 305/294-7775, 800/278-4552 ■ 818 Fleming St 33040 ■ full brkfst, hot tub ■ www.equatorresort.com

12 **Fleur de Key Guesthouse** [★M,SW,N,WC,GO] 305/296-4719, 800/932-9119 ■ 412 Frances St (at Eaton) ■ luxury guesthouse, hot tub, sundeck ■ www.fleurdekey.com

56 **Heartbreak Hotel** [MW,GO] 305/296-5558 ■ 716 Duval St (at Petronia) ■ kitchens ■ www.heartbreakhotel.org

24 **Heron House** [GF,SW,WC] 305/294-9227, 888/861-9066 ■ 512 Simonton St (at Fleming) ■ hot tub, evening wine ■ www.heronhouse.com

25 **Island House** [MO,F,SW,N,WC,SW,GO] 305/294-6284, 800/890-6284 ■ 1129 Fleming St (at White) ■ full brkfst, some shared baths, hot tub, sauna, steam, gym, very cruisy ■ www.islandhousekeywest.com

26 **Key Lodge Motel** [GF] 305/296-9915, 800/458-1296 ■ 1004 Duval St (at Truman)

27 **Key West Harbor Inn B&B** [MW,SW,NS,WC] 305/296-2978, 800/608-6569 ■ 219 Elizabeth St (at Greene) ■ hot tub ■ www.keywestharborinn.com

28 **Knowles House B&B** [GS,SW,N,NS,GO] 305/296-8132, 800/352-4414 ■ 1004 Eaton St (at Grinnell) ■ restored 1880s conch house, sundeck ■ www.knowleshouse.com

29 **La Casa de Luces** [GF,WC] 305/296-3993, 800/432-4849 ■ 422 Amelia St (at Whitehead) ■ early 1900s conch house, jacuzzi ■ www.keywestcubanclub.com

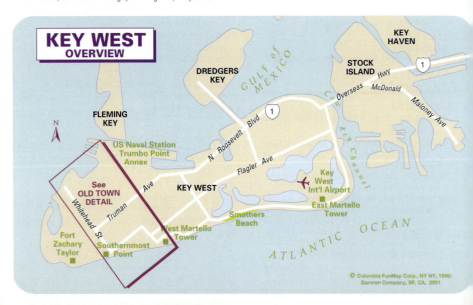

FLORIDA • USA

30 **La Te Da** [★MW,SW,N,S,WC,GO] 305/296-6706, 877/528-3320 ■ 1125 Duval St (at Catherine) ■ tropical setting, also restaurant & 3 bars, Sun T-dance ■ www.lateda.com

31 **Lightbourn Inn** [GF,SW,NS,WC,GO] 305/296-5152, 800/352-6011 ■ 907 Truman Ave (at Packer) ■ home of largest private teddy bear collection in Key West ■ www.lightbourn.com

32 **Lighthouse Court** [MO,SW,N] 305/294-9588 ■ 902 Whitehead St (at Olivia) ■ cottages & rooms, also tropical poolside cafe & bar, spa ■ www.lighthousecourt.com

33 **Marquesa Hotel** [GF,SW,WC] 305/292-1919, 800/869-4631 ■ 600 Fleming St (at Simonton) ■ also 'Cafe Marquesa' 6pm-11pm, full bar ■ www.marquesa.com

34 **Marrero's Guest Mansion** [GF,SW,NS] 305/294-6977, 800/459-6212 ■ 410 Fleming St (btwn Duval & Whitehead) ■ 1890 Victorian mansion, wknd sunset cocktails, hot tub ■ www.marreros.com

35 **Merlinn Inn** [GF,SW,NS,WC] 305/296-3336, 800/642-4753 ■ 811 Simonton St (at Petronia) ■ full brkfst ■ www.merlinnkeywest.com

36 **The Mermaid and the Alligator** [GS,SW,NS,GO] 305/294-1894, 800/773-1894 ■ 729 Truman Ave (at Elizabeth) ■ full brkfst ■ www.kwmermaid.com

37 **Nassau House** [GF,SW,NS] 305/296-8513, 800/296-8513 ■ 1016 Fleming St (at Grinnell) ■ sundeck, hot tub ■ www.nassauhouse.com

38 **Pearl's Rainbow** [★WO,SW,N,WC] 305/292-1450, 800/749-6696 ■ 525 United St (at Duval) ■ sundeck, hot tub, also bar, lesbian-owned/ run ■ www.pearlsrainbow.com

39 **Pier House Resort & Caribbean Spa** [GF,SW,NS,WC] 305/296-4600, 800/327-8340 ■ 1 Duval St (at Front) ■ private beach, hot tub, restaurants, bars, spa ■ www.pierhouse.com

40 **Pilot House Guest House** [GF,SW,N,WC] 305/293-6600, 800/648-3780 ■ 414 Simonton St (at Eaton) ■ Victorian mansion in Old Town, hot tub available ■ www.PilotHouseKeyWest.com

41 **Red Rooster Inn** [GF,SW,N,NS] 305/296-6558, 800/845-0825 ■ 709 Truman Ave (at Elizabeth) ■ 19th-century, 3-story inn ■ www.redroosterinn.com

42 **Sea Isle Resort** [★M,SW,N,WC,GO] 305/294-5188, 800/995-4786 ■ 915 Windsor Ln (at Olivia) ■ private courtyard, gym, sundeck, hot tub ■ www.seaisleresort.com

43 **Seascape Tropical Inn** [GF,SW,NS] 305/296-7776, 800/765-6438 ■ 420 Olivia St (at Duval) ■ guesthouse & cottages, hot tub, sundeck ■ www.seascapetropicalinn.com

Sheraton Suites—Key West [GF,SW,WC] 305/292-9800, 800/452-3224 ■ 2001 S Roosevelt Blvd ■ hot tub, also restaurant ■ www.sheratonkeywest.com

44 **Simonton Court Historic Inn & Cottages** [GF,SW] 305/294-6386, 800/944-2687 ■ 320 Simonton St (at Caroline) ■ 26 units, built in 1880s, 4 pools, hot tub, sundeck ■ www.simontoncourt.com

45 **Travelers Palm** [GF,SW] 305/295-9599, 800/294-9560 ■ 905-907 White St (at Truman) ■ www.whitestreetinn.com

46 **Tropical Inn** [GF,SW] 305/294-9977, 888/611-6510 ■ 812 Duval St (at Petronia) ■ old Conch house, rooms & cottages, hot tub, sundeck ■ www.tropicalinn.com

47 **Watson House** [GS,SW] 305/294-6712, 800/621-9405 ■ 525 Simonton St (btwn Fleming & Southard)

48 **William Anthony House** [GS,NS,WC,GO] 305/294-2887, 800/613-2276 ■ 613 Caroline St (at Simonton) ■ 1895 inn, social hour ■ www.WmAnthonyHse.com/gay.html

BARS

49 **801** [★MW,NH,D,S] 305/294-4737 ■ 801 Duval St (at Petronia) ■ 11am-4am, also 'Red Light Bar' (M,L)

50 **Bourbon Street Pub** [★M,S,V,WC] 305/296-1992 ■ 724 Duval St (at Angela) ■ noon-4am, popular daytime bar, start your 'Duval Crawl' here

51 **Diva's** [★MW,D,S] 305/292-8500 ■ 711 Duval St (at Angela) ■ noon-4am, also 'Shag' next door from 4pm, more straight

52 **Donnie's** [MW,NH,WC] 305/294-2655 ■ 900 Simonton St (at Olivia) ■ noon-4am

53 **Epoch** [★GF,D] 305/296-8521 ■ 623 Duval St (at Southard) ■ hrs vary (pls call), clsd Mon

30 **La Te Da** [★M,D,E] 305/296-6706 ■ 1125 Duval St ■ 5pm-9pm Sun, also piano bar ■ www.lateda.com

54 **Numbers** [M,NH,D,S,WC] 305/296-0333 ■ 1420 Simonton ■ 2pm-4am, male strippers, also restaurant ■ www.numberskeywest.org

38 **Pearl's Patio** [WO] 305/292-1450 ■ 525 United St (at Duval, at Pearl's Rainbow) ■ open during cocktail hour, till 10pm Sat ■ www.pearlsrainbow.com

NIGHTCLUBS

Tea on the Sea [MO,D,S,$] 305/294-5687 ■ 801 Duval (at Petronia) ■ 7pm-11pm Tue & Sat, meet at the bar for a drink, then take the party bus to the boat for a cruise

CAFES

Croissants de France [MW,BW] 305/294-2624 ■ 816 Duval St (at Petronia) ■ 7:30am-7pm, French pastries, patio

RESTAURANTS

Alice's [★] 305/296-6706 x39 ■ at 'La Te Da' accommodations ■ clsd Mon, fusion, home of award-winning chef Alice Weingarten ■ www.lateda.com

Antonia's [★] 305/294-6565 ■ 615 Duval St (at Southard) ■ 6pm-11pm, northern Italian, full bar ■ www.antoniaskeywest.com

Bo's Fish Wagon [★] 305/294-9272 ■ 801 Caroline (at Williams) ■ lunch, dinner in-season only, clsd Sun, 'seafood & eat it'

Cafe des Artistes 305/294-7100 ■ 1007 Simonton St (at Truman) ■ 6pm-11pm, tropical French, full bar

Camille's 305/296-4811 ■ 703 1/2 Duval St (at Angela) ■ 8am-3pm & 6pm-10pm, no dinner Sun-Mon, bistro, hearty brkfst ■ www.camilleskeywest.com

Kelly's Caribbean Bar Grill & Brewery [BW] 305/293-8484 ■ 301 Whitehead St (at Caroline) ■ lunch & dinner, owned by actress Kelly McGillis

La Trattoria Venezia [MW] 305/296-1075 ■ 524 Duval St (at Fleming) ■ 5:30pm-11pm, Italian, full bar

Lobos [BW] 305/296-5303 ■ 611 1/2 Duval St ■ 11am-6pm, sandwiches, plenty veggie

Louie's Backyard [★] 305/294-1061 ■ 700 Waddell Ave (at Vernon) ■ lunch & dinner, Sun brunch, fine dining, full bar from 11:30am-2am

Mangia Mangia [BW] 305/294-2469 ■ 900 Southard St ■ dinner only, fresh pasta, patio

Mangoes [WC] 305/292-4606 ■ 700 Duval St (at Angela) ■ 11am-11pm, 'Floribbean' cuisine, full bar

The Quay [E] 305/294-4446 ■ 12 Duval St (at Front) ■ lunch & dinner, gourmet, some veggie

Rooftop Cafe 305/294-2042 ■ 310 Front St (at Duval) ■ best Key Lime pie, full bar

Seven Fish [★] 305/296-2777 ■ 632 Olivia St (at Elizabeth) ■ 6pm-10pm, clsd Tue

Square One [WC] 305/296-4300 ■ 1075 Duval St (at Truman) ■ 6pm-10:30pm, American, full bar

ENTERTAINMENT & RECREATION

Bahia Honda State Park & Beach 35 miles N of Key West ■ Viking Beach is best

Brigadoon 305/923-7245 ■ 201 William St, Dock E ■ all-gay sails, sunset & snorkel cruises ■ www.captainstevekw.com

Fort Zachary Taylor Beach ■ more gay to the right

Mangrove Mistress [WO] 305/745-8886, 305/304-0806 ■ nature exploring & snorkeling, ceremonies, women-owned/ run

Moped Hospital 305/296-3344 ■ 601 Truman ■ forget the car—mopeds are a must for touring the island

Rude Awakening [W] 305/292-9403 ■ 92.5 FM WEOW ■ 6am-10am Mon-Fri, a morning zoo show with a lesbian twist; music, comedy, contests, news ■ www.keysradio.com

Venus Charters 305/292-9403, 305/744-8241 ■ snorkeling, light tackle fishing, dolphin watching, lesbian-owned/ run

Water Sport People 305/296-4546 ■ 1430 Thompson ■ scuba-diving instruction & group charters ■ divervicki@aol.com

BOOKSTORES

Blue Heron Books 305/296-3508 ■ 1018 Truman Ave (at Grinnell) ■ 10am-8pm, lgbt section

55 **Flaming Maggie's** 305/294-3931 ■ 830 Fleming St (at Margaret) ■ 10am-6pm, lgbt bookstore & coffeehouse

Key West Island Books 305/294-2904 ■ 513 Fleming St (at Duval) ■ 10am-9pm, new & used rare books, also lgbt section ■ kwbook@aol.com

RETAIL SHOPS

Fast Buck Freddie's [WC] 305/294-2007 ■ 500 Duval St (at Fleming) ■ 10am-6pm, till 10pm Sat, clothing, gifts

Fausto's Food Palace 305/296-5663 ■ 522 Fleming St (at Duval) ■ 8am-8pm, till 7pm Sun, cruisy grocery store

In Touch 305/292-7293 ■ 715 Duval St (at Angela) ■ 9:30am-11pm, gay gifts

Key West Aloe 305/294-5592, 800/445-2563 (mail order) ■ 524 Front St (at Duval) ■ 8:30am-8pm

Lido [GO] 305/294-5300 ■ 532 Duval St (at Fleming) ■ 10am-10pm, 11am-7pm Sun, clothing & gifts

PUBLICATIONS

Southern Exposure 305/294-6303 ■ gaykeywest.net

GYMS & HEALTH CLUBS

Bodies on South 305/292-2930 ■ 2740 N Roosevelt Blvd

Club Body Tech [MW] 305/292-9683 ■ 1075 Duval St (at Virginia) ■ full gym, steam room, massage therapy available

EROTICA

Leather Master 305/292-5051 ■ 418-A Appelrouth Ln (btwn Duval & Whitehead) ■ noon-11pm, till 6pm Sun, custom leather & more, also 'Annex'

Raincoat Willie's 305/293-9609 ■ 505 Southard St (at Duval) ■ videos, novelties & gifts

Miami

Miami—Greater Miami

ACCOMMODATIONS

56 **Miami River Inn** [GF,SW] 305/325-0045, 800/468-3589 ■ 118 SW S River Dr ■ B&B located in Miami's Little Havana district, jacuzzi ■ www.miamiriverinn.com

BARS

1 **The Boardwalk** [★M,MR,S] 305/949-4119 ■ 17008 Collins Ave (at 170th), Sunny Isles Beach ■ 6am-5am

2 **Cactus Bar & Grill** [M,MR,F,S,V] 305/438-0662 ■ 2041 Biscayne Blvd (at 20th Terr) ■ 4pm-2am, Latin night Sat, members night Th, 'Wall-to-Wall Men' Fri ■ www.thecactus.com

3 **Miami Eagle** [MO,PC,WC] 305/860-0056 ■ 1252 Coral Wy (at 3rd Ave) ■ 9pm-3am, till 4am wknds

4 **Power T Dance** [M,W,D] 305/576-1336 ■ 3701 NE 2nd Ave (near Biscayne Blvd) ■ 4pm-9pm Sun only ■ icandee@mindspring.com

5 **Sugar's** [M,NH,D,V,W] 305/940-9887 ■ 17060 W Dixie (at 172nd), North Miami Beach ■ 3pm-6am, more women Fri

NIGHTCLUBS

6 **Club Ozone** [M,D,S] 305/667-2888, 305/667-4684 ■ 6620 Red Rd/ SW 57th Ave ■ 9pm-5am, patio

7 **Fantasy Show** [D] 305/448-9009 ■ 3600 SW 8th Street ■ 9pm-close

7 **Oz Miami** [MW,D,MR] 305/444-0369 ■ 3470 SW 8th St (nr SW 35th Ave) ■ 5pm-5am Wed-Sun, women's night Fri

RESTAURANTS

The Bal Harbour Bistro [WC,GO] 305/861-4544 ■ 9700 Collins Ave (in the Bal Harbour Shops), Bal Harbour ■ 10am-10pm, full bar, patio

BOOKSTORES

8 **Lambda Passages Bookstore** 305/754-6900 ■ 7545 Biscayne Blvd (at 76th) ■ 11am-9pm, noon-6pm Sun, lgbt/feminist

PUBLICATIONS

Contax Guide 305/757-6333 ■ club listings & more

MEN'S CLUBS

▶ **Club Body Center Miami** [★SW,PC] 305/448-2214 ■ 2991 Coral Wy ■ 24hrs, monthly 'Mr Nude' contests, cookouts Sun

North Miami Clubhouse [MO,PC] 305/940-0086 ■ 22 NE 167th St (at N Miami Ave), North Miami ■ 24hrs ■ www.gayborhood.com/n.miamiclubhouse

EROTICA

Biscayne Books & Video 305/891-3475 ■ 117 Biscayne Blvd ■ 24hrs

Perrine Books & Video 305/233-3913 ■ 18093 S Dixie Hwy

Miami—Miami Beach/ South Beach

ACCOMMODATIONS

9 **Abbey Hotel** [GS] 305/531-0031, 888/612-2239 ■ 300 21st St (at Collins) ■ chic restored art deco, full brkfst, gym, rooftop lounge ■ www.abbeyhotel.com

10 **The Astor** [★GF,F,SW,WC] 305/531-8081, 800/270-4981 ■ 956 Washington Ave (at 10th St) ■ www.hotelastor.com

11 **The Bayliss** [MW] 305/538-5620, 888/305-4683 ■ 504 14th St ■ tropical art deco hotel, rooms & apts, nr beach ■ www.thebayliss.com

12 **The Beachcomber** [GF,F] 305/531-3755, 888/305-4683 ■ 1340 Collins Ave (at 13th St) ■ intimate art deco hotel, bar & bistro, nr beach ■ www.beachcombermiami.com

13 **The Blue Moon Hotel** [GF,F] 305/673-2262, 800/724-1623 ■ 944 Collins Ave ■ Mediterranean style hotel ■ www.bluemoonhotel.com

14 **The Bohemia** [MO,N,NS,GO] 305/534-1322, 888/883-4565 ■ 825 Michigan Ave (at 8th St) ■ apts, studios & rms, hot tub ■ www.bohemia825.com

15 **Brigham Gardens** [GS] 305/531-1331 ■ 1411 Collins Ave (at 14th) ■ art deco guesthouse, rooms & apts w/ kitchens, women-owned/ run ■ www.brighamgardens.com

16 **The Cardozo Hotel** [GF,F,WC] 305/535-6500, 800/782-6500 ■ 1300 Ocean Dr ■ Gloria Estefan's plush hotel ■ www.cardozohotel.com

17 **Castle Palms** [MO,SW,N,GO] 305/672-2080 ■ mansion, gym, sauna, hot tub

16 **Cavalier** [GS,WC] 305/604-5000, 800/688-7678 ■ 1320 Ocean Dr ■ beautiful restored art deco on the ocean ■ www.islandoutpost.com/Cavalier/

18 **The Century** [GF,F] 305/674-8855, 888/982-3688 ■ 140 Ocean Dr ■ restored art deco, rooms & suites, Joia restaurant, celebrity hangout ■ www.centuryhotelsobe.com

19 **Chesterfield Hotel** [GS] 305/531-5831, 800/244-6023 ■ 855 Collins Ave ■ animal-print decor

20 **Collins Plaza** [GF,F] 305/532-0849 ■ 318 20th St ■ no frills, 1 blk from ocean, restaurant

21 **The Colony Hotel** [GF,F,WC] 305/673-0088, 800/226-5669 ■ 736 Ocean Dr (at 7th St) ■ newly renovated art deco, ocean front ■ colonyhotel-sobe.com

22 **Deco Walk Hotel** [GS] 305/531-5511, 888/505-5027 ■ 928 Ocean Dr ■ restored art deco ■ www.decowalk.com

23 **Delano Hotel** [GF,F,SW] 305/672-2000, 800/555-5001 ■ 1685 Collins Ave ■ hip hotel designed by Phillipe Stark, great bar scene (see & be seen)

24 **Destinations International—Mantell** [MW,SW,GO] 305/532-9341, 800/277-4825 ■ 255 W 24th St ■ hotel reservation service for several art deco hotels & apts ■ www.colours.net

25 **Fairfax Hotel** [GF] 305/538-3787 ■ 1776 Collins Ave ■ newly renovated art deco, scenic view

Florida Hotel Network [★GO] 305/538-3616, 800/538-3616 ■ hotel reservations, vacation rentals ■ www.floridahotels.com

MIAMI

Miami Beach has a well-deserved reputation as a great vacation spot. The 'South Beach' area—with its vibrant club scene, fashionable circuit parties, and Art Deco style—offers an upbeat alternative for travelers in search of a fast-paced and culturally diverse milieu.

Queer Resources

COMMUNITY INFO
Switchboard of Miami 305/358-4357.

AIDS RESOURCES
SoBe AIDS Project 305/532-1033.

RECOVERY
Lambda Dade AA 305/573-9608. 410 NE 22nd St. (Carriage House), 8:30pm daily.

City Calendar

LGBT PRIDE
Spring. 305/358-8245, email: pridemiami@aol.com.

ANNUAL EVENTS
March - Winter Party 305/572-1841. AIDS benefit dance on the beach.
April/May - Gay & Lesbian Film Festival 305/534-9924, web: www.miamigaylesbianfilm.com.
November - White Party Vizcaya 305/667-9296. AIDS benefit.

Tourist Info

AIRPORT DIRECTIONS
Miami International. To South Beach, take 953 South to 836 East, to 395 East. 395 becomes 5th St in Miami Beach.

PUBLIC TRANSIT & TAXIS
Yellow Cab 305/444-4444.
Metro Taxi 305/888-8888.
Super Shuttle 305/871-2000.
Metro Bus 305/770-3131.

TOURIST SPOTS & INFO
Art Deco Welcome Center 305/672-2014.
Bayside Market Place 305/577-3344.
Miami Museum of Science & Space Transit Planetarium 305/854-4247.
Orchid Jungle.
Parrot Jungle and Gardens 305/666-7834.
Sanford L. Ziff Jewish Museum of Florida 305/672-5044.
Visitor's Center: Greater Miami Convention and Visitors Bureau, 701 Brickell Ave. 305/539-3000.

WEATHER
Warm all year. Temperatures stay in the 90°s during the summer and drop into the mid-60°s in the winter. Be prepared for sunshine!

BEST VIEWS
If you've got money to burn, a helicopter flight over Miami Beach is a great way to see the city. Otherwise, hit the beach.

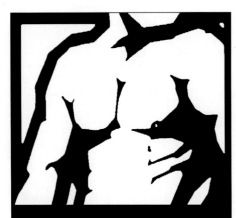

CLUB BODY CENTER MIAMI

Now in its 30th Year of Excellence

SENSUOUS SUNDAYS

begin at 2:00
with an amateur J/O show
2:30 pm
cookout with tropical drinks
3:00 pm
porn stars strip poolside and do a J/O in the V.I.P. Room

Tuesday & Friday
begin at 10:00 pm
with amateur safe sex show

OPEN 24 HOURS A DAY
7 DAYS A WEEK

**2991 CORAL WAY
MIAMI, FL
(305) 448-2214**

Florida Sunbreak 305/532-1516, 800/786-2732 ■ reservation service for condos & rentals ■ www.floridasunbreak.com

26 Fountainbleu Hilton Resort & Spa [GF,SW,WC] 305/538-2000, 800/445-6667 ■ 4441 Collins Ave ■ see overview map

9 The Governor Hotel [GF,SW] 305/532-2100, 800/542-0444 ■ 435 21st St ■ tropical courtyard, restaurant, nr ocean

19 the hotel [GF,F,SW] 305/531-2222, 877/843-4683 ■ 801 Collins Ave ■ interior design by Todd Oldham, restaurant, full bar ■ www.thehotelofsouthbeach.com

27 Hotel Impala [GF,F,WC] 305/673-2021, 800/646-7252 ■ 1228 Collins Ave ■ luxury hotel nr beach, also Italian restaurant ■ www.travelbase.com/destinations/miami-beach/impala/

19 Hotel Leon [GF,F,WC] 305/673-3767 ■ 841 Collins Ave (at 8th St) ■ stylish decor, popular w/ photo industry ■ www.hotelleon.com

28 Hotel Nash [GF,F,SW] 305/674-7800 ■ 1120 Collins Ave ■ sleek & modern new boutique hotel, also restaurant & spa ■ www.hotelnash.com

29 Hotel Ocean [★GF,F,WC] 305/672-2579, 800/783-1725 ■ 1230-38 Ocean Dr ■ great location ■ www.hotelocean.com

19 Hotel Shelley [GS,WC] 305/531-3341, 800/414-0612 ■ 844 Collins Ave ■ 1930s art deco hotel ■ www.hotelshelley.com

30 The Indian Creek Hotel [GF,F,SW,WC,GO] 305/531-2727, 800/491-2772 ■ 2727 Indian Creek Dr ■ simple & away from the action, 1 blk to ocean ■ www.indiancreekhotelmb.com

31 Island House Miami Beach [MO] 305/864-2422, 800/382-2422 ■ 715 82nd St ■ hot tub, patio, see overview map ■ www.islandhousesouthbeach.com

32 Island House South Beach [MO] 305/864-2422, 800/382-2422 ■ 1428 Collins Ave ■ www.islandhousesouthbeach.com

33 Jefferson House B&B [M,F,SW,GO] 305/534-5247, 877/599-5247 ■ 1018 Jefferson Ave ■ private tropical garden, full brkfst, nr beach ■ www.thejeffersonhouse.com

34 Kenmore Hotel [GS,SW,WC] 305/674-1930, 888/333-6719 ■ 1050 Washington Ave ■ 4 small art deco hotels ■ www.parkwashingtonresort.com

28 The Kent [GS,F,WC] 305/531-6771, 800/688-7678 ■ 1131 Collins Ave (at 11th St) ■ on the beach ■ www.islandoutpost.com/Kent/

29 The Leslie [GS] 305/531-8800, 800/688-7678 ■ 1244 Ocean Ave ■ art deco gem featured in 'The Birdcage,' outdoor cafe

19 Lily Guesthouse [MW,WC] 305/535-9900, 888/742-6600 ■ 835 Collins Ave ■ studios, suites, sundeck ■ www.lilyguesthouse.com

The Loft Hotel [GS] 305/534-2244 ■ 952 Collins Ave ■ affordable boutique hotel, 1 blk to beach ■ www.thelofthotel.com

35 Marlin Hotel [GS,WC] 305/531-8800, 800/688-7678 ■ 1200 Collins Ave ■ fabulous studios w/ full kitchens, stereo & WebTV, bar ■ www.islandoutpost.com/marlin/

32 The Nassau Suite Hotel [GF] 305/532-0043, 888/305-4683 ■ 1414 Collins Ave ■ renovated art deco, near beach ■ www.nassausuite.com

Damron Road Atlas 9 — Miami • Florida

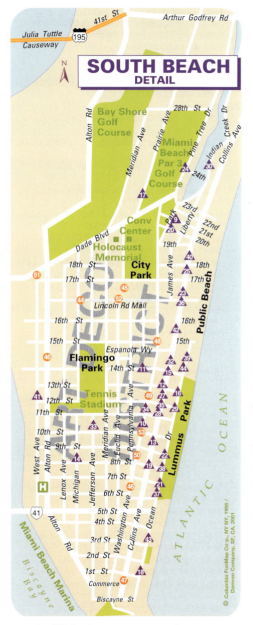

36 **The National Hotel** [GS,F,SW,WC] 305/532-2311, 800/327-8370 ■ 1677 Collins Ave ■ on beach ■ www.nationalhotel.com

54 **Ocean Surf Hotel** [GF,WC] 305/866-1648, 800/555-0411 ■ 7436 Ocean Terr (nr 75th St & Collins Ave) ■ beautiful restored art deco, in quiet North Beach, see overview map ■ www.oceansurf.com

37 **The Park Central** [GF,SW] 305/538-1611, 800/727-5236 ■ 640 Ocean Dr ■ ocean views

34 **Park Washington Resort** [GS,SW] 305/532-1930, 888/424-1930 ■ 1020 Washington ■ tiki bar ■ www.parkwashingtonresort.com

38 **The Pelican** [★GS,F] 305/673-3373, 800/773-5422 ■ 826 Ocean Dr (btwn 8th & 9th Sts) ■ designer theme rooms, restaurant w/ live DJ ■ www.pelicanhotel.com

39 **Penguin Hotel & Bar** [MW,F,WC] 305/534-9334, 800/235-3296 ■ 1418 Ocean Dr ■ renovated art deco ■ www.penguinhotel.com

25 **The Raleigh Hotel** [GS,SW] 305/534-6300, 800/848-1775 ■ 1775 Collins Ave ■ outdoor gym ■ www.raleighhotel.com

25 **Richmond Hotel** [GF,F,SW] 305/538-2331, 800/327-3163 ■ 1757 Collins Ave ■ full brkfst, hot tub, private beach access ■ www.richmondhotel.com

40 **The Shelborne Beach Resort** [GF,F,SW,WC] 305/531-1271, 800/327-8757 ■ 1801 Collins Ave (at 18th) ■ full brkfst, tropical gardens ■ www.shelborne.com

41 **South Beach Villas** [MW,SW,NS,GO] 305/673-9600, 888/429-7623 ■ 1201 West Ave (at 12th St) ■ www.beachvillasfla.com

25 **South Seas** [GF,F,SW] 305/538-1411, 800/345-2678 ■ 1751 Collins Ave ■ clean & basic, beach access, brkfst included ■ www.southbeachhotels.com

29 **The Tides** [GS,F,SW] 305/604-5000, 800/688-7678 ■ 1220 Ocean Dr ■ showcase Island Outpost hotel ■ www.islandoutpost.com/tides

42 **The Tropics Hotel & Hostel** [GS,SW] 305/531-0361 ■ 1550 Collins Ave (btwn 15th & 16th Sts) ■ modern hotel rooms & hostel, nr beach & attractions ■ www.tropicshotel.com

32 **Villa Paradiso Guesthouse** [MW] 305/532-0616 ■ 1415 Collins Ave ■ studios w/ full kitchens, courtyard ■ www.villaparadsiohotel.com

43 **The Wave Hotel** [GF,F] 305/673-0401, 800/501-0401 ■ 350 Ocean Dr ■ tropical-style newly renovated, popular for fashion shoots ■ www.wavehotel.com

44 **The Winterhaven** [GS,F] 305/531-5571, 800/395-2322 ■ 1400 Ocean Dr ■ ocean views ■ www.winterhavenhotelsobe.com

Bars

45 **Laundry Bar** [MW,NH,E] 305/531-7700 ■ 721 N Lincoln Ln ■ 7am-5am, also laundromat, cafe, Internet access ■ www.laundrybar.com

46 **Loading Zone** [M,L] 305/531-5623 ■ 1426-A Alton Rd (at 14th Ct) ■ 10pm-5am, heavy cruising, leather shop

Nightclubs

47 **Amnesia** [M,D] 305/531-5535 ■ 136 Collins Ave (at 1st St) ■ call for events

48 **Crobar** [★GF,D,WC] 305/531-5027 ■ 1445 Washington Ave (at the Cameo Theater) ■ 10pm-5am, gay Sun for 'Anthem'

49 **Level/ Federation 1235** [★M,D,S,$] 305/532-1525, 305/695-1834 ■ 1235 Washington Ave ■ 10pm-5am Fri only, huge dance club w/ live entertainment & dancers ■ www.levelnightclub.com

50 **Pump** [★M,D,WC] 305/538-7867 ■ 841 Washington Ave (btwn 8th & 9th) ■ 4am-close Fri-Sat, world-famous DJs & hot circuit crowd ■ www.pumpsouthbeach.com

51 **Salvation** [★M,D,A,$] 305/673-6508 ■ 1771 West Ave (at Alton Rd & 18th St) ■ Fri-Mon ■ www.salvationsobe.com

FLORIDA • USA

52 Score [★MW,D,S,V] 305/535-1111 ■ 727 Lincoln Rd (at Meridian) ■ lounge opens 1pm, dance club 10pm-5am, women's night Th ■ www.scorebar.com

53 Twist [★M,D,WC] 305/538-9478 ■ 1057 Washington Ave (at 11th) ■ 1pm-5am

Cafes
News Cafe [★] 305/538-6397 ■ 800 Ocean Dr ■ 24hrs, healthy sandwiches

Restaurants
11th Street Diner 305/534-6373 ■ 11th & Washington ■ 24hrs, full bar

A Fish Called Avalon [WC] 305/532-1727 ■ 700 Ocean Dr ■ 6pm-11pm, full bar

Balans 305/534-9191 ■ 1022 Lincoln Rd ■ 8am-2am, int'l, some veggie

El Rancho Grande 305/673-0480 ■ 1626 Pennsylvania Ave ■ 11:30am-11pm, Mexican

The Front Porch 305/531-8300 ■ 1420 Ocean Dr ■ 8am-10:30pm, healthy homecooking, full bar

Jeffrey's [★] 305/673-0690 ■ 1629 Michigan Ave (at Lincoln Rd) ■ dinner only, clsd Mon, romantic bistro

Joe's Stone Crab 305/673-0365 ■ 11 Washington Ave ■ lunch & dinner

Larios on the Beach 305/532-9577 ■ 820 Ocean Dr ■ 11:30am-11:30pm, till 2am Fri-Sat, Cuban

Nemos 305/532-4550 ■ 100 Collins Ave (at 1st St) ■ lunch & dinner, Sun brunch, chic decor, Pacific Rim & South American cuisine

Nexxt Cafe [★] 305/532-6643 ■ 700 Lincoln Rd ■ 9am-11pm

Ortanique on the Mile [★] 305/446-7710 ■ 278 Miracle Mile ■ lunch Mon-Fri, dinner 7 days, New World Caribbean, full bar

Pacific Time [BW] 305/534-5979 ■ 915 Lincoln Rd (btwn Jefferson & Michigan) ■ lunch & dinner wkdys, pan-Pacific

Palace Bar & Grill 305/531-9077 ■ 1200 Ocean Dr (at 12th) ■ 8am-midnight, till 1am wknds, salads & sandwiches, full bar, near gay beach

Spiga 305/534-0079 ■ 1228 Collins Ave (at 12th St) ■ lunch & dinner, tasty homemade pastas

Sushi Rock Cafe [★] 305/532-2133 ■ 1351 Collins Ave (at 14th) ■ full bar

Wolfie's Jewish Deli [★] 305/538-6626 ■ 2038 Collins Ave (at 21st St) ■ 24hrs

Yuca [E] 305/532-9822 ■ 501 Lincoln Rd (at Drexel Ave) ■ New Cuban cuisine, great afternoon tapas & cocktails

Entertainment & Recreation
Beach Scooter Rentals 305/532-0977 ■ 1461 Collins Ave

Fritz's Skate & Bike 305/532-1954 ■ 726 Lincoln Rd (at Euclid & Meridian) ■ rentals, in pedestrian mall

The Gay Beach 12th St & Ocean ■ where the boys are

Lincoln Rd Lincoln Rd (btwn West & Collins Aves) ■ pedestrian mall lined w/ fabulous restaurants, stores, galleries, museums, theaters, people at every step

Bookstores
The 9th Chakra 305/538-0671 ■ 811 Lincoln Rd (at Meridian) ■ metaphysical books, supplies, gifts

Retail Shops
GayMartUSA 305/535-1545 ■ 1200 Ocean Ave #2 (at 12th) ■ 10am-7pm ■ www.gaymartusa.com

Whittall & Shon 305/538-2606 ■ 1319 Washington (at 13th) ■ 11am-9:30pm, till midnight Fri-Sat, funky clothes & clubwear for boys

Publications
Miamigo 305/532-5051 ■ *miamigomag@aol.com*

She 954/474-0183 ■ Florida's hippest & hottest lesbian magazine, monthly ■ www.shemag.com

TWN (The Weekly News) 305/757-6333 ■ lgbt newspaper for South Florida ■ www.twnonline.org

Wire 305/538-3111

Gyms & Health Clubs
David Barton Gym [GF] 305/674-5757 ■ 1685 Collins Ave (in the 'Delano Hotel') ■ $20 day pass

Idol's Gym 305/532-0089 ■ 719 Lincoln Ln (behind Lincoln Rd) ■ 24hrs, $10 day pass

Ironworks Gym [★] 305/531-4743 ■ 1676 Alton Rd ■ 5:30am-11pm, $10 day pass

Erotica
Pleasure Emporium 305/673-3311 ■ 1019 5th St

Romantix Adult Emporium 305/226-8332 ■ 8831 SW 40th St

Romantix Emporium 305/255-2190 ■ 19800 S Dixie Hwy

Orlando

Accommodations
EO Inn & Spa [GS,F,NS] 407/481-8485, 888/481-8488 ■ 227 N Eola Dr (at Robinson) ■ rooftop terrace, sundeck, hot tub, cafe onsite ■ www.eoinn.com

Holiday Villas [GF,SW] 407/397-0700, 800/344-3959 ■ 2928 Vineland Rd (btwn SR 535 & 192), Kissimmee ■ 2 & 3-bdrm luxury villas just 5 miles from Walt Disney World ■ www.holidayvillas.com

Leora's B&B [WO,GO] 407/649-0009

1 ▶ **Parliament House Motor Inn** [★MW,D,MR,F,S,YC,SW,WC] 407/425-7571 ■ 410 N Orange Blossom Tr ■ also 5 bars (open at 8pm) ■ www.parliamenthouse.com

2 ▶ **Rick's B&B** [M,N,SW,GO] 407/396-7751, 407/414-7751 ■ full brkfst, patio, close to Walt Disney World ■ www.q-net.com/ricksbnb

---

Rick's Bed & Breakfast

RICK'S
BED & BREAKFAST

Experience Walt Disney World "Family Style" with Concierge Accommodations at a Bed and Breakfast Rate.

P.O. Box 22318, Lake Buena Vista, FL 32830. Telephone 24 hours a day: (407) 396-7751 or (407) 414-7751.
Email: RICKsBnB@aol.com

www.q-net.com/ricksbnb

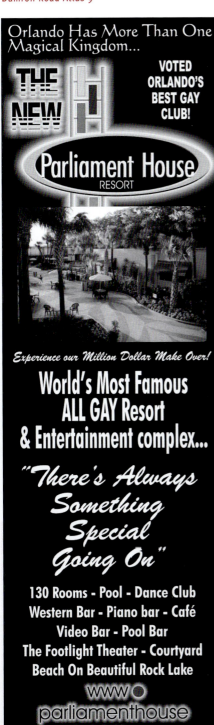

ORLANDO

For most travelers, Orlando is synonymous with Disney World (407/824-4321), but the Magic Kingdom is only one of the many theme parks in Orlando. In addition to Epcot Center and Disney-MGM Studios and the new Animal Kingdom, there's also Universal Studios Florida (407/363-8000), Gatorland (407/855-5496), and Sea World (407/351-3600). Primarily a family vacation area, Orlando will appeal to the kid in all of us.

Queer Resources

COMMUNITY INFO
▼ Gay/Lesbian Community Center 407/228-8272, web: glbcc.org. 946 N Mills, 11am-9pm, till 6pm Fri, noon-7pm Sat, noon-5pm Sun.

AIDS RESOURCES
Hope & Help 407/645-2577, 8am-5pm.
Centaur (crisis service) 407/849-1452.

RECOVERY
Free To Be 1901 E. Robinson St. (church) 407/898-3621, 8pm daily.

City Calendar

LGBT PRIDE
June.

ENTERTAINMENT
Orlando Gay Chorus 407/841-7464.

ANNUAL EVENTS
June (1st Sat) - Gay Day at Disney World 407/896-8431, web: gaydays.com.

Tourist Info

AIRPORT DIRECTIONS
Orlando International Airport. To get to Orange Blossom Trail, take 436 North from the airport to the East-West Expressway. Head west on the Expressway and take the Orange Blossom Trail exit.

PUBLIC TRANSIT & TAXIS
Yellow Cab 407/699-9999.
Gray Line 407/422-0744.
Lynx 407/841-8240.

TOURIST SPOTS & INFO
Sea World 407/351-3600.
Universal Studios 407/363-8000.
Walt Disney World 407/824-4321.
Wet & Wild Waterpark 407/351-3200.
Visitor's Center: 407/363-5871. 8723 International Dr, 8am-8pm.

WEATHER
Mild winters, hot summers.

FLORIDA • USA

Things Worth Remembering [GS,SW,NS,GO] 407/291-2127, 800/484-3585 (code: 6908) ■ 2603 Coventry Ln ■ near attractions, owners are former theme park employees w/ many behind-the-scenes stories ■ orlandob2b@aol.com

Topaz [MO,SW,NS,GO] 941/419-0627 ■ 1431 South Blvd, Kissimmee ■ dayintonightsap@webtv.net

3 **The Veranda B&B** [GF,SW,NS,WC] 407/849-0321, 800/420-6822 ■ 115 N Summerlin Ave ■ hot tub ■ www.TheVerandaBandB.com

Westside Inn & Suites [GF,SW,WC] 407/295-5270, 800/828-5270 ■ 3200 W Colonial Dr (at John Young Pkwy) ■ www.westsideorlando.com

BARS

4 **The Cactus Club** [M,P] 407/894-3041 ■ 1300 N Mills Ave ■ 3pm-2am, patio, more women wknds

5 **Copper Rocket** [GF,BW,WC] 407/645-0069 ■ 106 Lake Ave (at 17-92), Maitland ■ 11:30am-2am, 4pm-midnight Sun, microbrews, full restaurant

6 **Faces** [★W,NH,D,E,WC] 407/291-7571 ■ 4910 Edgewater Dr ■ 4pm-2am

7 **Full Moon Saloon** [M,CW,L] 407/648-3725 ■ 500 N Orange Blossom Tr ■ noon-2am, popular Sun afternoon, patio ■ www.fullmoonsaloon.com

8 **Hank's** [M,NH,BW,WC] 407/291-2399 ■ 5026 Edgewater Dr ■ noon-2am, patio

9 **Little Orphan Andy's** [MW,NH,S,WC] 407/299-7717 ■ 5700 N Orange Blossom Tr (in Rosemont Plaza) ■ 3pm-2am

1 **Stable** [M,CW,L] 407/425-7571 ■ 410 N Orange Blossom Tr (at 'Parliament House') ■ 8pm-2am

15 **Studz** [M,NH] 407/523-8810 ■ 4453 Edgewater Dr (at Thistledown) ■ 2pm-2am, from noon wknds

10 **Will's Pub** [GF,NH,F,BW,WC] 407/898-5070 ■ 1820-50 N Mills Ave ■ 4pm-2am; also 'Loch Haven Motor Inn,' 407/896-3611

11 **Wylde's** [M,NH,CW,K] 407/835-1889 ■ 3535 S Orange Blossom Tr ■ 2:30pm-2am

NIGHTCLUBS

Chaos [GF,D,TG,S,18+,WC,GO] 904/257-1967 ■ 745 Ridgewood Ave (at US 1 & 8th St), Holly Hill ■ 3pm-2am, till 6am Fri-Sat

12 **The Club** [★GS,D,S,V,18+] 407/872-0066 ■ 578 N Orange Ave ■ 9pm-3am, more gay Sat ■ www.clubatfirestone.com

13 **Club Quest** [GS,D,MR,S,18+] 407/228-8226 ■ 745 Bennett Rd ■ 10pm-3am Th-Sat only

16 **Empire** [M,D] 407/522-0411 ■ 4315 N Orange Blossom Trail (at Lee) ■ gay Sat night & at Sun T-dance only

1 ▶ **Parliament House Motor Inn** [★MW,D,MR,F,S,YC,SW,WC] 407/425-7571 ■ 410 N Orange Blossom Tr ■ 5 bars (open at 8pm) ■ www.parliamenthouse.com

14 **Southern Nights** [★MW,D,MR,S,WC] 407/898-0424 ■ 375 S Bumby Ave ■ 4pm-2am, Latin Mon, more women Wed & Sat, patio ■ www.southern-nights.com

CAFES

Shaffer Coffeehouse [WC] 407/740-7782 ■ 535 W New England Ave, Winter Park ■ 8am-10pm (clsd 5pm-7:30pm), 9am-4pm Sun

White Wolf Cafe & Antique Shop [E,BW,WC] 407/895-5590 ■ 1829 N Orange Ave (at Princeton) ■ 10am-10pm, till 11pm wknds, clsd Sun, salads & sandwiches

RESTAURANTS

Brian's 407/896-9912 ■ 1409 N Orange Ave (at Virginia) ■ 6am-4pm, popular Sun

Captain Mary's [GO] 407/599-9269 ■ 1881 W Fairbanks Ave ■ 11:30am-3pm & 6pm-10pm, clsd Sun, full bar

Harvey's Bistro 407/246-6560 ■ 390 N Orange Ave (in Nations Bank Tower) ■ popular cocktail hour ■ Water4@aol.com

Hemingway's at the Hyatt [★] 407/239-1234 ■ 1 Grand Cypress Blvd, Lake Buena Vista ■ lunch & dinner, cont'l

La Sontanella [BW,WC] 407/425-0033 ■ 900 E Washington ■ 11am-10pm, seafood/ Italian, patio

Le Provence [E] 407/843-1320 ■ 50 E Pine St ■ lunch & dinner, clsd Sun, French bistro, full bar till 2am, live jazz wknds ■ www.cenfla.com/res/leprovence

Nicole St Pierre [WC] 407/647-7575 ■ 1300 S Orlando Ave, Maitland ■ lunch & dinner, clsd Sun

The Rainbow Cafe [MW] 407/425-7571x711 ■ at 'Parliament House' ■ 24hrs Fri-Sat, till 11pm Sun-Th

Taqueria Quetzalcoatl [BW] 407/629-4123 ■ 350 W Fairbanks Ave, Winter Park ■ 11am-11pm, from noon Sun, some veggie

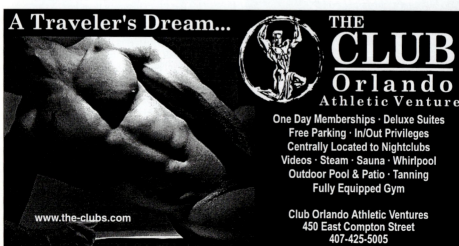

A Traveler's Dream...

THE CLUB
Orlando
Athletic Venture

One Day Memberships · Deluxe Suites
Free Parking · In/Out Privileges
Centrally Located to Nightclubs
Videos · Steam · Sauna · Whirlpool
Outdoor Pool & Patio · Tanning
Fully Equipped Gym

www.the-clubs.com

Club Orlando Athletic Ventures
450 East Compton Street
407-425-5005

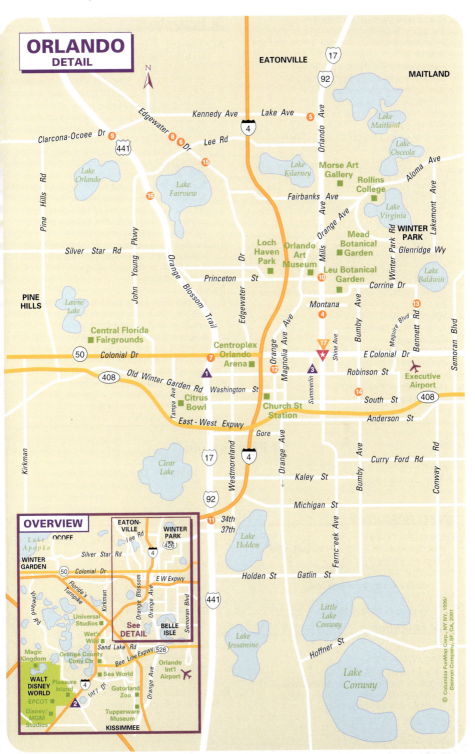

Florida • USA

ENTERTAINMENT & RECREATION
The Enzian Theater [BW] 407/629-0054 ■ 1300 S Orlando Ave (at Magnolia), Maitland ■ Central FL's only art house cinema & cafe

Family Values WPRK 91.5 FM ■ 3pm Fri, lgbt radio

Universal Studios Florida 407/363-8000, 800/232-7827 ■ 1000 Universal Studios Pl

Walt Disney World Resort 407/824-4321 ■ don't even pretend you came to Orlando for any other reason

BOOKSTORES
15 **Out & About Books** 407/896-0204 ■ 930 N Mills Ave (at E Marks St) ■ 10am-8pm, till 9pm Fri-Sat, noon-7pm Sun, lgbt bookstore ■ *bruceout@aol.com*

RETAIL SHOPS
Harmony Designs [WC] 407/481-9850 ■ 496 N Orange Blossom Tr ■ 1:30pm-11pm, pride store

Rainbow City [WC] 407/898-6096 ■ 936 N Mills Ave ■ 10am-9pm, noon-6pm Sun, lgbt giftshop

Twisted Palms 407/999-0111 ■ 1321 N Mills Ave ■ 11am-5pm, clsd Sun, new & gently worn clothing for men; also 'Twisted Palms Annex,' 498-B N Orange Blossom Tr, 407/835-8998 ■ *bustr@purplenet.net*

PUBLICATIONS
TLW Magazine 727/526-0585 ■ bi-weekly magazine for gay men ■ *www.tlwmen.com*

Watermark 407/481-2243 ■ bi-weekly lgbt newspaper ■ *www.watermarkonline.com*

MEN'S CLUBS
▶ **Club Orlando** [PC] 407/425-5005 ■ 450 E Compton St ■ 24hrs ■ *www.the-clubs.com*

EROTICA
Fairvilla Video 407/425-5352 ■ 1740 N Orange Blossom Tr

Midnight News 407/425-7571 ■ at 'Parliament House'

St Petersburg

ACCOMMODATIONS
1 **Bay Gables B&B** [GF,NS] 727/822-8855, 800/822-8803 ■ 340 Rowland Ct ■ 3-story Key West-style inn, smokefree, garden ■ *www.gulfcoastflorida.com/baygables*

2 **Boca Ciega** [WO,SW,GO] 727/381-2755 ■ B&B in private home ■ *worlddancer@aol.ocm*

22 **Changing Tides Cottages** [WO] 727/397-7706 ■ 225 Boca Ciega Dr, Madeira Beach ■ fully furnished rental cottages on harbor ■ *www.changingtidescottages.com*

3 **Dicken's House B&B** [GS,SW] 727/822-8622, 800/381-2022 ■ 335 8th Ave NE ■ newly restored 1900s home, nr beach, jacuzzi, massage ■ *www.dickenshouse.com*

Pass-A-Grille Beach Co-op [GF,SW] 727/367-4726 ■ 709 Gulf Way, St Petersburg Beach ■ *PAGBeachMotel@msn.com*

4 **Sea Oats by the Gulf** [GF,WC] 727/367-7568 ■ 12625 Sunshine Ln, Treasure Island 33706 ■ directly on the Gulf of Mexico ■ *www.flainns.com/seaoats*

5 **Suncoast Resort** [★MW,D,S,SW,WC,GO] 727/867-1111 ■ 3000 34th St S/ Hwy 19 S (at 32nd Ave S) ■ 5 bars, 2 restaurants, tennis, gay shopping mall ■ *www.suncoastresort.com*

BARS
6 **The Back Room Bar @ Surf & Sand Bar** [M,NH,K,WC] 727/391-2680 ■ 14601 Gulf Blvd, Madeira Beach ■ noon-2am, from 1pm Sun, beach access, patio

7 **Benders** [M,D,V,GO] 727/578-1606 ■ 10570 Gandy Blvd N (at 4th St N, next to Derby Ln) ■ 4pm-2am, from 1pm wknds, clsd Mon-Tue, CW Th, dancers Fri-Sat, retro T-dance Sun ■ *www.bendersbar.com*

8 **Common Ground** [MW,D,F,E,BW,WC] 727/522-7413 ■ 5571 4th St N (at 'Elsie's' restaurant) ■ 1pm-2am, live shows, Elsie's German restaurant till 9pm

ST PETERSBURG

Across the bay from its larger sister city, Tampa, St Petersburg is best known for its spectacular beaches.

Queer Resources

COMMUNITY INFO
Gay Information Line (The Line) 727/586-4297.

AIDS RESOURCES
PWA Coalition of Tampa Bay 813/238-2887, web: www.pwactampa.homepage.com.

RECOVERY
Pinellas County AA 727/530-0415.

City Calendar

LGBT PRIDE
June. 727/586-4297.

ANNUAL EVENTS
October - Film Festival & Gay Men's Chorus 800/729-2787, web: flagg.net/filmfestival/intro.htm.

Tourist Info

PUBLIC TRANSIT & TAXIS
Yellow Cab 727/821-7777.

TOURIST SPOTS & INFO
Great Explorations interactive kids museum 727/821-8992.
Salvador Dali Museum 727/823-3767.
Visitor's Center: Chamber of Commerce 727/821-6164. 8am-5pm Mon-Fri.

WEATHER
Some say it's the Garden of Eden—winter temperatures occasionally dip into the 40°s but for the rest of the year temperatures stay in the 70°-80°s.

BEST VIEWS
Pass-A-Grille Beach in Tampa.

St Petersburg • FLORIDA

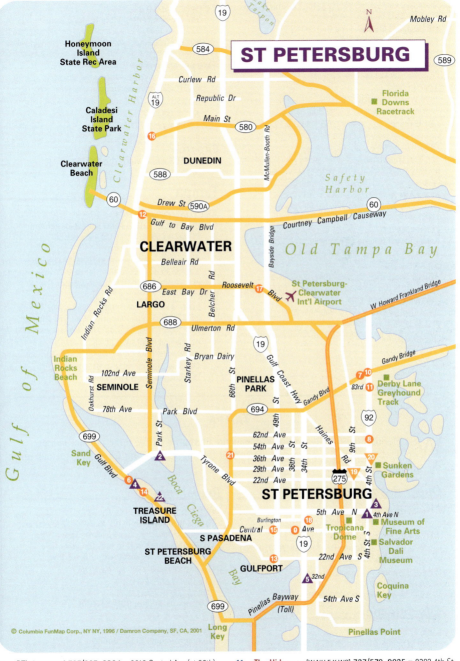

9 **DT's** [M,NH,WC] 727/327-8204 ■ 2612 Central Ave (at 26th) ■ 6pm-2am, male dancers Th-Sun, patio ■ dtsbar@aol.com

10 **Golden Arrow** [M,NH,B,L,WC] 727/577-7774 ■ 10504 Gandy Blvd (at 4th St) ■ noon-2am, from 1pm Sun, patio

11 **Haymarket Pub** [M,NH,P,WC] 727/577-9621 ■ 8308 4th St N (at 83rd) ■ 4pm-2am

11 **The Hideaway** [W,NH,E,K,WC] 727/570-9025 ■ 8302 4th St N (at 83rd) ■ 2pm-2am

12 **Pro Shop Pub** [★M,NH] 727/447-4259 ■ 840 Cleveland St (at Prospect), Clearwater ■ 11:30am-2am, from 1pm Sun

21 **Rafters** [M,K,F] 727/549-9041 ■ 4319 66th St N (at 43rd Ave) ■ 11am-2am

Florida • USA

13 **Sharp A's** [★MW,D,K,WC] 727/327-4897 ■ 4918 Gulfport Blvd S (at 49th), Gulfport ■ 4pm-2am
14 **VIP Lounge & Mexican Food Grill** [GF,WC] 727/360-5062 ■ 10625 Gulf Blvd ■ 9am-2am, food served 11am-10pm
15 **West Side Lounge** [MW,NH] 727/328-2636 ■ 4900 Central Ave (at 49th) ■ 1pm-2am, patio

Nightclubs
16 **1470 West** [MW,D,S,K,WC] 727/736-5483 ■ 325 Main St (at Alternate 19), Dunedin ■ 4pm-2am, patio
17 **Lost & Found** [M,D,K,S,WC] 727/539-8903 ■ 5858 Roosevelt Blvd (State Rd 686, at 58th), Clearwater ■ 4pm-2am, from 6pm Sat
18 **The New Connection** [M,NH,D,S,V,WC,GO] 727/321-2112 ■ 3100 3rd Ave N (at 31st St N) ■ 1pm-2am, 3 bars

Cafes
Beaux Arts [MW] 727/328-0702 ■ 2635 Central Ave ■ noon-5pm, 8pm Sat open mic, historic gallery w/ coffeehouse, sponsors events

Restaurants
Anna's Ravioli & Pasta Company [GO] 727/522-6627 ■ 5625 4th St N ■ 9am-5pm deli, 5pm-10pm dinner

Bookstores
19 **Affinity Books** [WC] 727/823-3662, 800/355-3662 ■ 2435 9th St N (at 25th Ave) ■ 10am-6pm, till 5pm Sat, noon-5pm Sun, lgbt, gifts
20 **Brigit Books** 727/522-5775, 800/566-2333 ■ 3434 4th St N #5 (at 34th Ave) ■ 10am-6pm, till 8pm Tue & Th, 1pm-5pm Sun, women's/ feminist ■ www.brigitbooks.com

Retail Shops
The MC Film Festival Video & Music Store 727/866-0904 ■ 3000 34th St S #30 (in Suncoast Resort) ■ noon-7pm, largest collection of nonerotic lgbt videos, CDs & pride gifts, also business ctr ■ mcfilmfest@aol.com

Publications
The Gazette 813/689-7566 ■ the Suncoast's monthly gay/ lesbian newsmagazine ■ gazette@tampabay.rr.com
MainStream 941/330-0888, 877/363-6246 ■ 1mstream@gte.net
TLW Magazine 727/526-0585 ■ bi-weekly magazine for gay men ■ www.tlwmen.com

Erotica
4th St Books & Video 727/821-8824 ■ 1427 4th St S (at Newton) ■ 24hrs

Tampa

Accommodations
1 **Gram's Place B&B & Artist Retreat** [GS,P,BYOB,N] 813/221-0596 ■ 3109 N Ola Ave ■ hot tub ■ www.Grams-Inn-Tampa.com
Ruskin House B&B [MW,P] 813/645-3842 ■ Victorian on 3 acres, 30 minutes south of Tampa & 30 minutes north of Sarasota, full brkfst ■ ruskinhouse.com

Bars
2 **2606** [★M,L,S,WC,GO] 813/875-6993 ■ 2606 Armenia Ave (at St Conrad) ■ 8pm-3am, from 6am Sun, also leather shop (opens after 9pm), strippers wknds ■ www.2606.com
3 **421 Saloon** [M,NH,BW,WC] 813/354-8797 ■ 421 S MacDill (btwn Swann & Azeele) ■ noon-3am, 1pm-2am Sun, patio
4 **City Side** [M,NH,P] 813/254-6466 ■ 3810 Neptune St (at Dale Mabry) ■ noon-3am, patio

Tampa

West Florida's largest city, Tampa is a relaxing alternative to the more popular Florida destinations. The slower pace of life is ideal for travelers looking for a place to soak up the sun in peace and quiet.

Queer Resources

Community Info
Gay Info Line 727/586-4297, 7pm-11pm.

AIDS Resources
PWA Coalition of Tampa Bay 813/238-2887, web: pwactampa.homepage.com.

Recovery
AA 813/933-9123.
MCC AA meetings 813/239-1951.

City Calendar

LGBT Pride
July. 813/854-8160 or 800/825-1000.

Entertainment
Tampa Bay Gay Men's Chorus 727/865-9004, web: www.tampabayarts.com.
Crescendo, Tampa Bay Womyn's Chorus 813/930-9055, web: www.crescendochorus.com

Tourist Info

Airport Directions
Tampa International. To get to most gay resorts and bars, follow signs to I-75 North. Take I-275 North and follow it to exits for either Dale Mabry Hwy, Nebraska Ave, or Busch Blvd.

Public Transit & Taxis
The Limo 727/572-1111.
Yellow Cab 813/253-0121.
Hartline Transit (bus) 813/254-4278.

Tourist Spots & Info
Busch Gardens 813/987-5082.
Florida Aquarium 813/273-4000.
Harbour Island.
Museum of Science & Industry 813/987-6100.
Ybor Square.
Visitor's Center: Greater Tampa Chamber of Commerce 813/228-7777, web: www.tampachamber.com
Tampa/Hillsborough Convention & Visitors Bureau 727/223-1111.

Tampa • FLORIDA

TAMPA BAY OVERVIEW

5 **Jungle** [★MW,NH] 813/877-3290 ■ 3703 Henderson Blvd (at Dale Mabry) ■ 3pm-3am

6 **Keith's Bar** [M,NH,S,GO] 813/971-3576 ■ 14905 N Nebraska (at Bearss) ■ 1pm-3am, strippers Fri

7 **Ki Ki Ki III** [M,BW] 813/254-8183 ■ 1908 W Kennedy Blvd (at Melville) ■ 11am-3am

8 **Klub Trendz** [W,D,MR,K,S,WC] 813/254-4188 ■ 2408 W Kennedy Blvd (at Armenia) ■ 5pm-3am, from 6pm Tue-Wed, clsd Sun-Mon, patio ■ www.rainbowcoin.com

9 **Metropolis** [MW,NH,WC] 813/871-2410 ■ 3447 W Kennedy Blvd (at Himes) ■ noon-3am, from 1pm Sun, shows Fri-Sat ■ www.metrotampa.com

FLORIDA • USA

10 **The Sahara** [W,NH,D,K,WC] 813/282-0183 ■ 4643 W Kennedy Blvd (at West Shore) ■ noon-3am, from 1pm Sun, Latin night Wed ■ saharalounge@aol.com

11 **The Tampa Brigg** [M,NH,S,GO] 813/931-3396 ■ 9002 N Florida Ave (at Busch) ■ 3pm-3am, strippers wknds

NIGHTCLUBS

12 **Chrome** [MW,D] 813/226-2476 ■ 901 N Franklin St (at Cass) ■ 10pm-3am Sat only

13 **Club Matrix** [★MW,D,F,S,GO] 813/237-8883 ■ 105 W Martin Luther King Blvd (at Tampa St) ■ 4pm-3am, theme nights, call for details, also restaurant, clsd Sun-Mon

14 **The Garage** [★M,D,S,18+] 813/221-2582 ■ 802 E Whiting St (at Jefferson) ■ 9:30pm-3am Fri & Sun only, strippers ■ www.factorytampa.com

15 **La Femme Buvette** [W,D,S] 813/247-9966 ■ 1328 E 9th Ave (at Republica de Cuba), Ybor City ■ 9pm-3am Fri-Sun only, call for events

16 **Pleasuredome** [GS,D,S,V,WC] 813/247-2711 ■ 1430 E 7th Ave (at 15th) ■ 9pm-3am Tue & Fri-Sat only, more gay Tue, 6 bars, drag shows ■ www.pleasuredomeonline.com

CAFES

Sacred Grounds [MW,E] 813/983-0837 ■ 4819 E Busch Blvd ■ 6:30pm-1am, till 2am Fri-Sat, till midnight Sun, live music & poetry slams

RESTAURANTS

Ho Ho Chinese [WC,GO] 813/254-9357 ■ 533 S Howard ■ 11:30am-10pm, full bar

Taqueria Quetzalcoatl [BW] 813/259-9982 ■ 402 S Howard Ave ■ 11am-11pm, from noon Sun, Mexican

ENTERTAINMENT & RECREATION

Sail More Life [GO] 727/328-2907 ■ 5000 13th Ave S (at 49th St S), Gulfport ■ sailboat charter, seasonal ■ www.sloyd.com

United Skates of America 813/876-5826 ■ 5121 N Armenia ■ lgbt skate 9pm-11:30pm Tue, seasonal

The Women's Show 813/238-8001 ■ WMNF 88.5 FM ■ 10am-noon Sat

BOOKSTORES

17 **Tomes & Treasures** [E] 813/251-9368 ■ 406-408 S Howard Ave (at Swann) ■ 11am-8pm, 1pm-6pm Sun, lgbt, also coffeehouse till midnight, till 10pm Sun, gallery

PUBLICATIONS

The Gazette 813/689-7566 ■ Florida's gay/ lesbian newsmagazine ■ thegazette@tampabay.rr.com

TLW Magazine 727/526-0585 ■ bi-weekly magazine for gay men ■ www.tlwmen.com

Watermark 407/481-2243 ■ bi-weekly lgbt newspaper ■ www.watermarkonline.com

GYMS & HEALTH CLUBS

Metro Flex Fitness 813/876-3539 ■ 2511 Swann Ave (at Armenia)

MEN'S CLUBS

Club Tampa [★PC] 813/223-5181 ■ 215 N 11th St ■ 24hrs

EROTICA

Buddies Video 813/876-8083 ■ 4322 W Crest Ave (at Hillsborough) ■ 24hrs

Playhouse Theatre 813/873-9235 ■ 4421 N Hubert (at Alva) ■ 24hrs

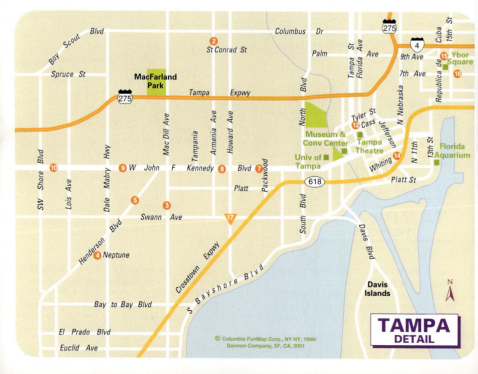

TAMPA DETAIL

Atlanta

Atlanta gained international attention as the host city of the 1996 Summer Olympics. Visitors and television viewers experienced the cosmopolitan atmosphere of this important growing southern city. Home to many great personalities, from Dr. Martin Luther King, Jr. to former president Jimmy Carter, as well as the national headquarters of CNN, Atlanta is the meeting-place of past and future.

Queer Resources

Community Info
▼ Atlanta Gay Center 404/523-7500, web: www.aglc.org. 159 Ralph McGill #600, 1:30pm-5:30pm Mon-Fri.
Gay Helpline 404/523-4357 6pm-11pm live.

AIDS Resources
AID Atlanta 404/872-0600, web: www.aidatlanta.org.

Recovery
Galano AA 404/881-9188. 585 Dutch Valley.

City Calendar

LGBT Pride
June. 404/876-3700, web: atlantapride.org.

Entertainment
Atlanta Feminist Women's Chorus 770/438-5823.
Lefont Screening Room 404/231-1924, gay film.

Annual Events
May - Armory Sports Classic 404/881-9280 (Armory Bar). Softball & many other sports competitions. Midtown Music Festival 404/577-8686.
August - Hotlanta 404/874-3796. Weekend of river rafting, pageants & parties for boys.
December - Women's Christmas Ball/Good Friends for Good Causes 770/938-1194.

Tourist Info

Airport Directions
Hartsfield International. Take 85 North, and get off at 14th to go downtown or to Midtown, or turn left on Piedmont to get to Ansley Sq. Or get off of 85 at the Piedmont exit and take a left onto Cheshire Bridge, or go back over the freeway, north, on Piedmont to Buckhead.

Public Transit & Taxis
Yellow Cab 404/521-0200.
Atlanta Airport Shuttle 404/524-3400.
Marta 404/848-5000.

Tourist Spots & Info
Atlanta Botanical Garden 404/876-5859.
CNN Center 404/827-1700.
Coca-Cola Museum.
Margaret Mitchell House 404/249-7015.
Martin Luther King Jr. Memorial Center.
Piedmont Park.
Underground Atlanta 404/523-2311.
Visitor's Center: 404/521-6600 or 800/285-2682 (in GA), web: www.atlanta.com

Weather
Summers are warm and humid (upper 80°s to low 90°s) with occasional thunderstorms. Winters are icy with occasional snow. Temperatures can drop into the low 30°s. Spring and fall are temperate – spring brings blossoming dogwoods and magnolias, while fall festoons the trees with Northeast Georgia's awesome fall foliage.

Best Views
70th floor of the Peachtree Plaza, in the Sun Dial restaurant. Also from the top of Stone Mountain.

GEORGIA

Atlanta

ACCOMMODATIONS
1 **Abbett Inn** [GS,NS,GO] 404/767-3708 ■ 1746 Virginia Ave ■ 1880s Victorian ■ www.abbettinn.com
2 ▶ **Ansley Inn B&B** [GS,NS,GO] 404/872-9000, 800/446-5416 ■ 253 15th St ■ full brkfst, nr gay nightlife in Midtown ■ www.ansleyinn.com
3 **Hello B&B** [MW,NS] 404/892-8111 ■ 1865 Windemere Dr ■ B&B in a private home, hot tub ■ members.aol.com/hellobnb
   Lynwood Place B&B [MO,SW,N,GO] 404/622-5622 ■ 767 Lynwood St SE (at Boulevard) ■ hot tub ■ www.lynwoodplace.com
4 **Midtown Manor** [GS,GO] 404/872-5846, 800/680-9234 ■ 811 Piedmont Ave NE ■ Victorian guesthouse ■ www.trdigital.com/midtown/manor
5 **Sheraton Atlanta Hotel** [GF,F,SW,WC] 404/659-6500, 800/325-3535 ■ 165 Courtland St (at International Blvd) ■ 3 restaurants, full bar, gym ■ www.sheraton.com

BARS
6 **Atlanta Eagle** [★M,D,B,L,GO] 404/873-2453 ■ 306 Ponce de Leon Ave NE (at Argonne) ■ 8pm-3am, from 5pm Sun, also 'American Bear Saloon' inside from 5pm, also leather store ■ www.atlantaeagle.com
7 **Blake's (on the Park)** [MW,NH,P,S,V] 404/892-5786, 888/441-8984 ■ 227 10th St (at Piedmont) ■ 3pm-2am
8 **Buddies** [M,NH,CW] 404/634-5895 ■ 2345 Cheshire Bridge Rd (at La Vista) ■ 1:30pm-4am, till 3am Sat
9 **Buddies Midtown** [MW,F,WC] 404/872-2655 ■ 239 Ponce de Leon (at Penn) ■ 3pm-4am, from noon wknds, sports bar
10 **Bulldogs** [★M,NH,D,L,MR,V] 404/872-3025 ■ 893 Peachtree St NE (btwn 7th & 8th) ■ 2pm-4am, till 3am Sat, cruise bar ■ members.aol.com/bulldognco
11 **Burkhart's Pub** [MW,NH,F,K,S,WC] 404/872-4403 ■ 1492-F Piedmont Ave (at Monroe, in Ansley Mall) ■ 4pm-4am, 2pm-3am wknds, patio ■ www.burkharts.com
12 **Eddie's Attic** [GS,E] 404/377-4976 ■ 515-B N McDonough St (at Trinity Place), Decatur ■ 4pm-close, rooftop deck, live music, gay comedy 4th Tue, restaurant, occasional lesbian hangout ■ www.eddiesattic.com
13 **Hoedowns** [★M,D,CW,S,WC] 404/876-0001 ■ 931 Monroe Dr #B (at Midtown Promenade) ■ 3pm-3am, clsd Mon, more women Th
14 **Kaya** [GS,D,MR-AF,F,S] 404/874-4460 ■ 1068 Peachtree St NE (at 12th) ■ call for hrs, more gay wknds, T-dance Sun, patio, also restaurant
   Le Buzz [MW,NH,D,F,K,S,WC] 770/424-1337 ■ 585 Franklin Rd A-10 (at S Marietta Pkwy, in Longhorn Plaza), Marietta ■ 7pm-3am, from 6pm Sat, clsd Sun, karaoke Tue & Th, drag shows & male dancers Wed, DJ Fri-Sat, patio
15 **Mary's** [MW,NH,V] 404/624-4411 ■ 1287 Glenwood Ave (at Flat Shoals) ■ 5pm-2am, till 3am Sat, 4pm-midnight Sun, friendly cocktail bar
16 **The Metro** [★M,D,MR,S,V] 404/874-9869 ■ 1080 Peachtree St (at 11th) ■ 4pm-4am, till 3am Sat, clsd Sun, go-go boys nightly, Latin night Tue
17 **Midtown Saloon & Grill** [★M,NH,F] 404/874-1655 ■ 738 Ponce de Leon Ave NE (at Ponce de Leon Plaza) ■ 2pm-4am, food served 5pm-10pm, patio
18 **Miss Q's** [M,NH] 404/875-6255 ■ 560-B Amsterdam (in Midtown Outlets) ■ 4pm-close, from noon wknds, big screen TV, popular happy hour
19 **Model T** [M,NH,K,S,OC,WC] 404/872-2209 ■ 699 Ponce de Leon NE (at Barnett) ■ noon-4am, shows Sat, cruisy
20 **The Moreland Tavern** [MW,NH,F,WC] 404/622-4650 ■ 1196 Moreland Ave SE (at Confederate) ■ noon-2am, patio
21 **My Sister's Room** [★W,D,F,E,K,YC] 404/370-1990 ■ 222 E Howard Ave (at E Trinity Pl), Decatur ■ 6pm-2am Tue-Th, till 3am Fri-Sat, 4pm-midnight Sun, clsd Mon, also restaurant, patio ■ www.mysistersroom.com
22 **New Order Lounge** [M,NH,E,OC,WC] 404/874-8247 ■ 1544 Piedmont Ave NE (at Monroe in Ansley Sq Ctr) ■ 2pm-2am, till 3am wknds
23 **Opus I** [M,NH,OC,WC] 404/634-6478 ■ 1086 Alco St NE (at Cheshire Bridge) ■ 9am-4am, from 12:30pm Sun
24 **The Oscar's** [M,V] 404/874-7748 ■ 1510-C Piedmont Ave (in Ansley Mall) ■ 2pm-4am, till 3am Sat, clsd Sun

from the INN-Side

ANSLEY INN
Atlanta's finest bed & breakfast

Experience Atlanta

an elegant english tudor located in the heart of midtown Atlanta's historic district

• 22 rooms w/ private bath, jacuzzi, cable TV, wet bar, coffee maker
• scrumptious full breakfast, afternoon snacks
• open all year round

253 Fifteenth Street • Atlanta, GA 30309
404-872-9000 • 800-446-5416 • FAX 404-892-2318
e-mail: reservations@ansleyinn.com • web: www.ansleyinn.com

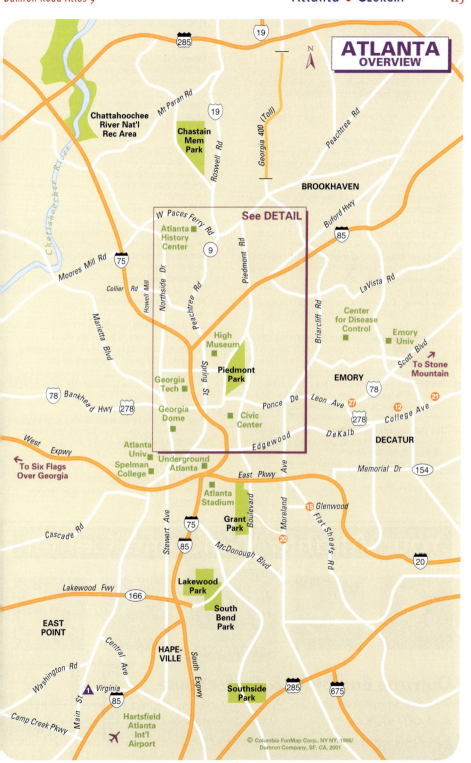

GEORGIA • USA

25 **The Palace** [M,D,MR-AF] 404/522-3000 ■ 91 Broad St ■ 5pm-close, 3 levels

26 **The Phoenix** [M,NH] 404/892-7871 ■ 567 Ponce de Leon (at Monroe) ■ 9am-4am, from 12:30pm Sun, hustlers

27 **Pin Up's** [GF,F,S,18+,WC] 404/373-3715 ■ 2788 E Ponce de Leon Ave, Decatur ■ 11am-3am, from 1pm Sat, from 6pm Sun, strip club, more gay for nude go-go boys Th-Sun

24 **Scandals** [★M,NH,K,WC] 404/875-5957 ■ 1510-G Piedmont Ave NE (in Ansley Mall) ■ 11:30am-4am, till 3am Sat, from 12:30pm Sun

28 **Swinging Richard's** [M,S,$] 404/352-0530 ■ 1400 Northside Dr NW (btwn I-75 & Northside Dr) ■ 5pm-3am, till 4am Fri, clsd Sun-Mon, gay strip club, gift shop ■ www.swingingrichards.com

29 **The Tower II** [W,NH,S,YC,WC] 404/523-1535 ■ 735 Ralph McGill Blvd NE ■ 5pm-2am, till 3am Fri-Sat, till midnight Sun, dancing/ DJ Fri

30 **Tripps** [M,NH] 404/724-0067 ■ 1931 Piedmont Circle (at Cheshire Bridge) ■ 9am-4am, till 3am Sun, from 12:30pm Sun, free buffet at 3pm

17 **The Upper Room** [GS,NH,K] 404/874-9934 ■ 736 Ponce de Leon, NE (at Ponce de Leon Pl) ■ 11am-2am, till midnight Sun, clsd Mon, rooftop patio

Nightclubs

31 **The Armory** [★MW,D,MR,F,S,V,YC,WC] 404/881-9280 ■ 836 Juniper St NE (at 7th) ■ 4pm-3am, till 4am Fri, 4 bars, also restaurant, patio

32 **Backstreet** [★GS,D,MR,S,V,YC,PC,$] 404/873-1986 ■ 845 Peachtree St NE (btwn 5th & 6th, enter rear) ■ 24hrs, 3 flrs, gift shop, home of 'Charlie Brown's XXX-Rated Cabaret' Th-Sat ■ www.backstreetatlanta.com

33 **The Chamber** [GF,D,S] 404/248-1612 ■ 2115 Faulkner Dr (at Cheshire Bridge) ■ 10pm-4am Th-Fri, till 3am Sat, fetish crowd, 18+ Th, also 'Glitterdome' 3rd Fri, queer glamrock club ■ www.theglitterdome.com

34 **The Chili Pepper** [GF,D,E,WC] 404/812-9266 ■ 208 Pharr Rd (btwn Piedmont & Peachtree in Buckhead) ■ 9pm-4am, till 3am Sat, clsd Sun-Mon

35 **Deux Plex** [GS,D,MR,F,S,18+,$] 404/733-5900 ■ 1789 Cheshire Bridge Rd ■ call for hours, also French bistro 5pm-2:30am, clsd Mon

36 **ESSO** [GF,D,MR,WC] 404/872-3776 ■ 489 Courtland St (at Pine) ■ 10pm-3am, clsd Sun-Wed, 3 flrs, rooftop deck, hip hop/ R&B

37 **Ground Zero** [★M,D,GO] 404/892-9325 ■ 582 Piedmont Ave (at North Ave) ■ 11pm-close Fri-Sat & 5pm-close Sun only, wknd warehouse circuit party, call for info

38 **The Heretic** [★M,D,L,F,S,WC] 404/325-3061 ■ 2069 Cheshire Bridge Rd (at Piedmont) ■ 9am-4am, from noon wknds, 3 bars, patio, call for theme nights, also 'Heretic Leathers' toy shop

39 **Ladies of the Night** [W,D,MR-AF,F,$] 404/874-5673, 800/970-5833 ■ 1231 W Peachtree (at Club Jaguar) ■ 11pm-4am Fri

40 **Masquerade** [GF,D,F,E,18+,$] 404/577-8178, 404/577-2002 ■ 695 North Ave NE ■ 10pm-4am Wed-Fri, till 3am Sat, 7pm-midnight Sun ■ masq@masq.com

17 **MJQ Concourse** [★GF,D,A,S,YC] 404/870-0575 ■ 736 Ponce de Leon Ave (at Ponce de Leon Pl) ■ 10pm-3am

41 **The Rarity** [★M,D,MR,F,S,V,WC] 404/875-5238 ■ 1924 Piedmont Rd NE (at Cheshire Bridge Rd) ■ 4pm-4am, till 3am Sat, till midnight Sun, clsd Mon, hip-hop Wed, go go boys ■ www.therarityatlanta.com

42 **The Warehouse/ Traxx** [GS,D,MR-AF,S,18+] 404/681-4422 ■ 339 Marietta St NW (at Simpson) ■ 10pm-3am, more gay Mon, Th & wknds ■ traxxatl@aol.com

Cafes

Caribou Coffee 404/733-5539 ■ 1551 Piedmont Ave (at Monroe) ■ 6am-11pm, 7am-midnight wknds

Innovox 404/872-4482 ■ 499 Ponce de Leon Ave NE ■ 7am-1am, 24hrs wknds, Internet coffeehouse

Intermezzo 404/355-0411 ■ 1845 Peachtree Rd NE ■ 11am-3am, till 4am Fri-Sat, classy cafe, full bar, great desserts

Restaurants

Agnes & Muriel's [★BW] 404/885-1000 ■ 1514 Monroe Dr (nr Piedmont) ■ 11am-11pm, till midnight Fri-Sat, from 10am wknds, patio

Apres Diem 404/872-3333 ■ 931 Monroe Dr #C-103 ■ lunch & dinner, French bistro, live jazz

The Big Red Tomato Bistro 404/870-9881 ■ 980 Piedmont Rd NE (at 10th St) ■ dinner & Sun brunch, Italian, full bar, patio

Your Atlanta Welcome Center

Outwrite Bookstore & Coffeehouse
991 Piedmont Ave @ 10th Street   Midtown Atlanta
404.607.0082   www.outwritebooks.com
SUN-THUR: 9AM-11PM   FRI-SAT: 9AM-MID

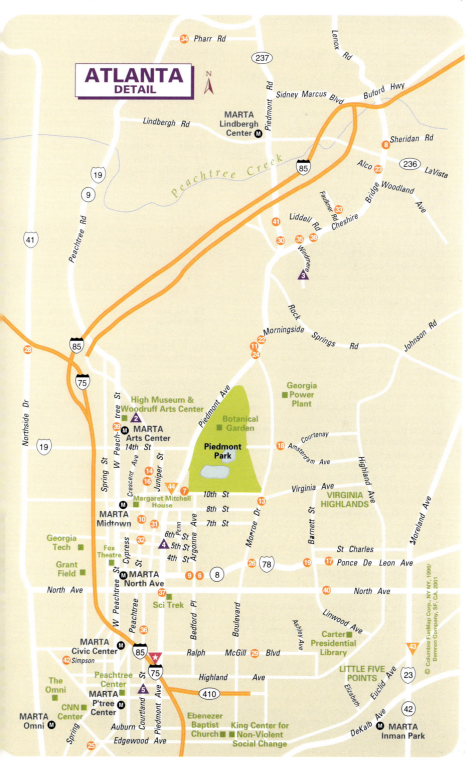

GEORGIA • USA

Bridgetown Grill [★WC] 404/873-5361 ■ 689 Peachtree (across from Fox Theater) ■ 11am-11pm, funky Caribbean, some veggie

Camille's [WC] 404/872-7203 ■ 1186 N Highland ■ dinner only, Italian ■ www.camilles.com

The Colonnade 404/874-5642 ■ 1879 Cheshire Bridge Rd NE ■ lunch & dinner, traditional Southern

Cowtippers [TG,WC] 404/874-3469 ■ 1600 Piedmont Ave NE (at Monroe) ■ 11:30am-11pm, steakhouse

Dunk N' Dine [★MW,TG] 404/636-0197 ■ 2277 Cheshire Bridge Rd (at Lenox) ■ 24hrs, downscale diner, queens abound

Einstein's [★WC] 404/876-7925 ■ 1077 Juniper (at 12th) ■ 11am-midnight, till 1am Fri-Sat, some veggie, Sun brunch, full bar, patio

The Flying Biscuit Cafe [★BW,WC,GO] 404/687-8888 ■ 1655 McLendon Ave (at Clifton) ■ 9am-10pm, clsd Mon, healthy brkfst all day, plenty veggie

Majestic Diner [★AYOR] 404/875-0276 ■ 1031 Ponce de Leon (at Clayton Terrace) ■ 24hrs, diner right from the '50s, cantankerous waitresses included

Murphy's [★WC] 404/872-0904 ■ 997 Virginia Ave (at N Highland Ave) ■ 11am-10pm, till midnight Fri, from 8am wknds, plenty veggie, best brunch in town

North Park Square 770/919-2693 ■ 23 N Park Sq (at Church St), Marietta ■ lunch Mon-Sat, dinner Tue-Sat, Sun brunch, upscale wine bar & bistro, eclectic cuisine ■ northpark.hypermart.net

R Thomas [★BW,WC] 404/872-2942 ■ 1812 Peachtree Rd NE ■ 24hrs, healthy Californian/ juice bar, plenty veggie

Swan Coach House 404/261-0636 ■ 3130 Slaton Dr NW, Buckhead ■ lunch & dinner

Veni Vidi Vici 404/875-8424 ■ 41 14th St ■ lunch Mon-Fri, dinner 5pm-11pm nightly, upscale Italian, some veggie

Watershed 404/378-4900 ■ 406 W Ponce de Leon, Decatur ■ 11am-10pm, clsd Sun, wine bar, also gift shop, owned by Emily Saliers of the Indigo Girls

ENTERTAINMENT & RECREATION

Alternative Talk 404/523-8989 (station #), 404/523-3471 (office #) ■ WRFG 89.3FM ■ 5pm-5:30pm Fri, radio program for Atlanta's African-American lgbt community

Atlanta Feminist Women's Chorus 770/438-5823

Funny That Way Theatre Company 404/893-3344, 404/627-6672 ■ lgbt theater company, seasonal musicals, call for schedule

Lambda Radio 404/523-8989 ■ WRFG 89.3 FM ■ 6pm Tue, lgbt radio program

Little 5 Points, Moreland & Euclid Ave S of Ponce de Leon Ave ■ hip & funky area w/ too many restaurants & shops to list

Martin Luther King, Jr. Center for Non-Violent Social Change 404/524-1956 ■ 449 Auburn Ave NE ■ 9am-5pm daily, includes King's birth home, the church where he preached in the 60s & his gravesite

BOOKSTORES

24 Brushstrokes 404/876-6567 ■ 1510-J Piedmont Ave NE (nr Monroe) ■ 10am-10pm, till 11pm Fri-Sat, lgbt variety store

43 Charis Books & More [WC] 404/524-0304 ■ 1189 Euclid Ave NE (at Moreland) ■ 10:30am-6:30pm, till 8pm Wed-Sat, noon-6pm Sun, feminist ■ Charisbook@aol.com

44 ▶ Outwrite Bookstore & Coffeehouse [F,WC] 404/607-0082 ■ 991 Piedmont Ave NE (at 10th) ■ 8am-11pm, till midnight Fri-Sat, lgbt, music, videos, gifts, cafe

RETAIL SHOPS

The Boy Next Door 404/873-2664 ■ 1447 Piedmont Ave NE (btwn 14th & Monroe) ■ 11am-7pm, noon-6pm Sun, clothing

The House of Warlords 404/315-9000, 877/993-7377 (orders) ■ 2111 Faulkner Rd ■ 11am-7pm, till 9pm Sat, clsd Sun-Mon, custom leather ■ www.thehouseofwarlords.com

In the Moment [GO] 404/817-7005 ■ 626 N Highland Ave (at North Ave) ■ noon-7pm, till 8pm Fri-Sat, till 6pm Sun, art, furnishings, gifts ■ itmstore@bellsouth.net

The Junkman's Daughter 404/577-3188 ■ 464 Moreland Ave (at Euclid) ■ 11am-7pm, till 8pm Sat, hip stuff

Metropolitan Deluxe [WC] 404/892-9337 ■ 1034 N Highland NE (at Virginia) ■ 10am-10pm, till 11pm Fri-Sat, till 7pm Sun, flowers & gifts

Piercing Experience 404/378-9100 ■ 1654 McLendon Ave NE (at Clifton) ■ noon-9pm, till 5pm Sun, clsd Mon

PUBLICATIONS

Clikque Magazine 404/817-3898 ■ 1117 Peachtree Walk NE, Ste 125 30309 ■ great glossy newsmagazine for lgbt African-Americans, some nat'l club listings ■ www.clikque.com

ETC Magazine 404/888-0063 ■ weekly entertainment guide & news resource for lgbt Atlanta & Southeast ■ www.etcmag.com

GYMS & HEALTH CLUBS

Boot Camp [GF] 404/876-8686 ■ 1544 Piedmont Ave NE #105 (in Ansley Mall) ■ full gym

The Fitness Factory [★GF] 404/815-7900 ■ 500 N Amsterdam (in 'Amsterdam Outlets') ■ full gym

Mid-City Fitness Center [MW] 404/321-6507 ■ 2201 Faulkner Dr NE (at Cheshire Bridge) ■ cruisy

MEN'S CLUBS

Flex [SW] 404/815-0456 ■ 76 4th St (at Spring St) ■ 24hrs ■ www.flexbaths.com

Fort Troff [LV,PC,GO] 303/329-0444 ■ 701 Edgehill (at 10th & Howell Mill) ■ theme parties ■ www.forttroff.com

IT [PC] 1244 Techwood Dr ■ 11pm-close Wed-Th, from midnight Fri-Sun, must have pass to enter, inquire locally

The Sanctuary [PC] 404/874-4838 ■ 1417 Dutch Valley Pl ■ dungeon, men's night Th & Sat, pansexual Fri, also 'Dark Angel Leather' 11am-11pm, 3pm-8pm Sun, clsd Mon ■ www.thesanctuary.net

SEX CLUBS

The Sanctuary [PC] 404/874-4838 ■ 1417 Dutch Valley Pl ■ women's night last Fri ■ www.thesanctuary.net

EROTICA

4skins 2 404/685-1700 ■ 593 Westminster Dr NE (at Monroe) ■ custom leather, also location inside Atlanta Eagle ■ www.foreskinsleather.com

Heaven 404/262-9113 ■ 2628 Piedmont (at Sidney Marcus Blvd)

Insercetion 404/888-0878 ■ 505 Peachtree St NE ■ call for other locations

The Poster Hut/ Scream Boutique 404/633-7491 ■ 2175 Cheshire Bridge Rd ■ clothing, toys

Starship 404/320-9101 ■ 2275 Cheshire Bridge Rd ■ leather & more, 7 locations in Atlanta

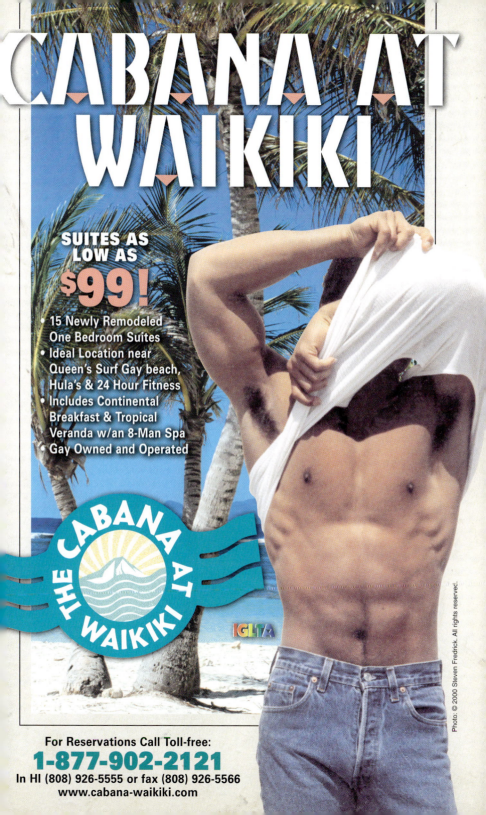

HAWAII

Honolulu

ACCOMMODATIONS
1 **Breakers Hotel** [GF,SW] 808/923-3181, 800/426-0494 ■ 250 Beachwalk ■ also bar & grill ■ www.breakers-hawaii.com

2 ▶**The Cabana at Waikiki** [★M,GO] 808/926-5555, 877/902-2121 ■ 2551 Cartwright Rd (off Kapahulu Ave) ■ 1-bdrm suites w/ kitchens & lanais, 8-man spa, 1 blk to gay Queen's Surf beach ■ www.cabana-waikiki.com

3 **The Coconut Plaza Hotel** [GF,SW,WC] 808/923-8828 ■ 450 Lewers St, Waikiki (at Ala Wai) ■ nr beach ■ www.aston-hotels.com

4 **Hale Plumeria** 808/732-7719 ■ 3044 Hollinger St ■ apt, 4 blks to Waikiki Beach ■ gledingh@aol.com

5 **Hawaiian Waikiki Beach Hotel** [GF,F,E,SW,WC] 808/922-2511, 800/877-7666 ■ 2570 Kalakaua Ave (at Paoakalani Ave) ■ ocean views ■ www.hawaiianwaikikibeach.com

Jerry's Vacation Condo [GS] 808/737-1281, 888/261-7092 ■ Waikiki

Outrigger Hotels & Resorts [GF] 808/921-6600, 800/688-7444 ■ many properties in Waikiki ■ www.outrigger.com

6 **Queen's Surf Vacation Rentals** [GS,SW,GO] 808/732-4368, 888/336-4368 ■ ocean views ■ www.ndhi.com/qs

7 **Waikiki GLBT Vacation Rentals** [GF,NS,WC] 808/922-1659, 800/543-5663 ■ 1580 Makaloa St, Ste 770 ■ reservation service, ask for Walt Flood ■ www.waikiki-vacation-GLBT-rentals.com

8 **Waikiki Joy Hotel** [GF,F,K,SW] 808/923-2300, 800/733-5569 ■ 320 Lewers St ■ boutique hotel, jacuzzis, nr beach ■ www.aston-hotels.com/display.cfm?p=waikikijoyhotel

9 **Waikiki Parkside Hotel** [GF,SW,WC] 808/955-1567, 800/237-9666 ■ 1850 Ala Moana Blvd (at Kalai & Ena) ■ www.waikikiparkside.com

6 **Waikiki Vacation Studio Condo** [GS,SW,NS,GO] 808/737-1281, 888/261-7092 ■ 134 Kapahulu Ave #722 ■ nr beach, 3-night minimum ■ www.cyberrentals.com/hi/hascOAHU.html

BARS
10 **Angles** [MW,NH,D,S,V] 808/926-9766, 808/923-1130 (infoline) ■ 2256 Kuhio Ave, 2nd flr, Waikiki (at Seaside) ■ 10am-2am, DJ Wed-Sun, free Internet access, more women Sun, male dancers Th-Sun ■ www.gayhawaii.com/angles

6 **Hula's Bar & Lei Stand** [★MW,D,TG,F,S,V,YC] 808/923-0669 ■ 134 Kapahulu Ave (2nd flr of Waikiki Grand Hotel) ■ 10am-2am, close to gay beach, Th & Sun go-go boys ■ www.hulas.com

11 **In Between** [GS,NH,K] 808/926-7060 ■ 2155 Lau'ula St, Waikiki (off Lewers, across from 'Planet Hollywood') ■ 2pm-2am

12 **Michelangelo's** [M,NH,F,K] 808/951-0008 ■ 444 Hobron Ln #P-8 (in Eaton Sq Shopping Ctr, Waikiki) ■ 10am-2am, from 6am wknds, sports bar, cruisy ■ gayhawaii.com/michelangelo

NIGHTCLUBS
13 **Fusion Waikiki** [★M,D,A,TG,S,K,V] 808/924-2422 ■ 2260 Kuhio Ave, upstairs (at Seaside) ■ 9pm-4am, from 8pm Fri-Sat, from 10pm Sun, go-go boys Wed, 18+ 1st & 3rd Sun ■ www.gayhawaii.com/fusion

14 **Venus Nightclub** [GS,D,MR-A,S,YC] 808/951-8671, 808/955-2640 ■ 1349 Kapiolani Blvd (below 'China House' restaurant, at Piikoi) ■ 8pm-4am, drag shows Tue & Sat, male dancers Wed, Fri-Sat ■ www.venusnightclub.com

CAFES
Caffe Giovannini [GO] 808/979-2299 ■ 1888 Kalakaua Ave, Waikiki (across from the 'Wave') ■ 8am-midnight, patio, great coffee, sandwiches & desserts

Mocha Java Cafe 808/591-9023 ■ 1200 Ala Moana Blvd (in Ward Ctr) ■ 8am-9pm, till 5pm Sun, plenty veggie

RESTAURANTS
A Pacific Cafe [WC] 808/593-0035 ■ 1200 Ala Moana Blvd (in Ward Ctr) ■ dinner nightly, Pacific Rim & Mediterranean, reservations req'd

Café Che Pasta [MW,D,K] 808/524-0004, 808/531-4140 (info line) ■ 1001 Bishop St (enter off Alakea St) ■ 11am-8pm, from 5pm Sat, clsd Sun, full bar, karaoke 7pm-2am Wed, 'Black Garter Cafe' for women 9pm-2am Fri

Cafe Sistina [WC] 808/596-0061 ■ 1314 S King St ■ lunch Mon-Fri, dinner nightly, northern Italian, some veggie, full bar

Eggs n' Things 808/949-0820 ■ 1911-B Kalakaua Ave ■ 11pm-2pm, diner, popular after-hours

Indigo 808/521-2900 ■ 1121 Nu'uanu Ave ■ lunch Tue-Fri, dinner Tue-Sat, Eurasian, live jazz Fri-Sat

Keo's Thai [★] 808/951-9355 ■ 2028 Kuhio Ave ■ 7:30pm-11pm, reservations advised ■ www.keosthaicuisine.com

La Cucaracha 808/922-2288 ■ 102 Nahua Rd (at Kuhio Ave) ■ 2pm-2am, Mexican, full bar

Lewers St. Steak & Seafood [WC] 808/926-1881 ■ 412 Lewers St (at the Marc Suites) ■ brkst & dinner, full bar

Singha Thai [E] 808/941-2898 ■ 1910 Ala Moana Blvd ■ 4pm-11pm

Sunset Terrace [E] 808/971-3595 ■ 2335 Kalakaua Ave (on 2nd Fl of Outrigger Waikiki on the Beach Hotel) ■ 7am-9:30pm, Asian-Pacific seafood & American

ENTERTAINMENT & RECREATION
LikeHike 808/455-8193 ■ gay hiking tours every other Sun, also gay kayaking trips, call for info & locations ■ www.gayhawaii.com/likehike/

Queens Surf Beach Kapiolani Park ■ popular gay beach

Rainbow Charters 808/943-2628 ■ PO Box 75422, Honolulu 96836 ■ whale watching, snorkling, sunset cocktails & commitment ceremonies, lesbian-owned/ run

Taking the Plunge 808/922-2600, 888/922-3483 ■ various diving trips, free hotel pickup ■ gayhawaii.com/div

RETAIL SHOPS
15 **Eighty Percent Straight** 808/923-9996 ■ 1917 Kalakaua Ave, Waikiki (at Ala Moana) ■ 10am-10pm, till 11pm Fri-Sat, lesbigay clothing, books, videos, cards, toys; also 2139 Kuhio Ave, 808/923-4222

PUBLICATIONS
DaKine Magazine 808/923-7378 ■ monthly lgbt newsmagazine for all islands, club & nightlife listings ■ dakinemagazine@hawaii.rr.com

Odyssey Magazine Hawaii 808/955-5959 ■ everything you need to know about gay Hawaii ■ www.odysseyhawaii.com

Pocket Guide to Hawaii 808/923-2400 ■ distributed free in the islands or $5 by mail order ■ gayhawaii.com

Honolulu • Hawaii

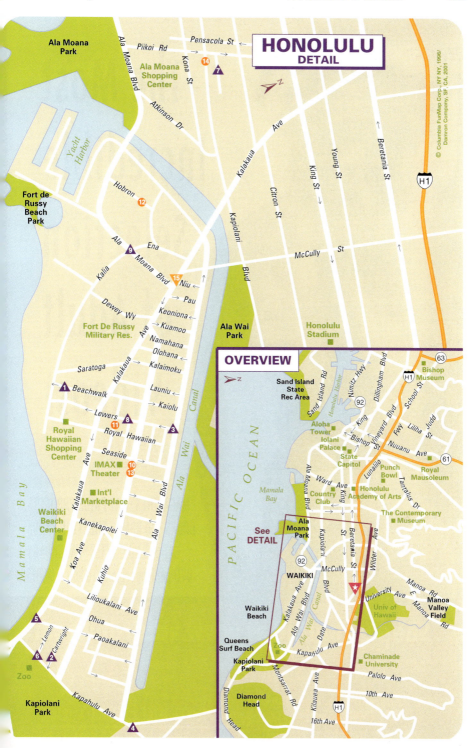

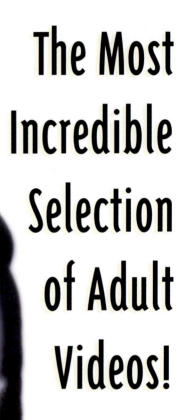

Honolulu

Visions of sparkling beaches, lush tropical flowers, magnificent sunsets, active volcanoes, and an easy-going attitude draw visitors from around the world to the Hawaiian Islands. Located on the island of Oahu, Honolulu and Waikiki beach offer a mixture of shopping, entertainment, and the natural beauty that makes Hawaii an earthly paradise.

Queer Resources

Community Info
▼ Gay/Lesbian Community Center 808/951-7000, web: www.glcc-hawaii.org. 2424 S Beretania, 10am-7pm, clsd Sun.
Helpful websites: www.gayhawaii.com & www.hawaiiscene.com/gayscene.

AIDS Resources
808/922-1313.

Recovery
808/946-1438, 277 Ohua (yes, it's Ohua!) (Waikiki Health Ctr), 8pm daily.

City Calendar

LGBT Pride
June. 808/951-7000 (GLCC).

Annual Events
April - Merrie Monarch Festival.
May - Golden Week, celebration of Japanese culture.
September - Aloha Week.

Tourist Info

Airport Directions
Honolulu International Airport—Take Nimitz Hwy South, which becomes Ala Moana South. Go right at Kalakaua into Waikiki.

Public Transit & Taxis
Charley's 808/955-2211.
The Bus 808/848-5555.

Tourist Spots & Info
Bishop Museum 808/848-4174.
Foster Botanical Gardens.
Hanauma Bay.
Honolulu Academy of Arts 808/532-8741.
Polynesian Cultural Center.
Waimea Falls Park.
Visitor's Center: 808/923-1811, web: www.gohawaii.com.

Weather
Usually paradise perfect, but humid. It rarely gets hotter than the upper 80°s.

Best Views
Helicopter tour.

Men's Clubs
Max's Gym [★V,18+,PC] 808/951-8232 ■ 444 Hobron Ln, 4th flr (at Ala Moana Blvd, in Eaton Sq) ■ 24hrs, also 'Cafe Max' ■ www.maxsgym.com

P-10A [S,V,18+,PC,$] 808/942-8536 ■ 444 Hobron Ln, #P-10A (next to 'Michelangelo') ■ 6pm-6am, 24 hrs wknds, low rates, drug/ alcohol-free, nude dancers midnight Fri-Sat

Erotica
▶ **Diamond Head Video** 808/735-6066 ■ 870 Kapahulu Ave (near 'Genki Sushi') ■ www.adultdhv.com

Risque II Theatre/ Bookstore [AYOR] 808/531-7318 ■ 32 N Hotel St, in Chinatown (upstairs) ■ 24hrs

Chicago

An energetic and exciting city, Chicago brings together the best of popular culture and fine art. The city boasts world-class museums and outdoor sculpture as well as jazz and house music, theater and nightclubs, baseball and beaches. A cruise on Lake Michigan—with themes from city history to wine-tasting—should top every visitor's to-do list.

Queer Resources

Community Info
▼ Horizons Community Services 773/472-6469. 961 W Montana, 9am-10pm Mon-Th, till 5pm Fri. web: www.horizonsonline.org. (See New Town map.)
Lesbian/Gay Helpline, 773/929-4357, 6pm-10pm.

AIDS Resources
800/243-2437 (in IL).

Recovery
New Town Alano Club (AA), 773/529-0321. 909 W Belmont St, 2nd flr (btwn Clark & Sheffield).

City Calendar

LGBT Pride
June. 773/348-8243, web: www.chicagopridecalendar.org.

Annual Events
February - Fireball circuit party 773/244-6000.
March - Women's Film Festival 773/907-0610.
May - International Mr. Leather 800/545-6753. Weekend of events and contest on Sunday. Bear Pride 773/248-1683.
June - Lambda Literary Awards 202/682-0952. The Oscars of lgbt writing & publishing. Chicago Blues Festival 312/744-3315.
August - Halsted Street Fair 773/868-3010 ext. 27.
November - Chicago Lesbian & Gay Film Festival 773/293-1447.

Tourist Info

Airport Directions
O'Hare International. The Kennedy Expressway heads toward the city. Or take Mannheim Rd to the Eisenhower Expressway. Inquire locally about which is currently the lesser of two evils.

Public Transit & Taxis
Yellow & Checker Cabs 312/ 829-4222.
Chicago Airport Shuttle Service 773/247-7678.
Chicago Transit Authority 312/836-7000.
Amtrak 312/655-2385.

Tourist Spots & Info
900 North Michigan Shops.
The Art Institute of Chicago 312/443-3600.
Historic Water Tower.
Museum of Science and Industry 773/684-1414.
Sears Tower Skydeck Observatory 312/875-9696.
Second City & the Improv Comedy Clubs.
Visitor's Center: Chicago Office of Tourism 312/744-2400. web: www.chicago.il.org.

Weather
'The Windy City' earned its name. Winter temperatures have been known to be as low as -46°. Summers are humid, normally in the 80°s.

Best Views
Skydeck of the 110-story Sears Tower.

ILLINOIS

Chicago

Chicago is divided into 5 geographical areas:
Chicago—Overview
Chicago—North Side
Chicago—New Town
Chicago—Near North
Chicago—South Side

Chicago—Overview

Entertainment & Recreation
Artemis Singers 773/764-4265 ■ lesbian feminist chorus ■ www.geocities.com/artemissingers
Bailiwick Arts Center 773/883-1090 ■ 1229 W Belmont ■ many lgbt-themed productions, including the popular Pride Series ■ www.bailiwick.org
Chicago Neighborhood Tours [GF] 312/742-1190 ■ 78 E Washington St (at the Chicago Cultural Ctr) ■ make the Windy City your kind of town ■ www.chgocitytours.com
The Hancock Observatory 888/875-8439 ■ 875 N Michigan Ave (in John Hancock Ctr) ■ renovated 94th-flr observatory w/ 'Skywalk' ■ www.hancock-observatory.com
Leather Archives & Museum 773/761-9200 ■ 6418 N Greenview ■ by appt ■ www.leatherarchives.org
Sears Tower Skydeck 312/875-9696 ■ 233 S Wacker Dr (enter at Jackson Blvd) ■ see the City from one of the world's tallest buildings ■ www.the-skydeck.com

Publications
The Alternative Phone Book 773/472-6319 ■ directory of local businesses ■ www.prairienet.org/apb/
BLACKlines 773/871-7610 ■ monthly news & features for Black lgbts ■ outlines@suba.com
Chicago Free Press 773/325-0005 ■ lgbt newspaper ■ www.chicagofreepress.com
En La Vida 773/871-7610 ■ monthly news & features for Latino/a lgbts ■ outlines@suba.com
Gab 773/248-4542 ■ has got the dirt on Chicago's club scene ■ gabmag@earthlink.net
Gay Chicago 773/327-7271 ■ weekly, extensive resource listings ■ gaychimag@aol.com
Pride Magazine 773/769-6328 ■ also publish Chicago Pink Pages ■ pridemag@aol.com
Windy City Times/ Outlines 773/871-7610 ■ weekly lgbt newspaper & calendar guide ■ www.outlineschicago.com

Chicago—North Side

ACCOMMODATIONS

A Sister's Place [WO,GO] 773/275-1319 ■ guestrooms in artist's flat, women-owned/ run

1. **The Ardmore House** [M,GO] 773/728-5414 ■ 1248 W Ardmore Ave (at Magnolia) ■ Victorian B&B, full brkfst wknds, hot tub ■ www.ardmorehousebb.com
2. **Gregory House** [GS,GO] 773/878-3019 ■ 1718 W Gregory St (btwn Clark & Foster) ■ 1925 bungalow in charming Andersonville, some shared baths ■ www.gregoryhousechicago.com

BARS

3. **Big Chicks** [MW,NH,D,V,WC] 773/728-5511 ■ 5024 N Sheridan (btwn Foster & Argyle) ■ 4pm-2am, from 2pm wknds, patio, Sun BBQ ■ www.bigchicks.com

Charmer's Lounge [M,NH] 773/465-2811 ■ 1502 W Jarvis (at Greenview) ■ 6pm-2am, 4pm-3am Sat

4. **Chicago Eagle** [MW,L,WC] 773/728-0050 ■ 5015 N Clark St (at Argyle) ■ 8pm-4am, till 5am Sat
5. **Clark's on Clark** [★M,NH] 773/728-2373 ■ 5001 N Clark St (at Argyle) ■ 4pm-4am, till 5am Sat, from 8pm Sun
6. **Different Strokes** [M,NH,MR,S] 773/989-1958 ■ 4923 N Clark St (at Argyle) ■ noon-2am, till 3am Sat, dancers Sat
7. **Granville Anvil** [M,NH,L] 773/973-0006 ■ 1137 W Granville (E of Broadway) ■ 9am-2am
8. **Jackhammer** [★M,NH,D,L,S,V] 773/743-5772 ■ 6406 N Clark St (at Devon) ■ 4pm-4am, till 5am Sat, dancers wknds, patio ■ www.jackhammer-chicago.com
9. **Legacy** [M,NH] 773/588-9405 ■ 3042 W Irving Park Rd (at Kedzie) ■ 8pm-4am, till 5am Sat, unconfirmed
10. **Lost & Found** [W,NH] 773/463-7599 ■ 3058 W Irving Park Rd (at Albany) ■ 7pm-2am, from 3pm Sat, clsd Mon
11. **Madrigal's** [MW,MR-L,S] 773/334-3033 ■ 5316 N Clark St (at Balmoral) ■ 5pm-2am, till 3am Sat, strippers Th-Sun
12. **Scot's** [MW,NH] 773/528-3253 ■ 1829 W Montrose (at Damen) ■ 3pm-2am, from 11am wknds
13. **Star Gaze** [W,NH,F,E] 773/561-7363 ■ 5419 N Clark (at Foster) ■ 5pm-2am, 3pm-3am Sat, from noon Sun
14. **Touché** [★M,L] 773/465-7400 ■ 6412 N Clark St (at Devon) ■ 5pm-4am, from 3pm wknds

CAFES

Mountain Moving Coffeehouse [WO,E] 312/409-0276 ■ 1700 W Farragut (in basement of Summerdale church) ■ 7:30pm Sat only, check local lgbt paper for dates ■ www.angelfire.com/il2/mmch

RESTAURANTS

Chicago Diner [BW] 773/935-6696 ■ 3411 N Halsted St ■ 11am-10pm, from 10am wknds, hip & vegetarian

Fireside 773/878-5942 ■ 5739 N Ravenswood (at Rosehill) ■ 11am-4am, from 10am Sat, Cajun, pizza, patio, full bar

Julie Mai's 773/784-6000 ■ 5025 N Clark (at Winnemac) ■ 4pm-10pm, till 11pm Fri-Sat, French/ Vietnamese, full bar

Lolita's Cafe [MW,MR-L,TG,S] 773/561-3356 ■ 4400 N Clark St (at Montrose) ■ 5pm-2am, clsd Mon, authentic Mexican, full bar, also club from 11pm Fri-Sat (D,S)

Tendino's [WC] 773/275-8100 ■ 5335 N Sheridan (at Broadway) ■ 11am-11pm, till midnight wknds, pizzeria, full bar

Tomboy [★BYOB,WC,GO] 773/907-0636 ■ 5402 N Clark (at Balmoral) ■ 5pm-10pm, till 11pm wknds, clsd Mon

ENTERTAINMENT & RECREATION

Hollywood Beach [★] at Hollywood & Sheridan Sts ■ 'the' gay beach

BOOKSTORES

KOPI: A Traveler's Cafe [E] 773/989-5674 ■ 5317 N Clark St (at Summerdale) ■ 8am-11pm, till midnight Fri, from 9am Sat, from 10am Sun

15. **Women & Children First** [WC] 773/769-9299, 888/923-7323 ■ 5233 N Clark St (at Foster) ■ 11am-7pm, till 9pm Wed-Fri, from 10am Sat, till 6pm Sun, women-owned/ run ■ womenchildren.booksense.com

RETAIL SHOPS

Gay Mart 773/929-4272 ■ 3457 N Halsted St (at Cornelius)

Specialty Video Films [GO] 773/878-3434 ■ 5307 N Clark St (at Foster) ■ 10am-10pm, till 11pm Fri-Sat, foreign, cult, art house, lesbigay & erotic videos

GYMS & HEALTH CLUBS

Cheetah Gym 773/728-7777 ■ 5248 N Clark St (at Foster) ■ 5:30am-11pm, till 10pm Fri, 8am-9pm wknds ■ cheetahfit@aol.com

MEN'S CLUBS

Man's Country [PC] 773/878-2069 ■ 5017 N Clark St (at Argyle) ■ 24hrs

Man's World [PC] 773/728-0400 ■ 4862 N Clark St (at Lawrence) ■ 24hrs Fri-Sat

EROTICA

Admiral Theater 773/478-8111 ■ 3940 W Lawrence

Chicago—New Town

ACCOMMODATIONS

1. **Best Western Hawthorne Terrace** [GF,WC] 773/244-3434, 888/675-2378 ■ 3434 N Broadway (at Hawthorne Pl) ■ located in the heart of Chicago's gay community ■ www.hawthorneterrace.com
2. **City Suites Hotel** [GF] 773/404-3400, 800/248-9108 ■ 933 W Belmont (btwn Clark & Sheffield) ■ accommodations w/ touch of European style ■ www.cityinns.com
3. **Majestic Hotel** [GF] 773/404-3499, 800/727-5108 ■ 528 W Brompton Pl (at Addison) ■ romantic 19th-century atmosphere ■ www.cityinns.com
4. **Villa Toscana B&B** [MW,GO] 773/404-2643, 800/404-2643 ■ 3447 N Halsted St ■ 1890s coach house ■ www.villa-toscana.net
5. **The Willows** [GF] 773/528-8400, 800/787-3108 ■ 555 W Surf St (at Broadway) ■ hotel w/ 19th-century French flare in Lincoln Park ■ www.cityinns.com

BARS

6. **Annex 3** [MW,NH,V,WC] 773/327-5969 ■ 3160 N Clark St (at Belmont) ■ noon-2am, till 3am Sat, sports bar
7. **Beat Kitchen** [GF,F,E] 773/281-4444 ■ 2100 W Belmont (btwn Hoyne & Damen) ■ noon-2am
8. **Berlin** [★MW,D,TG,S,V,WC] 773/348-4975 ■ 954 W Belmont (at Sheffield) ■ 5pm-4am, 8pm-5am Sat, from 8pm Mon, women's night Wed
9. **Big Daddies Bar & Grill** [MW,NH,F] 773/929-0922 ■ 2914 N Broadway (at Oakdale) ■ 7am-2am, till 3am Sat, from 11am Sun
10. **Blues** [★GF,E] 773/528-1012, 773/549-9436 ■ 2519 N Halsted ■ 8pm-2am, till 3am Sat, classic Chicago blues spot

Chicago—North Side/ New Town • ILLINOIS

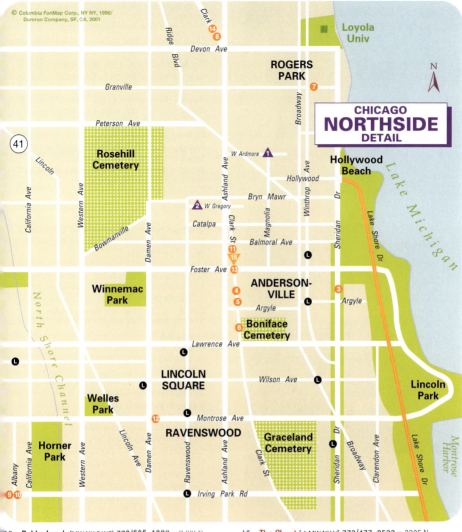

8 **Bobby Love's** [MW,NH,E,WC] 773/525-1200 ■ 3729 N Halsted St (at Waveland) ■ 3pm-2am, from noon wknds, till 3am Sat

1 **Buck's Saloon** [M,NH] 773/525-1125 ■ 3439 N Halsted St (btwn Cornelia & Newport) ■ 10am-2am, patio

2 **Buddies** [★MW,CW,F] 773/477-4066 ■ 3301 N Clark St (at Aldine) ■ 3pm-2am, from 9pm wknds, till 3am Sat, restaurant from 11am ■ www.buddiesrestaurantbar.com

3 **Cell Block** [M,D,B,L,WC] 773/665-8064 ■ 3702 N Halsted (at Waveland) ■ 4pm-2am, from 2pm wknds, also 'Holding Cell' from 10pm Th-Sun (strict leather/ latex/ uniform code), also 'Leather Cell' store ■ www.cellblock-chicago.com

4 **Charlie's Chicago** [M,D,CW] 773/871-8887 ■ 3726 N Broadway (btwn Waveland & Grace) ■ 3pm-4am, till 5am Sat

5 **Circuit** [GS,D,MR,K,S] 773/325-2233 ■ 3641 N Halsted St (at Addison) ■ 9pm-4am, till 5am Sat, clsd Mon-Tue, also 'Club Rehab' from 4pm, Latin Wed-Th ■ www.circuitclub.com

16 **The Closet** [★MW,NH,V] 773/477 8533 ■ 3325 N Broadway St (at Buckingham) ■ 2pm-4am, till 5am Sat, from noon wknds

17 **Cocktail** [MW,NH,D,V,WC] 773/477-1420 ■ 3359 Halsted St (at Roscoe) ■ 4pm-2am, from 2pm wknds, till 3am Sat, go-go dancers Tue & Th, more women Mon

19 **Dram Shop** [GF,NH] 773/525-9885 ■ 3040 N Broadway (at Barry) ■ 7am-2am

20 **Gentry on Halsted** [M,P,E] 773/348-1053 ■ 3320 N Halsted (at Aldine) ■ 4pm-2am, till 3am Sat, from 3pm Sun, piano bar

21 **Girlbar** [W,D,E,WC] 773/871-4210 ■ 2625 N Halsted St (btwn Fullerton & Diversey) ■ 7pm-2am, from 3pm Fri & Sun, till 3am Sat, clsd Mon, 'Boybar' Wed, salsa 2nd Th, 2 levels, patio

22 **Little Jim's** [★M,NH] 773/871-6116 ■ 3501 N Halsted St (at Cornelia) ■ 11am-4am, till 5am Sat

Illinois • USA

UNIVERSAL GEAR
UNIVERSALGEAR.COM
3153 N. BROADWAY
CHICAGO IL 773/296.1090

1601 17TH STREET NW
WASHINGTON DC 202/319.0136

136 8TH AVENUE NEW YORK
(OPENING OCTOBER 2001)

23 **Lucky Horseshoe** [M,NH,S] 773/404-3169, 800/443-3169 ■ 3169 N Halsted St (at Briar) ■ 2pm-2am, from noon wknds, dancers nightly, patio
24 **Manhandler** [★M,NH,V] 773/871-3339 ■ 1948 N Halsted St (at Armitage) ■ noon-4am, till 5am Sat, patio
25 **The North End** [M,NH,WC] 773/477-7999 ■ 3733 N Halsted St (at Grace) ■ 3pm-2am, till 3am Sat, from 11am wknds, sports bar
26 **Roscoe's** [★MW,NH,D,S,V] 773/281-3355 ■ 3354-56 N Halsted St (at W Roscoe) ■ 2pm-2am, noon-3am Sat, 6 bars, patio cafe in summer ■ www.roscoes.com
27 **Sidetrack** [★M,NH,V,WC] 773/477-9189 ■ 3349 N Halsted St (at Roscoe) ■ 3pm-2am, rooftop open in summer
28 **Spin** [GS,D,S,V] 773/327-7711 ■ 800 W Belmont (enter on Halsted) ■ 4pm-2am, till 3am Sat, from 2pm wknds, 3 bars, 80s Th ■ www.spin-nightclub.com

Nightclubs
29 **Manhole** [★M,D,L,V] 773/975-9244 ■ 3458 N Halsted St (at Cornelia) ■ 9pm-4am, till 5am Sat
30 **Smart Bar** [★GF,D,A] 773/549-4140 ■ 3730 N Clark St (downstairs at the 'Metro') ■ 10pm-4am, till 5am Sat, goth Tue, punk Wed

Cafes
Mike's Broadway Cafe [MW,WC] 773/404-2205 ■ 3805 N Broadway (btwn Grace & Halsted) ■ 7am-10pm, 24hrs Fri-Sat, popular brunch, American
Pick Me Up Cafe & All Nite Express Lounge 773/248-6613 ■ 3408 N Clark ■ 5pm-3am, 24hrs Fri-Sat

Restaurants
Angelina Ristorante [WC] 773/935-5933 ■ 3561 N Broadway (at Addison) ■ 5:30pm-11pm, Sun brunch, Italian, full bar
Ann Sather's [★] 773/348-2378 ■ 929 W Belmont Ave (at Sheffield) ■ 7am-10pm, Swedish diner & New Town fixture
Buddies Restaurant & Bar [★MW,WC] 773/477-4066 ■ 3301 N Clark St (at Aldine) ■ 11am-11pm, from 9am wknds, full bar, eye-catching menu ■ www.buddiesrestaurantbar.com
Cornelia's [WC] 773/248-8333 ■ 750 W Cornelia Ave (at Halsted) ■ clsd Mon, dinner nightly, upscale Italian, full bar ■ www.tribads.com/cornelias
The Pepper Lounge [MW] 773/665-7377 ■ 3441 N Sheffield (btwn Newport & Clark) ■ 6pm-1:30am, till midnight Sun, clsd Mon, supper club, gourmet Italian, full bar ■ www.pepperlounge.com
The Raw Bar & Grill [E,WC] 773/348-7291 ■ 3720 N Clark St (at Waveland) ■ 5pm-2am, seafood, also lounge
Technicolor Kitchen [WC] 773/665-2111 ■ 3210 N Lincoln Ave (at Belmont & Ashland) ■ dinner, clsd Mon, kitschy decor, eclectic fusion menu ■ www.TechnicolorKitchen.com
Zoom Kitchen 773/325-1400 ■ 620 W Belmont (at Broadway) ■ 11am-10pm, from 9am-9pm Sun, American, plenty veggie

Bookstores
31 **Unabridged Books** 773/883-9119 ■ 3251 N Broadway St (at Aldine) ■ 10am-10pm

Retail Shops
Specialty Video Films [GO] 773/248-3834 ■ 3221 N Broadway St (at Belmont) ■ 10am-10pm, till 11pm Fri-Sat, foreign, cult, art house, lgbt & erotic videos
32▶ **Universal Gear** 773/296-1090 ■ 3153 N Broadway (at Belmont) ■ 11am-10pm, till 11pm Fri-Sat, casual, club, athletic & designer clothing ■ www.universalgear.com

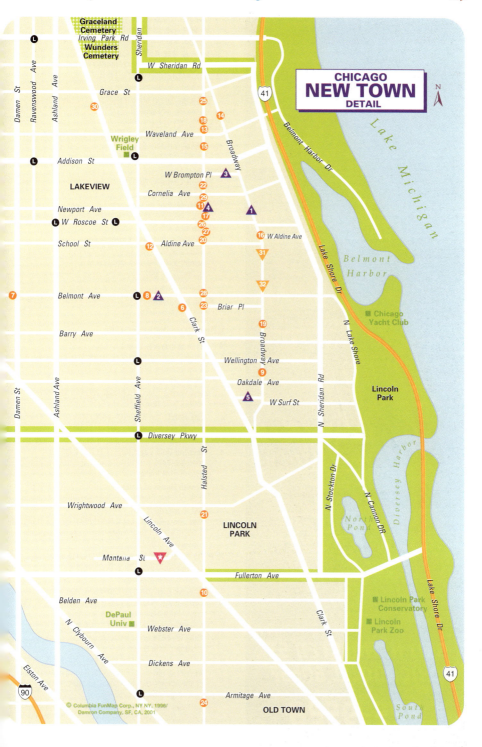

We're Everywhere [GO] 773/404-0590, 800/772-6411 ■ 3434 N Halsted St (at Newport) ■ noon-9pm, 11am-8pm wknds, also mail order catalog ■ www.wereeverywhere.com

GYMS & HEALTH CLUBS
The Body Shop [MO] 773/248-7717 ■ 3246 N Halsted St (btwn Clark & Belmont) ■ 24hrs ■ chicagoam@locker-rooms.com

Chicago Sweat Shop [GF] 773/871-2789 ■ 3215 N Broadway (at Belmont)

MEN'S CLUBS
The Steamworks Gym & Sauna [★PC] 773/929-6080 ■ 3246 N Halsted St (N of Belmont) ■ 24hrs ■ www.steamworksOnLine.com

EROTICA
Adult Fantasy 773/525-9705 ■ 2928 N Broadway (at Oakdale) ■ 24hrs

Batteries Not Included 773/935-9900 ■ 3420 N Halsted (btwn Roscoe & Addison) ■ 50% of all profits donated to charity ■ www.toysafterdark.com

Male Hide Leathers 773/929-0069 ■ 2816 N Lincoln Ave (at Diversey) ■ noon-8pm, 1pm-5pm Sun, clsd Mon, custom leather ■ www.malehide.com

The Pleasure Chest 773/525-7152 ■ 3155 N Broadway (at Belmont Ave)

▶ **The Ram Bookstore** 773/525-9528 ■ 3511 N Halsted St (at Cornelia) ■ 24hrs

Chicago—Near North

ACCOMMODATIONS
1. **Allegro** [GF,E,F,WC] 312/236-0123, 800/643-1500 ■ 171 W Randolph (at LaSalle) ■ upscale lounge & restaurant ■ www.allegrochicago.com
2. **Best Western Inn of Chicago** [GF,F,WC] 312/787-3100, 800/557-2378 ■ 162 E Ohio St (at Michigan Ave)
3. **Cass Hotel** [GF,F] 312/787-4030, 800/781-4030 ■ 640 N Wabash Ave (btwn Ontario & Erie) ■ full bar ■ www.casshotel.com
4. **Days Inn Gold Coast** [GF,WC] 312/664-3040, 800/329-7466 ■ 1816 N Clark St (at Lincoln) ■ also restaurant & lounge
5. **Flemish House of Chicago** [GS,GO] 312/664-9981 ■ 68 E Cedar St (btwn Rush & Lake Shore Dr) ■ B&B, studios & apts in greystone rowhouse ■ www.chicagobandb.com
6. **Gold Coast Guesthouse** [GF] 312/337-0361 ■ 113 W Elm St 60610 ■ 1873 townhouse, also 2 studios available ■ www.bbchicago.com
22. ▶ **The Hotel Burnham** [GF] 312/782-1111, 877/294-9712 ■ One W Washington St (at Dearborn) ■ www.burnhamhotel.com
7. **Hotel Monaco** [GF] 312/960-8500, 800/397-7661 ■ 225 N Wabash (at S Water & Wacker Pl) ■ upscale, gym, also restaurant ■ www.monaco-chicago.com
8. **Hyatt Regency Chicago** [GF] 312/565-1234, 800/233-1234 ■ 151 E Wacker Dr (at Michigan Ave) ■ restaurant, cafe & bar
9. **Knickerbocker Hotel** [GS,F,WC] 312/751-8100, 800/621-8140 ■ 163 E Walton Pl (Michigan Ave) ■ right off the Magnificent Mile, gym, restaurant & bar ■ www.regal-hotels.com/chicago

Old Town B&B [GS] 312/440-9268 ■ roof deck, gym ■ www.oldtownbandbchicago.com

Until the Taj Mahal has concierge service...

There's the Hotel Burnham Chicago. A National Historic Landmark adored by architects. Where oysters will arouse you. Dom will fulfill you. And evening carriage rides will keep you coming back for more. Something you can only imagine at the Taj Mahal.

One West Washington ◆ Chicago ◆ 312.782.1111 ◆ www.burnhamhotel.com

HOTEL BURNHAM
CHICAGO
Chicago's First Love™

MEMBER OF

KIMPTON GROUP

Chicago—Near North/ South Side • ILLINOIS

BARS
10 Artful Dodger [GF,D] 773/227-6859 ■ 1734 W Wabansia (at Hermitage, in Wicker Park) ■ 5pm-2am, 8pm-3am Sat

11 Club Foot [GF,NH,D,A] 773/489-0379 ■ 1824 W Augusta (in Wicker Park) ■ 8pm-2am, till 3am Sat, kitschy

12 Gentry on State [★M,P,E,V] 312/664-1033 ■ 440 N State (at Illinois) ■ 4pm-2am, till 3am Sat

13 Second Story Bar [M,NH] 312/923-9536 ■ 157 E Ohio St (at Michigan Ave) ■ noon-2am, till 3am Sat

NIGHTCLUBS
14 Baton Show Lounge [MW,S,WC] 312/644-5269 ■ 436 N Clark St (btwn Illinois & Hubbard) ■ 8pm-4am, clsd Mon-Tue ■ www.thebatonshowlounge.com

15 Boom Boom Room at Red Dog [★GF,D,S,$] 773/278-1009 ■ 1958 W North Ave (enter in alley behind 'Border Line Tap') ■ gay night 10:30pm-4am Mon, also 'Resurrection' Sat

16 Club Intimus [W,D,MR-AF,S,WC] 312/901-1703 ■ 312 W Randolph St (at 'Cafe Bacetti') ■ 9pm-3am Sat only

17 Condo Club [MW,D,MR,F,S] 773/235-5875 ■ 1931 N Milwaukee (at Western, in Wicker Park) ■ 9pm-2am, till 3am Sat, after hrs Fri, clsd Mon-Tue, 18+ Fri

18 The Crobar [★GF,D] 312/243-4800 ■ 1543 N Kingsbury (at Sheffield) ■ 10pm-4am, clsd Mon-Tue, more gay Sun for 'Glee Club' ■ www.crobarnightclub.com

19 The Rails [M,D,MR-AF,S,$] 708/802-1705, 312/486-2086 ■ 1675 N Elston Ave (at North Ave, at 'Prop House' in Wicker Park) ■ 11pm-4am Fri only ■ www.clubrails.com

20 Second City [GF,E] 312/337-3992, 877/337-4707 ■ 1608 N Wells St (at North) ■ legendary comedy club, call for reservations ■ www.secondcity.com

CAFES
Earwax Records 773/772-4019 ■ 1564 N Milwaukee Ave (in Wicker Park) ■ 11am-midnight, till 1am Fri-Sat, from 10am wknds, plenty veggie

Local Grind 773/489-3490 ■ 1585 N Milwaukee Ave (in Wicker Park) ■ 6am-1am, till 3am Fri-Sat, 7am-midnight Sun, popular brunch, plenty veggie

RESTAURANTS
The Berghoff 312/427-3170 ■ 17 W Adams St (at State) ■ 11am-9pm, till 10pm Sat, clsd Sun, German

Fireplace Inn 312/664-5264 ■ 1448 N Wells Ave (at North Ave) ■ 4pm-10pm, till 11pm Fri-Sat, from 11am Sun, bbq, full bar

Iggy's 312/829-4449 ■ 700 N Milwaukee, River North (at Chicago) ■ dinner nightly, till 4am Th-Sat, till 2am Sun, int'l, full bar, patio

Kiki's Bistro 312/335-5454 ■ 900 N Franklin St (at Locust) ■ French, full bar

Manny's 312/939-2855 ■ 1141 S Jefferson St (at Roosevelt) ■ 5am-4pm, clsd Sun, killer corned beef

The Mashed Potato Club [WC] 312/255-8579 ■ 316 W Erie St (at Orleans) ■ dinner nightly, till midnight wkdays, till 2am Fri-Sat, over 100 potato toppings, full bar

Shaw's Crab House [WC] 312/527-2722 ■ 21 W Hubbard (at State) ■ lunch & dinner, full bar

BOOKSTORES
21 Barbara's Bookstore [WC] 312/642-5044 ■ 1350 N Wells St (at Schiller, in Old Town) ■ 9am-10pm, 10am-9pm Sun, women's/ lgbt section; also 700 E Grand Ave at Navy Pier, 312/222-0890; also Oak Park, 708/848-9140

Quimby's Queer Store [WC] 773/342-0910 ■ 1854 W North Ave (at Wolcott, in Wicker Park) ■ noon-8pm, till 10pm Fri-Sat, till 6pm Sun, alternative literature & comics ■ www.quimbys.com

GYMS & HEALTH CLUBS
Thousand Waves Spa [WO] 773/549-0700 ■ 1212 W Belmont Ave (at Racine) ■ noon-9pm, 10am-7pm wknds, clsd Mon, health spa for women only, women-owned/run ■ www.thousandwaves.com/twspa

EROTICA
Bijou Theatre 312/943-5397 ■ 1349 N Wells St (at North Ave) ■ 24hrs ■ www.bijouworld.com

Erotic Warehouse [WC] 312/226-5222 ■ 1246 W Randolph (at Elizabeth) ■ 24hrs

Mimi's Adult Bookstore 773/283-0980 ■ 3203 N Cicero (at Belmont) ■ 24hrs

Chicago—South Side

BARS
Club Escape [MW,D,MR-AF,F] 773/667-6454 ■ 1530 E 75th St (at Stoney Island) ■ 4pm-2am, till 3am Sat, women's night Tue & Th

Inn Exile [M,D,V,WC] 773/582-3510 ■ 5758 W 65th St (at Menard, nr Midway Airport) ■ 8pm-2am, till 3am Sat

Jeffery Pub [★MW,D,MR-AF,E,WC] 773/363-8555 ■ 7041 S Jeffery (at 71st) ■ 4pm-4am, from 11am Fri-Sun

NIGHTCLUBS
Escapades [M,D,V] 773/229-0886 ■ 6301 S Harlem ■ 10pm-4am, till 5am Sat

BOOKSTORES
57th St Books 773/684-1300 ■ 1301 E 57th St, Hyde Park (at Kimbark St) ■ 10am-10pm, till 8pm Sun, lgbt section

INDIANA

Indianapolis

ACCOMMODATIONS
1 **Kurt's Bed & Breakfast Inn** [MO,SW,N] 317/291-5728 ■ 3212 Lupine Dr (nr 34th St & High School Rd)
2 **Renaissance Tower Historic Inn** [GF] 317/262-8648, 800/676-7786 ■ 230 E 9th St (btwn Delaware & Alabama) ■ studio suites, full kitchens ■ www.rentowerinn.com

BARS
3 **501 Eagle** [★M,D,L] 317/632-2100 ■ 608 E Market (at College) ■ 5pm-3am, clsd Sun, 'HiNRG' Fri-Sat (D), also 'Options', safer-sex info center ■ www.501eagle.com
4 **Brothers Bar & Grill** [MW,WC] 317/636-1020 ■ 822 N Illinois St (at St Clair) ■ 4pm-midnight, till 10pm Sun, also restaurant till 10pm ■ www.oaktree.net/brothers
5 **Illusions** [MW,D,K,S] 317/266-0535 ■ 1446 E Washington (at Arsenal) ■ 7am-3am, noon-12:30am Sun
6 **The Metro** [MW,D,S,WC] 317/639-6022 ■ 707 Massachusetts Ave (at College) ■ 4pm-3am, noon-12:30am Sun, patio, also restaurant & 'Colors' shop
7 **Varsity Lounge** [M,NH,F] 317/635-9998 ■ 1517 N Pennsylvania St (S of 16th) ■ 10am-3am, noon-midnight Sun

NIGHTCLUBS
8 **Our Place** [★M,D,V,WC] 317/638-8138 ■ 231 E 16th St (at Alabama) ■ 4pm-3am, clsd Sun, patio ■ www.ourplace.net
9 **The Ten** [★W,D,S,WC] 317/638-5802 ■ 1218 N Pennsylvania St (at 12th, enter rear) ■ 6pm-3am, clsd Sun
10 **The Unicorn Club** [★M,S,PC] 317/262-9195 ■ 122 W 13th St (at Illinois) ■ 8pm-3am, clsd Sun, male dancers ■ www2.oaktree.net/unicorn/
11 **Utopia** [★MW,D,F] 317/638-0215 ■ 924 N Pennsylvania St (at St Joseph's) ■ 6pm-1am, till 3am Fri-Sat, clsd Mon ■ www.utopiaindy.com

CAFES
Cath's Coffeehouse [E] 317/251-2677 ■ 5401 N College (at 54th) ■ 7am-7pm, 8am-3pm Sun
The MT Cup 317/639-1099 ■ 314 Massachusetts Ave (at New Jersey) ■ 7am-7pm, 8am-1am Sat, sandwiches & baked goods

RESTAURANTS
Aesop's Tables [BW,WC] 317/631-0055 ■ 600 N Massachusetts Ave (at East) ■ lunch & dinner, authentic Mediterranean
English Ivy's 317/822-5070 ■ 944 N Alabama (N of 9th St) ■ till 3am Mon-Sat, 11am-12:30am Sun, also full bar
Peter's 317/465-1155, 800/479-0909 ■ 8505 Keystone Crossing Blvd ■ dinner, clsd Sun, upscale dining, full bar

ENTERTAINMENT & RECREATION
Men's Chorus 317/931-9464 ■ www.indychoruses.org
Women's Chorus 317/931-9464 ■ www.indychoruses.org

INDIANAPOLIS

Indianapolis conjures up images of fast cars and midwestern hospitality. The capital of a largely rural state, 'Indy' may not be New York or Los Angeles, but it has an easy-going charm all its own.

Queer Resources

COMMUNITY INFO
The Switchboard 317/251-7955, web: www.gayindy.org/switchboard.

AIDS RESOURCES
AIDServe 317/920-1200.
Damien Center 317/632-0123.

RECOVERY
AA Gay/Lesbian 317/632-7864.

City Calendar

LGBT PRIDE
June.

ENTERTAINMENT
Women's Chorus 317/931-9464.
Men's Chorus at the Crossroads Performing Arts 317/931-9464.

ANNUAL EVENTS
Memorial Day Weekend - Indy 500 auto race.
June - National Women's Music Festival (in Muncie, IN) 317/927-9355.

Tourist Info

AIRPORT DIRECTIONS
Indianapolis International Airport. To get to downtown, take the Airport Expressway to I-70 East. Take I-70 East and then exit on Washington St or New York St.

PUBLIC TRANSIT & TAXIS
Yellow Cab 317/487-7777.
Metro Transit 317/635-3344.

TOURIST SPOTS & INFO
Indianapolis Museum of Art 317/923-1331.
Speedway 500 317/481-8500.
Zoo 317/630-2001.
Visitor's Center: Indianapolis Visitor's Bureau 317/639-4282, 800/323-4639, web: www.indy.org.

WEATHER
The spring weather is moderate (50's-60°s) with occasional storms. The summers are typically midwestern: hot (mid-90°s) and humid. The autumns are mild and colorful in southeastern Indiana. As for winter, it's the wind chill that'll get to you.

Indianapolis • INDIANA

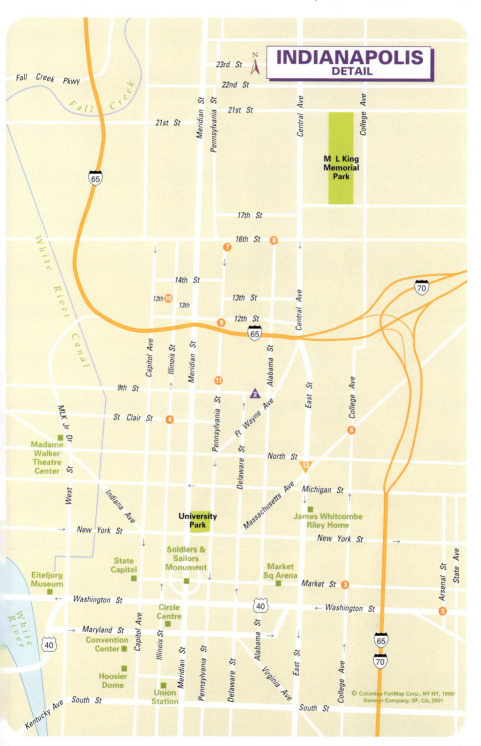

Indianapolis • INDIANA

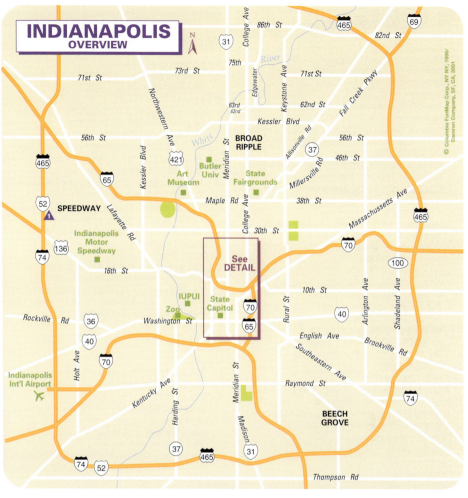

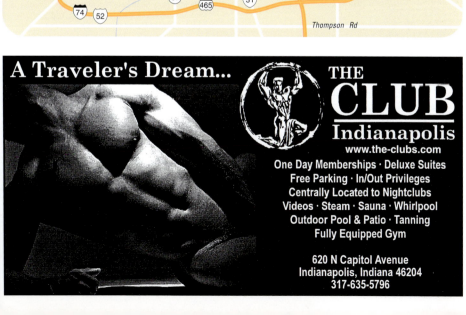

Indiana / Kansas • USA

Bookstores
Borders 317/849-8660 ■ 5612 Castleton Corner Ln (at 86th St) ■ 9am-10pm, 10am-8pm Sun, some lgbt titles

12 **Out Word Bound** 317/951-9100 ■ 625 N East St (at Massachusetts Ave) ■ 11:30am-9pm, till 10pm Fri-Sat, noon-6pm Sun, lgbt books & gifts, special events ■ www.owbbooks.com

Retail Shops
Colors Pride & Leather Shop 317/686-0984 ■ 707 Massachusetts Ave (upstairs at 'Metro') ■ hrs vary

Contours/ Torso 317/916-9054 ■ 719 Massachusetts (at College) ■ 2pm-11pm, till midnight Fri-Sat, 1pm-5pm Sun, clothing, gifts

Dawghouse Cards & Gifts [WC] 317/822-1757 ■ 222 E Market St (at Delaware) ■ 8am-6pm, clsd Sun

Gaia Wines [GO] 317/634-9463 ■ 608 Massachusetts Ave (at North) ■ 11am-8pm, noon-6pm Sun ■ www.gaiawines.com

Indy News 317/632-7680 ■ 20 E Maryland (at Meridian) ■ 6am-7pm, till 6pm wknds

Southside News 317/887-1020 ■ 8063 Madison Ave ■ 6am-9pm, till 7pm Sun

Publications
OUTlines—The Indiana Gay/Lesbian Newspaper 317/923-8550 ■ lgbt newsmagazine w/ extensive resources ■ www.indygaynews.com

The Sarj Guide Magazine 317/870-7275 ■ club guide for IN, KY, OH & TN, great maps ■ www.oaktree.net/sarjguide

The Word 317/725-8840 ■ lgbt newspaper ■ www.indword.com

Men's Clubs
▶ **Club Indianapolis** [SW,PC] 317/635-5796 ■ 620 N Capitol Ave (at North & Walnut) ■ 24hrs ■ www.the-clubs.com

▶ **The Works** [PC,GO] 317/547-9210 ■ 4120 N Keystone Ave (at 38th) ■ 24hrs ■ www.a1.com/theworks

Kansas

Wichita

Accommodations
1 **Hawthorn Suites** [GF,WC] 316/729-5700 ■ 2405 N Ridge Rd ■ buffet brkfst

Bars
2 **Dreamers II** [W,F,D,WC] 316/522-2028 ■ 4000 S Broadway (at MacArthur) ■ 4pm-2am Mon-Fri

3 **J Lounge** [MW,E,K,WC] 316/262-1363 ■ 513 E Central (at Emporia) ■ 4pm-2am, gay cabaret ■ www.J-Lounge.com

4 **Kirby's Beer Store** [GF,S] 316/685-7013 ■ 3227 E 17th (at Holyoke) ■ 2pm-2am, from 3pm wknds

6 **Ralph's** [MW,NH,K] 316/682-4461 ■ 3210 E Osie (at George Washington) ■ 3pm-2am ■ rickerick@webtv.net

7 **Side Street Saloon** [M,NH,WC] 316/267-0324 ■ 1106 S Pattie (nr Lincoln & Hydraulic) ■ 2pm-2am, patio

8 **The T-Room** [M,NH,WC] 316/262-9327 ■ 1507 E Pawnee (at K-15) ■ 3pm-2am

Nightclubs
9 **Club Vixon** [MW,D] 316/618-1756 ■ 223 S St Francis (at Waterman) ■ 9pm-2am, till 3am wknds, clsd Tue

10 **Fantasy Complex** [MW,D,CW,S,WC] 316/682-5494 ■ 3201 S Hillside (at 31st) ■ 8pm-2am, clsd Mon-Tue, also 'South Forty' (CW bar) from 3pm Tue-Sun

5 **Metro** [M,D,F,S,18+] 316/262-8130 ■ 458 N Waco (at Central) ■ 9pm-2am Th-Sun, 18+ Fri & Sun, also restaurant

Cafes
Riverside Perk 316/264-6464 ■ 1144 Bidding (at 11th) ■ 7am-10pm, till midnight Fri-Sat, from 10am Sun

Restaurants
Lexie D's 316/264-8280 ■ 430 E Douglas ■ 11am-11pm, some veggie

Moe's Sub Shop 316/524-5511 ■ 2815 S Hydraulic (at Wassall) ■ 11am-8pm, clsd Sun

Old Mill Tasty Shop 316/264-6500 ■ 604 E Douglas (at St Francis) ■ 11am-3pm, 8am-5pm Sat, clsd Sun, old-fashioned soda fountain, lunch menu

---

Wichita

Golfers take note: Wichita has more public golf holes per capita than any other US city.

Queer Resources

Community Info
Land of Awes Info Line 316/269-0913, touchtone info, web: www.awes.com.

Recovery
One Day At A Time 316/522-7411. 2821 S Hydraulic.

City Calendar

LGBT Pride
June.

Tourist Info

Airport Directions
Wichita Mid-Continent Airport. To get to most gay bars, take US 54 East and exit Hillside South.

Public Transit & Taxis
American Cab Co. 316/262-7511.
Metropolitan Transit Authority 316/265-7221.

Tourist Spots & Info
Old Cowtown Museum 316/264-6398.
Pyradomes.
Wichita Art Museum 316/268-4921.
Visitor's Center: Kansas Travel & Tourism Dept 800/252-6727, web: www.kansascommerce.com.

Wichita • Kansas

Wichita Detail
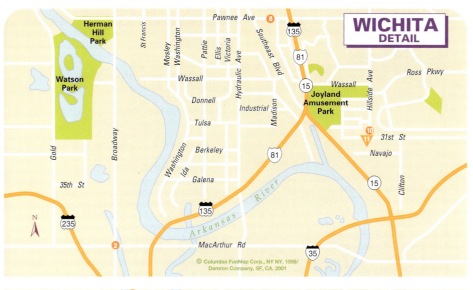

Wichita Overview

Kansas/Kentucky • USA

Tanya's Soup Kitchen 316/267-5349 ■ 725 E Douglas (behind Black Canyon Grill) ■ lunch Mon-Sat, dinner Wed-Sat, clsd Sun, eclectic cuisine, some veggie

The Upper Crust 316/683-8288 ■ 7038 E Lincoln ■ lunch only, clsd wknds, homestyle

Vientiane 316/618-6470 ■ 3141 S Hillside ■ 11am-8pm, Thai & Laotian food

Entertainment & Recreation
Cabaret Oldtown Theatre 316/265-4400 ■ 412 1/2 E Douglas (at Topeka) ■ edgy, kitschy productions ■ www.cabaretoldtown.com

Bookstores
The Dusty Bookshelf [GO] 316/262-7415 ■ 922 E Douglas (at Washington) ■ 10am-8pm, 1pm-5pm Sun, used books, lgbt books in gender section

Retail Shops
Holier Than Thou Body Piercing 316/266-4100 ■ 1111 E Douglas Ave (at Washington) ■ noon-8pm, till 6pm Sun ■ HTTBP@aol.com

11 **Mother's** 316/686-8116 ■ 3100 E 31st St S (at Hillside) ■ hrs vary, lgbt gifts

Erotica
Priscilla's 316/942-1244 ■ 6143 W Kellogg (at Dugan)

Xcitement Video 316/832-1816 ■ 220 E 21st St (at Broadway) ■ 24hrs; also 1515 S Oliver (at Harry), 316/688-5343 & 1306 E Harry (at Pattie), 316/269-9036

KENTUCKY

Louisville

Accommodations
1 **Columbine Inn** [GF] 502/635-5000, 800/635-5010 ■ 1707 S 3rd St (nr Leet St) ■ 1896 Greek revivial mansion, full brkfst ■ www.thecolumbin.com
2 **Holiday Inn Southwest** [GF,F,SW,WC] 502/448-2020 ■ 4110 Dixie Hwy (at I-264) ■ lounge ■ holinnswlouky@mindspring.com
3 **Inn at the Park** [GF] 502/637-6930, 800/700-7275 ■ 1332 S 4th St (at Park Ave) ■ restored mansion, full brkfst ■ www.innatpark.com

Bars
4 **Gypsies** [GS,D,F,S,K,WC] 502/561-0752 ■ 319 E Market (at Floyd) ■ 4pm-close, clsd Mon
5 **Magnolia Bar** [GF,NH,YC] 502/637-9052 ■ 1398 S 2nd St (at Magnolia) ■ noon-4am
6 **Teddy Bears Bar & Grill** [M,NH,WC] 502/589-2619 ■ 1148 Garvin Pl (at St Catherine) ■ 11am-4am, from 1pm Sun
7 **Tryangles** [M,CW,S,WC] 502/583-6395 ■ 209 S Preston St (at Market) ■ 4pm-4am, Levi's bar, strippers

LOUISVILLE

Beautiful Louisville (say 'Louavul') sits on the banks of the Ohio River and is home to the world-famous Kentucky Derby. The Belle of Louisville is the oldest operating steamboat on the Mississippi River system. Baseball fans will enjoy the Louisville Slugger Tour at Hillerich & Bradsby (502/585-5226), makers of baseball bats since 1884.

Queer Resources

Community Info
Gay/ Lesbian/ Bisexual/ Transgendered Hotline 502/454-7613, live info 6pm-10pm.
The GayLouisville.com Visitor's Center 812/941-5197 2pm-midnight.
Williams-Nichols Institute 502/636-0935, 6pm-9pm, lesbigay archives, referrals.

AIDS Resources
502/574-5490.

Recovery
502/454-7613.

City Calendar

LGBT Pride
June.

Entertainment
Community Chorus 502/327-4099.

Annual Events
May - Kentucky Derby.
June - Kentucky Shakespeare Festival 502/583-8738.
October - Halloween Cruise on the Ohio River.

Tourist Info

Airport Directions
Stadiford Field Airport (located at US 264 and US 65). To get to town take 65 North.

Public Transit & Taxis
Yellow Taxi 502/636-5511.
TARC Bus System 502/585-1234.
Toonerville II Trolley or Louisville Horse Trams 502/581-0100.

Tourist Spots & Info
Belle Of Louisville Steamboat 502/574-2992.
Farmington.
Hadley Pottery 502/584-2171.
Kentucky Derby 502/584-6383.
Locust Grove.
St. James Court.
West Main Street Historic District.
Visitor's Center: Louisville Visitor Center 800/792-5595.

Weather
Mild winters and long, hot summers!

Best Views
The Spire Restaurant and Cocktail Lounge on the 19th floor of the Hyatt Regency Louisville.

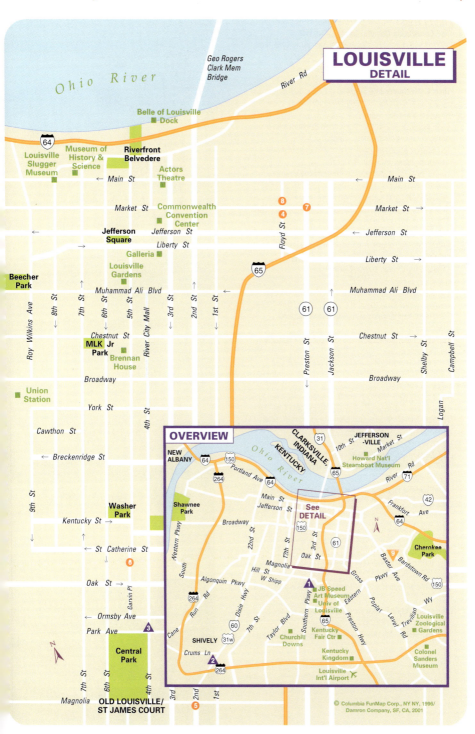

KENTUCKY / LOUISIANA • USA

NIGHTCLUBS
8 **The Connection Complex** [★MW,D,F,S,V,WC] 502/585-5752 ■ 120 S Floyd St (at Market) ■ 5pm-4am, includes piano bar, video bar, cabaret, gift shop ■ www.theconnection.net

CAFES
Days Coffeehouse [GO] 502/456-1170 ■ 1420 Bardstown Rd (at Edenside) ■ 8am-10pm, till 11pm wknds

RESTAURANTS
Cafe Mimosa 502/458-2233 ■ 1216 Bardstown Rd ■ lunch & dinner, Vietnamese, Chinese & sushi

El Mundo [★] 502/899-9930 ■ 2345 Frankfort Ave ■ 11:30am-10pm, clsd Sun, Mexican

Lynn's Paradise Cafe [MW,GO] 502/583-3447 ■ 984 Barret Ave (at Baxter) ■ 7am-10pm, clsd Mon, also bar

Queenie's Pizza & Such [GO] 502/636-3708 ■ 2622 S 4th St ■ 11am-10pm, till 11pm Fri-Sat, 4pm-8pm Sun, clsd Mon

Rudyard Kipling [E] 502/636-1311 ■ 422 W Oak St ■ lunch Mon-Fri, dinner from 5:30pm Mon-Sat, full bar

ENTERTAINMENT & RECREATION
Community Chorus 502/327-4099

BOOKSTORES
9 **Carmichael's** 502/456-6950 ■ 1295 Bardstown Rd (at Longest Ave) ■ 8am-10pm, till 11pm Fri-Sat, from 10am Sun, large lgbt section; also 2866 Frankfort Ave, 502/895-6950

Hawley Cooke Books 502/456-6660 ■ 3024 Bardstown Rd (in Gardiner Lane Shopping Ctr) ■ 9am-9pm, 10am-6pm Sun; also 27 Shelbyville Rd Plaza, 502/893-0133 & 2400 Lime Kiln Ln, 502/425-9100)

RETAIL SHOPS
8 **MT Closets** [WC] 502/587-1060, 800/606-4524 ■ 120 S Floyd (in the Connection Complex) ■ 4pm-1am, 7pm-3am Fri-Sat, 7pm-1am Sun, clsd Mon-Tue, clubwear, pride gifts ■ mtclosets.com

PUBLICATIONS
The Letter 502/636-0935 (news), 502/772-7570 (advertising) ■ statewide lgbt newspaper ■ www.theletter.net

The Rainbow Pages 502/899-3551 ■ lgbt resource guide

EROTICA
Arcade Adult Bookstore 502/637-8383 ■ 2822 7th St (at Arcade)

Blue Movies 502/585-4627 ■ 244 W Jefferson St (at 3rd) ■ 24hrs

The Erotic Touch 502/363-9448 ■ 3423 Taylor Blvd (at Longfield Ave)

Louisville Manor 502/449-1443 ■ 4600 Dixie Hwy/ US 61 ■ 24hrs

Showboat Adult Bookstore 502/361-0007 ■ 3524 S 4th St (at Berry Blvd) ■ hustlers

The Toy Store 502/366-7563 ■ 1857 Berry Blvd (at 7th)

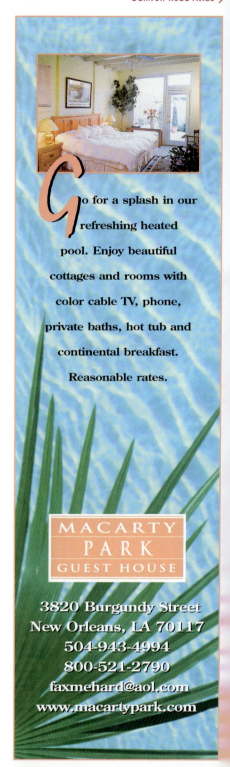

Go for a splash in our refreshing heated pool. Enjoy beautiful cottages and rooms with color cable TV, phone, private baths, hot tub and continental breakfast. Reasonable rates.

MACARTY PARK GUEST HOUSE

3820 Burgundy Street
New Orleans, LA 70117
504-943-4994
800-521-2790
faxmehard@aol.com
www.macartypark.com

New Orleans • LOUISIANA

LOUISIANA

New Orleans

ACCOMMODATIONS

1. **1227 Easton House** [GS,NS,GO] 504/488-5453, 877/311-1023 ■ 1227 N Rendon St (btwn Esplanade & Grand Rte St John) ■ b&b, full brkfst, some shared baths ■ www.eastonhouse1227.com
2. **A Creole House Hotel** [GS,NS] 504/524-8076, 800/535-7858 ■ 1013 St Ann (btwn Burgundy & Rampart) ■ 1830s building furnished in period style
3. **Alternative Accommodations/ French Quarter Accommodation Service** [GF] 504/949-5815, 800/209-9408 ■ 1001 Marigny St ■ 4 guesthouses ■ www.fqaccommodations.com
4. **Andrew Jackson Hotel** [GF] 504/561-5881, 800/654-0224 ■ 919 Royal St (btwn St Philip & Dumaine) ■ historic inn, rms & suites, tropical courtyard
5. **B&W Courtyards B&B** [GS,GO] 504/945-9418, 800/585-5731 ■ 2425 Chartres St (btwn Mandeville & Spain) ■ www.bandwcourtyards.com ■ hot tub
6. **Bed & Beverage Guest Apts** [GS,SW,WC] 504/588-1483, 800/809-7815 ■ 612 St Philip St ■ furnished studios in the French Quarter ■ bedandbeverage.com
7. **Big D's B&B** [MW] 504/945-8049 ■ 704 Franklin Ave (at Royal) ■ lesbian-owned/ run
   Big Easy/ French Quarter Lodging [GS,GO] 504/433-2563, 800/368-4876 ■ 233 Cottonwood Dr, Gretna ■ free reservation service ■ www.crescentcity.com/fql/
8. **The Big Easy Guest House** [GS] 504/943-3717, 800/679-0540 ■ 2633 Dauphine St (at Franklin) ■ 1830s private home, 8 blks from French Quarter ■ bigeasygh@aol.com

NEW ORLEANS

New Orleans is (in)famous for its Mardi Gras celebration, arguably the nation's best known street party. But the Big Easy is a good time all year long. The French Quarter is home to Bourbon Street with its round-the-clock bars and jazz clubs. One local establishment, Pat O'Brien's (504/525-4823), tops the nation's list for volume of alcohol sold, much of it in the form of the bar's signature drink, the Hurricane. For melt-in-your-mouth beignets, a local style of doughnut, Cafe du Monde (504/525-4544) is the place.

Queer Resources

COMMUNITY INFO
▼ Lesbian/Gay Community Center 504/945-1103, web: www.gayneworleans.com/the_center. 2114 Decatur, call for hours.

AIDS RESOURCES
504/821-6050.

RECOVERY
AA Lambda Center 504/947-0548. 2106 Decatur.

City Calendar

LGBT PRIDE
September. 504/522-0907.

ANNUAL EVENTS
February - Mardi Gras 504/566-5011. North America's rowdiest block party.
April - Gay Easter Parade 504/581-4173.
Gulf Coast Womyn's Festival at Camp SisterSpirit (in Ovett, MS) 601/344-1411.
April/May - New Orleans Jazz & Heritage Festival.
Labor Day - Southern Decadence 504/522-8047.
Gay mini-Mardi Gras.

Tourist Info

AIRPORT DIRECTIONS
New Orleans Int'l Airport. Take I-10 southeast.

PUBLIC TRANSIT & TAXIS
United Cab 504/522-9771.
Airport Shuttle 504/522-3500.
Regional Transit Authority 504/248-3900.

TOURIST SPOTS & INFO
Bourbon Street in the French Quarter.
Cafe du Monde for beignets 504/581-2914.
Garden District.
Moon Walk.
Pat O'Brien's for a hurricane 504/525-4823.
Preservation Hall 504/522-2841.
Top of the Market.
New Orleans Museum of Art 504/488-2631.
Visitor's Center: 504/566-5011, web: www.neworleanscvb.com.
Louisiana Office of Tourism 800/334-8626.

WEATHER
Summer temperatures hover in the 90°s with subtropical humidity. Winters can be rainy and chilly. The average temperature in February (Mardi Gras month) is 58° while the average precipitation is 5.23".

BEST VIEWS
Top of the Mart Lounge (504/522-9795) on the 33rd floor of the World Trade Center of New Orleans.

LOUISIANA • USA

9 **The Biscuit Palace** [GF,WC] 504/525-9949 ■ 730 Dumaine (btwn Royal & Bourbon) ■ 1820s Creole mansion in the French Quarter ■ www.biscuitpalace.com
Block-Keller House [GS,NS,GO] 504/483-3033, 877/588-3033 ■ 3620 Canal St (at Telemachus) ■ jellebry@msn.com

10 **Bon Maison Guest House** [★GF] 504/561-8498 ■ 835 Bourbon St (btwn Lafittes & Bourbon Pub) ■ 1833 townhouse, suites & apts, patio ■ www.bonmaison.com

11 **Bourbon Orleans Hotel** [★GF,F,SW] 504/523-2222, 800/521-5338 ■ 717 Orleans (at Bourbon St) ■ rms & suites, restaurant & lounge ■ www.bourbonorleans.com

10 **Bourgoyne Guest House** [★MW] 504/524-3621, 504/525-3983 ■ 839 Bourbon St (at Dumaine St) ■ 1830s Creole mansion, courtyard

12 **Bywater B&B** [GF,NS] 504/944-8438 ■ 1026 Clouet St ■ Victorian cottage, kitchen, fireplace, some shared baths ■ bywaterbnb.com

13 **Casa de Marigny Creole Guest Cottages** [GS,SW] 504/948-3875 ■ 818 Frenchmen St (at Dauphine) ■ private cottages, tropical courtyard ■ sayhello.com/marigny
The Chimes B&B [GF,NS] 504/488-4640, 800/729-4640 ■ Constantinople at Coliseum (in Garden District) ■ suites & rms in an 1876 home ■ www.historiclodging.com/chimes

14 **Crescent City Guest House** [M,N] 504/944-8722, 877/203-2140 ■ 612 Marigny St (at Chartres) ■ nr French Quarter, hot tub ■ www.crescentcitygh.com

15 **Dauzat House** [GF] 504/524-2075 ■ 1000 Conti St (at Burgundy) ■ jacuzzis, fireplaces

16 **Doubletree Hotel** [GF,F,SW] 504/581-1300, 888/874-9074 ■ 300 Canal St (btwn S Peters & Tchoupitoulas) ■ gym, restaurants & lounge ■ www.hilton.com/doubletree

17 **Empress Hotel** [GF] 504/529-4100, 888/524-9200 ■ 1317 Ursulines Ave (btwn Treme & Marais) ■ 2 blks to French Quarter ■ www.empreshotel.com

18 **Fourteen Twelve Thalia—A B&B** [GS,GO] 504/522-0453 ■ 1412 Thalia (btwn Prytania & Coliseum) ■ 1-bdrm apt in the Lower Garden District ■ grisgrisigs@yahoo.com

19 **French Quarter B&B** [MW,SW,GO] 504/525-3390 ■ 1132 Ursulines (btwn N Rampart & St Claude Ave) ■ apt
French Quarter Corporate Apts 504/524-7260 ■ 1-bdrm apts ■ dasalpha@aol.com
French Quarter Reservation Service 504/523-1246, 800/523-9091 ■ www.neworleansgay.com

20 **French Quarter Suites** [GF,SW,WC,GO] 504/524-7725, 800/457-2253 ■ 1119 N Rampart (at Ursulines) ■ apt & suites, kitchens, hot tub ■ frenchquartersuites.com

21 **The Frenchmen Hotel** [★GS,SW,NS,WC] 504/948-2166, 888/365-2775 ■ 417 Frenchmen St (where Esplanade, Decatur & Frenchmen intersect) ■ 1860s Creole townhouses, spa ■ www.french-quarter.org

22 **Glimmer Inn B&B** [GF] 504/897-1895 ■ 1631 7th St (at St Charles) ■ 1891 Victorian & cottage, some shared baths ■ www.bbonline.com/la/glimmer

23 **Green House Inn** [MW,SW,GO] 504/525-1333, 800/966-1303 ■ 1212 Magazine St (at Erato) ■ gym, hot tub ■ www.GreenInn.com

24 **HH Whitney House on Esplanade** [GS,NS,GO] 504/948-9448, 877/944-9448 ■ 1923 Esplanade Ave (at N Prieur St) ■ 1865 B&B, hot tub, some shared baths ■ www.hhwhitney.com
Historic Rentals [GS,GO] 800/537-5408 ■ 1-bdrm apts in French Quarter ■ www.historicrentals.com

25 **Hotel de la Monnaie** [GF,SW,WC] 504/947-0009 ■ 405 Esplanade Ave (btwn Decatur & N Peters) ■ all-suite hotel, hot tub, courtyard

26 **House of David** [MW,GO] 504/948-3438 ■ 735 Touro St (at Dauphine) ■ newly remodeled 1820s Creole cottage, jacuzzi, private courtyard ■ www.greatstays.com/sela1002.html

27 **Ingram Haus** [GS,GO] 504/949-3110 ■ 1012 Elysian Fields Ave (btwn N Rampart & St Claude) ■ apts, courtyard ■ sites.netscape.net/ingramhaus/flag
Inn The Quarter [GF] 888/523-5235 ■ 1840s townhouse, private courtyard ■ innthequarter@hotmail.com

28 **La Dauphine, Residence des Artistes** [GS,NS,GO] 504/948-2217 ■ 2316 Dauphine St (btwn Elysian Fields & Marigny) ■ free airport pickup (call for details) ■ www.ladauphine.com
La Gallery on Annunciation [MW,NS,GO] 504/522-8834 ■ 1235 Annunciation St ■ 2-rm suite w/ private balcony ■ LaGallery1235@aol.com

29 **La Maison Marigny B&B on Bourbon** [GF,NS,GO] 504/948-3638, 800/570-2014 ■ 1421 Bourbon St (at Esplanade) ■ on the quiet end of Bourbon St ■ www.lamaisonmarigny.com

30 **La Residence** [GS] 504/832-4131, 800/826-9718 x11 ■ Esplanade & Marais Sts ■ 1840s Creole cottage, 1 & 2-bdrm apts, tropical courtyard ■ www.laresidence.net

31 **Lafitte Guest House** [★GS,NS,GO] 504/581-2678, 800/331-7971 ■ 1003 Bourbon St (at St Philip) ■ elegant French manor house ■ www.lafitteguesthouse.com

32 **Lamothe House Hotel** [GS,SW,NS,GO] 504/947-1161, 800/367-5858 ■ 621 Esplanade Ave (btwn Royal & Chartres) ■ 1800s antique furnished Victorian guesthouse

33 **Lanata House** [GS,SW,GO] 504/522-0374 ■ 1220 Chartres St, #5 (at Gov Nicholls) ■ furnished residential accommodations ■ www.lanatahouseapts.com

34 **Lions Inn** [MO,SW,N,GO] 504/945-2339, 800/485-6846 ■ 2517 Chartres St (btwn Spain & Franklin) ■ handsome 1850s home, patio, hot tub ■ www.lionsinn.com
▶ **Macarty Park Guesthouse** [GS,SW,GO] 504/943-4994, 800/521-2790 ■ 3820 Burgundy St ■ rms, cottages & condos, hot tub ■ www.macartypark.com

35 **Maison Burgundy** [GS,SW,GO] 504/948-2355, 800/863-8813 ■ 1860 Burgundy St (on corner of Pauger, btwn Pauger & Burgundy) ■ rms & suites

36 **Maison Dauphine** [M,GO] 504/943-0861 ■ 2460 Dauphine St (btwn Spain & St Roch) ■ nr French Quarter, suites, hot tub ■ JimRod@aol.com

32 **Marigny Guest House** [GF,SW,NS] 504/944-9700, 800/367-5858 ■ 621 Esplanade (btwn Royal & Chartres) ■ quaint Creole cottage

37 **Mazant Guest House** [GF] 504/944-2662 ■ 906 Mazant (at Burgundy) ■ inexpensive 1880s Greek revival B&B

38 **The McKendrick-Breaux House** [GF] 504/586-1700, 888/570-1700 ■ 1474 Magazine St (at Euterpe) ■ 1860s restored Greek Revival, hot tub ■ www.mckendrick-breaux.com

39 **Mentone B&B** [GF,NS] 504/943-3019 ■ 1437 Pauger St (at Kerlerec) ■ ste in Victorian home ■ www.mentonebandb.com

40 **New Orleans Guest House** [GF] 504/566-1177, 800/562-1177 ■ 1118 Ursulines Ave (at N Rampart) ■ 1848 Creole cottage, courtyard, free parking ■ www.virtualcities.com/ons/la/r/lar7801.htm

New Orleans • Louisiana

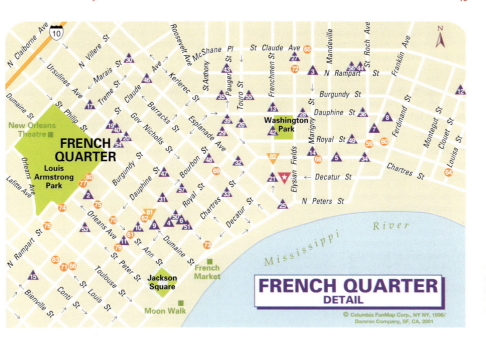

LOUISIANA • USA

3 **Olde Town Inn** [GS] 504/949-5815, 800/209-9408 ■ 1001 Marigny St ■ historic guesthouse, tropical courtyard, walk-ins welcome ■ www.fqaccommodations.com

42 **Parkview Marigny B&B** [GS,NS,GO] 504/945-7875, 877/645-8167 ■ 726 Frenchmen St (at Dauphine) ■ 1870s Creole townhouse, patio ■ www.neworleansbb.com

43 **Pauger Guest Suites** [GS,SW,GO] 504/944-2601 ■ 1722 Pauger St ■ nr French Quarter ■ gdelatte@aol.com

44 **Pecan Tree Inn of New Orleans** [M,GO] 504/943-6195, 800/460-3167 ■ 2525 N Rampart St (at Roch St) ■ courtyards, fireplaces, kitchens ■ www.pecantreeinn.com

45 **Radisson Hotel New Orleans** [GF,F,SW] 504/522-4500 ■ 1500 Canal St (at LaSalle St) ■ www.radisson.com

46 **The Rathbone Mansion Esplanade** [GS,GO] 504/947-2100, 800/947-2101 ■ 1227 Esplanade Ave (at St Claude) ■ 1850s Greek Revival mansion, rms & suites, hot tub, patio ■ www.rathboneinn.com

47 **Rober House Condos** [GS,SW,WC,GO] 504/529-4663, 800/523-9091 ■ 822 Ursulines Ave (at Dauphine) ■ courtyard ■ www.neworleansgay.com

48 **Royal Barracks Guest House** [MW,GO] 504/529-7269, 888/255-7269 ■ 717 Barracks St (at Bourbon) ■ jacuzzi, private patios ■ www.rbgh.com

49 **Royal St Courtyard** [MW,GO] 504/943-6818, 888/846-4004 ■ 2438 Royal St (at Spain) ■ historic 1884 guesthouse, full kitchens, hot tub ■ royalctyd@aol.com

50 **Rue Royal Inn** [GS,WC] 504/524-3900, 800/776-3901 ■ 1006 Royal St (at St Philip) ■ 1830s Creole townhouse, rms & suites ■ www.rueroyalinn.com

51 **Ruffino's Guest House** [GF,NS] 504/588-9004, 888/687-3900 ■ 631 St Philip (btwn Chartres & Royal) ■ in the French Quarter ■ www.vacationmanagement.net

Southern Comforts [GF,SW,WC,GO] 323/850-5623 (in CA), 800/889-7359 ■ French Quarter rentals, hot tub ■ www.SouthernComforts.com

52 **St Charles Guest House** [GF,SW] 504/523-6556 ■ 1748 Prytania St (at Felicity) ■ pensione-style guest house, some shared baths ■ www.stcharlesguesthouse.com

53 **St Peter Guest House** [GF] 504/524-9232, 888/604-6300 ■ 1005 St Peter St (at Burgundy) ■ antique-furnished early 1800s bldg, historic location ■ www.crescent-city.org

54 **Sun & Moon B&B** [GS] 504/529-4652, 800/638-9169 ■ 1037 N Rampart St (at Ursulines) ■ Creole cottage, fountain courtyard ■ www.sunandmoon.qpg.com

55 **Sun Oak Museum & Guesthouse** [GS,GO] 504/945-0322 ■ 2020 Burgundy St ■ Greek Revival Creole cottage, circa 1836, w/ gardens ■ members.aol.com/sunoakgh

56 **Sweet Olive B&B** [GF] 504/947-4332, 877/470-5323 ■ 2460 N Rampart (at Spain) ■ www.sweetolive.com

57 **Ursuline Guest House** [★GS,GO] 504/525-8509, 800/654-2351 ■ 708 Ursulines Ave (btwn Royal & Bourbon) ■ hot tub, evening socials

Vieux Carré Rentals [GF] 504/525-3983 ■ 841 Bourbon St ■ 1 & 2-bdrm apts

BARS

58 **Angles** [MW,NH,D,K,S,18+,WC] 504/834-7979 ■ 2301 N Causeway Blvd (at 34th), Metairie ■ 6pm-2am, till 4am Th-Sat, 4pm-midnight Sun, karaoke Th ■ www.gayneworleans.com/angles

59 **Another Corner** [M,NH,B,F,WC] 504/945-7006 ■ 2601 Royal St (at Franklin) ■ 24hrs, also restaurant

60 **Big Daddy's** [MW,NH,F,E,WC] 504/948-6288 ■ 2513 Royal (at Franklin) ■ 24hrs

61 **Bourbon Pub & Parade** [★M,D,V,YC] 504/529-2107 ■ 801 Bourbon St (at St Ann) ■ 24hrs, cruise bar, CW Tue, 18+, Th, T-dance Sun ■ www.bourbonpub.com

62 **Cafe Lafitte in Exile/ The Balcony Bar** [★M,D,S,V] 504/522-8397 ■ 901 Bourbon St (at Dumaine) ■ 24hrs, 'Balcony Bar' upstairs features area's first cyber bar ■ www.lafittes.com

83 **Club Park Ave** [W,D,S] 504/454-1120 ■ 3515 Hessmer (at Veterans) ■ 6pm-close, clsd Sun-Mon

63 **The Corner Pocket** [★M,NH] 504/568-9829 ■ 940 St Louis (at Burgundy) ■ 24hrs, male dancers Th-Sun ■ www.cornerpocket.net

64 **Country Club** [MW,NH,F,S,SW] 504/945-0742 ■ 634 Louisa St (at Chartres) ■ 11am-1am, from 4pm Mon-Fri in winter, hot tub ■ countryclubneworleans.com

65 **Cowpoke's** [M,NH,D,CW,E] 504/947-0505 ■ 2240 St Claude (at Elysian Fields) ■ noon-1am, dance lessons 8pm Th

59 **Double D's Half Moon Saloon** [M,NH,D,WC] 504/948-2300 ■ 706 Franklin Ave (at Royal) ■ 24hrs

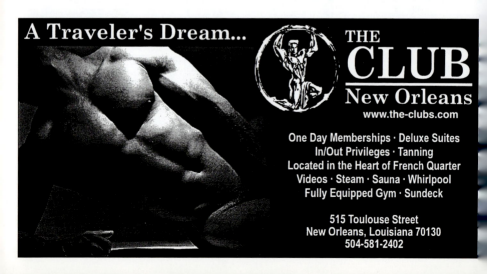

A Traveler's Dream...

THE CLUB
New Orleans

www.the-clubs.com

One Day Memberships · Deluxe Suites
In/Out Privileges · Tanning
Located in the Heart of French Quarter
Videos · Steam · Sauna · Whirlpool
Fully Equipped Gym · Sundeck

**515 Toulouse Street
New Orleans, Louisiana 70130
504-581-2402**

New Orleans • LOUISIANA

66 **The Double Play** [M,NH] 504/523-4517 ■ 439 Dauphine (at St Louis) ■ 24hrs
67 **The Four Seasons** [★MW,NH,F,E,K,S,18+,GO] 504/832-0659 ■ 3229 N Causeway Blvd (at 18th), Metairie ■ 3pm-4am, also the 'Outback Bar', patio
68 **The Friendly Bar** [★MW,NH,F,WC] 504/943-8929 ■ 2301 Chartres St (at Marigny) ■ 11am-3am
69 **Golden Lantern** [M,NH] 504/529-2860 ■ 1239 Royal St (at Barracks) ■ 24hrs ■ goldenlantern@aol.com
70 **Good Friends Bar** [★M,NH,P,E,WC] 504/566-7191 ■ 740 Dauphine (at St Ann) ■ 24hrs, good cocktails, also 'Queens Head Pub' Th-Sun, piano singalong ■ www.goodfriendsbar.com
65 **Hi-Ho Lounge** [GF,A,E,YC] 504/947-9334 ■ 2239 St Claude Ave (at Elysian Fields) ■ eves, casual cocktail lounge, live music some wknds
71 **Le Roundup** [M,NH,TG,CW] 504/561-8340 ■ 819 St Louis (at Dauphine) ■ 24hrs
72 **The Mint** [MW,NH,D,K,S] 504/944-4888 ■ 940 Elysian Fields Ave (at N Rampart) ■ 2pm-close ■ themintno@aol.com
73 **MRB** [★M,NH] 504/524-2558 ■ 515 St Philip (at Decatur) ■ 24hrs, patio ■ www.mrblive.com
74 **Ninth Circle** [M,NH,TG,S] 504/524-7654 ■ 700 N Rampart (at St Peter) ■ 24hrs, cabaret shows on wknds
72 **Phoenix** [★M,NH,B,L,GO] 504/945-9264 ■ 941 Elysian Fields Ave (at N Rampart) ■ 24hrs, cruise room, bear night Sun, also 'Eagle's Nest' (D,V) 9pm-5am & leather store ■ www.phoenixbar.com
75 **Rawhide 2010** [★M,NH,A,B,L,V] 504/525-8106 ■ 740 Burgundy (at St Ann) ■ 24hrs, underground sound ■ www.rawhide2010.com
76 **Society Page** [M,NH,TG,S] 504/593-9941 ■ 542 N Rampart (at Toulouse) ■ 3pm-3am, till 5am Fri-Sat, drag shows
77 **TT's** [M,NH,S,OC] 504/523-9521 ■ 820 N Rampart (at St Ann) ■ 11am-3am, male dancers Fri-Sat
74 **Voodoo at Congo Square** [M,NH] 504/527-0703 ■ 718 N Rampart (at Orleans) ■ 24hrs

NIGHTCLUBS

79 **735 Nightclub** [M,D,S] 504/581-6740 ■ 735 Bourbon St (at Orleans) ■ 24hrs ■ www.735bourbon.com
The Full Moon [M,D,L] 504/341-4396 ■ 424 Destrehan, Harvey ■ 9pm-close, clsd Mon
61 **Oz** [★M,D,S,V,YC,WC] 504/593-9491 ■ 800 Bourbon St (at St Ann) ■ 24hrs ■ www.ozneworleans.com
84 **Rainbows** [MW,D] 504/454-3200 ■ 3536 18th St (at Edenborn), Metairie ■ 6pm-close, from 3pm Sun, clsd Mon
80 **Venture-N** [M,D,L,S,WC] 504/596-2236 ■ 834 N Rampart (at St Ann) ■ 24hrs, patio, also leather shop ■ www.gayneworleans.com/wolfendales

CAFES

PJ's [★] 504/949-2292 ■ 634 Frenchmen St ■ 7am-11pm, till midnight Fri-Sat
Red Bike Bakery & Cafe 504/529-2453 ■ 746 Tchoupitoulas (off Julia) ■ lunch daily, dinner Tue-Sat, plenty veggie, outdoor dining

RESTAURANTS

Cafe Sbisa 504/522-5565 ■ 1011 Decatur ■ dinner & Sun brunch, French Creole, patio
Casamento's 504/895-9761 ■ 4330 Magazine (at Napoleon Ave) ■ 5:30pm-9pm, clsd Jun-Aug, best oyster loaf in city
Clover Grill [★] 504/523-0904 ■ 900 Bourbon St (at Dumaine) ■ 24hrs, diner fare
Commander's Palace 504/899-8221 ■ 1403 Washington Ave (in Garden District) ■ lunch & dinner, upscale Creole, Sun jazz brunch
Eve's Market 504/891-4015 ■ 4601 Freret (at Cadiz) ■ 10am-7pm, clsd Sun, healthy deli & natural food store, plenty veggie
Feelings Cafe [E] 504/945-2222 ■ 2600 Chartres St (at Franklin Ave) ■ dinner nightly, Fri lunch, Sun brunch, Creole, also piano bar wknds
Fiorella's Cafe 504/528-9566 ■ 45 French Market Pl (at Gov Nicholls & Ursulines) ■ 7am-5pm, clsd Sun, homecooking
La Peniche 504/943-1460 ■ 1940 Dauphine St (at Touro St) ■ 24hrs, diner
Lucky Cheng's [S] 504/529-2045 ■ 720 St Louis (btwn Bourbon & Royal) ■ lunch & dinner, Sun brunch, Asian Creole, full bar, cabaret shows, drag-queen waitresses
Mama Rosa 504/523-5546 ■ 616 N Rampart (at Toulouse & St Louis) ■ 11am-9pm, till 11pm wknds, Italian
Mona Lisa [BW] 504/522-6746 ■ 1212 Royal St (at Barracks) ■ 11am-10:30pm, till midnight wknds, Italian, some veggie
Nola [WC] 504/522-6652 ■ 534 St Louis St (btwn Chartres & Decatur) ■ lunch (except Sun) & dinner, fusion Creole
Old Dog New Trick Cafe [WC] 504/522-4569 ■ 307 Exchange Alley (btwn Royal & Chartres off Conti) ■ 11:30am-9pm, vegetarian, outdoor dining
Olivier's [WC] 504/525-7734 ■ 204 Decatur St ■ lunch & dinner, Creole
Petunia's [★] 504/522-6440 ■ 817 St Louis (at Bourbon) ■ 8am-11pm, Cajun/ Creole, full bar ■ www.petuniasrestaurant.com
Pontchartrain Cafe 504/524-0581 ■ 2031 St Charles Ave (in 'Grand Heritage Hotel') ■ lunch & dinner, Creole
Poppy's Grill [WC] 504/524-3287 ■ 717 St Peter (at Royal & Bourbon) ■ 24hrs, diner
Praline Connection 504/943-3934 ■ 542 Frenchmen St (at Chartres) ■ 10:30am-9pm, soul food, gospel jazz brunch Sun
Quarter Scene 504/522-6533 ■ 900 Dumaine St (at Dauphine) ■ 8am-midnight, dinner only Tue, homecooking, some veggie ■ www.quarterscene.com
Quartermaster 504/529-1416 ■ 1100 Bourbon St ■ 24hrs, sandwiches & more
Sammy's Seafood 504/525-8442 ■ 627 Bourbon St (across from Pat O' Brien's) ■ 11am-midnight, Creole/ Cajun
Secret Garden 504/524-2041 ■ 538 St Philip St (at Decatur) ■ 5:30pm-10pm, Sun brunch, Creole +
Vaqueros 504/891-6441 ■ 4938 Prytania (at Robert) ■ lunch & dinner, Southwestern-Mexican, good margaritas
Vera Cruz [WC] 504/866-1736 ■ 7537 Maple (at Hillard) ■ 5pm-11pm, clsd Sun, Mexican

ENTERTAINMENT & RECREATION

Café du Monde 504/587-0835, 800/772-2927 ■ 1039 Decatur St (Old Jackson Square) ■ till you've had a beignet—fried dough, powdered w/ sugar, that melts in your mouth—you haven't been to New Orleans & this is 'the' place to have them 24hrs a day
Gay Heritage Tour 504/945-6789 ■ 909 Bourbon St ■ call for details, departs from 'Alternatives' bookstore

LOUISIANA / MARYLAND • USA

Haunted History Tour 888/644-6787 ■ guided 2-1/2 hr tours of New Orleans' most famous haunts, including Anne Rice's home

Pat O'Brien's [GF] 800/597-4823 ■ 718 St Peter St (btwn Bourbon & Royal) ■ more than just a bar—come for the Hurricane, stay for the kitsch ■ www.patobriens.com

St Charles Streetcar 504/248-3900 (RTA #) ■ Canal St (btwn Bourbon & Royal Sts) ■ it's not named Desire, but you should still ride it if you want to see the Garden District, Blanche

BOOKSTORES

81 Alternatives 504/524-5222 ■ 907 Bourbon St (at Dumaine) ■ 11am-7pm, till 9pm Fri-Sat, clsd Tue, lgbt

Bookstar [WC] 504/523-6411 ■ 414 N Peters (in Jax Brewery Complex) ■ 9am-midnight

82 Faubourg Marigny Bookstore [WC] 504/943-9875 ■ 600 Frenchmen St (at Chartres) ■ 10am-8pm, till 6pm wknds, lgbt

Sidney's News Stand 504/524-6872 ■ 917 Decatur St (btwn St Philip & Dumaine) ■ 8am-9pm, till 10pm Sat, some lgbt titles

RETAIL SHOPS

Hit Parade [★] 504/524-7700 ■ 741 Bourbon St ■ 11am-midnight, till 2am Fri-Sat, lgbt books, designer circuit clothing & more

Postmark New Orleans 504/529-2052, 800/285-4247 ■ 631 Toulouse St (btwn Chartres & Royal) ■ 10am-6pm, from noon Sun, gay gifts, furniture, art, postcards

Rab-Dab 504/529-3577 ■ 508 St Philip St ■ 11am-6pm, men's clothing/ clubwear & gifts ■ rabdabno@aol.com

Rings of Desire 504/524-6147 ■ 1128 Decatur St, 2nd flr ■ piercing studio ■ www.ringsofdesire.com

Second Skin Leather 504/561-8167 ■ 521 St Philip St (btwn Decatur & Chartres) ■ noon-10pm, till 6pm Sun

Something Different [GO] 504/891-9056 ■ 5300 Tchoupitoulas (in Riverside Market) ■ 10am-9pm, till 7pm Sat, noon-6pm Sun ■ www.gayamerica.com/billy/

PUBLICATIONS

Ambush Mag 504/522-8049 ■ lgbt newspaper ■ www.ambushmag.com

Southern Voice 404/876-1819 ■ weekly lgbt newspaper for AL, FL (panhandle), GA, LA, MS, TN w/ resource listings ■ www.southernvoice.com

MEN'S CLUBS

▶ The Club New Orleans [★PC] 504/581-2402 ■ 515 Toulouse St (at Decatur) ■ 24hrs ■ www.the-clubs.com

Flex—New Orleans [V] 504/598-3539 ■ 700 Baronne St ■ 24hrs wknds ■ www.flexbaths.com

EROTICA

Airline Bookstore 504/468-2931 ■ 1404 26th St (off Bainbridge), Kenner ■ 24hrs

Chartres St Conxxxion 504/586-8006 ■ 107 Chartres St (off Canal St) ■ 24hrs

Gargoyles 504/529-4386 ■ 1201 Decatur St (at Gov Nicholls) ■ leather/ fetish shop ■ www.gargoylesclothing.com

Panda Bear [WC] 504/529-3593 ■ 415 Bourbon St (at St Louis) ■ leather & toys

Paradise [WC] 504/461-0000 ■ 41 W 24th St (at Crestview), Kenner

BALTIMORE

Baltimore, one of the 'hub' cities of the Chesapeake Bay, is a quaint, working-class city by the sea, with a friendly and diverse population. It's not far from Washington, DC, and, like the nation's capital, Baltimore is packed with museums and history. Baltimore does have its quirky side: it's the site of Edgar Allen Poe's home (and grave) and hometown of John Waters, the over-the-top filmmaker.

Queer Resources

COMMUNITY INFO

▼ Gay/Lesbian Community Center 410/837-5445. 241 W Chase St, 10am-4pm Mon-Fri.
Gay/Lesbian Switchboard 410/837-8888, 410/837-8529 (TDD), 7pm-10pm.

AIDS RESOURCES
AIDS Action Baltimore 410/837-2437.

RECOVERY
AA Gay/Lesbian 410/663-1922.

City Calendar

LGBT PRIDE
June. 410/837-5445 (GLCC).

Tourist Info

AIRPORT DIRECTIONS
Baltimore/Washington International. To get to downtown area, take 295 North approximately 8 miles.

PUBLIC TRANSIT & TAXIS
Yellow Cab 410/685-1212.
MBA Transit 410/539-5000.

TOURIST SPOTS & INFO
Baltimore Museum of Art 410/396-7100.
Fort McHenry 410/962-4299.
Harborplace.
National Aquarium 410/576-3800.
Poe House & Museum 410/396-7932.
Visitor's Center: Baltimore Tourism Office 410/659-7300 or 800/543-1036.

WEATHER
Unpredictable rains and heavy winds. In summer, the weather can be hot (90°s) and sticky.

BEST VIEWS
Top of the World Trade Center at the Inner Harbor.

Baltimore • Maryland

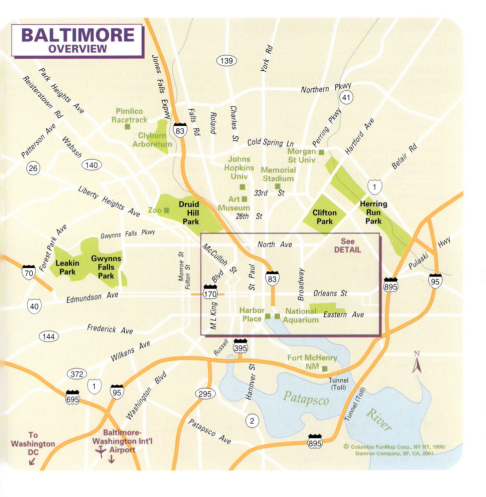

Visit Damron Online!

- search our online database
- get the latest updates
- direct web/ email links
- more categories (including websites)
- shop for discounted guides
- calendar of events
- tour operator listings
- gay travel links & more!

www.damron.com

MARYLAND • USA

Baltimore

ACCOMMODATIONS

1   **Abacrombie Badger B&B** [GS,NS,GO] 410/244-7727 ■ 58 W Biddle St (at Cathedral) ■ 1880s townhouse, also restaurant ■ www.badger-inn.com

2   **Biltmore Suites** [GF] 410/728-6550, 800/868-5064 ■ 205 W Madison St (at Park) ■ Victorian hotel ■ www.biltmoresuites.com

3   **Clarion Hotel—Mt Vernon Square** [GF,F,WC] 410/727-7101, 800/292-5500 ■ 612 Cathedral St (at W Monument) ■ restaurant, lounge, gym, jacuzzis ■ www.clarionhotel.com

4   **Harbor Inn Pier 5** [GS,F,WC] 410/539-2000 ■ 711 Eastern Ave (at President) ■ boutique hotel on waterfront, full brkfst, restaurant, cigar bar ■ www.harborinnpier5.com

5   **Mr Mole B&B** [★GS,GO] 410/728-1179 ■ 1601 Bolton (at McMechen) ■ suites on Bolton Hill ■ www.mrmolebb.com

BARS

6   **The Allegro** [M,D,S,V] 410/837-3906 ■ 1101 Cathedral St (at Chase) ■ 6pm-2am, 18+ Th ■ members.aol.com/theallegro/

7   **Atlantis** [M,S] 410/727-9099 ■ 615 Fallsway (at Centre St) ■ 5pm-2am, from 6pm Sun, clsd Mon, nude male dancers

8   **Baltimore Eagle** [★M,L,WC] 410/823-2453 ■ 2022 N Charles St (enter on 21st) ■ 3pm-2am, from 2pm wknds, leather store, patio ■ www.baltimoreeagle.com

9   **Central Station** [★MW,F,K,S,V] 410/752-7133 ■ 1001 N Charles St (at Eager) ■ 3pm-2am, 2 bars, karaoke Mon, also sidewalk cafe ■ www.centralstationpub.com

10 **Club Bunns** [MW,D,MR-AF,S] 410/234-2866 ■ 608 W Lexington St (at Greene St) ■ 5pm-2am, male strippers Wed, female strippers Sat

11 **Club Mardi Gras** [M,NH,MR-AF,S,WC] 410/783-9873 ■ 228 Park Ave (at Saratoga) ■ 4pm-2am

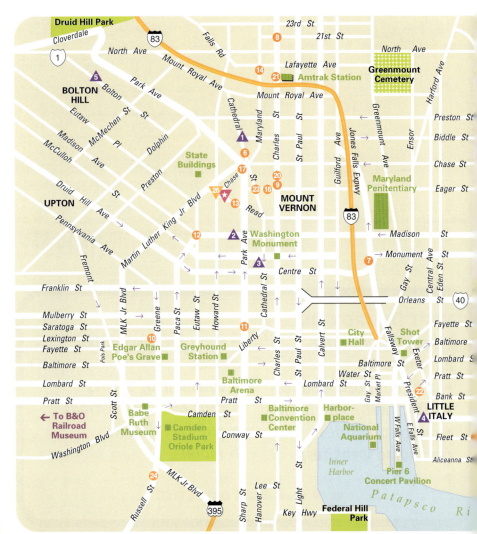

Baltimore • Maryland

12 **Coconuts Cafe** [★W,D,F,E,WC,GO] 410/383-6064 ■ 311 W Madison (at Eutaw) ■ 4pm-2am, from 6pm Mon, from 11am Fri ■ www.coconutscafe.com

13 **The Drinkery** [M,NH] 410/225-3100 ■ 203 W Read St (at Park)

14 **The Gallery Bar & Studio Restaurant** [MW,WC] 410/539-6965 ■ 1735 Maryland Ave (at Lafayette) ■ 2pm-1:30am, dinner nightly

15 **Harmon's Pub** [MW,NH,WC] 410/563-9417 ■ 3230 E Fairmont Ave (at N East Ave) ■ 2pm-1am, unconfirmed

16 **Hippo** [★MW,D,TG,E,K,V,WC] 410/547-0069, 410/576-0018 ■ 1 W Eager St (at Charles) ■ 4pm-2am, 3 bars, more women first wknd, piano bar ■ www.clubhippo.com

17 **Leon's** [M,NH,F,WC] 410/539-4993, 410/539-4850 ■ 870 Park Ave (at Chase) ■ 11:30am-2am, also 'Tyson's Place' restaurant

18 **Port in a Storm** [W,NH,D,F,WC] 410/732-5608 ■ 4330 E Lombard St (at Kresson) ■ 10am-2am

19 **The Quest** [M,NH] 410/563-2617 ■ 3607 Fleet St (at Conkling) ■ 4pm-2am

20 **Stagecoach** [MW,D,CW,F,K,S,WC] 410/547-0107 ■ 1003 N Charles St (at Eager) ■ 4pm-2am, Tex/Mex, free dance lessons

NIGHTCLUBS

21 **Club 1722** [M,D] 410/727-7431 ■ 1722 N Charles St (at Lafayette) ■ 1:45am-5am, clsd Mon-Wed, cruisy

22 **Orpheus** [GF,D,A,L,18+] 410/276-5599 ■ 1001 E Pratt St (at Exeter) ■ goth Th, fetish party Sat

23 **Paloma's** [GS,D,F,E] 410/783-9004 ■ 15 W Eager St (at Cathedral) ■ 8pm-4am, till 11pm Sun

24 **The Paradox** [★MW,D,MR-AF,F,E,V,WC] 410/837-9110 ■ 1310 Russell St (at 13th) ■ 10pm-4am, midnight-6am Fri-Sat, more gay Sat

25 **The Rainbow Room** [M,S] 410/276-1740 ■ 600 S Broadway (at Fleet) ■ 6pm-2am Wed-Sun, drag shows

CAFES

Donna's Coffee Bar [BW] 410/385-0180 ■ 2 W Madison (at Charles) ■ 7:30am-11pm, 9am-midnight wknds

Louie's the Bookstore Cafe [E,WC] 410/230-2998 ■ 518 N Charles (at Franklin) ■ 11am-midnight, till 2am wknds, also full bar

RESTAURANTS

Alonso's [WC] 410/235-3433 ■ 415 W Cold Spring Lake (at Keswick Rd) ■ 11am-midnight, till 1am Fri-Sat, Italian ■ www.alonsos.com

Cafe Hon [WC] 410/243-1230 ■ 1002 W 36th St (at Roland) ■ 7am-9pm, 9am-10pm wknds, some veggie

Gampy's [MW,WC] 410/837-9797 ■ 904 N Charles St (at Read) ■ 11:30am-1am, till 2am Wed-Th, till 3am wknds

Loco Hombre 410/889-2233 ■ 413 E Cold Spring Ln (at Roland) ■ 11am-5pm

The Millrace 410/448-3663 ■ 5201 Franklintown Rd (at Security) ■ dinner, clsd Sun, seafood

Mount Vernon Stable & Saloon 410/685-7427 ■ 909 N Charles St (btwn Eager & Read) ■ lunch & dinner, some veggie, also bar 11:30am-2am

Spike & Charlie's Restaurant/ Wine Bar 410/752-8144 ■ 1225 Cathedral St (at Preston) ■ 5:30pm-11:30pm, clsd Mon

BOOKSTORES

26 **Lambda Rising** [WC] 410/234-0069 ■ 241 W Chase St (at Read) ■ 10am-10pm, lgbt

PUBLICATIONS

The Baltimore Alternative 410/235-3401 ■ lgbt newspaper ■ www.baltalt.com

Gay Life 410/837-7748 ■ lgbt newspaper ■ www.bgp.org

Woman's Monthly 202/965-5399 ■ articles & calendar of community/ arts events for greater DC/ Baltimore area ■ www.womo.com

EROTICA

Big Top Books 410/547-2495 ■ 429 E Baltimore

Earle Theater 410/488-5134 ■ 4845 Belair Rd ■ www.earletheatre.com

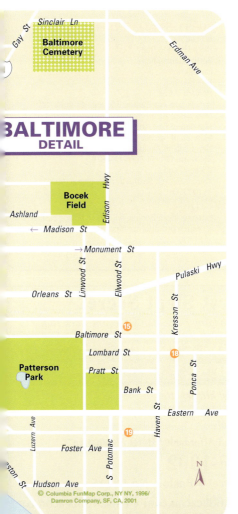

Boston

Home to 65 colleges and universities, Boston has long been an intellectual center for the continent. The result is a city whose character is both traditional and free-thinking, high-brow and free-wheeling. The various ethnic neighborhoods, like the Italian-American North End, have their own charm.

Queer Resources

COMMUNITY INFO
Gay/ Lesbian Helpline 617/267-9001. 6pm-11pm, 5pm-7:30pm Sat & 5pm-10pm Sun.
Cambridge Women's Center 617/354-8807.

AIDS RESOURCES
Fenway Community Health Center 617/267-0900.

RECOVERY
617/426-9444 (AA#).

City Calendar

LGBT PRIDE
June. 617/522-7890.

ENTERTAINMENT
Gay Men's Chorus 617/424-8900.
The Theatre Offensive 617/542-4214.
Tool Box Productions 617/497-9215.

ANNUAL EVENTS
May - Gay & Lesbian Film/Video Festival 617/369-3300 (MFA).
June - AIDS Walk, web: www.aidswalk.net.

Tourist Info

AIRPORT DIRECTIONS
Logan International. Take the Callahan Tunnel to I-93 south and exit Albany St/East Berkeley St. (Damron suggests not driving in Boston. Instead, take a shuttle, taxi, or the 'T.')

PUBLIC TRANSIT & TAXIS
Boston Cab 617/536-5010.
Instyle Transportation limo service 617/ 641-2400 or 877/ 64-STYLE (see display ad on page 156).
MBTA (the 'T') 800/392-6100.

TOURIST SPOTS & INFO
Beacon Hill.
Black Heritage Trail.
Boston Common.
Faneuil Hall.
Freedom Trail.
Harvard University.
Isabella Stewart Gardner Museum 617/566-1401.
Museum of Afro-American History 617/725-0022.
Museum of Fine Arts 617/267-9300.
Museum of Science 617/723-2500.
New England Aquarium 617/973-5281.
Old North Church 617/523-6676.
Walden Pond.
Visitor's Center: Boston Visitor's Bureau 800/447-6277.

WEATHER
Extreme—from freezing winters to boiling summers with a beautiful spring and fall.

Boston's Best Slept Secret
Nightly and Weekly Lodging in Boston's Elegant Back Bay

463 BEACON STREET GUEST HOUSE

- Private baths w/ kitchenettes
- Close to T & the Prudential Center
- Parking Available

A Comfortable and Affordable "Hotel Alternative"

(617) 536-1302
463 Beacon Street • Boston, MA 02115
E-mail: info@463beacon.com • www.463beacon.com

MASSACHUSETTS

Boston

ACCOMMODATIONS

▶ **463 Beacon St Guest House** [GF] 617/536-1302 ■ 463 Beacon St ■ residential area, minutes from Boston's heart ■ www.463beacon.com

82 Chandler B&B [GS,NS] 617/482-0408, 888/482-0408 ■ 82 Chandler St ■ historic townhouse in South End, great views ■ www.channel1.com/82chandler

't Amsterdammertje [MW,NS] 617/471-8454, 800/484-6401 x1676 ■ full brkfst, Euro-American B&B, nr Boston ■ www.bbonline.com/ma/am/

Carolyn's B&B [GF,NS] 617/864-7042 ■ 102 Holworthy St, Cambridge ■ full brkfst, nr Harvard Square ■ fantasiaca@aol.com

Chandler Inn [GF] 617/482-3450, 800/842-3450 ■ 26 Chandler St ■ centrally located ■ www.chandlerinn.com

Clarendon Square B&B [MW] 617/536-2229 ■ 198 W Brookline St (at Tremont/ Bolyston) ■ restored Victorian townhouse ■ www.clarendonsquare.com

Just Right Reservations 978/934-9931 ■ covers hotels & B&Bs in MA ■ www.justrightreservations.org

Logan B&B [MO,N,GO] 617/561-0985 ■ traveler747@webtv.net

Oasis Guest House [★GS,WC,GO] 617/267-2262 ■ 22 Edgerly Rd ■ Back Bay location, some shared baths ■ www.oasisgh.com

Rutland Square House B&B [GS,GO] 617/247-0018, 800/786-6567 ■ 56 Rutland Sq ■ Victorian townhouse

Taylor House B&B [GS,NS,GO] 617/983-9334, 888/228-2956 ■ 50 Burroughs St ■ Italianate Victorian ■ www.taylorhouse.com

Victorian B&B [WO,NS] 617/536-3285 ■ full brkfst, lesbian-owned/ run

BARS

5 **Boston Eagle** [★M,NH,F] 617/542-4494 ■ 520 Tremont St (nr Berkeley) ■ 3pm-2am, from noon Sun

6 **Boston Ramrod** [★M,L,D,V,YC,WC] 617/266-2986 ■ 1254-56 Boylston St (at Ipswich, 1 blk from Fenway Park) ■ noon-2am, pansexual fetish night open to all 3rd Fri; also 'Rubberworks' fetish store ■ www.ramrodboston.com

7 **Chaps/ Vapor** [★M,D,S] 617/695-9500 ■ 100 Warrenton St (at Stuart) ■ noon-2am, piano bar Mon, Latino night Wed, T-dance Sun, dancers ■ www.chapsofboston.com

8 **Club Cafe** [★MW,P,F,E,V,WC] 617/536-0966 ■ 209 Columbus (at Berkeley) ■ 11:30am-2am, from 2pm Sat, 3 bars including 'Moonshine' video bar, also restaurant ■ www.clubcafe.com

3 **Fritz** [★M,NH] 617/482-4428 ■ 26 Chandler St (in the 'Chandler Inn') ■ noon-2am, sports bar, popular Sun brunch

9 **Jacque's** [★M,TG,S] 617/426-8902 ■ 79 Broadway (at Stuart) ■ 11am-midnight, drag cabaret, live music Fri-Sat

10 **Lava Bar** [GS,D] 617/267-7707 ■ 575 Commonwealth, top flr (in Kenmore Sq) ■ 10pm-2am, clsd Mon-Wed, women's night Sat ■ www.lavabar.com

11 **Luxor** [★M,V] 617/423-6969 ■ 69 Church St (btwn Stuart & Arlington, in Theater District) ■ 4pm-1am, also '69 Church St' lounge & 'Mario's' Italian restaurant

6 **Machine** [★M,D,V,YC,WC] 617/536-1950 ■ 1254 Boylston St (beneath 'Boston Ramrod') ■ 10pm-2am Fri-Sat only ■ www.ramrodboston.com

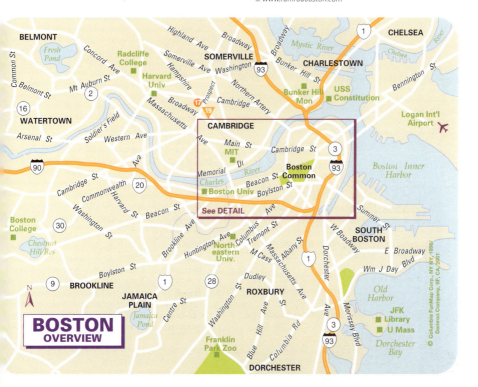

MASSACHUSETTS • USA

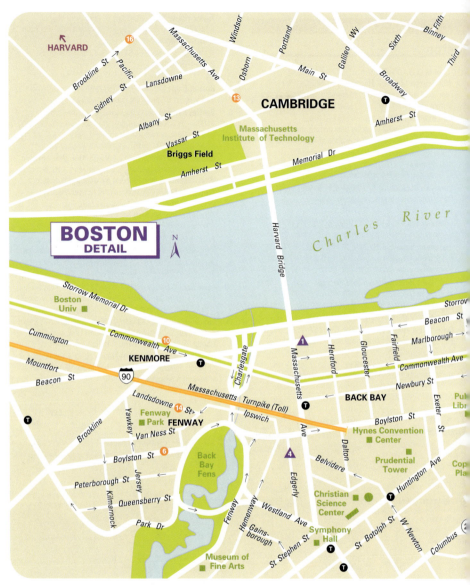

<u>Midway Cafe</u> [W,NH,D,E,YC,WC] 617/524-9038 ■ 3496 Washington St, Jamaica Plain ■ 9pm-2am Th ■ www.djdee.com/dykenite/

<u>Milky Way Lounge & Lanes</u> [GS,F,E] 617/524-3740 ■ 403 Centre St, Jamaica Plain ■ 6pm-1am, live music, women's poetry readings

12 **One Nineteen Merrimac** [M,NH,D,WC] 617/367-0713 ■ 119 Merrimac St (at Causeway) ■ 10:30am-2am, from noon Sun, cruisy ■ www.119merrimac.com

13 **Paradise** [M,D,S] 617/494-0700 ■ 180 Massachusetts Ave, Cambridge ■ 7pm-1am, till 2am Th-Sat, stripper bar, college night Th, T-dance Sun ■ www.paradisecambridge.com

<u>Upstairs at the Hideaway</u> [W,NH] 617/661-8828 ■ 20 Concord Ln, Cambridge ■ 6pm-2am Th & Sun only

NIGHTCLUBS

14 **Avalon** [★M,D,YC,$] 617/262-2424 ■ 15 Lansdowne St ■ 9pm-2am Th-Sun, more gay Sun ■ www.avalonboston.com

15 **Buzz** [★M,D,S,$] 617/267-8969 ■ 67 Stuart St ■ 10pm-2am Sat, go go boys ■ www.buzzboston.com

16 **Manray** [GS,D,A,19+,YC] 617/864-0400 ■ 21 Brookline St (off Mass Ave, in Central Sq), Cambridge ■ 9pm-2am, clsd Sun-Tue, more gay at 'Campus' Th & 'Liquid' Sat (disco/new wave), goth Wed, fetish Fri ■ www.manrayclub.com

Boston • MASSACHUSETTS

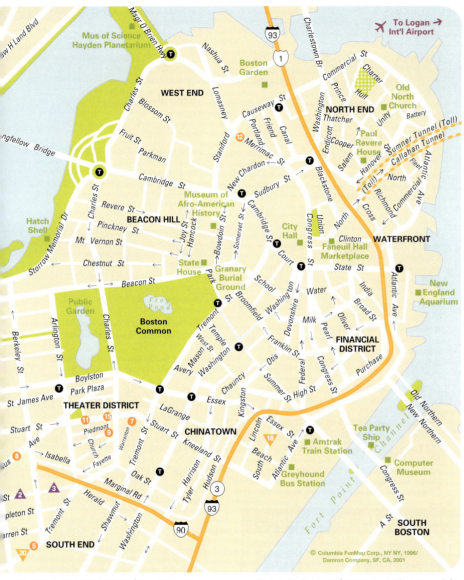

The Middle East [GF,A,F,E,YC] 617/497-0576 ■ 472 Massachusetts Ave (in Central Sq), Cambridge ■ 11am-1am, till 2am wknds, live music, also restaurant ■ www.mideastclub.com

Someplace Else at Ryles [W,D,F] 617/876-9330 ■ 212 Hampshire St (at Cambridge St, in Inman Sq), Cambridge ■ 5pm-2am Sun

Static [MW,D,S,18+] 617/262-2437 ■ 13 Lansdowne (at Axis) ■ 10pm-2am Mon ■ www.axisnightclub.com

CAFES

1369 Cafe 617/576-4600 ■ 757 Massachusetts Ave (in Central Sq), Cambridge ■ coffee & baked goods; also 1369 Cambridge St (Inman Sq) location, 617/576-1369

Designs for Living 617/536-6150 ■ 52 Queensberry St (at Jersey St) ■ 7am-6:30pm, till noon Wed, from 8am Sat, from 9am Sun, cybercafe & bookstore ■ www.bosnet.com

Diesel Cafe [GO] 617/629-8717 ■ 257 Elm St (in Davis Sq), Somerville ■ 7am-midnight, till 1am Fri-Sat, from 8am wknds, plenty veggie

Francesca's [★MW,WC] 617/482-9026 ■ 564 Tremont St (at Clarendon) ■ 8am-11pm, till midnight wknds, excellent pastries

Geoffrey's Cafe [BW,GO] 617/266-1122 ■ 578 Tremont St (at Dartmouth) ■ 9am-10pm, till 11pm wknds, great desserts

MASSACHUSETTS • USA

Restaurants

Biba [★WC] 617/426-7878 ■ 272 Boylston St (at Arlington) ■ lunch & dinner, upscale dining, eclectic California cuisine

Blackstone's on the Square [★GS,WC] 617/247-4455 ■ 1525 Washington St ■ lunch Mon-Fri, dinner nightly, brunch Sun, bistro fare, also martini bar till midnight Mon-Fri, till 1am wknds

Brandy Pete's 617/439-4165 ■ 267 Franklin St (at Congress) ■ Mon-Fri only, lunch & dinner

Buddha's Delight 617/451-2395 ■ 3 Beach St, 2nd flr ■ 11am-9:30pm, Chinese, vegetarian

Casa Romero 617/536-4341 ■ 30 Gloucester St ■ 5pm-10pm, till 11pm wknds, Mexican

City Girl Caffe [GO] 617/864-2809 ■ 204 Hampshire St (at Prospect), Cambridge ■ 11am-9pm, from 10am wknds, clsd Mon, Italian, plenty veggie, great sandwiches

Club Cafe [★MW,E,V,WC] 617/536-0966 ■ 209 Columbus (at Berkeley) ■ dinner & wknd brunch, also 3 bars ■ www.clubcafe.com

Icarus 617/426-1790 ■ 3 Appleton St (off Tremont) ■ dinner only, New American

Johnny D's [D,E] 617/776-2004 ■ 17 Holland St (in Davis Sq), Somerville ■ dinner Tue-Sat & wknd brunch, Southern, plenty veggie, live music nightly ■ www.johnnyds.com

Laurel 617/424-6711, 617/424-6664 ■ 142 Berkeley St (at Columbus) ■ lunch & dinner, Sun brunch

New Blue Diner [MW,WC] 617/695-0087 ■ 150 Kneeland St (at South St) ■ 7am-4pm, 24hrs Th-Sun, Southern bbq, plenty veggie

Rabia's [WC] 617/227-6637 ■ 73 Salem St (at Cross St) ■ lunch & dinner, fine Italian, some veggie

Ristorante Lucia 617/367-2353 ■ 415 Hanover St ■ lunch Fri-Sun, dinner nightly, great North End pasta, some veggie

Trattoria Pulcinella 617/491-6336 ■ 147 Huron Ave (at Concord), Cambridge ■ dinner, fine Italian, cash only

Entertainment & Recreation

Freedom Trail ■ start at the Visitor Information Center in Boston Common (at Tremont & West Sts), the most famous cow pasture & oldest public park in the US, & follow the red line to some of Boston's most famous sites

Instyle Transportation

Instyle Transportation is Boston's only gay owned & operated limo and sedan service. We will transport that VIP attending your next corporate event; take you to and from Logan Airport; help you with your commitment ceremony; get you to and from Provincetown, or simply a night out in our brand new luxury vehicles. Bottled water is complimentary. For more info, please call, or visit our website: instyletransportation.com. Remember: if you're going to do it, do it Instyle!

PHONE **617/641-2400 or 877/64-STYLE**

Gay Men's Chorus 617/424-8900 ■ PO Box 1390, 02117 ■ www.bgmc.org

Isabella Stewart Gardner Museum 617/566-1401 ■ 280 The Fenway ■ Venetian palazzo filled w/ Old Masters to Impressionists, gorgeous courtyard, clsd Mon ■ www.boston.com/gardner

John Hancock Observatory 617/247-1977 ■ 200 Clarendon St, 60th flr (at St James St)

Museum of Afro-American History/ Black Heritage Trail 617/425-0022 ■ 46 Joy St (at Smith Ct, on Beacon Hill) ■ exhibits in the African Meeting House, the oldest standing African-American church in the US

Theater Offensive 617/542-4214 ■ 'New England's foremost presenter of lgbt theater', 'Out on the Edge' festival in Sept ■ www.thetheateroffensive.org

Tool Box Productions 617/497-9215 ■ 60 Bishop Allen Dr #4, Cambridge 02139 ■ multimedia cabaret & events, women of all colors

Bookstores

18 **Calamus Bookstore** [★] 617/338-1931, 888/800-7300 ■ 92-B South St ■ 9am-7pm, noon-6pm Sun, 'New England's complete GLBT bookstore', also cards, music, jewelry, videos ■ www.calamusbooks.com

19 **New Words Bookstore** 617/876-5310, 800/928-4788 ■ 186 Hampshire St (at Prospect), Cambridge ■ noon-8pm, 10am-6pm Sat, noon-6pm Sun, clsd Mon, feminist ■ world.std.com/~newwords/

Trident Booksellers & Cafe [BW,WC] 617/267-8688 ■ 338 Newbury St (off Mass Ave) ■ 9am-midnight, good magazine browsing

Unicorn Books 781/646-3680 ■ 1210 Massachusetts Ave (at Appleton), Arlington Hts ■ 10am-9pm, till 5pm wknds, from noon Sun, spiritual titles

20 **We Think The World of You** [★] 617/574-5000 ■ 540 Tremont St (btwn Berkeley & Clarendon) ■ 10am-7pm, till 6:30pm Sat, 11:30am-5:50pm Sun, lgbt

Wordsworth 617/354-5201 ■ 30 Brattle St (at Mt Auburn in Harvard Sq), Cambridge ■ 9am-11pm, 10am-10pm Sun, some lgbt titles

Publications

Bay Windows 617/266-6670 ■ lgbt newspaper ■ www.baywindows.com

In Newsweekly 617/426-8246 ■ New England's lgbt newspaper ■ www.innewsweekly.com

Sojourner—The Women's Forum 617/524-0415 ■ monthly progressive paper ■ www.sojourner.org

Gyms & Health Clubs

Metropolitan Fitness [GF] 617/536-3006 ■ 209 Columbus

Mike's Gym II [★GO] 617/338-6210, 617/338-6677 ■ 560 Harrison Ave (at Waltham St) ■ www.MikesGymII.com

Erotica

Amazing Express 617/859-8911 ■ 1258 Boylston St (at Ipswich) ■ also 57 Stuart St, 617/ 338-1252

Eros Boutique 617/425-0345 ■ 581-A Tremont St, 2nd flr ■ fetishwear & toys ■ www.gis.net/~eros

Grand Opening! 617/731-2626 ■ 318 Harvard St, 2nd flr (at Beacon, in Arcade Bldg), Brookline ■ women's sex toy store ■ www.grandopening.com

Hubba Hubba 617/492-9082 ■ 534 Massachusetts Ave (at Brookline, in Central Sq), Cambridge ■ fetish gear

Marquis de Sade 617/426-2120 ■ 73 Berkeley St (at Chandler)

Provincetown • MASSACHUSETTS

PROVINCETOWN

The country's largest lesbian and gay resort is the quintessential New England whaling village on the very tip of Cape Cod. Sleepy in the winter months, Provincetown swarms with lesbian and gay tourists from Memorial Day through Labor Day weekend. A car is almost a liability on the crowded streets; bicycle rentals are a better choice.

Queer Resources

COMMUNITY INFO
Provincetown Business Guild 508/487-2313, 800/637-8696, web: www.ptown.org.

AIDS RESOURCES
508/487-9445.

City Calendar

LGBT PRIDE
May.

ANNUAL EVENTS
June - Golden Threads 802/848-8002. Gathering for lesbians over 50 & their admirers, at the Provincetown Inn. PO Box 60475, Northampton, MA 01060-0475.
August - Provincetown Carnival 800/637-8696.
October - Women's Week 800/637-8696. It's very popular, so make your reservations early! Fantasia Fair - for TS/TVs & their admirers.
December - Holly Folly.

Tourist Info

AIRPORT DIRECTIONS
Provincetown Airport (508/487-0241) handles commuter airlines from Logan International in Boston. It is appproximately a 3-hour drive from Logan in Boston or Green Airport in Providence.

PUBLIC TRANSIT & TAXIS
Mercedes Cab 508/487-3333.
Provincetown Taxi 508/487-8294.
Ferry Bay State Spray & Provincetown Steamship Co (from Boston, during summer) 617/723-7800.

TOURIST SPOTS & INFO
The beach.
Galleries.
Heritage Museum 508/487-7098.
Herring Cove Beach.
Pilgrim Monument.
Provincetown Museum 508/487-1310.
Whale watching.

WEATHER
New England weather is unpredictable. Be prepared for rain, snow or extreme heat! Otherwise, the weather during the season consists of warm days and cooler nights.

BEST VIEWS
People-watching from an outdoor cafe or on the beach.

Provincetown

ACCOMMODATIONS

1. **1807 House** [MW,WC] 508/487-2173, 888/522-1807 ▪ 54 Commercial St (btwn W Vine & Point St) ▪ rms, suites & apts, 50 ft from beach ▪ www.provincetown.com/1807
2. **Admiral's Landing Guest House** [M,GO] 508/487-9665, 800/934-0925 ▪ 158 Bradford St (btwn Conwell & Pearl) ▪ 1840s Greek Revival home & studio efficiencies ▪ www.admiralslanding.com
3. ▶**Aerie House & Beach Club** [MW,GO] 508/487-1197, 800/487-1197 ▪ 184 Bradford St (at Miller Hill) ▪ hot tub, sundeck ▪ www.aeriehouse.com
4. **Ampersand Guesthouse** [M,GO] 508/487-0959, 800/574-9645 ▪ 6 Cottage St ▪ 1880s Greek Revival, sundeck ▪ www.ampersandguesthouse.com
5. **Anchor Inn Beach House** [★GS,NS,WC] 508/487-0432, 800/858-2657 ▪ 175 Commercial St ▪ private beach, harbor view ▪ www.anchorinnbeachhouse.com
6. **The Archer Inn** [M,NS,GO] 508/487-2529, 800/263-6574 ▪ 26 Bradford St (at Pleasant) ▪ rooms & cottage, some shared baths, art deco 1930s theme ▪ archerinn.com
7. **Bayberry Accommodations** [MW,NS,GO] 508/487-4605, 800/422-4605 ▪ 16 Winthrop St ▪ newly renovated, award-winning home, hot tub ▪ www.bayberryaccommodations.com
8. **Bayshore** [GS,GO] 508/487-9133 ▪ 493 Commercial St (at Howland) ▪ apts, private beach ▪ www.provincetown.com/bayshore
   Beachfront Realty 508/487-1397 ▪ 151 Commercial St ▪ vacation rentals & housing ▪ beachfront@tiac.net
9. **Beaconlight Guest House** [★M,NS,GO] 508/487-9603, 800/696-9603 ▪ 12 Winthrop St ▪ award-winning guesthouse, rms & suites, hot tub, sundecks, parking ▪ www.beaconlightguesthouse.com
10. **Benchmark Inn & Central** [MW,SW,NS,GO] 508/487-7440, 888/487-7440 ▪ 6-8 Dyer St ▪ hot tub, sauna, fireplaces, harbor views, sundeck ▪ www.benchmarkinn.com
    Best Inn [GF,SW,WC] 508/487-1711, 800/422-4224 ▪ also restaurant & lounge ▪ www.capeinn.com
11. **Boatslip Beach Club** [★M,SW,GO] 508/487-1669, 800/451-7547 ▪ 161 Commercial St (at Atlantic) ▪ seasonal, also several bars & popular T-dance ▪ www.boatslipbeachclub.com
12. **The Bradford Carver House** [MW,GO] 508/487-4966, 800/826-9083 ▪ 70 Bradford St ▪ restored mid-19th-century home ▪ www.bradfordcarver.com
13. **Bradford Gardens Inn** [W,GO] 508/487-1616, 800/432-2334 ▪ 178 Bradford St ▪ 1820s Colonial & cottages, full brkfst ▪ www.bradfordgardens.com
14. **Bradford House & Motel** [GF,WC] 508/487-0173 ▪ 41 Bradford St ▪ www.bradfordhousemotel.com
15. **Brass Key Guesthouse** [★MW,SW,WC,GO] 508/487-9005, 800/842-9858 ▪ 67 Bradford St (at Carver) ▪ luxury inn w/ hot tub ▪ www.brasskey.com
16. **Burch House** [M] 508/487-9170 ▪ 116 Bradford St ▪ seasonal, studios
17. **The Captain & His Ship** [GS,GO] 508/487-1850, 800/400-2278 ▪ 164 Commercial St (btwn Winthrop & Central) ▪ seasonal, sundeck ▪ www.captainandhisship.com
18. **Captain Lysander's Inn** [GF] 508/487-2253 ▪ 96 Commercial St (at Mechanic) ▪ sundeck w/ harbor view, some shared baths

HAVE IT ALL!
1 800 648-0364

With over 10 years of experience, we represent the largest selection of accommodations in Provincetown. We can also make all your travel arrangements to anywhere in the world with our on-site ticketing service. Entertainment and Restaurants—one call and we'll take care of your tickets or reservations. It's so easy, when you want the best, call PRS.

PROVINCETOWN RESERVATIONS SYSTEM®

**TRAVEL
ACCOMMODATIONS
ENTERTAINMENT**

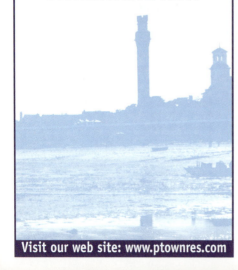

Visit our web site: www.ptownres.com

19 **Captain's House B&B** [M,NS,GO] 508/487-9353, 800/457-8885 ■ 350-A Commercial St (at Center) ■ patio ■ www.captainshouseptown.com

20 **Carl's Guest House** [MO,N,GO] 508/487-1650, 800/348-2275 ■ 68 Bradford St (at Court) ■ some shared baths, sundeck ■ www.carlsguesthouse.com

21 **Carpe Diem Guesthouse** [MW,NS,GO] 508/487-4242, 800/487-0132 ■ 12 Johnson St ■ also cottage, full German brkfst, hot tub ■ www.carpediemguesthouse.com

22 **The Carriage House Guesthouse** [GS,GO] 508/487-8855, 800/309-0248 ■ 7 Central St ■ 1700s guesthouse w/ luxurious modern rms, hot tub ■ www.thecarriagehse.com

23 **Check'er Inn** [WO] 508/487-9029, 800/894-9029 ■ 25 Winthrop St (btwn Bradford & Brown) ■ apts, hot tub, private decks, lesbian-owned/ run ■ www.sandtrapcc.com/checker/

24 **Chicago House** [M] 508/487-0537, 800/733-7869 ■ 6 Winslow St (at Bradford) ■ rms & apts ■ www.chicagohse.com

21 **Christopher's by the Bay** [MW,NS] 508/487-9263, 877/487-9263 ■ 8 Johnson St (at Bradford) ■ Victorian guesthouse, full brkfst, some shared baths, patio ■ www.christophersbythebay.com

25 **The Clarendon House** [GS,GO] 508/487-1645, 800/669-8229 ■ 118 Bradford St (btwn Ryder & Alden) ■ also cottage, hot tub, roof deck ■ www.clarendonhse.com

26 **Coat of Arms** [M] 508/487-0816, 800/224-8230 ■ 7 Johnson St ■ seasonal

27 **The Commons Guesthouse & Bistro** [GS] 508/487-7800, 800/487-0784 ■ 386 Commercial St (at Pearl) ■ deck w/ full bar, also restaurant ■ www.commonsghb.com

28 **Crown & Anchor** [MW,SW] 508/487-1430 ■ 247 Commercial St ■ also cabaret & poolside bars ■ www.thecrownandanchor.net

29 **Crowne Pointe Historic Inn** [MW,SW,WC,GO] 508/487-6767, 877/276-9631 ■ 82 Bradford St ■ 1800s mansion, full brkfst, hot tub ■ www.crownepointe.com

30 ▶ **Dexter's Inn** [MW,NS,GO] 508/487-1911, 888/521-1999 ■ 6 Conwell St (at Railroad) ■ sundeck ■ www.ptowndextersinn.com

The Dunes Motel & Apartments [MW] 508/487-1956, 800/475-1833 ■ seasonal, rooms & apts, decks ■ www.thedunesprovincetown.com

31 **Elephant Walk Inn** [★M,GO] 508/487-2543, 954/730-0664 (Nov-April), 800/889-9255 ■ 156 Bradford St (at Conwell) ■ sundeck, parking, seasonal ■ www.elephantwalkinn.com

32 **Fairbanks Inn** [★MW,GO] 508/487-0386, 800/324-7265 ■ 90 Bradford St ■ www.fairbanksinn.com

33 **Gabriel's Apartments & Guest Rooms** [★MW,N,NS,GO] 508/487-3232, 800/969-2643 ■ 104 Bradford St ■ full brkfst, hot tub, sundecks, gym ■ www.gabriels.com

34 **Gifford House Inn & Dance Club** [MW,GO] 508/487-0688, 800/434-0130 ■ 11 Carver St ■ seasonal also several bars & '11 Carver' restaurant (dinner only, seafood) ■ www.giffordhouse.com

35 **Gracie House** [MW,NS] 508/487-4808 ■ 152 Bradford St (at Conwell) ■ historic, restored Queen Anne ■ www.idealwebsites.com/gracie

36 **Grand View Inn** [MW,GO] 508/487-9193, 888/268-9169 ■ 4 Conant St ■ decks ■ www.ptownguide.com/grandviewinn

37 **The Gull Walk Inn** [WO,GO] 508/487-9027 ■ 300-A Commercial St ■ seasonal, shared baths, sundeck, garden ■ www.gullwalkinn.com

Provincetown • Massachusetts

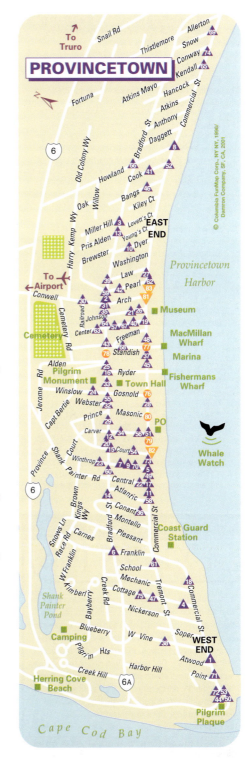

38 **Halle's** [W,GO,NS] 508/487-6310 ■ 14 W Vine St (at Tremont) ■ cottage & apts, sundeck ■ www.provincetown.com/halles

39 **Harbor Lights Guest Apartments** [GS,NS,GO] 508/487-8246 ■ 163 Bradford St (at Law St) ■ studio & 1-bdrm apt, parking

40 **Heritage House** [★MW] 508/487-3692 ■ 7 Center St ■ lesbian-owned/ run, shared baths ■ www.heritageh.com

41 **The Inn at Cook Street** [GF,NS,GO] 508/487-3894, 888/266-5655 ■ 7 Cook St ■ intimate & quiet ■ www.innatcookstreet.com

42 **Ireland House** [MW,GO] 508/487-7132 ■ 18 Pearl St (at Arch) ■ 1820s B&B, garden ■ www.irelandhse.com

43 **John Randall House** [MW,GO] 508/487-3533, 800/573-6700 ■ 140 Bradford St (at Standish) ■ open year-round ■ www.johnrandallhouse.com

44 **Land's End Inn** [GF,NS] 508/487-0706, 800/276-7088 ■ 22 Commercial St ■ rms & apts ■ cimarron.net/usa/ma/lei.html

45 **Lotus Guest House** [MW,GO] 508/487-4644, 888/508-4644 ■ 296 Commercial St (at Standish) ■ seasonal, decks, garden ■ www.provincetown.com/lotus

46 **Mayflower Apartments & Cottages** [GF] 508/487-1916 ■ 6 Bangs St (at Commercial St) ■ kitchens

45 **Moffett House** [M,L,GO] 508/487-6615, 800/990-8865 ■ 296-A Commercial St ■ seasonal, levi/ leather-friendly, women very welcome

47 **The Oxford** [MW,NS,GO] 508/487-9103, 888/456-9103 ■ 8 Cottage St ■ newly renovated 1850 Revival, parking ■ www.oxfordguesthouse.com

Pilgrim Colony Inn [GS,GO] 508/487-1100 ■ 670 Shore Rd Rte 6-A, North Truro ■ seasonal, private beach ■ www.pilgrimcolony.com

48 **Pilgrim House Inn** [W,WC] 508/487-6424 ■ 336 Commercial St ■ seasonal, also 'Café Crudité' restaurant & 'Vixen' bar/ dance club ■ www.provincetown.com/pilgrimhouse/

49 **The Prince Albert Guest House** [M,NS,GO] 508/487-0859, 800/992-0859 ■ 166 Commercial St ■ Victorian ■ www.princealbertguesthouse.net

50 **Provincetown Inn** [GS,SW,WC] 508/487-9500, 800/942-5388 ■ 1 Commercial St (at Rotary) ■ waterfront, private beach, poolside bar & grill, theater ■ provincetowninn.com

51 **The Ranch Guestlodge** [M,NS] 508/487-1542, 800/942-1542 ■ 198 Commercial St ■ shared baths, sundeck, also bar ■ www.capecodaccess.com/ranch/

52 **Ravenwood Guest House** [MW,GO] 508/487-3203 ■ 462 Commercial St (at Cook) ■ 1830 Greek Revival, also apts & cottage, patio, private beach ■ www.provincetown.com/ravenwood/

53 **Red Inn** [MW,GO] 508/487-0050 ■ 15 Commercial St (at Point) ■ elegant waterfront dining & lodging

54 **Revere Guesthouse** [MW,NS] 508/487-2292, 800/487-2292 ■ 14 Court St (btwn Commercial & Bradford) ■ restored 1820s captain's home, also apt ■ www.reverehouse.com

55 **Romeo's Holiday** [MW,N,GO] 508/487-6636, 877/MY-ROMEO ■ 97 Bradford St (btwn Gosnold & Masonic) ■ hot tub ■ www.romeosholiday.com

56 **Roomers** [M,GO] 508/487-3532 ■ 8 Carver St (at Commercial) ■ seasonal, Greek Revival guesthouse

57 **Rose Acre** [WO] 508/487-2347 ■ 5 Center St (at Commercial) ■ rms, apts & cottage, decks, gardens ■ roseacreguests.com

MASSACHUSETTS • USA

58 **Rose & Crown Guest House** [GS,GO] 508/487-3332 ■ 158 Commercial St ■ also cottage, lavish gardens ■ www.provincetown.com/rosecrown

Sandbars Motel [GS] 508/487-1290 ■ 570 Shore Rd, Beach Pt, North Truro ■ seasonal, all oceanfront rooms, private beach ■ www.sandbarsmotel.com

11 **Sandpiper Beach House** [★GS,SW,NS,GO] 508/487-1928, 800/354-8628 ■ 165 Commercial St ■ Victorian, sundeck, private beach ■ www.sandpiperbeachhouse.com

59 **Season's, An Inn for All** [MW,SN] 508/487-2283, 800/563-0113 ■ 160 Bradford St (at Pearl) ■ Victorian B&B, full brkfst ■ www.provincetownseasons.com

60 **Shamrock Motel, Cottages & Apartments** [GS,SW,WC,GO] 508/487-1133, 888/554-7474 ■ 49 Bradford St (at Central) ■ rms, apts & cottages, hot tub ■ www.myshamrock.com

61 **Shiremax Inn** [MW,GO] 508/487-1233, 888/744-7362 ■ 5 Tremont St (btwn Franklin & School) ■ 1900s guesthouse, seasonal, children allowed, sundeck, also apts

3 **Snug Cottage** [GS,GO] 508/487-1616, 800/432-2334 ■ 178 Bradford St ■ boutique B&B ■ www.snugcottage.com

62 **Somerset House** [★MW,GO] 508/487-0383, 800/575-1850 ■ 378 Commercial St (at Pearl) ■ Victorian mansion ■ www.somersethouseinn.com

63 **The Stationmaster's House** [WO,GO] 508/487-1329 ■ 27 Center St ■ 1800s guesthouse w/ railroad motif, shared bath, 3 night min ■ www.provincetown.com/stationmaster

64 **Sunset Inn** [MW,N,GO] 508/487-9810, 800/965-1801 ■ 142 Bradford St (at Center) ■ seasonal, some shared baths ■ www.sunsetinnptown.com

65 **Surfside Inn** [GS,SW,GO] 508/487-1726, 800/421-1726 ■ 543 Commercial (at Kendall Ln) ■ seasonal, waterfront motel w/ lots of amenities, private beach ■ www.surfsideinn.cc

66 **Three Peaks Guest House** [MW,GO] 508/487-1717, 800/286-1715 ■ 210 Bradford St (at Howland) ■ 1870s Victorian, sundeck ■ www.threepeaks.com

Truro Vineyards [GF] 508/487-6200 ■ Rte 6-A, North Truro ■ seasonal, inn, patio, also wine tasting & store

67 **The Tucker Inn** [MW,NS] 508/487-0381, 800/477-1867 ■ 12 Center St ■ 1870s guesthouse, rms & cottage, lesbian-owned/ run ■ www.provincetown.com/tucker

68 **Victoria House** [MW,GO] 508/487-4455 ■ 5 Standish St ■ www.provincetownusa.com/victoriahouse

69 **Watermark Inn** [GF] 508/487-0165 ■ 603 Commercial St ■ suites w/ kitchens, beachside ■ Watermark-Inn.com

70 **Watership Inn** [★M,GO] 508/487-0094, 800/330-9413 ■ 7 Winthrop St ■ sundeck ■ www.watershipinn.com

71 **West End Inn** [GF,GO] 508/487-9555, 800/559-1220 ■ 44 Commercial St ■ seasonal, rms, suites & apts ■ www.westendinn.com

72 **Westwinds Condominium** [MW,SW,GO] 508/487-1841 ■ 28 Commercial St (at Point) ■ seasonal, apts & cottages, private beach ■ www.provincetown.com/westwinds

73 **White Wind Inn** [★MW,GO] 508/487-1526 ■ 174 Commercial St (at Winthrop) ■ well-appointed Provincetown landmark ■ www.whitewindinn.com

74 **Windamar House** [W,GO] 508/487-0599 ■ 568 Commercial St (at Conway) ■ 1840s sea captain's home, also apts ■ www.provincetown.com/windamar/

75 **Windsor Court** [MW,SW,GO] 508/487-2620 ■ 15 Cottage St ■ suites w/ kitchens, hot tub ■ www.windsorcourtptown.com

BARS

76 **The Antro** [M,D,S,WC] 508/487-8800 ■ 258 Commercial St ■ 8pm-1am, clsd Nov-April, cabaret & restaurant, call for events

11 **The Boatslip Beach Club** [★MW,D,F,YC] 508/487-1669, 800/451-7547 ■ 161 Commercial St (at Central) ■ seasonal, popular T-dance 3:30pm daily, special events, also restaurant, seafood ■ www.boatslipbeachclub.com

77 **Chaser's** [S,NH,D,S,K] 508/487-7200 ■ 293 Commercial St (at Standish) ■ 4pm-1am, also sports bar ■ www.chasersbar.qpg.com

77 **Governor Bradford** [GF,F,K,S] 508/487-2781 ■ 312 Commercial St (at Standish) ■ 11am-1am, 'drag karaoke', also restaurant

78 **The Jungle Cabaret** [MW,F,S,GO] 508/487-9941 ■ 135 Bradford St (above 'Tropical Joe's' restaurant) ■ seasonal, shows at 7pm, 8:30pm & 10pm ■ thejungle@aol.com

79 **Pied Piper** [★MW,D] 508/487-1527 ■ 193-A Commercial St ■ noon-1am, more men 6:30pm-9:30pm during 'After Tea T-Dance', also 'Venus' for women Fri-Sat ■ www.thepied.com

---

Dexter's Inn

DEXTER'S INN

A traditional Cape Cod Guest House. The perfect place for your all-season vacation, located in the heart of downtown Provincetown, just a short walk to Commercial St., shops, restaurants, art galleries, and clubs. Or relax on our spacious sun deck. 15 Cape Cod style rooms, 12 with private baths. Our unique clustering of rooms allows for private entrance from deck or patio. In-room phones, color cable TV, refrigerators, AC, daily maid service, continental breakfast, ample free parking, patios, and flowering gardens. Open year round.

www.ptowndextersinn.com   e-mail: dextersinn@aol.com

PHONE **508/487-1911 or 888/521-1999**

Aerie House and Beach Club

Some of the best harbor views in Provincetown from either our Guesthouse perched atop Miller Hill or our bay front Beach Club. Offering a complete range of accommodations including rooms with either shared or private baths, an efficiency apartment, and our spectacular "Eagle's Nest" two-bedroom suite at the Guesthouse, and luxury apartments at our Beach Club. Private beach, hot tub, large sundeck, bicycles, home gym, fireplaces, airport/pier pick up, parking. Open year round.

www.aeriehouse.com

PHONE **800/487-1197**

Provincetown • MASSACHUSETTS

34 **Porchside Lounge** [M,NH] 508/487-0688 ■ 11 Carver St (in the 'Gifford House' accommodations) ■ 5pm-1am
28 **Rooster Bar** [MW,NH,D,S,V] 508/487-1430 ■ 247 Commercial St (in the 'Crown & Anchor') ■ 6pm-1am, also 'Lobby Bar' from 11am ■ www.thecrownandanchor.net
77 **Steve's Alibi** [★GS,NH,S] 508/487-2890 ■ 291 Commercial St ■ 11am-1am, drag shows Wed-Mon, local favorite ■ www.stevesalibi.com
28 **Vault** [MO,L] 508/487-1430 ■ 247 Commercial St (at 'Crown & Anchor') ■ 9pm-1am ■ www.thecrownandanchor.net
48 **Vixen** [W,D,E] 508/487-6424 ■ 336 Commercial St (at Pilgrim House Inn) ■ 4pm-1am, from 11am Fri-Sat, from noon Sun ■ www.provincetown.com/vixen/

NIGHTCLUBS
80 **Atlantic House (The 'A-House')** [★M,D] 508/487-3821 ■ 6 Masonic Pl ■ 9pm-1am, weekly theme parties, also 'The Little Bar' (M,NH) & the 'Macho Room' (M,L) ■ www.ahouse.com
76 **Club Antro** [★M,D,WC] 508/487-8800 ■ 258 Commercial St (at 'The Antro') ■ after 11pm, theme nights, circuit crowd on Sat
34 **Club Purgatory** [M,D,L] 508/487-8442 ■ 9-11 Carver St (at Bradford St) ■ 9pm-1am, theme nights, popular Sun for 'Bound' ■ www.giffordhouse.com
28 **Crown & Anchor Ballroom** [★MW,D,YC] 508/487-1430 ■ in the 'Crown & Anchor' accommodations ■ 10:30pm-1am, seasonal ■ www.thecrownandanchor.net

CAFES
No Ordinary Joe 508/487-6656 ■ 148-A Commercial St ■ 7:30am-11pm, great coffee w/ a view
Post Office Cafe Cabaret [MW,E] 508/487-3892 ■ 303 Commercial St (upstairs) ■ 8am-midnight (brkfst till 3pm), call for off-season hrs, some veggie

RESTAURANTS
Bayside Betsy's [WC] 508/487-0120 ■ 177 Commercial St ■ brkfst, lunch & dinner on waterfront, also 'Mixers Cocktails' 11:30am-1am ■ www.baysidebetsys.com
Bubala's by the Bay [★] 508/487-0773 ■ 183-185 Commercial ■ seasonal, 8am-11pm, bar till 1am, patio ■ www.capecodaccess.com/bubala's/
Café Blasé 508/487-9465 ■ 328 Commercial St ■ brkfst, lunch & dinner, patio, full bar
Café Crudité 508/487-6237 ■ 336 Commercial St #6 (upstairs) ■ seasonal, lunch & dinner, vegetarian, vegan & macrobiotic ■ www.cafecrudite.com
Chester [★] 508/487-8200 ■ 404 Commercial St ■ dinner from 6pm
Ciro & Sal's 508/487-6411 ■ 4 Kiley Ct (btwn Bangs St & Lovett's Ct) ■ dinner from 5:30pm, Italian ■ www.ciroandsals.com
Clem & Ursie's 508/487-2333 ■ 89 Shank Painter Rd ■ 11am-8pm, affordable outdoor dining, cuisine theme nights, also fish market, deli & grocery
Front Street Restaurant [MW] 508/487-9715 ■ 230 Commercial St ■ seasonal, 6pm-10:30pm, bistro, bar till 1am
Gallerani's [★MW,BW] 508/487-4433 ■ 133 Commercial St ■ dinner, Italian, pizza
Grand Central [★] 508/487-7599 ■ 5 Masonic St ■ dinner, seasonal, int'l/ seafood, full bar
Lobster Pot [WC] 508/487-0842 ■ 321 Commercial St (harborside) ■ noon-10pm, seafood, some veggie ■ www.provincetown.com/lobsterpot

Martin House 508/487-1327 ■ 157 Commercial St ■ 6pm-close, clsd Wed, outdoor dining (summers)
The Mews Restaurant & Cafe [★WC] 508/487-1500 ■ 429 Commercial St (btwn Lovett's & Kiley) ■ dinner, lunch wknds, also 'Cafe Mews' upstairs ■ www.mews.com
Napi's Restaurant [WC] 508/487-1145, 800/571-6274 ■ 7 Freeman St ■ dinner, lunch Oct-April, int'l/ seafood, plenty veggie ■ www.napisrestaurant.com
Pucci's Harborside [★WC] 508/487-1964 ■ 539 Commercial St ■ seasonal, lunch & dinner, some veggie, full bar, on the water, great Bloody Marys
Sal's Place [★] 508/487-1279 ■ 99 Commercial St ■ seasonal, seafood/ Italian, publisher's choice: cheese & butter pasta, deck, on the water
Spiritus Pizza [★] 508/487-2808 ■ 190 Commercial St ■ noon-2am, great espresso shakes & late night hangout
Tropical Joe's [GO] 508/487-9941 ■ 135 Bradford St (at Standish) ■ seasonal, 10am-4pm & 6pm-close, lunches to go, outdoor dining, also bar ■ tropicaljoes@aol.com

ENTERTAINMENT & RECREATION
Art's Dune Tours [GO] 508/487-1950 ■ day trips, sunset tours, and charters ■ www.artsdunetours.com
Off the Coast Kayak [GO] 508/487-2692, 877/785-2925 ■ 3 Freeman St ■ rentals & guided tours for P-town, Truro & Wellfleet ■ www.offthecoastkayak.com
Ptown Bikes [GO] 508/487-8735 ■ 42 Bradford ■ rentals ■ www.ptownbikes.com

BOOKSTORES
81 **Now, Voyager** 508/487-0848 ■ 357 Commercial St ■ 10am-11pm (11am-5pm off-season), lgbt ■ www.nowvoyagerbooks.com
Provincetown Bookshop 508/487-0964 ■ 246 Commercial St ■ 10am-11pm (till 5pm off-season)

RETAIL SHOPS
City Video 508/487-4493 ■ 193 Commercial St ■ 10am-11pm, lgbt section ■ ddanded@aol.com
Don't Panic 508/487-1280 ■ 192 Commercial St ■ seasonal, 10am-10pm, lgbt gifts
GayMartUSA 508/487-7517 ■ 176 Commercial St ■ from 10am, clothes & gifts ■ www.gaymartusa.com
82 **Pride's** 508/487-1127 ■ 182 Commercial St ■ 10am-11pm (in summer), call for off-season hrs, lgbt gifts
Recovering Hearts [WC] 508/487-4875 ■ 2-4 Standish St ■ 10am-11pm (in summer), call for off-season hrs
83 **Womencrafts** 508/487-2501 ■ 376 Commercial St ■ 10am-11pm (in summer), call for off-season hrs

PUBLICATIONS
In Newsweekly 617/426-8246 ■ New England's lgbt newspaper ■ www.innewsweekly.com
Provincetown Banner 508/487-7400 ■ newspaper ■ www.provincetown.com/banner/
Provincetown Magazine 508/487-1000 ■ seasonal, P-Town's oldest weekly magazine ■ www.ptownmag.com

GYMS & HEALTH CLUBS
Mussel Beach [MW] 508/487-0001 ■ 35 Bradford St (btwn Montello & Conant) ■ 6am-9pm
Provincetown Gym [MW] 508/487-2776 ■ 82 Shank Painter Rd (at Winthrop) ■ www.provincetowngym.com

EROTICA
Wild Hearts 508/487-8933 ■ 244 Commercial St ■ 11am-11pm (in summer) & noon-5pm, till 11pm wknds (off-season), toys for women ■ www.wildhearts.com

MICHIGAN • USA

DETROIT

Known for its cars and stars, 'Motown' is the home of living legends like Aretha Franklin, Diana Ross & the Supremes, the Temptations, Stevie Wonder, Anita Baker, and Madonna. Detroit is also rich in African-American culture. Noteworthy sights include the Museum of African-American History, the Motown Museum, and just under the river—via the Detroit/ Windsor Tunnel—is the North American Black Historical Museum in Windsor, Canada.

Queer Resources

COMMUNITY INFO
▼ Affirmations Lesbian/Gay Community Center 248/398-7105, web: www.comnet.org/affirmations. 195 W 9-Mile Rd #106, Ferndale, 9am-9pm, till 4pm Sat, 1pm-9pm Sun.
Lesbian/Gay Switchboard 248/398-4297, 800/398-4297. 4pm-10pm, clsd wknds.

AIDS RESOURCES
800/590-2437.

RECOVERY
248/541-6565.

City Calendar

LGBT PRIDE
May/June. 248/547-5878 (Just for Us).

ANNUAL EVENTS
January - Lesbian & Gay Film Festival 248/547-5878.
August - Michigan Womyn's Music Festival 231/757-4766, 616/898-3707. One of the biggest annual gatherings of lesbians on the continent, in Walhalla.

Tourist Info

AIRPORT DIRECTIONS
Detroit International. To get downtown, take I-94 E. Take the exit for Federal Hwy 10 and head south until Hwy 10 runs into I-75 and E Jefferson Ave.

PUBLIC TRANSIT & TAXIS
Shuttle 734/283-4800.
DOT (bus service) 313/933-1300.
Detroit People Mover 313/962-7245.

TOURIST SPOTS & INFO
Belle Isle Park.
Detroit Institute of Arts 313/833-7900.
Greektown.
Motown Historical Museum 313/875-2264.
Museum of African-American History 313/494-5800.
Renaissance Center 313/568-8000.
Visitor's Center: 313/202-1800 or 800/338-7648, www.visitdetroit.com.

WEATHER
Be prepared for hot, humid summers and cold, dry winters.

BEST VIEWS
From the top of the 73-story Westin Hotel at the Renaissance Center.

MICHIGAN

Detroit

ACCOMMODATIONS
1 The Antheneum Suite Hotel [GF,WC] 313/962-2323, 800/772-2323 ■ 1000 Brush St (at Lafayette) ■ luxury hotel, restaurant & lounge, gym ■ www.antheneumsuitehotel.com
2 Millner Hotel [GF] 313/963-3950, 800/521-0592 ■ 1538 Centre St ■ downtown ■ www.millner-hotels.com
3 Shorecrest Motor Inn [GF,WC] 313/568-3000 ■ 1316 E Jefferson Ave ■ downtown, also restaurant

BARS
4 Adam's Apple [M,NH] 313/240-8482 ■ 18937 W Warren (at Artesian) ■ 3pm-2am
5 Back Pocket [★M,F] 313/272-8374 ■ 8832 Greenfield Rd (at Joy) ■ 2pm-2am
6 Club Gold Coast [★M,D,S,WC] 313/366-6135 ■ 2971 E 7-Mile Rd (at Conant) ■ 7pm-2am
7 The Continental [M,NH,D,MR-AF] 313/964-4077 ■ 156 Monroe (at Broadway) ■ noon-2am, from 6pm wknds
8 The Deck [M,NH,S] 313/822-1991 ■ 14901 E Jefferson (at Alter) ■ 4pm-2am, from 8pm Mon-Tue
9 Detroit Eagle [★M,D,CW,L,WC] 313/873-6965 ■ 1501 Holden (at Trumbull) ■ 8pm-2am, from 5pm Fri & Sun, clsd Mon-Tue ■ www.detroiteagle.com
10 Gigi's [M,D,TG,S,GO] 313/584-6765 ■ 16920 W Warren (at Clayburn, enter rear) ■ noon-2am, from 2pm wknds, dancers Mon & Fri, drag shows Wed & Sat ■ hometown.aol.com/gigisbar/

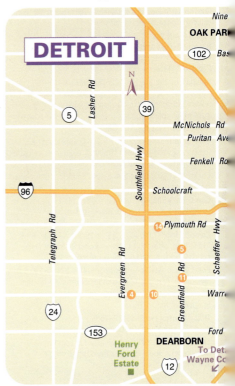

Detroit • Michigan

11 **Hayloft Saloon** [M,NH,L,OC,WC] 313/581-8913 ■ 8070 Greenfield Rd (S of Joy Rd) ■ 3pm-2am, levi/ leather bar

12 **Male Box** [M,NH,D,GO] 313/892-5420 ■ 3537 E 7-Mile Rd (btwn Conant & Ryan) ■ 2pm-2am, CW Wed, leather night Sat, Sun T-dance ■ malebox@ameritech.net

13 **Menjo's** [★M,D,V,YC] 313/863-3934 ■ 928 W McNichols (at Hamilton) ■ noon-8pm, till 2am Th-Sun, popular 'happy hour'

14 **The Other Side** [MW,NH,F,K,WC] 313/836-2324 ■ 16801 Plymouth (at Southfield) ■ noon-2am, karaoke Tue

15 **R&R Saloon** [M,D,L] 313/849-2751 ■ 7330 Michigan Ave (at Central) ■ 2pm-2am

16 **Stingers Lounge** [MW,NH,F,K,GO] 313/892-1765 ■ 19404 Sherwood (at 7-Mile) ■ 6pm-5am, from 8pm wknds, karaoke Wed-Th

17 **Sugarbakers** [W] 313/892-5203 ■ 3800 E 8-Mile Rd (at Ryan Ave) ■ 6pm-2am, sports bar & grill

18 **The Temple** [GS,D,F,WC] 248/414-7400 ■ 344 W 9-Mile Rd (2 blks W of Woodward), Ferndale ■ 5pm-2am, clsd Mon, more gay Wed & Fri, patio ■ www.thetempleferndale.com

19 **The Woodward Bar & Grill** [★M,F,K,WC] 313/872-0166 ■ 6426 Woodward Ave (at Milwaukee, rear entrance) ■ 11am-2am, from 2pm wknds, lounge, karaoke Mon ■ thrwoodward@aol.com

20 **The Works** [M,D,V] 313/961-1722 ■ 1846 Michigan Ave (at Rose Parks) ■ 9pm-close

Nightclubs

21 **Backstreet** [★M,D,YC,WC,$] 248/358-9844 ■ 415 E Congress (next to St Andrews Hall) ■ 9pm-4am Sat, 5 levels ■ backstdet@aol.com

20 **Club 450** [MW,D,18+] 734/727-0000 ■ 450 S Merriman, Westland ■ 8pm-2am Th-Sun

22 **Cobalt** [★M,D,S,WC,GO] 248/591-0106 ■ 22061 Woodward Ave, Ferndale ■ 9pm-2am, clsd Mon-Tue, T-dance Sun ■ www.clubcobalt.net

4 **Diamond Jim's Saloon** [MW,NH,D,CW,F] 313/336-8680 ■ 19650 Warren (E of Evergreen) ■ 6pm-2am, dance lessons ■ diamondjimsaloon@aol.com

23 **Numbers** [M,D,MR,F,V,YC] 313/868-9145, 313/869-9524 ■ 17518 Woodward (at McNichols) ■ 10pm-4am, clsd Mon

24 **Off Broadway East** [M,D,MR,YC] 313/521-0920 ■ 12215 Harper St (at Dickerson) ■ 9pm-2am, Wed & Sat popular

25 **One-X** [M,D,MR,18+.YC,WC] 313/964-0580 ■ 2575 Michigan Ave (at 17th) ■ 10pm-2am, clsd Tue, 'Strongarm Sat' hosts 'the largest Black Gay dance party in Midwest' ■ www.onexdetroit.com

26 **The Rainbow Room** [MW,D,S] 313/891-1020 ■ 6640 E 8-Mile Rd (at Mound) ■ 7pm-2am Wed-Sat, from 5pm Sun ■ www.rainbowpet.com/rainbowroom

Stiletto's [W,D,S] 734/729-8980 ■ 1641 Middlebelt Rd (at Michigan Ave), Inkster ■ 8pm-2am, clsd Mon

27 **Temple** [M,D,MR-AF,WC] 313/832-2822 ■ 2906 Cass Ave (btwn Charlotte & Temple) ■ noon-2am, popular wknds ■ thetemplebar@aol.com

28 **Times Square** [GS,D,$] 313/961-0232 ■ 1431 Times Square (at Grand River Ave) ■ 10pm-close Fri-Sat only ■ www.timessquaredetroit.com

29 **Zippers** [★MW,D,MR-AF,S,WC] 313/892-8120 ■ 6221 E Davison ■ 9pm-2am Th-Sat, more women Sat

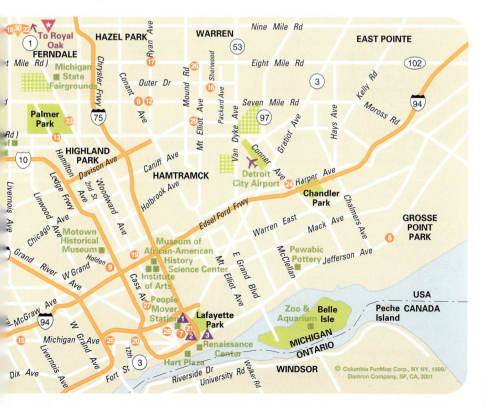

MICHIGAN • USA

CAFES
Avalon Bakery 313/832-0008 ■ 422 W Willis (at Cass) ■ 6am-6pm, clsd Sun-Mon, lesbian-owned/ run

RESTAURANTS
Como's [WC] 248/548-5005 ■ 22812 Woodward (at 9-Mile), Ferndale ■ 11am-2am, till 3:30am Fri-Sat, from 2pm wknds, Italian, full bar ■ www.comospizza.com

La Dolce Vita [MW,WC] 313/865-0331 ■ 17546 Woodward Ave (at McNichols) ■ dinner, Sun brunch, clsd Mon-Tue, Italian, patio, full bar

Pronto 248/544-7200 ■ 608 S Washington (at 6th), Royal Oak ■ 11am-10pm, till midnight Fri-Sat, from 9am wknds

Rhinoceros [E] 313/259-2208 ■ 265 Riopelle (off Jefferson) ■ 5pm-2am, jazz club, full bar

Sweet Lorraines [WC] 248/559-5985 ■ 29101 Greenfield Rd (at 12-Mile), Southfield ■ 11am-10pm, till midnight Fri-Sat, modern American

Twingo's [GS,GO] 313/832-3832 ■ 4710 Cass Ave ■ 11am-11pm, till 2am Th-Sat, till 8pm Sun, nouvelle French, full bar, live jazz Fri-Sat

Vivio's 313/393-1711 ■ 2460 Market St (btwn Gratiot & Russell) ■ lunch & dinner, clsd Sun, Italian, some veggie

ENTERTAINMENT & RECREATION
Detroit Women's Coffeehouse [F,E,S] 313/833-9107 ■ 4605 Cass Ave (at 1st Unitarian Church) ■ 2nd Sat, except in August ■ www.angelfire.com/mi2/detwomcof/

BOOKSTORES
30 **A Woman's Prerogative Bookstore** [WC] 248/545-5703 ■ 175 W 9-Mile Rd (at Woodward), Ferndale ■ noon-7pm, till 9pm Th, till 5pm Sat & till 4pm Sun, lesbian, some gay men's titles ■ lesbobook@aol.com

Chosen Books [WC] 248/543-5758 ■ 120 W 4th St (btwn Main St & Woodward), Royal Oak ■ noon-10pm, lgbt

30 **Just 4 Us** 248/547-5878 ■ 211 W 9-Mile Rd (at Woodward), Ferndale ■ noon-8pm, clsd Sun, also espresso bar ■ just4usmi@aol.com

RETAIL SHOPS
The Dressing Room 810/286-0412 ■ 42310 Hayes, Clinton Township ■ 1pm-8pm, noon-5pm Sat, clsd Sun, cross-dressing boutique ■ www.mslisasdressingroom.com

PUBLICATIONS
Between the Lines 248/615-7003, 888/615-7003 ■ statewide lgbt weekly ■ www.pridesource.com

Cruise Magazine 248/545-9040 ■ statewide gay entertainment listings ■ www.cruisemagazineonline.com

Metra 248/543-3500 ■ covers IN, IL, MI, OH, PA, WI & Ontario, Canada ■ www.metramagazine.com

Out Post 313/702-0272 ■ bi-weekly newspaper for metro Detroit ■ opost@aol.com

MEN'S CLUBS
Body Zone [★V,PC] 313/366-9663 ■ 1617 E McNichols (at I-75) ■ 24hrs, gym, steam, sauna & tanning, $7 day pass

EROTICA
24hr Video 313/869-2955 ■ 17438 Woodward Ave (N of McNichols Rd) ■ 11am-4am

Escape Adult Bookstore 313/336-6558 ■ 18740 W Warren (8 blks W of Southfield)

Fifth Wheel Adult Books 313/846-8613 ■ 9320 Michigan Ave (at Wyoming)

Noir Leather [WC] 248/541-3979 ■ 124 W 4th (at Center), Royal Oak

Uptown Book Store 313/869-9477 ■ 16541 Woodward Ave

Saugatuck

ACCOMMODATIONS
Campit Campground [MW,GO] 616/543-4335, 877/226-7481 ■ seasonal, campsites & RV hookups, also B&B ■ www.saugatuckweekends.com

Deerpath Lodge [WO,SW] 888/DEER-PATH, 616/857-DEER ■ on 45 secluded acres, full brkfst, hot tub, kayaks

1 **Douglas House B&B** [GS,GO] 616/857-1119, 313/922-4220 ■ 41 Spring St, Douglas ■ nr gay beach

3 **Driftwood Cottages** [W,GO] 616/857-2586 ■ 2731 Lakeshore Dr, Fennville ■ short drive to Saugatuck, kitchenettes

2 **The Dunes Resort** [MW,D,TG,F,E,S,SW,WC,GO] 616/857-1401 ■ 333 Blue Star Hwy, Douglas ■ motel & cottages, swimming, open year-round ■ www.dunesresort.com

Hillby Thatch Cottages [GF] 847/864-3553 ■ 71st St, Glenn ■ 15 mins from Saugatuck ■ www.hillbythatch.com

4 **Kirby House** [GF,SW,NS,GO] 616/857-2904, 800/521-6473 ■ 294 W Center (at Blue Star Hwy) ■ Queen Anne Victorian ■ www.kirbyhouse.com

The Lighthouse Motel [GS,SW,WC,GO] 616/857-2271 ■ Douglas

5 **Moore's Creek Inn** [GS,NS,GO] 616/857-2411, 800/838-5864 ■ 820 Holland St (at Lucy) ■ old-fashioned farmhouse ■ cimarron.net/usa/mi/moore.html

6 **The Newnham SunCatcher Inn** [GF,SW] 616/857-4249 ■ 131 Griffith (at Mason) ■ full brkfst, hot tub, lesbian-owned/ run ■ www.bbonline.com/mi/suncatcher

The Spruce Cutter's Cottage [GS,GO] 616/543-4285, 800/493-5888 ■ 6670 126th Ave (at Blue Star Hwy & M-89), Fennville ■ full brkfst ■ sprucecutters@teleweb.net

Sturdy Girls B&B [MW,GO] 616/543-4335, 877/226-7481 ■ full access to Campit Campground amenities (see listing) ■ www.saugatuckweekends.com

SAUGATUCK

Saugatuck is a quaint resort town on the shores of Lake Michigan. The main tourists sites are its beaches, dunes and orchards. The historic city of Holland, home of the Wooden Shoe Factory, is also nearby.

Tourist Info

AIRPORT DIRECTIONS
Kent County Airport in Grand Rapids, Michigan.

PUBLIC TRANSIT & TAXIS
Interurban bus service 616/857-1418.

TOURIST SPOTS & INFO
Red Barn Playhouse.
Saugatuck Dunes State Park.
Visitor's Center: Saugatuck-Douglas Convention & Visitors Bureau 616/857-1701, web: www.saugatuck.com.

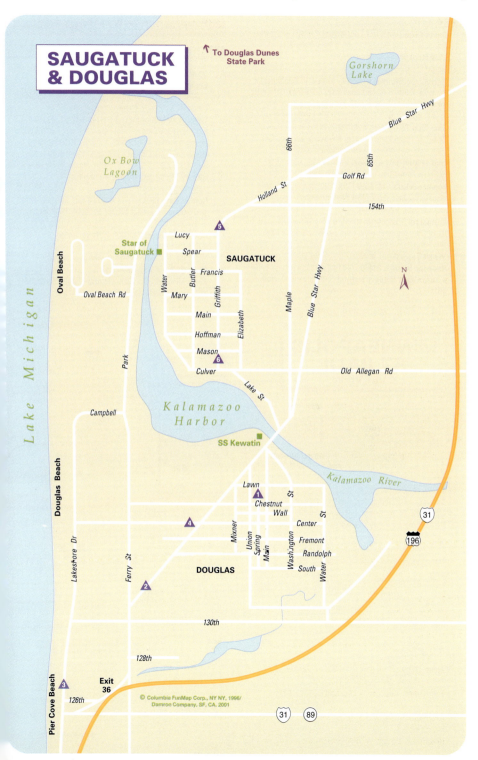

MICHIGAN / MINNESOTA • USA

BARS
2 **Dunes Disco** [MW,D,TG,E,S,GO] 616/857-1401 ▪ 333 Blue Star Hwy (at the 'Dunes Resort') ▪ 9am-2am, 3 bars, cabaret, patio ▪ www.dunesresort.com

CAFES
Uncommon Grounds 616/857-3333 ▪ 127 Hoffman (at Water) ▪ 7:30am-10pm, open later on wknds, coffee & juice bar

RESTAURANTS
Blue Frog To Go [MW] 616/857-5711 ▪ in the 'Dunes Resort' ▪ 11am-7pm, till 9pm Fri-Sat, open May-Oct only, take-out only ▪ www.dunesresort.com

Loaf & Mug [BW] 616/857-2974 ▪ 236 Culver St (at Butler) ▪ 8am-3pm, clsd Tue, some veggie

Pumpernickel's 616/857-1196 ▪ 202 Butler St (at Mason) ▪ seasonal, 8am-3pm (clsd Wed in winter), sandwiches & fresh breads, some veggie

Restaurant Toulouse [WC] 616/857-1561 ▪ 248 Culver St (at Griffith) ▪ dinner only, country French, some veggie, full bar

RETAIL SHOPS
Hoopdee Scootee 616/857-4141 ▪ 133 Mason (at Butler) ▪ 10am-9pm, till 6pm Sun (till 5pm in winter), clothing, gifts

MINNESOTA

Minneapolis / St Paul

ACCOMMODATIONS
Country Guest House [MW] 715/247-3520, 888/893-9991 ▪ 1673 38th St, Somerset, WI ▪ secluded romantic get-away, lesbian-owned/ run

Cover Park Manor [GF,WC] 651/430-9292, 877/430-9292 ▪ 15330 58th St N (at Peller), Stillwater ▪ full brkfst, in-room jacuzzi & fireplace ▪ www.coverpark.com

Eagle Cove B&B [GF,WC] 715/448-4302, 800/467-0279 ▪ W 4387 120th Ave (at 452nd St), Maiden Rock, WI ▪ country retreat, expanded cont'l brkfst ▪ eglcove@cannon.net

1 **Garden Gate B&B** [GF] 612/227-8430, 800/967-2703 ▪ 925 Goodrich Ave (at Milton), St Paul ▪ 1907 Victorian, massage available

2 ▶ **Hotel Amsterdam** [MW,GO] 612/288-0459, 800/649-9500 ▪ 828 Hennepin Ave (btwn 8th & 9th), Minneapolis ▪ shared baths ▪ www.gaympls.com

3 **Nan's B&B** [GF] 612/377-5118 ▪ 2304 Fremont Ave S (at 22nd), Minneapolis ▪ 1895 Victorian family home, full brkfst ▪ www.virtualcities.com/mn/nan/htm

4 **Regal Minneapolis Hotel** [GF,F,SW,WC] 612/332-6000, 800/522-8856 ■ 1313 Nicollet Mall (btwn W Grant & 13th St), Minneapolis ■ www.milennium-hotels.com

BARS

5 **19 Bar** [M,NH,BW,WC] 612/871-5553 ■ 19 W 15th St (at La Salle), Minneapolis ■ 3pm-1am, from 1pm wknds

6 **Bev's Wine Bar** [GF] 612/337-0102 ■ 250 3rd Ave N (at Washington Ave), Minneapolis ■ 4:30pm-1am, from 6pm Sat, clsd Sun-Mon, light food menu, patio

7 **Boom** [M,F,V,GO] 612/378-3188 ■ 401 E Hennepin Ave (at 4th), Minneapolis ■ 4pm-1am, from noon wknds, clsd Mon-Tue, also 'Oddfellows' restaurant, dinner nightly

8 **Brass Rail** [★M,S,V,WC] 612/333-3016 ■ 422 Hennepin Ave (at 4th), Minneapolis ■ noon-1am, from 11am Sun, dancers Th-Sat ■ www.gaympls.com

9 **Bryant Lake Bowl** [GF,A,F,E,WC] 612/825-3737 ■ 1810 W Lake St (at corner of Bryant), Minneapolis ■ 8am-1am, bar, theater, restaurant & bowling alley

10 **Minneapolis Eagle** [M,L,F] 612/338-4214 ■ 515 Washington Ave S (btwn Portland & 5th Ave), Minneapolis ■ 11am-1am, from noon wknds, patio, dress code enforced from 9pm Fri-Sat ■ www.minneapoliseagle.com

11 **Over the Rainbow** [MW,D,F,K,S,GO] 651/487-5070 ■ 719 N Dale St (at Minnehaha), St Paul ■ 11am-1am ■ www.overthebow.com

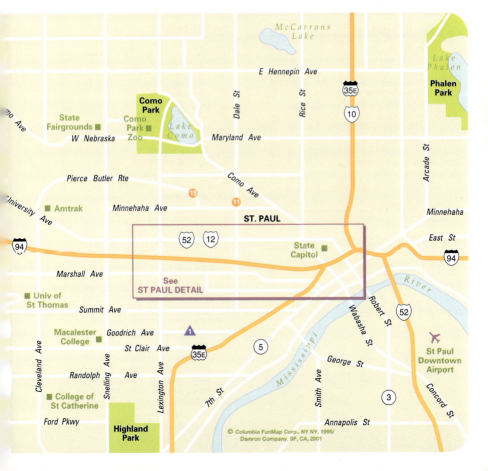

MINNESOTA • USA

12 **The Saloon** [★M,D,F,K,WC,GO] 612/332-0835 ■ 830 Hennepin Ave (at 9th), Minneapolis ■ 8am-1am, till 3am Fri-Sun, from 10am Sun, Latin Tue, also 'The Tank' (L,V) Wed & Sun from 9pm ■ www.gaympls.com

13 **The Town House** [★MW,D,E] 651/646-7087 ■ 1415 University Ave (at Elbert), St Paul ■ 3pm-1am, from noon wknds, theme nights, also 'Blanche's Cabaret' piano bar from 8pm Tue-Sat ■ www.townhousebar.com

14 **Trikkx** [M,D,F,S,WC] 651/224-0703 ■ 490 N Robert St (at 9th St), St Paul ■ 4pm-1am, noon-2am wknds, Latin 3rd Wed, male dancers Fri-Sat, also restaurant ■ www.trikkx.com

NIGHTCLUBS

15 **Club Metro** [★MW,D,TG,F,E,K,WC,$] 651/489-0002 ■ 733 Pierce Butler Rte (at Minnehaha), St Paul ■ 4pm-1am, 3pm-3am Fri-Sat, from 2pm Sun, patio

8 **Gay 90s** [★MW,D,MR,E,K,WC] 612/333-7755 ■ 408 Hennepin Ave (at 4th), Minneapolis ■ 8am-1am (dinner 5pm-9pm nightly), 8-bar complex, also 'Men's Room (MO,L) ■ www.gay90s.com

16 **Ground Zero/ The Front** [★GS,D,S,WC] 612/378-5115, 612/857-1012 ■ 15 NE 4th St (at Hennepin), Minneapolis ■ pm-1am, clsd Sun-Tue, 'Bondage a Go Go' Th, more gay Sat for 'Creation', also 'The Front' from 8pm

MINNEAPOLIS/ST PAUL

The 'Twin Cities' of Minneapolis and St Paul are a liberal oasis in the northern midwest. Located on the banks of the Mississippi River, the cities share 936 lakes, 513 parks, and a history of Native American and Northern European settlements. If you want more than glimpses into the various cultures of Minnesota, visit the Minneapolis American Indian Center or the American Swedish Institute.

Whatever you do, don't stay indoors the whole time. In the summer, boating, fishing, sunbathing, water-skiing, walking, jogging, and bicycling are all popular. With winter, you can enjoy snowmobiling, ice hockey, cross-country skiing or snuggling by a fire.

Queer Resources

COMMUNITY INFO
Gay/Lesbian Infoline 612/822-0127 or 800/800-0350, info line.
Chrysalis Women's Center 612/871-0118. 2650 Nicollet Ave, Minneapolis. 9am-9pm, till 5pm Fri, till 1pm Sat, clsd Sun.
Quatrefoil Library, Lesbigay Library & Resource Center 651/641-0969. 1619 Dayton Ave, St Paul.

AIDS RESOURCES
Minnesota AIDS Project 612/341-2060, web: www.mnaidsproject.org.

RECOVERY
AA Intergroup 612/922-0880.

City Calendar

LGBT PRIDE
July. 952/996-9250.

ANNUAL EVENTS
September - Gay Night at Knott's Camp Snoopy in Mall of America.

Tourist Info

AIRPORT DIRECTIONS
Minneapolis/St Paul International. To get to downtown Minneapolis, get on I-494W to I-35W North. Follow I-35W until you come to the downtown exits.
To get to the State Capitol in St Paul, take I-494E to I-35E North. Follow I-35E to the Kellogg Blvd exit. Take Kellogg Blvd to W 7th St and turn left. Follow W 7th to 8th St and Robert, turn left and follow to University Ave. Turn left on University.

PUBLIC TRANSIT & TAXIS
Town Taxi (Minn) 612/331-8294.
Yellow Cab (St Paul) 651/222-4433.
Airport Express 612/827-7777.
MTC 612/349-7000.

TOURIST SPOTS & INFO
Mall of America (the largest mall in the US w/indoor theme park) 952/883-8800.
Minneapolis Institute of Arts 612/870-3131.
Museum of Questionable Medical Devices 612/379-4046.
Walker Art Center/Minneapolis Sculpture Garden 612/375-7622.
Frederick R Weisman Art Museum 612/625-9494.
Visitor's Center: 800/445-7412, web: www.minneapolis.org.

WEATHER
Winters are harsh. If driving, carry extra blankets and supplies. The average temperature is 19°, and it can easily drop well below 0°, and then there's the wind chill! Summer temperatures are usually in the upper-80°s to mid-90°s and HUMID.

BEST VIEWS
Observation deck of the 32nd story of Foshay Tower (closed in winter).

Minneapolis/ St Paul • MINNESOTA

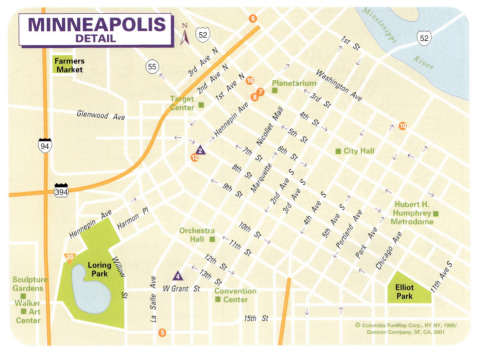

17 **Lucy's** [MW,D,K,S,GO] 651/228-9959 ■ 601 N Western Ave (at Thomas Ave), St Paul ■ 3pm-1am, from noon wknds, CW Th, go-go boys Fri

18 **Margarita Bella** [GS,MR-L,D,F] 612/331-7955 ■ 1032 3rd Ave NE (at Central), Minneapolis ■ 9pm-1am, more gay Wed, also restaurant 11am-9pm

CAFES

Anodyne at 43rd [E,WC] 612/824-4300 ■ 4301 Nicollet Ave (at 43rd), Minneapolis ■ 6:30am-10pm, from 7am Sat, from 8am Sun, till midnight wknds

Cafe Wyrd [MW] 612/827-5710 ■ 1600 W Lake St (at Irving), Minneapolis ■ 7am-1am

Cahoots 651/644-6778 ■ 1562 Selby Ave (at Snelling), St Paul ■ 7am-9:30pm, 7:30am-11pm wknds, coffee bar

Moose & Sadie's 612/371-0464 ■ 212 3rd Ave N (at 2nd St), Minneapolis ■ 7:30am-11pm, till 1:30am wknds, 9am-10pm Sun, warehouse district cafe

Ruby's Cafe [★MW] 612/338-2089 ■ 1614 Harmon Pl (at Loring Park), Minneapolis ■ 7am-2pm, from 10am Th-Sat, from 8am Sun, outdoor seating

Uncommon Grounds [GS] 612/872-4811 ■ 2809 Hennepin Ave (at 28th Ave), Minneapolis ■ 10am-1am, outdoor seating

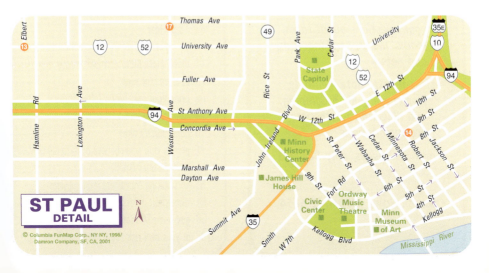

MINNESOTA • USA

It's like a thousand brochures!

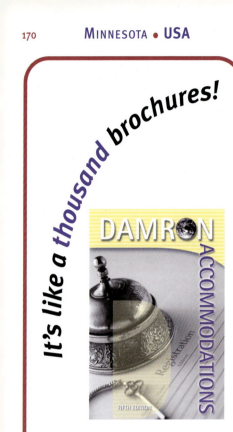

- full-color photographs speak louder than words
- over 1800 international listings cover gay-friendly hotels, B&Bs, and accommodations across the globe!
- detailed listings answer all your questions about rates, rooms, meals, smoking, kids, and pets
- cross-indexes note Men-only, Women-only, RV & Camping, and Wheelchair-accessible accommodations
- over 550 pages, only $22.95!

➤ ORDER NOW: (800) 462-6654

Damron Codes

➤	advertiser
★	popular
MO	men only
GF	gay-friendly (mostly straight)
GS	gay/straight (evenly mixed)
MW	lesbians/gay men
M	mostly men
W	mostly women (listing names in this color)
WO	women only (listing names in this color)
NH	neighborhood bar
D	live DJ & dancing
A	alternative (grunge babes, goths)
B	bears
CW	country western (music, dancing and/or dress)
L	leather, fetish (often a dress code)
P	professional crowd
MRC	multiracial clientele
MR-AF	African-American clientele
MR-A	Asian clientele
MR-L	Latino/a clientele
TG	transgender-friendly
F	hot food served
E	live entertainment (piano, bands, comedy)
K	karaoke
S	shows (drag, strip, or cabaret)
V	videos
18+	18 & older
YC	young crowd (mostly 20-somethings)
OC	older/more mature crowd (mostly over 40)
BW	beer and/or wine
BYOB	bring your own bottle (often "private" clubs)
SW	swimming onsite (usually a pool)
N	public nudity okay
PC	private club (membership open to out-of-towners; often BYOB)
NS	no smoking (anywhere inside business)
WC	wheelchair access (includes bathrooms)
GO	gay-owned/ operated
AYOR	at your own risk (beware of bashers or cops)

Minneapolis/ St Paul • Minnesota

The Urban Bean [E] 612/824-6611 ■ 3255 Bryant Ave S (at 33rd), Minneapolis ■ 7am-11pm, patio

Restaurants

Al's Breakfast [★] 612/331-9991 ■ 413 14th Ave SE (at 4th), Minneapolis ■ 6am-1pm, from 9am Sun, great hash

Bobino Cafe & Wine Bar 612/623-3301 ■ 222 E Hennepin Ave, Minneapolis ■ lunch Mon-Fri, dinner nightly, classic bistro

Campiello 612/825-2222 ■ 1320 W Lake St (at Hennepin), Minneapolis ■ dinner & Sun brunch, Italian

D'Amico Cucina [E] 612/338-2401 ■ 100 N 6th St (btwn 1st & 2nd Aves), Minneapolis ■ dinner nightly, a la carte, full bar

Goodfellows 612/332-4800 ■ 40 S 7th (at Hennepin), Minneapolis ■ lunch & dinner, clsd Sun, full bar, upscale American

King & I Thai 612/332-6928 ■ 1346 LaSalle Ave (at W Grant) ■ 11am-1am, from 5pm Sat, clsd Sun, full bar, plenty veggie ■ kingandithai.citysearch.com

La Covina Café [WC] 651/645-5288 ■ 1570 Selby Ave (at Snelling), St Paul ■ lunch & dinner, Mexican

Mud Pie Vegetarian Restaurant [BW] 612/872-9435 ■ 2549 Lyndale Ave S (at 25th St W), Minneapolis ■ 11am-10:30pm, till 11:30pm Fri-Sat, from 10am wknds, patio

Murray's 612/339-0909 ■ 26 S 6th St (at Hennepin), Minneapolis ■ lunch Mon-Fri, dinner nightly, steak & potatoes

Palomino Euro Bistro 612/339-3800 ■ 825 Hennepin Ave (at 9th St), Minneapolis ■ 11am-1am, 5pm-12:30am Sun, Italian/ Mediterranean

Rudolph's Bar-B-Que [WC] 612/871-8969 ■ 1933 Lyndale (at Franklin), Minneapolis ■ 11am-midnight, full bar

Entertainment & Recreation

32nd St Beach E side of Lake Calhoun (33rd & Calhoun Blvd), Minneapolis ■ gay beach

Fresh Fruit 612/341-0980 ■ KFAI 90.3 FM, Minneapolis ■ 7:30pm-8:30pm Th, gay radio program, also a variety of lgbt programs 9pm-midnight Sun

Twin Lake Beach [N] in Wirth Park (33rd & Calhoun Blvd), Minneapolis ■ hard to find, inquire locally

Vulva Riot [W,TG,NS] 612/375-7657 ■ 2822 Lyndale Ave S (at 28th), Minneapolis ■ 7pm 1st Sat, women's art & performance ■ www.mtn.org/vulvariot

Bookstores

19 A Brother's Touch [WC] 612/377-6279 ■ 2327 Hennepin Ave (at 24th), Minneapolis ■ 11am-7pm, till 6pm Sat, noon 5pm Sun, lgbt ■ www.brotherstouch.com

20 Amazon Bookstore Co-operative [WC] 612/821-9630 ■ 4432 Chicago Ave S, Minneapolis ■ 8am-9pm, from 9am Sat, from 10am Sun, till 6pm wknds, feminist bookstore since 1970 (no relation to Seattle's amazon.com), women-owned/ run, open mic Fri, also cafe ■ www.amazonbookstorecoop.com

Magus Books, Ltd 612/379-7669, 800/996-2387 ■ 1316 SE 4th St (at 13th/ 14th), Minneapolis ■ 10am-9pm, till 6pm wknds, from noon Sun, alternative spirituality books & supplies, also mail order ■ www.magusbooks.com

Retail Shops

The Rainbow Road [WC] 612/872-8448 ■ 109 W Grant (at LaSalle), Minneapolis ■ 10am-10pm, lgbt retail & video

Publications

Lavender Magazine 612/871-2237, 877/515-9969 ■ lgbt newsmagazine ■ www.lavendermagazine.com

Minnesota Women's Press 651/646-3968 ■ 771 Raymond Ave, St Paul ■ 9am-6pm, till 3pm Sat, clsd Sun, newspaper, also bookshop & library ■ www.womenspress.com

Gyms & Health Clubs

Body Quest [MW] 612/377-7222 ■ 245 Aldrich Ave N (at Glenwood), Minneapolis

Erotica

Denmark Books 651/222-2928 ■ 459 W 7th St, St Paul

Fantasy House [WC] 612/824-2459 ■ 709 W Lake (at Lyndale), Minneapolis ■ adult gifts

Fit 2 A T Leather 651/487-0513 ■ 733 Pierce Butler Route (in 'Club Metro'), St Paul ■ Th-Sat evenings

Lickety Split 612/333-0599 ■ 251 3rd Ave S, Minneapolis

Triangle @ SexWorld 612/317-1086 ■ 241 2nd Ave N, 3rd Fl (at Washington), Minneapolis ■ 24hrs
■ www.sexworld.com

Kansas City

Kansas City is famous for barbecue, baseball, and the blues. But visitors will find many other attractions, like the Nelson-Atkins Museum of Art (816/751-1278) and the Black Archives of Mid-America (816/483-1300).

Queer Resources

Community Info
Gay/Lesbian Community Center 816/374-5945. 1615 W 39th St (2nd flr of 'Supreme Bean' coffeehouse), 7pm-9pm Fri.
Gay/Lesbian Info Hotline 816/753-0700, web: www.currentnews.com.

AIDS Resources
Hotline 816/471-1186.

Recovery
AA Central Office 816/471-7229.
Live & Let Live AA 816/531-9668.

City Calendar

LGBT Pride
June. 816/420-0100, web: www.prideproductions.org.

Tourist Info

Airport Directions
Kansas City International. To get downtown, take I-29 approximately 20 miles south.

Public Transit & Taxis
Yellow Cab 816/471-5000.
KCI Shuttle 800/243-6383.
Metro 816/221-0660.

Tourist Spots & Info
Historic 18th & Vine District (includes Kansas City Jazz Museum & the Negro Leagues Baseball Museum).
Nelson-Atkins Museum of Art 816/561-4000.
Thomas Hart Benton Home & Studio 816/931-5722.
Harry S Truman Nat'l Historical Site (in Independence, MO) 816/254-2720.
Visitor's Center: Convention & Visitors Bureau 816/691-3800.

MISSOURI

Kansas City

Accommodations
B&B in KC [W,NS,GO] 913/648-5457 ■ 9215 Slater, Overland Park, KS ■ full brkfst ■ m8fish@aol.com
1   LaFontaine Inn 816/753-4434, 888/832-6000 ■ 4320 Oak St ■ www.lafontainebb.com
2   Southmoreland on the Plaza [GF,NS] 816/531-7979 ■ 116 E 46th St ■ 1913 B&B, full brkfst, hot tub, sundeck ■ www.southmoreland.com
    Su Casa B&B [GF,SW,NS] 816/965-5647 ■ 9004 E 92nd St ■ Southwest style home, full brkfst wknds ■ www.sucasabb.com

Bars
3   Balanca's [MW,NH] 816/221-9220 ■ 1007 Grand Ave (at 11th) ■ 4pm-1:30am, clsd Sun
4   Buddies [M,NH] 816/561-2600 ■ 3715 Main St (at 37th) ■ 6am-3am, clsd Sun
    Club Evos [MW,D,F,S,18+] 913/321-6100, 816/753-0700 ■ 47 Central Ave (at James), KS ■ 9pm-2am, also restaurant from 10am
5   Dixie Belle Complexx [★M,D,B,L,F,WC] 816/471-1575 ■ 1915 Main St (at 20th) ■ 11am-3am, 5 bars, also leather shop & bar ■ www.dixiebelle.net
6   Missie B's [M,NH,D,TG,S,K] 816/561-0625 ■ 805 W 39th St (at Southwest Trafficway) ■ 6am-3am, clsd Sun ■ www.missiebs.com
7   The Other Side [M,NH,E,V,WC] 816/931-0501 ■ 3611 Broadway (at 36th/ Valentine) ■ 4:30pm-1:30am, clsd Sun, piano bar wknds
8   Sidekicks [MW,D,CW,S,WC] 816/931-1430 ■ 3707 Main St (at 37th) ■ 2pm-3am, clsd Sun
9   Soakie's [MW,D,MR,F,S,WC] 816/221-6060 ■ 1308 Main St (at 13th) ■ 9am-1:30am, till 3am Fri-Sat, from 11am Sun
10 Tootsie's [W,D,F,S,WC] 816/471-7704 ■ 1822 Main (at 18th) ■ noon-3am wknds, clsd Mon
11 Wetherbee's [W,D,F,K,S,WC] 816/454-2455 ■ 2510 NE Vivian Rd (at Antioch) ■ 6pm-3am ■ www.kcbar.com

Nightclubs
12 Club Cabaret [M,D,F,S,YC,WC] 816/753-6504 ■ 5024 Main St (at 51st) ■ 6pm-3am, from 3pm Sun, clsd Mon-Tue
13 The Hurricane [GF,D,E] 816/753-0884 ■ 4048 Broadway (at Westport Rd) ■ 3pm-3am, live bands
14 XO [GS,D,K] 816/753-0112 ■ 3954 Central (btwn Westport & Broadway) ■ 9pm-3am, gay Th only ■ www.kcclubs.com

Cafes
Broadway Cafe 816/531-2432 ■ 4106 Broadway Blvd (at Westport) ■ 7am-midnight, from 8:30am wknds
Muddy's [BW,WC] 816/756-1997 ■ 1719 W 39th St (at Bell) ■ 7am-midnight, 8am-6pm Sun
Planet Cafe [★GO,E] 816/561-7287 ■ 3535 Broadway Blvd (at 35th) ■ 7am-11pm, till midnight Fri-Sat, from 10am wknds

Restaurants
Classic Cup Cafe [WC] 816/753-1840 ■ 301 W 47th St (at Central) ■ 7am-10pm
The Corner Restaurant [WC] 816/931-6630 ■ 4059 Broadway (at Main) ■ 7am-3pm daily & 5pm-8pm Mon-Fri
Metropolis [★MW,F,WC] 816/753-1550 ■ 303 Westport Rd (at Central) ■ dinner only, clsd Sun-Mon

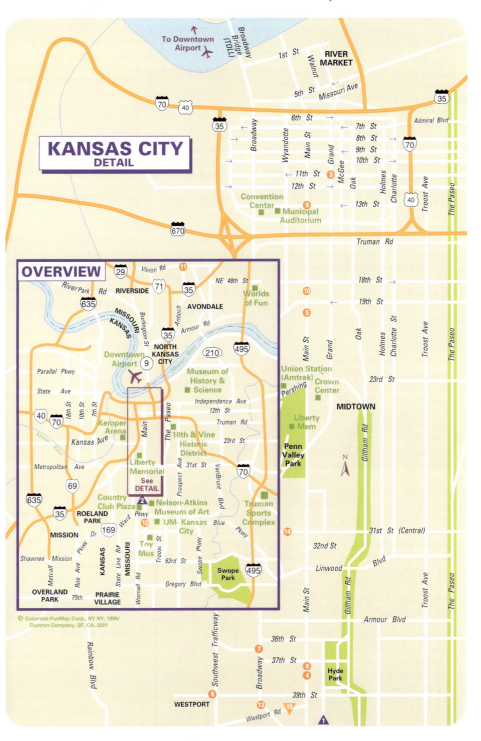

MISSOURI • USA

Otto's Malt Shop 816/756-1010 ■ 3903 Wyoming (at 39th) ■ 11am-10pm, till midnight wknds

Sharp's 63rd St Grill [BW,WC] 816/333-4355 ■ 128 W 63rd St ■ 7am-10pm, till 11pm Fri-Sat, from 8am Sat, from 9am Sun

Strouds 816/333-2132 ■ 1014 E 85th St (btwn Troost & Holmes) ■ 4pm-10pm, lunch Fri-Sun, fried chicken

ENTERTAINMENT & RECREATION

Heartland Men's Chorus 816/931-3338 ■ www.hmckc.org

Unicorn Theatre 816/531-3033 ■ 3820 Main ■ contemporary American theater

RETAIL SHOPS

15 Larry's Gifts & Cards 816/753-4757 ■ 205 Westport Rd (btwn Main & Broadway) ■ 10am-7pm, till 6:30pm Sat, till 5pm Sun, lgbt

Lion's Den 816/523-5070 ■ 7719 Wornall ■ tattoos & piercing

PUBLICATIONS

CN Magazine 816/561-2679 ■ www.CurrentNews.com

EXP 816/753-4242, 877/397-6244 ■ bi-monthly gay magazine for MO, IL & KS ■ www.expmag.com

The Liberty Press Kansas City 816/931-3060 ■ lgbt newspaper serving Kansas City ■ www.libertypress.net

MEN'S CLUBS

Hydes KC 816/561-1010 ■ hrs vary, call for location

EROTICA

Erotic City 816/252-3370 ■ 8401 E Truman Rd (at I-435) ■ 24hrs, arcade

Hollywood at Home 913/649-9666 ■ 9063 Metcalf (at 91st), Overland Park, KS

Ray's Video & Newsstand 816/753-7692 ■ 3324 Main St (at 34th) ■ 24hrs

St Louis

ACCOMMODATIONS

1 ➤ A St Louis Guesthouse [M,N,NS] 314/773-1016 ■ 1032-38 Allen Ave (at Menard) ■ in historic Soulard district, hot tub ■ stlouisgh@aol.com

2 Brewers House B&B [MW,GO] 314/771-1542, 888/767-4665 ■ 1829 Lami St (at Lemp) ■ 1860s home, jacuzzi ■ brewerhse@aol.com

3 Lafayette House B&B [GF] 314/772-4429, 800/641-8965 ■ 2156 Lafayette Ave (at Jefferson) ■ Queen Anne Victorian, full brkfst, hot tub, lesbian-owned/ run ■ www.bbonline.com/mo/lafayette/

MotherSource Travels [W,GO] 314/973-1890, 618/462-4051 ■ 187 W 19th St, Alton, IL ■ reservation service ■ www.mothersourcesolutions.com

4 Napoleon's Retreat B&B [GS,NS,GO] 314/772-6979, 800/700-9980 ■ 1815 Lafayette Ave (at Mississippi) ■ restored 1880s townhouse, full brkfst ■ www.napoleansretreat.com

5 Two Boys Inn B&B [MW,GO] 314/773-6700 ■ 2712 S Compton Ave (at Magnolia) ■ full brkfst ■ www.twoboysinn.com

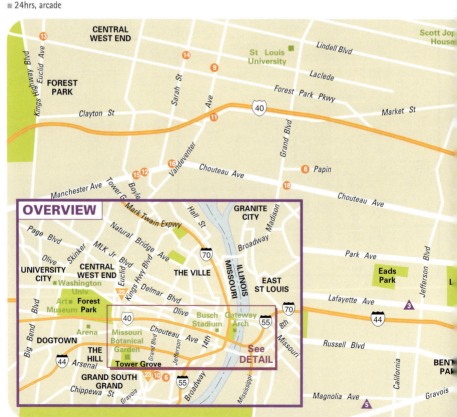

St Louis • Missouri

Bars

6 Alibi's [M,TG,S,F,WC] 314/772-8989 ▪ 3016 Arsenal (at Minnesota) ▪ 1pm-3am, also dinner & Sun brunch, patio

7 Clementine's [★M,L,F,WC] 314/664-7869 ▪ 2001 Menard (at Allen) ▪ 10am-1:30am, from 8:30am Sat, 11am-midnight Sun, patio

Club Escapades [MW,D,K,S] 618/222-9597 ▪ 113 W Main St, Belleville, IL ▪ 5pm-2am

8 The Drake Bar [MW,E,WC] 314/865-1400 ▪ 3502 Papin St (at Theresa, 1 blk NE of Grand & Chouteau) ▪ 4pm-1:30am, clsd Sun, piano bar, patio ▪ www.thedrakebar.com

9 Eagle in Exile [M,NH,B,L] 314/652-0171 ▪ 17 S Vandeventer (at Forest Park Pkwy) ▪ 6pm-1:30am, clsd Sun ▪ www.magsbar.com/eagle.htm

10 Grey Fox Pub/ Spanky's Restaurant [MW,NH,TG,F,S] 314/772-2150 ▪ 3501 S Spring (at Potomac) ▪ 11am-1:30am, from 9am Sat, clsd Sun, patio

Inside Out [MW,F,S,V] 618/797-0700 ▪ 3145 W Chain of Rocks Rd, Granite City, IL ▪ 8pm-2am Th-Fri, till 3am Sat, from 2pm Sun ▪ www.insideout000.homestead.com

11 JJ's Clubhouse & Bar [M,NH,B,L,F,WC] 314/535-4100 ▪ 3858 Market St (at Vandeventer) ▪ 4pm-1:30am, clsd Sun, bear/ levi/ leather bar

12 Knightz Too [MW,NH,F,K,S,V] 314/531-5850 ▪ 4112-14 Manchester Ave ▪ 4pm-1:30am, clsd Mon, video bar, karaoke Wed-Th

13 Loading Zone [★MW,V,WC] 314/361-4119 ▪ 16 S Euclid (at Forest Park Pkwy) ▪ 2pm-1:30am, clsd Sun

14 Nero Bianco [M,D,MR-AF,WC] 314/531-4123 ▪ 6 S Sarah (btwn Laclede & Forest Park) ▪ 4pm-1am, clsd Sun, jazz Fri ▪ nero4me@cs.com

15 Novak's Bar & Grill [MW,E,K,S,WC] 314/531-3699 ▪ 4146 Manchester ▪ 4pm-1:30am, patio ▪ www.novaksbar.com

16 Rainbow's End [MW,NH,F,S,WC] 314/652-8790 ▪ 4060 Chouteau (at Manchester) ▪ 9am-close, patio, also leather shop

17 Tangerine [GF,D,F,S] 314/621-7335 ▪ 1405 Washington Ave (at 14th) ▪ 11am-2pm Tue-Fri & 6pm-3am Tue-Sat, hipster lounge, also restaurant, mostly veggie

Nightclubs

12 Attitudes [MW,D,F] 314/534-3858 ▪ 4100 Manchester ▪ 6pm-3am, clsd Sun-Mon

18 The Complex/ Angles [★MW,D,F,S,V,WC] 314/772-2645 ▪ 3511 Chouteau (at Grand) ▪ 5pm-3am, from 9pm Sun-Tue, multiple bars, patio ▪ www.complexnightclub.com

19 Faces Complex [MW,D,F,S,V,18+] 618/271-7410 ▪ 130 4th St (at Missouri), East St Louis, IL ▪ 3pm-6am, 3 levels, patio ▪ www.facesnolimits.com

20 The Galaxy [GF,A,L,E,$] 314/231-2404 ▪ 1227 Washington Ave ▪ hrs vary, fetish night Mon

Mabel's Budget Beauty Shop & Chainsaw Repair [M,D,S,WC] 618/465-8687 ▪ 602 Belle St (at 6th St), Alton, IL ▪ 4pm-2am, patio

9 Magnolia's [★M,D,CW,F,S,K,WC] 314/652-6500 ▪ 5 S Vande-venter (at Forest Park Pkwy) ▪ 4pm-3am, from 3pm Sun, cabaret wknds, leather Fri-Sun ▪ www.magsbar.com

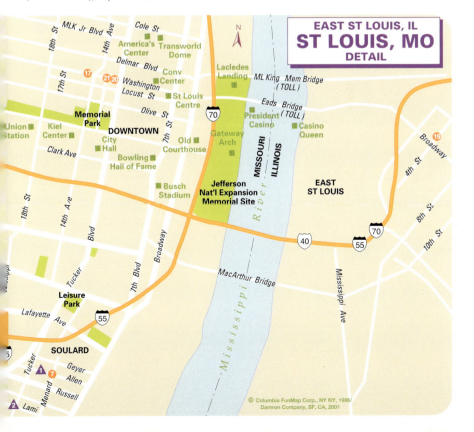

St Louis

Most visitors come to St Louis to see the famous Gateway Arch (314/655-1700), the tallest monument in the US at 630ft, designed by renowned architect Eero Saarinen. After you've ridden the elevators in the Arch and seen the view, take a trip to the historic Soulard, the 'French Quarter of St Louis.' Established in 1779 by Madame and Monsieur Soulard as an open air market, it's now the place for great food and jazz. And the Market still attracts crowds—lesbigay and straight—on the weekends. While down by the Arch, enjoy riverfront dining aboard any of the several riverboat restaurants on the Mississippi. The Central West End (on and around Euclid) is homebase for the lesbigay community.

Queer Resources

Community Info
Gay/Lesbian Hotline 314/367-0084. 6pm-10pm only, clsd Sun.

AIDS Resources
Hotline 314/647-1144.

Recovery
Steps Alano Club 314/436-1858, www.step-salanostl.org. 1935-A Park Ave, Lafayette Square, 8pm nightly.

City Calendar

LGBT Pride
June. 314/772-8888

Annual Events
June- Six Flags St Louis Gay Day 636/938-4800.

Tourist Info

Airport Directions
Lambert-St Louis International. To get downtown, take I70 approximately 17 miles east.

Public Transit & Taxis
County Cab 314/991-5300.
GEM Shuttle 314/427-3311.
The Bi-State Bus System 314/231-2345.

Tourist Spots & Info
Anheuser-Busch Brewery.
Argosy Casino 800/336-7568.
Cathedral Basilica of St Louis (world's largest collection of mosaic art).
Dave & Buster's dining & entertainment center 314/209-8015.
Gateway Arch (duh).
Grant's Farm 314/843-1700.
St Louis Art Museum 314/721-0072.
Stone Hill Winery (in Hermann) 800/909-9463.
The extremely quaint town of St. Charles.
Visitor's Center: 421-1023 or 800/ 888-3861, web: www.explorestlouis.com.

Weather
100% midwestern. Cold—little snow and the temperatures can drop below 0°. Hot, muggy summers raise temperatures back up into the 100°s. Spring and fall bring out the best in Mother Nature.

Best Views
Where else? Top of the Gateway Arch in the Observation Room.

21 **Velvet Lounge** [GS,D] 314/241-8178, 314/241-2997 ■ 1301 Washington Ave (at 13th Ave) ■ 9pm-3am Th-Sun

CAFES
Coffee Cartel [★] 314/454-0000 ■ 2 Maryland Plaza (at Euclid) ■ 24hrs

MokaBe's [★S,WC] 314/865-2009 ■ 3606 Arsenal (at S Grand) ■ 11am-1am, plenty veggie, shows wknds

RESTAURANTS
Busch's Grove 314/993-0011 ■ 9160 Clayton Rd (at Price) ■ lunch & dinner, full bar till 1am, clsd Sun-Mon

Cafe Balaban [★WC] 314/361-8085 ■ 405 N Euclid Ave (at McPherson) ■ pizza, Sun brunch, full bar

Dressel's 314/361-1060 ■ 419 N Euclid (at McPherson) ■ great Welsh pub food, full bar

Duff's [WC] 314/361-0522 ■ 392 N Euclid Ave (at McPherson) ■ lunch & dinner, clsd Mon, wknd brunch, fine dining, full bar

Kirk's Bistro & Bar 314/361-1456 ■ 512 N Euclid (at Washington) ■ 5pm-10pm, till 11pm Fri-Sat, Sun brunch

Majestic Bar & Restaurant 314/361-2011 ■ 4900 Laclede (at Euclid) ■ 6am-1:30am, diner fare

On Broadway Bistro [WC] 314/421-0087 ■ 5300 N Broadway (at Grand) ■ 11am-3am, full bar

Ted Drewes Frozen Custard [★] 314/481-2652 ■ 6726 Chippewa (at Jameson) ■ 11am-11pm, seasonal, a St Louis landmark; also 4224 S Grand Blvd, 314/352-7376

Tomatillo Mexican Grill 314/991-4995 ■ 9641 Olive Blvd (at Warson) ■ 11am-10pm, till midnight wknds

Tony's 314/231-7007 ■ 410 Market St (at Broadway) ■ dinner only, clsd Sun, Italian fine dining

Zinnia 314/962-0572 ■ 7491 Big Bend Blvd (at Shrewsbury), Webster Groves ■ lunch Tue-Fri & dinner Tue-Sun, California-style bistro

ENTERTAINMENT & RECREATION
Anheuser-Busch Brewery Tours/ Grant's Farm 314/577-2626, 314/843-1700 ■ all-American kitsch: see the Clydesdales in their air-conditioned stables, or visit the Busch family estate that was once the home of Ulysses S Grant ■ www.budweisertours.com

Int'l Bowling Museum & Hall of Fame 314/231-6340 ■ 111 Stadium Plaza (across from Busch Stadium) ■ 5,000 yrs of bowling history (!) & 4 free frames

Planet Proud Books & Gifts

3194 S. Grand Avenue

St. Louis' community source for books, magazines, gifts, stickers, jewelry, stationery, videos, and safer-sex supplies!! Gay owned and operated. Visit our website: www.planetproud.com.

PHONE **314/772-GLBT**

A ST. LOUIS GUESTHOUSE

Accommodations With Phone, Private Bath, and Hot Tub in Courtyard

Located in Historic Soulard Next Door To Clementines

(314) 773-1016

1032-38 Allen Ave.
St. Louis, MO 63104

MISSOURI • USA

Lavender Limelight Radio Show 314/664-3688 ■ KDHX 88.1FM ■ 7pm Th, lgbt radio show
Wired Women, Inc 314/352-9473 ■ concerts & events for the women's community ■ wiredwomen@aol.com

BOOKSTORES
22 Left Bank Books 314/367-6731 ■ 399 N Euclid Ave (at McPherson) ■ 10am-10pm, 11am-6pm Sun, feminist & lgbt titles ■ www.left-bank.com
23▶ Planet Proud Books & Gifts 314/772-4528 ■ 3194 S Grand (at Wyoming) ■ 10am-8pm, till 9pm Fri-Sat, from noon wknds, till 5pm Sun ■ www.planetproud.com

RETAIL SHOPS
▶ Boxers 314/454-0209 ■ 310 N Euclid Ave (at Maryland) ■ 11am-6pm, 1pm-5pm Sun, men's underwear ■ eboxersonline.com
Daily Planet News 314/367-1333 ■ 243 N Euclid Ave (at Maryland) ■ 7am-9pm
Friends & Luvers 314/771-9405 ■ 3550 Gravois (at Grand) ■ 10am-10pm, noon-7pm Sun, fetish clothes, toys, videos, dating service

Heffalump's 314/361-0544 ■ 387 N Euclid Ave (at McPherson) ■ 11am-8pm, till 10pm Fri-Sat, noon-5pm Sun, gifts

PUBLICATIONS
EXP 314/367-0397, 877/397-6244 ■ bi-monthly gay magazine for MO, IL & KS ■ www.expmag.com
Vital Voice 314/865-3787 ■ PO Box 170138 63117 ■ bi-monthly news & feature publication ■ vitalvoicenews@aol.com
Women's Yellow Pages of Greater St Louis 314/567-0487 ■ www.wypstlouis.com

MEN'S CLUBS
▶ Club St Louis [PC,SW] 314/533-3666 ■ 2625 Samuel Shepard Dr (at Jefferson) ■ 24hrs ■ www.the-clubs.com

EROTICA
Cheap Trx 314/664-4011 ■ 3211 S Grand Blvd ■ body piercing, sex supplies ■ www.cheaptrx.com
Ngamson's 314/772-5819 ■ 2822 Cherokee (at Oregon) ■ www.ngamson.com

Damron Codes

- ➤ advertiser
- ★ popular
- **MO** men only
- **GF** gay-friendly (mostly straight)
- **GS** gay/straight (evenly mixed)
- **MW** lesbians/gay men
- **M** mostly men
- **W** mostly women (listing names in this color)
- **WO** women only (listing names in this color)
- **NH** neighborhood bar
- **D** live DJ & dancing
- **A** alternative (grunge babes, goths)
- **CW** country western (music, dancing and/or dress)
- **B** bears
- **L** leather, fetish (often a dress code)
- **P** professional crowd
- **MRC** multiracial clientele
- **MR-AF** African-American clientele
- **MR-A** Asian clientele
- **MR-L** Latino/a clientele
- **TG** transgender-friendly
- **F** hot food served
- **E** live entertainment (piano, bands, comedy)
- **K** karaoke
- **S** shows (drag, strip, or cabaret)
- **V** videos
- **18+** 18 & older
- **YC** young crowd (mostly 20-somethings)
- **OC** older/more mature crowd (mostly over 40)
- **BW** beer and/or wine
- **BYOB** bring your own bottle (often "private" clubs)
- **SW** swimming onsite (usually a pool)
- **N** public nudity okay
- **NS** no smoking (anywhere inside business)
- **PC** private club (membership open to out-of-towners; often BYOB)
- **WC** wheelchair access (includes bathrooms)
- **GO** gay-owned/ operated
- **AYOR** at your own risk (beware of bashers or cops)

Las Vegas

Shows, slots, and shiny lights: that's the allure of Las Vegas. A glittering oasis in the middle of the desert, Las Vegas is the home of 24-hr entertainment.

Queer Resources

COMMUNITY INFO
▼ Gay/Lesbian Community Center 702/733-9800, web: www.thecenter-lasvegas.com. 912 E Sahara Ave (at Maryland Pkwy), 11am-7pm, till 3pm Sat, clsd Sun.

AIDS RESOURCES
702/474-2437.
Aid for AIDS of Nevada 702/382-2326.

RECOVERY
Alcoholics Together 702/737-0035. 953 E Sahara #233, 12:15pm & 8pm daily.

City Calendar

LGBT PRIDE
May. 702/225-3389 (SNAPI Hotline), web: www.vegaspride.com.

ANNUAL EVENTS
March - NGRA (Nat'l Gay Rodeo Assn) Bighorn Rodeo 888/643-6472, web: members.aol.com/ngra99.

Tourist Info

AIRPORT DIRECTIONS
McCarran International. To get to the bars, take Swenson St to Tropicana Ave. Turn left on Tropicana. At Paradise Rd, turn right. Take Paradise to Sahara Ave or to Las Vegas Blvd (The Strip).

PUBLIC TRANSIT & TAXIS
Western Cab 702/382-7100.
Yellow Cab 702/873-2000.
Various resorts have their own shuttle service.
CAT Citizens Area Transit 702/228-7433.

TOURIST SPOTS & INFO
Bellagio Art Gallery 702/693-7111.
Guinness World Records Museum 702/792-3766.
Hoover Dam.
Imperial Palace Auto Collection 702/731-3311.
King Tut Museum (at the Luxor) 702/262-4000.
La Cage at the Riveria 702/794-9433.
Las Vegas Art Museum 702/360-8000.
Liberace Museum 702/798-5595.
Museum of Natural History 702/384-3466.
StarTrek: The Experience.
Visitor's Center: Convention & Visitors Authority 702/892-0711.

BEST VIEWS
Top of the Stratosphere. Or hurtling through the loops of the rollercoaster atop the New York New York Hotel. (Note: Do not ride immediately after visiting the buffet.)

NEVADA

Las Vegas

ACCOMMODATIONS
   Blue Moon Resort [MO,SW,GO] 702/896-1124 ■ hot tub ■ www.bluemoonlv.com
1 **Chapman Guest House** [MO,SW,N] 702/312-4625 ■ near E Sahara Ave & Maryland Pkwy ■ hot tub ■ www.chapmanguesthouse.com
▶ **Las Vegas B&B–Lucky You** [M,SW,N,GO] 702/384-1129 ■ hot tub, sauna, shared baths ■ members.aol.com/haven00069/
2 **Las Vegas Rainbow** [MO,SW,N,WC,GO] 702/699-8977, 866/DOROTHY ■ 1800 Chapman Dr (at Oakey/ 15th St) ■ decadent b&b, full brkfst, bar, jacuzzi ■ www.lasvegasrainbow.com
3 **Oasis Guesthouse** [MO,SW] 702/369-1396 ■ 662 Rolling Green Dr ■ full brkfst, jacuzzi ■ ruintoit@aol.com
4 **Viva Las Vegas Villas** [GF,NS] 702/384-0771, 800/574-4450 ■ 1205 Las Vegas Blvd ■ campy themed rms & suites, onsite disco, also commitment ceremonies ■ www.vivalasvegasvillas.com

BARS
5 **Angles Lounge** [MW,NH,V,WC] 702/791-0100 ■ 4633 Paradise Rd (at Naples) ■ from 3pm daily, also 'Club Lace' from 10:30pm Wed-Sat (D), more women Fri
6 **Backdoor Lounge** [MW,NH,D,S,SW,WC] 702/385-2018 ■ 1415 E Charleston (nr Maryland Pkwy) ■ 24hrs, patio, Latin night Fri
7 **Backstreet** [★MW,D,CW,WC] 702/876-1844 ■ 5012 S Arville Rd (at Tropicana) ■ 24hrs, DJ Wed-Sun
8 **Badlands Saloon** [M,NH,D,CW,WC,GO] 702/792-9262 ■ 953 E Sahara #22 (in Commercial Ctr) ■ 24hrs
5 **The Buffalo** [★M,L,V,WC] 702/733-8355 ■ 4640 Paradise Rd (at Naples) ■ 24hrs
9 **Cobalt Las Vegas** [M,F,S,V,WC] 702/693-6567 ■ 900 E Karen Ave #H-102 (in Commercial Ctr) ■ 24hrs, women always welcome ■ www.cobaltlv.com
10 **Flex** [MW,D,K,S] 702/385-3539 ■ 4371 W Charleston (at Arville) ■ 24hrs ■ www.gay-lasvegas.com/flex.htm

11 **Freezone** [MW,NH,D,TG,F,K,S,YC,GO] 702/794-2300 ■ 610 E Naples ■ 24hrs, women's night Tue, Latin Wed, also restaurant
12 **Goodtimes** [M,NH,D,K,WC] 702/736-9494 ■ 1775 E Tropicana (at Spencer, in Liberace Plaza) ■ 24hrs, DJ Fri, Sat & Mon, more women Mon & Wed ■ www.gayworldguide.com/goodtimes
13 **Keys** [MW,F,E,S,GO] 702/731-2200 ■ 1000 E Sahara Ave ■ 10am-4am, piano bar, dinner Wed-Sat, also restaurant ■ www.keys-lv.com
14 **The Las Vegas Eagle** [M,L] 702/458-8662 ■ 3430 E Tropicana (at Pecos) ■ 24hrs, DJ Wed, Fri & Sat, also 'The Annex' bar 8pm-4am Wed & Fri
9 **Las Vegas Lounge** [NH,TG,F,E,S,GO] 702/737-9350 ■ 900 E Karen Ave ■ 24hrs, also 2 restaurants
15 **Phoenix** [MW] 702/438-3050 ■ 40 N Nellis ■ 24hrs
15 **Snick's Place** [M,NH,WC] 702/385-9298 ■ 1402 S 3rd St (at Oakey) ■ 24hrs
16 **The Spotlight Lounge** [★M,NH,D,F,S] 702/696-0202 ■ 957 E Sahara (at Commerical Center's entrance) ■ 24hrs, buffet wknds ■ www.spotlightlv.com

NIGHTCLUBS
17 **The Bird Cage** [MW,D,TG,F,S,V,WC] 702/598-2030 ■ 207 N 3rd (at Ogden) ■ 9pm-5am, also restaurant & juice bar
18 **The Gipsy** [★M,D,S,V,YC] 702/731-1919 ■ 4605 S Paradise Rd (at Naples) ■ 10pm-close, Latin night Mon
19 **House of Blues** [GF,D,F,S,$] 702/632-7600 ■ 3950 Las Vegas Blvd S (at Hacienda Ave in 'Madalay Bay') ■ more gay from 11pm Sun & Th ■ www.hob.com

CAFES
   Cool Beans [F,WC,GO] 702/693-6327 ■ 900 E Karen Ave #H108 ■ 7am-midnight, from 11am Sun, sandwiches & desserts, Internet access, women's night Fri
   Espresso Roma Cafe [E] 702/369-1540 ■ 4440 S Maryland Pkwy ■ 7am-midnight, from 8am wknds, open mic Sun-Mon
   Mermaid Cafe [BW,F,E] 702/240-6002 ■ 2910 Lake East Dr (off Canyon Gate) ■ open till 11pm, till midnight Fri-Sat

RESTAURANTS
   Café Luna [GO] 702/875-5858 ■ 4647 Paradise Rd ■ dinner, clsd Mon
   Coyote Cafe [WC] 702/891-7349, 888/757-2572 ■ 3799 S Las Vegas Blvd (in 'MGM Grand') ■ 8:30am-11pm, the original Santa Fe chef ■ www.coyote-cafe.com
   Mama Jo's 702/869-8099 ■ 3655 S Durango ■ lunch & dinner, Italian
   The Raw Truth 702/450-9007 ■ 3620 E Flamingo ■ 9am-9pm, 11am-6pm Sun, organic vegan, juice bar ■ www.rawfoodists.com/rawtruth
   Sushi Boy Desu 702/736-8234 ■ 4632 S Maryland Pkwy #12 ■ 11am-10pm

ENTERTAINMENT & RECREATION
   Crystal Palace Skating Rink 702/458-7107 ■ 4680 Boulder Hwy ■ 8:30pm-11pm 3rd Mon, lgbt skate
   Cupid's Wedding Chapel 702/598-4444, 800/543-2933 ■ 827 Las Vegas Blvd ■ commitment ceremonies, "Have the Vegas wedding you've always dreamed of!" ■ www.cupidswedding.com
   The Forum Shops at Caesars 3570 Las Vegas Blvd S (in 'Caesars Palace') ■ you saw it in Showgirls & many other movies, now come shop in it for yourself

Lucky You B&B

Las Vegas' oldest gay B&B. Located two blocks from the Vegas Strip and within minutes of nightlife and attractions. 5 minutes from downtown. Clothing-optional, European-style guest house with elegant appointments and tropical pool, hot tub, and patio. TV and VCR in every room, with a full American breakfast prepared by former chef to Liberace.

PHONE & FAX **702/384-1129**

Las Vegas • Nevada

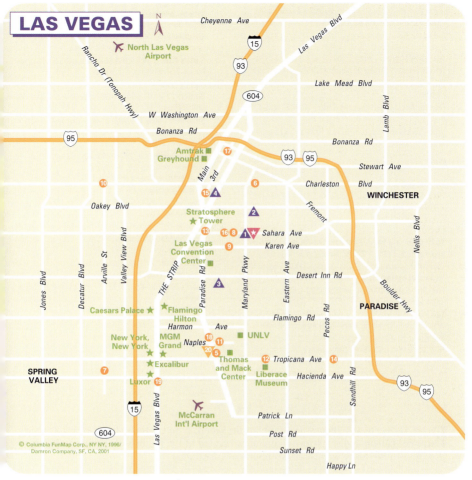

King Tutankhamun's Tomb & Museum 702/262-4555 ■ 3900 Las Vegas Blvd S (in the 'Luxor Las Vegas') ■ exact replica of the tomb when Howard Carter opened it in 1922

La Cage 702/794-9433 ■ 2901 Las Vegas Blvd (at the Riviera) ■ the biggest drag show in town, Frank Marino & friends impersonate the divas, from Joan Rivers to Tina Turner ■ www.theriviera.com

Las Vegas Gay & Lesbian Chorus 702/594-3393

Liberace Museum 702/798-5595 ■ 1775 E Tropicana Ave ■ this is one queen's closet you have to look into— especially if you love your pianos, clothes & cars covered w/ diamonds

The Volcano at The Mirage 3400 Las Vegas Blvd S ■ see the gimmick that inspired the rest of the showstoppers along the Strip—erupts every few minutes after dark

Bookstores

Borders [WC] 702/258-0999 ■ 2323 S Decatur (at Sahara) ■ 9am-11pm, till 9pm Sun, lgbt section, cafe

Get Booked 702/737-7780 ■ 4640 Paradise #15 (at Naples) ■ 10am-midnight, till 2am Fri-Sat, lgbt ■ getbooked1@aol.com

Retail Shops

The Fig Leaf [M] 702/259-5510 ■ 4367 W Charleston ■ 10am-6pm, noon-5pm Sun, unique fashions

Sin City 702/387-6969 ■ 1013 Charleston (at Main) ■ piercing & tattoo studio

Publications

Las Vegas Bugle 702/369-6260 ■ lgbt newspaper ■ www.lvbugle.com

Lesbian Voice 702/650-0636 ■ monthly magazine ■ lesbianvoice@hotmail.com

Out Las Vegas 702/650-0636 ■ monthly lgbt entertainment newspaper ■ www.outlasvegas.com

Men's Clubs

Apollo Spa & Health Club [MO,SW] 702/650-9191 ■ 953 E Sahara Ave #A19 (nr Paradise & Maryland, at Commercial Ctr entrance) ■ 24hrs ■ www.apollospa.com

Erotica

Adult Super Store 702/798-0144 ■ 3850 W Tropicana ■ 24hrs, cruisy theaters

NEVADA • USA

Bare Essentials Fantasy Fashions [GO] 702/247-4711 ■ 4029 W Sahara Ave (nr Valley View Blvd) ■ men's and women's, also toys ■ www.xoticdancer.com/bareessentials
Industrial Road Adult Books 702/734-7667 ■ 3427 Industrial Rd (at Spring Mtn) ■ 24hrs
Pal Joey's 702/734-7589 ■ 3084 S Highland #C ■ fetishwear, also tattoos & piercing ■ www.pal-joeys.com
Price Video 702/734-1342 ■ 700 E Naples Dr #102 (at Swenson)
Rancho Adult Entertainment Center 702/645-6104 ■ 4820 N Rancho #D (at Bone Mtn) ■ 24hrs
Video West [GO] 702/248-7055 ■ 5785 W Tropicana (at Jones)

Reno

ACCOMMODATIONS
1   **Holiday Inn & Diamonds Casino** [GF,SW,WC] 775/786-5151, 800/648-4877 ■ 1000 E 6th St (at Wells Ave) ■ www.hireno.com

BARS
2   **1099 Club** [★MW,NH,S,V,WC] 775/329-1099 ■ 1099 S Virginia St (at Vassar) ■ 24hrs, patio
3   **Carl's Pub** [MW,NH,D] 775/829-8886 ■ 3310 S Virginia St (at Moana) ■ 11am-3am, patio
4   **Five Star Saloon** [M,NH,D,F,WC] 775/329-2878 ■ 132 West St (at 1st) ■ 24hrs
5   **The Patio** [MW,NH] 775/323-6565 ■ 600 W 5th St (btwn Washington & Ralston) ■ 11am-2am, more women Fri
6   **The Quest** [M,D,TG,S] 775/333-2808 ■ 210 W Commercial Row (at West) ■ noon-5am, 24hrs wknds

NIGHTCLUBS
7   **Visions** [★M,D,F,E,YC] 775/786-5455 ■ 340 Kietzke Ln (btwn Glendale & Mill) ■ noon-6am, patio, 'Glitter Palace' gift shop Wed-Sun

CAFES
Sassy's Cafe & Deli 775/856-3501 ■ 195 N Edison (at Mill) ■ 7:30am-4pm, clsd wknds

BOOKSTORES
Borders 775/448-9999 ■ 4995 S Virginia St ■ 9am-11pm, lgbt section
Sundance Books 775/786-1188 ■ 1155 W 4th St (at Keystone) ■ 9am-9pm, 10am-6pm wknds

PUBLICATIONS
Reno Informer 775/747-8833, 877/387-3385 ■ northern Nevada's lgbt newspaper
■ www.reno-informer.com

MEN'S CLUBS
Steve's [PC] 775/323-8770 ■ 1030 W 2nd St (at Keystone) ■ 24hrs, spa

EROTICA
The Chocolate Walrus [★] 775/825-2267 ■ 160 E Grove ■ clsd Sun
Fantasy Faire 775/323-6969 ■ 1298 S Virginia (at Arroyo) ■ leather & fetish
Suzie's 775/786-8557 ■ 195 Kietzke Ln (at E 2nd St) ■ 24hrs

RENO

Reno, known as the 'Biggest Little City in the World,' is an exciting mixture of Vegas-style casino gaming and small-town hospitality. Located at the foothills of the Sierras, Reno is also close to the many world-class ski resorts of Lake Tahoe.

Queer Resources

COMMUNITY INFO
▼ A Rainbow Place lgbt center 775/789-1780, www.arainbowplacenv.org. 33 St Lawrence Ave, call for hrs.
24 hr infoline 800/ 627-1168.

AIDS RESOURCES
Nevada AIDS Foundation 775/786-4673.

RECOVERY
AA Central Office 775/355-1151.
Cornerstones Gay/Lesbian AA 775/359-5658, 2850 Wrondel Way #J.

City Calendar

LGBT PRIDE
August-775/ 825-2117, www.renopride.com

Tourist Info

AIRPORT DIRECTIONS
Reno-Cannon International Airport. To get dowtown, take Plumb Ln from terminal to Virginia St. Turn right on Virginia and head north.

PUBLIC TRANSIT & TAXIS
Bell Limo 775/786-3700.
Reno/Sparks Cab 775/333-3333.
City Fare (bus) 775/348-7433.

TOURIST SPOTS & INFO
Casinos.
Lake Tahoe.
Virginia City.
Visitor's Center: Greater Reno-Sparks Chamber of Commerce 775/686-3030.
Reno/Sparks Convention & Visitors Authority 775/827-RENO or 800/FOR-RENO, web: www.reno-sparkschamber.org.

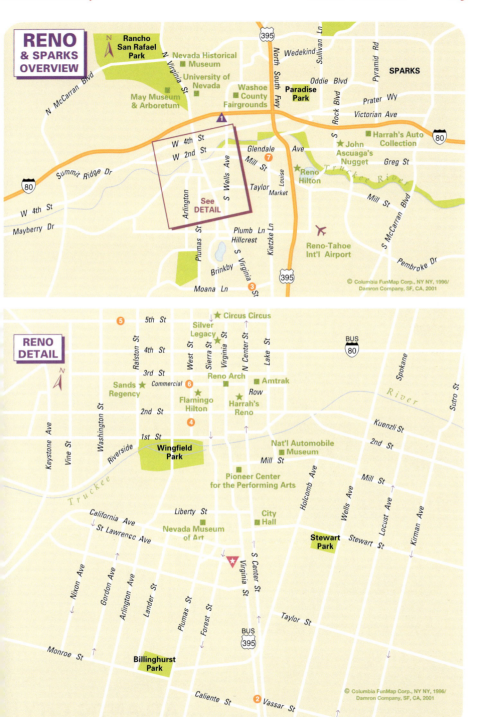

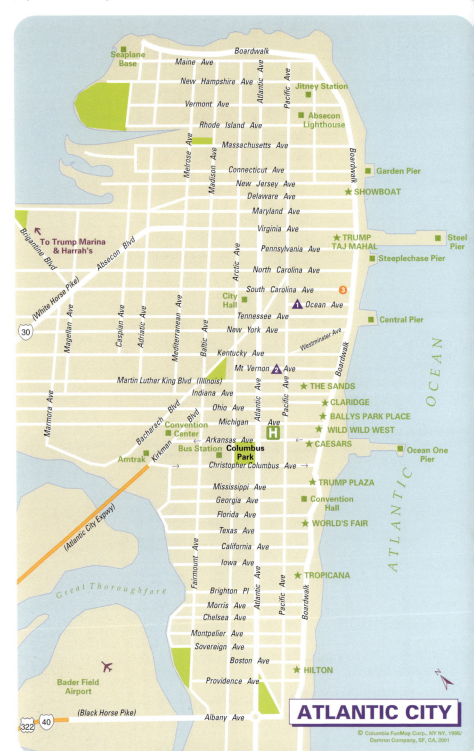

NEW JERSEY
Atlantic City

ACCOMMODATIONS
1. **Ocean House** [MO,V,SW,N,GO] 609/345-0198 ■ 127 S Ocean Ave ■ shared baths
2. **Surfside Resort Hotel** [MW,SW,GO] 609/347-0808, 888/277-7873 ■ 18 S Mt Vernon Ave (at Pacific) ■ small, upscale straight-friendly hotel, sundeck ■ www.studiosix.com

BARS
2. **Brass Rail Bar & Grill** [★MW,NH,F,K,S,GO] 609/348-0192 ■ at 'Surfside Resort Hotel' ■ 24hrs ■ www.studiosix.com
2. **Oak Room** [GF,E,GO] 609/347-7873 ■ at 'Surfside Resort Hotel' ■ 9pm-1:30am Fri-Sat only, upscale piano lounge ■ www.studiosix.com
3. **Reflections** [MW,NH,W] 609/348-1115 ■ 130 South Carolina Ave (at Pacific) ■ 5pm-4am

NIGHTCLUBS
2. **Studio Six Video Dance Club** [★MW,D,E,V] 609/348-3310 ■ upstairs at 'Brass Rail' ■ 10pm-close ■ www.studiosix.com

RESTAURANTS
Mama Mott's [WC] 609/345-8218 ■ 151 S New York Ave (at Pacific) ■ dinner nightly, Italian & seafood
White House Sub Shop 609/345-1564 ■ 2301 Arctic Ave (at Mississippi) ■ 10am-10pm, till 11pm Fri-Sat, from 11am Sun

EROTICA
Atlantic City News 609/344-9444 ■ 101 S Martin Luther King Jr Blvd (at Pacific) ■ 24hrs

ATLANTIC CITY

Once the East Coast's most posh resort, Atlantic City still attracts visitors with its famous casinos. Anyone who's ever played Monopoly will enjoy seeing the original Boardwalk and Park Place.

Queer Resources

COMMUNITY INFO
Gay Helpline of NJ 973/285-1595, live 7:30pm-10:30pm.

AIDS RESOURCES
NJ Women & AIDS Network 732/846-4462 or 800/747-1108.

Tourist Info

AIRPORT DIRECTIONS
Atlantic City International. To get to the Boardwalk, simply take Atlantic City Expressway to Atlantic or Pacific.

PUBLIC TRANSIT & TAXIS
Yellow Cab 609/344-1221.
Sterling Transportation 609/347-7711.
New Jersey Transit 800/582-5946 (in NJ).

TOURIST SPOTS & INFO
Absecon lighthouse.
Visitor's Center: 609/348-7100. Chamber of Commerce 609/345-5600.

- *full-color photographs speak louder than words*
- *over 1800 international listings cover gay-friendly hotels, B&Bs, and accommodations across the globe!*
- *detailed listings answer all your questions about rates, rooms, meals, smoking, kids, and pets*
- *cross-indexes note Men-only, Women-only, RV & Camping, and Wheelchair-accessible accommodations*
- *over 550 pages, only $22.95!*

ORDER NOW: (800) 462-6654

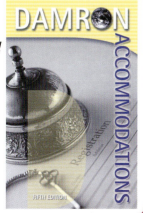

Albuquerque

The mission city of Albuquerque will celebrate its tricentennial in a few years, but visitors can enjoy the historic Old Town now. Just west of the city lies an even more ancient tribute to the region's history: Petroglyph National Monument, a volcanic outcropping decorated with hundreds of rock carvings left by the indigenous people of the area.

Queer Resources

Community Info
Common Bond Info Line 505/891-3647, web: members.aol.com/gayinformation/index.html.

AIDS Resources
505/388-4784.

Recovery
AA Gay/Lesbian 505/266-1900 (AA#).

City Calendar

LGBT Pride
June. 505/856-0871.

Entertainment
New Mexico Gay Rodeo Association, web: www.nmgra.com.

Annual Events
September - Albuquerque AIDS Walk 505/938-7100, email: aidswalk@aol.com.
October - Kodak Int'l Hot Air Balloon Fiesta 505/828-2887 or 888/422-7277, web: www.balloonfiesta.com.

Tourist Info

Tourist Spots & Info
Albuquerque Museum 505/243-7255.
Indian Pueblo Cultural Center 505/843-7270 or 800/766-4405 (outside NM).
New Mexico Museum of Natural History 505/841-2802.
Old Town.
Rattlesnake Museum 505/242-6569.
Wildlife West Nature Park & Chuckwagon 505/281-7655.
Visitor's Center: 800/733-6396, web: www.newmexico.com.
Albuquerque Lesbian & Gay Chamber of Commerce 505/243-6767.

Weather
Sunny and temperate. Warm days and cool nights in summer, with average temperatures from 65° to 95°. Winter is cooler, from 28° to 57°.

Best Views
Sandia Peak Tram (505/856-7325) at sunset.

New Mexico

Albuquerque

Accommodations
1 **Brittania & W E Mauger Estate B&B** [GF,NS] 505/242-8755, 800/719-9189 ■ 701 Roma Ave NW (at 7th) ■ intimate Queen Anne, full brkfst ■ www.maugerbb.com
Casa de Alegria B&B [GS,WC,GO] 505/890-0176, 888/320-3456 ■ 5 Alegria Ln (at Old Church Rd), Corrales ■ full brkfst, hot tub ■ www.new-mexico-inn.com
2 **Casitas at Old Town** [GS,NS,GO] 505/843-7479 ■ 1604 Old Town Rd NW ■ suites in a classic adobe bldg, private patios ■ www.oldtowncasitas.com
El Peñasco [W,GO] 505/771-8909, 888/576-2726 ■ adobe guest house, full brkfst, 30 miles from Albuquerque ■ www.q-net.com/elpeñasco
3 **Golden Guesthouses** [MW] 505/344-9205, 888/513-GOLD ■ 2645 Decker NW ■ individual & shared units ■ www.gaynewmexico.com
4 **Hacienda Antigua B&B** [GS,SW,NS,GO] 505/345-5399, 800/201-2986 ■ 6708 Tierra Dr NW (close to corner of 2nd & Osuna) ■ full brkfst, hot tub ■ www.haciendantigua.com
Mountain View [W,WC,GO] 505/296-7277 ■ full brkfst wknds, hot tub ■ needles65@juno.com
5 **Nuevo Dia** [GF] 505/856-7910 ■ 11110 San Rafael Ave NE (at Browning) ■ guesthouse, hot tub ■ www.helmassoc.com
6 **Taracotta** [GS,NS,GO] 505/344-9443 ■ 3118 Rio Grande Blvd NW (at Candelaria) ■ hot tub, patio ■ ricknbarry@earthlink.net
7 **W J Marsh House** [GF] 505/247-1001, 888/956-2774 ■ 301 Edith SE (nr Central & Broadway) ■ full brkfst ■ www.marshhouse.com
8 **Wyndham Albuquerque Hotel** [GF,SW] 505/843-7000, 800/227-1117 ■ 2910 Yale Blvd SE (at Gibson) ■ 4-star hotel, also 'Rojo Bar & Grill' ■ wyndhamalbuquerque.com

Bars
9 **Albuquerque Mining Co (AMC)** [★M,D,S,V,WC,GO] 505/255-4022 ■ 7209 Central Ave NE (at Louisiana) ■ 3pm-2am, till midnight Sun, also 'Pit Bar' (M,L), patio bar
10 **Albuquerque Social Club** [★MW,D,PC] 505/255-0887 ■ 4021 Central Ave NE (enter rear) ■ noon-midnight, till 2am Fri-Sat ■ hometown.aol.com/albsocclub
11 **Foxes Lounge** [M,D,S] 505/255-3060 ■ 8521 Central Ave NE (btwn Wisconsin & Wyoming) ■ 10am-2am, noon-midnight Sun, home bar of the Royal Court
12 **The Ranch** [M,D,CW,B,L,WC] 505/275-1616 ■ 8900 Central SE (at Wyoming) ■ 11am-2am, till midnight Sun
13 **Renea's** [W,NH,D,F,K] 505/343-1554 ■ 6132 4th NW (near Osuna) ■ 4pm-midnight, till 2am wknds, clsd Mon ■ www.homestead.com/reneas/welcome.html

Nightclubs
14 **Pulse** [★M,D,A,E,$] 505/255-3334 ■ 4100 Central Ave SE (at Montclaire, in Nob Hill) ■ 9pm-2am, clsd Mon-Tue, 18+ Wed-Th, goth Th ■ www.pulsenightclub.com

Restaurants
Artichoke Café 505/243-0200 ■ 424 Central Ave ■ lunch Mon-Fri & dinner Mon-Sat, bistro, plenty veggie
Chef du Jour [WC] 505/247-8998 ■ 119 San Pasquale SW (at Central) ■ lunch Mon-Fri, dinner Fri-Sat, plenty veggie
Double Rainbow [WC] 505/255-6633 ■ 3416 Central SE (2 blks W of Carlisle) ■ 6am-midnight, plenty veggie

Albuquerque • New Mexico

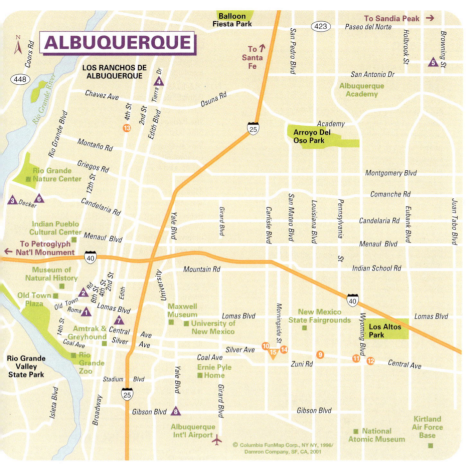

Frontier 505/266-0550 ■ 2400 Central SE (at Cornell) ■ 24hrs, good breakfast burritos

Romano's Macaroni Grill 505/881-3400 ■ 2100 Louisiana NE (at Winrock Mall) ■ lunch & dinner, Italian

Sadie's Cocinita [★] 505/345-5339 ■ 6230 4th St NW (nr Osuna) ■ 11am-10pm, till 9pm Sun, New Mexican

Entertainment & Recreation

Hugs & Hot Air Ballooning [GF,GO] 505/450-8692 ■ 12272 N Hwy 14, Cedar Crest ■ scenic balloon rides, woman-owned/ run ■ members.aol.com/FlyHugs

Women in Movement in NewMexico (WIMIN) 505/899-3627 ■ www.wiminfest.org

Bookstores

Bird Song 505/268-7204 ■ 139 Harvard SE (nr Central) ■ 11am-7pm, used, lgbt section ■ www.abebooks.com/home/birdsong

Page One 505/294-2026, 800/521-4122 ■ 11018 Montgomery NE ■ 7am-11pm ■ www.page1book.com

Sisters & Brothers Bookstore 505/266-7317, 800/687-3480 (orders only) ■ 4011 Silver Ave SE (btwn Morningside & Montclair) ■ 10:30am-7pm, till 6pm Sun, clsd Mon, lgbt ■ www.sistersandbrothers.com

Retail Shops

In Crowd [WC,GO] 505/268-3750 ■ 3106 Central SE (at Richmond) ■ 10am-6pm, noon-4pm Sun, local & folk art

Publications

Out! Magazine 505/243-2540 ■ lgbt newsmagazine ■ www.outmagazine.com

Gyms & Health Clubs

Betty's Bath & Day Spa [N] 505/341-3456 ■ 1865 Candelaria NW ■ full service spa w/ separate women-only hot tub, men's night Th ■ www.bettysbath.com

Pride Gym [MO,N,PC] 505/242-7810 ■ 1803 3rd St NW (4 blks S of I-40) ■ www.pride-gym.com

Erotica

Castle Superstore 505/262-2266 ■ 5110 Central Ave SE (at San Mateo)

Mr Peepers 505/343-8063 ■ 4300 Edith Blvd NE (at Candelaria) ■ 24hrs

Video Maxxx 505/341-4000 ■ 810 Comanche NE (at I-25) ■ leather, novelties, books, etc

Viewpoint [★] 505/268-6373 ■ 6406 Central Ave SE (at San Pedro) ■ 24hrs

NEW YORK

Fire Island

ACCOMMODATIONS
Belvedere Hotel [MO,SW,WC] 631/597-6448 ▪ Venetian-style palace, hot tub, jacuzzi, gym ▪ www.belvederefireisland.com

Black Sheep in Exile B&B [M,NS] 631/597-6565 ▪ 71 Bay Walk E, Fire Island Pines ▪ full brkfst, gourmet dinner available ▪ www.blacksheep-ny.com

Boatel [M,F,SW,WC] 631/597-6500 ▪ The Pines ▪ also restaurant

Bob Howard Realtor 631/597-9400, 212/819-9400 ▪ The Pines ▪ great source for rentals

Dune Point Guesthouse [MW,WC,GO] 631/597-6261 ▪ hot tub

Grove Hotel [M,SW,N,WC,GO] 631/597-6600 ▪ Dock Walk, Cherry Grove ▪ 4 bars on premises ▪ www.grovehotel.com

Holly House [MW,NS] 631/597-6911 ▪ Holly Walk nr Bayview Walk, Cherry Grove ▪ seasonal, shared abths

Pines Place [M,SW] 631/597-6162 ▪ guesthouse offers rooms in 2 locations, some shared baths ▪ www.pinesplace.com

BARS
Cherry's [★MW,F,E,S] 631/597-6820 ▪ 158 Bayview Walk, Cherry Grove ▪ seasonal, noon-4am, patio, also restaurant

The Island Club & Grille [M,D,E] 631/597-6001 ▪ 36 Fire Island Blvd, The Pines ▪ seasonal, 6pm-4am, from 4pm wknds, grille open 6pm-11pm, clsd Wed, also piano bar

NIGHTCLUBS
Grove Hotel (formerly the 'Ice Palace') [MW,D,S,YC,WC] 631/597-6600 ▪ Cherry Grove ▪ www.grovehotel.com

The Pavilion [★MW,D,WC] 631/597-6131 ▪ Fire Island Blvd, The Pines ▪ seasonal, noon-8am, also 'Yacht Club' restaurant

RESTAURANTS
Cherry Grove Pizza 631/597-6766 ▪ Dock Walk (under the 'Grove Hotel'), Cherry Grove ▪ 11am-11pm

Michael's 631/597-6555 ▪ Dock Walk, Cherry Grove ▪ seasonal, 7am-midnight, upscale diner fare

Rachel's at the Grove [MW] 631/597-4174 ▪ Lewis Walk, Cherry Grove ▪ brkfst, lunch & dinner, outdoor seating, ocean views, also bar

Top of the Bay [★MW] 631/597-6699 ▪ Dock Walk at Bay Walk, Cherry Grove ▪ seasonal, 7pm-midnight, scenic outdoor dining

ENTERTAINMENT & RECREATION
Invasion of the Pines the Pines dock (July 4th wknd) ▪ come & enjoy the annual fun as boatloads of drag queens from Cherry Grove arrive to terrorize the posh Pines

RETAIL SHOPS
All American Boy 631/597-7758 ▪ Harbor Walk, The Pines ▪ noon-5:30pm, 10am-7:30pm wknds, clothing

GYMS & HEALTH CLUBS
Island Gym [★M] 631/597-7867 ▪ Harbor Walk, The Pines ▪ where the boys of Fire Island work out

FIRE ISLAND

Queer Resources

COMMUNITY INFO
Gay & Lesbian Switchboard of Long Island (GLSB of LI) 516/737-1615

RECOVERY
Fire House in Cherry Grove 516/654-1150.

Tourist Info

AIRPORT DIRECTIONS
Long Island Airport in Islip. Service from NYC and other US cities, then taxi to Sayville.
Seaplane service from E 23rd St in Manhattan Th-Fri, return Sun-Mon, $239+ cash, one way. 800/468-8639.

PUBLIC TRANSIT & TAXIS
South Bay Water Taxi 516/665-8885. Service from Sayville to Fire Island.
Ferry service to The Pines and Cherry Grove from Sayville takes 20 minutes. Call 631/589-0810 for schedule.
By car: go east on the Long Island Expressway to exit 59 to Ocean Ave, then head south to Lakeland Ave and the town of Sayville. The ferry is located on River Rd.

Long Island

Long Island is divided into 2 geographical areas:
Long Island—Nassau County
Long Island—Suffolk County

Long Island—Nassau

BARS

Auntie M's [MW,NH,S] 516/679-8280 ■ 3546 Merrick Rd (at Blockbuster Shopping Plaza), Seaford ■ 5pm-4am, from 3pm Sun

Blanche [M,NH,E,S] 516/694-6906 ■ 47-2 Boundary Ave, South Farmingdale ■ 7pm-4am, from 3pm Sun, dancers Fri-Sat ■ hometown.aol.com/blanchesli

Pal Joey's [M,NH] 516/785-9301 ■ 24-57 Jerusalem Ave (at Newbridge Rd), North Bellmore ■ 4pm-4am, from 8pm Sat ■ members.aol.com/paljoeys/

RESTAURANTS

Rattlesnake Jones 516/378-7177 ■ 153 Merrick Ave (off Sunrise), Merrick ■ dinner, clsd Mon

ENTERTAINMENT & RECREATION

Jones Beach Field #6

Long Island—Suffolk

ACCOMMODATIONS

132 North Main [M,SW,NS,WC] 516/324-2246 ■ 132 N Main, East Hampton ■ seasonal mini-resort ■ tm132nmain@aol.com

Centennial House of East Hampton [GS,SW,NS,GO] 516/324-9414 ■ 13 Woods Ln, East Hampton ■ full brkfst, also 3-bdrm cottage ■ www.centhouse.com

Cozy Cabins Motel [MW,GO] 631/537-1160 ■ seasonal, hot tub, sundeck

House on Newtown B&B [GS] 631/324-1858 ■ 172 Newtown Ln (at McGuirk St), East Hampton ■ www.hamptonsvacations.com

Summit Motor Inn [GF] 631/666-6000, 800/869-6363 ■ 501 E Main St (at Brentwood Rd), Bay Shore

Sunset Beach [GF,F] 631/749-2001 ■ 35 Shore Rd, Shelter Island ■ seasonal ■ www.sunsetbeachli.com

BARS

Club 608 [MW] 631/661-9580 ■ 608 Sunrise Hwy (at Belmont Ave), West Babylon ■ 2pm-4am ■ www.club608.com

Forever Green [W,NH,D,E,K,GO] 631/226-8280 ■ 841 N Broome Ave, Lindenhurst ■ 8pm-4am, from 5pm Fri, from 7pm Sun ■ www.liforevergreen.com

Long Island Eagle [M,NH,L] 631/968-2750 ■ 94 N Clinton Ave (at Union Blvd), Bay Shore ■ 9pm-4am, from 4pm Sun

NIGHTCLUBS

Bunkhouse [★M,D,K,S,WC,GO] 631/567-2865 ■ 192 N Main St/ Montauk Hwy (at Foster Ave), Sayville ■ 7pm-4am

Nocturnal [M,D] 54 Montauk Hwy, Southampton ■ Sat only

Shi [W,D,S,WC] 516/486-9516 ■ 121 Woodfield Rd, West Hempstead ■ 8pm-4am, clsd Mon

The Swamp [M,D,YC,WC] 631/537-3332 ■ 378 Montauk Hwy (at Eastgate Rd), East Hampton ■ 6pm-4am, clsd Tue-Wed in winter, also 'Annex' restaurant, cont'l/ seafood

Thunders [★MW,D,E,S,GO] 631/423-5241 ■ 1017 E Jericho Tpke, Huntington Station ■ 9pm-4am, clsd Mon, 18+ wknds, male dancers Sat, huge outdoor area, piano bar Tue & Fri ■ www.thunders.com

RESTAURANTS

Babette's 631/329-5377 ■ 66 Newtown Ln, East Hampton ■ brkfst, lunch & dinner, healthy

ENTERTAINMENT & RECREATION

Fowler Beach Southampton

EROTICA

Heaven Sent Me 631/434-4777 ■ 108 Cain Dr, Hauppauge Industrial Pk, Brentwood ■ 24hrs

New York City

It would take a lifetime to experience New York in all its contradictory glory. Glamorous and gritty, refined and rude, dirty and dazzling: New York is all this and more. Whatever your pleasure, New York has it in abundance, from history, theater and art, to shopping, nightlife, and dining.

Queer Resources

Community Info
Lesbian & Gay Switchboard of NY 212/989-0999.
▼ Lesbian & Gay Community Services Center 212/620-7310, web: www.gaycenter.org. One Little West 12th St, 9am-11pm. See Greenwich Village map.
East End Gay Organization (EEGO) 516/324-3699.

AIDS Resources
New York State 800/541-2437 (in NY only).

Recovery
Intergroup Gay AA 212/647-1680, web: www.royy.com/begmtgs.html.

City Calendar

LGBT Pride
Last Sunday in June. 212/807-7433, web: www.nycpride.org.
Bronx Pride - June. 718/670-3396.
Brooklyn Pride - June. 718/670-3337.

Annual Events
March - Saint-at-Large Black Party.
May - AIDS Walk-a-thon 212/807-9255.
June - New York Int'l Gay/Lesbian Film Festival 212/254-7228.
September - Wigstock 212/439-5139. Outrageous wig/drag/performance festival in Tompkins Square Park in the East Village.
New York Lesbian/Gay Experimental Film/Video Fest 212/571-4242. Film, videos, installations & media performances.

Tourist Info

Airport Directions
John F Kennedy International. 1 hr/$45+ taxi ride to Manhattan.
LaGuardia: 45 min/$35+ taxi ride.

Public Transit & Taxis
Wave an arm on any streetcorner for a taxi.
Public transit MTA 718/330-1234.

Tourist Spots & Info
Broadway.
Carnegie Hall 212/903-9600.
Central Park.
Ellis Island.
Empire State Building 212/736-3100.
Greenwich Village.
Guggenheim Museum 212/423-3600.
Lincoln Center 212/546-2656.
Metropolitan Museum of Art.
Museum of Modern Art 212/708-9400.
Radio City Music Hall 212/247-4777.
Rockefeller Center.
Statue of Liberty.
Times Square.
United Nations.
Wall Street.
World Trade Center 212/435-4170.
Visitor's Center: 212/397-8222.
nycvisit.com

Weather
A spectrum of extremes with pleasant moments thrown in. Spring and fall are the best times to visit.

Best Views
Coming over any of the bridges into New York, the Empire State Building, or the World Trade Center.

New York City

New York City is divided into 8 geographical areas:
- NYC—Overview
- NYC—Soho, Greenwich & Chelsea
- NYC—Midtown
- NYC—Uptown
- NYC—Brooklyn
- NYC—Queens
- NYC—Bronx
- NYC—Staten Island

NYC—Overview

NIGHTCLUBS
Sea Tea [M,D,F,S] 212/675-4357 ■ leaves from Pier 40 ■ seasonal sailing T-dance ■ www.seatea.com

ENTERTAINMENT & RECREATION
Before Stonewall 212/439-1090 ■ lesbian/ gay history tour ■ www.bigonion.com

Dyke TV (Free Speech TV) 212/989-8310 ■ 'TV show produced by lesbians for lesbians,' also do public screenings every other month ■ dyketv.org

Pro Musica Tours 212/541-5122, 800/916-0312 ■ performing arts itineraries

Think It's Not When It Is 718/949-5162 ■ theater company promoting positive lgbt images ■ tinwii@aol.com

Townhouse Tours 212/539-2683 ■ tours of New York's gay history ■ www.townhousetours.com

PUBLICATIONS
Empire 212/352-3535 ■ stylish glossy for gay New York ■ www.hx.com

HX Magazine 212/352-3535 ■ complete weekly guide to gay New York at night ■ www.hx.com

LGNY (Lesbian & Gay New York) 212/691-1100 ■ lgbt newspaper ■ www.lgny.com

New York Blade News 212/268-2701 ■ 242 W 30th St, 4th flr ■ weekly lgbt newspaper ■ www.nyblade.com

Next 212/627-0165 ■ party paper ■ www.nextmagazine.net

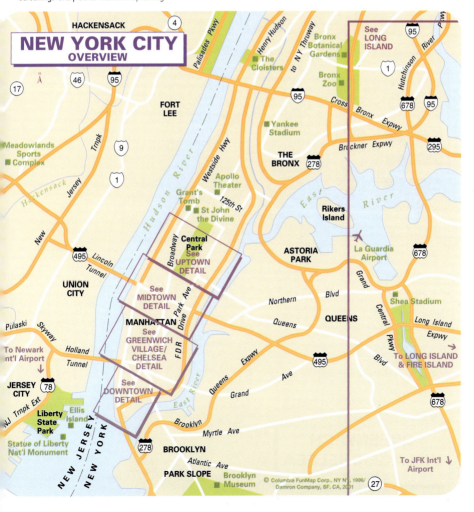

NEW YORK • USA

NYC — Soho, Greenwich & Chelsea

ACCOMMODATIONS

1 **Abingdon Guesthouse** [GS,NS,WC] 212/243-5384 ■ 13 8th Ave (at W 12th St) ■ quiet, mature clientele ■ www.abingdonguesthouse.com

2 **Chelsea Inn** [GF] 212/645-8989, 800/640-6469 ■ 46 W 17th St (btwn 5th & 6th Aves) ■ European-style inn ■ www.chelseainn.com

3 **Chelsea Mews Guest House** [MO,NS,GO] 212/255-9174 ■ 344 W 15th St (btwn 8th & 9th Aves) ■ some shared baths

4 ▶ **Chelsea Pines Inn** [MW,GO] 212/929-1023 ■ 317 W 14th St (btwn 8th & 9th Aves) ■ some shared baths ■ cpiny@aol.com

5 **The Chelsea Savoy Hotel** [GS,WC] 212/929-9353 ■ 204 W 23rd St (at 7th Ave) ■ www.chelseasavoy.qpg.com

6 **Colonial House Inn** [M,N,GO] 212/243-9669, 800/689-3779 ■ 318 W 22nd St (btwn 8th & 9th Aves) ■ rooftop patio ■ www.colonialhouseinn.com

East Village B&B [WO,NS,GO] 212/260-1865 ■ 244 E 7th St ■ in the heart of the Village ■ bcsellen@juno.com

7 **The Gramercy Park Hotel** [GF] 212/475-4320, 800/221-4083 ■ 2 Lexington Ave (at E 21st St) ■ aging hotel across from Gramercy Park ■ www.gramercyparkhotel.com

8 **Holiday Inn** [GF,F] 212/966-8898 ■ 138 Lafayette St (btwn Canal & Howard, in Chinatown) ■ www.holidayinn-nyc.com

Home Suite Hom ■ hospitality & home exchanges, contact Mark Schall ■ www.gaytrip.com

9 **Hotel Washington Square** [GF,F] 212/777-9515, 800/222-0418 ■ 103 Waverly Pl (at MacDougal St) ■ renovated 100-yr-old hotel, 'C3' restaurant 7:30am-10:30pm ■ www.washingtonsquarehotel.com

10 **Incentra Village House** [MW,GO] 212/206-0007 ■ 32 8th Ave (at W 12th St)

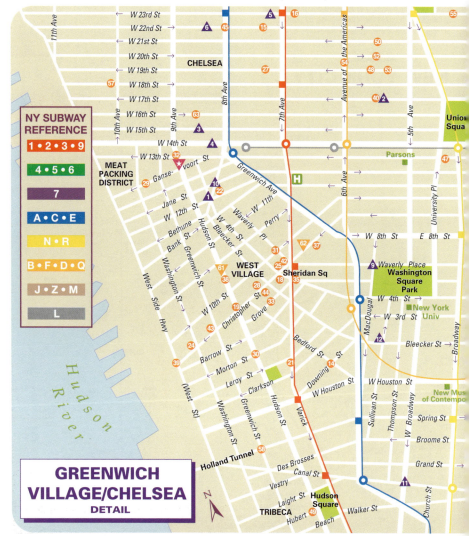

GREENWICH VILLAGE/CHELSEA DETAIL

11 **Soho Grand Hotel** [GF,WC] 212/965-3000, 800/965-3000 ■ 310 W Broadway (at Canal St) ■ big, glossy, over-the-top hotel ■ www.sohogrand.com

12 **Southern Comforts** [GS,WC,GO] 323/850-5423, 800/889-7359 ■ handsome condo in the heart of the Village ■ www.SouthernComforts.com

BARS

13 **The Bar** [M,NH] 212/254-5766 ■ 68 2nd Ave (at 4th St) ■ 4pm-4am

14 **Bar d'O** [GF,S] 212/627-1580 ■ 29 Bedford St (at Downing St) ■ 7:30pm-3am, theme nights, women's night Mon

15 **Barracuda** [★M,S] 212/645-8613 ■ 275 W 22nd St (at 8th Ave) ■ 4pm-4am, live DJs

16 **Blu** [M,D] 212/633-6113 ■ 161 W 23rd St (at 7th Ave) ■ 4pm-4am, DJ Tue-Sun, Internet access

17 **The Boiler Room** [★M,NH] 212/254-7536 ■ 86 E 4th St (at 2nd Ave) ■ 4pm-4am

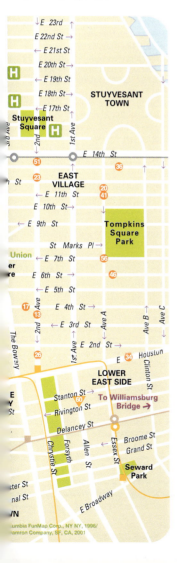

NEW YORK CITY

Winner Out & About Editor's Choice Award

Outstanding Achievement in Gay Travel

CHELSEA PINES INN

The Cozy Bed and Breakfast in the Heart of Gay New York

SHELDON POST, Founder

CHARMING ROOMS FROM $89

Private or Semi-private baths
Telephone/Cable TV with Free HBO
Refrigerator/Hair Dryer/Irons &
Ironing Boards in all rooms
Air Conditioning/Central Heating
Expanded Continental Breakfast
featuring Homemade Bread,
Krispy Kreme Donuts & Fresh Fruit
Walk to Christopher Street, all
bars, clubs, shops

**Advance Reservations Suggested
All Major Credit Cards Accepted**

317 West 14th Street
New York City 10014
Tel: 212.929.1023 Fax: 212.620.5646
E.Mail: cpiny@aol.com
Website: www.q-net.com/chelseapines

NEW YORK • USA

It's like a thousand brochures!

DAMRON ACCOMMODATIONS
FIFTH EDITION

- full-color photographs speak louder than words
- over 1800 international listings cover gay-friendly hotels, B&Bs, and accommodations across the globe!
- detailed listings answer all your questions about rates, rooms, meals, smoking, kids, and pets
- cross-indexes note Men-only, Women-only, RV & Camping, and Wheelchair-accessible accommodations
- over 550 pages, only $22.95!

▶ ORDER NOW: (800) 462-6654

---

18 **Boots & Saddle** [M,NH] 212/929-9684 ■ 76 Christopher St (at 7th Ave S) ■ 8am-4am, noon-4pm Sun

19 **Chi Chiz** [M,NH,MR] 212/462-0027 ■ 135 Christopher St (at Hudson) ■ 4pm-4am

20 **The Cock** [M,K,S] 212/946-1871 ■ 188 Ave 'A' (at 12th St) ■ 10:30pm-4am, a 'sleazy rock 'n roll bar', DJs, strippers

21 <u>Crazy Nanny's</u> [W,D,TG,E,K,V] 212/929-8356, 212/366-6312 (event line) ■ 21 7th Ave S (at Leroy) ■ 4pm-4am, DJ Th-Sat ■ www.crazynannys.com

22 <u>Cubbyhole</u> [W,NH] 212/243-9041 ■ 281 W 12th St (at 4th St) ■ 4pm-3am, from 2pm wknds ■ cubby4w12@aol.com

23 **Dick's Bar** [M] 212/475-2071 ■ 192 2nd Ave (at 12th St) ■ 2pm-4am, porno nights Tue & Th

24 **The Dugout** [M,NH,B,WC] 212/242-9113 ■ 185 Christopher St (at Weehawken) ■ 4pm-4am, from 1pm Sun, sports bar

25 **Duplex** [GF,E,$] 212/255-5438 ■ 61 Christopher St (at 7th Ave) ■ 4pm-4am, piano bar & cabaret from 9pm, from 4pm on wknds, cover charge + 2 drink minimum

26 **Fat Cock 29** [M,V] 212/946-1871 ■ 2nd Ave (btwn 1st & 2nd Sts) ■ 6pm-4am, nice & sleazy

Foot Friends/ Boot Bros [M,$] 212/760-5952 ■ 8pm-2am Mon at 'The Lure' (409 W 13th St, look for the bootprint on the door), call for dates; also 8pm-midnight 2nd Sat at 'J's Hangout' (675 Hudson St) ■ www.footfriends.com

27 **g** [★M] 212/929-1085 ■ 223 W 19th St (at 7th Ave) ■ 4pm-4am, lounge, live DJs, juice bar

28 **The Hangar** [M,NH] 212/627-2044 ■ 115 Christopher St (at Bleecker) ■ 3pm-4am, live DJs

29 **hell** [MW] 212/727-1666 ■ 59 Gansevoort St (at Washington) ■ 7pm-4am, from 5pm Fri, swanky lounge, DJ Tue-Th & Sun

30 <u>Henrietta Hudson</u> [W,NH,WC] 212/924-3347 ■ 438 Hudson (at Morton) ■ 4pm-4am, from 1pm wknds

31 **Julius** [M,NH,F,OC] 212/929-9672 ■ 159 W 10th St (at Waverly) ■ 8am-4am

32 **The Lure** [★M,B,L] 212/741-3919 ■ 409 W 13th (at 9th Ave) ■ 8pm-4am, from 5pm Sun, theme nights ■ thelure.com

33 **Marie's Crisis** [MW,E] 212/243-9323 ■ 59 Grove St (at 7th Ave) ■ 4pm-4am, piano bar from 9:30pm, from 5pm wknds

34 <u>Meow Mix</u> [★W,D,E] 212/254-0688 ■ 269 E Houston St (at Suffolk) ■ 7pm-4am, 'Fey' lounge 11pm Sun ■ www.meowmixchix.com

35 **The Monster** [★M,D,WC] 212/924-3558 ■ 80 Grove St (at W 4th St, Sheridan Sq) ■ 4pm-4am, from 2pm wknds, piano bar & cabaret, T-dance Sun, 'Sabor Latino' Mon, disco Tue ■ www.manhattan-monster.com

36 **Phoenix** [MW,NH] 212/477-9979 ■ 447 E 13th (at Ave A) ■ 4pm-4am, patio

37 **Pieces** [M,NH,K,S] 212/929-9291 ■ 8 Christopher St ■ 2pm-4am, karaoke Tue, drag shows Wed, DJ Fri-Sat

38 <u>Rubyfruit Bar & Grill</u> [W,F] 212/929-3343 ■ 531 Hudson St (at Charles St) ■ 3pm-2am, till 4am Fri-Sat, full menu served 5pm-11pm, till midnight Fri-Sat

39 **Sneaker Bar** [M,NH,B,MR,WC] 212/242-9830 ■ 392 West St (at Christopher) ■ noon-4am, DJ Wed & Fri-Sun, bears Tue

40 **Splash** [★MO,D,S,V,YC] 212/691-0073 ■ 50 W 17th St (at 6th Ave) ■ 4pm-4am ■ www.splashbar.com

41 **Starlight Bar & Lounge** [MW,E] 212/475-2172 ■ 167 Ave 'A' (at 11th St) ■ 9pm-3am, clsd Mon-Wed, live DJs, more women Sun for 'Starlette'

NYC—Soho, Greenwich & Chelsea • NEW YORK

42 **Stonewall Inn** [M,D] 212/463-0950 ■ 53 Christopher St (at 7th Ave) ■ 2:30pm-4am

43 **Two Potato** [M,NH,MR-AF,S] 212/255-0286 ■ 143 Christopher St (at Greenwich St) ■ noon-4am, strip shows Wed & Sun, drag Fri-Sat, karaoke Th

44 **Ty's** [M,NH,L,GO] 212/741-9641 ■ 114 Christopher St (btwn Bleecker & Hudson) ■ 2pm-4am, from 1pm wknds ■ www.citysearch.com/nyc/tys

45 **The View** [★M,V] 212/929-2243 ■ 232 8th Ave (at 22nd St) ■ 3pm-4am, from 1pm wknds, art show Th

46 **Wonder Bar** [★MW,V,WC] 212/777-9105 ■ 505 E 6th St (at Ave 'A') ■ 6pm-4am, cocktail lounge DJ

63 **XL** [M,D] 212/995-1400 ■ 357 W 16th St (btwn 8th & 9th) ■ 4pm-4am, impressive lighting system, gorgeous bartenders ■ www.xlnewyork.com

NIGHTCLUBS

47 **13 Bar & Lounge** [GF,D] 212/979-6777 ■ 35 E 13th St (at University Pl) ■ 10pm-4am, lounge from 5pm, more gay Th

48 **Big Apple Ranch** [MW,D,CW,BW,$] 212/358-5752 ■ 39 W 19th St, 5th flr (btwn 5th & 6th, at 'Dance Manhattan') ■ 8pm-1am Sat only, two-step lessons

49 **Body & Soul at Vinyl** [GS,D,MR,$] 212/330-9169 ■ 6 Hubert St (at Hudson) ■ 3pm Sun, classic house, a NYC must; also 'Shelter' 11pm Sat, alcohol-free dance party

50 **Centro Fly** [GS,D,F] 212/627-7770 ■ 45 W 21st St (btwn 5th & 6th) ■ www.centro-fly.com

51 **Clit Club** [★W,D,MR,E,WC] 212/533-2860 ■ 219 2nd Ave (at the Flamingo) ■ 10pm-4am Fri ■ dagger3@aol.com

51 **Flamingo East** [W,D] 212/533-2860 ■ 219 2nd Ave (at 13th St) ■ 'Clit Club' Fri

52 **Fourplay** [W,D] 212/627-7867 ■ 28 W 20th St (btwn 5th & 6th Aves, at Lava] ■ Mon only, boys welcome

53 **Hush** [M,D] 212/989-4874 ■ 17 W 19th St (btwn 5th & 6th Aves) ■ 11pm-close Mon only ■ www.fagtag.com

21 **Legendary Buddha Bar Party** [W,D,MR,$] 888/784-8538 ■ 28 7th Ave (at Leroy, at 'Neva Lounge') ■ 9pm Sun only ■ www.girlzparty.com

54 **Limelight** [★GF,D,$] 212/807-9109 ■ 660 6th Ave (at W 20th St) ■ 10pm-4am Wed-Sun, after hrs Fri-Sat, more gay Sun at 'Drama!') ■ www.limelight-tunnel.com

55 **LoverGirl NYC** [W,D,S,$] 212/631-1000, 212/726-8302 ■ 28 E 23rd St (btwn Broadway & Park, at 'True') ■ 10pm-4:30am Sat

21 **Nowbar** [M,TG,S,$] 212/802-9502 ■ 22 7th Ave S (at Leroy St) ■ drag shows Th-Sat ■ www.fetishplanetnyc.com

56 **Pyramid** [GF] 212/462-9077 ■ 101 Ave 'A' (at 7th St) ■ 10pm-4am, more gay Fri at '1984', New Wave party

57 **Roxy** [★GS,D,A,S,$] 212/645-5156 ■ 515 W 18th St (at 10th Ave) ■ 11pm-4am Fri-Sat, rollerdisco from 7pm Wed, gay Sat ■ www.roxynyc.com

Saint-At-Large [★M,D] 212/674-8541 ■ huge circuit parties: White Party in Feb & Black Party in March ■ www.saintatlarge.com

Shescape [WO,D] 212/686-5665 ■ women's dance parties in various locations

58 **Squeeze Box** [GS,D,A,S,$] 212/334-1390 ■ 511 Greenwich St (at Spring St, at 'Don Hill's') ■ queer rock 'n' roll from 10pm last Fri, call for other events

CAFES

Big Cup [★M] 212/206-0059 ■ 228 8th Ave (at 22nd St) ■ 7am-2am, boy central

Caffe Raffaella 212/929-7247 ■ 134 7th Ave S (at Charles St) ■ 11am-2am, armchair cafe

RESTAURANTS

7A [★] 212/673-6583 ■ 109 Ave 'A' (at 7th St) ■ 24hrs

Around the Clock 212/598-0402 ■ 8 3rd Ave (at 9th St) ■ 24hrs

Benny's Burritos 212/254-2054 ■ 93 Ave 'A' (at 6th St) ■ 11:30am-midnight, cheap & huge; also 113 Greenwich (at Jane), 212/727-0584

Blue Ribbon [WC] 212/274-0404 ■ 97 Sullivan St (at Spring St) ■ 4pm-4am, clsd Mon, cont'l/ American, chef hangout

Brunetta's [★MW] 212/228-4030 ■ 190 1st Ave (btwn 11th & 12th Sts) ■ affordable Italian, some veggie, patio

Chelsea Bistro & Bar 212/727-2026 ■ 358 W 23rd St (at 9th Ave) ■ 5pm-11pm, trendy French, full bar

The Cloister Cafe 212/777-9128 ■ 238 E 9th St (at 2nd Ave) ■ 11am-midnight, garden dining

Cola's [★] 212/633-8020 ■ 148 8th Ave (at 17th St) ■ 4:30pm-11:30pm, affordable Italian

East of Eighth 212/352-0075 ■ 254 W 23rd St (at 8th) ■ lunch, dinner till midnight, till 2am wknds

Eighteenth & Eighth 212/242-5000 ■ 159 8th Ave ■ boys, boys, boys

Empire Diner 212/243-2736 ■ 210 10th Ave (at 22nd St) ■ 24hrs

First 212/674-3823 ■ 87 1st Ave (at 6th St) ■ 6pm-2am, till 3am Fri-Sat, 11am-1am Sun, cont'l, hip crowd

Flamingo East [D] 212/533-2860 ■ 219 2nd Ave (at 13th St) ■ also bar w/ dancing & 'offbeat rec room'

Florent [★] 212/989-5779 ■ 69 Gansevoort St (at Washington) ■ 9am-5am, 24hrs Fri-Sat, French diner

Food Bar 212/243-2020 ■ 149 8th Ave (at 17th St) ■ Mediterranean

Garage [E] 212/645-0600 ■ 99 7th Ave S (at Grove St) ■ plenty veggie, live jazz

Global 33 212/477-8427 ■ 99 2nd Ave (at 5th St) ■ 5pm-midnight, int'l tapas, trendy

La Nouvelle Justine 212/673-8908 ■ 101 E 2nd St ■ doms & slaves serve it up in this SM-themed restaurant

---

Creative Vision Books

548 Hudson Street, NYC

NYC's GLBT Bookstore, stocks 5000+ books, videos, DVD's, greeting cards, unique gifts, CD's, posters, art work, Gay Pride wear, rare magazines, photos, film. Part of every sale is donated to our community. Come say hello, munch on free, home baked cookies, listen to our own electric music mix and browse. At home, order by phone (1-800-997-9899) fax, (1-212-645-0395), Email (vince@123internetme.net) or at www.creativevisionsbooks.com.

PHONE **800/997-9899**

NEW YORK • USA

"This is nothing like the 'green sign' hotel your parents stayed in!"

- **The easiest business decision on Wall Street.**
- **The most technologically advanced rooms among any business hotel.**
- **Your closest commute to Wall Street.**
- **Location, Location, Location.**

Holiday Inn®
Wall Street District
**15 Gold Street • New York, NY 10023
tel: 212.232.7700 • fax: 212.425.7800
Reservations: 212.232.7800**

Life Cafe 212/477-8791 ■ 343 E 10th St (at Ave 'B') ■ 11am-1am, till 3am Fri-Sat, vegetarian artist hangout

Lips [S] 212/675-7710 ■ 2 Bank St (at Greenwich) ■ 6pm-midnight, till 3am Sat, 'Disco Fever Brunch' noon-6pm Sun, Italian/ American served by queens

Lucky Cheng's [★K,S] 212/473-0516 ■ 24 1st Ave (at 2nd St) ■ 5pm-midnight, 'The Goldfish Pond' drag lounge & bar from 9pm

Mary's Restaurant 212/741-3387 ■ 42 Bedford St (at 7th Ave S) ■ 6pm-midnight, brunch Sun (except summers)

Miracle Grill 212/254-2353 ■ 112 1st Ave (at 6th St) ■ garden dining

Restivo [GO] 212/366-4133 ■ 209 7th Ave (at 22nd St) ■ noon-midnight, Italian, intimate ambiance

Sacred Chow [WC] 212/337-0863 ■ 522 Hudson St (at 10th St) ■ 7:30am-11pm, gourmet vegan

Sazerac House Bar & Grill 212/989-0313 ■ 533 Hudson (at Charles) ■ noon-11pm, Cajun, full bar

Stingy Lulu's 212/674-3545 ■ 129 St Marks Pl (at Ave 'A') ■ 11am-4am, funky American diner, popular brunch, drag queen servers

The Viceroy [★] 212/633-8484 ■ 160 8th Ave (at 18th St) ■ noon-midnight, fusion, full bar

ENTERTAINMENT & RECREATION

DrédKing—Drag King/Gender-Illusionist 212/946-4475 ■ one of the best known Drag Kings since 1995, call for performance dates/ details ■ www.dredking.com

Leslie-Lohman Gay Art Foundation Gallery 212/673-7007 ■ 127-B Prince St, lower level ■ 1pm-6pm, clsd Sun-Mon ■ www.leslie-lohman.org

PS 122 212/477-5288, 212/477-5029 ■ 150 1st Ave (at E 9th St) ■ it's rough, it's raw, it's real New York performance art ■ www.ps122.org

Wessel & O'Connor 212/242-8811 ■ 242 W 26th St (btwn 7th & 8th Aves) ■ open Tue-Sun in winter, Mon-Fri in summer, gay photography gallery ■ www.wesseloconnor.com

WOW Cafe Cabaret 212/777-4280 ■ 59 E 4th St, 4th fl (btwn 2nd Ave & Bowery) ■ open Th-Sat, women's theater

BOOKSTORES

Bleecker Street Books 212/675-2084 ■ 350 Bleecker St (at W 10th St) ■ 10:30am-11:30pm

60 **Bluestockings Women's Bookstore** [E] 212/777-6028 ■ 172 Allen St (btwn Stanton & Rivington) ■ noon-8pm, from 2pm Sun, also cafe ■ www.bluestockings.com

61 ▶ **Creative Visions Books** 212/645-7573, 800/997-9989 ■ 548 Hudson St (btwn Perry & Charles) ■ noon-10pm, till 11pm Fri-Sat, lgbt ■ www.creativevisionsbooks.com

62 **Oscar Wilde Memorial Bookshop** 212/255-8097 ■ 15 Christopher St (at 7th Ave) ■ 11am-8pm, noon-7pm Sun, lgbt ■ wildebooks@aol.com

Soho Books 212/226-3795 ■ 351 W Broadway (at Grant) ■ 10am-midnight

RETAIL SHOPS

DeMask 212/352-2850 ■ 135 W 22nd St (btwn 6th & 7th Aves) ■ 11am-7pm, European fetish fashion ■ demask.com

DV8 [GO] 212/337-9744 ■ 211 W 20th St (at 7th Ave) ■ noon-8pm, till 7pm Sat, clsd Sun-Mon, fetishwear ■ www.dv8newyork.com

Flight 001 212/691-1001 ■ 96 Greenwich (btwn Jane & 12th) ■ noon-8pm, clsd Sun, travel gear

Rainbows & Triangles 212/627-2166 ■ 192 8th Ave (at 19th St) ■ 11am-9pm, till 10pm Fri-Sat ■ www.rainbowsandtriangles.com

NYC—Soho/Downtown • NEW YORK

GYMS & HEALTH CLUBS
19th St Health & Fitness [MW] 212/929-6789 ■ 22 W 19th St (btwn 5th & 6th) ■ 8am-11pm, day passes available
David Barton Gym [MW] 212/727-0004 ■ 552 6th Ave (btwn 15th & 16th) ■ 6am-midnight, 10am-9pm wknds
New York Sports Club [M] 212/627-0065 ■ 128 8th Ave (btwn 16th & 17th) ■ 6am-midnight

MEN'S CLUBS
The Manhole 212/647-1726 ■ 28 9th Ave (btwn 13th & 14th, in the Triangle Bldg) ■ S/M playspace w/ dungeon, hosts 'NY Jacks' JO club
West Side Club [★M,PC] 212/691-2700 ■ 27 W 20th St, 2nd flr (at 6th Ave) ■ 24hrs

SEX CLUBS
Hellfire [GS,TG] 212/647-0063 ■ 28 9th Ave (btwn 13th & 14th, in the Triangle Bldg) ■ 8pm-2am Th, 10pm-5am Fri-Sat, pansexual playspace w/ dungeon ■ www.clubhellfire.com
J's Hangout [M,D,BYOB,$] 212/242-9292 ■ 675 Hudson St (at 14th St) ■ call for events/ theme nights
Throb [WO,$] 718/788-5122 ■ 8pm-1am 1st Th, women-only play party, call for location ■ throbparty@aol.com
The Vault [L] 212/255-6758 ■ 146 W 28th St (at 6th Ave) ■ sex & fetish club, call for events & hrs ■ clubvault.com

EROTICA
Ann St Entertainment Center 212/267-9760 ■ 21 Ann St (at Broadway)

Christopher St Book Shop 212/463-0657 ■ 500 Hudson St (at Christopher)
Leather Man 212/243-5339 ■ 111 Christopher St
The Noose 212/807-1789 ■ 261 W 19th St (at 8th Ave)
Pleasure Chest 212/242-2158 ■ 156 7th Ave S (at Charles)
Toys in Babeland 212/375-1701 ■ 94 Rivington (btwn Orchard & Ludlow) ■ noon-10pm, till 8pm Sun ■ www.babeland.com
Unicorn Bookstore 212/924-2921 ■ 277-C W 22nd St (at 7th Ave)

NYC—Downtown

ACCOMMODATIONS
1 ▶ **Holiday Inn Wall Street District** [GS,WC] 212/232-7700, 800/465-4329 ■ 15 Gold St ■ all suites & rms have 'virtual offices' w/ T1 connectivity: just plug in & log on ■ holidayinnwsd.com

NIGHTCLUBS
2 **After Work Wednesdays** [W,D,MR,F,K] 888/784-8538 ■ 27 Park Pl (at Church, at 'Club B-52') ■ 6pm-2am Wed, networking & karaoke 6pm-10pm, dancing/DJ from 10pm ■ www.girlzparty.com

MEN'S CLUBS
Wall Street Sauna [★] 212/233-8900 ■ 1 Maiden Ln, 11th flr

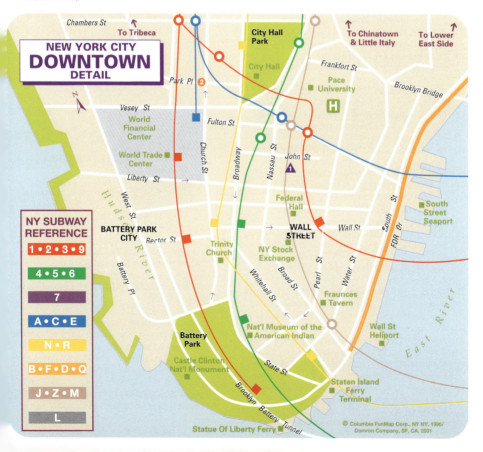

NEW YORK • USA

NYC—Midtown

ACCOMMODATIONS

1 **Gershwin Hotel** [GF] 212/545-8000 ▪ 7 E 27th St (at 5th Ave) ▪ artsy, seedy hotel w/ model's floor dorms & rooms, bar 6pm-2am, cafe 7am-11am, jazz room & art gallery ▪ www.gershwinhotel.com

2 **Habitat Hotel** [GF] 212/753-8841, 800/255-0482 ▪ 130 E 57th St (at Lexington) ▪ upscale budget hotel ▪ www.habitatny.com

3 **Holiday Inn Martinique on Broadway** [GS] 212/736-3800, 888/694-6543 ▪ 49 W 32nd St (btwn Broadway & 5th) ▪ also restaurant ▪ www.holidayinnbroadway.com

4 **The Hotel Metro** [GF] 212/947-2500, 800/356-3870 ▪ 45 W 35th St (at 5th Ave) ▪ slick art deco hotel, 1 blk from Empire State Bldg ▪ www.hotelmetronyc.com
Ivy Terrace 516/662-6862 ▪ private studio rental w/ terrace ▪ www.ivyterrace.com

5 **Park Central Hotel** [GF,WC] 212/247-8000, 800/346-1359 ▪ 870 7th Ave (at 56th St) ▪ also restaurant ▪ www.parkcentralny.com

6 **Travel Inn** [GF,SW] 212/695-7171, 800/869-4630 ▪ 515 W 42nd St (at 10th Ave) ▪ www.newyorkhotel.com/travelinn/travelinn.htm

BARS

7 **Barrage** [M] 212/586-9390 ▪ 401 W 47th St (at 9th Ave) ▪ 4pm-close

8 **BS New York** [M,NH,V] 212/684-8376 ▪ 405 3rd Ave (at 29th St) ▪ 3pm-4am, theme nights

9 **Chase** [GS] 212/333-3400 ▪ 255 W 55th St (at 8th Ave) ▪ cocktail lounge & cafe

10 **Chase Hell's Kitchen** [M,WC] 212/582-2200 ▪ 359 W 54th St (btwn 8th & 9th) ▪ 6pm-4am, also downstairs lounge

11 **Cleo's Saloon** [M,NH] 212/307-1503 ▪ 656 9th Ave (at 46th St) ▪ 8am-4am, from noon Sun

12 **Danny's Skylight Room** [GF,$] 212/265-8133 ▪ 346 W 46th St (at 9th Ave) ▪ 4pm-midnight, brunch Wed & wknds, piano bar from 6pm, cover + 2 drink minimum

13 **Don't Tell Mama** [★GF,S,YC,$] 212/757-0788 ▪ 343 W 46th St (at 9th Ave) ▪ 4pm-4am, piano bar & cabaret, cover + 2 drink minimum, call for shows

14 **Dusk** [GS] 212/924-4490 ▪ 147 W 24th St (btwn 6th & 7th) ▪ 6pm-close, clsd Sun

15 **Hannah's Lava Lounge** [MW] 212/974-9087 ▪ 923 8th Ave (at 55th St) ▪ noon-4am, art exhibits

16 **Julie's** [W,P,E] 212/688-1294 ▪ 305 E 53rd St, 2nd Fl (btwn 2nd & 3rd Ave) ▪ 5pm-4am, DJ Wed-Sun, piano bar, theme nights

17 **Oscar Wilde** [M,P] 212/486-7309 ▪ 221 E 58th St (at 2nd Ave) ▪ 4pm-4am

18 **Pegasus** [M,E] 212/888-4702 ▪ 119 E 60th St (at Lexington) ▪ open mic Fri-Sat, piano bar, 'Asian lounge' Sat

19 **Posh** [M] 212/957-2222 ▪ 405 W 51st St (at 9th Ave) ▪ 4pm-4am, theme nights

20 **Regents** [M,E] 212/593-3091 ▪ 317 E 53rd St (at 2nd Ave) ▪ 5pm-4am, also restaurant, plenty veggie

21 **Stella's** [M,S] 212/575-1680 ▪ 266 W 47th St (at 8th Ave) ▪ noon-4am, go-go boys

22 **The Web** [M,D,MR-A,K,S] 212/308-1546 ▪ 40 E 58th St (at Madison) ▪ 4pm-3am, theme nights, go-go boys

23 **Xth Ave Lounge** [M,F] 212/245-9088 ▪ 642 10th Ave (at 45th St) ▪ 4pm-4am, from 6pm wknds

NIGHTCLUBS

24 **Escuelita** [M,D,MR-L,TG,S,$] 212/631-0588 ▪ 301 W 39th St (at 8th Ave) ▪ 10pm-4am Th-Sat, T-dance 5pm Sun, mostly women Fri for 'Spicy Fridays' ▪ www.escuelita.com

25 **Female Fridaze** [W,D,MR] 888/784-8538 ▪ 133 W 33rd St (btwn 6th & 7th, at 'Club Midtown 133') ▪ 10pm Fri only ▪ www.girlzparty.com

24 **Her/ She Bar** [W,D,$] 212/631-1093 ▪ 301 W 39th St (at 8th Ave, at 'Escuelita') ▪ 10pm-4am Fri

25 **The Tunnel** [M,D,S,$] 212/695-4682 ▪ 27th St (btwn 11th & 12th Aves) ▪ 11pm Fri-Sat

26 **Twilo** [★GS,D,E,$] 212/268-1600 ▪ 530 W 27th St (at 10th Ave) ▪ 11pm Fri-Sat, more gay Sat at 'Junioverse'

CAFES

Cafe Un Deux Trois [★] 212/354-4148 ▪ 123 W 44th St (at Broadway) ▪ noon-midnight, bistro

NYC—Midtown • New York

Restaurants

Bar Nine 212/399-9336 ■ 807 9th Ave (at W 53rd St) ■ 5pm-4am

Comfort Diner 212/867-4555 ■ 216 E 45th St (at 3rd Ave) ■ 7am-10pm, reasonable '50s diner

Martino's 212/751-0029 ■ 230 E 58th St (btwn 2nd & 3rd Ave) ■ dinner, Sun brunch, Italian, near 'Julie's' bar

Revolution 212/489-8451 ■ 611 9th Ave (at 43rd St) ■ 5pm-midnight, trendy video dining, bar till 3am

Rice & Beans 212/265-4444 ■ 744 9th Ave (at 50th St) ■ 11am-10pm, Latin/ Brazilian, plenty veggie

Scopa [★] 212/686-8787 ■ 27 E 28th St (at Madison) ■ great Italian deli from 8am, lunch & dinner daily in the main dining room, full bar

Townhouse Restaurant [★MW] 212/826-6341 ■ 206 E 58th St (at 3rd Ave) ■ lunch & dinner, Sun brunch, open late wknds, plenty veggie

Gyms & Health Clubs

Spa 227 [MO] 212/754-0277 ■ 227 E 56th St (btwn 2nd & 3rd) ■ 6am-midnight, 8am-10pm wknds, $20 day pass

Men's Clubs

East Side Club [★PC] 212/753-2222, 212/888-1884 ■ 227 E 56th St, 6th flr ■ 24hrs, day passes available

Erotica

Come Again 212/308-9394 ■ 353 E 53rd St (at 2nd Ave) ■ clsd Sun, woman-owned erotica store ■ www.comeagainnyc.com

Eve's Garden 212/757-8651 ■ 119 W 57th St #1201 (btwn 6th & 7th) ■ 11am-7pm, clsd Sun, women's sexuality boutique, men must be escorted by a woman

Gaiety Burlesk 212/221-8868 ■ 201 W 46th St (at Broadway) ■ famed strip shows—you never know which celebrity you'll see on stage or in the crowd

NEW YORK • USA

NYC—Uptown

ACCOMMODATIONS
1 **333 West 88th Associates** [GF,GO] 212/724-9818, 800/724-9888 ■ 333 W 88th St (at Riverside Dr) ■ weekly rental apts & B&B rooms ■ www.333w88.com

BARS
2 **Brandy's Piano Bar** [M] 212/650-1944 ■ 235 E 84th St (at 2nd Ave) ■ 4pm-4am
3 **Bridge Bar** [M] 212/223-9104 ■ 309 E 60th St (at 2nd Ave) ■ 4pm-4am
4 **Candle Bar** [★M,NH] 212/874-9155 ■ 309 Amsterdam (at 74th St) ■ 2pm-4am, cruisy
5 **Eight of Clubs** [M,NH,V] 212/580-7389 ■ 230 W 75th St (at Broadway) ■ noon-4am, from 4pm Mon-Tue, tiny cruise bar
   Saints [M,NH] 212/961-0599 ■ 992 Amsterdam (at 109th St) ■ 4pm-4am
6 **Tool Box** [M,NH,V] 212/348-1288 ■ 1742 2nd Ave (at 91st St) ■ 8pm-4am, cruisy
7 **The Works** [★M,V] 212/799-3245 ■ 428 Columbus Ave (at 81st St) ■ 2pm-4am, live jazz Wed, great 'beer bust' Sun ■ www.theworksnyc.com

NIGHTCLUBS
151 Dance Party [M,D,MR-L,S] 718/991-9830 ■ 2nd Fri only, Latin, R&B & house, call for location
Intimate Collaborations [W,D,18+,MR,F,WC,GO] 212/894-3724 x 1285 ■ 2611 Frederick Douglas Blvd/ 8th Ave (at 139th St) ■ 7pm-close Th ■ www.girlzparty.com

RESTAURANTS
Carnegie Delicatessen 212/757-2245 ■ 854 7th Ave (nr 55th St) ■ 7am-4am, one of NYC's most famous delis

RETAIL SHOPS
Gremlik Leather 212/769-8969, 877/473-6545 ■ 2pm-8pm Mon-Fri, unique leather wear & harnesses, online store ■ www.GremlikLeather.com

EROTICA
Les Hommes Book Shop 212/580-2445 ■ 217 W 80th St, 2nd flr (at Broadway)

NYC—Brooklyn

BARS
The Abbey [GS,NH,D] 718/599-4400 ■ 536 Driggs Ave (btwn N 7th & 8th), Williamsburg ■ from 4pm, more gay Sun
Bar 4 [GS,NH,E] 718/832-9800 ■ 444 7th Ave (at 15th St, in Park Slope) ■ 6pm-4am, DJ Sat
Excelsior [MW] 718/832-1599 ■ 390 5th Ave (btwn 6th & 7th), Brooklyn ■ 6pm-4am, from 2pm wknds, more women Th, patio
Friend's Tavern [MW,NH] 718/834-0069 ■ 97 Atlantic Ave (btwn Henry & Hicks, across from LI College Hospital), Brooklyn Heights ■ 6pm-2am
Ginger's Bar [MW,NH] 718/788-0924 ■ 363 5th Ave (btwn 5th & 6th Sts, in Park Slope) ■ 6pm-4am, from 2pm wknds
Rising Cafe [W] 718/789-6280 ■ 186 5th Ave (at Sackett) ■ 5pm-midnight, from 1pm Fri, from 10am-2am wknds, live music, performances & poetry

NIGHTCLUBS
Club Ovations [W,D,MR] 888/784-8538 ■ 860 Atlantic Ave (btwn Vanderbilt & Clinton), Brooklyn ■ Sat only ■ www.girlzparty.com
Spectrum [MW,D,K,S] 718/238-8213 ■ 802 64th St (at 8th Ave) ■ 9:30pm-4am Th-Sat, karaoke Fri

CAFES
Halcyon [F,BW] 718/260-9299 ■ 227 Smith (at Butler), Carroll Gardens ■ noon-midnight, also antiques & records

RESTAURANTS
200 Fifth [E] 718/638-0023, 718/638-2925 ■ 200 5th Ave (btwn Union & Sackett) ■ 4pm-close, eclectic, full bar
Aunt Suzie [E] 718/788-2868 ■ 247 5th Ave (at Garfield Pl) ■ dinner only, Italian
Johnny Mack's [E] 718/832-7961 ■ 1114 8th Ave (btwn 11th & 12th) ■ 4pm-11pm, till 1am Fri-Sat, brunch noon-3:30pm Sun
Max & Moritz [E] 718/499-5557 ■ 426-A 7th Ave (btwn 14th & 15th) ■ 5:30pm-close, wknd brunch, French/American
Santa Fe Grill 718/636-0279 ■ 62 7th Ave (at Lincoln) ■ 5:30pm-close, also bar
Sweet Mama's 718/768-8766 ■ 168 7th Ave (nr 1st St), Brooklyn ■ dinner only

ENTERTAINMENT & RECREATION
Sing Out! Brooklyn 718/769-1421 ■ concerts & special events

NYC—Brooklyn/Queens/Bronx • New York

NYC—Queens

Bars

Albatross [W,NH,GO] 718/274-9164 ■ 36-19 24th Ave (at 37th), Astoria ■ 6pm-close

BS East [M,NH,E,V,WC] 718/263-0300 ■ 113-24 Queens Blvd (at 76th), Forest Hills ■ 5pm-4am, go-go dancers Sat

Friend's Tavern [M,NH,MR-L] 718/397-7256 ■ 78-11 Roosevelt Ave, Jackson Hts ■ 4pm-4am, DJ Wed-Sun

Music Box [M,MR-L] 718/429-9356 ■ 40-08 74th St (at Roosevelt Ave), Jackson Hts ■ 4pm-4am, drag Sun

Zodiacs Tavern [M,S] 718/899-4724 ■ 69-19 Roosevelt Ave (at 69th St), Jackson Hts ■ 9pm-4am, clsd Mon & Wed, DJ Fri-Sat, drag shows, go-go boys

Nightclubs

Atlantis 2010 [MW,D,MR-L,S] 718/457-3939 ■ 76-19 Roosevelt Ave (at 77th St), Jackson Hts ■ 10pm-4am Fri-Sun only

Krash [MW,D,MR,S] 718/937-2400 ■ 34-48 Steinway St, Astoria ■ open Mon & Th-Sat, DJ Fri-Sat, more women Sat

Men's Clubs

82nd Street Club [MO,MR-L] 718/396-3945 ■ 40-33 82nd St, Jackson Heights ■ 2pm-2am

Northern Men's Sauna [PC] 718/445-9775 ■ 3365 Farrington St, Flushing

NYC—Bronx

Nightclubs

G-Vibe [MW,D] 914/422-0024 ■ 1854 Westchester Ave ■ 9pm-4am Mon & Wed only

Negra's Way [W,D] 718/822-9274 ■ 1306 Union Port Rd (at Westchester Ave) ■ 9pm-4am Wed only

The Warehouse [M,D,S] 718/992-5974 ■ 141 E 140th St (btwn Grand Concourse & Walton) ■ 11pm Fri-Sat

NORTH CAROLINA
Charlotte

Accommodations
1 **Chez Arlaine B&B** [GS,NS,GO] 704/643-1211 ■ 425 Pecan Ave (at 7th) ■ elegant 1920 house, full brkfst ■ www.arlaineinc.com
2 **The Morehead Inn** [GF,WC,GO] 704/376-3357, 888/667-3432 ■ 1122 E Morehead St ■ antique-filled suites in historic neighborhood, full brkfst ■ www.moreheadinn.com
3 **Vanlandingham Estate** [GS,NS,WC,GO] 704/334-8909, 888/524-2020 ■ 2010 The Plaza ■ Bungalow-style estate on 4 acres of gardens, full brkfst ■ www.vanlandinghamestate.com

Bars
4 **Brass Rail** [★M,NH,B,L,PC,WC] 704/399-4313 ■ 3707 Wilkinson Blvd (at Morehead) ■ 5pm-2:30am, from 3pm Sun, also patio bar ■ www.brassrail.8m.com
5 **Central Station** [MW,NH,MR,PC] 704/377-0906 ■ 2131 Central Ave (at The Plaza) ■ 5pm-2am
6 **Hartigan's Irish Pub** [★GS,NH,F,GO] 704/347-1841 ■ 601 S Cedar St ■ 11am-10pm, till 2am wknds, from 5pm Sun, lesbian hangout
7 **Have a Nice Day Cafe** [GF,D,18+] 704/373-2233 ■ 314 N College St (btwn 6th & 7th) ■ 9pm-2am, from 8pm Sat
8 **Liaisons** [★MW,NH,F,V,PC] 704/376-1617 ■ 316 Rensselaer Ave (at South Blvd) ■ 5pm-1am, restaurant Wed-Sun ■ www.pinkhousenc.com

Nightclubs
9 **300 Stonewall** [★M,D,S] 704/347-4200 ■ 300 E Stonewall (at South Blvd) ■ 9pm-close Wed & Fri-Sat only, 3 bars, male dancers, patio ■ www.300stonewall.com
10 **Chaser's** [M,D,S,V,PC,WC] 704/339-0500 ■ 3217 The Plaza (at 36th) ■ 5pm-2am, till 10pm Sun, strippers
11 **Club Myxx** [MW,D,MR-AF,S,PC] 704/525-5001 ■ 3110 S Tryon St ■ 10pm-4am Sat & from 9pm Sun
12 **Genesis** [M,D] 704/358-0322 ■ 605 W 5th St (at N Graham) ■ Fri-Sat nights
7 **Mythos** [★GF,D,A,S,18+,PC,WC] 704/375-8765, 704/559-5959 (info line) ■ 300 N College St (at 6th) ■ 10pm-3am, till 4am wknds, 11pm-4am Sun, clsd Mon, more gay Th & Sun ■ www.mythosclub.com
13 **Salamandra** [GF,D,MR-L,$] 704/559-4141 ■ 300 E Morehead ■ 9pm-3am Fri-Sat, Latin dance club, Wed 18+, dress code, patio
14 **Scorpios** [★MW,D,CW,MR,K,S,V,18+,PC,WC] 704/373-9124 ■ 2301 Freedom Dr ■ 9pm-3:30am, clsd Mon, Latin night Fri, also 'Diva's' show bar & 'Queen City Saloon' ■ www.scorpios.com

Cafes
Caribou Coffee 704/334-3570 ■ 1531 East Blvd (nr Scott) ■ 6am-11pm, till midnight Fri-Sat
Tic Toc Coffeeshop [F] 704/375-5750 ■ 512 N Tryon St (btwn 8th & 9th) ■ 7am-3pm, clsd wknds, plenty veggie

Restaurants
300 East 704/332-6507 ■ 300 East Blvd (at Cleveland) ■ 11:30am-10pm, till 11pm Tue-Th, till midnight Fri-Sat, New American, some veggie, full bar
Alexander Michaels 704/332-6789 ■ 401 W 9th St (at Pine) ■ lunch & dinner, clsd Sun, pub fare, full bar
Cafe Dada 704/373-0001 ■ 1220 Thomas St (at Pecan) ■ 11am-midnight, till 2am Fri-Sat, full bar, Southwestern wraps, plenty veggie ■ coffeehouse@aol.com
Cosmos Cafe 704/372-3553 ■ 300 N College (at 6th) ■ 11am-2am, from 5pm wknds, new world cuisine, also 'Thirsty Camel' cigar/ martini lounge & 'Microcosm' art gallery
Fat City 704/343-0240 ■ 3127 N Davidson St (at 35th) ■ noon-2am, from 2pm Sun
Lupie's Cafe 704/374-1232 ■ 2718 Monroe Rd (nr 5th St) ■ 11am-11pm, from noon Sat, clsd Sun, homestyle cookin'

Bookstores
Paper Skyscraper [WC] 704/333-7130 ■ 330 East Blvd (at Euclid Ave) ■ 10am-7pm, till 6pm Sat, noon-5pm Sun, books & funky gifts
15 **White Rabbit Books & Things** 704/377-4067 ■ 834 Central Ave (at 7th) ■ 11am-9pm, 1pm-6pm Sun, lgbt, also magazines, T-shirts & gifts ■ www.whiterabbitbooks.com

Retail Shops
Urban Evolution 704/332-8644 ■ 1329 East Blvd (at Scott) ■ 10am-9pm, 1pm-6pm Sun, clothing & more

Publications
The Front Page 919/829-0181 ■ lgbt newspaper for the Carolinas ■ www.frontpagenews.com
Q Notes 704/531-9988 ■ biweekly lgbt newspaper for the Carolinas ■ www.q-notes.com

Gyms & Health Clubs
Charlotte 24-Hour Fitness Center [GF] 704/537-9060 ■ 3900 E Independence Blvd

Erotica
Carolina Video Source 704/566-9993 ■ 8829 E Harris Blvd
Hwy 74 Video & News 704/399-7907 ■ 3514 Barry Dr
Independence News 704/332-8430 ■ 3205 The Plaza (at 36th)
Queen City Video & News 704/344-9435 ■ 2320 Wilkinson Blvd ■ 24hrs

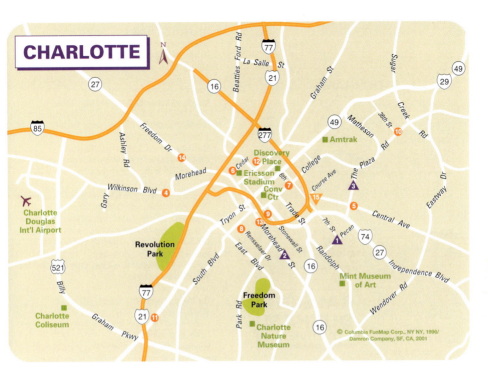

Charlotte

With big-city attractions surrounded by breath-taking scenery, Charlotte has been voted one of the top ten US cities to live in. It is home to some superb museums, ranging from Discovery Place (704/372-0471 for tickets)—a major science center, complete with its own tropical rain forest—to the Mint Museum of Art (704/337-2000), a fine arts collection housed in the first branch of the US Mint outside Washington, DC.

Queer Resources

Community Info
Gay/Lesbian Switchboard 704/535-6277. 6:30pm-10:30pm Sun-Th.

AIDS Resources
AIDS Hotline 704/333-2437.

Recovery
AA Central Office 704/332-4387, 3200 Park Rd, 8pm Fri.

City Calendar

LGBT Pride
May. web: www.charlottepride.com.

Tourist Info

Airport Directions
Charlotte-Douglas International. To get downtown, take Hwy 74/29 east to I-277.

Public Transit & Taxis
Yellow Cab 704/332-6161.
S&S Airport Shuttle 704/534-4131.
Charlotte Transit 704/336-7433.

Tourist Spots & Info
Discovery Place 704/372-0471 (for tickets).
Mint Museum of Art 704/337-2000.
Visitor's Center: Convention & Visitors Bureau 704/334-2282 or 800/231-4636, web: charlottecvb.org.

NORTH CAROLINA • USA

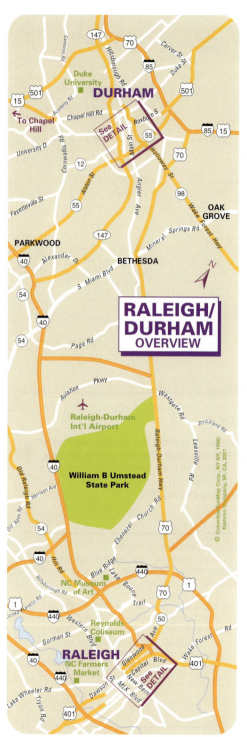

Raleigh/Durham/Chapel Hill

ACCOMMODATIONS
Joan's Place [GS,NS,WC] 919/942-5621 ■ shared baths, lesbian-owned/ run ■ mjoanbs@aol.com
Mineral Springs Inn [M,SW,N,NS] 919/596-2162 ■ 718 S Mineral Springs Rd (nr Hwy 70), Durham ■ full brkfst, jacuzzi ■ mineralspringsinn.com
1 **Morehead Manor B&B** [GS] 919/687-4366, 888/437-6333 ■ 914 Vickers Ave (at Morehead), Durham ■ splendidly decorated Colonial home, full brkst ■ www.moreheadmanor.com
2 **The Oakwood Inn B&B** [GF] 919/832-9712, 800/267-9712 ■ 411 N Bloodworth St (at Oakwood), Raleigh ■ full brkfst ■ members.aol.com/oakwoodbb

BARS
Backdoor [W,D,18+,PC] 919/872-6818 ■ 4801 Leigh Dr (at Green Rd), Raleigh ■ 9pm-2:30am Sat only
3 **Chambers** [GS,F,E] 919/834-1938 ■ 19 W Hargett St (at Salisbury), Raleigh ■ 5:30pm-11pm, till midnight wknds, clsd Sun, dinner, 'retro American', 'Family' night Th
4 **Flex** [★M,B,L,E,S,PC] 919/832-8855 ■ 2 S West St (at Hillsborough), Raleigh ■ 5pm-close, from 2pm Sun, 18+ Mon & Th ■ www.flex-club.com

NIGHTCLUBS
5 **The Capital Corral (CC)** [M,D,MR,S,18+,PC,WC] 919/755-9599 ■ 313 W Hargett St (at Harrington), Raleigh ■ 8pm-close, from 6pm Sun, also piano bar, more diverse Th ■ www.cc-raleigh.com
Insomnia [MW,D,18+] 919/967-2852 ■ 306 W Franklin St (at 'Gotham' nightclub), Chapel Hill ■ 10pm-3am Fri ■ www.clubgotham.com
6 **Legends** [MW,D,S,YC,PC,WC] 919/831-8888 ■ 330 W Hargett St (at Harrington), Raleigh ■ 9pm-close, deck ■ www.legends-club.com
7 **Power Company** [MW,D,MR-AF,F,S,18+,WC,$] 919/683-1151 ■ 315 W Main St (at Ramseur, enter rear), Durham ■ 11pm-close 2nd & 4th Fri, male & female dancers
8 **Visions** [W,D,E,K,PC] 919/688-3002 ■ 711 Rigsbee Ave, Durham ■ call for hrs, deck, volleyball court ■ visions.citysearch.com

CAFES
Caffe Trio [★] 919/928-8575 ■ 201 E Franklin (at Henderson), Chapel Hill ■ 7am-11pm, from 9am wknds

RESTAURANTS
The Artist's Escape [MW] 919/960-3717 ■ 137 E Franklin St, Chapel Hill ■ noon-2am, from 5pm wknds, also bar
Crooks Corner [WC] 919/929-7643 ■ 610 Franklin St (at Merritt Mill Rd), Chapel Hill ■ 5:30pm-10:30pm Mon-Sat, brunch Sun, Southern cooking, full bar ■ www.crookscorner.com
Elmo's Diner 919/929-2909 ■ 776 9th St (in the Carr Mill Mall), Chapel Hill ■ 6:30am-10pm, till 11pm wknds, some veggie
Irregardless Cafe 919/833-8898 ■ 901 W Morgan St (at Hillsborough), Raleigh ■ lunch Mon-Fri, dinner Mon-Sat, brunch Sun, plenty veggie
Magnolia Grill [WC] 919/286-3609 ■ 1002 9th St (at Knox), Durham ■ 6pm-9:30pm, clsd Sun-Mon, upscale Southern, full bar
Rathskeller [WC] 919/821-5342 ■ 2412 Hillsborough St (at Chamberlain), Raleigh ■ 11:30am-10pm, till 11pm Wed-Sat, from noon Sun, comfort food, plenty veggie, full bar

Raleigh/Durham/Chapel Hill • North Carolina

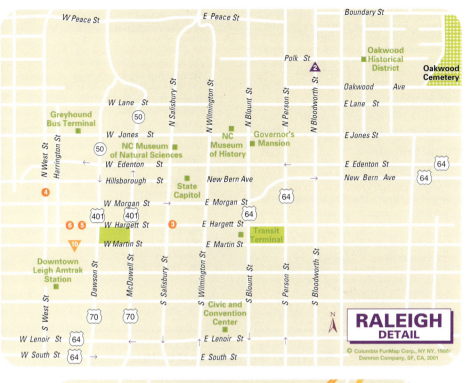

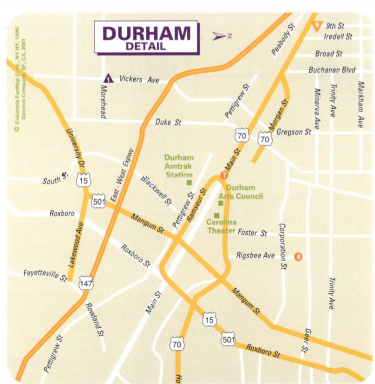

North Carolina • USA

Vertigo Diner 919/832-4477 ■ 426 S McDowell St (at Cabarrus), Raleigh ■ lunch Tue-Fri, dinner Wed-Sat, brunch Sun, also bar till 2am, retro chic

Weathervane Cafe [WC] 919/929-9466 ■ Eastgate Shopping Ctr, Chapel Hill ■ 10am-9pm, till 10pm Fri-Sat, till 6pm Sun, patio, full bar, great brunch ■ www.southernseason.com

Bookstores

Internationalist Books 919/942-1740 ■ 405 W Franklin St (at Columbia), Chapel Hill ■ 11am-8pm, noon-6pm Sun, from 2pm Mon, progressive/ alternative, readings & events ■ www.internationalistbooks.com

Quail Ridge Books 919/828-1588, 800/672-6789 ■ 3522 Wade Ave (at Ridgewood Ctr), Raleigh ■ 9am-9pm, lgbt section

Reader's Corner 919/828-7024 ■ 3201 Hillsborough St (at Rosemary), Raleigh ■ 10am-8pm, noon-6pm wknds, used books

9 **Regulator Bookshop** 919/286-2700 ■ 720 9th St (btwn Hillsborough & Perry), Durham ■ 9am-9pm, till 6pm Sun, also cafe ■ www.regbook.com

10 **White Rabbit Books & Things** [WC] 919/856-1429 ■ 309 W Martin St (btwn Dawson & Harrington), Raleigh ■ 11am-9pm, till 7pm Sat, 1pm-6pm Sun, lgbt, gifts ■ www.whiterabbitbooks.com

Retail Shops

Innovations 919/833-4833 ■ 517 Hillsborough St (at Glenwood), Raleigh ■ 11am-7pm, from 1pm Sun, clsd Mon, leather, fetishwear, piercings ■ www.sinshop.com

Publications

The Front Page 919/829-0181 ■ lgbt newspaper for the Carolinas ■ www.frontpagenews.com

Hotspots Magazine 304/782-3358 ■ serving the Carolinas ■ www.hotspotsimag.com

Erotica

Atlantis Video & News 919/682-7469 ■ 522 E Main St (nr Dillard), Durham

Capitol Blvd News 919/831-1400 ■ 2236 Capitol Blvd, Raleigh

Castle Video & News 919/836-9189 ■ 1210 Capitol Blvd, Raleigh ■ 24hrs

Movie Town 919/489-9945 ■ 3615 Chapel Hill Blvd (at University), Durham ■ 24hrs

Our Place 919/833-8968 ■ 327 W Hargett (at Harrington), Raleigh ■ 24hrs

Videos for the Mature 919/787-0016 ■ 9016 Glenwood Ave, Raleigh ■ 24hrs

Raleigh/Durham/Chapel Hill

The cities of Raleigh and Durham are only 8 miles apart, so most people think of them (along with nearby Chapel Hill) as a unit. Located in the gorgeous heartland of North Carolina, these cities and their universities provide cultural events and historic sites galore.

Queer Resources

Community Info
Gay & Lesbian Helpline of Wake County 919/821-0055. 7pm-10pm.
Orange County Women's Center 919/968-4610, 210 Henderson, Chapel Hill, 9am-7pm Mon-Th, till 2pm Fri, clsd wknds.

AIDS Resources
AIDS Info for Wake County 919/250-3950.

Recovery
AA Raleigh 919/783-6144.
AA Durham 919/286-9499. 4907 Gacy Gamet Rd, 8pm Fri.

Tourist Info

Airport Directions
Raleigh-Durham International. Take US 40 toward Raleigh and use the Wade Ave exit. At Capital Ave (US 1), turn right. Head south toward downtown. The street will change to Dawson at W Martin. Turn right here. Take US 40 towards Durham to 147 North (Durham Fwy). Take Swift Ave exit toward Duke east Campus. Go right, turns into Broad St, which will lead you to Main St.

Public Transit & Taxis
Bus (Capital Area Transit) 919/828-7228.
Triangle Transit Authority 919/549-9999.

Tourist Spots & Info
Duke University, Durham.
Exploris (interactive global learning center), Raleigh 919/834-4040.
NC Museum of Art, Raleigh 919/839-6262.
NC Museum of Life & Science, Durham 919/220-5429.
Oakwood Historic District, Raleigh.
University of North Carolina, Chapel Hill.
Visitor's Center: 919/834-5900 or 800/849-8499, web: www.raleighcvb.org.

Cincinnati

Cincinnati holds the distinction of having the largest number of chili parlors per capita in the world. Served over spaghetti, Cincinnati-style chili is mild and can be enjoyed with grated cheese, onions, and beans. The city is also home to the 'sexiest zoo' in the country, according to Newsweek.

Queer Resources

Community Info
Gay/Lesbian Community Switchboard 513/591-0222.
▼ Gay & Lesbian Community Center 513/591-0200, web: www.glbtcentercincinnati.com. 4119 Hamilton Ave, 6pm-9pm Mon-Fri, noon-4pm Sat, clsd Sun & holidays.

AIDS Resources
800/332-2437.

Recovery
AA Lesbian/Gay 513/961-1938.

City Calendar

LGBT Pride
September. 513/591-0200 (GLCC).

Tourist Info

Airport Directions
Greater Cincinnati International (in Kentucky). To get to downtown, take I-275 East to I-75/I-71 North over the Ohio River. Follow I-75 North or I-71 East, and look for downtown exits.

Public Transit & Taxis
Yellow Cab 513/241-2100.
Queen City Metro 513/621-4455.

Tourist Spots & Info
The Beach waterpark (in Mason) 513/398-2040.
Carew Tower 513/241-3888.
Cincinnati Art Museum 513/721-5204.
Fountain Square.
Krohn Conservatory 513/421-4086.
Museum Center at Union Terminal 513/287-7000.
Paramount King's Island (24 miles N of Cincinnati) 513/754-5800.
Visitor's Center: 513/621-2142 or 800/344-3445 (in OH), web: www.cincyusa.com.

Best Views
Mt. Adams & Eden Park.

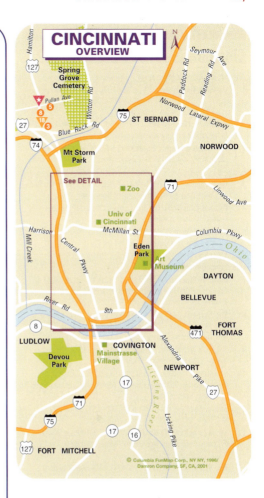

The Dock

The Dock is the place to dance in Cincinnati. Open daily, the Dock boasts an incredible sound with 14,000 watts per beat, hi-NRG dancing and a dazzling light show in the dance bar. The video bar opens at 8pm with 17 video screens for your viewing pleasure. In the summer, come join us at 5pm for sand volleyball on our patio bar. Terrific shows every Sunday & Tuesday and after hours until 4am every Friday & Saturday.

Phone **513/241-5623**

Ohio

Cincinnati

Accommodations
1. **Cincinnatian Hotel** [GF] 513/381-3000, 800/942-9000 ■ 601 Vine St (nr 8th) ■ restaurant & lounge ■ www.cincinnatianhotel.com
   City View Hide-A-Way [MO,N,GO] 513/244-2469 ■ 2628 Maryland Ave (at Grand Ave) ■ hot tub
2. **The Vernon Manor Hotel** [GF,F] 513/281-3300, 800/543-3999 ■ 400 Oak St ■ gym ■ www.vernon-manor.com

Bars
3. **Bullfishes** [W,NH,D,E] 513/541-9220 ■ 4023 Hamilton Ave (at Blue Rock) ■ 7pm-close, from 5pm Sun
4. **Golden Lion** [M,NH,D,S] 513/281-4179 ■ 340 Ludlow (at Telford), Clifton ■ 4pm-2:30am
5. **Junkers Tavern** [GF,NH] 513/541-5470 ■ 4156 Langland (at Pullan) ■ 7:30am-1am
6. **Milton's** [GF,NH] 513/784-9988 ■ 301 Milton St (at Sycamore) ■ 4pm-2:30am
7. **Plum St Pipeline** [★M,NH,D,S,V] 513/241-5678 ■ 241 W Court (at Plum) ■ 4pm-2:30am, DJ wknds on 3rd flr ■ www.pipelinebar.com
8. **The Serpent** [M,L] 513/681-6969 ■ 4042 Hamilton Ave (at Blue Rock) ■ 7pm-2:30am, clsd Mon, dress code Fri-Sat ■ www.serpentbar.com
9. **Shirley's** [W,NH,D,WC] 513/721-8483 ■ 2401 Vine St ■ 8pm-2:30am, from 4pm Sun, clsd Mon
10. **Shooters** [M,D,CW,K,S] 513/381-9900 ■ 927 Race St (at Court) ■ 4pm-2:30am, karaoke Wed, dance lessons 8pm Th, more women Th
11. **Simon Says** [★M,NH,P,WC] 513/381-7577 ■ 428 Walnut (at 5th) ■ 11am-2:30am, from 1pm Sun
12. **Spurs** [★M,B,L,F,WC] 513/621-2668 ■ 1119 Race St ■ 4pm-2:30am, bear night Wed, also 'Acme Leather & Toy Co' ■ www.spursbar.com
13. **The Subway** [M,NH,D,F,S] 513/421-1294 ■ 609 Walnut St (at 6th) ■ 6am-2:30am, from noon Sun

Nightclubs
14. ▶ **The Dock** [★MW,D,K,S,19+,WC] 513/241-5623 ■ 603 W Pete Rose Wy (nr Central) ■ 5pm-2:30am, till 4am wknds, (from 8pm winter), clsd Mon ■ www.thedock-cincy.com
15. **DV8** [GF,D,A] 513/723-0700 ■ 1120 Walnut St ■ 10am-3am Th & 11am-4am Fri-Sat
3. **Jacobs on the Avenue** [M,NH,D,K,S] 513/591-2100 ■ 4029 Hamilton Ave (at Blue Rock) ■ 5pm-2:30am, from 7pm Sat-Mon, till 1am Sun-Mon ■ www.jacobsbar.com
16. **Oscar's** [GS,D] 513/421-3007 ■ 700 Pete Rose Way ■ 5pm-wknds only, more gay Sun
17. **Warehouse** [GF,D,A,F,V,18+] 513/684-9313 ■ 1313 Vine St (2 blks N of Central Pkwy) ■ 10pm-2:30am Wed, till 4am Fri-Sat, patio

Cafes
Kaldi's Cafe & Books [E,WC] 513/241-3070 ■ 1204 Main St (at 12th) ■ 9am-1am, 10am-2am Fri-Sat, 10am-midnight Sun, full bar

Restaurants
Boca 513/542-2022 ■ 4034 Hamilton Ave (btwn Knowlton St & Broadway) ■ lunch & dinner, clsd Mon, nouvelle int'l, patio, full bar
Carol's on Main [★WC,GO] 513/651-2667 ■ 825 Main St (btwn 8th & 9th) ■ 11am-1am, till 2:30am Th-Sat, from 4pm wknds, bistro ■ www.carolsonmain.com
The Diner on Sycamore [WC] 513/721-1212 ■ 1203 Sycamore (at 12th) ■ 11am-midnight, till 1am Fri-Sat, full bar, great meatloaf
Mullane's Parkside Café [BW,WC] 513/381-1331 ■ 723 Race St (btwn 7th & Garfield) ■ 11:30am-11pm, till midnight Fri-Sat, from 5pm Sat, clsd Sun

Entertainment & Recreation
Alternating Currents 513/333-9243, 513/961-8900 ■ WAIF 88.3 FM ■ 3pm Sat, lgbt public affairs radio program ■ www.alternatingcurrents.org

Bookstores
18. **Crazy Ladies Bookstore** [★] 513/541-4198 ■ 4039 Hamilton Ave (at Blue Rock) ■ 11am-8pm, till 6pm Sat, noon-4pm Sun, women's ■ www.crazyladies.org

Retail Shops
19. **Pink Pyramid** 513/621-7465 ■ 907 Race St (btwn 9th & Court) ■ 11am-10:30pm, till midnight Fri-Sat, 1pm-8pm Sun, pride store ■ www.pinkpyramid.com
Spotlight Inc 513/721-0808 ■ 633 Main St ■ noon-5pm, till 7pm wknds, clothing

Erotica
Pyramid Leather Crypt & Art Gallery 513/591-1700 ■ 4040 Hamilton ■ fetish clothing & toys

---

VISIT DAMRON ONLINE!

- search our online database
- get the latest updates
- direct web/ email links
- more categories (including websites)
- shop for discounted guides
- calendar of events
- tour operator listings
- gay travel links & more!

www.damron.com

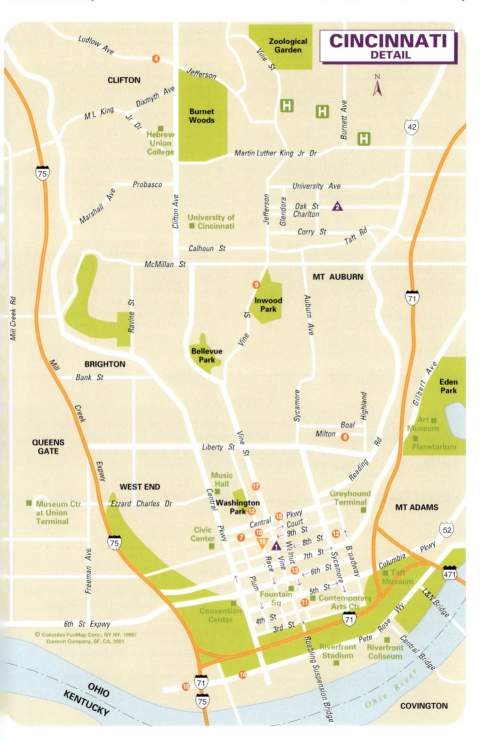

Cleveland

ACCOMMODATIONS

1. **Bourbon House** [GS,NS,GO] 216/939-0535 ■ 6116 Franklin Blvd (at W 65th) ■ 1901 Victorian, full brkfst ■ www.bbchannel.com/bbc/p602971.asp
2. **Clifford House** [GS,NS,GO] 216/589-9432, 216/589-0121 ■ 1810 W 28th St (at Jay) ■ 1868 historic brick home, close to downtown, fireplaces ■ www.cliffordhouse.com
3. **Edgewater Estates** [GS] 216/961-1764 ■ 9803 Lake Ave ■ English Tudor on Lake Erie, full brkfst, patio, nr beaches ■ www.bedandbreakfast.com/bbc/p616727.asp
   Grandmother's Haven [MW] 216/631-1231 ■ 3560 W 45th St (at Fulton) ■ 2-bdrm suite ■ c-suite.hypermart.net
4. **Greystone B&B** [GS,GO] 216/939-0405 ■ 10405 Lake Ave (at W 104th St) ■ weekly rates available

BARS

5. **A Man's World** [MW,D] 216/574-2203 ■ 2909 Detroit Ave (at 29th St) ■ noon-2:30am, DJ wknds, patio
6. **Deco** [M,NH,D,S] 216/221-8576 ■ 11213 Detroit Ave ■ 3pm-2:30am, strippers
7. **The Hawk** [MW,NH,WC] 216/521-5443 ■ 11217 Detroit Ave (at 112th St) ■ 10am-2:30am, from noon Sun
8. **Hi & Dry Inn** [GF] 216/621-6166 ■ 2207 W 11th St (at Fairfield) ■ 11:30am-2am, clsd Sun, jazz club & restaurant, patio
9. **Leather Stallion Saloon** [★M,B,L,F,S] 216/589-8588 ■ 2205 St Clair Ave (nr E 21st St) ■ 3pm-2:30am, DJ wknds, patio ■ www.leatherstallion.com
10. **Locker Room** [M,NH,D,WC] 216/781-9191 ■ 2032 W 25th St (at Lorain & 24th) ■ 4pm-2:30am
11. **MJ's Place** [★MW,NH,P,K,S] 216/476-1970 ■ 11633 Lorain Ave (at W 117th St) ■ 4pm-2:30am, clsd Sun, women very welcome at 'the gay Cheers', piano bar Mon ■ www.mjsplace.com
12. **Muggs** [GF,NH] 216/398-7012 ■ 3194 W 25th St (nr Clark) ■ 11am-2:30am, from 9:30am wknds
13. **The Nickel/ Five Cent Decision** [W,NH,D] 216/661-1314 ■ 4365 State Rd (Rte 94, at Montclair) ■ 6pm-2:30am, food served Th
14. **Paradise Inn** [W,NH] 216/741-9819 ■ 4488 State Rd (Rte 94, at Rte 480) ■ 11am-close, till 1am wknds
15. **Rockies Bar** [★M,D,K,F,S,V] 216/961-3115 ■ 9208 Detroit Ave (at W 93rd St) ■ 4pm-2:30am, patio, Cleveland's only Sun T-dance ■ www.rockies-clev.com
16. **Scarlet Rose's Lounge** [GF,NH] 216/351-7511 ■ 2071 Broadview Rd (at Roanoke) ■ noon-2am
17. **Twist** [★MW,D,P] 216/221-2333 ■ 11633 Clifton (at 117th St) ■ 9am-2:30am, from noon Sun
18. **Victory's** [MW,NH,D,WC] 216/228-5777 ■ 13603 Madison Ave (at W 85th St) ■ 7pm-2:30am, from 5pm Fri, clsd Sun

NIGHTCLUBS

19. **Aunt Charley's The Cage** [★M,D,TG,K,S] 216/651-0727 ■ 9506 Detroit Ave (at W 95th) ■ 8pm-2:30am
20. **Club Atlantis** [GS,D,A,MR,V,WC] 216/621-6900 ■ 620 Frankfort ■ 9pm-2:30am, 10pm-4am Sat, clsd Mon-Tue, fetish Fri, more gay Sat

---

CLEVELAND

An historic industrial center, Cleveland also offers all the best in culture and nightlife. The riverfront area known as 'The Flats' houses clubs and restaurants, while University Circle is home to the Cleveland Museum of Art and the Museum of Natural History, among many others.

Queer Resources

COMMUNITY INFO
▼ Cleveland Lesbian/Gay Community Center 216/651-15428, web: www.lgcsc.org. 6600 Detroit Ave, noon-10pm, 6pm-9pm Sun.
Lesbian/Gay Hotline 216/651-6452.
Women's Center 216/651-1450, web: www.womensctr.org. 6209 Storer Ave.

AIDS RESOURCES
Task Force of Greater Cleveland 216/621-0766.

RECOVERY
216/241-7387 call 9am-5pm Mon-Fri.

City Calendar

LGBT PRIDE
June. 216/371-0214, web: www.clevelandpride.org

Tourist Info

AIRPORT DIRECTIONS
Cleveland Hopkins International. To get downtown, take the Berea Freeway to I-71 and continue on until it merges with I-90 and follow into downtown.

PUBLIC TRANSIT & TAXIS
Yellow Cab 216/623-1500.
AmeriCab 216/881-1111.
Regional Transit Authority (RTA) 216/621-9500.
Lolly the Trolley 216/771-4484.

TOURIST SPOTS & INFO
Cleveland Metroparks Zoo 216/661-6500.
Cleveland Museum of Art 216/421-7340.
Coventry Road district.
Cuyahoga Valley National Recreation Area.
The Flats.
Rock and Roll Hall of Fame 216/781-7625.
Visitor's Center: 216/621-4110, web: www.travelcleveland.com.

Cleveland • Ohio

211

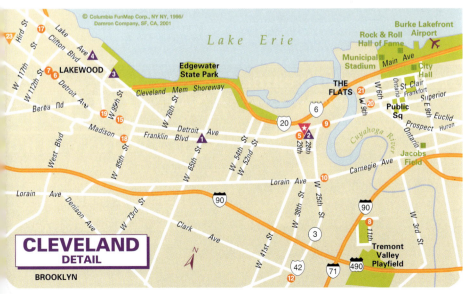

Ohio • USA

21 The Grid [★M,D,S,V] 216/623-0113 ■ 1281 W 9th (at St Clair) ■ 5pm-2:30am, from 4pm Sun, male strippers Wed & Fri-Sun ■ www.thegrid.com

22 The Rec Room [W,D,F,WC] 216/433-1669 ■ 15320 Brookpark Rd ■ 6pm-1am

5 Tool Shed [M,NH,D,CW,L,18+,WC] 216/771-7812 ■ 2901 Detroit Ave (enter on W 29th St) ■ 7pm-2:30am, cruise bar, CW Sun, also 'Crossover' (MO,L) downstairs from 10pm Fri-Sat, strict dress code

CAFES

Johnny Mango [WC] 216/575-1919 ■ 3120 Bridge Ave (btwn Fulton & W 32nd) ■ 11am-10pm, till 11pm Fri-Sat, from 9am wknds, healthy world food & juice bar, also full bar

Lonesome Dove Cafe [BW] 216/397-9100 ■ 3093 Mayfield Rd (at Lee) ■ 7am-6pm, till 5pm Sat, clsd Sun

RESTAURANTS

Cafe Tandoor 216/371-8500, 216/371-8569 ■ 2096 S Taylor Rd (at Cedar), Cleveland Hts ■ lunch & dinner, Indian, plenty veggie

Club Isabella [E] 216/229-1177 ■ 2025 University Hospital Rd (at Euclid Ave) ■ lunch Mon-Fri & dinner nightly, clsd Sun, Italian, live jazz nightly

Harmony Bar & Grille [E] 216/398-5052 ■ 3359 Fulton ■ lunch & dinner, clsd Mon (also clsd Sun summers), eclectic

Hecks [★WC] 216/861-5464 ■ 2927 Bridge Ave (at W 30th) ■ lunch & dinner, gourmet burgers

The Inn on Coventry [WC] 216/371-1811 ■ 2785 Euclid Heights Blvd (at Coventry), Cleveland Hts ■ 7am-9pm, from 8:30am Sat, 9am-3pm Sun, 8am-3pm Mon, popular Bloody Marys

ENTERTAINMENT & RECREATION

Rock & Roll Hall of Fame 216/781-ROCK ■ 1 Key Plaza ■ even if you can't stand rock, be sure to stop by & check out IM Pei's architectural gift to Cleveland ■ www.rockhall.com

BOOKSTORES

Bookstore on W 25th St 216/566-8897 ■ 1921 W 25th St (at Lorain) ■ 10am-6pm, noon-5pm Sun, lgbt section

Borders Bookshop & Espresso Bar 216/292-2660 ■ 2101 Richmond Rd (at Cedar, in LaPlace Mall), Beachwood ■ 9am-11pm, till 9pm Sun

23 Diverse Universe [WC,GO] 216/227-9830 ■ 12011 Detroit Ave (at Hopkins), Lakewood ■ 10am-9pm, noon-6pm Sun, lgbt books, videos, clothing & pride gifts ■ www.diverse-universe.com

RETAIL SHOPS

Bank News 216/281-8777 ■ 4025 Clark Ave (at W 41st St) ■ 10:30am-8:30pm, clsd Sun

Body Language 216/251-3330, 888/429-7733 ■ 3291 W 115th St (at Lorain Ave) ■ 11am-10pm, till 6pm Sun, 'an educational store for adults in alternative lifestyles' ■ www.body-language.com

Body Work Productions 216/623-0744 ■ 2710 Detroit Ave (at W 28th) ■ 1pm-8pm, piercing

City Dweller [GO] 216/226-7106 ■ 12005 Detroit Ave, Lakewood ■ 10am-9pm, gifts & home decorations

The Clifton Web 216/961-1120 ■ 11512 Clifton Blvd (at W 117th) ■ 11am-8pm, from 10am Sat, till 5pm Sun, cards & gifts

PUBLICATIONS

Exposé Magazine 800/699-6781 ■ covers Cleveland, Akron, Canton, Warren, Youngstown & Lorain ■ exposeusa@earthlink.net

Gay People's Chronicle 216/631-8646, 800/426-5947 ■ Ohio's largest weekly lgbt newspaper w/ extensive listings ■ www.gaypeopleschronicle.com

Hotspots Magazine 304/782-3358 ■ serving all of Ohio ■ www.hotspotsimag.com

MEN'S CLUBS

▶ **The Club Cleveland** [★PC] 216/961-2727 ■ 1448 W 32nd St (off Detroit Ave) ■ 24hrs ■ www.the-clubs.com

Flex [V,PC] 216/696-0595 ■ 1293 W 9th St (btwn Lakeside & St Clair) ■ 24hrs ■ www.flexbaths.com

EROTICA

Brookpark News & Video [AYOR] 216/267-9019 ■ 16700 Brookpark Rd (at W 150th) ■ 24hrs

Hide Park Leather 216/529-9699 ■ 15521 Detroit Ave, Lakewood ■ clsd Sun-Mon

Laws Leather Shop 216/961-0544 ■ 1112 Clifton Blvd ■ hrs vary, clsd Mon-Tue

Rocky's Entertainment & Emporium [AYOR] 216/267-4936 ■ 13330 Brookpark Rd (at W 130th) ■ 24hrs

A Traveler's Dream...

THE CLUB Cleveland
www.the-clubs.com

One Day Memberships · Deluxe Suites
Free Parking · In/Out Privileges
Centrally Located · Tanning
Videos · Steam · Sauna · Whirlpool
Sundeck · Fully Equipped Gym

1448 West 32nd Street
Cleveland, Ohio 44113
216-961-2727

Columbus

ACCOMMODATIONS
The Brewmaster's House [MO] 614/449-8298 ■ full brkfst, historic house ■ www.damron.com/homepages/BrewmastersHouse/

Columbus B&B [GF,GO] 614/444-8888 ■ 763 S 3rd St ■ in historic district

1 **Courtyard by Marriott** [GF,WC] 614/228-3200, 800/321-2211 ■ 35 W Spring St (at Front St) ■ hot tub

2 **The Gardener's House** [M,NS,GO] 614/444-5445 ■ 556 Frebis Ave (at Ann St) ■ hot tub ■ villfloral@msn.com

Summit Lodge Resort & Guesthouse [★GF,F,SW] 740/385-3521 ■ clothing optional resort, 45 miles to Columbus, camping, hot tub, swimming, also restaurant ■ www.uniquelynx.com/summitlodge

BARS

3 **AWOL** [M,NH,F,WC] 614/621-8779 ■ 49 Parsons Ave (at Oak) ■ 1pm-2:30am

4 **Blazer's Pub** [W,NH] 614/299-1800 ■ 1205 N High St (at 5th) ■ 4pm-2:30am, 3pm-9pm Sun

5 **Club 20** [M,NH] 614/261-5575 ■ 20 E Duncan (at High) ■ noon-2:30am, from 1pm Sun, patio

6 **Club Diversity** [MW,E] 614/224-4050 ■ 124 E Main (btwn 3rd & 4th Sts) ■ 5pm-2am, from 6pm Fri-Sat, clsd Sun-Mon, piano bar, also coffeehouse

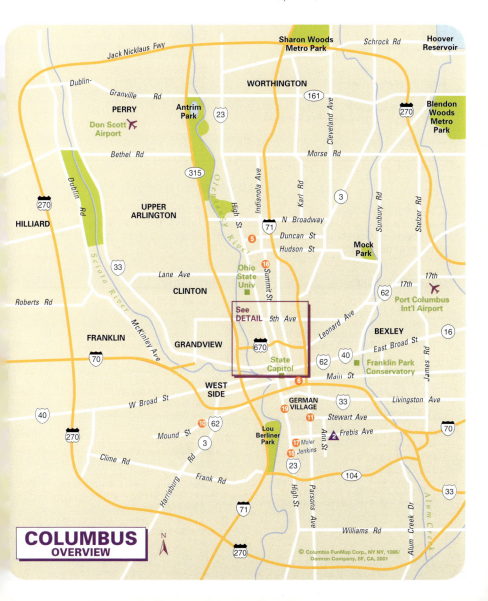

7 **Columbus Eagle Bar** [★M,D,WC] 614/228-2804 ■ 232 N 3rd St (at Hickory) ■ 8pm-2:30am

8 **Downtown Connection** [M,NH] 614/299-4880 ■ 1126 N High St (at 4th Ave) ■ 5pm-2am, from 3pm wknds, sports bar

9 **Eagle in Exile (Patrick's)** [M,NH,WC] 614/294-0069 ■ 893 N 4th St (at 2nd Ave) ■ 9pm-2:30am Wed-Sun

10 **The Far Side** [W,NH,E] 614/276-5817 ■ 1662 W Mound St (at Reed) ■ 5pm-1am, till 2:30am Fri-Sat, from 6pm Sun, live bands wknds

11 **Garrett's Saloon** [M,NH,CW,K,S] 614/449-2351 ■ 1071 Parsons Ave (at Stewart) ■ 11am-2:30am, CW in the day, Top 40 at night, karaoke Mon

12 **Havana Video Lounge** [★MW,NH,V] 614/421-9697 ■ 862 N High (at 1st Ave) ■ 5pm-2:30am, male strippers Sun

13 **Kelly's** [MW,WC] 614/221-8463 ■ 73 E Gay St (at 3rd St) ■ 5pm-2:30am

14 **The Pyramid Night Club** [M,NH,S] 614/228-6151 ■ 196-1/2 E Gay St (at 5th St, enter rear) ■ 4pm-2:30am, from 1pm wknds, strippers Tue & Sun

15 **Remo's** [MW,NH,K,S] 614/443-4224 ■ 1409 S High St (at Jenkins) ■ 11am-2:30am, clsd Sun

16 **Slammers Pizza Pub** [MW,F,WC] 614/469-7526 ■ 202 E Long St (at 5th St) ■ 11am-2:30am, from 2:30pm wknds, patio

17 **The South Bend Tavern** [M,NH,WC] 614/444-3386 ■ 126 E Moler St (at 4th St) ■ noon-2:30am

18 **Summit Station** [W,NH,K,S] 614/261-9634 ■ 2210 Summit St (btwn Allen & Oakland) ■ 4pm-2:30am

19 **Tremont II** [M,NH,OC] 614/445-9365 ■ 708 S High St (at Frankfort) ■ noon-2:30pm, 1pm-11:30pm Sun

20 **Union Station Video Cafe** [★MW,P,F,V,WC] 614/228-3740 ■ 630 N High St (at Goodale) ■ 11am-2am, video bar, Internet access, also full menu

Nightclubs

21 **Axis** [★M,D,WC,GO] 614/291-4008 ■ 775 N High St (at Hubbard) ■ 10pm-2:30am, 18+, Varsity Night Th w/ dancers

22 **Club Utopia** [MW,D,F,S,WC] 614/470-2272 ■ 115 Parsons Ave (at Franklin) ■ 2pm-2:30am, from noon Sun, CW Wed, strippers most nights

23 **Tradewinds II** [M,D,B,L,V,WC] 614/461-4810 ■ 117 E Chestnut (at 3rd St) ■ 4pm-2:30am, clsd Mon, 3 bars & restaurant, Columbus Ursine Brotherhood 6pm 2nd Sat

24 **Wall Street** [★MW,D,CW,P,S,YC,WC] 614/464-2800 ■ 144 N Wall St (at Long) ■ 8pm-2:30am, from 9pm Wed, clsd Mon-Tue, more men Wed, CW Th, drag Sun
■ www.outinohio.com

Columbus

Columbus is both Ohio's largest city and its capital. It offers a wide variety of attractions, from the Columbus Jazz Orchestra to the Brewery District. The Short North, the area on High Street just north of downtown, hosts the very popular 'Gallery Hop' on the first Saturday of the month.

Queer Resources

Community Info
▼ Stonewall Columbus Hotline/Community Center 614/299-7764, web: www.stonewall-columbus.org. 1160 N High St (at 4th Ave), 10am-7pm, till 5pm Fri, clsd wknds.

AIDS Resources
Columbus AIDS Task Force 614/299-2437.

Recovery
614/253-8501.

City Calendar

LGBT Pride
June. 614/299-7764 (Stonewall).

Annual Events
June - Pagan Spirit Gathering in Athens campground, 1.5 hrs south of Columbus 608/924-2216 (Wisconsin office).
September - Ohio Lesbian Festival 614/267-3953.

Tourist Info

Airport Directions
Port Columbus International. To get to downtown, take 17th Ave to Hwy 62 South. Follow Hwy 62 until it comes to Hwy 40 West. Follow 40 West as it runs right through downtown.

Public Transit & Taxis
Yellow Cab 614/444-4444.
Northway Taxicab 614/299-4118, 614/299-1191.
Independent 614/235-5551.
Airport Express Shuttle 614/476-3004.
Central Ohio Transit Authority (COTA) 614/228-1776.

Tourist Spots & Info
Columbus Museum of Modern Art 614/221-6801.
Columbus Zoo 614/645-3550.
German Village district.
Wexner Center for the Arts 614/292-0330.
Visitor's Center: 614/221-2489, web: www.ohiotourism.com.

Weather
Truly midwestern. Winters are cold, summers are hot.

Columbus • Ohio

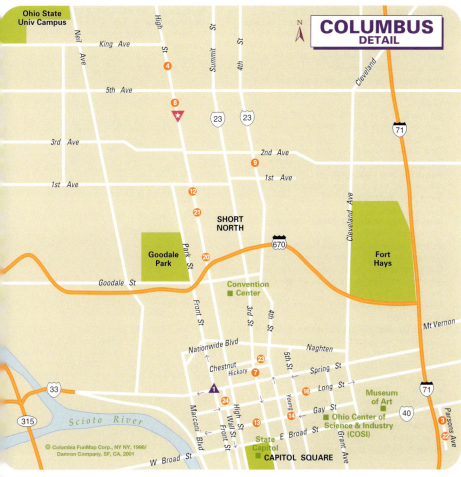

CAFES

The Coffee Table [MW] 614/297-1177 ■ 731 N High St (at Buttles) ■ 7:30am-midnight, till 1am wknds, 8am-10pm Sun

Cup-O-Joe Cafe 614/221-1563 ■ 627 3rd St (at Sycamore) ■ 6:30am-11pm, till midnight Fri-Sat, from 7:30am Sun

RESTAURANTS

Chinese Village 614/297-7979 ■ 2124 Lane St (at High) ■ 11am-10pm

Fresno's [★] 614/298-0031 ■ 782 N High St (at Buttles Ave) ■ 11am-11pm, from 4pm Sat, clsd Sun

L'Antibes [WC,GO] 614/291-1666 ■ 772 N High St #106 (at Warren) ■ dinner from 5pm, clsd Sun-Mon, French ■ users.aol.com/lantibes

Lemon Grass [★] 614/224-1414 ■ 641 N High (N of Goodale St) ■ lunch & dinner, from 3pm Sat, clsd Sun, Pacific Rim Asian cuisine, reservations advised

Nacho Mama's 740/548-5655 ■ 5277 US Hwy 23

No Attitude Bar & Grill [★GO] 614/464-3663 ■ 53 Parsons Ave (at Oak) ■ 11am-2pm & 5pm-10pm, clsd Sat-Sun, some veggie, full bar

Out on Main [★MW,E,V,WC] 614/224-9510 ■ 122 E Main (btwn 3rd & 4th) ■ 5pm-10pm, till 11pm Fri-Sat, brunch 11am-2:30pm Sun, upscale casual dining, piano wknds, full bar ■ www.outonmain.com

ENTERTAINMENT & RECREATION

The Reality Theatre 614/294-7541 ■ 736 N Pearl St (btwn Lincoln & Warren) ■ lgbt plays & new releases, call for show dates ■ www.realitytheatre.com

BOOKSTORES

The Book Loft of German Village 614/464-1774 ■ 631 S 3rd St (at Sycamore) ■ 10am-11pm, till midnight Fri-Sat, lgbt section

The Shadow Realm [WC] 614/262-1175 ■ 3347 N High St (1 blk S of N Broadway) ■ metaphysical & occult bookstore, readings & workshops, sponsors the annual 'Witch's Ball' in Oct

RETAIL SHOPS

ACME Art Company 614/299-4003 ■ 1129 N High St (at 4th Ave) ■ alternative art space, call for hrs

Creative-A-Tee 614/297-8844 ■ 874 N High St ■ noon-7pm, till 5pm Sat, clsd Sun-Mon, pride T-shirts, silkscreening

Hausfrau Haven 614/443-3680 ■ 769 S 3rd St (at Columbus) ■ 10am-6:30pm, till 5pm Sun, greeting cards, wine & gifts
KRT (Kukula's Rainbow Tribe) 614/228-8337 ■ 636 N High St (at Russell) ■ noon-9pm, till midnight Fri-Sat, till 6pm Sun, lgbt gifts & tanning
Metro Video 614/291-7962 ■ 848 N High St (at Hubbard) ■ 11am-midnight, from noon Sun, large selection of lgbt videos
Pierceology 614/297-4743 ■ 872 N High St (S of 1st) ■ noon-9pm, till 10pm Fri-Sat, 1pm-7pm Sun, body piercing studio
Torso 614/421-7663 ■ 772 N High St (at Warren) ■ 1pm-9pm, noon-10pm Sat, till 5pm Sun, men's clothing
Wallich Gallery 614/291-2787 ■ 745 N High St (btwn Buttles & Hubbard) ■ 11am-7pm, till 5pm Sat, clsd Sun-Mon ■ gds517@yahoo.com

North Campus Video 614/268-4021 ■ 2465 N High St (at Hudson) ■ 24hrs
Zodiac 614/252-0281 ■ 1565 Alum Creek Dr (at Livingston) ■ 24hrs

PUBLICATIONS
Hotspots Magazine 304/782-3358 ■ serving all of Ohio ■ www.hotspotsimag.com
Outlook 614/268-8525, 866/452-3697 ■ lgbt newspaper, good resource pages ■ www.outlooknews.com
Spotlight Magazine 614/805-5664 ■ bi-weekly lgbt paper for Central Ohio ■ spotlight@columbus.rr.com
The Stonewall Journal 614/299-7764 ■ www.stonewall-columbus.org

MEN'S CLUBS
► **The Club Columbus** [SW] 614/291-0049 ■ 795 W 5th Ave (at Olentangy Rd) ■ gym, steam, sauna ■ www.the-clubs.com

EROTICA
Bexley Video 614/235-2341 ■ 3839 April Ln (at Courtright)
Garden 614/294-2869 ■ 1186 N High St (at 5th Ave) ■ adult toys
IMRU 614/228-9660 ■ 235 N Lazelle (at Hickory, above the 'Eagle') ■ leather, pride & fetish store
The Lion's Den Adult Bookstore 614/475-1943 ■ 3015 Morse ■ 24hrs
The Lion's Den Adult Bookstore 614/861-6770 ■ 4315 Kimberly Pkwy (off Hamilton Rd) ■ 24hrs

A Traveler's Dream...

THE CLUB Columbus
www.the-clubs.com

One Day Memberships · Free Parking
Private Dressing Rooms
In/Out Privileges · Centrally Located
Steam · Sauna · Whirlpool · Tanning
Heated Pool & Patio
Fully Equipped Gym

795 West Fifth Avenue
Columbus, Ohio 43211
614-291-0049

OKLAHOMA

Oklahoma City

ACCOMMODATIONS
American Crossroads B&B [M,GO] 405/495-1111 ■ reservation service

1 ▶ Habana Inn [★MW,SW,WC] 405/528-2221, 800/988-2221 (reservations only) ■ 2200 NW 39th Expwy (at Youngs) ■ gay resort, also 3 clubs, piano bar, restaurant, gift shop ■ www.habanainn.com

Tommy's Ranch [GS,SW,WC,GO] 405/216-8669 ■ 13700 S Sooner Rd, Edmond ■ 20 min from OK City, cabins, full brkfst, camping, horseback riding ■ www.tommysranch.com

BARS
2 Copper Penny Lounge [M,NH,GO] 405/947-9361 ■ 3201 N May Ave (30th) ■ 10:30am-2am, from noon Sun, 'tacky little beer joint,' patio ■ www.copperpenny.org

3 Coyote Club [W,D,S,GO] 405/521-9533 ■ 2120 NW 39th St (at Youngs) ■ 8pm-close Th-Sat, from 2pm Sun, shows Fri ■ www.anglesclub.com

1 The Finishline [MW,D,CW,WC] 405/525-2900 ■ at 'Habana Inn' ■ noon-2am, CW lessons 7pm Tue-Wed, poolside bar ■ www.habanainn.com/finish.shtml

4 Hi-Lo Club [MW,NH,E] 405/843-1722 ■ 1221 NW 50th St (btwn Western & Classen) ■ noon-2am, live bands weekly

5 KA's [W,NH,D,WC] 405/525-3734 ■ 2024 NW 11th (at Pennsylvania) ■ 3pm-2am, beer bar, live entertainment monthly

1 The Ledo [MW,F,E,K,S,WC] 405/525-0730 ■ at 'Habana Inn' ■ 4pm-close, cabaret & lounge, piano bar, live shows Sat, karaoke Th ■ www.habanainn.com

6 Levi's [M,NH,L,WC] 405/947-1155 ■ 2807 NW 36th St (at May Ave) ■ noon-2am, patio, cruise bar

7 Partners [★W,NH,D,E,S,WC] 405/942-2199 ■ 2805 NW 36th St (at May Ave) ■ 5pm-close, from 6pm Fri, from 7pm Sat, clsd Mon-Tue, patio ■ www.partners4club.com

8 Tramps [★M,D,S,WC] 405/521-9888 ■ 2201 NW 39th St (at Barnes) ■ noon-2am, from 10am wknds

NIGHTCLUBS
9 Angles [★MW,D,S,WC] 405/524-3431 ■ 2117 NW 39th St (at Pennsylvania) ■ 9pm-2am, clsd Mon-Wed ■ www.anglesclub.com

OKLAHOMA • USA

OKLAHOMA CITY

First settled in 1889, Oklahoma City maintains its 'Old West' roots. In keeping with its history of rugged individualism and invention, Oklahoma City is home to the National Cowboy Hall of Fame...and to a monument commemorating the inventor of the shopping cart, OKC resident Sylvan Goldman.

Queer Resources

COMMUNITY INFO
▼ The Center 405/525-2437 or 405/524-6000. 2135 NW 39th St, 11am-7pm Mon-Thurs, till midnight Fri, clsd Sat/Sun.
Herland Sister Resources 405/521-9696.

AIDS RESOURCES
405/748-9933.

RECOVERY
Live & Let Live 405/947-3834, 3405 N Villa.

City Calendar

LGBT PRIDE
June. 405/525-2437 (The Center).

ANNUAL EVENTS
May - Herland Spring Retreat 405/521-9696. Music, workshops.
September - Herland Fall Retreat.

Tourist Info

AIRPORT DIRECTIONS
Will Rogers World Airport. To get to the area within the detail map, take I-44 North. Exit on Pennsylvania Ave.

PUBLIC TRANSIT & TAXIS
Yellow Cab 405/232-6161.
Airport Express 405/681-3311.
Metro Transit 405/235-7433.

TOURIST SPOTS & INFO
Historic Paseo Arts District.
Myriad Gardens' Crystal Bridge 405/297-3995.
National Cowboy Hall of Fame 405/478-2250.
National Softball Hall of Fame 405/424-5266.
Omniplex 405/602-6664.
Will Rogers Park.
Visitor's Center: 405/297-8912, web: www.okccvb.org.

1 The Copa [MW,D,S,WC,$] 405/525-0730 ■ at 'Habana Inn' ■ 9pm-2am, clsd Mon, cover charge Sun ■ www.habanainn.com

10 The Park [M,D,S,V,WC] 405/528-4690 ■ 2125 NW 39th St (at Barnes/ Pennsylvania) ■ 5pm-2am, from 3pm Sun, patio, cruisy ■ www.anglesclub.com

11 Wreck Room [★MW,D,S,YC] 405/525-7610 ■ 2127 NW 39th St (at Pennsylvania) ■ 10pm-close Th-Sat, juice bar, 18+ after 1am ■ www.anglesclub.com

CAFES
Grateful Bean Cafe & Soda Fountain [E] 405/236-3503 ■ 1039 Walker ■ 11am-5pm, clsd wknds, plenty veggie, 'Seattle-style' espresso

RESTAURANTS
Bricktown Brewery Restaurant 405/232-2739 ■ 1 N Oklahoma (at Sheridan) ■ 11am-10pm, till 2am Fri-Sat, live bands Fri-Sat ■ www.bricktownbrewery.com

Gusher's Bar & Grill [WC] 405/528-2221 x411 ■ at 'Habana Inn' ■ 11am-10:30pm, from 8am wknds, till 3:30am Fri-Sat for after-hours brkfst ■ www.habanainn.com

Painted Desert 405/524-5925 ■ 3700 N Shartel (at NW 36th St) ■ 11am-2:30am, pizza, sandwiches, full bar

Terra Luna Grille 405/879-0009 ■ 7408 N Western (at 73rd) ■ lunch & dinner

RETAIL SHOPS
23rd St Body Piercing 405/524-6824 ■ 411 NW 23rd St (at N. Hudson)

Ziggyz 405/521-9999 ■ 4005 N Pennsylvania (at I-240) ■ novelty gifts & smokeshop; also 3426 SW 29th, 405/682-2299

PUBLICATIONS
Gayly Oklahoman 405/528-0800 ■ lgbt newspaper ■ www.gayly.com

The Herland Voice 405/521-9696 ■ newsletter

EROTICA
Christie's Toy Box 405/946-4438 ■ 3126 N May Ave (at 30th) ■ also 1039 S Meridian, 405/948-3333

Jungle Red [WC] 405/524-5733 ■ at 'Habana Inn' ■ 1pm-close, from noon wknds, novelties, leather, gifts ■ www.habanainn.com

Naughty & Nice 405/686-1110 ■ 3121 SW 29th St (at I-44) ■ 24hrs

Randi's Playthings 405/681-0308 ■ 4711 S Pennsylvania (at 44th) ■ adult toys, lingerie, some plus sizes

OKLAHOMA CITY'S HABANA INN

The Southwest's Largest All Gay Resort

175 Guest Rooms ★ Two Swimming Pools
Poolside Rooms ★ Suites ★ Cable TV

Park Once And Party All Night!
Located In The Habana Inn Complex

THE COPA

OKC's Hottest Dance Club
Newly Redecorated

- Tuesday Amatuer Strip-Off
- Wednesday Kitty's Comedy Capers
- Thursday Open Talent Dong Show
- Friday HOT-HOT Male Dancers
- Saturday HOT-HOT Male Dancers
- Sunday The COPA Show

Open 9pm - 2am   Closed Mondays

Finishline

OKC's Only Country Dance Floor
OPEN 7 days a week

COUNTRY MUSIC & DANCING
POOL BAR during season

Darts **Noon - 2am** Pool

GUSHER'S Bar & Grill

Finest Prime Rib in OKC

OPEN
Mon - Fri 11am
Sat & Sun 9am

SERVING UNTIL
Sun - Thurs 10:30pm
Fri & Sat 3:30am

The Ledo Cabaret & Lounge

Open 4pm Daily

Karaoke
Every Thursday & Friday from 9pm
Join the Fun Sing Along!

OKC'S Only Piano Bar
Best Martini's in Town

ShowBiz Saturday's 10:00pm
OKC's Top Female Impersonators
with host Ginger Lamar

2200 NW 39th Expressway, Oklahoma City, OK 73112
Call for rates and information
(405) 528-2221   Reservations only: 1-800-988-2221
Website: www.habanainn.com

OREGON • USA

Portland

ACCOMMODATIONS

1. **The Clyde Hotel** [MW,GO] 503/224-8000 ■ 1022 SW Stark St (at 10th) ■ some shared baths ■ *clydehotel.com*
2. **Fifth Avenue Suites Hotel** [GF] 503/222-0001, 800/711-2971 ■ 506 SW Washington (at 5th Ave) ■ also restaurant, gym ■ *www.5thavenuesuites.com*
3. **Hotel Vintage Plaza** [★GF,WC] 503/228-1212, 800/263-2305 ■ 422 SW Broadway ■ upscale hotel, also restaurant & lounge ■ *www.vintageplaza.com*
4. **MacMaster House** [GF,NS] 503/223-7362, 800/774-9523 ■ 1041 SW Vista Ave (at Park Pl) ■ historic inn nr Rose Gardens ■ *www.macmaster.com*
5. **The Mark Spencer Hotel** [GF] 503/224-3293, 800/548-3934 ■ 409 SW Eleventh Ave (nr Stark) ■ *www.markspencer.com*
6. **Sullivan's Gulch B&B** [MW,GO] 503/331-1104 ■ 1744 NE Clackamas St (at 17th) ■ 1907 Portland home, decks ■ *www.sullivansgulch.com*

BARS

7. **Bar of the Gods** [GS,NH,BW,WC] 503/232-2037 ■ 4801 SE Hawthorne (at 48th Ave) ■ 5pm-2:30am
8. **Boxxes** [★M,D,K,V,WC] 503/226-4171 ■ 1035 SW Stark (at SW 11th Ave) ■ 11:30am-2:30am, from 3pm wknds, also 'Brig' (MW,D) 9pm-2:30am, also 'Red Cap Garage' restaurant, noon-2:30am
9. **Candlelight Room** [GF,F,E] 503/222-3378 ■ 2032 SW 5th (at Lincoln) ■ 10am-2:30am, from 11am wknds, burgers
10. **CC Slaughter's** [★M,D,CW,F,K,V] 503/248-9135 ■ 219 NW Davis (at 3rd) ■ 11am-2:30am, CW Wed & Fri ■ *www.eaglepdx.com/slaughters*
11. **Darcelle XV** [GS,F,S,WC] 503/222-5338 ■ 208 NW 3rd Ave (at NW Davis St) ■ 5pm-11pm, 6pm-2am Sat, clsd Sun-Tue
12. **Eagle PDX** [M,L,V] 503/241-0105 ■ 1300 W Burnside (at 13th Ave) ■ 4pm-2:30am ■ *www.eaglepdx.com*
13. **The Egyptian Club** [★W,D,F,S,WC] 503/236-8689 ■ 3701 SE Division (at SE 37th Ave) ■ 11:30am-2:30am, from 4pm Sat-Sun, DJ & karaoke Th-Sat, strippers Tue
14. **Fox & Hound** [M,K,WC] 503/243-5530 ■ 217 NW 2nd Ave (btwn Everett & Davis) ■ 9:30am-2am, from 8:30am wknds, poker bar, also restaurant, brunch Sun

PORTLAND

At the foot of Mt Hood, sprawling along the Columbia River, lies Portland, the 'City of Roses'. The mild, often rainy weather gives the area its lush greenery. An ecologically and ideologically progressive city, Portland has perhaps the cleanest city air and water in the nation, attracting many visitors to become residents.

Queer Resources

COMMUNITY INFO
Lesbian Community Project 503/233-3913. 1001 E Burnside, call for hrs.

AIDS RESOURCES
Cascade AIDS Project 503/223-5907.
AIDS and STD Hotline 503/223-2437.

RECOVERY
Live & Let Live 503/238-6091, 2940-A SE Belmont St.

City Calendar

LGBT PRIDE
June. 503/295-9788.

ANNUAL EVENTS
June - The Gathering. Annual pagan camp in the Oregon Woods.
August - Annual Women's Softball 503/233-3913 (LCP).
September - Northwest Women's Music Celebration.

Tourist Info

AIRPORT DIRECTIONS
Portland International. Take 205 South, then 84 West to City Center/Morrison Bridge exit. Cross the bridge, take Washington St into town.

PUBLIC TRANSIT & TAXIS
Radio Cab 503/227-1212.
Raz 503/684-3322.
Tri-Met System 503/238-7433.

TOURIST SPOTS & INFO
Microbreweries.
Mt. Hood Festival of Jazz.
Old Town.
Pioneer Courthouse Square.
Rose Festival.
Washington Park.
Visitor's Center: 503/222-2223 or 877/678-5263.
Oregon Tourism Commission 800/547-7842, web: www.pova.com.

WEATHER
The wet and sometimes chilly winter rains give Portland its lush landscape that bursts into beautiful colors in the spring and fall. Summer brings sunnier days. (Temperatures can be in the 50°s one day and the 90°s the next.)

BEST VIEWS
International Rose Test Gardens at Washington Park.

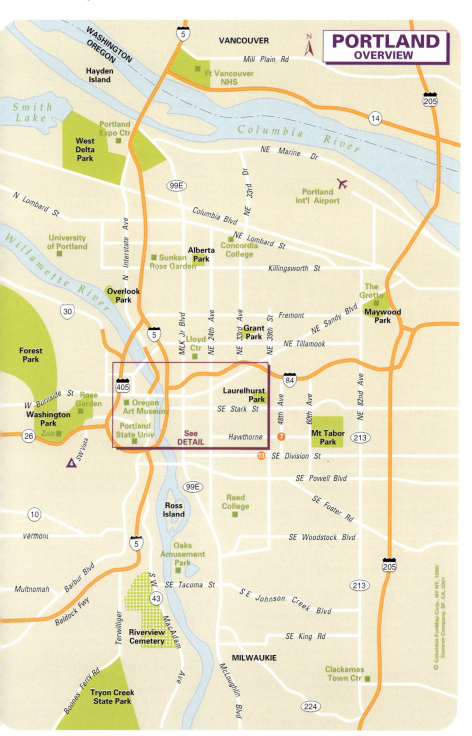

OREGON • USA

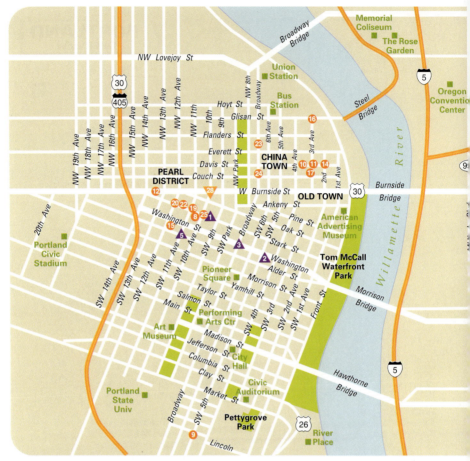

15 The Frontline [M,NH,F] 503/243-2181 ■ 1135 SW Washington (at 12th) ■ 11am-midnight, bar till 2:30am Fri-Sat, restaurant till 5am

16 Gail's Dirty Duck Tavern [M,NH,B,L,OC,WC] 503/224-8446 ■ 439 NW 3rd (at Glisan) ■ 3pm-1:30am, from noon wknds, 'home of the bears,' hanky night & leather social 1st & 3rd Fri

17 Hobo's [GS,E,WC] 503/224-3285 ■ 120 NW 3rd Ave (btwn Davis & Couch) ■ 4pm-2:30am, piano bar, also restaurant, some veggie

18 JOQ's Tavern [M,NH,F,WC] 503/287-4210 ■ 2512 NE Broadway (at NE 24th Ave) ■ 11am-2:30am

19 Scandals Tavern [M,NH,F,WC,GO] 503/227-5887 ■ 1038 SW Stark St (at SW 11th Ave) ■ 11:30am-2:30am, friendly bar, restaurant from 7pm

20 Silverado [★M,D,S,K,WC] 503/224-4493 ■ 1217 SW Stark St (btwn SW 11th & 12th Aves) ■ 9am-2:30am, dancers, also restaurant ■ www.silveradopdx.com

21 Starky's [★MW,NH,F,WC] 503/230-7980 ■ 2913 SE Stark St (at SE 29th Ave) ■ 11am-2am, patio, also restaurant

22 Three Sisters Tavern [M,NH,D,S] 503/228-0486 ■ 1125 SW Stark St (at 12th) ■ 1pm-2:30am, DJ & strippers Wed-Sat

23 Tiger Bar [★GF,WC] 503/222-7297 ■ 317 NW Broadway (btwn Everett & Flanders) ■ 5pm-2:30am, open for lunch Tue-Fri

Nightclubs

24 Embers [★M,D,F,S,WC] 503/222-3082 ■ 110 NW Broadway (at NW Couch St) ■ 11:30am-2:30am, also restaurant

25 Panorama [★GF,D,BW,WC] 503/221-7262 ■ 341 SW 10th Ave (at Stark) ■ 9pm-4am Fri-Sat only, call for events

Cafes

Bread & Ink Cafe [★BW,WC] 503/239-4756 ■ 3610 SE Hawthorne Blvd (at 36th) ■ 7am-9pm, till 10pm Fri-Sat, from 9am Sun (clsd btwn lunch & dinner)

Cafe Lena [★E,WC] 503/238-7087 ■ 2239 SE Hawthorne Blvd (at SE 23rd) ■ 8am-9:30pm, till 3pm Sun, clsd Mon

Cup & Saucer Cafe [★NS] 503/236-6001 ■ 3566 SE Hawthorne Blvd (btwn 34th & 36th) ■ 7am-9pm

Marco's Cafe & Espresso Bar 503/245-0199 ■ 7910 SW 35th (at Multnomah Blvd), Multnomah ■ 7am-9:30pm, from 8am wknds, till 2pm Sun

The Pied Cow 503/230-4866 ■ 3244 SE Belmont ■ 4pm-midnight, till 1am wknds, funky Victorian, great desserts, patio

Portland • OREGON

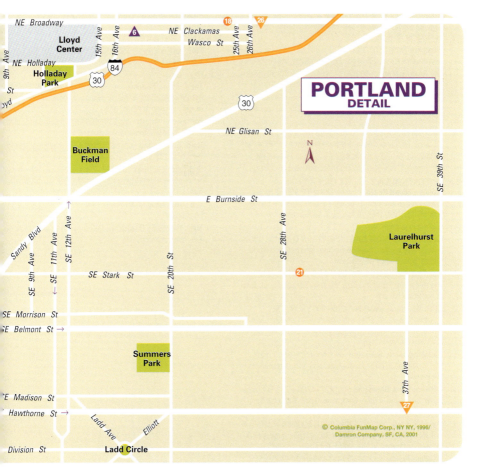

Saucebox [MW,WC] 503/241-3393 ■ 214 SW Broadway (at Stark) ■ 11:30am-1:30pm & 6pm-10pm, clsd Sun-Mon, pan-Asian, plenty veggie, full bar

Touchstone Coffee House [GO,E] 503/262-7613 ■ 7631 NE Glisan St ■ 7am-9pm, till 10pm Th-Fri, 8am-10pm Sat, till 3pm Sun ■ www.touchstonecoffeehouse.com

RESTAURANTS

The Adobe Rose [BW] 503/235-9114 ■ 1634 SE Bybee Blvd (at Milwaukee) ■ 11:30am-2pm, also 5pm-9pm Fri-Sat, clsd Sun-Mon, New Mexican cuisine

Assaggio [BW] 503/232-6151 ■ 7742 SE 13th (at Lambert) ■ 5pm-9:30pm, clsd Sun-Mon, Italian, plenty veggie

Bastas Trattoria 503/274-1572 ■ 410 NW 21st (at Flanders) ■ lunch Mon-Fri & dinner nightly, northern Italian, full bar till 1am

Bijou Cafe [★] 503/222-3187 ■ 132 SW 3rd Ave (at Pine St) ■ 7am-2pm, from 8am wknds, also 6pm-10pm Tue-Sat, plenty veggie

Brasserie Montmartre 503/224-5552 ■ 626 SW Park (at Alder) ■ lunch & dinner, Sun brunch, bistro menu, live jazz, full bar

Daydream Cafe [★GO] 503/233-4244 ■ 1740 SE Hawthorne (at 17th) ■ 7am-7:30pm, till 5pm wknds

Delta [WC] 503/771-3101 ■ 4607 SE Woodstock ■ 5pm-10pm, from noon wknds, Southern, plenty veggie

Dot's Cafe [★] 503/235-0203 ■ 2521 SE Clinton ■ lunch & dinner till 2am, full bar, eclectic American, plenty veggie

Esparza's Tex-Mex Cafe [★] 503/234-7909 ■ 2725 SE Ankeny St (at 28th) ■ 11:30am-10pm, clsd Sun-Mon

Fish Grotto [★] 503/226-4171 ■ 1035 SW Stark (at SW 11th Ave, at 'Boxxes') ■ 5pm-close, clsd Mon, some veggie, full bar

Hobo's [★E,WC] 503/224-3285 ■ 120 NW 3rd Ave (btwn Davis & Couch) ■ 4pm-2:30am

Majas Taqueria 503/226-1946 ■ 1000 SW Morrison ■ 11am-9:30 pm

Montage [★WC] 503/234-1324 ■ 301 SE Morrison ■ lunch & dinner, Louisiana-style cookin'

Nicholas' 503/235-5123 ■ 318 SE Grand ■ 10am-9pm, noon-8pm Sun, Middle Eastern

Old Wives Tales [BW,WC] 503/238-0470 ■ 1300 E Burnside St (at 13th) ■ 8am-9pm, till 10pm Fri-Sat, multiethnic vegetarian

The Original Pancake House 503/246-9007 ■ 8600 SW Barbur Blvd ■ 7am-3pm, clsd Mon-Tue, great brkfst

Paradox Cafe [★] 503/232-7508 ■ 3439 SE Belmont ■ 8am-9pm, till 10pm Fri-Sat, healthy vegetarian diner grub, killer Reuben

Pizzacato [★BW] 503/242-0023 ■ 505 NW 23rd (at Glisan) ■ 11:30am-10pm, till 11pm Fri-Sat, plenty veggie

The Roxy [★MW,WC] 503/223-9160 ■ 1121 SW Stark St ■ 24hrs, clsd Mon, American

Starky's [MW] 503/230-7980 ■ 2913 SE Stark St ■ 11am-2pm & 5:30pm-9:30pm, from 9:30am Sun, full bar till 2:30am

Vista Spring Cafe [BW] 503/222-2811 ■ 2440 SW Vista (at Spring) ■ 11am-10pm, from noon wknds, till 9pm Sun

Wildwood [★] 503/248-9663 ■ 1221 NW 21st Ave (at Overton) ■ 11am-9pm (reservations advised), full bar

ENTERTAINMENT & RECREATION
Sauvie's Island Beach 25 miles NW (off US 30) ■ follow Reeder Rd to the Collins beach area, park at the farthest end of the road, then follow path to beach

BOOKSTORES
Countermedia 503/226-8141 ■ 927 SW Oak (btwn 9th & 10th) ■ 11am-7pm, noon-6pm Sun, alternative comics, vintage gay books/ periodicals

26 **Gai-Pied** 503/331-1125 ■ 2544 NE Broadway (at 26th) ■ 11am-8pm, till 9pm Fri-Sat, till 7pm Sun, gay bookstore ■ www.gaipied.com

27 **In Other Words** [WC,E] 503/232-6003 ■ 3734 SE Hawthorne Blvd (at 37th) ■ 10am-9pm, 11am-6pm Sun, women's books, music & resource ctr ■ www.inotherwords.org

Laughing Horse Bookstore [WC] 503/236-2893 ■ 3652 SE Division (at 37th) ■ 11am-7pm, clsd Sun, alternative/ progressive

Looking Glass Bookstore 503/227-4760 ■ 318 SW Taylor (btwn 3rd & 4th) ■ 9am-6pm, from 10am Sat, clsd Sun, general, some lgbt titles

28 **Powell's Books** [WC] 503/228-4651, 800/878-7323 ■ 1005 W Burnside St (at 10th) ■ 9am-11pm, largest new & used bookstore in the world, cafe

Reading Frenzy [WC] 503/274-1449 ■ 921 SW Oak St ■ 11am-7pm, noon-6pm wknds, zines, comics, lgbt section

Twenty-Third Ave Books [WC] 503/224-5097 ■ 1015 NW 23rd Ave (at Lovejoy) ■ 9:30am-9pm, from 10am Sat, 11am-7pm Sun, general, lgbt section

RETAIL SHOPS
In Her Image Gallery [WC] 503/231-3726 ■ 3208 SE Hawthorne (at 32nd) ■ 11am-6pm, 10am-5pm wknds, clsd Mon-Tue

It's My Pleasure 503/280-8080 ■ 3106 NE 64th Ave (at Sandy Blvd) ■ books, erotica, toys, gifts, workshops, call for hours ■ www.teleport.com/~pleasure

The Jellybean [WC] 503/222-5888 ■ 721 SW 10th Ave (at Morrison) ■ 10am-6pm, noon-5pm Sun, cards, T-shirts, gifts

Presents of Mind [WC] 503/230-7740 ■ 3633 SE Hawthorne (at 37th Ave) ■ 10am-7pm, jewelry, unique gifts

PUBLICATIONS
Just Out 503/236-1252 ■ lgbt newspaper, extensive resource directory ■ justout@justout.com

GYMS & HEALTH CLUBS
Inner City Hot Tubs [GF] 503/238-1065 ■ 2927 NE Everett St (btwn 29th & 30th) ■ 10am-11pm, from 1pm Sun, wellness ctr, reservations req'd

Princeton Athletic Club [GF] 503/222-2639 ■ 614 SW 11th Ave (at Alder)

MEN'S CLUBS
Club Portland [★18+,PC] 503/227-9992 ■ 303 SW 12th Ave ■ 24hrs

EROTICA
The Crimson Phoenix [WC] 503/228-0129 ■ 1876 SW 5th Ave (btwn Harrison & Hall) ■ 'sexuality bookstore for lovers', condoms, herbs, gifts

Fantasy for Adults 503/239-6969 ■ 3137 NE Sandy Blvd (nr NE 39th) ■ 24hrs

Hard Times Video 503/223-2398 ■ 311 NW Broadway (at Everett) ■ 24hrs

Spartacus Leathers 503/224-2604 ■ 302 SW 12th Ave (at Burnside) ■ 10am-11pm, till midnight Fri-Sat, till 9pm Sun

Tim's Hideaway 503/771-9774 ■ 4229 SE 82nd Ave, #3 (at Holgate)

Tim's Hideaway Downtown 503/224-2338 ■ 330 SW 3rd Ave (btwn Stark & Oak)

Philadelphia • PENNSYLVANIA

ACCOMMODATIONS

1 **The Alexander Inn** [GS,GO] 215/923-3535, 877/253-9466 ■ Spruce (at 12th) ■ www.alexanderinn.com
2 **Antique Row B&B** [GF] 215/592-7802 ■ 341 S 12th St (at Pine) ■ 1820s townhouse, full brkfst ■ bp341@aol.com
3 **Doubletree Hotel** [GF] 215/893-1600, 800/222-8733 ■ 237 S Broad St (at Locust)
4 **Embassy Suites Center City** [GF] 215/561-1776, 800/362-2779 ■ 1776 Ben Franklin Pkwy (at 18th) ■ www.embassysuitesdowntown.com
5 **Gaskill House** [GS,NS,GO] 215/413-0669 ■ 312 Gaskill St (btwn Lombard & South St) ■ full brkfst, fireplaces, on Society Hill ■ www.gaskillhouse.com
  Glen Isle Farm [GF,F,NS] 610/269-9100, 800/269-1730 ■ 30 miles out of town, in Downingtown ■ full brkfst
6 **Latham Hotel** [GF] 215/563-7474, 800/528-4261 ■ 135 S 17th St (at Walnut)
7 **Rittenhouse Hotel** [GF,F] 215/546-9000, 800/635-1042 ■ 210 W Rittenhouse Sq (at 19th)
8 **Rodeway Inn** [GF] 215/546-7000, 800/887-1776 ■ 1208 Walnut St (btwn 12th & 13th)
9 **Spring Garden Manor** [GS,GO] 215/567-2484 ■ 2025 Spring Garden St (at 20th) ■ full brkfst, in city center
11 **Uncles Upstairs Inn** [M,GO] 215/546-6660 ■ 1220 Locust St (at 12th) ■ downtown townhouse

BARS

12 **12th Air Command Headquarters for Men** [M,D,A,F] 215/545-8088 ■ 254 S 12th St (btwn Locust & Spruce) ■ 4pm-2am, from 2pm Sun, free buffet Wed-Fri
13 **Key West** [MW,NH,D,S,WC] 215/545-1578 ■ 207-209 S Juniper (btwn Walnut & Locust) ■ 4pm-2am, from 2pm Sun, also piano bar
14 **The Khyber** [GF,F,E] 215/238-5888 ■ 56 S 2nd St (btwn Market & Chestnut) ■ also restaurant (lunch only)
15 **Love Lounge** [GS] 215/922-0499 ■ 232 South St (btwn 2nd & 3rd) ■ 10pm-close wknds only, call first
16 **The Post** [M,NH,S,WC] 215/985-9720 ■ 1705 Chancellor St (at 17th) ■ noon-2am, brunch Sun, dancers Fri-Sat ■ www.thepostbar.com

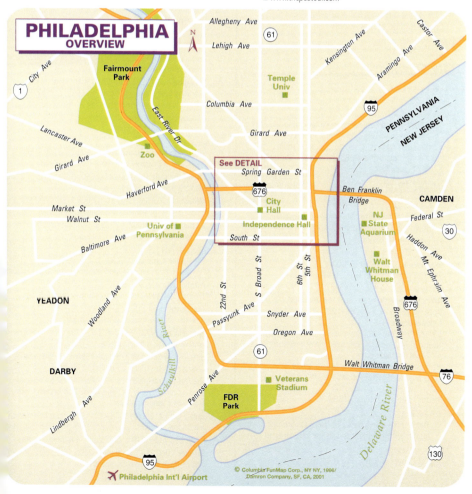

PENNSYLVANIA • USA

PHILADELPHIA

Though it's packed with sites of rich historical value, Philadelphia also has a multicultural present. Between visits to the Liberty Bell and Betsy Ross's home, travelers will enjoy the Reading Terminal Market —an historic and quaint farmer's market preserved within the new Convention Center, the Afro-American Historical and Cultural Museum, and the National Museum of American Jewish History.

Queer Resources

COMMUNITY INFO
▼ William Way LGBT Community Center 215/732-2220, web: www.waygay.org. 1315 Spruce St, noon-10pm, till 7pm Sat.
The Attic Youth Center 215/545-4331, web: www.critpath.org/attic. 419 S 15th St.
Women in Transition Hotline 215/751-1111.

AIDS RESOURCES
Choice Hotline 215/985-3300.

RECOVERY
215/923-7900.

City Calendar

LGBT PRIDE
June. 215/875-9288.

ANNUAL EVENTS
April/May - PrideFest America Philadelphia 215/732-3378, web: www.pridefest.org. Weekend of lgbt film, performances, sports, parties & more.
June - Womongathering 856/694-2037. Women's spirituality fest.

Tourist Info

AIRPORT DIRECTIONS
Philadelphia International. Take I-95 North to downtown. To go directly through downtown, take I-95 to Hwy 611.

PUBLIC TRANSIT & TAXIS
Quaker City Cab 215/728-8000.
Transit Authority (SEPTA) 215/580-7800.

TOURIST SPOTS & INFO
African American Museum 215/574-0380.
Betsy Ross House 215/686-1252.
Independence Hall.
Liberty Bell Pavilion.
National Museum Of American Jewish History 215/923-3811.
Norman Rockwell Museum 215/922-4345.
Philadelphia Museum of Art 215/763-8100.
Rodin Museum 215/763-8100.
Visitor's Center: 215/636-1666.

WEATHER
Winter temperatures hover in the 20's. Summers are humid with temperatures in the 80's and 90's.

BEST VIEWS
Top of Center Square, 16th & Market.

17 **Tavern on Camac** [MW,D,F,K] 215/545-0900 ■ 243 S Camac St (at Spruce) ■ noon-2am, piano bar, DJ wknds
18 **Tyz** [M,D] 215/546-4195 ■ 1418 Rodman St (nr 15th & Richmond) ■ 11pm-3am
11 **Uncle's** [M,NH] 215/546-6660 ■ 1220 Locust St (at 12th) ■ 11am-2am
19 **Venture Inn** [M,F,OC] 215/545-8731 ■ 255 S Camac (at Spruce) ■ noon-2am, from 11am Sun
20 **The Westbury** [M,NH,F,WC] 215/546-5170 ■ 261 S 13th (at Spruce) ■ 10am-2am, dinner till 10pm, till 11pm wknds
21 **Woody's** [★M,D,CW,F,V,YC,WC] 215/545-1893 ■ 202 S 13th St (at Walnut) ■ 11am-2am, videos Mon, 18+ Wed, cover some nights ■ www.woodysbar.com

NIGHTCLUBS
22 **2-4 Club** [M,D,PC,$] 215/735-5772 ■ 1221 St James St (off 13th & Locust) ■ 1am-3am Mon-Tue, from midnight Wed & Sun, from 10pm Fri-Sat
23 **Bike Stop** [★M,D,L] 215/627-1662, 800/859-8480 ■ 204-206 S Quince St (at St James) ■ 4pm-2am, from 2pm wknds, cruisy, also leather shop ■ www.thebikestop.com
24 **Fluid** [GF,D,S,$] 215/629-3686 ■ 613 S 4th St (at South) ■ 10pm-2am, more gay wknds, theme nights
25 **Gasoline** [GS,D] 215/925-1900 ■ Eighth St (at Callowhill St) ■ 9pm-2am Fri-Sat, from 10pm Sun
26 **Palmer Social Club** [GF,D,PC] 215/925-5000 ■ 601 Spring Garden St (at 6th) ■ late-night Th-Tue, 3 flrs
27 **Proto Lounge** [GS,D,$] 215/351-9026 ■ 125 S 2nd St (at Chestnut) ■ 8pm-close Th-Sat
28 **Shampoo** [GF,D,A] 215/922-7500 ■ 417 N 8th St (at Willow) ■ 9pm-2am, more gay Fri ■ shampoooonline.com
29 **Sisters** [W,D,K,S,WC] 215/735-0735 ■ 1320 Chancellor St (at Juniper) ■ 5pm-2am, also restaurant, dinner Wed-Sun ■ www.sistersnightclub.com

CAFES
10th Street Pour House 215/922-5626 ■ 262 S 10th St (at Spruce) ■ 7:30am-3pm, from 8:30am wknds
Cheap Art Cafe [★] 215/735-6650 ■ 260 S 12th St (btwn Locust & Spruce) ■ 24hrs
Millennium Coffee 215/731-9798 ■ 212 S 12th (btwn Locust & Walnut) ■ open till midnight
Stellar Coffee 215/625-7923 ■ 1101 Spruce St (at 11th) ■ 6:30am-9pm

RESTAURANTS
The Adobe Cafe [E] 215/483-3947 ■ 4550 Mitchell St (at Greenleaf), Roxborough ■ lunch & dinner, till 11pm Fri-Sat
Astral Plane 215/546-6230 ■ 1708 Lombard St (btwn 17th & 18th) ■ lunch & dinner, some veggie, full bar
The Continental 215/923-6069 ■ 138 Market St (at 2nd) ■ dinner nightly, brunch wknds, also bar
Frangelica 215/731-9930 ■ 200 S 12th St (at Walnut) ■ lunch Mon-Fri, dinner nightly
Harmony Vegetarian 215/627-4520 ■ 135 N 9th St (at Cherry) ■ 11am-10pm, till midnight Fri-Sat
The Inn Philadelphia 215/732-2339 ■ 251 S Camac St (btwn Locust & Spruce) ■ 5pm-10pm, Sun brunch, clsd Mon, some veggie, full bar
Judy's Cafe 215/928-1968 ■ 627 S 3rd St (at Bainbridge) ■ 5:30pm-midnight, Sun brunch from 10:30am, full bar
L2 [E] 215/732-7878 ■ 2201 South St ■ dinner nightly
Latimer's Deli 215/545-9244 ■ 255 S 15th St (at Latimer) ■ 9am-9pm, till 11pm Fri, Jewish deli

Philadelphia • PENNSYLVANIA

Liberties [E] 215/238-0660 ■ 705 N 2nd St (at Fairmount) ■ lunch & dinner, Sun brunch, full bar

My Thai 215/985-1878 ■ 2200 South St (at 22nd) ■ 5pm-10pm, till 11pm Fri-Sat

Palladium/ Gold Standard [WC] 215/387-3463 ■ 3601 Locust Walk (at 36th) ■ lunch & dinner, bar till 12:30am

Roosevelt's Pub 215/636-9722 ■ 2222 Walnut (at 23rd) ■ lunch & dinner, some veggie, full bar

Shing Kee [BYOB,GO] 215/829-8983 ■ 52 N 9th St ■ lunch & dinner

Striped Bass 215/732-4444 ■ 1500 Walnut (at 15th) ■ lunch, dinner & Sun brunch, upscale dining

Swanky Bubbles 215/928-1200 ■ 10 S Front St (at Market) ■ dinner nightly, also bar

Valanni [MW] 215/790-9494 ■ 1229 Spruce St ■ dinner only, also bar ■ www.valanni.com

Waldorf Cafe [WC] 215/985-1836 ■ 20th & Lombard Sts ■ dinner, clsd Mon, some veggie, full bar

White Dog Cafe 215/386-9224 ■ 3420 Sansom St (at Walnut) ■ lunch & dinner, full bar

Entertainment & Recreation

Amazon Country 215/898-6677 ■ WXPN-FM 88.9 ■ 9pm Sun, lesbian radio

'Q Zine' 215/898-6677 ■ WXPN-FM 88.5 ■ 10pm Sun, lgbt radio

The Walt Whitman House 856/964-5383 ■ 328 Mickle Blvd (btwn S 3rd & 4th Sts), Camden, NJ ■ the last home of America's great & controversial poet, just across the river

Bookstores

30 **Afterwords** 215/735-2393 ■ 218 S 12th St (btwn Locust & Walnut) ■ 11am-10pm

31 **Giovanni's Room** [★] 215/923-2960 ■ 345 S 12th St (at Pine) ■ open daily, lgbt ■ www.giovannisroom.com

Retail Shops

Infinite Body Piercing 215/923-7335 ■ 626 S 4th (at South)

Publications

Cafe Magazine [GO] 215/627-0791 ■ essays, poetry, short fiction along w/ local listings & photos ■ cafemag.com

Greater Philadelphia Women's Yellow Pages 610/446-4747

PGN (Philadelphia Gay News) 215/625-8501 ■ lgbt newspaper w/ extensive listings ■ www.epgn.com

Swirl Magazine 215/625-8501 ■ nightlife guide

Gyms & Health Clubs

12th St Gym [GF] 215/985-4092 ■ 204 S 12th St (btwn Locust & Walnut) ■ 5:30am-11pm

Men's Clubs

Club Body Center [PC] 215/735-9568 ■ Chancellor St ■ 24hrs ■ www.clubbodycenter.com

LR Fitness 215/564-0225 ■ 105 S 18th (at Sansom) ■ 24hrs

Sex Clubs

Philly Jacks [MO,PC] 215/618-1519 ■ 1318 Walnut (at 13th)

Erotica

Adonis Cinema Complex 215/557-9319 ■ 2026 Sansom St

Condom Kingdom 215/829-1668 ■ 437 South St (at 5th) ■ safer sex materials & toys

Danny's New Adam & Eve Books 215/925-5041 ■ 133 S 13th St (at Walnut) ■ 24hrs

Fetishes Boutique 215/829-4986, 877/2-CORSET ■ 704 S 5th (at Bainbridge) ■ noon-10pm ■ fetishesboutique.com

The Pleasure Chest 215/561-7480 ■ 2039 Walnut (btwn 20th & 21st) ■ clsd Sun-Mon

Pittsburgh

Long associated with steel mills and heavy industry, Pittsburgh is coming into its own as a major American city. Industry magnates like Carnegie and Westinghouse have left their mark, but not only in economic terms: visitors can enjoy the Carnegie Museum of Art and Westinghouse Park. Carnegie-Mellon University and the University of Pittsburgh add their own collegiate culture to the city.

Queer Resources

COMMUNITY INFO
Gay/Lesbian Community Center Phoneline 412/422-0114. 5808 Forward Ave, 2nd flr, 6:30pm-9:30pm, 3pm-6pm Sat, clsd Sun.

AIDS RESOURCES
800/662-6080.

RECOVERY
Lambda AA 412/471-7472.

City Calendar

LGBT PRIDE
June. 412/422-0114 (GLCC #).

Tourist Info

AIRPORT DIRECTIONS
Greater Pittsburgh International. To get to downtown, take Hwy 60 to I-279. Follow I-279 through Ft Pitt Tunnels and across Ft Bridge. Once across bridge, take exit for Liberty Ave.

PUBLIC TRANSIT & TAXIS
Yellow Cab 412/665-8100.
Airline Transportation Co. 412/321-4990.
Port Authority Transit (PAT) 412/442-2000.

TOURIST SPOTS & INFO
Andy Warhol Museum 412/237-8300.
Carnegie Museums of Pittsburgh 412/622-3131.
Fallingwater (in Mill Run) 724/329-8501.
Frick Art & Historical Center 412/371-0600.
Golden Triangle district.
National Aviary 412/323-7235.
Phipps Conservatory 412/622-6914.
Rachel Carson Homestead (in Springdale) 724/274-5459.
Station Square.
Visitor's Center: 412/281-7711 or 800/359-0758, web: www.pittsburgh-cvb.org.

Pittsburgh

ACCOMMODATIONS
The Arbors Guesthouse [MO,NS,GO] 412/321-4376 ■ 745 Magnin St ■ hot tub ■ arbormen@gateway.net

1   The Inn on the Mexican War Streets (at Bogg's Mansion) [MW,F,GO] 412/231-6544 ■ 604 W North Ave ■ located on the historic & gay-friendly North Side ■ hometown.aol.com/innwarst/collect/index.htm

2   The Priory [GF] 412/231-3338 ■ 614 Pressley (nr Cedar Ave) ■ 24-rm Victorian ■ www.thepriory.com

BARS

3   Brewery Tavern [GF] 412/681-7991 ■ 3315 Liberty Ave (at Herron Ave) ■ 10am-2am, from noon Sun

4   Holiday Bar [★M,NH,S] 412/682-8598 ■ 4620 Forbes Ave (at Craig) ■ 4pm-2am, from 2pm wknds, patio

5   Images [M,K,V] 412/391-9990 ■ 965 Liberty Ave (at 10th St) ■ 2pm-2am, from 7pm Sat, from 9pm Sun, karaoke Mon & Th

6   Leather Central [★M,L,F,V] 412/682-9869 ■ 1226 Herron Ave (at Liberty, in 'Donny's' basement) ■ 8pm-midnight Th, 9pm-2am Fri-Sat, 5pm-midnight Sun

7   Liberty Avenue Saloon [MW,NH,S] 412/338-1533 ■ 941 Liberty Ave (at Smithfield) ■ 11am-2am, from 5pm wknds, also restaurant

    New York, New York [★MW,F] 412/661-5600 ■ 5801 Ellsworth Ave (at Maryland) ■ 4pm-2am, from 2pm Sun, also restaurant

8   Pittsburgh Eagle [★M,D,L,WC] 412/766-7222 ■ 1740 Eckert St (nr Beaver) ■ 9pm-2am, clsd Sun-Tue ■ www.pitteagle.com

9   Real Luck Cafe [MW,NH,F,WC] 412/566-8988 ■ 1519 Penn Ave (at 16th) ■ 3pm-2am

10 Senator's [MW,F] 412/362-1600 ■ 401 Hastings St (at Reynolds) ■ 4pm-2am, clsd Sun

Pittsburgh • PENNSYLVANIA

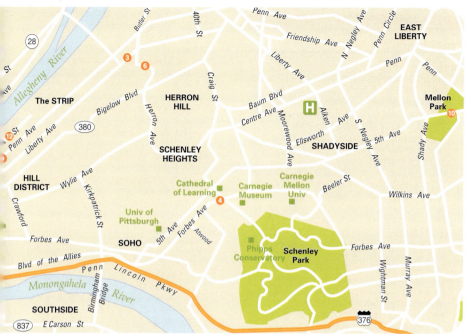

7 Sidekicks [MW,F,S] 412/642-4535 ■ 931 Liberty Ave (at Smithfield) ■ 5pm-midnight, clsd Sun, also restaurant

NIGHTCLUBS
CJ Deighan's [W,D,F,S,WC] 412/561-4044 ■ 2506 W Liberty Ave, Brookline ■ 8pm-2am, clsd Sun-Mon, men welcome

6 Donny's Place [★MW,D,L,F,E] 412/682-9869 ■ 1226 Herron Ave (at Liberty) ■ 4pm-2am, from 3pm Sun, also leather bar

7 House of Tilden [MW,D,PC] 412/391-0804 ■ 941 Liberty Ave, 2nd flr (at Smithfield) ■ 10pm-3am

12 M [★GF,D,A,E,WC] 412/261-4512 ■ 1600 Smallman St ■ 8pm-2am Wed-Sun, lesbigay night Th w/ 'Babylon'

13 Pegasus Lounge [★M,D,S,YC] 412/281-2131 ■ 818 Liberty Ave (at 9th) ■ 9pm-2am, clsd Sun-Mon

CAFES
Tuscany Cafe 412/488-4475 ■ 1501 E Carson St (at 15th) ■ 7am-2am, from 8am wknds, full bar

RESTAURANTS
Rosebud [E,WC] 412/261-2221 ■ 1650 Smallman St ■ dinner only, clsd Mon

ENTERTAINMENT & RECREATION
Andy Warhol Museum 412/237-8300 ■ 117 Sandusky St ■ clsd Mon-Tue, is it soup or is it art—see for yourself

BOOKSTORES
The Bookstall 412/683-2644 ■ 3604 5th Ave (at Meyran) ■ 9:30am-5pm, till 4:30pm Sat, clsd Sun

St Elmo's Books & Music 412/431-9100 ■ 2208 E Carson St (at 22nd St) ■ 10am-9pm

RETAIL SHOPS
A Pleasant Present [WC] 412/421-7104 ■ 2301 Murray Ave (at Nicholson) ■ 10am-7pm, till 8:30pm Th, till 6pm Fri, clsd Sun-Mon

Joe's Closet 412/201-9001 ■ 945 Liberty Ave (at Smithfield) ■ 11am-8pm, till midnight Fri-Sat, clsd Sun

Slacker [WC] 412/381-3911 ■ 1321 E Carson St (btwn 13th & 14th) ■ 11am-9pm, till 11pm Fri-Sat, noon-6pm Sun, magazines, clothing, leather, piercing

PUBLICATIONS
Hotspots Magazine 304/782-3358 ■ free monthly lgbt guide to bars, clubs & the scene in Pittsburgh

Out 412/243-3350 ■ lgbt newspaper ■ www.outpub.com

MEN'S CLUBS
Arena Health Club [PC] 412/471-8548 ■ 2025 Forbes Ave (at Seneca) ■ 24hrs

EROTICA
Boulevard Videos & Magazines 412/261-9119 ■ 346 Blvd of the Allies (at Smithfield) ■ 24hrs, leather, toys

Golden Triangle News 412/765-3790 ■ 816 Liberty Ave (at 9th) ■ 24hrs

RHODE ISLAND • USA

RHODE ISLAND

Providence

BARS
1. **Deville's** [★W,NH,D,WC] 401/751-7166 ■ 1 Allens Ave (at Eddy) ■ 7pm-1am, till 2am Fri-Sat, clsd Mon-Tue
2. **The Providence Eagle** [M,L,WC] 401/421-1447 ■ 200 Union St (at Weybosset) ■ 3pm-1am, from noon wknds, till 2am Fri-Sat ■ www.providenceeagle.com
3. **Union Street Station** [M,D,S,WC] 401/331-2291 ■ 69 Union St (at Washington) ■ noon-1am, till 2am Fri-Sat ■ www.69unionstreetstation.com
4. **Wheels** [MW,D,K,V,WC] 401/272-6950 ■ 125 Washington (at Mathewson) ■ noon-1am, till 2am Fri-Sat, DJ wknds
5. **Yukon Trading Co** [★M,D,B,L] 401/274-6620 ■ 124 Snow St (at Weybosset) ■ 5pm-1am, till 2am Fri-Sat, from 4pm wknds, uniform & bear bar

NIGHTCLUBS
6. **Bar One** [GS,D,18+] 401/621-7112 ■ 1 Throop Alley (off S Main St) ■ gay Sun, call for events
7. **Gerardo's** [GS,D,E,K,WC] 401/274-5560 ■ 1 Franklin Sq (btwn Allens & Eddy) ■ 8pm-1am, till 2am Fri-Sat
8. **Mirabar** [M,D,K,S,WC] 401/331-6761 ■ 35 Richmond St (at Weybosset) ■ 3pm-1am, till 2am Fri-Sat
9. **Pulse** [MW,D,K,S,18+,$] 401/272-2133 ■ 86 Crary St (at Plain) ■ 9pm-close, from 6pm Sun, clsd Mon-Tue ■ www.pulseprovidence.com

CAFES
The Castro 401/421-1144 ■ 77 Ives (at Wickenden) ■ 7am-11pm, from 8am Sun, till midnight Fri-Sat, pizza, salads, sandwiches

Coffee Cafe [GO] 401/421-0787 ■ 257 S Main St (at Power) ■ 7am-5pm, 8am-4pm Sat, clsd Sun, patio

RESTAURANTS
Al Forno [★] 401/273-9760 ■ 577 S Main St ■ dinner only, clsd Sun-Mon, Little Rhody's best dining experience

Camille's 401/751-4812 ■ 71 Bradford St (at Atwell's Ave) ■ lunch & dinner, dinner only Sat, full bar

Down City Diner [WC] 401/331-9217 ■ 151 Weybosset St ■ lunch & dinner, popular Sun brunch (very gay), full bar

Julian's 401/861-1770 ■ 318 Broadway (at Vinton) ■ 9am-2pm Wed-Sun & 6pm-10pm Wed-Sat, clsd Mon-Tue

Rue de l'Espoir [★] 401/751-8890 ■ 99 Hope St (at John) ■ lunch & dinner, clsd Mon, full bar

Trent [BYOB] 401/861-5363 ■ 748 Hope St ■ 11:30am-9pm, clsd Sun-Mon

Viola's 401/861-5766 ■ 58 DePasquale Plaza (on Federal Hill) ■ lunch Wed-Sun, dinner Wed-Mon, patio

BOOKSTORES
Books on the Square 401/331-9097 ■ 471 Angell St (at Wayland) ■ 9am-9pm, till 10pm Fri-Sat, 10am-6pm Sun, some lgbt

RETAIL SHOPS
Esta's on Thayer St 401/831-2651 ■ 257 Thayer St (across from Avon cinema) ■ videos, pride items & Tarot readings

PUBLICATIONS
In Newsweekly 617/426-8246 ■ New England's lgbt newspaper ■ www.innewsweekly.com

Metroline 860/233-8334 ■ regional newspaper & entertainment guide, covers CT, RI & MA ■ www.metroline-online.com

PROVIDENCE

Located only an hour from Boston, Providence blends the best of big city culture and cuisine with the charm and history of old New England. Providence is also home of prestigious Brown University and the innovative Rhode Island School of Design (RISD).

Queer Resources

COMMUNITY INFO
Gay/Lesbian Helpline of Rhode Island 401/751-3322. 7pm-10pm Mon, Wed & Fri.
Sarah Doyle Women's Center of Brown University 401/863-2189.

AIDS RESOURCES
800/235-2331 (in Rhode Island only).
AIDS Care Ocean State 401/521-3603.

RECOVERY
Sisters In Sobriety AA 401/438-8860. 25 Pomona, 7pm Sat.

City Calendar

LGBT PRIDE
June. 401/467-2130.

Tourist Info

AIRPORT DIRECTIONS
TF Green. To get downtown, take right at terminal exit. Then take US 95 North for approximately 15 minutes. To get to Providence from Boston's Logan Airport, take 93 South to 95 South for approximately 1 hour.

PUBLIC TRANSIT & TAXIS
Yellow Cab 401/941-1122.
RIPTA Bus Service 401/781-9400.

TOURIST SPOTS & INFO
Newport.
RISD Museum 401/454-6500, web: www.risd.edu.
Waterfire (on Providence River every 3rd Sat).
Visitor's Center: 401/274-1636 (in RI) or 800/233-1636, web: www.providencecvb.com.

Providence • RHODE ISLAND

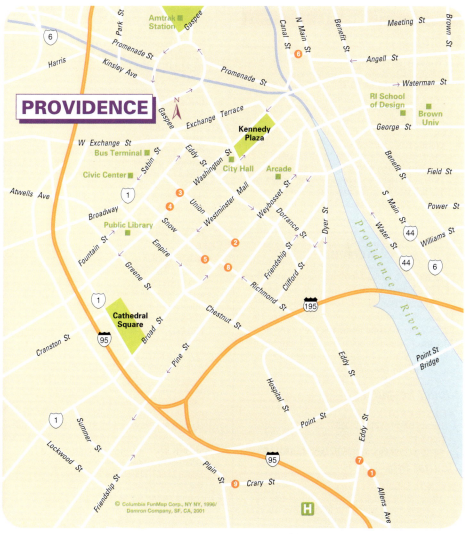

Options 401/831-4519 ■ extensive resource listings ■ gayoptions@aol.com

MEN'S CLUBS
Club Providence [PC] 401/274-0298 ■ 257 Weybosset (at Richmond) ■ 24hrs ■ www.clubbodycenter.com

The Gay Mega-Plex [PC,WC,GO] 401/780-8769 ■ 257 Allens Ave ■ 24hrs ■ www.themega-plex.com

EROTICA
Adult Video & News 401/785-1324 ■ 255 Allens Ave (at Point)

Airborne 401/273-0610 ■ 262 Charles St (at Orms)

Amazing Express 401/438-3070 ■ 155 Newport Ave/ Rte 1A (at New) ■ also 15 Thurbers Ave, 401/467-7631

Corner Discount Outlet 401/861-0739 ■ 1954 Westminster (at Manton Ave)

Flickers Adult Emporium 401/780-0771 ■ 257 Allens Ave (beside 'The Gay Mega-Plex') ■ video arcade, nude male dancers 9pm-1am Th-Sat

Miko 401/421-6646 ■ 653 N Main St (at Doyle) ■ fetish wear ■ www.mikoexoticwear.com

Video Expo 401/274-4477 ■ 75 Empire St (at Weybosset)

TENNESSEE

Memphis

ACCOMMODATIONS
French Quarter Suites [GF] 901/728-4000, 800/843-0353 ■ 2144 Madison ■ also 'Bourbon St Cafe'
1 **Talbot Heirs Guesthouse** [GF,NS] 901/527-9772, 800/955-3956 ■ 99 S 2nd St (btwn Union & Peabody Pl) ■ suites w/ kitchens, funky decor ■ www.talbothouse.com

BARS
2 **Crossroads** [MW,NH,CW,S] 901/276-8078 ■ 1278 Jefferson (at Claybrook) ■ noon-3am, beer & set-ups only
3 **J Wags Bar** [M,D,F,S] 901/725-1909 ■ 1268 Madison (btwn Claybrook & Montgomery) ■ 24hrs, beer & set-ups only, patio
4 **The Jungle** [M,NH,L,F] 901/278-4313 ■ 1474 Madison (at McNeil) ■ 2pm-3am, from noon Sat, beer & set-ups only

Memphis

To most travelers, Memphis means one thing: Elvis. While no trip to Memphis would be complete without a visit to Graceland, the city also boasts a number of other attractions. The Beale Street Historic District is the cradle of 'Mississippi Delta' blues music, and nighttime still finds plenty of traditional blues, jazz, and rock 'n' roll in the area.

Queer Resources

AIDS RESOURCES
Friends For Life 901/272-0855.
RECOVERY
Memphis Lambda Center 901/276-7379, 1488 Madison.

Tourist Info

AIRPORT DIRECTIONS
Memphis International. To get downtown, take US 240 West and head north to Union Ave exit. Follow Union Ave for approximately 20 minutes.
PUBLIC TRANSIT & TAXIS
Yellow Cab 901/526-2121.
MATA 901/274-6282.
TOURIST SPOTS & INFO
Beale Street.
Graceland 800/238-2000, web: www.elvis-presley.com.
Mud Island.
Nat'l Civil Rights Museum 901/521-9699.
Overton Square.
Sun Studio 901/521-0664.
Visitor's Center: 901/543-5333, web: memphistravel.com.
WEATHER
Suth'n. H-O-T and humid in the summer, cold (30°s-40°s) in the winter, and a relatively nice (but still humid) spring and fall.
BEST VIEWS
A cruise on any of the boats that ply the river.

5 **Lorenz** [MW,D,CW,S] 901/274-8272 ■ 1528 Madison Ave (at Avalon) ■ 11am-midnight, from 9:30am Sun, 'Aftershock' 9pm-11am, patio
6 **Madison Flame** [MW,NH,D] 901/278-9839 ■ 1588 Madison (at Avalon) ■ 7pm-3am Wed, Fri-Sat only, more women Sat
7 **The Metro** [MW,D,F,K,S,WC] 901/274-8010 ■ 1349 Autumn St (at Cleveland) ■ 6pm-3am, karaoke Tue, drag shows wknds, T-dance 3pm Sun, patio
8 **One More** [GF,NH,MR,F] 901/278-6673 ■ 2117 Peabody Ave (at Cooper) ■ 11am-3am, from noon Sun, patio

NIGHTCLUBS
9 **Amnesia** [★MW,D,A,F,YC,SW,WC,$] 901/454-1366 ■ 2866 Poplar (nr Walnut Grove) ■ 8pm-3am, clsd Mon-Wed, patio
10 **Backstreet** [MW,D,WC] 901/276-5522 ■ 2018 Court Ave (at Morrison) ■ 8pm-3am, till 6am wknds, clsd Tue-Th, beer & set-ups only ■ www.backstreetmemphis.com
11 **N-cognito** [MW,D,MR-AF,S] 901/523-0599 ■ 338 S Front (at Vance) ■ 10pm-3:30am Th-Fri, till 5am Sat, 4pm-midnight Sun, theme nights
12 **Pumping Station** [M,D] 901/272-7600 ■ 1382 Poplar

CAFES
Buns on the Run 901/278-2867 ■ 2150 Elzey Ave (at Cooper) ■ 7am-2pm, till 1:30pm Sat, clsd Sun
Java Cabana 901/272-7210 ■ 2170 Young Ave (at Cooper) ■ 11am-10pm, till midnight Fri, noon-midnight Sun
Otherlands Coffee Bar 901/278-4994 ■ 641 S Cooper ■ 7am-8pm
P&H Cafe [BW,WC] 901/726-0906 ■ 1532 Madison (at Adeline) ■ 11am-3am, from 5pm Sat, clsd Sun

RESTAURANTS
Automatic Slim's Tonga Club [WC] 901/525-7948 ■ 83 S 2nd St (at Union) ■ lunch & dinner Mon-Fri, dinner Mon-Sat, Caribbean & Southwestern, plenty veggie, full bar
Cafe Society [WC] 901/722-2177 ■ 212 N Evergreen Ave (btwn McLean & Belvedere) ■ lunch & dinner, full bar
Lilly's [★] 901/276-9300 ■ 903 S Cooper (at Oliver) ■ 11am-9pm, till 10pm Fri-Sat, noon-6pm Sun, pan-Asian, dim sum
Melange 901/276-0002 ■ 948 S Cooper (at Young) ■ dinner till 10:30pm, bar till 3am
Saigon Le 901/276-5326 ■ 51 N Cleveland ■ 11am-9pm, clsd Sun, pan-Asian

ENTERTAINMENT & RECREATION
Aphrodite ■ women's performance group ■ www.geocities.com/wellesley/5999/
Center for Southern Folklore 901/525-3655 ■ 119 S Main St (at Peabody Pl) ■ 11am-7pm, till 11pm Th-Sat, live music, gallery, also cyber cafe ■ www.southernfolklore.com

BOOKSTORES
Davis Kidd Booksellers 901/683-9801 ■ 397 Perkins Rd Ext (at Poplar & Walnut Grove) ■ 9am-10pm, 10am-8pm Sun, some lgbt titles, also cafe

RETAIL SHOPS
Inz & Outz [WC] 901/728-6535 ■ 553 S Cooper ■ 10am-6pm, from 1pm Sun, pride items, books & gifts

PUBLICATIONS
Family & Friends 901/682-2669 ■ lgbt newsmagazine ■ members.aol.com/familymag/homepage.html
Triangle Journal News 901/454-1411 ■ lgbt newspaper, w/ resource listings ■ www.memphistrianglejournal.com

EROTICA
Cherokee Books 901/744-7494 ■ 2947 Lamar ■ 24hrs
Paris Theater 901/323-2665 ■ 2432 Summer Ave ■ 24hrs

Damron Road Atlas 9 — Memphis • TENNESSEE — 233

Nashville

Accommodations

IDA [MW,GO] 615/597-4409 ■ 904 Vickers Hollow Rd, Dowelltown ■ rural queer arts community 1hr SE of Nashville, camping May-Sept (no RV hookups), veggie meals included ■ www.rfdmag.org/idaland

NASHVILLE

Before Branson, before 'new country,' there was Nashville. Home of the Grand Ole Opry concert hall and the Country Music Hall of Fame, Nashville is still the mecca of country music. Kitsch lovers should stop by Bongo Java (615/385-5282) to view the 'Nun Bun,' a cinnamon roll that bears a remarkable—some would say miraculous—resemblance to Mother Teresa.

Queer Resources

Community Info
▼ Nashville Center 615/297-0008. 703 Berry Rd, 6pm-9pm.

AIDS Resources
Nashville Cares 615/259-4866, 800/845-4266.

Recovery
615/831-1050.

City Calendar

LGBT Pride
September.

Tourist Info

Airport Directions
Nashville International. To get to most of the gay bars, take I-40 West and follow signs toward Memphis. Exit on Broadway.

Public Transit & Taxis
Yellow Cab 615/256-0101.
Music City Taxi 615/889-0038.
Gray Line Airport Shuttle 615/275-1180.
MTA 615/862-5950.

Tourist Spots & Info
Country Music Hall of Fame 615/416-2001.
Grand Ole Opry & Opryland USA 615/889-6611.
Jack Daniel Distillery 615/327-1551.
The Parthenon 615/862-8431.
Ryman Auditorium 615/254-1445.
Tennessee Antebellum Trail 931/486-9055.
Visitor's Center: 615/259-4730,
web: www.nashvillecvb.com.

Weather
See Memphis.

Best Views
Try a walking tour of the city.

Rainbow Falls Resort [MW,SW,GO] 615/876-9194, 877/545-2433 ■ 6251 Marrowbone Lake Rd, Joelton ■ chalets, cabins & campsites, restaurant, hot tub, private lake, closed Tue-Wed ■ rainbow-falls.com

1 **Savage House** [GS,GO] 615/244-2229 ■ 165 8th Ave N (btwn Church & Commerce) ■ full brkfst, 1840s Victorian townhouse, also 'Gas Lite Lounge'

Bars

10 **The Cabaret: Episode 2** [MW,D,S] 615/367-1995 ■ 833 Murfreesboro Rd ■ 8pm-3am, clsd Mon ■ www.tnthecabaret.com

2 **Chez Collette** [W,NH,D,K,S] 615/256-9134 ■ 300 Hermitage Ave (at Lea) ■ 6pm-3am, clsd Mon-Tue

1 **The Gas Lite Lounge** [MW,F,E] 615/254-1278 ■ 167-1/2 8th Ave N (btwn Church & Commerce) ■ 4:30pm-1am, till 3am Fri-Sat, from 3pm wknds, piano bar

3 **George's Pub** [M,NH] 615/259-4006 ■ 1501 Second Ave (at Carney) ■ 3pm-3am, from 2pm Sun

4 **Illusions/ Tool Box** [M,S] 615/361-3616 ■ 339 Wilhagen Rd (at Murfeesboro) ■ 4pm-3am, cruise bar, also pride store

5 **Jungle Lounge & Restaurant** [M,D,S] 615/256-9411 ■ 306 4th Ave S (at Molloy) ■ 11am-3am, noon-1am Sun, patio

6 **TC's Triangle** [MW,NH,F,WC] 615/242-8131 ■ 1401 4th Ave (btwn Lafayette & Chestnut) ■ 1pm-3am, from noon wknds

Nightclubs

7 **The Chute Complex** [★M,D,CW,L,K,S,WC] 615/297-4571 ■ 2535 Franklin Rd (at Wedgewood) ■ 5pm-3am, 6 bars, patio, also restaurant w/ piano bar

8 **Connection Complex** [★MW,D,CW,S,V,WC] 615/742-1166 ■ 901 Cowan St (at Jefferson) ■ 8pm-3am, clsd Mon, 3 clubs, restaurant & gift shop ■ www.theconnection.net

Restaurants

Calypso Cafe 615/321-3878 ■ 2305 Elliston Pl ■ 11am-9pm, Caribbean

International Market 615/297-4453 ■ 2010 Belmont Blvd (at International) ■ lunch & dinner, Thai/ Chinese, plenty veggie

The Mad Platter [WC] 615/242-2563 ■ 1239 6th Ave N (at Monroe) ■ lunch Tue-Sat, dinner by reservation only, clsd Mon

Radio Cafe 615/262-1766 ■ 1313 Woodland St (at 14th) ■ 11am-close Mon-Fri, from 8am wknds

Towne House Tea Room 615/254-1277 ■ 165 8th Ave N (btwn Church & Commerce) ■ brkfst & lunch Mon-Fri, clsd wknds, buffet

World's End [MW] 615/329-3480 ■ 1713 Church St (at 17th & 18th) ■ 4pm-1am, clsd Mon, cruisy

Bookstores

Davis-Kidd Booksellers 615/385-2645 ■ 4007 Hillsboro Rd (at Abbot-Martin) ■ 9am-10pm, till 11pm Fri-Sat, 10am-7pm Sun, lgbt section

9 **Outloud Books & Gifts** 615/340-0034 ■ 1709 Church St (at 18th Ave) ■ 11am-9pm, till 10pm Fri-Sat, noon-6pm Sun, lgbt ■ OUTLOUD1@aol.com

Publications

Query 615/259-4135 ■ lgbt newspaper

Xenogeny/ Southern X-posure 615/831-1806 ■ lgbt newspaper & bar guide ■ www.gaytn.com

Erotica

Purple Onion 615/259-9229 ■ 2807 Nolansville Rd (at SE Jeep Eagle) ■ 24hrs; also 2702 Dickerson Rd location, 615/227-8833

Regina's Books 615/256-5775 ■ 700 Division (at 8th Ave S)

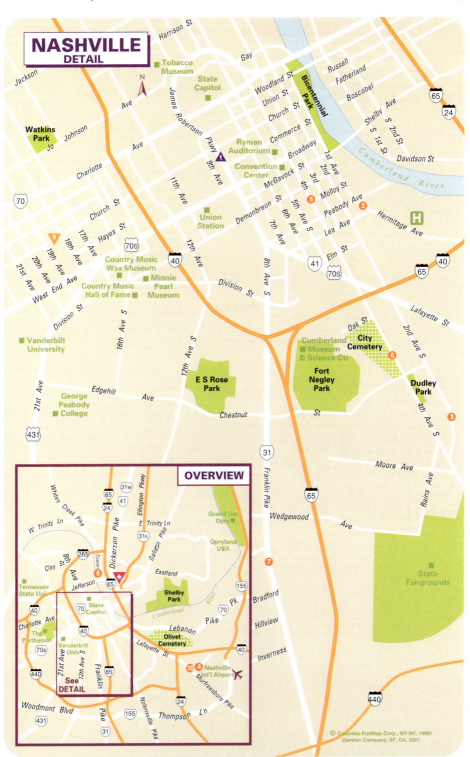

Texas

Austin

Accommodations
1. **1888 Miller Crockett House** [GF,WC,GO] 512/441-1600, 888/441-1641 ■ 112 Academy Dr (at Congress Ave) ■ New Orleans style estate, full brkfst, near outdoor recreation ■ www.millercrockett.citysearch.com
2. **Carrington's Bluff** [GF] 512/479-0638, 800/871-8908 ■ 1900 David St (at W 22nd St) ■ full brkfst ■ www.governorsinnaustin.com
3. **Days Inn North** [GF,SW,WC] 512/835-4311, 800/DAYSINN ■ 820 E Anderson Ln (Hwy 183) ■ www.austindaysinn.com
4. **Driskill Hotel** [GF,F,WC] 512/474-5911, 800/252-9367 ■ 604 Brazos St (at 6th) ■ even if you don't stay in this landmark hotel, be sure to check out the lobby
5. **Governor's Inn** [GF] 512/477-0711, 800/871-8908 ■ 611 W 22nd St (at Rio Grande) ■ neo-classical Victorian, full brkfst ■ www.governorsinnaustin.com
6. **Hotel San Jose** [GS,SW,WC] 512/444-7322, 800/574-8897 ■ 1316 S Congress Ave ■ small boutique hotel ■ www.sanjosehotel.com
7. **Lazy Oak Inn** [GF] 512/447-8873, 877/947-8873 ■ 211 W Live Oak (btwn S 1st & Congress) ■ 1911 plantation-style farmhouse, full brkfst, hot tub ■ www.lazyoakbandb.com
8. **Omni Hotel** [GF,F,SW,WC] 512/476-3700, 800/843-6664 ■ 700 San Jacinto (at 8th) ■ rooftop pool, also health club
9. **Park Lane Guest House** [MW,SW,WC] 512/447-7460, 800/492-8827 ■ 221 Park Ln (at Drake) ■ also cottage, lesbian-owned/ run
10. **Summit House B&B** [MW,SW,NS,GO] 512/445-5304 ■ 1204 Summit St (at Lupine) ■ reservations req'd, full brkfst ■ summit.home.texas.net

Bars
11. **'Bout Time** [★MW,NH,TG,S,WC] 512/832-5339 ■ 9601 N IH-35 (at Rundberg) ■ 2pm-2am, drag shows, volleyball court
12. **The Boyz Cellar** [M,D] 512/479-8482 ■ 213 W 4th (at Colorado) ■ 6pm-2am, till 4am Fri-Sat, clsd Mon-Tue ■ www.boyzcellar.com

Austin

Music lovers know Austin as the home of the South by Southwest (SXSW) music festival. This college town has a definite left-wing slant and a more liberal social climate than many other Texan cities.

Queer Resources

Community Info
Austin Latina/o Lesbian & Gay Organization 512/472-2001, web: members.tripod.com/~allgo.

AIDS Resources
AIDS Services of Austin 512/458-2437.

Recovery
Live & Let Live AA 512/453-1441, 2700 W Anderson Ln #412, 8pm nightly and at 1pm Sun.
AA Central Office 512/837-9362.

City Calendar

Annual Events
May & Labor Day - Splash Days. Weekend of parties in clothing-optional Hippie Hollow.
August/September - Austin G/L Int'l Film Festival 512/302-9889.

Tourist Info

Airport Directions
Mueller Municipal. To get to the State Capitol, take Manor Rd west until it runs into I-35. Go south on I-35. Take exits for the State Capitol around 11th & 12th Sts.

Public Transit & Taxis
Yellow-Checker 512/472-1111.
Various hotels have their own shuttles.
Capital Metro 512/474-1200.

Tourist Spots & Info
Aqua Festival.
Elisabet Ney Museum 512/458-2255.
George Washington Carver Museum 512/472-4809.
Hamilton Pool.
Laguna Gloria Art Museum 512/458-8191.
McKinney Falls State Park.
Mount Bonnell.
Museo del Barrio de Austin.
Zilker Park/Barton Springs.
Visitor's Center: Texas Tourist Division 800/888-8839.
Greater Austin Chamber of Commerce 512-478-9383.

Weather
Summers are real scorchers (high 90°s—low 100°s) and last forever. Spring, fall and winter are welcome reliefs.

Best Views
State Capitol.

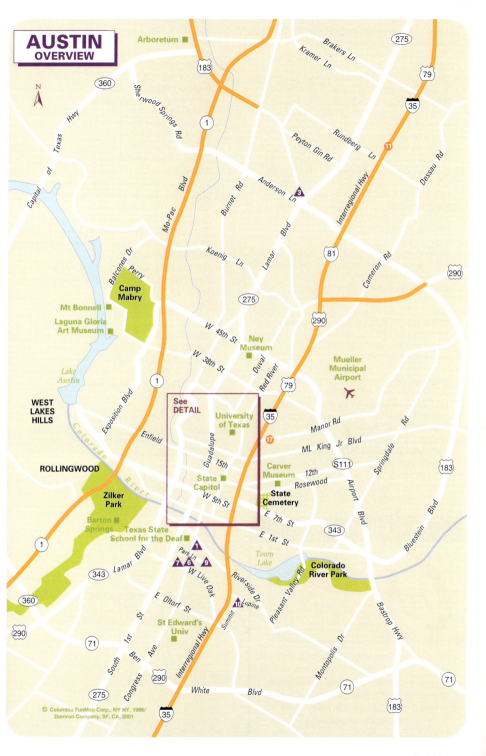

TEXAS • USA

13 **Casino El Camino** [GF,NH,F] 512/469-9330 ■ 516 E 6th St (at Red River) ■ 4pm-2am, psychedelic punk jazz lounge

14 **Chain Drive** [M,L,WC] 512/480-9017 ■ 504 Willow St (at Red River) ■ 2pm-2am, grill 4pm-8pm Sun, 'Bear Bust' 2nd Sun

15 ▶ **Charlie's** [★M,D,MR-LS,YC,WC] 512/474-6481 ■ 1301 Lavaca (at 13th) ■ 2pm-2am, patio ■ www.charliesaustin.com

16 **The Forum** [★M,D,S] 512/476-2900 ■ 408 Congress Ave (at 4th) ■ 2pm-2am, afterhours Th-Sat, clsd Sun (seasonal), patio ■ www.theforumaustex.com

17 **Gaby & Mo's** [W,NH,MR,F,E,18+,BW,WC] 512/457-9027 ■ 1809 Manor Rd (at Chicon) ■ 7am-midnight, from 9am wknds, brunch Sun, also cafe ■ www.gabynmos.com

18 **Rainbow Cattle Company** [MW,D,CW] 512/472-5288 ■ 305 W 5th St (btwn Guadalupe & Lavaca) ■ 2pm-2am, steak night Th ■ www.rainbowcattleco.com

19 **Splash Video Bar** [M,V] 512/477-6969 ■ 406 Brazos St (at 4th) ■ 3pm-2am Mon-Fri, from 2pm wknds, patio ■ www.splashvideobar.com

NIGHTCLUBS

20 **1920's Club** [F] 512/479-7979 ■ 918 Congress Ave (at E 11th St) ■ jazz club, 5pm-midnight, till 2am wknds, from 6pm Sun ■ www.1920s.com

21 **Dick's Dejà Disco** [M,D] 512/457-8010 ■ 113 San Jacinto Blvd (btwn 1st & 2nd) ■ 2pm-2am, from noon wknds, patio

22 **Oil Can Harry's** [★M,D,A,YC,WC] 512/320-8823 ■ 211 W 4th St (btwn Lavaca & Colorado) ■ 2pm-2am, till 4am Fri-Sat, cookout 5pm-8pm Sun, patio ■ www.oilcanharrys.com

CAFES

Joe's Bakery & Coffeeshop 512/472-0031 ■ 2305 E 7th St ■ 7am-3pm, clsd Mon, Tex-Mex

Little City Espresso Bar & Cafe 512/476-2489 ■ 916 Congress Ave (at E 11th St) ■ 7am-midnight, from 9am Sat, till 10pm Sun, popular gay hangout

RESTAURANTS

Castle Hill Cafe 512/476-0728 ■ 1101 W 5th St (at Baylor) ■ lunch & dinner, clsd Sun

City Grill [BW,GO] 512/479-0817 ■ 401 Sabine St ■ 5pm-close

Eastside Cafe [BW,WC] 512/476-5858 ■ 2113 Manor Rd (at Coleto, by bright yellow gas station) ■ lunch & dinner, some veggie

El Sol y La Luna [E,WC,GO] 512/444-7770 ■ 1224 S Congress Ave (at Academy) ■ 7am-3pm, till 10pm Wed-Sat, great brkfst, live music Fri-Sat

Fonda San Miguel [GO] 512/459-4121 ■ 2330 W North Loop ■ dinner only, popular Sun brunch, interior & coastal Mexican, full bar ■ www.fondasanmiguel.com

Jo's Coffee Shop [GO] 512/444-3800 ■ 1300 S Congress Ave ■ 7am-7pm

Katz's [WC] 512/472-2037 ■ 618 W 6th St (at Rio Grande) ■ 24hrs, NY-style deli, full bar

Romeo's [BW,WC] 512/476-1090 ■ 1500 Barton Springs Rd (nr Lamar) ■ lunch & dinner, Italian, some veggie

Suzi's Chinese Kitchen 512/441-8400 ■ 1152 S Lamar (at Treadwell) ■ lunch & dinner, clsd Sun

Threadgill's 512/451-5440 ■ 6416 N Lamar (at Koenig) ■ 11am-10pm, till 9pm Sun, great chicken-fried steak

West Lynn Cafe [BW] 512/482-0950 ■ 1110 W Lynn (at W 12th St) ■ vegetarian

ENTERTAINMENT & RECREATION

Barton Springs [N] Barton Springs Rd ■ natural swimming hole

Bat Colony Congress Ave Bridge (at Barton Springs Dr) ■ everything's bigger in Texas—including the colony of bats that flies out from under this bridge every evening March-Oct ■ www.batcon.org

Historic Austin Tours 512/478-0098, 800/926-2282 x4577 ■ 201 E 2nd St (in the Visitor Information Center) ■ free guided & self-guided tours of the Capitol, Congress Ave & 6th St, Texas State Cemetery, Hyde Park

BOOKSTORES

23 **Book Woman** [WC] 512/472-2785 ■ 918 W 12th St (at Lamar) ■ 10am-9pm, noon-6pm Sun

24 **Lobo** [WC] 512/454-5406 ■ 3204-A Guadalupe (btwn 32nd & 33rd) ■ 10am-10pm, till 11pm Fri-Sat, lgbt ■ loboaustin@aol.com

RETAIL SHOPS

Celebration! 512/453-6207 ■ 108 W 43rd (at Speedway) ■ 10am-6:30pm, clsd Sun, eclectic gift shop

PUBLICATIONS

Texas Triangle 512/476-0576 ■ weekly lgbt newspaper w/ arts calendar & statewide resource list ■ www.txtriangle.com

MEN'S CLUBS

Midtowne Spa—Austin [PC] 512/302-9696 ■ 5815 Airport Blvd (at Koenig) ■ 24hrs

EROTICA

Austin Six 512/385-5328 ■ 521 Thompson Ln (at Hwy 183) ■ 24 hrs

Forbidden Fruit 512/478-8358 ■ 512 Neches (btwn 5th & 6th)

Oasis Bookstore 512/835-7208 ■ 9601 N IH-35 (at Rundberg) ■ 24hrs

Charlie's

Austin's oldest and most popular bar every night of the week. Top 40 dance music played most of the time with one night of oldies. Great patio with separate sound system. Lots of free parking and risk-free walking to & from the parking areas. Open every day 2pm-2am, with Happy Hour til 9pm.

www.charliesaustin.rr.com

PHONE **474-6481**

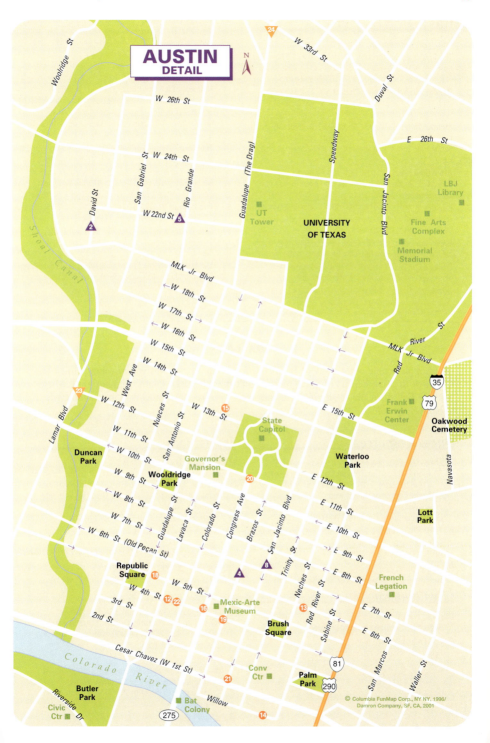

Dallas

Accommodations

1. **The Courtyard on the Trail** [GS,SW,NS,GO] 214/553-9700, 800/484-6260 x0465 ■ 8045 Forest Trail (at White Rock Trail) ■ full brkfst ■ www.courtyardonthetrail.com
2. **Holiday Inn Select Dallas Central** [GS] 214/373-6000, 888/477-STAY ■ 10650 N Central Expwy (at Meadow) ■ www.holiday-inn.com/dal-central
3. **Melrose Hotel** [GF,SW,WC] 214/521-5151, 800/635-7673 ■ 3015 Oak Lawn Ave (at Cedar Springs) ■ full brkfst, piano bar, lounge & 4-star restaurant, smokefree rms available

Bars

4. **After Dark** [MW,E,WC] 214/219-1099 ■ 4026 Cedar Springs (at Throckmorton) ■ 4pm-2am, piano & jazz bar ■ csafterdark@aol.com
5. **Buddies II** [W,D,CW,S] 214/526-0887 ■ 4025 Maple Ave (at Throckmorton) ■ 11am-2am, from noon Sun, clsd Mon, volleyball court, CW wknds
6. **Crews Inn** [★M,D,S,WC] 214/526-9510 ■ 3215 N Fitzhugh (at Travis) ■ noon-2am, popular Tue nights, patio
7. **Dallas Eagle** [M,L] 214/357-4375 ■ 2515 Inwood #107 (at Maple, enter rear) ■ 4pm-2am, after hrs Sat
8. **Dewayne's Oasis** [M,NH,D,F,K,S] 214/528-6234 ■ 5334 Lemmon Ave (at Hudnall) ■ 11am-2am
9. **The Fraternity House** [M,K,S,WC] 214/252-9071 ■ 2525 Wycliff (at Dallas Tollway) ■ noon-2am, show bar, male dancers Fri-Sat, karaoke Sun, also game room ■ www.thefraternityhouse.com
10. **Hidden Door** [M,NH,L] 214/526-9211 ■ 5025 Bowser ■ 7am-2am, from noon Sun
11. **Hideaway Club** [MW,P,E,OC] 214/559-2966 ■ 4144 Buena Vista (at Fitzhugh) ■ 8am-2am, from noon Sun, piano bar
12. **JR's Bar & Grill** [★M,F,WC] 214/559-0650 ■ 3923 Cedar Springs Rd (at Throckmorton) ■ 11am-2am, grill till 4pm ■ www.caven.com
31. **The Keep Tavern & Grill** [M,P,F,18+,WC,GO] 214/969-6900 ■ 1914 Laws St (1 blk E of Lamar & Munger) ■ 24hrs, Sun brunch
13. **Moby Dick** [MW,V,WC] 214/520-6629 ■ 4011 Cedar Springs Rd (btwn Douglas & Throckmorton) ■ noon-2am
6. **Pub Pegasus** [M,NH,WC] 214/559-4663 ■ 3326 N Fitzhugh (at Travis) ■ noon-2am, from 11am Sat
15. **Side 2 Bar** [M,NH,WC] 214/528-2026 ■ 2615 Oak Lawn Ave (btwn Fairmount & Brown) ■ 8am-2am, from noon Sun
16. **The Studio** [MW,NH] 214/521-7079 ■ 3851 Cedar Springs Rd (at Reagan) ■ 9am-2am, from noon Sun, male dancers Mon, strippers Tue

Dallas

Although people often think of Dallas as a conservative city, this young, vibrant town has much to offer. If you enjoy live music, don't miss the Deep Ellum neighborhood, where you can find great music any night of the week. The Oak Lawn area is home to the city's lesbigay community.

Queer Resources

Community Info
▼ John Thomas Gay/Lesbian Community Center 214/528-9254. 2701 Reagan (at Brown). Resource Center of Dallas, web: www.resourcecenterdallas.org. Gay/Lesbian Info Line 214/520-8781.

AIDS Resources
AIDS Services of Dallas 214/941-0523.
AIDS ARMS 214/521-5191.

Recovery
Lambda AA 214/267-0222. 2438 Butler, #106.

City Calendar

LGBT Pride
September, web: www.dallaspride.org.

Annual Events
February - Black Gay/Lesbian Conference.

Tourist Info

Airport Directions
Dallas/Ft Worth International. To get to the heart of Cedar Springs Rd, take Hwy 114 to Hwy 183. Take Hwy 183 to I-35 E. Go south on I-35 and exit on Oaklawn. Go north on Oaklawn to Cedar Springs. Turn left on Cedar Springs.

Public Transit & Taxis
Yellow Cab 214/426-6262.
Dallas Area Rapid Transit (DART) 214/979-1111.

Tourist Spots & Info
Dallas Arboretum & Botanical Garden 214/327-8263.
Dallas Museum of Art 214/922-1200.
Dallas Theatre Center/ Frank Lloyd Wright.
Texas State Fair & State Fair Park 214/565-9931.
Visitor's Center: 214/571-1000, web: www.dallascvb.com.

Weather
Can be unpredictable. Hot summers (90°s–100°s) with possible severe rain storms. Winter temperatures hover in the 20°s through 40°s range.

Best Views
Hyatt Regency Tower.

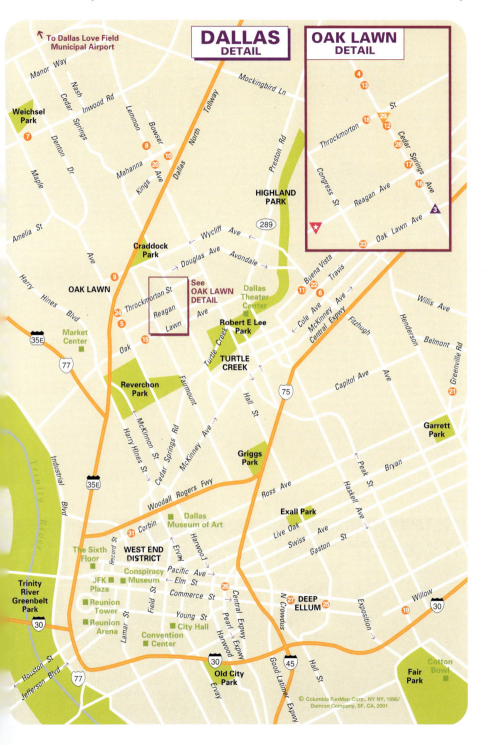

Texas • USA

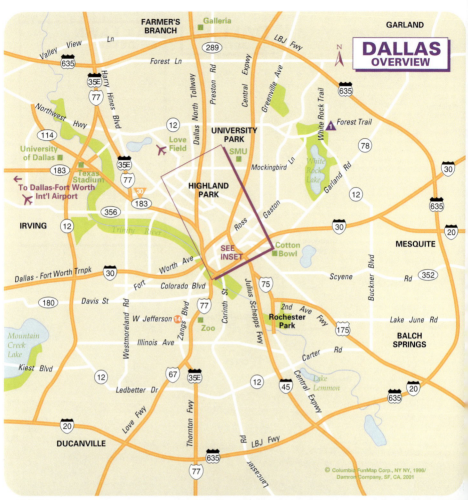

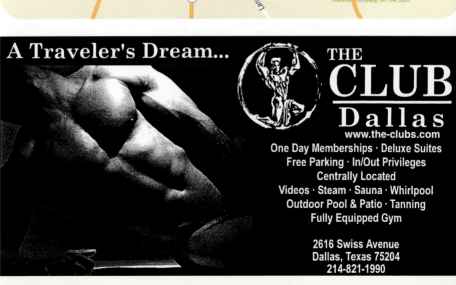

Dallas • Texas

17 Sue Ellen's [★W,D,E,WC] 214/559-0650 ■ 3903 Cedar Springs Rd (at Reagan) ■ 3pm-2am, from noon wknds, patio, 'Sue Ellen's Variety Show' Th, Sun bbq/ volleyball ■ www.caven.com

18 Throckmorton Mining Co [★M,L] 214/559-0650 ■ 3014 Throckmorton (at Cedar Springs) ■ 1pm-2am ■ www.caven.com

19 Trestle [M,NH,L] 214/826-9988 ■ 412 S Haskell ■ 8pm-2am

20 Twisted Lemmon Club [M,NH] 214/219-5006 ■ 5006 Lemmon Ave ■ 2pm-2am

21 Upstaged [GF,$] 214/827-7070 ■ 1802-A Greenville Ave ■ 5pm-2am, clsd Mon-Tue, stand-up comedy & improv after 8pm

22 Zippers [M,NH] 214/526-9519 ■ 3333 N Fitzhugh (at Travis) ■ noon-2am, dancers

23 The Zone [M,NH,WC] 214/559-0880 ■ 3810 Congress ■ 2pm-2am, patio

Nightclubs

20 Bamboleo's [MW,D,MR-L,WC] 214/520-1124 ■ 5027 Lemmon Ave ■ 9pm-2am, clsd Mon-Wed

24 The Brick [M,D,WC,$] 214/521-2024 ■ 4117 Maple Ave (at Throckmorton) ■ 9pm-4am, patio

25 Club NV [W,D,P,MR-AF,E,23+] 214/742-2708 ■ 3100 Main St. #208 (corner of Indiana & Malcom X) ■ 9pm-2am, from 8pm Sun, bbq/ more men Sun

26 The Metro [M,D,MR-AF,S,18+,WC] 214/742-2101 ■ 2204 Elm (at Pearl St) ■ 9:30pm-2am Th-Sun, drag shows, more women Sun

27 One [GS,D,A] 214/741-1111 ■ 3025 Main (in Deep Ellum) ■ 10pm-4am, more gay Fri, clsd Sun-Wed

28 Round-Up Saloon [★M,D,CW,WC] 214/522-9611 ■ 3912-14 Cedar Springs Rd (at Throckmorton) ■ 3pm-2am, from noon wknds

28 Village Station [★M,D,S,V] 214/559-0650 ■ 3911 Cedar Springs Rd ■ 9pm-3am, T-dance from 5pm Sun, also 'Rose Room' cabaret ■ www.caven.com/village.htm

Cafes

Dream Cafe [WC] 214/954-0486 ■ 2800 Routh St (in the 'Quadrangle') ■ 7am-10pm, till 11pm Fri-Sat, till 3pm Mon-Tue, plenty veggie

Restaurants

Ali Baba Cafe 214/823-8235 ■ 1905 Greenville Ave (nr Ross) ■ lunch & dinner, clsd Sun-Mon, Middle Eastern

Black-Eyed Pea [WC] 214/521-4580 ■ 3857 Cedar Springs Rd (at Reagan) ■ 11am-10pm, Southern homecookin', some veggie

Blue Mesa Grill 972/934-0165 ■ 5100 Beltline Rd (at Tollway), Addison ■ 11am-10pm, great fajitas, full bar

The Bronx Restaurant & Bar [WC,GO] 214/521-5821 ■ 3835 Cedar Springs Rd (at Oak Lawn) ■ lunch & dinner, Sun brunch, clsd Mon, some veggie

Cremona Bistro & Cafe 214/871-1115 ■ 3136 Routh St (at Cedar Springs) ■ 5pm-10pm Mon-Th, Italian, full bar

Fresh Start Market & Deli [WC,GO] 214/528-5535 ■ 4108 Oak Lawn (nr Avondale) ■ 7am-7pm, 9am-6pm Sat, noon-6pm Sun, organic, plenty veggie

Hunky's [★BW,WC,GO] 214/522-1212 ■ 4000 Cedar Springs Rd (at Throckmorton) ■ 11am-10pm, till 11pm Fri-Sat, from noon Sun, patio

Mansion on Turtle Creek 214/526-2121 ■ 2821 Turtle Creek Blvd (at Gillespie) ■ lunch & dinner, Sun brunch, fancy Southwestern

Monica Aca y Alla [★TG,E,WC] 214/748-7140 ■ 2914 Main St (at Malcolm X) ■ clsd Mon, Tex-Mex, full bar, shows Fri-Sat

Sushi on McKinney [WC] 214/521-0969 ■ 4500 McKinney Ave (at Armstrong) ■ lunch & dinner, till 11pm Fri-Sat, full bar

Thai Soon 972/234-6111 ■ at Coit & Beltline ■ lunch & dinner, till midnight Fri-Sat

Vitto's [BW,WC,GO] 214/946-1212 ■ 316 W 7th St (at Bishop) ■ lunch & dinner, Italian

Zizikis's [WC] 214/521-2233 ■ 4514 Travis St, #122 (in Travis Walk) ■ 11am-11pm, till midnight Fri-Sat, Sun brunch, Greek, full bar

Entertainment & Recreation

Conspiracy Museum 214/741-3040 ■ 110 S Market (in the Katy Bldg) ■ dedicated to infamous US assassinations since 1835 & their cover-ups

Lambda Weekly 214/823-8930 ■ KNON 89.3 FM ■ 8pm-10pm, lgbt radio show for northern TX

Turtle Creek Chorale (TCC) 214/526-3214 ■ 3630 Harry Hines Blvd (at Sammons Ctr for the Arts) ■ world-famous male choir w/ several subscription concerts yearly & many CDs ■ www.turtlecreek.org

The Women's Chorus of Dallas (TWCD) 214/520-7828 ■ 3630 Harry Hines Blvd (at Sammons Ctm for the Arts) ■ several subscription concerts throughout year & 'beaucoup CDs' ■ www.twcd.org

Bookstores

29 Crossroads Market Bookstore/ Cafe [WC] 214/521-8919 ■ 3930 Cedar Springs Rd (at Throckmorton) ■ 9am-11pm, lgbt ■ crossrds@onramp.net

Retail Shops

An Occasional Piece 214/520-0868 ■ 3922 Cedar Springs Rd (at Throckmorton) ■ gifts, cards, collectibles

Off the Street 214/521-9051 ■ 4001-B Cedar Springs (at Throckmorton) ■ 10am-9pm, noon-6pm Sun, lgbt gifts

29 Tapelenders [GO] 214/528-6344 ■ 3946 Cedar Springs Rd (at Throckmorton) ■ 9am-midnight, from 11am Sun, lgbt T-shirts, books, video rentals

Publications

Dallas Voice 214/754-8710 ■ lgbt newspaper w/ extensive resource listings ■ www.dallasvoice.com

Gyms & Health Clubs

Centrum Sports Club [GF,SW] 214/522-4100 ■ 3102 Oak Lawn (at Cedar Springs) ■ $15 day pass

Men's Clubs

▶ Club Dallas [★SW,PC] 214/021-1990 ■ 2616 Swiss Ave (at Good Latimer) ■ 24hrs ■ www.the-clubs.com

Midtowne Spa-Dallas [★PC] 214/821-8989 ■ 2509 Pacific (at Hawkins) ■ 24hrs

Erotica

30 Alternatives 214/630-7171 ■ 1720 W Mockingbird Ln (at Hawes)

Shades of Grey Leather [WC] 214/521-4739 ■ 3930-A Cedar Springs Rd (at Throckmorton)

Leather by Boots-Dallas 214/528-3865 ■ 2525 Wycliff #124 (at Maple) ■ 10am-6pm, till 8pm Th-Sat

TEXAS • USA

HOUSTON

Houston, the largest city in the bigger-than-life state of Texas, is home to the Astrodome, a fine collection of historical and fine arts museums, and the 570-ft San Jacinto Monument commemorating the independence of the Lone Star Republic.

Queer Resources

COMMUNITY INFO
Gay/Lesbian Switchboard 713/529-3211. 8am-10pm Mon-Fri.
Women's Center Hotline 713/528-2121, 9am-9pm Mon-Fri.

AIDS RESOURCES
Hotline 713/524-2437, 24 hrs.

RECOVERY
Lambda AA Center 713/521-1243. 1201 W. Clay, noon-midnight, from 8pm Sat.

City Calendar

LGBT PRIDE
June. 713/529-6979.

ANNUAL EVENTS
May/June - Gay & Lesbian Film Festival, web: www.hglff.org.

Tourist Info

AIRPORT DIRECTIONS
Houston Intercontinental & Houston Hobby Airport.
To get from Hobby to Montrose, take Broadway to I-45 North. Exit on the Allen Parkway and turn left. Take the Allen Parkway to Montrose and turn left.
To get from Houston International to Montrose, take south exit on Hwy 59. Take Hwy 59 to I-45 South. Follow I-45 to the Allen Parkway. Take the Allen Parkway to Montrose and turn left.

PUBLIC TRANSIT & TAXIS
Yellow Cab 713/236-1111.
Metropolitan Transit Authority 713/635-4000.

TOURIST SPOTS & INFO
Astroworld 713/799-1234.
Contemporary Arts Museum 713/284-8250.
The Galleria.
Menil Museum 713/525-9400.
Museum of Fine Arts 713/639-7300.
Rothko Chapel 713/524-9839.
Visitor's Center: 713/227-3100.

WEATHER
Humid all year round—you're not that far from the Gulf. Mild winters, although there are a few days when the temperatures drop into the 30°s. Winter also brings occasional rainy days. Summers are very hot.

BEST VIEWS
Spindletop, the revolving cocktail lounge on top of the Hyatt Regency.

Houston

ACCOMMODATIONS
1 **Angel Arbor B&B Inn** [GF,NS] 713/868-4654, 800/722-8788 ■ 848 Heights Blvd (at 9th) ■ full brkfst, close to downtown ■ www.angelarbor.com

2 **Gar-Den Suites** [MO,SW,NS,GO] 713/528-2302, 800/484-1036 x2669 ■ 2702 Crocker St #1 (at Westheimer) ■ nudity ok at hot tub ■ www.gar-densuites.com

3 **The Lovett Inn** [★GS,SW,GO] 713/522-5224, 800/779-5224 ■ 501 Lovett Blvd, Montrose (at Whitney) ■ historic home of former Houston mayor & Federal Court judge, sundeck, hot tub ■ www.HoustonGayLodging.com

4 **Montrose Inn** [M] 713/520-0206, 800/357-1228 ■ 408 Avondale (at Taft) ■ full brkfst, 'our motto: basic & butch' ■ www.montroseinn.com

5 **Patrician B&B Inn** [GF] 713/523-1114, 800/553-5797 ■ 1200 Southmore Blvd (at San Jacinto) ■ 1919 three-story mansion, full brkfst ■ www.texasbnb.com

Rainbow Reflections B&B [WO,GO] 409/763-2450 ■ 1426 Ave N 1/2, Galveston ■ friendly home atmosphere only 1/2 blk from beach & many restaurants ■ val409.email@msn.com

BARS
6 **The 611 Club** [★M,NH] 713/526-7070 ■ 611 Hyde Park (at Stanford) ■ 7am-2am, from noon Sun

7 **Brazos River Bottom (BRB)** [★M,D,CW] 713/528-9192 ■ 2400 Brazos (btwn Hadley & McIlhenny) ■ 7am-2am, from noon Sun

8 **Briar Patch** [M,NH,E] 713/665-9678 ■ 2294 W Holcombe (at Greenbriar) ■ 2pm-2am, piano bar

9 **The Bricks II** [M,NH,CW] 713/528-8102 ■ 617 Fairview (at Stanford) ■ 10am-2am, from noon Sun, patio

10 **Chances** [MW,D,E,WC] 713/523-7217 ■ 1100 Westheimer (at Waugh) ■ 2pm-2am, from noon wknds

11 **Cousins** [MW,NH,S] 713/528-9204 ■ 817 Fairview (at Converse) ■ 11am-2am, from noon Sun

12 **Decades** [MW,NH] 713/521-2224 ■ 1205 Richmond (btwn Mandel & Montrose) ■ 11am-2am, from noon Sun

13 **EJ's** [M,NH,E] 713/527-9071 ■ 2517 Ralph (at Westheimer) ■ 7am-2am, from noon Sun, hustlers

14 **Guava Lamp** [M,K,S,WC] 713/524-3359 ■ 2159 Portsmouth (btwn Shepherd & Greenbriar, in Shepherd Plaza) ■ 4pm-2am, swanky lounge w/ martinis & more, karaoke Wed & Sun, drag shows Sat ■ www.clubpicasso.com

15 **JR's** [★M,S,V,WC] 713/521-2519 ■ 808 Pacific (at Grant) ■ noon-2am, more women Sun, patio

16 **Mary's** [★M,NH,L,WC] 713/527-9669 ■ 1022 Westheimer (at Waugh) ■ 7am-2am, from 10am Sun, patio

32 **Meteor** [M,P,V,GO] 713/521-0123 ■ 2306 Genesee (at Fairview) ■ 4pm-2am

17 **Michael's Outpost** [M,NH] 713/520-8446 ■ 1419 Richmond (at Mandell) ■ 11am-2am, from noon Sun

18 **Montrose Mining Co** [★M,L] 713/529-7488 ■ 805 Pacific (at Grant) ■ 4pm-2am, from 1pm wknds, patio

10 **The New Barn** [MW,D,CW] 713/521-9533 ■ 1100 Westheimer (at Waugh) ■ 2pm-2am, from noon wknds

Rainbow Room [W,D] 281/872-0215 ■ 527 Barren Springs Dr (at Ella Blvd) ■ noon-2am

19 **Ripcord** [M,L,WC] 713/521-2792 ■ 715 Fairview (at Crocker) ■ 1pm-2am, till 4am Fri-Sat

Houston • TEXAS

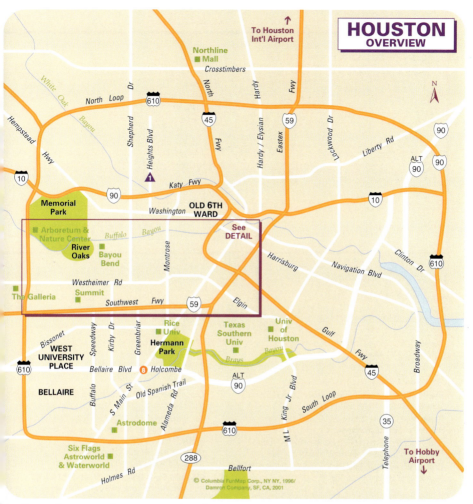

HOUSTON OVERVIEW

20 **Venture 'N** [M,NH,B,L] 713/522-0000 ■ 2923 S Main (btwn Anita & Elgin) ■ 3pm-2am, cruisy

NIGHTCLUBS

10 **Charlie's** [MW,D,WC] 713/522-4065 ■ 1100 Westheimer (at Montrose) ■ 7pm-2am Wed-Sat

21 **Club Nsomnia** [M,D,BYOB] 713/522-6100 ■ 202 Tuam Ave (at Helena St) ■ 2am-5am Wed-Th & Sun, till 6am Fri-Sat ■ ahch@pdq.net

22 **Club Rainbow** [W,D,S] 713/522-5166 ■ 1417-B Westheimer ■ 8pm-2am, clsd Mon-Tue, 2 levels

23 **Incognito** [MW,MR-AF,S] 713/237-9431 ■ 2524 McKinney (at Live Oak) ■ 9pm-2am, from 6pm Sun, clsd Tue-Th

24 **Inergy** [★MW,D,MR-L,E] 713/666-7310 ■ 5750 Chimney Rock (at Glenmont) ■ 8pm-2am, clsd Mon-Tue, dancers wknds

25 **Numbers** [GF,D,E,YC] 713/526-6551 ■ 300 Westheimer (at Taft) ■ live music venue

26 **Pacific Street** [★M,D,L,S,V,WC] 713/523-0213 ■ 710 Pacific St (at Crocker) ■ 9pm-2am, from 7pm Fri & Sun, patio

27 **Rascals** [MW,D,MR-AF,S,V,18+] 713/942-2582 ■ 1318 Westheimer (at Commonwealth) ■ 10pm-2am, clsd Mon-Wed

28 **Rich's** [★M,D,A,E,V,18+] 713/759-9606 ■ 2401 San Jacinto (at McIlhenny) ■ 9pm-2am, from 7pm Sun, clsd Mon-Wed

29 **Toyz** [M,D,MR-L,S] 713/668-4892 ■ 5322 Glenmont (at Chimney Rock)

Viviana's Night Club [M,D,MR] 713/862-0203 ■ 5219 Washington ■ 5pm-2am

CAFES

Diedrich Coffee 713/526-1319 ■ 4005 Montrose (btwn Richmond & W Alabama) ■ 6am-midnight

Java Java Cafe [★] 713/880-5282 ■ 911 W 11th (at Shepherd) ■ open till midnight Fri-Sat

RESTAURANTS

Baba Yega's [★WC] 713/522-0042 ■ 2607 Grant (at Pacific) ■ 11am-10pm, till 11pm Fri-Sat, patio, full bar

Barnaby's Cafe [★BW,WC] 713/522-0106 ■ 604 Fairview (at Stanford) ■ 11am-10pm, till 11pm Fri-Sat, clsd Mon; also 1701 S Shepard, 713/520-5131

Texas • USA

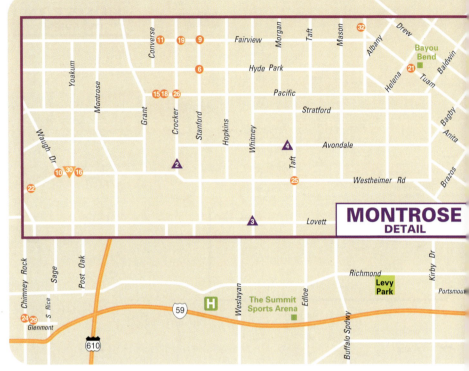

Black-Eyed Pea [★WC] 713/523-0200 ■ 2048 W Grey (at Shepherd) ■ 11am-10pm, Southern
Brasil [BW] 713/528-1993 ■ 2604 Dunlavy (at Westheimer) ■ 9am-2am, bistro, plenty veggie
Cafe Annie 713/840-1111 ■ 1728 Post Oak Blvd (at San Felipe) ■ lunch Mon-Fri, dinner Mon-Sat, clsd Sun
Captain Benny's Half Shell [BW] 713/666-5469 ■ 8506 S Main ■ lunch & dinner, clsd Sun
Chapultepec [BW] 713/522-2365 ■ 813 Richmond (btwn Montrose & Main) ■ 24hrs, Mexican, some veggie
Fox Diner [BW,NS,GO] 713/523-5369 ■ 2815 S Shepherd Dr ■ lunch & dinner Mon-Fri, dinner Sat, brunch Sun ■ www.foxdiner.com
House of Pies [★] 713/528-3816 ■ 3112 Kirby (at Richmond/ Alabama) ■ 24hrs
Magnolia Bar & Grill [WC] 713/781-6207 ■ 6000 Richmond Ave (at Fountain) ■ Cajun, full bar

Houston • Texas

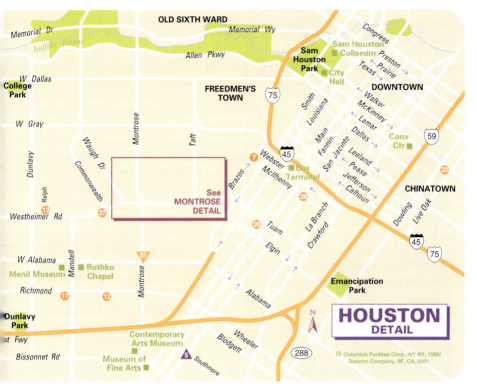

Ming's Cafe 713/529-7888 ■ 2703 Montrose (at Westheimer) ■ 11am-10pm, Chinese

Mo Mong 713/524-5664 ■ 1201 Westheimer #B (at Montrose) ■ 11am-11pm, till midnight Fri-Sat, Vietnamese, full bar

Ninfa's [★] 713/228-1175 ■ 2704 Navigation ■ 11am-10pm, Mexican, full bar

Ninos 713/522-5120 ■ 2817 W Dallas (btwn Montrose & Waugh) ■ lunch Mon-Fri, dinner Mon-Sat, clsd Sun, Italian, some veggie, full bar

Pot Pie Pizzeria [BW,GO] 713/528-4350 ■ 2207 Richmond ■ 11am-11pm, till 10pm Sun, some veggie

Spanish Flower [BW] 713/860-1706 ■ 4701 N Main (at Airline) ■ 24hrs, till 10pm Tue, Mexican

Tango [E] 713/521-7888 ■ 224 Westheimer ■ lunch Tue-Fri, dinner Tue-Sun, clsd Mon, also bar, women's night Fri

Entertainment & Recreation

'After Hours' 713/526-4000 ■ KPFT 90.1 FM ■ midnight-3am Sat, lgbt radio, also 'Lesbian/ Gay Voices', 8pm Mon ■ www.kpft.org

Bookstores

Crossroads Market Bookstore/ Cafe [F,WC] 713/942-0147 ■ 1111 Westheimer (at Yoakum) ■ 7am-midnight, lgbt ■ crossrds@onramp.net

Lobo—Houston [WC] 713/522-5156 ■ 3939 Montrose Blvd (at Alabama) ■ 9am-midnight, lgbt books & videos, also cafe

Retail Shops

Basic Brothers [WC] 713/522-1626 ■ 1232 Westheimer (at Commonwealth) ■ 10am-9pm, noon-6pm Sun, lgbt gifts, clothes ■ www.eroticattire.com

Lucia's Garden 713/523-6494 ■ 2942 Virginia (at W Alabama) ■ 10am-6pm, till 7pm Tue & Th, clsd Sun, spiritual herb center

Publications

Houston Voice 713/529-8490, 800/729-8490 ■ lgbt newspaper ■ www.houstonvoice.com

OutSmart 713/520-7237 ■ free monthly lgbt newsmagazine ■ www.outsmartmagazine.com

Gyms & Health Clubs

Fitness Exchange [GF] 713/524-9932 ■ 4040 Milam

YMCA Downtown [GF,SW] 713/659-8501 ■ 1600 Louisiana St (at Pease)

Men's Clubs

▶ The Club Houston [★SW,PC] 713/659-4998 ■ 2205 Fannin (at W Gray) ■ 24hrs ■ www.the-clubs.com

Midtowne Spa–Houston [★SW,PC] 713/522-2379 ■ 3100 Fannin (at Elgin) ■ 24hrs

Erotica

BJ's 24 Hour News 713/649-9241 ■ 6314 Gulf Fwy

Diners News 713/522-9679 ■ 240 Westheimer (at Mason) ■ 24hrs

Eros 1207 [GO] 713/944-6010 ■ 1207 Spencer Hwy (at Allen Genoa) ■ 10am-midnight ■ www.eros1207.com

Leather Forever 713/526-6940 ■ 604 Westheimer ■ noon-8pm

Damron Codes

- ➤ advertiser
- ★ popular
- **MO** men only
- **GF** gay-friendly (mostly straight)
- **GS** gay/straight (evenly mixed)
- **MW** lesbians/gay men
- **M** mostly men
- **W** mostly women (listing names in this color)
- **WO** women only (listing names in this color)
- **NH** neighborhood bar
- **D** live DJ & dancing
- **A** alternative (grunge babes, goths)
- **CW** country western (music, dancing and/or dress)
- **B** bears
- **L** leather, fetish (often a dress code)
- **P** professional crowd
- **MRC** multiracial clientele
- **MR-AF** African-American clientele
- **MR-A** Asian clientele
- **MR-L** Latino/a clientele
- **TG** transgender-friendly
- **F** hot food served
- **E** live entertainment (piano, bands, comedy)
- **K** karaoke
- **S** shows (drag, strip, or cabaret)
- **V** videos
- **18+** 18 & older
- **YC** young crowd (mostly 20-somethings)
- **OC** older/more mature crowd (mostly over 40)
- **BW** beer and/or wine
- **BYOB** bring your own bottle (often "private" clubs)
- **SW** swimming onsite (usually a pool)
- **N** public nudity okay
- **NS** no smoking (anywhere inside business)
- **PC** private club (membership open to out-of-towners; often BYOB)
- **WC** wheelchair access (includes bathrooms)
- **GO** gay-owned/ operated
- **AYOR** at your own risk (beware of bashers or cops)

SAN ANTONIO

Remember the Alamo in San Antonio. This old Spanish mission town has grown into a cultural center showcasing the fine and performing arts, as well as the native arts. Many of the 18th-century missions are preserved and open to the public.

Queer Resources

COMMUNITY INFO
▼ Gay/Lesbian Community Center 210/732-4300, web: glccsa.org. 3126 N St Mary's (at Hwy 281), 1pm-8pm Mon-Sat, till 6pm Sun.
Lesbian Information Line (LISA) 210/828-5472.

AIDS RESOURCES
AIDS Resource Ctr. 210/222-2437. 800 Lexington 9am-5pm Mon-Fri.

RECOVERY
Lambda Club AA 210/732-4300 (Ctr #). 923 E Mistletoe (off N St Mary's).

City Calendar

LGBT PRIDE
June. 210/732-4300 (Center).

ANNUAL EVENTS
Late April - Fiesta San Antonio.

Tourist Info

AIRPORT DIRECTIONS
San Antonio International.

PUBLIC TRANSIT & TAXIS
Yellow Cab 210/226-4242.
Via Info 210/362-2020.

TOURIST SPOTS & INFO
The Alamo 210/225-1391.
Hemisfair Park.
El Mercado.
Plaza de Armas.
River Walk.
San Antonio Museum of Art 210/978-8100.
Visitor's Center: 210/270-8748, 800/447-3372, web: www.sanantoniocvb.com.

WEATHER
60°s-90°s in the summer, 40°s-60°s in the winter.

BEST VIEWS
From the deck of the Inn on Broadway.

San Antonio • TEXAS

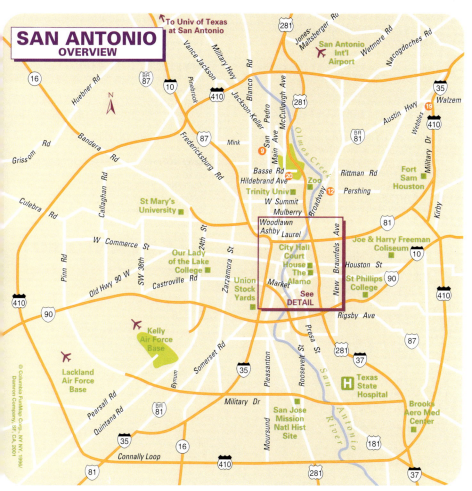

San Antonio

ACCOMMODATIONS

1. **Adams House B&B** [GF] 210/224-4791, 800/666-4810 ■ 231 Adams St (at S Alamo) ■ full brkfst, also carriage house ■ www.adams-house.com
2. **Arbor House Inn & Suites** [GS,GO] 210/472-2005, 888/272-6700 ■ 540 S St Mary's St (btwn Alamo & St Mary's)
3. **Desert Hearts Cowgirl Club** [WO,F,SW,GO] 830/796-7446 ■ 10101 Hwy 173 N, Bandera ■ 2-bdrm cabin on 30-acre ranch ■ members.aol.com/cowgirlj/
4. **The Garden Cottage** [GF,SW] 210/828-7815 ■ private cottage ■ lookit.home.texas.net/cottage
5. **The Painted Lady Inn on Broadway** [★MW] 210/220-1092 ■ 620 Broadway (at 6th) ■ full brkfst, private art deco suites, rooftop deck & spa ■ www.thepaintedladyinn.com
6. **Villager Lodge** [GF] 210/222-9463, 800/584-0800 ■ 1126 E Elmira (at Wilmington)

BARS

6. **2015 Place** [M,NH] 210/733-3365 ■ 2015 San Pedro (at Woodlawn) ■ 4pm-2am, from 2pm wknds, patio
7. **The Annex** [M,NH,WC] 210/223-6957 ■ 330 San Pedro Ave (at Euclid) ■ 4pm-2am, patio
8. **Cobalt Club** [MW,NH,S,WC] 210/734-2244 ■ 2022 McCullough ■ 4pm-2am, from 2pm wknds
9. **Copa SA** [M,NH,WC] 210/342-2276 ■ 119 El Mio (at San Pedro) ■ 4pm-2am, DJ wknds, also large game room
20. **The Hideout** [MW,NH,WC] 210/828-4222 ■ 5307 McCullough (nr Basse) ■ 4pm-2am, patio
10. **The Metropolis** [M,NH,WC] 210/527-1707 ■ 140 E Houston (on the Riverwalk) ■ 11am-2am, from noon Sun
12. **One-Oh-Six Off Broadway** [M,NH,OC] 210/820-0906 ■ 106 Pershing St (at Broadway) ■ noon-2am
13. **Pegasus** [M,E] 210/299-4222 ■ 1402 N Main (btwn Laurel & Evergreen) ■ 2pm-2am
14. **Petticoat Junction** [W,D,S,WC] 210/737-2344 ■ 1818 N Main (at Dewey) ■ 7pm-2am, patio
15. **Silver Dollar Saloon** [M,D,CW,K,S,WC] 210/227-2623 ■ 1418 N Main Ave (at Laurel) ■ 2pm-2am, 2-story patio bar

NIGHTCLUBS

16. **The Bonham Exchange** [★MW,D,V,18+,GO] 210/271-3811 ■ 411 Bonham St (at 3rd/ Houston) ■ 4pm-2am, from 8pm wknds, till 4am Fri-Sat ■ www.bonhamexchange.com

Texas • USA

17 **El Torro** [GS,D,MR-L,E] 210/732-3150 ■ 3000 N St Mary's (at Rte 281) ■ call for theme nights, more gay Fri

18 **The Saint** [MW,D,A,S,18+] 210/225-7330 ■ 1430 N Main (at Evergreen) ■ 9pm-2am, till 4am Sat

19 **Sparks** [M,D,S,V] 210/653-9941 ■ 8011 Webbles St (at Walzem) ■ 3pm-2am, hot oil dancers Tue

Cafes

Candlelight Coffeehouse 210/738-0099 ■ 3011 N St Mary's (at Rte 281) ■ 4pm-midnight, till 1am Fri-Sat, clsd Mon

Restaurants

Giovanni's Pizza & Italian Restaurant 210/212-6626 ■ 913 S Brazos (at Guadalupe) ■ 10am-8pm Mon-Fri

Madhatter's Tea [BYOB,WC] 210/821-6555 ■ 3606 Ave 'B' (at Mulberry) ■ 7am-10pm, from 9am wknds, till 3pm Sun, patio

Retail Shops

Backbone Body Mods 210/349-6337 ■ 4741 Fredericksburg Rd (off Loop 10) ■ 1pm-8pm, till 10pm Fri-Sat, piercing

Dark Fire Gallery 210/682-3500 ■ 7126 Eckert Rd, Ste 8 ■ pride, BDSM & fetish items ■ www.darkfiregallery.com

FleshWorks/ Skins & Needles 210/472-0313 ■ 110 Jefferson (at Houston) ■ clsd Mon

On Main 210/737-2323 ■ 2514 N Main (btwn Woodlawn & Mistletoe) ■ 10am-6pm, till 5pm Sat, clsd Sun, gifts, cards & T-shirts

Zebra'z 210/472-2800, 800/788-4729 ■ 1608 N Main ■ 11am-9pm, lgbt dept store, also online ■ www.zebraz.com

Men's Clubs

Alternative Clubs [SW,PC] 210/223-2177 ■ 827 E Elmira St (at St Mary's) ■ 24hrs wknds

Executive Spa [PC] 210/732-4433 ■ 1121 Basse Rd ■ 24hrs

Erotica

Apollo News 210/653-3538 ■ 2376 Austin Hwy (at Walzem) ■ 24hrs

Broadway News 210/223-2034 ■ 2202 Broadway

Encore Video 210/821-5345 ■ 1031 NE Loop 410

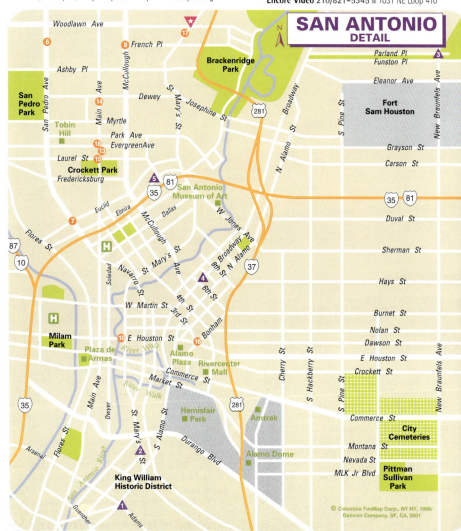

Salt Lake City

Utah

Accommodations

1. **Anton Boxrud B&B** [GF] 801/363-8035, 800/524-5511 ■ 57 S 600 E (at S Temple) ■ full brkfst, hot tub, some shared baths ■ www.netoriginals.com/antonboxrud
2. **Hotel Monaco Salt Lake City** [GF,WC] 801/595-0000, 877/294-5110 ■ 15 W 200 S ■ rms & suites, restaurant & bar, gym ■ www.monaco-saltlakecity.com
3. **Maple Grove B&B** [GF,NS,GO] 801/322-5372 ■ 539 E 3rd Ave ■ hot tub, shared baths ■ members.aol.com/maplebandb/main.html
4. **Parrish Place** [GS,NS,GO] 801/832-0970, 888/832-0869 ■ 720 E Ashton Ave ■ Victorian mansion, hot tub ■ www.parrishpl.com
5. **Peery Hotel** [★GF,WC] 801/521-4300, 800/331-0073 ■ 110 W 300 S ■ full brkfst, also 2 restaurants & bar ■ www.peeryhotel.com
6. **Ric's Place** [MO,NS,GO] 801/466-6747 ■ 1272 E 1300 S (at 13th E) ■ private home ■ www.theinnkeeper.com/ricsplace
7. **Saltair B&B/ Alpine Cottages** [★GF,NS] 801/533-8184, 800/733-8184 ■ 164 S 900 E ■ full brkfst, hot tub, cottages from 1870s ■ www.saltlakebandb.com

Bars

8. ▶ **Club Blue** [MO,D,PC,GO] 801/517-4074 ■ 60 E 800 S (at State St) ■ 7pm-2am, from 8pm Sat, 3pm-2am Sun, underwear Th, leather night Fri, T-dance Sun, patio ■ www.clublue.com
9. **Deer Hunter** [M,NH,D,L,PC,WC] 801/363-1802 ■ 636 S 300 W (at 7th St S) ■ 4pm-2am, from noon wknds, levi/ leather bar, patio ■ www.thedeerhunter.net
10. **Paper Moon** [W,D,CW,F,E,K,PC,WC] 801/466-8517 ■ 3424 S State St ■ 3pm-1am ■ www.thepapermoon.com
11. **Radio City** [M,WC] 801/532-9327 ■ 147 S State St (btwn 1st & 2nd) ■ 11am-1am, beer only
12. **The Trapp** [MW,D,CW,PC,WC] 801/531-8727 ■ 102 S 600 W (at 1st S S) ■ 11am-1am, patio, food Sun ■ www.thetrapp.com

Nightclubs

13. **Bricks Tavern** [★GS,D,K,V,18+,PC] 801/328-0255 ■ 579 W 200 S (at 600 W) ■ 9:30pm-2am, clsd Sun-Mon, more gay Th-Fri, patio ■ www.bricksclub.com
14. **Club Axis** [★GS,D,S,V,18+,PC] 801/519-2947 ■ 100 S 500 W (at 100 S) ■ 9:30pm-close, gay night Fri, women's night Wed ■ www.clubaxis.com
15. **Club Manhattan** [GF,D,F] 801/364-7651 ■ 5 East 400 S, Salt Lake City ■ lunch & dinner, live jazz, more gay Th after 11 pm
16. **ZipperZ** [M,D,K,V,PC,GO] 801/521-8300 ■ 155 W 200 S (at 200 W) ■ 11am-2am, karaoke Mon, brunch wknds, 2-week membership available for $5 ■ www.zipperz.com

Cafes

Coffee Garden [WC] 801/355-3425 ■ 898 E 900 S ■ 6:30am-11pm, till midnight wknds

Cup of Joe 801/363-8322 ■ 353 W 200 S (btwn 300 & 400 S) ■ 7am-midnight, Internet access

Restaurants

Baci Trattoria [WC] 801/328-1333 ■ 134 W Pierport Ave ■ lunch Mon-Fri, dinner Mon-Sat, clsd Sun, full bar

Lambs Restaurant [WC] 801/364-7166 ■ 169 S Main St ■ 7am-9pm, till 8pm Sat, clsd Sun

Market St Grill [WC] 801/322-4668 ■ 48 W Market St ■ lunch & dinner, Sun brunch, seafood/ steak, full bar

Rio Grande Cafe [★] 801/364-3302 ■ 270 S Rio Grande ■ lunch & dinner, Mexican, full bar

Santa Fe 801/582-5888 ■ 2100 Emigration Canyon ■ dinner, Sun brunch

Entertainment & Recreation

Concerning Gays & Lesbians 801/363-1818 ■ KRCL 90.9 FM ■ 12:30pm-1pm Wed

Lambda Hiking Club 801/532-8447 ■ 700 E 200 S (in MacFrugal's parkling lot) ■ 10am 1st & 3rd Sat ■ info@gayhike.org

Bookstores

Golden Braid Books [GS] 801/322-1162, 801/322-0404 (cafe) ■ 151 S 500 E ■ 10am-9pm, till 10pm Fri-Sat, till 6pm Sun, also 'Oasis Cafe', 7am-9:30pm Mon-Fri

SALT LAKE CITY

Renowned as the world center of Mormonism, Salt Lake City is home to one of the largest genealogical research databases in the country (801/240-4085). Salt Lake City is also a great home base for those who want to take advantage of the area's excellent skiing.

Queer Resources

COMMUNITY INFO
▼ Utah Gay & Lesbian Center 801/539-8800 or 888/874-2743, web: www.glccu.org. 361 N 300 W.
Community Events/AIDS Hotline 801/487-2100 or 800/366-2437.
Utah Women's Resource Center 801/581-8030.

AIDS RESOURCES
801/487-2323.

RECOVERY
Gay/Lesbian AA 801/322-5869.

City Calendar

LGBT PRIDE
June. 801/461-5002, web: www.utahpride.org

ANNUAL EVENTS
Winterfest Utah Gay ski weekend (call Center).

Tourist Info

AIRPORT DIRECTIONS
Salt Lake City International. To get to the area covered by the detail map, take I-80 East to 15 North. Take the North Temple St exit.

PUBLIC TRANSIT & TAXIS
Yellow Cab 801/521-2100.
Utah Transit Authority (UTA) 801/287-4636.

TOURIST SPOTS & INFO
Great Salt Lake.
Temple Square.
Trolley Square.
Visitor's Center: 801/521-2868, web: www.saltlake.org.

RETAIL SHOPS
17 **Cahoots** [WC,GO] 801/538-0606 ■ 878 E 900 S (at 900 E) ■ 10am-8pm, noon-5pm Sun, unique gift shop
Gypsy Moon Emporium 801/521-9100 ■ 1011 E 900 S ■ hrs vary, clsd Sun, metaphysical ■ www.aros.net/~gypsymn/

PUBLICATIONS
The Pillar of the Gay/Lesbian Community 801/265-0066 ■ 'Utah's true alternative newspaper' ■ members.aol.com/pillarslc

EROTICA
All For Love [WC] 801/487-8358 ■ 3072 S Main St (at 33rd St S) ■ clsd Sun, leather/SM boutique
Blue Boutique 801/485-2072 ■ 2106 S 1100 E (at 2100 S) ■ www.blueboutique.com
Hayat's Magazines & Gifts 801/486-9925 ■ 1350 S State St (at 13th St S)
Mischievous 801/530-3100 ■ 559 S 300 W (at 6th St S) ■ clsd Sun
Video One 801/524-9883 ■ 484 S 900 W ■ also cult & art films

- full-color photographs speak louder than words
- over 1800 international listings cover gay-friendly hotels, B&Bs, and accommodations across the globe!
- detailed listings answer all your questions about rates, rooms, meals, smoking, kids, and pets
- cross-indexes note Men-only, Women-only, RV & Camping, and Wheelchair-accessible accommodations
- over 550 pages, only $22.95!

ORDER NOW: (800) 462-6654

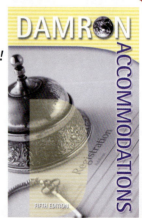

Damron Road Atlas 9 — Salt Lake City • UTAH — 253

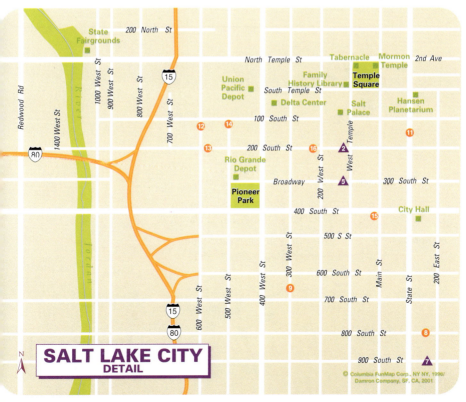

NORFOLK

With its historic waterfront and a climate ranked among the most desireable in the country by the National Weather Service, Norfolk makes a great vacation spot.

Queer Resources

COMMUNITY INFO
Hampton Roads Gay Info Line 757/495-9597.

AIDS RESOURCES
AIDS Resource Center 757/446-6170 or 800/999-8385.

RECOVERY
757/495-3113.

City Calendar

LGBT PRIDE
June. 757/456-1972, web: www.hamptonroadspride.com.

Tourist Info

AIRPORT DIRECTIONS
Norfolk International. To get to Civic Center, take a left on to Norview Ave. Take Norview Ave for about 4 miles and continue past Chesapeake Blvd. Once at Tidewater Dr, turn left and follow toward Civic Center.

PUBLIC TRANSIT & TAXIS
Yellow Cab 757/622-3232.
Norfolk Airport Shuttle 757/857-1231.
Hampton Roads Transit 757/222-6000.

TOURIST SPOTS & INFO
Busch Gardens (in Williamsburg) 757/253-3350.
The Chrysler Museum of Art 757/664-6200.
Douglas Macarthur Memorial 757/441-2965.
Hermitage Foundation Museum 757/423-2052.
Historic Williamsburg.
Norfolk Naval Base 757/444-7955.
St Paul's Episcopal Church 757/627-4353.
Waterside Festival Marketplace.
Visitor's Center: 800/368-3097, web: www.vgnet.com.

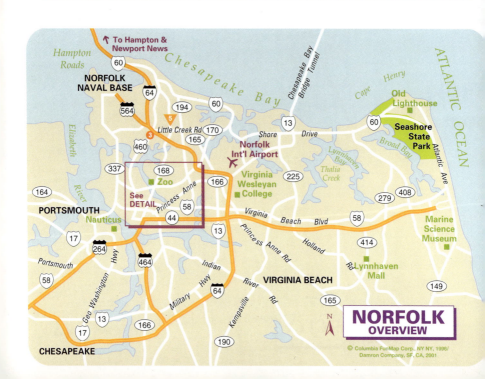

Norfolk • VIRGINIA

Norfolk

BARS
1. **The Garage** [M,NH,F,WC] 757/623-0303 ■ 731 Granby St (at Brambleton) ■ 8am-2am, from noon Sun
2. **Hershee Bar** [W,D,F,E,K,WC] 757/853-9842 ■ 6117 Sewells Pt Rd (at Norview) ■ 4pm-2am, from noon wknds
3. **Nutty Buddy's** [★M,D,F,S,WC] 757/588-6474 ■ 143 E Little Creek Rd ■ 4pm-2am, Sun brunch, also restaurant
4. **The Wave** [M,D,F,S,WC] 757/440-5911 ■ 4107 Colley Ave (at 41st St) ■ 4pm-2am, from 5pm Sat, clsd Tue & Th, also restaurant, male dancers Wed

CAFES
Oasis Cafe [GO] 757/627-6161 ■ 142 W York St #101A (in York Center bldg) ■ 7:30am-5pm Mon-Fri

RESTAURANTS
Charlie's Cafe [BW] 757/625-0824 ■ 1800 Granby St (at 18th) ■ 7am-3pm

Uncle Louie's [E,K,WC] 757/480-1225 ■ 132 E Little Creek Rd (at Granby) ■ 8am-11pm, till midnight Fri-Sat, till 10pm Sun, Jewish fine dining, also bar & deli

BOOKSTORES
5. **Lambda Rising** [WC] 757/480-6969 ■ 9229 Granby St (at Tidewater) ■ 10am-10pm, lgbt
6. **Phoenix Rising East** 757/622-3701 ■ 619B Colonial Ave (at Olney) ■ noon-9pm, till 7pm Sun, lgbt

PUBLICATIONS
Shout! 540/529-6363 ■ entertainment & personals for the Virginias & Carolinas ■ www.shoutmag.com

EROTICA
Leather & Lace 757/583-4334 ■ 149 E Little Creek Rd (at Granby) ■ 11am-9pm, clsd Sun

WASHINGTON

Seattle

ACCOMMODATIONS

1 **Ace Hotel** [GS,GO] 206/448-4721 ■ 2423 1st Ave (at Wall St) ■ modern & stylish, some shared baths ■ www.theacehotel.com
2 **Alexis Hotel** [GF,WC] 206/624-4844, 800/426-7033 ■ 1007 1st Ave (at Madison) ■ luxury hotel w/ Aveda spa ■ www.alexishotel.com
3 **Amaranth Inn** [GS,NS] 206/322-5574, 800 /720-7161 ■ 1451 S Main St (at 16th) ■ 1890s mansion, full brkfst
   Artist's Studio Loft B&B [GF,NS] 206/463-2583 ■ 16529 91st Ave SW, Vashon Island ■ hot tub ■ www.asl-bnb.com
4 **Bacon Mansion** [GS,WC] 206/329-1864, 800/240-1864 ■ 959 Broadway E (at E Prospect) ■ Edwardian-style Tudor ■ baconmansion.com
5 **Chambered Nautilus B&B** [GF] 206/522-2536, 800/545-8459 ■ 5005 22nd Ave NE (at N 50th St) ■ colonial home, full brkfst, sundecks ■ www.chamberednautilus.com
6 **Gaslight Inn** [★GS,SW,NS,GO] 206/325-3654 ■ 1727 15th Ave (at E Howell St) ■ also 'Howell St Suites' next door ■ www.gaslight-inn.com
7 **Gypsy Arms B&B** [GS,L,GO] 206/547-8194 ■ 3628 Palatine Ave N ■ Victorian inn w/ full dungeon, hot tub ■ www.gypsyarms.com
8 **Hawthorn Inn & Suites** [GF,NS,WC] 206/624-6820, 800/437-4867 ■ 2224 8th Ave (at Blanchard) ■ hotel, full brkfst ■ www.hospitalityassociates.net/seattle.html
9 **Hill House B&B** [GF,NS] 206/720-7161, 800/720-7161 ■ 1113 E John St (at 12th Ave) ■ full brkfst ■ www.seattlebnb.com
10 **Hotel Monaco** [GF,WC] 206/621-1770, 800/945-2240 ■ 1101 4th Ave (at Spring St) ■ www.monaco-seattle.com
11 **Hotel Vintage Park** [GF] 206/624-8000, 800/853-3914 ■ 1100 5th Ave (at Spring) ■ ultra luxe sleep in Seattle, also restaurant ■ www.vintagepark.com
12 **Inn at Queen Anne** [GS] 206/282-7357, 800/952-5043 ■ 505 1st Ave N (at Republican) ■ kitchenettes ■ www.innatqueenanne.com
13 **Landes House B&B** [MW,GO] 206/329-8781, 888/329-8781 ■ 712 11th Ave E (at Aloha) ■ two 1906 houses joined by deck, hot tub ■ www.landeshouse.com

SEATTLE

Nicknamed the 'Emerald City,' Seattle's mild climate—with less rain than New York City—is only one of its many charms. The city has burgeoned in the last decade, but the quirky style that spawned grunge is still there. Seattle's collective obsession with java gives a whole new meaning to 'counter-culture.'

Queer Resources

COMMUNITY INFO
Lesbian Resource Center 206/322-3953, web: www.lrc.net. 2214 S Jackson, noon-7pm Tue-Fri, till 5pm Sat.
TEN (The Eastside Network) 425/450-4890.

AIDS RESOURCES
Seatle AIDS Hotline 206/443-1208.

RECOVERY
Capitol Hill Alano 206/322-9590. 1222 E Pine St 2nd fl, daily meetings.
Intergroup 206/587-2838.

City Calendar

LGBT PRIDE
Last Sunday in June. 206/324-0405.

ENTERTAINMENT
Team Seattle 206/322-7769, a 35-team gay network.

ANNUAL EVENTS
September - AIDSwalk 206/329-6923.
  Power Surge, biannual women's SM conference 206/233-8429.
October - Seattle Gay & Lesbian Film Festival 206/323-4274.

Tourist Info

AIRPORT DIRECTIONS
Seattle-Tacoma International (Sea-Tac). To get to the Capitol Hill District, take I-5 North and exit on Madison St. Take Madison St to Broadway. At Broadway, turn left.

PUBLIC TRANSIT & TAXIS
Farwest 206/622-1717.
Gray Top Cab 206/622-4800.
Airport Shuttle Express 206/622-1424.
Metropolitan Transit 206/553-3000.

TOURIST SPOTS & INFO
International District.
Pike Place Market.
Pioneer Square.
Seattle Art Museum 206/654-3100.
Space Needle 206/443-9800.
Woodland Park Zoo 206/684-4800.
Visitor's Center: 206/461-5800, web: www.seattle.com.

WEATHER
Winter's average temperature is 50° while summer temperatures can climb up into the 90°s. Be prepared for rain at any time during the year.

BEST VIEWS
Top of the Space Needle, but check out the World's Fair Monorail too.

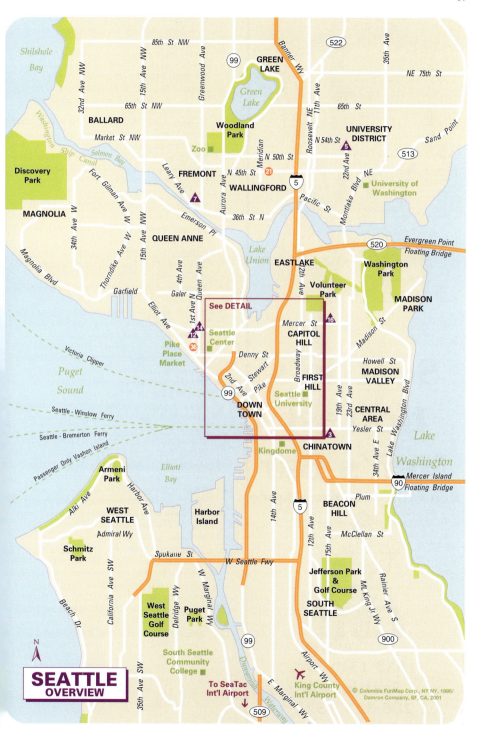

WASHINGTON • USA

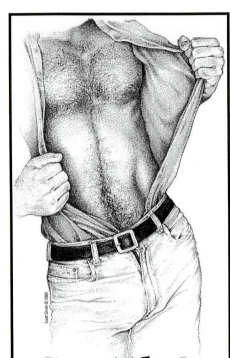

Seattle's Hottest Men's Bar

Men * Party * Cruise * Dance

**1533 13th Ave.
Seattle, WA
206-323-1525**

For more information visit our web site at:
www.TheCuff.com

14 **MarQueen Hotel** [GS] 206/282-7407, 888/445-3076 ■ 600 Queen Anne Ave N (btwn Roy & Mercer) ■ www.marqueen.com

15 **Pioneer Square Hotel** [GF,WC] 206/340-1234, 800/800-5514 ■ 77 Yesler Wy (at 1st St) ■ gym, restaurants & saloon ■ www.pioneersquare.com

16 **Salisbury House B&B** [GF,NS] 206/328-8682 ■ 750 16th Ave E (at Roy) ■ full brkfst, jacuzzi, women-owned/ run ■ www.salisburyhouse.com

17 **The Shafer-Baillie Mansion** [GF] 206/322-4654, 800/922-4654 ■ 907 14th Ave E (at Aloha) ■ some shared baths ■ www.shaferbaillie.com

Wild Lily Ranch B&B [★MW,SW,NS,GO] 360/793-2103 ■ cabins & authentic Sioux tipis on Skykomish River, 1 hr from Seattle, hot tub ■ www.wildlilyranch.com

BARS

18 **Bad Juju Lounge** [GS,D,F] 206/709-9951 ■ 1518 11th Ave (at Pike) ■ 3pm-2am, 'Estrogen Lounge' for women Mon

19 **The Baltic Room** [GS,E] 206/625-4444 ■ 1207 Pine St (at Melrose) ■ 5pm-2am, clsd Mon, piano bar

20 **CC Attle's** [★M,NH,V,WC] 206/726-0565 ■ 1501 E Madison (at 15th Ave) ■ 6am-2am, patio, also 'Veranda Room' bar, 206/320-1162

21 **Changes** [M,NH,K,V,F,WC] 206/545-8363 ■ 2103 N 45th St (at Meridian) ■ noon-2am

22 ▶ **The Cuff** [★M,D,L,F,WC] 206/323-1525 ■ 1533 13th Ave (at Pine) ■ 11am-2am, 4 bar areas, also patio, always busy, popular wknd nights ■ www.thecuff.com

23 **Double Header** [M,NH] 206/464-9918 ■ 407 2nd Ave (at Washington) ■ 10am-midnight, till 2am wknds, 'one of the oldest gay bars in the US'

24 **Elite Tavern** [MW,NH,BW,WC] 206/324-4470 ■ 622 Broadway Ave (at Roy) ■ 10am-2am

25 **Hana's Restaurant & Lounge** [M,D,F,WC] 206/340-1591 ■ 1914 8th Ave (at Stewart) ■ noon-2am, Korean food 11am-6pm

27 **Madison Pub** [★M,NH,OC,WC] 206/325-6537 ■ 1315 E Madison St (at 13th) ■ noon-2am

28 **Manray** [M,D,F,V] 206/568-0750 ■ 514 E Pine (at Belmont) ■ 4pm-2am, Sun brunch ■ www.manrayvideo.com

29 **R Place** [M,NH,F,K,WC] 206/322-8828 ■ 619 E Pine (at Boylston) ■ 2pm-2am, video sports bar ■ www.rplaceseattle.com

30 **Rendezvous** [GF,NH] 206/441-5823 ■ 2320 2nd Ave (at Battery) ■ 6am-2am, live bands Th-Sat

31 **The Seattle Eagle** [M,L,WC] 206/621-7591 ■ 314 E Pike St (at Bellevue) ■ 2pm-2am, patio ■ www.SeattleEagle.com

32 **The Seawolf Saloon & Gallery** [M,NH,F,WC] 206/323-2158 ■ 1413 14th Ave (at Madison) ■ 11am-2am, from 6am wknds

33 **Sonya's Bar & Grill** [M,NH] 206/441-7996 ■ 1919 1st Ave (btwn Virginia & Stewart) ■ 11am-2am

34 **Thumpers** [★M,V,WC,GO] 206/328-3800 ■ 1500 E Madison St (at 15th) ■ 11am-2am, also restaurant

35 **Timberline Tavern** [MW,D,CW,BW] 206/883-0242 ■ 2015 Boren Ave (nr Fairview & Denny) ■ 6pm-2am, from 4pm Sun, clsd Mon, dance lessons Tue-Wed, disco T-dance Sun

36 **Watertown** [GF,D] 206/284-5003 ■ 106 1st Ave N (at Denny) ■ 4pm-2am, from 8pm Sat, till 3am wknds

37 **Wildrose Tavern & Restaurant** [W,NH,D,F,K,S,WC] 206/324-9210 ■ 1021 E Pike St (at 11th) ■ 3pm-midnight, from noon Th-Fri, till 1am Tue-Th, till 2am Fri-Sat

Seattle • Washington

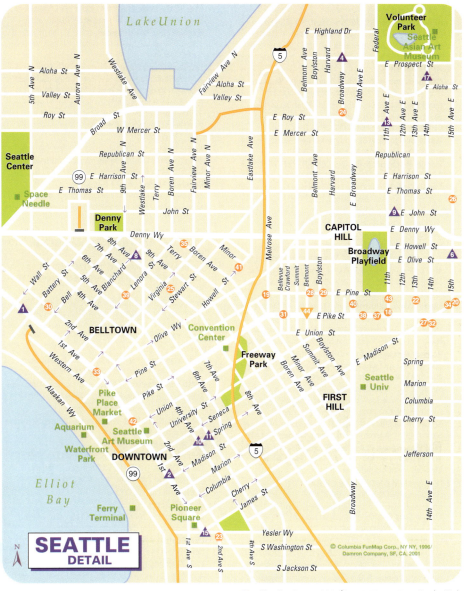

Nightclubs

38 **Ego** [GS,D] 206/709-2227 ■ 916 E Pike (at Broadway) ■ 10pm-2am Wed-Fri, till 4am Sat, from 7pm Sun, more women Wed, more gay Sat ■ www.getego.com

39 **Jazz Alley** [GF,F,E,$] 206/441-9729 ■ 2033 6th Ave (at Lenora) ■ call for events & reservations ■ www.jazzalley.org

40 **Neighbours Restaurant & Dance Club** [★MW,D,YC,WC] 206/324-5358 ■ 1509 Broadway (at E Pike, enter in alley) ■ 3pm-2am, till 4am Fri-Sat, 2 flrs

41 **Re-bar** [★GS,D,E] 206/233-9873 ■ 1114 Howell (at Boren Ave) ■ open till 2am, cabaret/ theater, DJ Th-Sun, women's night Sat

42 **Showbox** [GF,D,E,$] 206/628-3151 ■ 1426 1st Ave (at Pike) ■ 'Zoot Suit Sundays' w/ swing lessons

43 **The Vogue** [GF,D,A,S] 206/324-5778 ■ 1516 11th Ave (at Pine) ■ 9pm-2am, theme nights

Cafes

2 Galz Java & Juice 206/789-2233 ■ 102 15th Ave E (at Denny) ■ open early, cafe & bakery, call for events, lesbian-owned/ run; also Ballard location: 5905 15th Ave NW ■ www.2galz.com

Addis Cafe [★] 206/325-7805 ■ 61224 E Jefferson (at 12th) ■ 8am-10pm, Ethiopian

Espresso Vivace 206/860-5869 ■ 901 E Denny Wy #100 ■ 6:30am-11pm

WASHINGTON • USA

RESTAURANTS

Al Boccalino 206/622-7688 ■ 1 Yesler Wy (at Alaskan) ■ lunch Mon-Fri, dinner nightly, classy southern Italian

Broadway New American Grill [★] 206/328-7000 ■ 314 Broadway E (at E Harrison) ■ 9am-1:30am, from 8am wknds, full bar

Cafe Septieme [★MW] 206/860-8858 ■ 214 Broadway Ave E (at Thomas & John) ■ 9am-midnight, also bar

Campagne 206/728-2800 ■ 86 Pine St (at 1st) ■ 5:30pm-10pm, French, reservations advised, also 'Cafe Campagne,' brkfst, lunch & dinner

Dahlia Lounge 206/682-4142 ■ 1904 4th Ave (at Virginia) ■ lunch & dinner, New American, full bar

Frontier Restaurant & Bar [WC] 206/441-4377 ■ 2203 1st Ave (at Blanchard) ■ 10am-2am, best cheap food in town

Giorgina's Pizza 206/329-8118 ■ 131 15th Ave E (at John) ■ 11am-10pm, from 5pm wknds

Gravity Bar [WC] 206/325-7186 ■ 415 Broadway E (at Harrison) ■ 10am-10pm, till 11pm Fri-Sat, vegetarian/juice bar

Kokeb [BW] 206/322-0485 ■ 9261 12th Ave ■ 5pm-10pm, till 11pm Fri-Sat, clsd Sun, Ethiopian, some veggie

Mae's Phinney Ridge Cafe [★WC] 206/782-1222 ■ 6410 Phinney Ridge N (at 65th) ■ 7am-3pm, brkfst menu, some veggie ■ www.maescafe.com

Mama's Mexican Kitchen 206/728-6262 ■ 2234 2nd Ave (in Belltown) ■ lunch & dinner, funky crowd

Queen City Grill [★WC] 206/443-0975 ■ 2201 1st Ave (at Blanchard) ■ noon-11pm, from 5pm wknds, fresh seafood

Rosebud Restaurant & Bar 206/323-6636 ■ 719 E Pike St (at Harvard Ave) ■ lunch Mon-Fri, dinner nightly, brunch wknds ■ www.halcyon.com/sage/

Sunlight Cafe [BW,WC] 206/522-9060 ■ 6403 Roosevelt Wy NE (at 64th) ■ 7am-9:30pm, vegetarian ■ www.sunlightcafe.com

Szmania's 206/284-7305 ■ 3321 W McGraw St (in Magnolia Bluff) ■ lunch Tue-Fri, dinner Tue-Sun, clsd Mon

Wild Ginger Asian Restaurant & Satay Bar [★] 206/623-4450 ■ 1400 Western Ave (at Union) ■ lunch Mon-Sat, dinner nightly, bar till 1am

ENTERTAINMENT & RECREATION

Gay Bingo 206/323-0069, 206/328-8979 ■ 15th & E Union (at Temple De Hirsch Sinai) ■ monthly, run by the Chicken Soup Brigade ■ www.csbrigade.org

Harvard Exit 206/323-8986 ■ 807 E Roy St ■ repertory film theater

House of Dames Productions 206/720-5252, 206/720-1729 ■ women's theater group ■ www.houseofdames.com

Northwest Lesbian & Gay History Museum Project 206/903-9517 ■ exhibits & free newsletter

Pro Homo Voci ■ gay/ straight musical theater troupe ■ www.prohomovoci.com

Seattle Gay Men's Chorus 206/323-0750 ■ www.seattlemenschorus.org

Tacky Tourist Clubs 206/679-3960 ■ fabulous social events ■ www.ttca.org

BOOKSTORES

Bailey/ Coy Books [WC] 206/323-8842 ■ 414 Broadway Ave E (at Harrison) ■ 10am-10pm, till 11pm Fri-Sat

Beyond the Closet Bookstore 206/322-4609 ■ 518 E Pike (at Belmont) ■ 10am-10pm, lgbt ■ www.beyondthecloset.com

Edge of the Circle 206/726-1999 ■ 701 E Pike (at Boylston) ■ noon-9pm, alternative spirituality store

Fremont Place Book Company 206/547-5970 ■ 621 N 35th (at Fremont Ave N) ■ 10am-8pm, till 9pm Wed-Sat, till 6:30pm Sun

Left Bank Books 206/622-0195 ■ 92 Pike St (at 1st Ave) ■ 10am-7pm, noon-6pm Sun, new & used books, lgbt section, worker-owned ■ www.leftbankbooks.com

Pistil Books & News 206/325-5401 ■ 1013 E Pike St (at 11th) ■ 10am-10pm, till 8pm Sun, new & used lgbt books ■ pistil@speakeasy.org

RETAIL SHOPS

Archie McPhee 206/297-0240 ■ 2428 NW Market (in Ballard) ■ 9am-7pm, 10am-6pm Sun, weird & wonderful toys & trinkets ■ www.mcphee.com

Broadway Market [★] 401 E Broadway (at Harrison & Republican) ■ mall full of funky, queer & hip stores

Metropolis 206/782-7002 ■ 7220 Greenwood Ave N (at 73rd) ■ 10am-8pm, cards & gifts

The Pink Zone 206/325-0050 ■ 211 Broadway (at John) ■ 10am-10pm, tattoos & piercings, also pride items ■ www.pinkzone.com

Sunshine Thrift Shops [WC] 206/324-9774 ■ 1718 12th Ave (at Pike/ Broadway) ■ 10am-6:30pm, nonprofit for AIDS groups

Venus [TG] 206/322-5539 ■ 1015 E Pike St (btwn 12th & Broadway) ■ noon-7pm, clsd Sun-Mon, plus-size consignment clothing, leather & corsets, lesbian-owned/ run ■ www.venusclothes.com

PUBLICATIONS

Pride Magazine 773/769-6328 ■ also publish Seattle Pink Pages ■ pridemag@aol.com

Seattle Gay Standard 206/322-9027 ■ weekly lgbt paper

SGN (Seattle Gay News) 206/324-4297, 206/322-7188 ■ weekly lgbt newspaper ■ www.sgn.org

The Stranger 206/323-7101 ■ queer-positive alternative weekly ■ www.thestranger.com

GYMS & HEALTH CLUBS

Hothouse Spa & Sauna [WO] 206/568-3240 ■ 1019 E Pike St #HH (at 11th, 2 blks E of Broadway) ■ noon-midnight, clsd Tue, baths, hot tub, massage

World Gym [GF] 206/583-0640 ■ 825 Pike St (at 8th Ave)

MEN'S CLUBS

Basic Plumbing 206/323-2799 ■ 1505 10th Ave (btwn Pike & Pine) ■ 6pm-5am, from 1pm wknds

Club Seattle [★PC] 206/329-2334 ■ 1520 Summit Ave (btwn Pine & Pike) ■ 24hrs

Club Z [PC] 206/622-9958 ■ 1117 Pike St (at Boren) ■ 4pm-9am, 24hrs wknds, discounts for out-of-towners

EROTICA

Castle Superstore 206/621-7236 ■ 613 Fairview Ave N ■ 24hrs

The Crypt 206/325-3882 ■ 1113 10th Ave E (at Denny)

Deja Vu Love Boutique 206/624-1784 ■ 1510 1st Ave (at Pike) ■ 24hrs

Fantasy Unlimited 206/682-0167 ■ 2027 Westlake Ave (at 7th) ■ 24hrs

Onyx Leather 206/328-1965 ■ 1605 12th Ave #8 ■ by appt only

Toys in Babeland [WC,GO] 206/328-2914 ■ 707 E Pike (btwn Harvard & Boylston) ■ 11am-10pm, noon-8pm Sun ■ www.babeland.com

Wisconsin

Milwaukee

ACCOMMODATIONS

1 **Layton Guest House** [M,GO] 414/389-0900 ■ 2146 S Layton Blvd (at Grant) ■ full brkfst ■ www.LaytonGuestHouse.com

2 **The Milwaukee Hilton** [GF,F,SW] 414/271-7250, 800/445-8667 ■ 509 W Wisconsin Ave (at 5th St)

3 **Park East Hotel** [GF,NS,WC] 414/276-8800, 800/328-7275 ■ 916 E State St (at Marshall) ■ also restaurant, some veggie

BARS

4 **1100 Club** [M,F] 414/647-9950 ■ 1100 S 1st St (at E Washington) ■ 7am-2am

5 **Ballgame** [M,NH] 414/273-7474 ■ 196 S 2nd St (at Pittsburgh) ■ 2pm-2am, from 11am wknds

6 **Boot Camp Saloon** [M,NH,L] 414/643-6900 ■ 209 E National Ave (at Barclay) ■ 4pm-2am, from 9pm Sat

7 **C'est La Vie** [M,S] 414/291-9600 ■ 231 S 2nd St (at Pittsburgh) ■ 5pm-2:30am, 2pm-2am Sun

8 **Club 219** [MW,D,MR,S] 414/276-2711 ■ 219 S 2nd St (btwn Florida & Pittsburgh) ■ 7pm-2am, from 4pm wknds

9 **Dish** [★W,D,S,WC] 414/273-3474 ■ 235 S 2nd St (at Oregon) ■ 8pm-close, hours vary Tue

10 **Fannie's/ The Club** [W,NH,D,WC] 414/649-9003 ■ 200 E Washington St ■ 7pm-2am, clsd Sun-Wed

11 **Harbor Room** [M,L] 414/672-7988 ■ 117 East Greenfield Ave ■ 10am-2am ■ www.harbor-room.com

12 **Henry's Pub & Grill** [GS,F,WC] 414/332-9690 ■ 2523 E Belleview Pl (at Downer) ■ 3pm-2am, full menu

13 **In Between** [MW,NH,WC] 414/273-2693 ■ 625 S 2nd St (at Bruce) ■ 5pm-2am, from 3pm wknds

14 **Kathy's Nut Hut** [W,NH] 414/647-2673 ■ 1500 W Scott (at 15th St) ■ 2pm-2am, from noon Fri-Sun

15 **M&M Club** [M,F,E,WC] 414/347-1962 ■ 124 N Water St (at Erie) ■ 11am-2am, from 10:30am Sun

16 **The Nomad** [GF,E] 414/224-8111 ■ 1401 E Brady St (at Warren) ■ 1pm-2am, from noon wknds

17 **South Water Street Dock** [M,NH,WC] 414/225-9676 ■ 354 E National (at Water St) ■ 5pm-2am, from 3pm wknds

18 **Station 2** [W,NH] 414/383-5755 ■ 1534 W Grant (at 15th Pl) ■ 6pm-2am, from 3pm Sun, clsd Mon-Tue

19 **Switch** [MW,NH] 414/220-4340 ■ 124 W National Ave (at 1st) ■ 5pm-2am, from 2pm wknds, patio

WISCONSIN • USA

20 **Taylor's Bar** [GS,WC,GO] 414/271-2855 ▪ 795 N Jefferson St (at Wells) ▪ 4pm-2am, from 5pm wknds, patio

21 **This Is It** [★M] 414/278-9192 ▪ 418 E Wells St (at Jefferson) ▪ 3pm-2am

22 **Triangle Bar** [M,NH,WC] 414/383-9412 ▪ 135 E National Ave (at Barclay) ▪ noon-2am

23 **Woody's** [MW,NH] 414/672-0806 ▪ 1579 S 2nd St (at Lapham St) ▪ 4pm-2am, from 2pm wknds

Nightclubs

24 **Club Boom** [MW,D,V] 414/277-5040 ▪ 625 S 2nd ▪ 8pm-2am Tue-Sun

25 **Fluid Lounge** [MW,MR-AF,E] 414/645-8330 ▪ 819 S 2nd St (at National) ▪ 5pm-2am, live jazz/DJ

26 **La Cage (Dance, Dance, Dance)** [★M,D,F,S,V,YC,WC] 414/383-8330 ▪ 801 S 2nd St (at National) ▪ 9pm-2am, 2-bar complex

Cafes

Alterra Coffee Roasters 414/273-3753 ▪ 2211 N Prospect Ave (at North) ▪ 7am-10pm, 8am-11pm Fri-Sat, 8am-9pm Sun

Fuel Cafe 414/374-3835 ▪ 818 E Center St ▪ 7am-midnight, from 9am wknds, infamous for their strong coffee

Wild Thyme Cafe 414/276-3144 ▪ 231 E Buffalo (btwn Water & Broadway) ▪ lunch till 3pm

Restaurants

Cafe Vecchio Mondo 414/273-5700 ▪ 1137 N Old World Third St (at Juneau) ▪ lunch & dinner, full bar

Coquette Cafe 414/291-2655 ▪ 316 N Milwaukee St (btwn Buffalo & St Paul) ▪ lunch Mon-Fri, dinner Mon-Sat, clsd Sun

The Knick [★WC] 414/272-0011 ▪ 1030 E Juneau Ave (at Waverly) ▪ 11am-midnight, from 9am wknds, some veggie, full bar

La Perla 414/645-9888 ▪ 734 S 5th St (at National) ▪ 11am-10:30pm, till 11:30pm Fri-Sat, 10am-10pm Sun, Mexican

Sanford Restaurant 414/276-9608 ▪ 1547 N Jackson St ▪ dinner only, clsd Sun, elegant Milwaukee Euro-style

Entertainment & Recreation

Boerner Botanical Gardens 414/529-1870 ▪ 5879 S 92nd St (in Whitnall Park), Hales Corners ▪ 8am-dusk, 40-acre garden & arboretum, garden clsd in winter

Mitchell Park Domes 414/649-9830 ▪ 524 S Layton Blvd (at Pierce) ▪ 9am-5pm, botanical gardens

Pridefest Milwaukee 414/645-3378 ▪ www.pridefestmilwaukee.com

Bookstores

27 **OutWords** [WC] 414/963-9089 ▪ 270 N Murray (at Park) ▪ 11am-10pm, till 6pm Sun, lgbt

---

MILWAUKEE

This unpretentious midwestern city is home to both the Miller Brewing Company and Harley Davidson. Its many ethnic communities—German, Italian, Irish, Polish—hold annual festivals that charm visitors and residents alike.

Queer Resources

Community Info
▼ Milwaukee LGBT Community Center 414/271-2656, web: www.mkelgbt.org. 170 S 2nd St.
Gay Information & Services 414/444-7331. 24 hr referral service.
Gay People's Union Hotline 414/562-7010. 7pm-10pm.
Lesbian Alliance 414/272-9442.

AIDS Resources
Aids Resource Center of Wisconsin (ARCW) 414/273-1991.

Recovery
AA Galano Club 414/276-6936. 2408 N Farwell Ave.

City Calendar

LGBT Pride
June. 414/645-3378, web: www.pridefest.com

Annual Events
September - AIDS Walk.

Tourist Info

Airport Directions
General Mitchell Field. To get to many of the gay bars take I-49 North to the W National Ave exit. Head east on W National to either S 2nd or S 1st St.

Public Transit & Taxis
Yellow Cab 414/271-6630.
Milwaukee Transit 414/344-6711.

Tourist Spots & Info
Annunciation Greek Orthodox Church.
Breweries.
Grand Avenue.
Mitchell Park Horticultural Conservatory.
Pabst Theatre 414/286-3665.
Summerfest.
Visitor's Center: 414/273-7222 or 800/231-0903.

Weather
Summer temperatures can get up into 90°s. Spring and fall are pleasantly moderate but too short. Winter brings snow, cold temperatures, and even colder wind chills.

Best Views
41st story of Firstar Center. Call 414/765-5733 to arrange a visit to the top floor observatory.

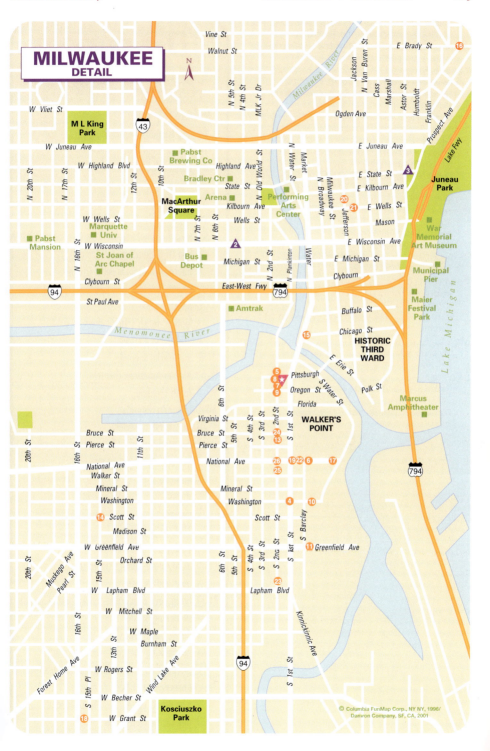

Wisconsin • USA

Peoples' Books 414/962-0575 ■ 2122 E Locust St (at Maryland) ■ 11am-7pm, till 6pm Sat, clsd Sun

Schwartz Bookstore 414/332-1181 ■ 2559 N Downer Ave ■ 9am-10pm, till 11pm Fri-Sat, till 9pm Sun

Retail Shops

Adambomb Gallery 414/276-2662 ■ 524 S 2nd St (at Bruce) ■ 11am-9pm, till 6pm Sat, clsd Sun-Mon, tattoo studio

Designing Men 414/389-1200 ■ 1200 S 1st St (at Scott) ■ noon-7pm, till 9pm Fri-Sat, till 6pm Sun

Miss Groove [GO] 414/298-9185 ■ 1225 E Brady (btwn Arlington & Franklin) ■ 11am-6pm, noon-4pm Sun, clsd Mon, accessories & gifts

Out of Solitude [GO] 414/223-3101 ■ 918 E Brady (at Astor) ■ 11am-6pm, till 4pm Sat, clsd Sun, jewelry & gifts

Yellow Jacket 414/372-4744 ■ 2225 N Humboldt Ave (at North Ave) ■ noon-7pm, till 5pm Sun, clsd Mon in summer, vintage clothes

You Should Be Dancing 414/258-2705 ■ 6421 W North Ave ■ 11am-7pm, noon-6pm Sat, clsd Sun ■ www.youshouldbedancing.org

Publications

IN Step 414/278-7840 ■ lgbt newspaper ■ www.instepnews.com

Quest 800/578-3785, 920/433-0611 ■ good bar list ■ www.quest-online.com

Men's Clubs

Midtowne Milwaukee [PC,WC] 414/278-8989 ■ 315 S Water Street ■ 24hrs ■ www.midtowne-spa.com/milwaukee/

Erotica

Booked Solid 414/774-7210 ■ 7035 W Greenfield Ave (at 70th), West Allis

Popular News 414/278-0636 ■ 225 N Water St (at Buffalo) ■ toys & videos

Damron Codes

- ➤ advertiser
- ★ popular
- MO men only
- GF gay-friendly (mostly straight)
- GS gay/straight (evenly mixed)
- MW lesbians/gay men
- M mostly men
- W mostly women (listing names in this color)
- WO women only (listing names in this color)
- NH neighborhood bar
- D live DJ & dancing
- A alternative (grunge babes, goths)
- CW country western (music, dancing and/or dress)
- B bears
- L leather, fetish (often a dress code)
- P professional crowd
- MRC multiracial clientele
- MR-AF African-American clientele
- MR-A Asian clientele
- MR-L Latino/a clientele
- TG transgender-friendly
- F hot food served
- E live entertainment (piano, bands, comedy)
- K karaoke
- S shows (drag, strip, or cabaret)
- V videos
- 18+ 18 & older
- YC young crowd (mostly 20-somethings)
- OC older/more mature crowd (mostly over 40)
- BW beer and/or wine
- BYOB bring your own bottle (often "private" clubs)
- SW swimming onsite (usually a pool)
- N public nudity okay
- NS no smoking (anywhere inside business)
- PC private club (membership open to out-of-towners; often BYOB)
- WC wheelchair access (includes bathrooms)
- GO gay-owned/ operated
- AYOR at your own risk (beware of bashers or cops)

BRITISH COLUMBIA

Vancouver

ACCOMMODATIONS
1. **The Albion Guest House** [GF,NS] 604/873-2287, 877/873-2287 ■ 592 W 19th Ave (at Ash) ■ full brkfst, hot tub ■ www.albionguesthouse.com
2. **Apricot Cat Guest House** [GF] 604/215-9898 ■ 628 Union St (4 blks E of Main) ■ restored 1898 character home ■ www.apricotcat.com
3. **Barclay House B&B** [GS,GO] 604/605-1351, 800/971-1351 ■ 1351 Barclay St (at Jervis) ■ restored Victorian, full brkfst ■ www.barclayhouse.com
4. **Barefoot Moon Guesthouse** [MW,NS] 604/251-9774 ■ 1620 Adanac St (at Commercial Dr) ■ healthy full brkfst
5. **The Buchan Hotel** [GF] 604/685-5354, 800/668-6654 ■ 1906 Haro St (btwn Denman & Gilford) ■ some shared baths ■ www.buchanhotel.com
6. **The Chelsea Cottage B&B** [GF,NS] 604/266-2681 ■ 2143 W 46th Ave (at West Blvd) ■ full brkfst, hot tub ■ www.vancouver-inn.com
7. **Colibri B&B** [MW,GO] 604/689-5100, 877/312-6600 ■ 1101 Thurlow St (at Pendrell) ■ deck ■ www.q-net.com/colibri
8. **Columbia Cottage** [GF,NS] 604/874-5327 ■ 205 W 14th Ave (at Manitoba) ■ 1920s Tudor, full brkfst ■ www.columbiacottage.com
   Downtown Accommodations/ Furnished Suites [GF] 604/454-8179, 877/454-8179 ■ 1415 W Georgia St (at Broughton) ■ gay-friendly ■ info@downtownaccom.com
9. **Dufferin Hotel** [GS,K,S] 604/683-4251, 877/683-5522 ■ 900 Seymour St (at Smithe) ■ also 3 bars (M) ■ www.dufferinhotel.com
10. **Hawks Ave B&B** [WO,NS] 604/253-0989, 604/728-9441 ■ 734 Hawks Ave ■ townhouse, full brkfst, nr downtown
11. **Heather Cottage** [GF] 604/261-1442 ■ 5425 Trafalgar St (btwn 38th & 39th) ■ full brkfst, hot tub ■ www.vancouver-bc.com/heathercottage
12. **Hotel Dakota/ Comfort Inn** [GF,F,GO] 604/605-4333, 888/605-5333 ■ 654 Nelson St (at Granville) ■ hip boutique-style hotel in the heart of entertainment district, ask for IGLTA Pride rate ■ www.hoteldakota.com
13. **The Johnson Heritage House B&B** [GF,NS] 604/266-4175 ■ 2278 W 34th Ave (at Vine) ■ full brkfst ■ www.johnsons-inn-vancouver.com

VANCOUVER

Vancouver is Canada's hip West Coast capital. This multicultural city is set in spectacular natural surroundings and boasts a 1000-acre rainforest in the middle of downtown. Vancouver is also a convenient 90-minute drive from Whistler's ski resort.

Queer Resources

COMMUNITY INFO
▼ The Centre 604/684-5307, web: www.intergate.bc.ca/business/thecentre. 1170 Bute St (btwn Davie & Pendrell), 9am-4pm. The Pride Line 604/684-6869. 7pm-10pm.

AIDS RESOURCES
Pacific Aids Resource Centre 604/681-2122.

RECOVERY
604/434-3933, 604/434-2553 (TDD).

City Calendar

LGBT PRIDE
August. 604/687-0955.

ENTERTAINMENT
Wreck Beach (great gay beach).

ANNUAL EVENTS
January - New Year's Day Polar Bear Swim.
May - Vancouver International Marathon 604/872-2928.
June - Dragon Boat Festival 604/688-2382.
   Du Maurier Jazz Festival Vancouver 604/872-5200.
   Stonewall Festival in the Park 604/684-6869.
July - Folk Music Festival 604/602-9798.
September/October - International Film Festival 604/685-0260, web: www.viff.org.
November - Vancouver Lesbian Week 604/669-9110.

Tourist Info

AIRPORT DIRECTIONS
Vancouver International. To get to Gastown or the West End, take Hwy 99 north and exit at Seymour St.

PUBLIC TRANSIT & TAXIS
Yellow Cab 604/681-1111.
Vancouver Airporter 604/946-8866.
BC Transit 604/521-0400.
A Visitors' Map of all bus lines is available through the tourist office listed below.

TOURIST SPOTS & INFO
Capilano Suspension Bridge
Chinatown.
Gastown.
Science World 604/443-7440.
Stanley Park.
Van Dusen Botanical Gardens 604/878-9274.
Visitor's Center: 604/683-2000, web: www.tourism-vancouver.org.
Vancouver Travel Info Center 604/683-2000.

WEATHER
It's cold and wet in the winter (32-45°F), but it's absolutely gorgeous in the summer (52-75°F)!

BEST VIEWS
Biking in Stanley Park, or on a ferry between peninsulas and islands. Atop one of the surrounding mountains.

BRITISH COLUMBIA • CANADA

14 **The Langtry** [GS,NS,GO] 604/687-7798 ■ 968 Nicola, Ste 1 ■ b&b apts in West End, full brkfst ■ www.thelangtry.com

15 **Listel Vancouver** [GS,F,SW] 604/684-8461, 800/663-5491 ■ 1300 Robson St (at Jervis) ■ boutique hotel, restaurant & bar, gym, hot tub ■ www.listel-vancouver.com

16 **The Manor Guest House** [GF,SW] 604/876-8494 ■ 345 W 13th Ave (at Alberta) ■ full brkfst, hot tub, some shared baths ■ www.manorguesthouse.com

17 **Nelson House B&B** [MW] 604/684-9793 ■ 977 Broughton St (btwn Nelson & Barclay) ■ Edwardian mansion, full brkfst ■ www.bbcanada.com/nelsonhousebnb

18 **'O' Canada House** [GS,GO] 604/688-0555, 877/688-1114 ■ 1114 Barclay St (at Thurlow) ■ restored 1897 Victorian home, full brkfst ■ www.ocanadahouse.com

15 **Pacific Palisades Hotel** [GF,SW] 604/688-0461, 800/663-1815 ■ 1277 Robson St (at Jervis) ■ suites, hot tub ■ www.pacificpalisadeshotel.com

19 **Penny Farthing Inn** [GF,NS] 604/739-9002 ■ 2855 W 6th Ave (at MacDonald) ■ 1912 heritage house in Kitsilano, full brkfst ■ pennyfarthinginn.com

Penny's [GF,NS] 604/254-2229 ■ 810 Commercial Dr (at Venables) ■ antique filled b&b, kitchens ■ www.pennysplacevancouver.com

20 **Pillow and Porridge Guest Suites** [GF,WC] 604/879-8977 ■ 2859 Manitoba St (btwn 12th & 13th Aves) ■ apts w/ private entrances, kitchens ■ www.pillow.net

River Run Cottages [GF,WC] 604/946-7778 ■ 4551 River Rd W, Ladner ■ on the Fraser River, full brkfst ■ www.riverruncottages.com

21 **Royal Hotel** [GS,GO] 604/685-5335, 877/685-5337 ■ 1025 Granville St ■ boutique-style, also 'Royal Pub' bar ■ www.attheroyal.com

Rural Roots B&B [MW,NS,N,WC,GO] 604/856-2380 ■ 4939 Ross Rd, Mt Lehman ■ full brkfst, hot tub, 1 hr from Vancouver ■ cimarron.net/canada/bc/rdrr.html

Sunshine Hills B&B [GF] 604/596-6496 ■ 11200 Bond Blvd, North Delta ■ full brkfst, shared bath ■ www.vancouver-bc.com/sunshinehillsbb

22 **Treehouse B&B** [GF] 604/266-2962 ■ 2490 W 49th Ave (btwn Larch & Balsam) ■ full brkfst, jacuzzi ■ www.treehousebb.com

23 **The West End Guest House** [GS,GO] 604/681-2889 ■ 1362 Haro St (at Broughton) ■ 1906 Victorian, full brkfst ■ www.westendguesthouse.com

BARS

9 **Avenue Lounge** [MW,K] 604/683-4251 ■ 900 Seymour St (at 'Dufferin Hotel') ■ 5pm-2:30am, till midnight Fri-Sat

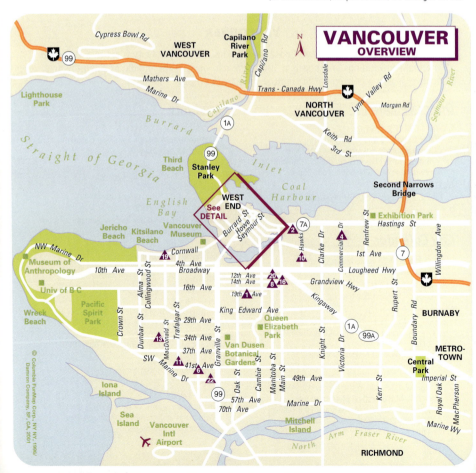

BRITISH COLUMBIA • CANADA

24 **Chuck's Pub** [M,D,S] 604/685-7777 ■ 455 Abbott St (at Heritage House Hotel) ■ noon-midnight, clsd Sun, leather Sat

25 **The Fountainhead Pub** [M,NH] 604/687-2222 ■ 1025 Davie St ■ 11am-midnight, till 1am Fri-Sat, patio

26 **Global Beat** [MW,F,BW,GO] 604/689-2444 ■ 1249 Howe St ■ 4pm-2am, restaurant & lounge

24 **Lotus Club** [D] 604/685-7777 ■ 455 Abbott St (at Heritage House Hotel) ■ straight club except for fetish night 9:30pm-2am last Sat

28 **The PumpJack Pub** [M,NH,CW,L,18+,WC] 604/685-3417 ■ 1167 Davie St (off Bute) ■ 2pm-midnight, till 1am Fri-Sat ■ www.pumpjackpub.com

21 **The Royal Pub** [★M,NH,E,S] 604/685-5335 ■ 1025 Granville St (at 'Royal Hotel') ■ noon-midnight, popular Fri happy hour ■ www.attheroyal.com/bar.htm

NIGHTCLUBS

29 **Chameleon Lounge** [GS,D,S] 604/669-0806 ■ 801 W Georgia ■ 9pm-close, more gay Sun

30 **Moulin Rouge** [D,$] 604/669-9333 ■ 860 Denman (btwn Haro & Robson) ■ 8pm-2am, till midnight Sun, gay on Wed only, cover charge

31 **Ms T's Cabaret** [MW,D,TG,K] 604/682-8096 ■ 339 W Pender St ■ 8pm-2am

32 **Numbers** [★M,D,S,V] 604/685-4077 ■ 1042 Davie (btwn Thurlow & Burrard) ■ 8pm-2am, till midnight Sun, 5 levels

26 **The Odyssey** [★M,D,S,YC] 604/689-5256 ■ 1251 Howe St (at Davie) ■ 9pm-2am

33 **Sublime** 816 Granville ■ 1am-6am Fri-Sat ■ sublimenightclub@hotmail.com

CAFES

Delany's 604/662-3344 ■ 1105 Denman St ■ 6am-11pm, coffee shop

Melriches Coffeehoue 604/689-5282 ■ 1244 Davie St ■ 7am-11pm

Moonbeans [★MW] 604/632-0032 ■ 1262 Davie ■ 7am-11pm, till midnight Fri-Sat, patio

Sneakers 1148 Davie St (btwn Bute & Thurlow) ■ 7am-4am, till 3am Sun, popular after-hrs spot

RESTAURANTS

Cafe S'il Vous Plaît 604/688-7216 ■ 500 Robson St (at Richards) ■ lunch & dinner, clsd Sun

Chianti's 604/738-8411 ■ 1850 W 4th St (at Burrard) ■ lunch & dinner

Cincin 604/688-7338 ■ 1154 Robson (off Bute) ■ lunch & dinner only wknds, Italian/ Mediterranean, full bar

Delilah's [WC] 604/687-3424 ■ 1789 Comox St (at Denman) ■ 5:30pm-11pm, some veggie, full bar

The Dish [GO] 604/689-0208 ■ 1068 Davie St ■ 7am-9pm, from 9am Sun, lowfat veggie fast food

Elbow Room Café 604/685-3628 ■ 560 Davie St (at Seymour) ■ 8am-4pm, till 5pm wknds, great brkfst

Hamburger Mary's 604/687-1293 ■ 1202 Davie St (at Bute) ■ 7am-3am, till 4am Fri-Sat, till 2pm Sun, some veggie, full bar

Henry's Landing 604/854-3679 ■ 2607 Ware St (at S Fraser Wy) ■ lunch & dinner, full bar

India Gate 604/684-4617 ■ 616 Robson St (at Granville) ■ lunch & dinner

Luxy Bistro [WC] 604/669-5899 ■ 1235 Davie St (btwn Bute & Jervis) ■ 11am-10pm, till 11pm wknds, some veggie, full bar

Mario's 604/852-6919 ■ 33555 S Fraser Wy (at Kent Ave) ■ lunch & dinner, Italian

Martini's 604/873-0021 ■ 151 W Broadway (btwn Cambie & Main) ■ 11am-2am, 3pm-3am Sat, till 1am Sun, great pizza & full bar

Milestone's 604/682-4477 ■ 1145 Robson St (at Thurlow) ■ lunch & dinner, full bar

Naam [WC] 604/738-7151, 604/738-7180 ■ 2724 W 4th St (at MacDonald) ■ 24hrs, vegetarian

Riley Cafe [WC] 604/684-3666 ■ 1661 Granville St (at Beech) ■ 11:30am-10pm, from 10:30am wknds, full bar

ENTERTAINMENT & RECREATION

Lotus Land Tours 604/684-4922, 800/528-3531 ■ 1251 Cardero St, Ste 2005 ■ day paddle trips, whale-watching trips, no experience necessary (price includes pick-up & meal) ■ www.lotuslandtours.com

Rockwood Adventures 604/926-7705 ■ 1330 Fulton Ave, West Vancouver ■ rain forest walks for all levels w/ free hotel pick-up ■ www.cool.mb.ca/rockwood

Sunset Beach right in the West End

BOOKSTORES

34 **Little Sister's** [★WC] 604/669-1753, 800/567-1662 (in Canada only) ■ 1238 Davie St (btwn Bute & Jervis) ■ 10am-11pm, lgbt (please support this great store in their ongoing legal battle against Canadian Customs by buying a book today) ■ www.lsisters.com

Spartacus Books 604/688-6138 ■ 311 W Hastings (at Hamilton) ■ 10am-8:30pm, 11am-7pm Sat, noon-7pm Sun, progressive titles

Women in Print [WC] 604/732-4128 ■ 3566 W 4th Ave (at Dunbar/ Collingwood) ■ 10am-6pm, noon-5pm Sun, women's bookstore

RETAIL SHOPS

Mack's Leathers 604/688-6225 ■ 1043 Granville (at Nelson) ■ 11am-7pm, till 8pm Th-Fri, also body piercing

Next Body Piercing 604/684-6398 ■ 1068 Granville St (at Nelson) ■ noon-6pm, also tattooing

State of Mind 604/682-7116 ■ 1100 Davie St (at Thurlow) ■ 9am-8pm, designer queer clothes

TopDrawers [WC] 604/684-4861 ■ 1030 Denman St #115 ■ 10am-7pm, till 9pm Th-Sat, men's clothing & underwear ■ www.topdrawers.com

PUBLICATIONS

Rainbow Choices Directory 416/762-1320, 888/241-3569 (Canada only) ■ lgbt entertainment & business directory for Canada ■ www.interlog.com/~rnbchoic

Xtra! West 604/684-9696 ■ lgbt newspaper ■ www.xtra.ca

MEN'S CLUBS

Club Vancouver [★] 604/681-5719 ■ 339 W Pender St (at Homer) ■ 24hrs

Fahrenheit 212° [PC] 604/689-9719 ■ 1048 Davie (at Burrard) ■ 24hrs; also 430 Columbia St, 604/540-2117 ■ www.F212.com

Hastings Steam & Sauna 604/251-5455 ■ 766 E Hastings (at Headley)

Richards St Service Club [PC] 604/684-6010 ■ 1169 Richards St 2nd floor (at Davie) ■ 24hrs

EROTICA

Love's Touch 604/681-7024 ■ 1069 Davie St

Womyn's Ware [GO] 604/254-2543, 888/WYM-WARE (orders only) ■ 896 Commercial Dr (at Denables, in East End) ■ noon-6pm, till 7pm Th-Fri, till 5pm Sun, toys for men too ■ www.womynsware.com

TORONTO

Toronto is more than just the capital city of Ontario, eh! It's the cultural and financial center of English-speaking Canada. And though it's not far from Buffalo, New York, and Niagara Falls, Toronto has a European ambiance. Its eclectic architecture, peaceful diversity of cultures, world-class nightlife, and excellent dining make it a great vacation getaway. Toronto is also well-known for its repertory film scene, so try not to miss the two-week Lesbian Gay Film Fest in the spring, or the Film Festival of Festivals in September.

Queer Resources

COMMUNITY INFO
▼ Community Centre 416/392-6874. 519 Church St (at Dundonald).
Xtra! Gay/Lesbian Info Line 416/925-9872 (touchtone info).

AIDS RESOURCES
AIDS Action Now 416/977-5903.
Hassle Free Clinic 416/922-0566 (women's), 416/922-0603 (men's).

RECOVERY
AA Gay/Lesbian 416/487-5591. 234 Edmonton Ave E #202.

City Calendar

LGBT PRIDE
June/July. 416/927-7433, web: www.torontopride.com.

ANNUAL EVENTS
May - International Gay & Lesbian Comedy and Music Festival, web: members.aol.com/werefunny. Inside Out: Lesbian & Gay Film and Video Festival 416/977-6847, web: insideout.on.ca.
June - duMaurier Downtown Jazz Festival 416/928-2033, web: www.tojazz.com.
International Dragon Boat Race Festival 416/364-0046.
July - Caribana Caribbean festival 416/969-3110.
September - International Film Festival 416/968-3456, web: www.bell.ca/filmfest.

Tourist Info

AIRPORT DIRECTIONS
Lester B Pearson International. To get to many of the gay bars, take 427 South to Queen Elizabeth Way (QEW) East. QEW becomes Gardiner Expressway. From Gardiner, exit on York St or Bay St.

PUBLIC TRANSIT & TAXIS
Co-op Taxi 416/504-2667.
Grey Coach 416/393-7911.
TTC 416/393-4636, web: www.city.toronto.on.ca/ttc.

TOURIST SPOTS & INFO
Art Gallery of Ontario 416/979-6648.
Bata Shoe Museum.
CN Tower 416/868-6937, www.cntower.ca.
Dr Flea's International Flea Market 416/745-3532.
Gardiner Museum of Ceramic Art, 416-586-8080.
Harbourfront Centre 416/973-3000, web: www.harbourfront.on.ca.
Hockey Hall of Fame 416/360-7735.
Kensington Market.
Ontario Place 416/314-9900.
Royal Ontario Museum 416/586-8000, web: www.rom.on.ca.
SkyDome 416/341-2300.
Underground City.
Visitor's Center: 800/363-1990, web: www.tourism-toronto.com.

WEATHER
Summers are hot (upper 80°s–90°s) and humid. Spring is gorgeous. Fall brings cool, crisp days. Winters are cold and snowy, just as you'd imagined they would be in Canada!

BEST VIEWS
The top of one of the world's tallest buildings, of course: the CN Tower. Or try a sightseeing air tour or a three-masted sailing ship tour.

ONTARIO • CANADA

ONTARIO

Toronto

ACCOMMODATIONS

213 Carlton Street - Toronto Townhouse [GS,WC,GO] 416/323-8898, 877/500-0466 ■ upscale townhouse, full brkfst, some shared baths ■ www.toronto-townhouse.com

1 **Allenby B&B** [GF,NS] 416/461-7095 ■ 223 Strathmore Blvd (nr Danforth & Greenwood) ■ shared bath

2 **Amazing Space B&B** [MW] 416/968-2323, 800/205-3694 ■ 246 Sherbourne St (at Dundas) ■ also 'Immaculate Reception' on Cawthra Park ■ www.immaculate-reception.com

3 **Amblecote B&B** [GF,NS] 416/927-1713 ■ 109 Walmer Rd (at Bernard) ■ www.amblecote.com

4 **Banting House B&B** [MW] 416/924-1458 ■ 73 Homewood Ave (at Wellesley) ■ Edwardian home, garden ■ www.bantinghouse.com

5 **Cawthra Park B&B** [GS,GO] 416/351-1503, 877/580-5015 ■ 10 Monteith St (nr Church & Wellesley) ■ Victorian townhouse, some shared baths, garden, deck ■ www.geocities.com/thetropics/equator/6581/

6 **Cawthra Square B&B–Great Inns of Toronto** [MW,NS,GO] 416/966-3074, 800/259-5474 ■ includes 'Ten Cawthra' & '512 Jarvis', some shared baths ■ www.sleepwithfriends.com

7 **Dundonald House** [M,GO] 416/961-9888, 800/260-7227 ■ 35 Dundonald St M4Y 1K3 ■ full brkfst, hot tub, sauna, gym, bicycles, shared baths ■ www.dundonaldhouse.com

8 **House on McGill** [GS,NS] 416/351-1503, 877/580-5015 ■ 110 McGill St (at Church & Carlton) ■ Victorian townhouse, shared baths, garden w/ deck ■ www.interlog.com/~mcgillbb/

9 **Huntley House** [GF] 416/923-6950 ■ 65 Huntley St (at Bloor) ■ 1871 historic house, full brkfst ■ 1871hist@interlog.com

10 **Immaculate Reception B&B** [MW,GO] 416/925-4202, 800/335-9190 ■ 34 Monteith St (at Church) ■ full brkfst ■ www.immaculate-reception.com

11 **The Mansion** [GS] 416/963-8385 ■ 46 Dundonald St (at Church) ■ elegant Victorian ■ mansion@istar.ca

12 **Mike's on Mutual** [MW,NS,GO] 416/944-2611 ■ 333 Mutual St (at Maitland) ■ B&B-private home ■ www.trends.net/~bif

13 **Muther's** [MO,N,GO] 416/466-8616 ■ 508 Eastern Ave (btwn Carlaw & Logan) ■ above 'Tool Box' bar ■ www.torque.net/~toolbox/

14 **Pimblett's Rest B&B** [GS,GO] 416/929-9525, 416/921-6898 ■ 242 Gerrard St E ■ Victorian, hot tub, theme rooms ■ members.attcanada.ca/~pimblett/pimblett.htm

Toronto B&B [GF] 416/588-8800 or 905/ 403-9399 ■ Box 269, 253 College St ■ reservation service ■ torontobandb.com

15 **Toronto Downtown B&B** [GS,GO] 416/921-3533, 877/950-6200 ■ 572 Ontario St (at Dundas) ■ luxurious, full brkfst, in gay village ■ www.tdbab.com

16 **Victoria's Mansion Inn & Guest House** [GF] 416/921-4625 ■ 68 Gloucester St ■ converted mansion ■ www3.sympatico.ca/victorias.mansion

5 **'With Friends' B&B** [GS] 416/925-2798 ■ 12 Monteith St (at Church & Wellesley) ■ restored 1877 terrace house overlooking Cawthra Square Park, deck ■ www.withfriendsbandb.com

BARS

17 **Bar 501** [MW,NH,S] 416/944-3272 ■ 501 Church (at Wellesley) ■ 11am-2am, infamous 'Window Show' Sun

18 **The Black Eagle** [M,B,L,F] 416/413-1219 ■ 457 Church St (btwn Maitland & Alexander) ■ 2pm-2am, from noon Sun (brunch), 3 bars, theme nights, bears Th, dress code Fri-Sat, rooftop patio ■ www.blackeagletoronto.com

19 **Carrington's** [M,NH] 416/944-0559 ■ 618 Yonge, upstairs (at St Joseph) ■ 11am-2am, sports bar

20 **The Cellblock/ Yard** [M,D,S] 416/921-0066 ■ 72 Carlton St (behind 'Zipperz') ■ drag shows Mon & Wed, DJ Th-Sun

21 **Ciao Edie** [GS,F] 416/927-7774 ■ 489 College St (at Markham) ■ 8pm-2am, 'Here Kitty Kitty' women's night Sun, oh-so-nice cocktail lounge w/ DJ

22 **Crews/ Tango** [M,N,D,S] 416/972-1662 ■ 508 Church ■ noon-3am, deck overlooking Church St, also 'Tango' (W) from 8pm Tue-Sat, popular Sat

23 **The Hair of the Dog** [MW,NH,F] 416/964-2708 ■ 425 Church St ■ 11:30am-2am, pub & restaurant, patio

24 **The House On Parliament Pub** [GS,NH,F] 416/925-4074 ■ 456 Parliament St ■ patio

45 **The Lounge** [MW,K] 416/469-5002 ■ 940 Danforth Ave (E of Donlands, above Replay Sports Bar) ■ wknds only, above gay-friendly sports bar

25 **Midtown** [MW,NH] 416/920-4533 ■ 552 College St (W of Euclid) ■ 5pm-2am, from 3pm Fri, from 1pm wknds, pool bar

26 **Pegasus Billiard Lounge** [MW,NH] 416/927-8832 ■ 489-B Church St (at Wellesley, upstairs) ■ 11am-2am ■ www.pegasusonchurch.com

27 **Queen's Head Pub (aka Pimblett's Pub)** [GS,NH,WC,GO] 416/ 929-9525 ■ 263 Gerrard St E (btwn Seaton & Parliament) ■ 4pm-3am, friendly pub, also restaurant, patio

28 **Red Spot Lounge & Bar** [MW,NH,F,E,K] 416/967-7768 ■ 459 Church St (at Carlton) ■ 4pm-2am

29 **Remington's Men of Steel** [MO,S,WC,GO] 416/977-2160 ■ 379 Yonge St (at Gerrard) ■ 3pm-2am, strip bar ■ www.remingtons.com

22 **Slack Alice** [★MW,F] 416/969-8742 ■ 562 Church St (at Wellesley) ■ 4pm-2am, from 11am wknds, also restaurant ■ www.slackalice.com

30 **Sneakers** [M,NH] 416/961-5808 ■ 502-A Yonge St (at Alexander) ■ 11am-2am, cruise bar, hustlers ■ www.gaytoronto.com/sneakers

31 **Survivors** [MW,NH,D,F] 905/453-2116 ■ 1 Nelson St W (at Hwy 10/ Queen St, across from the bus station) ■ 7pm-2am, from 4pm Sun, ladies' night Th, clsd Mon-Tue

13 **Toolbox** [★M,B,L,F,NS] 416/466-8616 ■ 508 Eastern Ave ■ 5pm-2am, from 2pm Fri, from noon wknds, Sun brunch, theme nights, cruisy patio ■ www.torque.net/~toolbox/

32 **Trax V** [★M,S,OC,WC] 416/963-5196 ■ 529 Yonge St (at Maitland) ■ 11am-2am, drag shows nightly, bingo

33 **Woody's/ Sailor** [★M,NH,F,WC] 416/972-0887 ■ 465-467 Church (at Maitland) ■ noon-2am, brunch from 10am wknds ■ www.woodystoronto.com

20 **Zipperz** [M,D,S] 416/921-0066 ■ 72 Carlton St (at Church) ■ noon-3am, drag shows, piano bar, patio

NIGHTCLUBS

34 **5ive** [★M,D,F,$] 416/964-8685 ■ 5 St Joseph St (at Yonge) ■ 10pm-2am, clsd Mon, also 'Life Lounge', open from 5pm

Toronto • ONTARIO

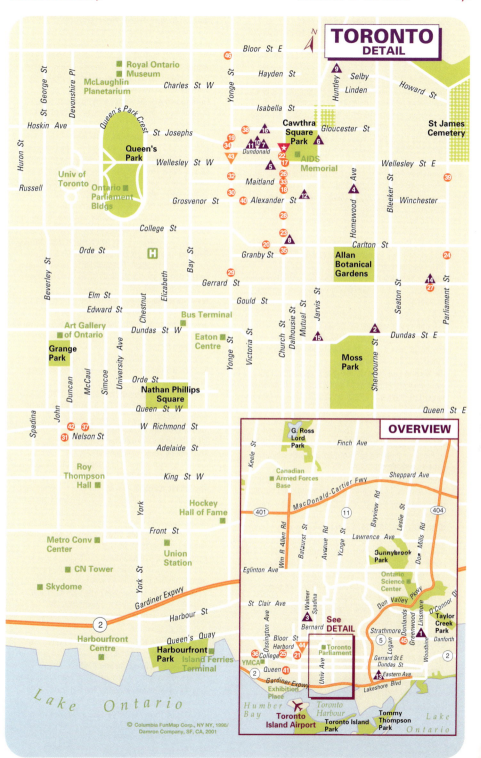

ONTARIO • CANADA

35 The Barn [★M,D,L,V] 416/977-4684 ■ 418 Church (at Granby) ■ 9pm-3am, till 4am Fri-Sat, from 4pm Sun, 3 flrs, also 'Stables,' 416/977-4702

36 El Convento Rico [★MW,D,MR,TG,S,$] 416/588-7800 ■ 750 College St (at Crawford) ■ 8pm-4am Fri-Sat only, drag shows at 1am ■ www.elconventorico.com

37 Fluid [GS,D,WC,$] 416/593-6116 ■ 217 Richmond St W ■ 10pm-4am, clsd Mon, more gay wknds, dress code

38 Fly [★M,D,$] 416/410-5246 ■ 6-8 Gloucester St (at Yonge) ■ 9pm-close Sat only, circuit crowd

39 Kitty Kitty Bang Bang [WO,D] ■ 19 Balmuto St (at 'Manhattan Club') ■ 9pm-2am 3rd Fri ■ dykedance@hotmail.com

38 Manhattan Club [GS,D,MR] 416/920-9119 ■ 19 Balmuto St (nr Yonge & Bloor) ■ queer night Sat

39 Pope Joan [W,D,F,E] 416/925-6662, 416/925-9990 ■ 547 Parliament (at Winchester) ■ 7pm-close, clsd Sun-Wed, popular Fri, brunch from noon summer wknds, big outdoor patio

40 Tallulah's Cabaret [M,S] 416/975-8555 ■ 12 Alexander St (at 'Buddies in Bad Times' theater) ■ cabaret Fri-Sat only, 'Sissy Saturdays' are popular

42 Whiskey Saigon [GF,D,S,$] 416/593-4646 ■ 250 Richmond W (at Duncan) ■ 9pm-3am Fri-Sun, huge club, rooftop patio, dress code

CAFES

Cafe Diplomatico [★] 416/534-6377 ■ 594 College (at Clinton, in Little Italy) ■ 8am-2am, patio

The Joy of Java [E] 416/465-8855 ■ 884 Queen St E ■ 8am-11pm, live jazz Sat, patio

The Second Cup [★] 416/964-2457 ■ 548 Church St (at Wellesley) ■ 24hrs (except Mon-Wed), coffee & desserts

Sweet City Bakery 416/962-0358 ■ 24 Wellesley St W (at Yonge) ■ 6:30am-5:30pm, 8am-4pm Sat, clsd Sun ■ www.sweetcitybakery.com

RESTAURANTS

Allen's Restaurant [E] 416/463-3086 ■ 143 Danforth Ave (at Broadview) ■ lunch & dinner, great scotch selection, patio ■ www.allens.to

Avalon 416/979-9918 ■ 270 Adelaide St W (at John) ■ dinner nightly, lunch Th only, clsd Sun, intimate dining

Babylon 416/923-2626 ■ 553 Church St ■ 3pm-2am, also martini bar

Bistro 422 416/963-9416 ■ 422 College St ■ 4pm-2am

Byzantium [M] 416/922-3859 ■ 499 Church St (S of Wellesley) ■ 5:30pm-11pm, chic, Continental/ global, also martini bar till 2am, patio ■ www.interlog.com/~byz

Cafe Jambalaya 416/922-5262 ■ 501 Yonge St (at Alexander, in Little Italy) ■ 11:30am-10pm, clsd Sun, Cajun, Caribbean & vegetarian, patio

Cafe Volo 416/928-0008 ■ 587 Yonge St (at Dundonald) ■ 11am-11pm, Italian, some veggie

Ethiopian House 416/923-5438 ■ 4 Irwin Ave (2 blks N of Wellesley, off Yonge) ■ noon-1am

Fly 416/410-5246 ■ 6-8 Gloucester St (at Yonge) ■ clsd Mon, fantastic buffet brunch Sun

Golden Thai 416/868-6668 ■ 105 Church St (at Richmond) ■ 11:30am-10:30pm, from 5pm wknds

The Gypsy Co-Op 416/703-5069 ■ 817 Queen St W (W of Bathurst) ■ noon-2am, 6pm-2am Mon, clsd Sun, also bar, eclectic & kitschy, women's night Wed ■ www.bandofgypsies.com

Hughie's Burgers, Fries & Pies 416/977-2242 ■ 777 Bay St (at College) ■ 11:30am-11pm, Sun brunch, full bar, patio

Il Fornello 416/920-7347 ■ 1560 Yonge St (1 blk N of St Clair) ■ 11:30am-10:30pm, no lunch Sat, Italian, plenty veggie; also 214 King W (at Simcoe), 416/977-2855 & 576 Danforth Ave (at Carlaw), 416/466-2931 ■ www.ilfornello.com

La Hacienda 416/703-3377 ■ 640 Queen St W (nr Bathurst) ■ lunch & dinner, sleazy, loud & fun Mexican restaurant

The Living Well Restaurant & Bar [MW,S] 416/922-6770 ■ 692 Yonge St (at Isabella) ■ 11:30am-1am, plenty veggie, also bar, open 6pm-2am, live DJ, patio ■ www.lwcafe.on.ca

Mary's Bar & Grill [GO] 416/598-4544 ■ 399 Church St (at Carlton) ■ 11am-11pm, till midnight Fri-Sat, burgers, salads, pasta, full bar

Oasis [E] 416/975-0845 ■ 294 College St (at Spadina) ■ 5pm-2am, eclectic tapas, also bar ■ oasisrest@sprint.ca

PJ Mellon's [WC] 416/966-3241 ■ 489 Church St (at Wellesley) ■ 11:30am-11pm, some veggie, wine bar

Rashnaa 416/929-2099 ■ 307 Wellesley St E (at Parliament) ■ 11:30am-11:30pm, buffet lunch till 3pm, inexpensive & good South Indian/ Sri Lankan, plenty veggie/ vegan, full bar

Rivoli Cafe 416/597-0794 ■ 332 Queen St W (at Spadina) ■ 10am-11:30pm, bar till 1am, some veggie

Solo on Yonge 416/920-0607 ■ 605 Yonge St ■ creative seafood & pasta dishes, int'l wine list, reservations recommended wknds

Splendido [WC] 416/929-7788 ■ 88 Harbord St (at Spadina) ■ 5pm-11pm, clsd Sun, great decor & gnocchi, full bar

The Superior Restaurant [WC] 416/214-0416 ■ 253 Yonge St (across from Eaton Ctr) ■ 11:30am-midnight, oysters, full bar

Tantra 416/926-0313 ■ 634 Church St (at Isabella) ■ lunch & dinner, also bar & lounge, patio

Trattoria Al Forno 416/944-8852 ■ 459 Church St (at Carlton) ■ lunch Mon-Fri & dinner nightly, full bar ■ rbranco@followme.com

The Village Rainbow 416/961-0616 ■ 477 Church St (at Maitland) ■ 7am-midnight, till 1am Th-Sat, from 8am Sun, full bar, big patio

Wilde Oscars [MW] 416/921-8142 ■ 518 Church St (at Maitland) ■ 11am-2am, Mediterranean, huge patio, also lounge (clsd summer) upstairs

Zelda's [★MW] 416/922-2526 ■ 542 Church St ■ 11am-2am, full drag service Sat, all-you-can-eat brunch wknds, full bar, big patio ■ www.zeldas.on.ca

Zelda's Satellite Lounge [MW] 416/922-4221 ■ 76 Wellesley St E ■ cafe & bar ■ www.zeldas.on.ca

ZiZi Trattoria 416/533-5117 ■ 456 Bloor St W (E of Bathurst) ■ 5pm-close

ENTERTAINMENT & RECREATION

AIDS Memorial in Cawthra Park

Buddies in Bad Times Theatre 416/975-8555 ■ 12 Alexander St ■ lgbt theater, also bar ■ www.buddies.web.ca

Gay/ Lesbian History Walking Tour 416/515-7155 ■ 2-hour tour, meets at 519 Church St Community Centre

Get Out of Town 416/994-1699 ■ day trips w/ in 2 hrs of Toronto: outdoor activities, winery tours, beaches, theater ■ www.getoutoftown.to

Iris: Toronto Women's Chorus 416/463-0017

Toronto • Ontario

Bookstores

A Different Booklist 416/538-0889 ■ 746 Bathurst St (at Bloor) ■ 10am-6pm, till 7pm Th-Fri, clsd Sun, multicultural titles & authors

Glad Day Bookshop [★] 416/961-4161, 877/783-3725 ■ 598-A Yonge St (at Wellesley, upstairs) ■ 10am-7pm, till 9pm Th-Fri, from noon Sun, great selection of lgbt books, mags & videos ■ gdbooks@on.aibn.com

The Omega Centre 416/975-9086, 888/663-6377 (in Canada) ■ 29 Yorkville Ave (btwn Yonge & Bay) ■ 10am-9pm, till 6pm Sat, 11am-5pm Sun, spiritual books ■ www.omegactr.com

This Ain't The Rosedale Library 416/929-9912 ■ 483 Church St (at Wellesley) ■ 10am-10pm, till 11pm Fri-Sat, 1pm-9pm Sun, lgbt books & magazines

Toronto Women's Bookstore 416/922-8744, 800/861-8233 ■ 73 Harbord St (at Spadina) ■ 10:30am-6pm, till 8pm Th-Fri, 10:30am-6pm Sat, noon-5pm Sun ■ www.womensbookstore.com

Wonderworks 416/323-3131 ■ 79-A Harbord St (at Spadina) ■ 10:30am-6pm, books & gifts ■ wonderworksonline.net

Retail Shops

Out in the Street 416/967-2759, 800/263-5747 ■ 551 Church St ■ 10am-8pm, from 11am Sun, lgbt accessories ■ outinthestreet@aol.com

Passage Body Piercing 416/929-7330 ■ 473 Church St ■ noon-7pm, clsd Sun-Mon, also tattoos & scarification

Planet Earth 416/929-2007, 877/503-7374 (mail-order) ■ 473 Church St ■ 10am-6pm, all-natural body care products

Secrets From Your Sister... [WC] 416/538-1234 ■ 476 Bloor St W ■ 11am-6pm, till 7pm Th-Sat, from noon Sun, 'beautiful lingerie in realistic sizes for the modern woman' ■ www.sfysister.com

Stargazer Studios 416/928-3579 ■ 460 Parliament St #1 ■ body piercing by appointment only

Take a Walk On the Wild Side [TG] 416/921-6112 ■ 161 Gerrard St E (at Jarvis) ■ 10am-7pm, till 11pm Sat, noon-4pm Sun, drag emporium ■ www.wildside.org

Vixon 416/960-6464 ■ 620 Yonge St ■ 11am-8pm, clubwear

Publications

The Pink Pages 416/972-7418 ■ annual lgbt directory ■ www.pinkpages.org

Rainbow Choices Directory 416/762-1320, 888/241-3569 (Canada only) ■ lgbt entertainment & business directory for Canada ■ www.interlog.com/~rnbchoic

Siren 416/778-9027 ■ lesbian newsmagazine ■ sirenmag@interlog.com

Xtra! 416/925-6665 ■ lgbt newspaper ■ www.xtra.ca

Gyms & Health Clubs

The Bloor Valley Club [GF,SW] 416/961-4695 ■ 555 Sherbourne St (at Bloor) ■ squash & fitness club

Men's Clubs

The Barracks [L] 416/593-0499 ■ 56 Widmer St (at Richmond) ■ 24hrs, spa, theme nights ■ www.barracks.com

The Bijou [AYOR] 416/971-9985 ■ 370 Church St (btwn Granby & Gerrard) ■ 9pm-4am, bathhouse

Central Spa 416/588-6191 ■ 1610 Dundas St W ■ noon-2am

Club Toronto Baths & Health Club [SW,PC] 416/977-4629 ■ 231 Mutual St (at Carlton) ■ 24hrs, gym equipment ■ www.clubtoronto.com

Spa Excess [★] 416/260-2363, 877/867-3301 ■ 105 Carlton St ■ 24hrs, 4 flrs ■ www.spaexcess.com

The Spa on Maitland 416/925-1571 ■ 66 Maitland, 2nd flr (at Church) ■ 24hrs ■ www.thespaonmaitland.com

St Marc Sauna [★WC] 416/927-0210 ■ 543 Yonge St, 4th flr (at Wellesley) ■ 24hrs ■ www.thebestspa.com

Erotica

Aslan Leather 416/306-0462 ■ 135 Tecumseth St, Unit 4 (rear) ■ 10am-7pm Tue-Sat by appt only, fine bondage gear ■ www.ASLANleather.com

Barbwire XXX Cinema 416/934-1359 ■ 543 Yonge St, 1st flr (below 'St Marc Spa') ■ 10pm-4am, from 11pm Sun-Mon, also private booths & cruise area ■ barbwireXXX@members.gayweb.com

Body Exotic Lingerie 416/597-3953 ■ 357-1/2 Yonge St (at Gould)

Come As You Are 416/504-7934 ■ 701 Queen St W (at Bathurst) ■ co-op owned sex store ■ www.comeasyouare.com

Good For Her [WC] 416/588-0900, 877/588-0900 ■ 175 Harbord St (nr Bathurst) ■ 11am-7pm, till 8pm Fri, till 6pm Sat, women-only till 2pm Th & noon-5pm Sun ■ www.goodforher.com

North Bound Leather [WC] 416/972-1037 ■ 586 Yonge ■ toys & clothing ■ www.northbound.com

Priape [★] 416/586-9914, 800/461-6969 ■ 465 Church St (at Wellesley, above Woody's) ■ clubwear, leather, books, toys & more ■ www.priape.com

Seduction 416/966-6969 ■ 577 Yonge St ■ www.seduction.ca

Montréal

This 350-year-old city is one of the largest French-speaking cities in the world. Its cosmopolitan atmosphere and Old World charm make it an ideal vacation spot.

Queer Resources

Community Info
- ▼ Centre Communautaire des Gais et Lesbiennes 514/528-8424, web: www.ccglm.qc.ca. 2075 rue Plessis.
- Women's Centre of Montréal 514/842-4780. 9am-5pm Mon-Fri.
- Gay Info Line 514/866-5090 (English), 514/866-0103 (French).

AIDS Resources
ABBAPS 514/521-8720.

Recovery
514/376-9230.

City Calendar

LGBT Pride
July/August. 514/285-4011.

Entertainment
Info Gay Events Hotline 514/252-4429.

Annual Events
- June - Festival International de Jazz de Montréal 514/871-1881, www.montrealjazzfest.com.
- August - Montréal World Film Festival 514/848-9933.
- October - Black & Blue Party 514/875-7026. AIDS benefit dance & circuit party.

Tourist Info

Airport Directions
Dorval International. To get to downtown, take Hwy 20 North and use the downtown exit.

Public Transit & Taxis
- Diamond Cab 514/273-6331.
- Montréal Urban Transit 514/280-5100.

Tourist Spots & Info
- Bonsecours Market 514/872-7730.
- Latin Quarter.
- Montréal Botanical Garden & Insectarium 514/872-1400.
- Montréal Museum of Fine Arts 514/285-2000.
- Old Montréal & Old Port.
- Olympic Park.
- Underground City.
- Visitor's Center: 514/844-5400, web: www.tourism-montreal.org.

Weather
It's north of New England so winters are for real. Beautiful spring and fall colors. Summers get hot and humid.

Best Views
From a caleche ride (horse-drawn carriage), from the top of the Montréal Tower, or from the patio of the old hunting lodge atop Mont Royal.

Province of Québec

Montréal

Accommodations

1. **Angelica Blue B&B** [GS] 514/844-5048, 800/878-5048 ■ 1213 Ste-Elisabeth (at Ste-Catherine) ■ theme rms, full brkfst, some shared baths, lesbian-owned/ run ■ www.angelicablue.com

   Au Stade B&B [MW] 514/254-1250 x1 ■ PO Box 60542 H1V 3T8 ■ be-brief@sympatico.ca

2. **Auberge Cosy** [★MO,GO] 514/525-2151 ■ 1274 Ste-Catherine Est (at la Visitation) ■ in the heart of the Village, hot tub ■ www.aubergecosy.com

3. **Auberge de la Fontaine** [GF,WC] 514/597-0166, 800/597-0597 ■ 1301 rue Rachel Est (at Chambord) ■ www.aubergedelafontaine.com

Montréal • PROVINCE OF QUÉBEC

4 ▶ **Auberge du Centre-Ville** [★MO] 514/938-9393, 800/668-6253 ■ 1070 rue Mackay (at René Lévèsque) ■ high sexual atmosphere, also bar & sauna ■ www.auxberges.ca

5 **Auberge Guyz B&B** [MW,GO] 514/521-9998 ■ 1407 Panet #2 ■ located in the gay village ■ www.auberge-guyz.qc.ca

6 **Aubergell.com** [MO,F,GO] 514/597-0878, 514/525-7744 ■ 1641 Amherst (at de Maisonneuve) ■ also full bar & restaurant, rooftop terrace ■ www.aubergell.com

7 **Aux Chambres au Village** [GS,GO] 514/844-6941 ■ 850 de la Gauchetière Est (at St-Hubert) ■ B&B ■ www.chambresauvillage.ca

8 **BBV (B&B du Village)** [M] 514/522-4771, 888/228-8455 ■ 1279 rue Montcalm (at Ste-Catherine) ■ jacuzzi ■ www.bbv.qc.ca

9 **Le Chasseur B&B** [M] 514/521-2238, 800/451-2238 ■ 1567 rue St-André (at Maisonneuve) ■ 1920s European townhouse, summer terrace

10 **Chateau Cherrier** [MW] 514/844-0055, 800/816-0055 ■ 550 rue Cherrier (at St-Hubert) ■ seasonal, full brkfst ■ chateau.cherrier@sympatico.ca

11 **Chez Roger Bontemps** [GS] 514/598-9587, 888/634-9090 ■ 1441 Wolfe (at Ste-Catherine) ■ B&B & furnished apts in two 1873 homes ■ www.bbcanada.com/2058.html

12 ▶ **La Conciergerie Guest House** [★MO,N,NS] 514/289-9297 ■ 1019 rue St-Hubert (at Viger) ■ hot tub, gym & sundeck ■ www.laconciergerie.ca

13 **Crowne Plaza Metro Centre** [GF,SW,WC] 514/842-8581, 800/561-4644 ■ 505 rue Sherbrooke Est (at Berri) ■ breathtaking views, full brkfst, hot tub, also restaurant & full bar ■ www.crowneplaza-montreal.com

14 **Darling B&B** [M,GO] 514/524-2381 ■ 2540 Darling St #7 (at Hochelaga) ■ hot tub ■ canadiannational@yahoo.com

15 **Le Dortoir B&B** [M,GO] 514/597-2688 ■ 2042 rue de la Visitation (at Ontario) ■ shared baths ■ rubywell@sympatico.ca

16 **La Douillette** [WO] 514/376-2183 ■ 7235 rue de Lorimier (at Jean Talon) ■ full brkfst, homey & cozy

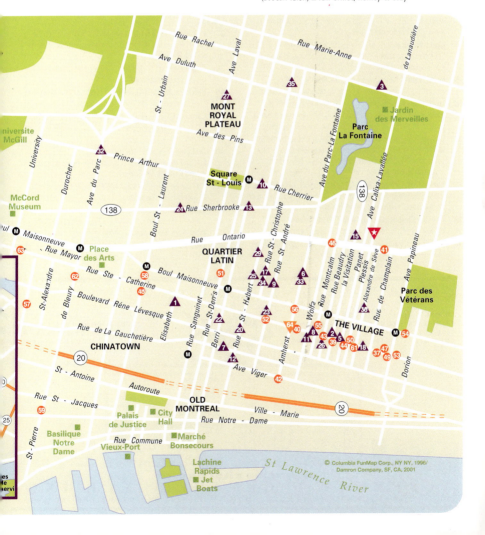

17 Ginger Bread House [MW,NS,GO] 514/597-2804 ■ 1628 St-Christophe (at Maisonneuve) ■ full brkfst, shared bath ■ www.gaylib.com/gingerbreadhouse

Hébergement Touristique du Plateau Mont-Royal [GF] 514/527-2394, 800/597-0597 ■ 1131 rue Rachel Est ■ reservation service ■ www.toujoursdimanche.com

Home Suite Hom [MW] 514/523-4642, 800/429-4983 ■ home exchange ■ www.gaytrip.com

18 Hotel Bourbon [★M] 514/523-4679, 800/268-4679 ■ 1574 rue Ste-Catherine Est (at Champlain) ■ also 'Bar Cajun' & popular 'La Track' disco, also 'Club Sandwich' 24hrs, also sauna, cybercafe, theater & more ■ www.bourbonmontreal.com

19 Hotel du Fort [GS,WC] 514/938-8333, 800/565-6333 ■ 1390 rue du Fort (at Ste-Catherine) ■ www.hoteldufort.com

20 Hotel Kent [GF] 514/845-9835 ■ 1216 rue St-Hubert (at Ste-Catherine)

22 Hotel Lord Berri [GF] 514/845-9236, 888/363-0363 ■ 1199 rue Berri (at Ste-Catherine) ■ also Italian restaurant ■ www.lordberri.com

23 Hotel Manoir des Alpes [GF] 514/845-9803, 800/465-2929 ■ 1245 rue St-André (at Ste-Catherine) ■ www.hotelmanoirdesalpes.qc.ca

24 Hotel Pierre [GF] 514/288-8519, 877/288-8577 ■ 169 Sherbrooke Est (btwn St-Denis & St-Laurent) ■ kitchen ■ www.pjca.com/hotelpierre

25 Hotel Visitel Network 514/529-0990 ■ 1617 rue St-Hubert (at Maisonneuve) ■ hotel & reservation service

26 Le Houseboy B&B [M,GO] 514/525-1459 ■ 1281 rue Beaudry (at Ste-Catherine Est) ■ full brkfst, shared baths, garden & patio, in the gay village ■ www.lehouseboy.com

27 Lindsey's B&B [★WO] 514/843-4869, 888/655-8655 ■ 3974 av Laval (nr Duluth) ■ charming townhouse close to Square St-Louis & rue Prince Arthur, full brkfst ■ www.lindseysmontreal.com

28 Loews Hotel Vogue [★GF] 514/285-5555, 800/465-6654 ■ 1425 rue de la Montagne (nr Ste-Catherine) ■ full-service 5-star hotel ■ www.loewshotels.com/voguehome.html

29 Maison Chablis [MO,F] 514/527-8346 ■ 1641 rue St-Hubert (at Maisonneuve) ■ some shared baths

30 Le Pension Vallières [WO,GO] 514/729-9552 ■ 6562 de Lorimier St (at Beaubien) ■ full brkfst

31 The Rainbow B&B/ L'Arc-en-ciel [MO,GO] 514/528-7501 ■ 3552 rue Ste-Catherine Est (at Joliette) ■ shared baths ■ www.bb-rainbow.qc.ca

32 Renaissance Montreal Hotel [GF,SW] 514/288-6666, 800/363-0735 ■ 3625 av Du Parc (at Prince Arthur) ■ www.renaissancehotels.com

33 Le Roy d'Carreau Guest House [MW,NS,GO] 514/524-2493 ■ 1637 rue Amherst (at Maisonneuve) ■ in Gay Village, hot tub ■ www.leroydcarreau.com

5 Ruta Bagage [GS] 514/598-1586 ■ 1345 rue Ste-Rose (at Panët) ■ Victorian B&B, full brkfst, shared baths ■ www.rutabagage.qc.ca

34 Le St-Christophe [MO,N] 514/527-7836 ■ 1597 St-Christophe (at Maisonneuve) ■ full brkfst, sundeck, hot tub ■ www.stchristophe.com

35 Le Traversin [GS,NS] 514/597-1546 ■ 4124 rue St-Hubert H2L 4A8 ■ full brkfst, some shared baths, hot tub ■ www.homeniscience.com/le_traversin

36 Turquoise B&B [M,GO] 514/523-9943, 877/707-1576 ■ 1576 rue Alexandre de Sève (at Maisonneuve) ■ Victorian B&B, shared baths ■ www.turquoisebb.com

Bars

37 L' Adonis [MO,S] 514/521-1355 ■ 1681 rue Ste-Catherine Est (at Papineau) ■ 3pm-3am, nude dancers, couples shows Th-Sun

38 Agora [M,NH,K] 514/934-1428 ■ 1160 Mackay (at Réné Lévesque) ■ 4pm-3am

39 Black Eagle Bar (Aigle Noir) [M,L] 514/529-0040 ■ 1315 Ste-Catherine Est (at Visitation) ■ 8am-4am, theme nights

40 Cabaret L'Entre Peau [★MW,S,WC] 514/525-7566 ■ 1115 Ste-Catherine Est (below 'Le Campus') ■ 1pm-3am, drag shows

40 Le Campus [M,S] 514/526-3616 ■ 1111 rue Ste-Catherine Est, 2nd flr (at Amherst) ■ 3pm-3am, nude dancers, couples shows Th-Sun

41 Citibar [GS,NH] 514/525-4251 ■ 1603 Ontario Est (at Champlain) ■ 11am-3am

42 Club Bolo [MW,D,CW,PC,$] 514/849-4777 ■ 960 rue Amherst (at Viger) ■ 8pm-1am Fri, 9pm-2am Sat, T-dance from 4pm Sun ■ www.clubbolo.com

43 Club Date [MW,NH,K,S] 514/521-1242 ■ 1218 rue Ste-Catherine Est (at Beaudry) ■ 8am-3am, singers

Montréal • Province of Québec

44 **Le Drugstore** [★MW,F] 514/524-1960 ■ 1366 rue Ste-Catherine Est (at Panêt) ■ 9am-3am, many bars & many flrs overlooking the Village's main drag ■ www.bourbonmontreal.com

45 **Foufounes Electriques** [GF,D,E] 514/844-5539 ■ 87 Ste-Catherine Est (at St-Laurent) ■ 3pm-3am, patio

46 **Fun Spot** [M,NH,D,TG,K,S] 514/522-0416 ■ 1151 rue Ontario Est (at Wolfe) ■ 11am-3am, poker machines, drag shows

47 **Météor** [MW,D,F,K,OC] 514/523-1481 ■ 1661 rue Ste-Catherine Est (at Champlain) ■ 11am-3am, '60s themed bar, ballroom dancing

48 **Le Mystique** [M,NH] 514/844-5711 ■ 1424 rue Stanley (at Maisonneuve) ■ 4pm-3am, English underground pub

39 **La Relaxe** [M,NH] 514/523-0578 ■ 1309 Ste-Catherine Est, 2nd flr ■ noon-3am, open to the street—as the name implies, a good place to relax & people-watch

49 **Rocky** [MO,V,OC] 514/521-7865 ■ 1673 rue Ste-Catherine Est (at Papineau) ■ 3pm-3am, ballroom & line dancing

50 **Sisters** [★WO,D,F] 514/522-4717 ■ 1333 rue Ste-Catherine Est, 2nd flr (at Panêt) ■ 6pm-3am Th-Sat, above 'Le Saloon Café,' men welcome on Tue

51 **Le St-Sulpice** [★GS,D,F] 514/844-9458 ■ 1680 rue St-Denis (at Ontario) ■ 11:30am-3am, cafe-bar, patio

52 **Stock Bar** [MO,S] 514/842-1336 ■ 1278 rue St-André (at Ste-Catherine) ■ 8pm-3am, clsd Mon-Tue, nude dancers

53 **Stud Bar** [M,B,L,K] 514/598-8243 ■ 1812 rue Ste-Catherine Est (at Papineau) ■ 10am-3am, karaoke Mon, DJ Tue, leather party Fri-Sat ■ www.studbar.com

54 **Taboo** [MO,S] 514/597-0010 ■ 1950 boul de Maisonneuve Est (at Dorion) ■ 7pm-3am, nude dancers

55 **Unity Pub** [MW,NH] 514/523-4429 ■ 1171 Ste-Catherine Est (below 'Unity Club') ■ terrace ■ www.unity-surf.com

56 **Vox Pub** [M,NH,V] 514/522-2766 ■ 1295 Amherst (at Ste-Catherine) ■ 11am-midnight, terrace, one of Montréal's oldest taverns

57 **West Side** [M,S] 514/866-4963 ■ 1071 Beaver Hall (at Belmont) ■ 4pm-3am, from 7pm wknds, nude dancers, ladies night Wed & Sat ■ www.westsidebar.com

Nightclubs

18 **Club Mississippi** [MW,D,TG,S] 514/521-1419 ■ 1584 rue Ste-Catherine Est (at 'Hotel Bourbon') ■ www.bourbonmontreal.com

Club Studio 54 [GF,D,$] 450/463-4553 ■ 8080 boul Taschereau, Brossard ■ Fri-Sat only

58 **Disco Cleo/ Chez Cleopatra** [M,D,TG,S] 514/871-8065 ■ 1230 boul St-Laurent (at Ste-Catherine) ■ 8pm-3am, drag shows

59 **Exotica** [MW,D,MR-L] 514/281-1773 ■ 417 rue St-Pierre (in Old Montreal) ■ 10pm-3am Th-Sun

Red Light [★GF,D] 450/967-3057 ■ 195 rue Notre-Dame de Fatima, Laval ■ wknds only, after-hours club

61 **Sky Club** [★MW,D,A,L,S] 514/529-6969 ■ 1474 rue Ste-Catherine Est ■ 10pm-3am, 'Sky Pub' on 1st flr, disco upstairs, T-dance Sun from 4pm, also 'Sky Jack' (leather bar) & the 'Suite' (drag shows)

62 **Sona** [GS,$] 514/282-1000 ■ 1439 rue Bleury (at Place des Arts, across from the Imperial Cinema) ■ wknds only, after-hours club ■ www.clubsona.com

63 **Stéréo** [MW] 514/282-3307 ■ 858 rue Ste-Catherine Est ■ after-hours, inquire locally

18 **La Track** [★M,D,L,S] 514/521-1419 ■ 1584 Ste-Catherine Est (at 'Hotel Bourbon') ■ 3pm-3am, 3 flrs w/ large back patio ■ www.bourbonmontreal.com

55 **Unity Club** [★MW,D,S,YC] 514/523-4429 ■ 1400 rue Montcalm (above 'Unity Pub') ■ Th-Sun, 4 flrs & great rooftoop terrace, more men Th for 'Boysnight,' more women Fri, T-dance Sun ■ www.unity-surf.com

Cafes

Café Titanic [★] 514/849-0894 ■ 445 St-Pierre (in Old Montréal) ■ 7am-5pm, clsd wknds, salads & soups

The Second Cup [NS] 514/285-4468 ■ 1351 Ste-Catherine Est ■ coffee shop

Restaurants

L' Ambiance (Salon de thé) 514/939-2609 ■ 1874 Notre-Dame Ouest (at des Seigneurs) ■ 11am-4pm Mon-Fri, dinner for large groups only, by reservation

L' Anecdote l [MW] 514/526-7967 ■ 801 rue Rachel Est (at St-Hubert) ■ 8am-10pm, burgers, plenty veggie; also 3751 av des Pins et St-Urbain, 514/282-0972 (more women at this location)

Après le Jour [MW] 514/527-4141 ■ 901 rue Rachel Est (at St-Andre) ■ dinner only, from 4pm Sun, Italian/ French, seafood

Looking for more of the globe?

Check out *Damron Online*

- user-friendly searchable database w/ more than 10,000 listings
- listings for Australia, Asia, Eastern Europe, Africa & European destinations like Italy & Greece
- updated monthly
- more categories: info lines, websites, travel agents & cruisy areas

But wait! There's more...
- a calendar of events
- worldwide lgbt+ tours
- travel links
- online bookstore

http://www.damron.com

Montréal • Province of Québec

L' Armoricain 514/523-2551 ■ 1550 Fullum (at Maisonneuve) ■ lunch & dinner
Aubergell.com 514/597-0878 ■ 1641 rue Amherst ■ 7am-10pm, from 5pm wknds, bistro, full bar ■ www.aubergell.com
Bacci 514/844-3929 ■ 4205 rue St-Denis (at Rachel) ■ 11am-3am, full bar
Bato Thai [★MW,BW] 514/524-6705 ■ 1310 rue Ste-Catherine Est ■ lunch & dinner
Bazou 514/982-0853 ■ 2004 Hôtel de Ville (at Ontario) ■ 5pm-11pm, Californian
La Campagnola [★BW] 514/866-3234 ■ 1229 rue de la Montagne (at Ste-Catherine) ■ 11am-1am, Italian, some veggie, great eggplant!
Chablis 514/523-0053 ■ 1639 rue St-Hubert (at Maisonneuve) ■ 11am-11pm, from 5pm wknds, Spanish/ French, terrace, full bar ■ www.restaurant-chablis.com
Le Christopher [★] 514/527-5666 ■ 1800 rue Ste-Catherine Est (at Papineau) ■ 11am-10pm, till 11pm Th-Fri, from 9am wknds
Chuchai 514/843-4194 ■ 4088 rue St-Denis (at Rachel) ■ lunch & dinner, veggie-only Thai, full bar
Commensal 514/845-2627 ■ 1720 St-Denis ■ open till 10pm, vegetarian
Da Salossi [BW,WC] 514/843-8995 ■ 3441 St-Denis (at Sherbrooke) ■ lunch & dinner, dinner only Sat, lunch only Mon, Italian, some veggie
L' Exception 514/282-1282 ■ 1200 rue St-Hubert (at Réné-Lévesque) ■ burgers & sandwiches, plenty veggie, terrace
L' Express [★] 514/845-5333 ■ 3927 rue St-Denis (at Duluth) ■ 8am-2am, 1pm-10pm Sun, French bistro & bar, great pâté
La Paryse [MW] 514/842-2040 ■ 302 rue Ontario Est (nr Sanguinet) ■ 11am-11pm (from 2pm in July), 50s-style diner
Piccolo Diavolo [★] 514/526-1336 ■ 1336 rue Ste-Catherine Est (at Panêt) ■ 5pm-2am, lunch Tue & Fri, Italian, charming waiters
Le Planète [YC,BW] 514/528-6953 ■ 1451 rue Ste-Catherine Est ■ lunch & dinner, brunch only Sun, global cuisine
Le Queen 514/526-6011 ■ 1329 rue Ste-Catherine Est (at Panêt) ■ noon-midnight, live shows Sat
Le Saloon Café [★] 514/522-1333 ■ 1333 rue Ste-Catherine Est (at Panêt) ■ 11am-midnight, till 2am Fri-Sat, int'l cuisine, big dishes & even bigger drinks; 'Sisters' upstairs
Thai Grill 514/270-5566 ■ 5101 boul St-Laurent

Entertainment & Recreation
Ça Roule 514/866-0633 ■ 27 rue de la Commune Est ■ in case you want to join all the other beautiful & buffed ones inline skating up & down Ste-Catherine
Cinéma du Parc 514/281-1900 ■ 3575 Parc (btwn Milton & Prince Arthur) ■ repertory film theater
Prince Arthur Est at boul St-Laurent, not far from Sherbrooke Métro station ■ closed-off street w/ tons of outdoor restaurants & cafés—it's touristy but oh-so-European

Bookstores
64 **L' Androgyne** [★WC] 514/842-4765 ■ 1436 Amherst (at Ste-Catherine) ■ 9am-6pm, till 9pm Th-Fri, 10am-5pm Sun, lgbt bookstore w/ English & French titles ■ info@androgyne.ca

Retail Shops
Priape [★] 514 /521-8451 ■ 1311 Ste-Catherine Est (at Visitation) ■ 10am-9pm, noon-9pm Sun, clubwear, leather, books, toys & more ■ www.priape.com
Screaming Eagle 514/849-2843 ■ 1424 boul St-Laurent ■ leather shop

Publications
Fugues 514/848-1854 ■ glossy lgbt bar/ entertainment guide ■ www.fugues.com
Rainbow Choices Directory 416/762-1320, 888/241-3569 (Canada only) ■ lgbt entertainment & business directory for Canada ■ www.interlog.com/~rnbchoic
RG 514/523-9463 ■ monthly newsmagazine ■ rgmag@colba.net

Gyms & Health Clubs
Body Tech [★] 514/849-7000 ■ 1010 Ste-Catherine Est (at Amherst)
Physotech [MW] 514/527-7587 ■ 1657 rue Amherst (nr Maisonneuve)

Men's Clubs
5018 Sauna [V] 514/277-3555 ■ 5018 boul St-Laurent (at St-Joseph) ■ 24hrs, hot tub ■ www.le5018.com
Aux Berges 514/938-9393 ■ 1070 rue Mackay (at 'Auberge du Centre-Ville') ■ also hotel
The Bronx [★L,E,V,PC] 514/525-8404 ■ 1166 Ste-Catherine Est ■ 24hrs, hot tub, specials for leather crowd, also 'Millennium' ■ www.thebestspa.com
Colonial Bath 514/285-0132 ■ 3963 av Colonial (at Napoléon) ■ 1pm-6am, 24hrs Sun
L' Oasis [★V,PC] 514/521-0785 ■ 1390 Ste-Catherine Est ■ 24hrs, jacuzzi ■ www.thebestspa.com/oasiseng.html
Sauna 456 [★SW,PC] 514/871-8341 ■ 456 rue de la Gauchetière Ouest (at Metro Sq) ■ 24hrs, 3 flrs, hot tub, also gym ■ www.le456.ca
Sauna Centre-Ville 514/524-3486 ■ 1465 rue Ste-Catherine Est (at Plessis) ■ 24hrs
Sauna du Plateau 514/528-1679 ■ 961 rue Rachel Est (at Boyer) ■ 24hrs ■ www.saunaduplateau.com
Sauna St-Hubert [V] 514/277-0176 ■ 6527 rue St-Hubert (at Beaubien) ■ 24hrs Th-Sun

Erotica
La Capoterie 514/845-0027 ■ 2061 St-Denis ■ condoms
Il Bolero 514/270-6065 ■ 6842-46 St-Hubert (btwn St-Zotique & Bélanger) ■ fetish & clubwear emporium, ask about monthly fetish party ■ www.ilbolero.com
Wega Cinema 514/987-5993, 800/361-9929 ■ 930 Ste-Catherine Est (at St-Timothy) ■ www.wegavideo.com

Québec

Accommodations

1 **727 Guest House** [MW] 418/648-6766, 800/652-6766 ■ 727 rue d'Aiguillon (btwn St-Augustin & côte Ste-Geneviève)
 Apts & Studios Ste-Angèle [GF] 418/648-1000 ■ 30 rue Ste-Angèle ■ actour@gbc.clic.net
2 **L' Auberge du Quartier** [GF] 418/525-9726, 800/782-9441 (in Québec only) ■ 170 Grande Allée Ouest (at av Cartier) ■ buffet brkfst ■ www.quebecweb.com/ADQ/
3 **Le Coureur des Bois Guest House** [MW,GO] 418/692-1117, 800/269-6414 ■ 15 rue Ste-Ursule (at St-Jean, in Old Québec) ■ also apts, shared baths ■ lecoureurdesbois@gayquebec.net
4 **Le Gîte de la Jeunesse** [GF] 418/648-9497 ■ 772 côte Ste-Geneviève (nr St-Jean)
5 **Hôtel Dominion 1912** [GF] 418/692-2224, 888/833-5253 ■ 126 rue St-Pierre ■ boutique hotel in city's 1st skyscraper ■ www.hoteldominion.com
6 **Loews Le Concorde** [GF,SW] 418/647-2222, 800/463-5256 ■ 1225 cour du Général-De Montcalm ■ 4-stars, located on Grand Allée, w/ revolving restaurant
 La Lucarne Enchantée [GF,SW] 418/829-3792 ■ 225 Chemin Royal, St Jean-De-L'Ile d'Orléans ■ full brkfst, nr beach, animals on premises, lesbian-owned/ run

Bars

7 **L' Amour Sorcier** [★MW,NH,F,V] 418/523-3395 ■ 789 côte Ste-Geneviève (at St-Jean) ■ 2pm-3am, cafe-bar, terrace
8 **Bar 321** [M,TG,S] 418/525-5107 ■ 321 de la Couronne (at La Salle) ■ 8am-3am
9 **Bar 889** [MW,NH,S] 418/524-5000 ■ 889 côte Ste-Geneviève ■ 8am-3am, patio
10 **Bar de la Couronne** [★M,S] 418/525-6593 ■ 310 rue de la Couronne (btwn rues de la Reine & de la Salle) ■ 8pm-3am, nude dancers, men only Th-Sat
 Bar L' Eveil [W,NH] 418/628-0610 ■ 670 rue Bouvier #118 ■ 3pm-close, from 8pm Sat, clsd Mon-Wed, patio
4 **Bar Mâle** [M,CW,LV] 418/648-9497 ■ 770 côte Ste-Geneviève (at d'Aiguillon) ■ 3pm-close Th-Sat, cruisy, theme nights
11 **Paradisio Café-Bar** [W,NH] 418/522-6014 ■ 161 rue St-Jean (at Turnbull) ■ 2pm-midnight, clsd Mon
12 **Pub La Malette** [MW] 418/523-8279 ■ 698 rue D'Aiguillon ■ 3pm-3am
13 **Taverne Le Drague** [★M,NH,D,F,S,BW,WC] 418/649-7212 ■ 815 rue St-Augustin (at St-Joachim) ■ 8am-3am, DJ Fri-Sun, drag shows, terrace ■ www.ledrague.com

Restaurants

Le Commensal 418/647-3733 ■ 860 rue St-Jean ■ 11am-10pm, vegetarian/ vegan
Le Hobbit 418/647-2677 ■ 700 rue St-Jean (at Ste-Geneviève) ■ 8am-close, some veggie
La Playa [GO] 418/522-3989 ■ 780 rue St-Jean (at St-Augustin) ■ lunch Th-Fri, dinner nightly, 'West Coast cuisine,' martini bar, heated terrace
Poisson d'Avril 418/692-1010 ■ 115 rue St-André (at St-Paul) ■ lunch & dinner, name is French for 'April Fools'
Restaurant Diana [★] 418/524-5794 ■ 849 rue St-Jean (at St-Augustine) ■ 8am-1am, till 2am Fri-Sat, Italian/ Greek
Zorba Grec [BYOB,WC] 418/525-5509 ■ 854 rue St-Jean (near Dufferin) ■ 24hrs, Canadian, Greek & Italian

Entertainment & Recreation

Le Château Frontenac [GF,SW] 418/692-3861, 800/441-1414 ■ 1 rue des Carrières ■ this hotel disguised as a castle remains the symbol of Québec—even if you can't afford the princess' ransom to stay the night, you can come & enjoy the view from outside ■ www.chateaufrontenac.com
Ice Hotel [GF] 418/661-4522, 877/505-0423 ■ Jan-March only—check it out before it melts away, 9 km E of Québec City in Montmorency Falls Park
■ www.icehotel-canada.com

Men's Clubs

Bloc 225 [PC] 418/523-2562, 877/523-2562 ■ 225 St-Jean (at Turnbull) ■ 24hrs, also 'Capital Gym'
Sauna Backboys [V] 418/521-6686, 877/523-6686 ■ 264 rue de la Couronne (at Prince Edward) ■ 24hrs during week ■ www.backboy.qc.ca
Le Sauna Hippocampe [★V,PC] 418/692-1521, 888/388-1521 ■ 31 rue McMahon ■ 24hrs, bar
■ www.clubsauna.com

QUÉBEC

The old quarter of Québec City was declared a world heritage site in 1985—and no wonder! With its colorful narrow streets and glorious architecture, it's easy to forget you're in North America.

Queer Resources

Community Info
▼ **Relais d'espérance** 418/522-3301 (info in French). 617 rue Montmartre. Gay center & coffeehouse.

AIDS Resources
Le Reseau (CATIE) 800/263-1638.

City Calendar

LGBT Pride
September. 418/836-6066.

Annual Events
January/February - Carnaval (Winter Celebration) 418/626-3716, web: www.carnaval.qc.ca.
March - Ski Out.
July - Summer Festival.

Tourist Info

Airport Directions
Québec City Aéroport. To get downtown, follow Boulevard Aéroport to Hwy Charest 440 East. Take Hwy Charest 440 East to downtown.

Public Transit & Taxis
Taxi Québec 418/525-8123.
Autobus La Quebecoise 888/872-5525, web: www.autobus.qc.ca
CTCUQ (bus service) 418/627-2511.

Tourist Spots & Info
Change of Guards at the Citadel.
Chateau Frontenac 418/692-3861.
Grand Allée.
Hôtel du Parlement.
Notre-Dame-de-Québec Basilica.
Old Québec.
Quartier du Petit-Champlain.
Visitor's Center: 800/363-7777, web: www.tourisme.gouv.qc.ca.

Québec • Province of Québec

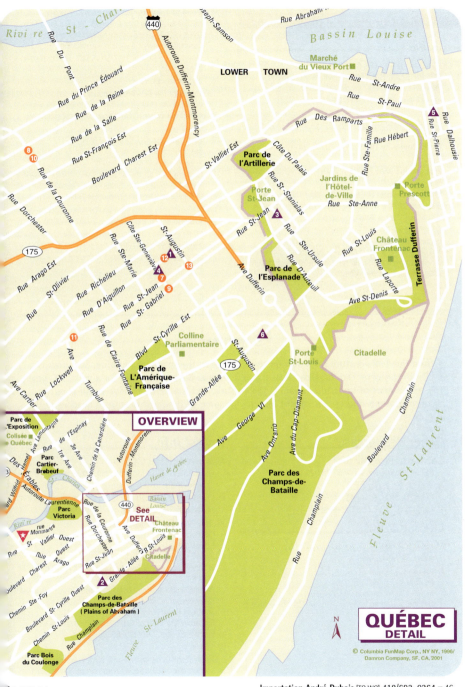

EROTICA

Empire Lyon 418/648-2301 ■ 873 rue St-Jean (at St-Augustin) ■ videos, toys, books, clothing, leather, perfumes, jewelry, gay paintings ■ gayvideocollection.com

Importation André Dubois [TG,WC] 418/692-0264 ■ 46 côte de la Montagne (at Frontenac Castle)

Importation Delta 418/647-6808, 877/647-6808 ■ 875 rue St-Jean ■ videos, magazines, books & more

PUERTO RICO

San Juan

ACCOMMODATIONS
1. **Atlantic Beach Hotel** [★MW,F,SW] 787/721-6900, 888/611-6900 ■ Calle Vendig 1, Condado (off Av Ashford) ■ rooftop deck w/ hot tub, some shared baths ■ www.atlanticbeachhotel.net
2. **Casa del Caribe Guest House** [GF] 787/722-7139 ■ Calle Caribe 57, Condado
3. **Casita Bonita By The Sea** [MW] 787/728-1241 ■ Calle Histella 3
4. **Condado Inn** [MW] 787/724-7145 ■ Av Condado 6 (at Av Ashford) ■ also bar
5. **El San Juan Hotel & Casino** [GF,F,SW] 787/791-1000, 800/468-2818 ■ Av Isla Verde 6063 (at Baldorioty de Castro), Isla Verde ■ Asian restaurant & cigar bar ■ www.wyndham.com/ElSanJuanResort/default.cfm
6. **Embassy Guest House** [GS,SW] 787/725-8284, 787/724-7440 ■ Calle Seaview 1126, Condado (off Calle Vendig) ■ across the street from beach, also bar & grill ■ home.att.net/~embassyguesthouse/
7. **Hotel El Convento** [★GF,SW] 787/723-9020, 800/468-2779 ■ Calle Cristo 100, Old San Juan (btwn Caleta de las Monjas & Calle Sol) ■ 17th-century former Carmelite convent ■ www.elconvento.com
8. **Hotel Iberia** [GS,GO] 787/722-5380, 787/723-0200 ■ Av Wilson 1464, Condado (btwn Avs de Diego & Washington) ■ also restaurant & bar
9. **L' Habitation Beach Guesthouse** [MW,GO] 787/727-2499 ■ Calle Italia 1957, Ocean Park (nr Santa Ana) ■ also restaurant & bar ■ www.freeyellow.com/members5/guesthouse/
10. **Marriott Resort & Casino** [GF,F,SW] 787/722-7000, 800/223-6388 ■ Av Ashford 1309 (at Av Condado) ■ www.marriothotels.com/SJUPR
11. **Numero Uno on the Beach** [GS,SW,WC] 787/726-5010, 787/727-9687 ■ Calle Santa Ana 1, Ocean Park (nr Calle Italia) ■ also 'Pamela's' restaurant & bar

BARS
1. **Atlantic Beach Bar** [★MW,F,S] 787/721-6900 ■ Calle Vendig 1 (at 'Atlantic Beach Hotel') ■ 11am-1am, T-dance Sun w/ strippers & show ■ www.atlanticbeachhotel.com
12. **Baccheus** [W,NH] Calle Parque 609, Local LM-9, Santurce ■ Th-Sun

SAN JUAN

From the 16th-century forts that grace its shores to the sparkling nightlife, San Juan is a Caribbean gem. Old San Juan lives up to its name: it's been around for almost 500 years. The resort areas of Condado, Miramar, Ocean Park, and Isla Verde provide world-class accommodations and entertainment along with some of the most delightful beaches in the Caribbean.

Queer Resources

COMMUNITY INFO
GEMA Hotline (en español) 787/723-4538.

AIDS RESOURCES
CONCRA 787/753-9443.
Fundacion SIDA 787/782-8888.

City Calendar

LGBT PRIDE
June. 787/261-2590.

ANNUAL EVENTS
February - Ponce Carnival.
June - Casals Festival 787/728-5744.
October - Bomba y Plena (African-Caribbean music festival).

Tourist Info

AIRPORT DIRECTIONS
Luis Muñoz Marin International. Take Hwy. 26 or 37 west to Condado.

PUBLIC TRANSIT & TAXIS
Metro Bus 787/763-4141.

TOURIST SPOTS & INFO
Condado Beach.
La Fortaleza.
Historic Old San Juan.
El Morro Fortress & Fort San Cristobal 787/729-6960.
Pablo Casals Museum 787/723-9185.
Quincentennial Plaza.
San José Church.
San Juan Museum of Art & History 787/724-1875.
Visitor's Center: 800/223-6530.

WEATHER
Tropical sunshine year-round, with temperatures that average in the mid-80°s from November to May. Expect more rain on the northern coast.

BEST VIEWS
From El Morro or alternatively, one of the harbor cruises that depart from Pier 2 in Old San Juan.

San Juan • Puerto Rico

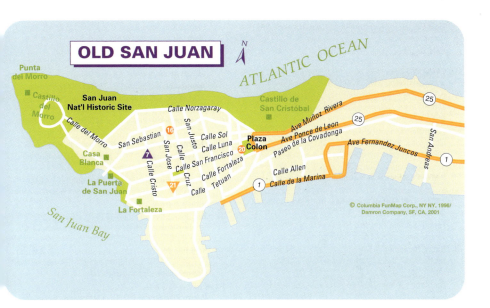

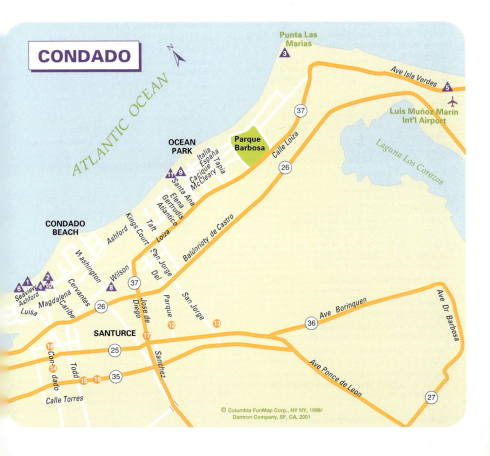

PUERTO RICO • CARIBBEAN

Bebo's Playa [MW,NH,D,S,V] Piñones, Isla Verde ■ noon-close Wed-Sun, beachfront, fun crowd, strippers Wed, drag shows Sun

7 **Café Bohemio** [GF,P] 787/723-9200 ■ Calle Cristo 100, Old San Juan (in 'Gran Hotel El Convento') ■ 11am-2am, popular Tue, also restaurant, food till 11pm ■ www.elconvento.com

13 **Cups** [W] 787/268-3570, 787/268-5640 ■ Calle San Mateo 1708, Santurce (btwn Calles Barbe & San Jorge) ■ 7pm-close, clsd Mon-Tue

4 **Downstairs Lounge** [M] 787/724-7145 ■ Av Condado 6 (at 'Condado Inn') ■ noon-4am, nr beach

14 **Junior's** [MW,NH,S] 787/723-9477 ■ Calle Condado 602, Santurce (btwn Calle Benito Alonso & Av Ponce de León) ■ 5:30pm-6:30am, drag & strip shows, local crowd

15 **Nuestro Ambiente** [W] 787/724-9093 ■ Av Ponce de León 1412, Santurce (across from Central High School) ■ 8pm-close, live music wknds

Paraiso del Mar [MW,NH,D,F,S] Carretera 187, Piñones, Isla Verde ■ 2pm-close Fri-Sun, beachfront dance bar

16 **Rivera Hermanos** [GF] 787/724-5828 ■ Calle San Sebastián 157, Old San Juan ■ 10am-7pm, clsd Sun, liquor shop & bar

17 **Tia Maria's** [★MW] 787/724-4011 ■ Av Jose de Diego 326, Stop 22, Santurce (at Ponce de León) ■ 10am-midnight, till 1am Th-Sun, liquor shop & bar

NIGHTCLUBS

18 **Bachelor** [M,D,S] ■ Av Condado 112, Santurce (behind Egypto) ■ 10pm-close, clsd Mon-Tue, drag & strip shows, theme nights, rooftop garden, nightly buffet, unconfirmed

Concepts (The Downtown Club) [MW,D,E] 787/763-7432 ■ Av Chardón 9 (in 'Le Chateau'), Hato Rey ■ Sun only, popular drag shows

19 **Eros** [★MW,D,S,V,GO] 787/722-1131 ■ Av Ponce de León 1257, Santurce (btwn Calles Villamil & Labra) ■ 10pm-5am, from 9pm Sun, clsd Mon-Tue, theme nights ■ www.erostheclub.com

Laguna Club [★M,D,S] Calle Barranquitas 53, Condado (btwn Calle Mayagüez & Av Ashford) ■ 11pm-late, strippers

Paraiso [MW,D] Av Eleanor Roosevelt (across from TeleVideo), Hato Rey ■ wknds only

CAFES

20 **Café Berlin** [★] 787/722-5205 ■ Calle San Francisco 407, Plaza Colón, Old San Juan (btwn Calles Norzagary & O'Donnel) ■ 9am-11pm, plenty veggie

RESTAURANTS

Al Dente 787/723-7303 ■ Calle Recinto S, Old San Juan ■ lunch & dinner, Italian

La Bombonera [★] 787/722-0658 ■ Calle San Francisco 259, Old San Juan ■ 7:30am-8pm, come for the strong coffee & pastries, since 1903!

Café Amadeus [★GO] 787/722-8635 ■ Calle San Sebastián 104, Old San Juan (btwn Calles San José & del Cristo) ■ lunch & dinner, bar noon-midnight Tue-Sat

Fussion 787/721-7997 ■ Calle Fortaleza 317, Old San Juan ■ lunch & dinner, Sun brunch, French/ Latin, also bar

The Gallery Cafe [E] 787/725-8676 ■ Calle Fortaleza 305, Old San Juan ■ lunch Mon-Fri, dinner Tue-Sat, also swanky & hip 'Gallery Lounge' upstairs ■ www.gallerycafe.net

Golden Unicorn 787/728-4066 ■ Calle Laurel 2415 ■ 11am-11pm, Chinese

The Parrot Club [E] 787/725-7370 ■ Calle Fortaleza 363, Old San Juan (btwn Plaza Colón & Callejón de la Capilla) ■ lunch & dinner, chic Nuevo Latino bistro & bar, live music Tue, Th & Sat

Sam's Patio 787/723-1149 ■ Calle San Sebastián 102, Old San Juan ■ lunch & dinner, Mexican

Transylvania Restaurant [E] 787/977-2328 ■ Recinto Sur 317, Old San Juan ■ lunch Tue-Sat & dinner nightly, Romanian, also bar & gallery, live music

Villa Appia 787/725-8711 ■ Av Ashford 1350, Condado ■ 11am-11pm, Italian

ENTERTAINMENT & RECREATION

Animation Cruises [MW,D] 787/725-3500 ■ gay cruises Th eves, call for reservations

Condado Bicycle 787/722-6288, 888/721-0066 ■ Av Ashford 1106 ■ tours & rentals ■ condadob@coqui.net

BOOKSTORES

21 **The Book Store** 787/724-1815 ■ Calle San José 255, Old San Juan (btwn Calles Tetuán & Fortaleza) ■ 9am-7pm, Spanish & English titles, lgbt section, also cafe

Scriptum 787/724-1123 ■ Av Ashford 1129-B, Condado (at Calle Vendig) ■ Spanish & English titles, lgbt section, also newspapers & magazines, cafe

PUBLICATIONS

Puerto Rico Breeze 787/724-3411 ■ lgbt newspaper ■ tkoontz@pr-plaza.net

GYMS & HEALTH CLUBS

Muscle Factory [GS] 787/721-0717 ■ Av Ashford 1302, Condado (btwn Avs Cervantes & Caribe) ■ 6am-10pm

MEN'S CLUBS

Steamworks [V,PC] 787/725-4993 ■ Calle Luna 205, 2nd flr, Old San Juan (btwn Calle San Justo & Calle de la Cruz, ring to enter) ■ 24hrs, sauna & spa ■ www.steamworksOnLine.com

EROTICA

Condom World 787/722-5348 ■ Calle San Francisco 353, Old San Juan (btwn Calles O'Donnel & Tamarindo) ■ condoms, toys, videos & more—13 locations in Puerto Rico

Pleasure Paradise 787/706-0855 ■ Av Roosevelt 1367 (in Plazoleta Julio Garriga) ■ www.pleasureparadise.net

London

London is an amalgam of the most staid and traditional elements of English society and the most innovative in youth culture. Visitors can easily spend several weeks on only the best known tourist attractions and still miss the spirit of London. Like New York, London is really a collection of smaller towns and neighborhoods, each with a distinct feel.

Queer Resources

Community Info
London Lesbian & Gay Switchboard
 44-207/837.73.24, web: www.lgs.org.uk.
London Lesbian Line 44-207/251.69.11.

AIDS Resources
National AIDS Helpline 0800/56.71.23.
London helpline 44-207/242.10.10.

Recovery
44-207/837.33.37.

City Calendar

LGBT Pride
July. web: www.pridelondon.org.

Annual Events
March/April - Lesbian & Gay Film Festival
 44-020/7928-3232, web: www.bfi.org.uk.
May - Soho Pink Weekend.
 Mr Gay UK Contest.
June - Mardi Gras 44-020/7494-2225.
August - Summer Rites 44-020/7737-2629.
October - Stonewall Equality Show 44-020/7336-8860. Huge charity concert.

Tourist Info

Airport Directions
London has 4 airports: Heathrow, Gatwick, Stansted & London City. All are well connected to Central London by rail and bus; Heathrow's Terminal 4 has its own Underground station (Piccadilly line).

Public Transit & Taxis
Freedom Cars 44-020/7734-1313.
Ladycabs 44-020/7254-3501.
London Travel Information (Tube & buses)
 44-020/7222-1234, 24hr info.

Tourist Spots & Info
British Museum 44-020/7323-8000.
Buckingham Palace 44-020/7839-1377.
Globe Theatre 44-020/7401-9919.
Kensington Palace 44-020/7937-9561.
Madame Tussaud's 44-020/7935-6861.
National Gallery 44-020/7839-3321.
Oscar Wilde's house (34 Tite Street).
St Paul's Cathedral 44-020/7236-4128.
Tate Gallery 44-020/7887-8000.
Tower of London 44-020/7680-9004.
Westminster Abbey 44-020/7222-5152.
Visitor's Center: 44-020/7824-8844, web: www.LondonTown.com.

Weather
London is warmer and less rainy than you may have heard. Summer temperatures reach the 70°s and the average annual rainfall is about half of that of Atlanta, GA or Hartford, CT.

Best Views
From Tower Bridge (Tower Hill Tube).

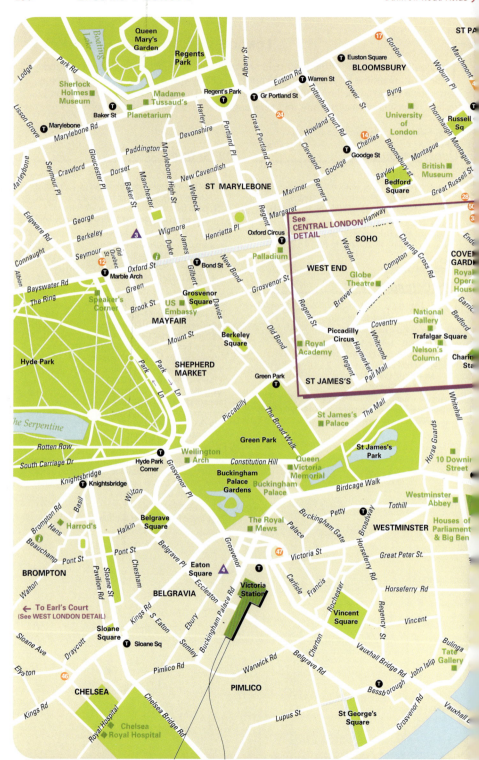

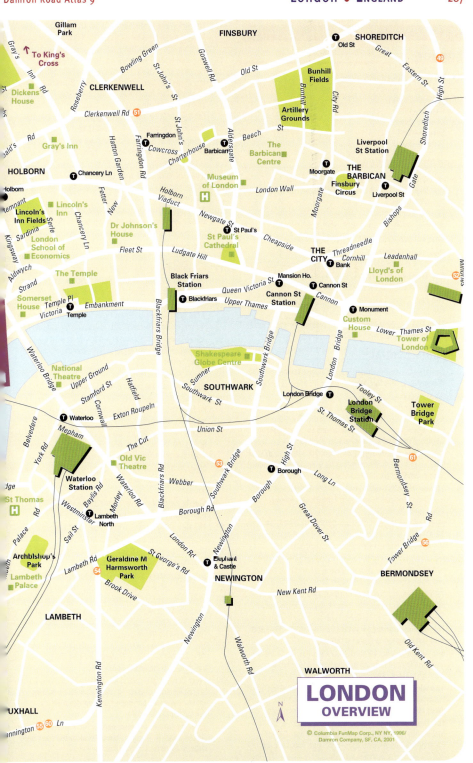

ENGLAND

London

London is divided into 6 regions:
London—Overview
London—Central
London—West
London—North
London—East
London—South

London—Overview

ENTERTAINMENT & RECREATION
Gay Sweatshop Limited 44-020/7242-1168 ■ gay theater troupe

PUBLICATIONS
Attitude 44-020/7308-5290 ■ attitude@norshell.co.uk
Boyz 44-020/7296-6000 ■ free weekly scene guide
Diva 44-020/7482-2576 ■ monthly glossy lesbian magazine ■ www.gaytimes.co.uk
Gay Times 44-020/7482-2576, 44-020/7267-0421 ■ gay glossy ■ www.gaytimes.co.uk
The Pink Paper 44-020/7296-6000 ■ free lgbt newspaper ■ editorial@pinkpaper.co.uk
Time Out 44-020/7813-3000 ■ weekly city scene guide w/ gay section ■ www.timeout.com

London—Central

London—Central includes Soho, Covent Garden, Bloomsbury, Mayfair, Westminster, Pimlico & Belgravia

ACCOMMODATIONS
1 **Central London Guestrooms & Apartments** [MW,NS,GO] 44-020/7497-7000 ■ Tottenham Court Rd (at Charing Cross Rd) ■ superior accommodations in Soho, Covent Garden, West End ■ www.go.to/londonapts
2 **Clone Zone Luxury Apts** [MW] 44-020/7287-3530 ■ 64 Old Compton St (at Whitcomb) ■ fully equipped apt above 'Clone Zone' retail store ■ www.clonezone.co.uk
3 **Manors & Co** [GF] 44-020/7486-5982, 800/454-4385 ■ 1 Baker St ■ luxury apts in the heart on London ■ www.manors.co.uk
4 **Noel Coward Hotel** [GF,SW] 44-020/7730-2094, 44-020/7730-9005 ■ 111 Ebury St (off Eccleston St, Belgravia) ■ some shared baths ■ www.noelcowardhotel.com

BARS
■ Note: 'Pub hours' usually means 11am-11pm Mon-Sat and noon-3pm & 7pm-10:30pm Sun
5 **79 CXR** [★M,WC] 44-020/7734-0769 ■ 79 Charing Cross Rd (Soho) ■ 1pm-2am, till 3am Fri-Sat, pub hrs Sun, 2 flrs, cruisy
6 **The Admiral Duncan** [★MW,NH,TG] 44-020/7437-5300 ■ 54 Old Compton St (Soho) ■ pub hrs
7 **Bar Aquda** [★MW] 44-020/7577-9891 ■ 13-14 Maiden Ln (btwn Bedford & Southampton, Covent Garden) ■ midnight-11pm, 3pm-10:30pm Sun, cafe-bar
8 **Barcode** [M,F,V] 44-020/7734-3342 ■ 3-4 Archer St (btwn Windmill & Rupert, off Shaftesbury, Soho) ■ pub hrs, karaoke Wed; also Earl's Court location (181 Finborough Rd)
9 **The Box** [★MW,D,F,V,WC] 44-020/7240-5828 ■ 32-34 Monmouth St, Seven Dials (nr Shaftesbury Ave, Covent Garden) ■ 5:30pm-3am, 3pm-midnight Sun, cafe-bar
10 **The Brief Encounter** [★MO,D] 44-020/7557-9851 ■ 42 St Martin's Ln (off Charing Cross, nr National Gallery, Covent Garden) ■ pub hrs, cruise bar
11 **The Candy Bar** [★W,D,F,S] 44-020/7437-1977 ■ 23-24 Bateman St (at Greek, in Soho) ■ 5pm-1am, till 3am Wed-Fri, 3pm-3am Sat, till midnight Sun, 2 flrs, men welcome as guests, call for events, outdoor seating
12 **The City of Quebec** [M,NH,B,OC] 44-020/7629-6159 ■ 12 Old Quebec St (at Marble Arch) ■ pub hrs, live DJs Th-Sun, 'Chubs & Chasers' Sun ■ quebec@all-man.com
13 **Compton's of Soho** [★M,L,F,WC] 44-020/7479-7961 ■ 53 Old Compton St ■ noon-11pm, 7pm-10:30pm Sun
14 **Drill Hall Theater & Bar** [GS,S,WC] 44-020/7637-8270, 44-020/7631-5107 ■ 16 Chenies St (btwn Alfred Pl & Ridgmount, Bloomsbury) ■ 5pm-11pm, women only Mon, also vegetarian restaurant
15 **The Edge** [★MW,D,WC] 44-020/7439-1313 ■ 11 Soho Sq ■ midnight-late, noon-10:30pm Sun, 4 flrs, cafe-bar, live music, outdoor seating ■ www.edgesoho.com
16 **The Escape** [★M,D,V] 44-020/7734-2626 ■ 10 Brewer St (nr Regent St) ■ 11am-3am, noon-11:30pm Sun
17 **Glass Bar** [WO,PC] 44-020/7387-6184 ■ West Lodge, 190 Euston Rd ■ 5:30pm-close, from 7:30pm Mon, from 6:30pm Sat, clsd Sun, 2 flrs, theme nights & events
18 **Halfway 2 Heaven** [★MO,B,L,MR,F,K,GO] 44-020/7321-2791 ■ 7 Duncannon St (at Charing Cross, West End) ■ pub hrs, cruise bar, theme nights ■ www.halfway2heaven.co.uk
19 **Jonathan's** [M,E,PC] 44-020/7930-4770 ■ 16 Irving St (off Charing Cross, above restaurant) ■ 3pm-11pm, pub hrs Sun, theater bar
20 **King's Arms** [MW,NH,B,K,F,V] 44-020/7734-5907 ■ 23 Poland St (Soho) ■ pub hrs, bears 8pm Fri
21 **Ku Bar** [MW,YC] 44-020/7437-4303 ■ 75 Charing Cross Rd (at Shaftesbury, Soho) ■ pub hrs, trendy cafe-bar ■ www.ku-bar.co.uk
22 **Kudos** [★MW,P,F,WC,GO] 44-020/7379-4573 ■ 10 Adelaide St (off the Strand) ■ pub hrs, trendy cafe-bar, basement video bar open from 4pm ■ www.kudos-bar.co.uk
23 **Loose** [WO,S] 30 Dean St (at 'Sunset Strip') ■ 9pm-1am Tue only, strippers/ dancers perform for women-only audience
24 **Matrix** [M,D,F] 44-020/7637-5352 ■ 125 Cleveland St ■ 5pm-11pm Mon-Fri, clsd wknds
25 **The Retro Bar** [MW,NH,D,K] 44-020/7839-4012 ■ 2 George Ct (off the Strand) ■ pub hrs
26 **Rupert Street Cafe-Bar** [MW,F,WC] 44-020/7734-5614 ■ 50 Rupert St (off Brewer) ■ pub hrs
27 **Soho's Strippers** [M,S] 44-020/7734-1593 ■ 7-12 Walkers Ct (off Brewer St) ■ Sun only, strippers
28 **Vespa Lounge** [WO,E,PC] 44-020/7836-8956 ■ Centre Point House, St Giles High St (upstairs, across the way from 'First Out') ■ 6pm-11pm, till 10:30pm Sun, theme nights, comedy last Sun ($)
29 **The Village Soho** [★M,YC,WC] 44-020/7434-2124, 44-020/7436-2468 ■ 81 Wardour St (at Old Compton) ■ pub hrs, cafe menu till 5pm
30 **West Central** [MW,D,TG,S] 44-020/7479-7981 ■ 29-30 Lisle St (behind Leicester Sq cinemas) ■ pub hrs, drag shows, basement bar open 10:30pm-3am Fri ■ westcentral@aol.com
Wow Bar [WO] ■ organize parties for women, including '100% babe' & '4 u girl', check local media for venue/ dates ■ www.users.dircon.co.uk/~wowbar/

London • ENGLAND

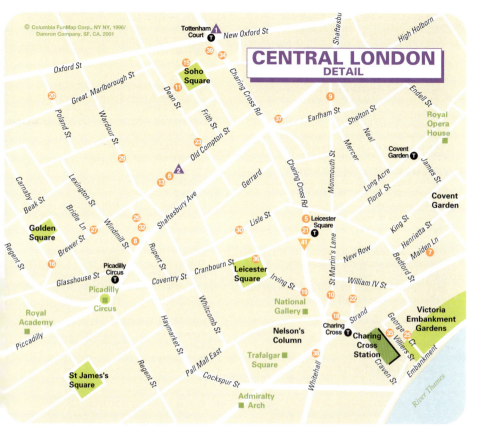

CENTRAL LONDON DETAIL

32 **The Yard** [MW,F,E,YC,WC] 44-020/7437-2652 ■ 57 Rupert St (off Brewer) ■ pub hrs, queer comedy night Wed upstairs at 'Screamers'

NIGHTCLUBS

33 **Atelier** [★M,D,$] 44-020/7419-9199 ■ 18 W Central St (at 'The End') ■ 9pm-3:30am Th, trendy ■ www.cocolatte.net

8 **Factor 25** [★M,D,$] at 'Rock', Hungerford House (Victoria Embankment) ■ 7pm-late Sun only

34 **G.A.Y.** [★M,D,E,YC,$] 44-020/7434-9592, 44-020/7734-6963 ■ 157 Charing Cross Rd (at Oxford St, in London Astoria theatre complex) ■ 10:30pm-late Mon & Th-Sat, this is a HUGE club ■ www.g-a-y.co.uk

35 **Heaven** [★M,D] 44-020/7930-2020, 00 44 20/7930-8306 ■ The Arches (off Villiers St) ■ the mother of all London gay clubs, call for hrs/ events ■ www.heaven-london.com

36 **Home** [GF,D,S,$] 44-0900/102-0107 (info line) ■ 1 Leicester Sq ■ open Th-Sat, gay Sun from 4pm, huge club on 7 flrs ■ www.homecorp.co.uk

37 **The Limelight** [★MW,D] 44-020/7437-4303, 44-020/7434-0572 ■ at 'The Sound Club', Swiss Centre (Leicester Square) ■ 6pm-midnight Sun only, T-dance ■ www.soundonsunday.co.uk

38 **Off the Hook** [★M,D,$] 44-020/0973-628585 ■ 143 Charing Cross Rd (at 'Velvet Underground') ■ 10pm-3am Mon, diverse crowd & funky music

35 **SubStation Soundshaft** [M,D,PC,$] 44-020/7278-0995 ■ Hungerford Ln (behind 'Heaven') ■ theme parties, call for details

39 **The Tube** [MW,D,S] 44-020/7287-3726 ■ 5-6 Falconberg Court (off Charing Cross, behind the 'Astoria') ■ 10:30pm-3:30am, till 5am Fri-Sat, theme nights

CAFES

First Out [MW] 44-020/7240-8042 ■ 52 St Giles High St (btwn Charing Cross & Shaftesbury) ■ 10am-11pm, 11am-10:30pm Sun, cont'l cafe, full bar, WO from 8pm Fri

Freedom Cafe-Bar [S,YC] 44-020/7734-0071 ■ 60 66 Wardour St (off Old Compton St) ■ 9am-11pm, till 10:30pm Sun, trendy scene cafe, also downstairs bar open till 2am Mon-Sat

Old Compton Cafe [★MW] 44-020/7439-3309 ■ 34 Old Compton St ■ 24hrs, all-day brkfst, salads & sandwiches, terrace

RESTAURANTS

Balans [P,TG,S,WC] 44-020/7437-5212 ■ 60 Old Compton St ■ 8am-5am, till 6am Fri-Sat, till 2am Sun, popular, cafe-bar, all-day/ night brunch

Food for Thought 44-020/7836-0239, 44-020/7836-9072 ■ 31 Neal St, downstairs (Covent Garden) ■ noon-8pm, vegetarian

The Gay Hussar [WC] 44-020/7437-0973 ■ 2 Greek St (on Soho Sq) ■ lunch & dinner, clsd Sun, Hungarian

ENGLAND • EUROPE

Mildred's 44-020/7494-1634 ■ 58 Greek St (off Shaftesbury) ■ noon-11pm, clsd Sun, plenty veggie/ vegan

Steph's 44-020/7734-5976 ■ 39 Dean St ■ lunch Mon-Fri & dinner Mon-Sat, clsd Sun, English

The Stockpot 44-020/7287-1066 ■ 18 Old Compton St ■ 11:30am-11:30pm, cheap!

Therapy [MW] 44-020/7499-5554 ■ 10-11 Lancashire Ct (off New Bond St) ■ lunch & dinner, clsd Sun, contemporary, plenty veggie/ vegan

Wagamama Noodle Bar [NS] 44-020/7292-0990, 44-020/7631-3140 ■ 10a Lexington St ■ noon-11pm, till 10pm Sun, Japanese; also locations in Bloomsbury and Covent Garden ■ www.wagamama.com

ENTERTAINMENT & RECREATION

Gay Film Night 44-020/7437-8181 ■ at Prince Charles Cinema (Leicester Pl) ■ every Mon, discount tickets available at 'Ku Bar'

Laughing Cows/ Hersterics 44-020/7836-8956 ■ at Vespa Lounge, under Centre Point House (St Giles Circus) ■ 8pm-11pm Sun, lesbian comedy club

SOHO Gay and Lesbian Walk 44-020/7437-6063 ■ 56 Old Compton St ■ www.kairos-soho.demon.co.uk

BOOKSTORES

40 **Gay's the Word** 44-020/7278-7654 ■ 66 Marchmont St (nr Russell Sq) ■ 10am-6:30pm, 2pm-6pm Sun, lgbt ■ gaystheword.co.uk

41 **Silver Moon Women's Bookshop** [WC] 44-020/7836-7906 ■ 64-68 Charing Cross Rd ■ lesbian/ feminist ■ www.silvermoonbookshop.co.uk

RETAIL SHOPS

American Retro 44-020/7734-3477 ■ 35 Old Compton St ■ 10:15am-7pm, clsd Sun, clothing & gifts ■ www.americanretro.com

Metal Morphosis 44-020/7434-4554 ■ 10-11 Moor St (at Old Compton St) ■ piercing studio, body jewelry ■ www.metalmorphosis.co.uk

Prowler [★] 44-020/7734-4031 ■ 3-7 Brewer St (behind 'Village Soho' bar) ■ large gay department store ■ www.prowler.co.uk

GYMS & HEALTH CLUBS

Covent Garden Health Spa 44-020/7836-2236 ■ 29 Endell St ■ sauna, steam, solarium, jacuzzi, holistic services, also bar ■ www.thesaunabar.com

London Central YMCA [GF,SW] 44-171/343-1700 ■ 112 Great Russell St

Soho Athletic Club [★,M] 44-020/7242-1290 ■ 10-14 Macklin St (at Drury Ln, Covent Garden)

EROTICA

RoB London [WC] 44-020/7735-7893 ■ 24-25 Wells St (nr Berwick St) ■ leather/ fetish shop ■ www.rob.nl

London — West

London—West includes Earl's Court, Kensington, Chelsea & Bayswater

ACCOMMODATIONS

Bailey's Hotel [GF] 44-020/7373-6000 ■ 140 Gloucester Rd (at Old Brompton Rd, Kensington) ■ 4-star hotel, also restaurant & bar ■ www.mill-cop.com

Comfort Inn Kensington [GF,F] 44-020/7373-3300 ■ 22-32 West Cromwell Rd (Earl's Court) ■ also bar ■ www.comfortinn.com/hotel/gb043

43 **George Hotel** [GF] 44-020/7387-8777 ■ 58-60 Cartwright Gardens (N of Russell Sq) ■ full brkfst, some shared baths ■ www.georgehotel.com

44 **The Philbeach Hotel** [M] 44-020/7373-1244 ■ 30-31 Philbeach Gardens (Earl's Court) ■ restaurant & bar, some shared baths ■ www.philbeachhotel.freeserve.co.uk

Prince William Hotel [GS] 44-020/7724-7414 ■ 42-44 Gloucester Ter (Windsor) ■ centrally located townhouse, some shared baths

Redcliffe Hotel [MW,F] 44-020/7823-3494 ■ 268 Fulham Rd (Chelsea) ■ also bar

Reeves Hotel [WO] 44-020/8740-1158 ■ 48 Shepherd's Bush Green (Hammersmith)

BARS

Champion [M,NH,S] 44-020/7229-5056, 44-020/7243-9531 ■ 1 Wellington Ter (at Bayswater Rd) ■ pub hrs, cruisy

45 **The Coleherne/ Leather Attic** [★M,NH,L,WC] 44-020/7244-5951 ■ 261 Old Brompton Rd (at Coleherne Rd) ■ pub hrs, industrial look, leather bar upstairs (dress code)

The George Music Bar [M,S] 44-020/8560-1456 ■ 114 Twickenham Rd ■ 5pm-11pm, from noon wknds, till 10:30pm Sun, 'George Cabaret' Fri-Sat & every other Sun

The Penny Farthing [★MW,NH,F,S,WC] 44-020/8600-0941, 44-020/8748-7045 ■ 135 King St (Hammersmith) ■ noon-midnight, till 10:30pm Sun, cabaret

46 **Queen's Head** [M,NH,OC] 44-020/7589-0262 ■ 27 Tryon St (btwn King's Rd & Sloane Ave, Chelsea) ■ pub hrs

Richmond Arms [M,D,P,S] 44-020/8940-2118 ■ 20 The Square (at Princess) ■ pub hrs

The Rocket [MW,D,S] 44-020/8992-1545 ■ 10-13 Churchfield Rd (Acton) ■ 6pm-11pm, from noon wknds, till 10:30pm Sun, 2 bars: 'Kirk's' cruise bar upstairs & cabaret bar downstairs

47 **The Stag** [M] 44-020/828-7287 ■ 15 Bressenden Pl (nr Victoria Stn) ■ noon-midnight, till 2am Fri, from 5pm Sat, till 10pm Sun

Ted's Place [M,D,TG,S,V,PC] 44-020/7385-9359 ■ 305a North End Rd ■ 7pm-11pm, men-only Mon, Tue, Wed & Fri, clsd Sat, cruisy

West Five (W5) [M,S,F] 44-020/8579-3266 ■ 5 Popes Ln (Ealing) ■ pub hrs, till 1am Fri-Sat, lunch served Sun, piano bar, lounge & cabaret, garden

NIGHTCLUBS

48 **Bromptons** [M,D,F,S] 44-020/7370-1344 ■ 294 Old Brompton Rd (at Warwick Rd) ■ 10:30pm-2am, 5:30pm-midnight Sun, MO Tue (strippers), cabaret Th, 'Privates on Parade,' strippers Sun, also 'Warwick' bar upstairs from 6pm, karaoke Mon & Th ■ BromptonCL@aol.com

RESTAURANTS

Balans West [MW] 44-020/7244-8388 ■ 239 Old Brompton Rd ■ 8am-1am, English

Phoenicia 44-020/7937-0120 ■ 11-13 Abingdon Rd ■ Lebanese/ Mediterranean

Wilde About Oscar [MW,WC] 44-020/7835-1858, 44-020/7373-1244 ■ at the 'Philbeach Hotel' ■ 7pm-11pm, eclectic/ French, garden

Willi's 44-020/7724-7414 ■ at the 'Prince William Hotel' ■ English

RETAIL SHOPS

Clone Zone 44-020/7373-0598 ■ 266 Old Brompton Rd (Earl's Court) ■ 11am-9pm, noon-6pm Sun, magazines, videos, toys; also Soho location (64 Old Compton St, 44-020/7287-3530) ■ www.clonezone.co.uk

London • ENGLAND

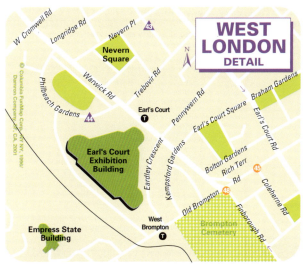

The Flag [MW,NH] 44-020/7272-4748 ■ 29 Crouch Hill ■ friendly pub

King Edward VI [★M,NH,F,WC] 44-020/7704-0745 ■ 25 Bromfield St (at Parkfield St, Islington) ■ noon-midnight, till 11:30pm Sun, lunch 2pm-5pm Sun, cafe-bar, terrace ■ edwardvi.8m.com

King William IV [MW,NH,TG,F,S,WC] 44-020/7435-5747 ■ 77 Hampstead High St (Hampstead) ■ pub hrs, drag shows

The Oak Bar [MW,D,F,K,S] 44-020/7354-2791 ■ 79 Green Lanes ■ 5pm-midnight, till 2am Fri-Sat, from 1pm wknds, cabaret/disco wknds, women only Fri & last Sat, 'Hoppa' for Cypriots, Greeks, Turks & friends 3rd Sat

The Ram Club Bar [M,WC] 44-020/7354-0576 ■ 39 Queen's Head St ■ pub hrs, terrace ■ www.geocities.com/WestHollywood/Heights/5073/rambar.htm

Gyms & Health Clubs

Soho Athletic Club [GF] 44-020/7370-1402 ■ 254 Earls Ct Rd ■ also Camden Town location: 193 Camden High St, 44-020/7482-4524

Men's Clubs

Holland Park Sauna (HPS 156) [V,SW] 44-020/8743-3264 ■ 156 Shepherd's Bush Shopping Ctr (Hammersmith) ■ jacuzzi, gym equipment, snackbar

London—North

London—North includes Paddington, Regents Park, Camden, St Pancras & Islington

Accommodations

Rainbowstay Guest House [MW,GO] 44-020/7713-5287 ■ 14 Thornhill Bridge Wharf (Islington) ■ www.rainbowstay.freeserve.co.uk

The Town House [M,GO] 44-020/7609-9082 ■ Caledonian Rd (Islington) ■ www.sbr22.dircon.co.uk

Bars

The Artful Dodger [MO,S,PC] 44-020/7226-0841 ■ 139 Southgate Rd (Islington) ■ 6pm-midnight, till 1am Th, till 2am Fri-Sat, from 1pm Sun, cruise bar, Towel Party Wed, men of color night Th, dancing/DJ & strippers Fri-Sat, 'Undies on Sundays'

Bar Fusion [MW,NH,F] 44-020/7688-2882 ■ 45 Essex Rd (at Queen's Head St, Islington) ■ 1pm-midnight, trendy cafe-bar

The Black Cap [MW,D,TG,F,S] 44-020/7428-2721 ■ 171 Camden High St (Camden Town) ■ noon-2am, 1pm-3am Fri-Sat, till midnight Sun, London's leading cabaret

Blush [MW,NH,F] 44-020/7923-9202 ■ 8 Cazenove Rd (Stoke Newington) ■ 5pm-midnight, brunch from noon wknds, clsd Mon, women only Fri from 8pm, friendly cafe-bar

Due South [MW,NH,F,K] 44-020/7249-7543 ■ 35 Stoke Newington High St (at Arcola St, Stoke Newington) ■ 5pm-midnight, from noon wknds, women only Th, beer garden, also restaurant

Duke of Wellington [MW,NH] 44-020/7254-4338 ■ 119 Balls Pond Rd (Islington) ■ noon-midnight, till 11:30pm Sun

Nightclubs

The Block [M,L,PC,$] 44-020/8988-0257 ■ 28 Hancock Rd (at Three Mill Ln, Bow) ■ 10pm-4am, till 6am Fri-Sat, till 3am Sun, clsd Mon-Wed, cruisy ■ www.the-block.co.uk

Central Station/ Underground [★M,D,TG,F,S,V] 44-020/7278-3294, 44-020/7833-8925 ■ 37 Wharfedale Rd (King's Cross) ■ 5pm-2am, till 3am Th, till 5am Fri-Sat, noon-midnight Sun, cabaret, strippers, theme nights including 'Strictly Handbag' Fri ■ www.centralstation.co.uk

Club Kali [★MW,D,$] 44-020/7272-8153 (Dome #) ■ 1 Dartmouth Park Hill (at 'The Dome') ■ 10pm-3am 1st & 3rd Fri, South Asian music

Fiction at The Cross [★MW,D,$] 44-020/7251-8778 ■ Bagleys Yard (Kings Cross) ■ 10:30pm-late Fri, see-and-be-seen ■ www.club-fiction.co.uk

The Liquid Lounge [MW,D,A,$] 44-020/7837-3218 ■ 257 Pentonville Rd (Kings Cross) ■ theme nights, 'Miss-Shapes' indie/ alternative women's night Sat

Popstarz [★MW,D,$] 44-020/7833-9988 ■ at 'Scala', 275 Pentonville Rd (Kings Cross) ■ 10pm-5am Fri ■ www.popstarznightclub.com

Bookstores

Compendium 44-020/7485-8944 ■ 234 Camden High St (Camden Town) ■ lgbt

Men's Clubs

Pacific 33 [V] 44-020/7609-8133, 44-020/7609-8011 ■ 33 Hornsey Rd (Holloway) ■ 24hrs wknds, bar

Erotica

Regulation 44-020/7226-0665 ■ 17a St Albans Pl (Islington Green) ■ fetish gear & toys 'made to measure' ■ www.regulation-ltd.co.uk

Sh! Women's Erotic Emporium 44-020/7613-5458 ■ 39 Coronet St (off Old St & Pitfield St, Shoreditch) ■ clsd Sun

Zipper Store 44-020/7284-0537, 44-020/7267-0021 (mail order) ■ 283 Camden High St (Camden Town) ■ fetishwear, books, videos, sex toys & more ■ www.zipper.co.uk

London—East

London—East includes City, Tower, Clerkenwell & Shoreditch

Accommodations

Leather Bear Den [MO,GO] 44-020/8800-9293 ■ 109 Clapton Common ■ renovated Victorian, home & playground for 'bears, bearded bikers & leathermen,' den available for parties ■ www.leatherbearden.com

Bars

Backstreet [MO,PC] 44-020/8980-8557, 44-020/8980-7880 ■ Wentworth Mews, Burdett Rd (at Mile End Rd, Bow) ■ 10pm-3am, 9pm-1am Sun, clsd Mon-Wed, strict leather/ rubber dress code ■ www.thebackstreet.com

BJ's White Swan [M,D,TG,F,S,V,WC] 44-020/7780-9870, 44-020/7791-0747 ■ 556 Commercial Rd (nr Bromley St) ■ 9pm-2am, till 1am Mon-Tue, till 3am Fri-Sat, T-dance 5:30pm-1am Sun, amateur male strip contest Mon & Wed

The Black Horse [M,NH,S,WC] 44-020/7790-1684 ■ 168 Mile End Rd (across from the Globe Centre, Stepney Green) ■ 8pm-1am, till 3am Fri-Sat, 4pm-midnight Sun, cabaret

Cock & Comfort [M,S] 44-020/7729-1090 ■ 359 Bethnal Green Rd ■ pub hrs, till 2am Fri-Sat, drag shows wknds

The Coronet [MW,D,K,S] 44-020/8522-0811 ■ 119 The Grove (Stratford) ■ 3pm-midnight, till 2am Fri-Sat, clsd Sun, cabaret nights, disco wknds, also 'Room 101' (men only), upstairs Sat, cruise bar

The Joiner's Arms [MW,NH,S] 44-020/7739-9654 ■ 116-118 Hackney Rd (nr Shoreditch) ■ 6pm-2am, noon-10:30pm Sun, after-hrs party Sun (dancing/DJ)

The Old Ship [MW,NH,S,WC] 44-020/7790-4082 ■ 17 Barnes St (in Stepney) ■ 6pm-11pm, from 7:30pm Sat, 1:30pm-10:30pm Sun, drag shows

Royal Oak [★MW,NH,TG,F] 44-020/7739-8204 ■ 73 Columbia Rd (Bethnal Green, in the flower market) ■ 11am-late, from 8am Sun

The Spiral [MW,NH,D,V] 44-020/7613-1351 ■ 138 Shoreditch High St (across from Shoreditch Church) ■ 10pm-2am, 9pm-4am Fri-Sat, till 3:30am Sun, clsd Mon-Tue, 'Trash Disco' Th, karaoke Fri, cabaret Sat, piano bar Sun

Nightclubs

Benjy's 2000 [★MW,D,YC] 44-020/8980-6427 ■ 562-A Mile End Rd ■ 9pm-1am Sun only

Club Travestie Extraordinaire [MW,D,TG,S,WC] 44-020/8788-4154 ■ at 'Stepneys', 373 Commercial Rd (Stepney) ■ TV/TS night 9pm-2am 2nd & 4th Sat

DTPM [★MW,D,YC,$] 44-020/7251-8778 (info line) ■ 77a Charterhouse St, Smithfield Mkt (at 'Fabric') ■ 8pm-late Sun, huge, stylish techno club ■ www.dtpm.net

Turnmills [★M,D,PC,$] 44-020/7250-3409 ■ 63B Clerkenwell Rd (Clerkenwell) ■ after-hrs club, call for events, 'Trade' 4am-1pm Sun & 'Habit' 10pm-7am Sun are very popular

Way Out Club [MW,D,TG,S,PC,$] 44-020/8363-0948 ■ 9 Crosswall (at 'Charlie's') ■ 9pm-4am Sat only, TV/TS & their friends

Men's Clubs

Chariots I [★SW,F] 44-020/7247-5333 ■ Chariots House, Fairchild St ■ 24hrs wknds, sauna, steam, jacuzzi, gym equipment, also 'Chariots Café-Bar' ■ www.gaysauna.co.uk

Chariots III 44-020/251-5553 ■ 57 Cowcross St (across from Farringdon tube) ■ 24hrs wknds ■ www.gaysauna.co.uk

The Health Club [TG] 44-020/8556-8082 ■ 800 Lea Bridge Rd (Walthamstow) ■ jacuzzi, steam

---

It's like a thousand brochures!

- full-color photographs speak louder than words
- over 1800 international listings cover gay-friendly hotels, B&Bs, and accommodations across the globe!
- detailed listings answer all your questions about rates, rooms, meals, smoking, kids, and pets
- cross-indexes note Men-only, Women-only, RV & Camping, and Wheelchair-accessible accommodations
- over 550 pages, only $22.95!

▶ **Order Now: (800) 462-6654**

Sailors Sauna 44-020/7791-2808 ■ 572-574 Commercial Rd (nr Limehouse tube) ■ open late, steam, tanning, jacuzzi

EROTICA

Centaurus 44-020/7251-3535 ■ 100 Old St (Clerkenwell) ■ clsd Sun, videos, books, photos, gallery, video cabins ■ www.centaurus.co.uk

Expectations 44-020/7739-0292 ■ 75 Great Eastern St (Shoreditch) ■ London's premier leather/ rubber store & mail order company ■ www.expectations.co.uk

The Penthouse: Private B&B [MO] 44-020/7251-3535 ■ centrally located, single, dbl & triple rms available ■ www.GayAccom.co.uk

London—South

London—South includes Southwark, Lambeth, Kennington, Vauxhall, Battersea, Lewisham & Greenwich

BARS

53 The A Bar [★MO,L,$] 44-020/7928-3223 ■ 82 Great Suffolk St ■ 8pm-1am, open later Fri-Sat, from 2pm Sat, 2pm-midnight Sun, theme nights, call for info

Bar 68 [M,S] 44-020/8665-0683 ■ 68 Brigstock Rd (Thornton Heath)

Buzz Bar [MW] 44-020/7207-3895 ■ 136 Battersea High St ■ bar & restaurant, food served noon-8pm ■ www.buzzbar.gayone.net

Centre Stage [M,NH,S] 44-020/7394-9766 ■ 118 Lower Rd (Rotherhithe) ■ 7pm-midnight, quiz night Tue, piano bar Wed, 'Trash Disco' Th till 1am, 'Fresh' (D) Fri till 2am, 'Showtime' Sat till 2am, lunch served 3pm-7pm Sun

54 The Cock [M,F,S] 44-020/7735-1013 ■ 340 Kennington Rd (nr Lambeth Rd, Kennington) ■ pub hrs, strippers Th, drag shows Sat, free pool for women Sun

55 Dukes [M,NH,B,L,S] 44-020/7793-0903 ■ 349 Kennington Ln (Vauxhall) ■ 8pm-1am, 9pm-2am Wed-Sat, 2pm-10:30pm Sun

56 The Fort [M,L] 44-020/7237-7742 ■ 131 Grange Rd (off Tower Bridge Rd, Bermondsey) ■ pub hrs, darkroom, theme nights, strict dress code

The Gloucester [M,NH,F,E,WC] 44-020/8858-2666 ■ 1 King William Walk (btwn Greenwich Pk & Footway Tunnel, Greenwich) ■ pub hrs

57 The Hoist [M,L] 44-020/7735-9972 ■ Railway Arch 47c, S Lambeth Rd (Vauxhall) ■ 10pm-3am Fri-Sat & 9pm-1am Sun, S/M club w/strict dress code ■ www.thehoist.co.uk

Kazbar [M,TG] 44-020/7622-0070 ■ 50 Clapham High St (Clapham) ■ 4pm-midnight, from noon Sat, till 11:30pm Sun, cafe-bar ■ www.kudosgroup.com/kazbar

58 The Little Apple [MW,D,TG,F,WC] 44-020/7735-2039 ■ 98 Kennington Ln ■ noon-midnight, till 11pm Sun, terrace

The Queen's Arms [MW,NH,D,S,WC] 44-020/8318-7305 ■ 63 Court Hill Rd (Lewisham) ■ 4pm-11pm, upscale cabaret bar, DJ Fri, beer garden

The Roebuck [MW,NH,D,F,K,S] 44-020/8852-1705 ■ 25 Rennell St (off Lewisham High St) ■ 11am-midnight, till 1am Th-Sat, till 11pm Sun

The Skinner's Arms [M,S] 44-020/8582-3397 ■ 60 Camberwell New Rd ■ open late

The Two Brewers [MW,D,S] 44-020/7498-4971, 44-020/7622-3621 ■ 114 Clapham High St (Clapham) ■ 6pm-1am, noon-3am Fri-Sat, lunch noon-6pm Sun, cabaret

NIGHTCLUBS

59 Crash [★M,D,V,$] 44-020/7278-0995 ■ Arch 66, Goding St ■ 10:30pm-late Sat, also 'Barracks' Mon (dress code) & 'Men's Room' Th ■ www.crashlondon.co.uk

60 Royal Vauxhall Tavern [M,NH,D,TG,S,WC] 44-020/7582-0833 ■ 372 Kennington Ln (Vauxhall) ■ 8pm-1am, till 2am Sat, noon-midnight Sun, popular Sat eves & Sun afternoons, drag shows

The Substation South [★M,D,L,PC] 44-020/7737-2095 ■ 9 Brighton Terr (Brixton) ■ 10:30pm-2am, till 3am Wed-Th, till 5am Fri, till 6am Sat, 9pm-3am Sun, men only Mon-Th & 3rd Sat, also 'Queer Nation' (multiracial crowd) Sat, strict fetish dress code some nights

CAFES

Surf.Net Cafe 44-020/8488-1200 ■ 13 Deptford Church St (at Deptford Broadway) ■ 11am-9pm, till 7pm Sat, clsd Sun, cybercafe ■ www.surfnet.co.uk

RESTAURANTS

Fileric 44-020/7720-4844 ■ 12 Queenstown Rd ■ French

Il Pinguino 44-020/7735-3822 ■ 62 Brixton Rd ■ Italian

ENTERTAINMENT & RECREATION

Oval Theatre Cafe Bar 44-020/7582-7680 ■ 52-54 Kennington Oval ■ 6pm-8pm, till 11pm Th-Sun, clsd Wed

RETAIL SHOPS

London Piercing Clinic 44-020/8656-7180 ■ 13 Portland Rd (S Norwood) ■ 11am-7pm, 2pm-6pm Sun ■ www.lpcpat.demon.co.uk

GYMS & HEALTH CLUBS

Paris Gymnasium [M] 44-020/7735-8989 ■ Arch 73, Goding St (behind 'Vauxhall Tavern') ■ £6.50 day pass

MEN'S CLUBS

Chariots II 44-020/8696-0929, 44-020/8696-7257 ■ 292 Streatham High Rd (at Babington Rd, enter rear) ■ 24hrs wknds, bears Tue ■ www.gaysauna.co.uk

The Locker Room [V] 44-020/7582-6288 ■ 8 Cleaver St (Kennington)

Pleasuredrome [NS] 44-020/7633-9194 ■ 125 Alaska St (Waterloo) ■ 24hrs, also gym, $7 day pass ■ www.pleasuredrome.co.uk

Star Steam [V] 44-020/7924-2269 ■ 38 Lavender Hill (Battersea) ■ seasonal terrace

Steamworks [V] 44-020/8694-0316/ 0606 ■ 309 New Cross Rd ■ 24hrs wknds

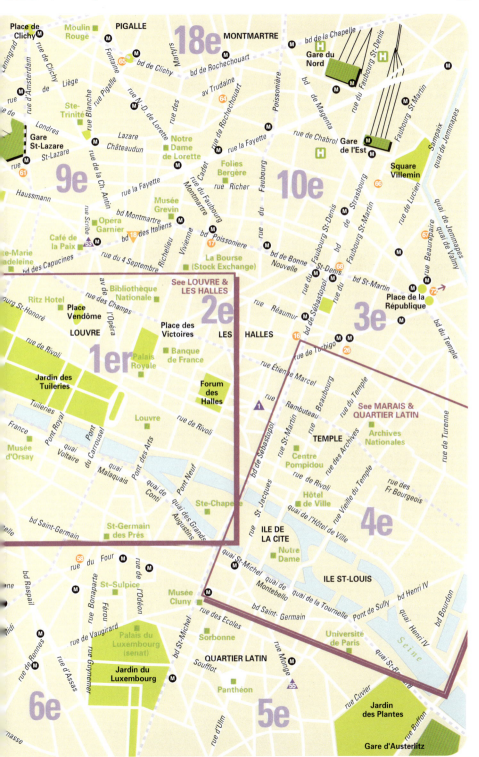

France

Paris

Note: M°=Métro station

Paris is divided by arrondissements (city districts); 01=1st arrondissement, 02=2nd arrondissement, etc ■ the detail maps have been designed around region names which include several arrondissements

Note: When phoning Paris from the US, dial the country code + the city code + the local phone number

Paris—Overview

Accommodations

A Parisian Home 33-1/47.03.02.25 ■ furnished apts in Paris ■ www.aparisianhome.com

Insightful Travelers [GF] 617/859-0720 (US#) ■ short-term apt rentals, 5-day minimum stay ■ www.latoile.com

Marais and Left Bank Historic Rentals [GF] 800/537-5408 (US#) ■ 25 rue des Rosiers (at rue des Ecouffes) ■ 1-bdrm apts ■ www.historicrentals.com

Paris Séjour Réservation [GF] 312/587-7707 (US#), 800/582-7274 ■ short-term apt rentals ■ www.psryourhomeinparis.com

Paris

Who doesn't adore Paris? The most romantic city in the world, Paris is a capricious lover. Beautiful and witty, dignified and grand, flirtatious and coy, Paris is worthy of lifelong devotion. It's hardly surprising, then, that so many artists and thinkers have made Paris their home. Not to mention plenty of lesbians and gay men! The Marais is the city's gayest neighborhood, offering great shopping, dining, cafes, and nightlife, in a charming and bustling maze of narrow streets. As of the year 2001, we now have two more reasons to love Paris—their recently elected, openly gay mayor and the legal recognition of lesbian and gay marriages (PACS).

Queer Resources

Community Info

▼ Centre Gai et Lesbien de Paris 33-1/43.57.21.47, web: www.cglparis.org. 3 rue Keller (11e, see Marais map), drop-in 2pm-8pm, till 7pm Sun.
Ecoute Gaie 33-1/44.93.01.02 (helpline). 6pm-10pm Mon-Fri & 6pm-8pm Sat.

AIDS Resources

SIDA Info Service, 0800/36.66.36.

City Calendar

LGBT Pride

June. 33-1/47.70.01.50, web: www.gaypride.fr. Lesbian Pride. 33-1/40.37.79.87, web: www.multimania.com/fiertelesbienne.

Annual Events

July 13 - Bastille Ball.
December - Paris Gay & Lesbian Film Festival.

Tourist Info

Airport Directions

Parisian drivers make Bostonians look tame. Damron recommends the many excellent public transit options from both Orly (Orlyrail/Orlybus) and Charles de Gaulle (Roissyrail/Roissybus) Airports into Paris. Air France also provides bus service.

Public Transit & Taxis

Alpha Taxi 33-1/45.85.85.85.
Taxi Bleu 33-1/49.36.10.10.
Taxi-Radio Étoile 33-1/42.70.41.41.
RATP (bus and Métro) 33-8/44.68.20.20 (in French), 33-8/36.68.41.14 (in English), web: www.ratp.fr.

Tourist Spots & Info

Arc de Triomphe 33-1/43.80.31.31.
Notre Dame Cathedral 33-1/42.34.56.10.
Eiffel Tower 33-1/44.11.23.45.
Louvre 33-1/40.20.51.51.
Musée d'Orsay 33-1/40.49.48.14.
Picasso Museum 33-1/42.71.25.21.
Rodin Musuem 33-1/44.18.61.10.
Sacre-Coeur Basilica 33-1/53.41.89.00.
Sainte-Chapelle 33-1/53.73.78.41.
Visitor's Center: 33-1/49.52.53.54, 127 av des Champs-Elysées (8e), web: www.paris.org.

Weather

Paris really is beautiful in the springtime. Chilly in the winter, the temperatures reach the 70°s during the summer.

Best Views

Eiffel Tower (of course!) and Sacre Coeur.

Paris • FRANCE

RentParis.com [MW] 415/255-8270 (US#) ■ 27 rue Rossini, Vitry sur Seine ■ fully furnished studios & apts ■ www.RentParis.com

PUBLICATIONS

Double Face 33-1/48.04.58.00 ■ lifestyle magazine, event/ party listings, free at venues around Paris

e.m@le 33-1/53.35.98.54 ■ weekly magazine w/ events & club listings, free at venues around Paris ■ emaleredac@netgate.fr

Housewife 33-1/40.26.60.31 ■ monthly satirical club scene 'zine for lesbians, free at venues around the Marais ■ housewife@lemel.fr

Illico 33-1/48.04.58.00 ■ free monthly newsmagazine w/ listings of events ■ groupeillico@mail2.imaginet.fr

Lesbia 33-1/43.48.89.54 ■ monthly glossy magazine

Têtu 33-1/56.80.20.80 ■ stylish & intelligent lgbt monthly ■ www.tetu.com

Paris—01

ACCOMMODATIONS

1   **Agora** [GF] 33-1/42.33.46.02, 33-1/42.33.80.90 ■ 7 rue de la Cossonerie (at rue St-Denis, M°Châtelet) ■ hotel.agora.fr@wanadoo.fr

2   **Castille** [GF,WC] 33-1/44.58.44.58, 800/448-8355 (US#) ■ 37 rue Cambon ■ ultra-luxe hotel

3   **Hôtel Louvre Richelieu** [GF,GO] 33-1/42.97.46.20 ■ 51 rue de Richelieu (M°Palais-Royal) ■ perso.club-internet.fr/joelgill

The Ritz [GF] 33-1/43.16.30.70, 800/223-6800 (US#) ■ 15 place Vendôme (M°Tuileries) ■ ultra-luxe hotel ■ www.ritz.com

BARS

4   **Le Banana Café** [★MW,D,S,YC,WC] 33-1/42.33.35.31 ■ 13-15 rue de la Ferronnerie (nr rue St-Denis, M°Châtelet) ■ 4pm-dawn, tropical decor, theme nights, Latina/o night Sun, terrace

5   **Le Cap Horn** [MW,D,F] 33-1/40.28.03.08 ■ 37 rue des Lombards (M°Châtelet) ■ noon-2am, cafe-bar, naval decor

7   **Le Stonewall** [M,D,S] 33-1/40.28.04.05 ■ 46 rue des Lombards (M°Châtelet) ■ 6:30pm-late, T-dance late Sun, strippers Wed

8   **Le Transfert** [M,L,V] 33-1/42.60.48.42 ■ 3 rue de la Sourdière (at rue du Faubourg St-Honoré, M°Tuileries) ■ midnight-dawn, small cruisy bar, theme nights, selective door

9   **Le Tropic Café** [MW,TG,F,YC,WC] 33-1/40.13.92.62 ■ 66 rue des Lombards (M°Châtelet) ■ noon-5am, tapas, terrace

10 **Le Vagabond** [M,F] 33-1/42.96.27.23 ■ 14 rue Thérèse (at av de l'Opera, M°Pyramides) ■ 6pm-close, clsd Mon, oldest gay bar & restaurant in Paris

NIGHTCLUBS

11 **Club 18** [M,D,PC,$] 33-1/42.97.52.13 ■ 18 rue du Beaujolais (at rue Vivienne, M°Palais-Royal) ■ midnight-dawn Th-Sun ■ site.voila.fr/club18

PARIS DETAIL
LOUVRE & LES HALLES

12 **L' Insolite** [★M,D] 33-1/40.20.98.53 ■ 33 rue des Petits-Champs (at rue du Beaujolais, enter through back courtyard, M°Pyramides) ■ 11pm-5am Th-Sun, cover Fri-Sat, 'vive le disco'

13 **Le Club** [M,D,MR,F,YC,PC,$] 33-1/45.08.96.25 ■ 14 rue St-Denis (at rue des Lombards, M°Châtelet) ■ midnight-close, theme nights, 'Butch' Fri, strippers Sun

14 **Le London** [M,D,F,$] 33-1/42.33.41.45 ■ 33 rue des Lombards, in basement (M°Châtelet) ■ 11pm-5am, till 7am Fri-Sat, clsd Mon, theme nights, Asian night Tue, also restaurant/ bar upstairs from 8:30pm

Restaurants

L' Amazonial [MW,S,WC] 33-1/42.33.53.13 ■ 3 rue Ste-Opportune (at rue Ferronnerie, M°Châtelet) ■ lunch Mon-Fri & dinner nightly, brunch wknds, Brazilian/ int'l, bingo Mon-Tue, cabaret Th, drag shows Sat, heated terrace

Au Diable des Lombards 33-1/42.33.81.84 ■ 64 rue des Lombards (at rue St-Denis, M°Châtelet) ■ 10am-1am, brunch till 6pm daily, American, full bar, terrace ■ www.diable.com

Au Petit Bonheur [MW,S] 33-1/42.21.17.12 ■ 9 rue St-Germain-d'Auxerrois (M°Châtelet) ■ lunch Tue-Fri & dinner Tue-Sun, clsd Mon, traditional French

Au Rendez-Vous des Camioneurs [M] 33-1/43.54.88.74 ■ 72 quai des Orfèvres (M°Pont Neuf) ■ lunch & dinner, traditional bistro

Chez Max 33-1/45.08.80.13 ■ 47 rue St-Honoré (M°Châtelet) ■ lunch Mon-Fri & dinner Mon-Sat, clsd Sun, clsd Aug, North African

Le Comptoir [★] 33-1/40.26.26.66 ■ 14 rue Vauvilliers (M°Châtelet) ■ noon-2am, till 4am Fri-Sat, int'l, also bar

Le Gut [M] 33-1/42.36.14.90 ■ 64 rue J-J-Rousseau (M°Châtelet) ■ 8am-7pm, clsd Sun, French bistro, also bar

La Poule au Pot 33-1/42.36.32.96 ■ 9 rue Vauvilliers (M°Les Halles) ■ 7pm-5am, clsd Mon, clsd Aug, traditional French

Yvan sur Seine [M] 33-1/42.36.49.52 ■ 26 quai du Louvre (M°Pont-Neuf) ■ 8pm-1am, till 4am Fri-Sat, 'Bad Boy Party' Sun

Entertainment & Recreation

Les Halles ■ underground sports/ entertainment complex w/ museums, theater, shops, clubs, cafes & more

Gyms & Health Clubs

Gymnase Club [GF] 33-1/40.20.03.03 ■ 147b rue St-Honoré (M°Louvre) ■ day passes available, many locations throughout city

Men's Clubs

Til't Sauna [V] 33-1/42.96.07.43 ■ 41 rue Ste-Anne (nr av de l'Opera, M°Pyramides) ■ 6pm-7am, bar

Top Sauna [M,V] 33-1/40.13.09.26 ■ 117 rue St-Denis (M°Etienne-Marcel) ■ also sex shop

L' Univers Gym & Sauna [S,V] 33-1/42.61.24.83 ■ 20-22 rue des Bons Enfants (M°Palais Royal) ■ gym equipment, bar, theme parties, strippers Sat ■ www.univers.net

Erotica

Big Shop 33-1/42.21.47.02 ■ 2 rue de la Cossonnerie (M°Châtelet) ■ videos, toys & fetish gear, also sex club

IEM Les Halles 33-1/42.96.05.74 ■ 43 rue de l'Arbre Sec (nr rue de Rivoli, M°Louvre) ■ www.iem.fr

Yanko 33-1/42.60.55.28 ■ 54 rue de l'Arbre Sec (nr rue de Rivoli, M°Louvre) ■ noon-10pm, toys & videos

Paris — 02

Bars

15 **La Champmeslé** [★W,S,WC] 33-1/42.96.85.20 ■ 4 rue Chabanais (at rue des Petits Champs, M°Pyramides) ■ 5pm-late, clsd Sun, cabaret Th, theme nights

16 **L' Impact** [MO,V] 33-1/42.21.94.24 ■ 18 rue Grenéta (M°Châtelet) ■ 10pm-6am, till 8am Fri-Sat, from 4pm Sun, cruise bar, backroom, theme nights, 'Hot Under the Towel' party 4pm Sun, free brkfst wknds

Nightclubs

17 **Le Pulp** [★W,D] 33-1/40.26.01.93 ■ 25 bd Poissonnière (M°Grands-Blvds) ■ 11pm-close, clsd Sun-Mon, theme nights, cover Fri-Sat, men welcome as guests

17 **Le Scorp** [M,D,S,YC] 33-1/40.26.01.50, 33-1/40.26.28.30 ■ 25 bd Poissonnière (M°Grands-Blvds) ■ midnight-7am, shows Sun-Tue, disco Wed, cover Fri-Sat

Cafes

Lezard Café 33-1/42.33.22.73 ■ 41 rue Tiquetonne (M°Etienne-Marcel) ■ noon-4pm & 7pm-midnight, tarts, also bar, open 9am-2am, terrace

Restaurants

Aux Trois Petits Cochons [MW,GO] 33-1/42.33.39.69 ■ 31 rue Tiquetonne (at rue St-Denis, M°Etienne-Marcel) ■ 8pm-midnight, gourmet French, reservations recommended ■ www.aux-trois-petits-cochons.fr

Le Dénicheur 33-1/42.21.31.01 ■ 4 rue Tiquetonne (M°Etienne-Marcel) ■ noon-midnight, from 7pm Mon, seafood

L' Homosapiens 33-1/40.26.94.85 ■ 29 rue Tiquetonne (M°Etienne-Marcel) ■ lunch Mon-Fri & dinner Mon-Sat, clsd Sun, French

Le Loup Blanc [★MW] 33-1/40.13.08.35 ■ 42 rue Tiquetonne (M°Etienne-Marcel) ■ 7:30pm-midnight, till 1am Sat, brunch 11am-4:30pm Sun, French/ int'l

Matinée-Soirée 33-1/42.21.18.00 ■ 5 rue Marie Stuart (M°Etienne-Marcel) ■ noon-2:30pm & 7pm-10:30pm, clsd Sun, French, terrace

Le Monde à l'envers [M] 33-1/40.26.13.91 ■ 35 rue Tiquetonne (M°Etienne-Marcel) ■ lunch Tue-Fri, dinner Tue-Sun, traditional French

Entertainment & Recreation

Cour et Jardin 33-1/39.75.19.08 ■ 2 impasse St-Denis ■ amateur lgbt theater group, performances 7pm Th & 5pm Sun

Bookstores

18 **Le Kiosque des Amis** 33-1/42.65.00.94 ■ 29 bd des Italiens (M°Opéra) ■ 10am-10pm, lgbt, French & int'l magazines

Paris — 03

Accommodations

19 **Hôtel de Saintonge** [GF] 33-1/42.77.91.13 ■ 16 rue de Saintonge (off rue du Perche btwn rue Charlot & rue Vieille du Temple, M°Filles-du-Calvaire)

Bars

20 **Le Dépôt** [M,D,S,$] 33-1/44.54.96.96 ■ 10 rue aux Ours (btwn bd de Sébastopol & rue St-Martin, M°Rambuteau) ■ 2pm-8am, huge cruise bar on 3 flrs, T-dance 5pm Sun, go-go boys ■ www.ledepot.com

21 **Le Duplex** [MW,NH,S] 33-1/42.72.80.86 ■ 25 rue Michel-le-Comte (at rue Beaubourg, M°Rambuteau) ■ 8pm-2am, friendly bar w/ Internet access

… Paris • France

20 **Ladies Room** [WO,D,$] 33-1/44.54.96.96 ■ 10 rue aux Ours (at 'Le Dépôt') ■ 11pm-dawn Wed only ■ www.ladiesroomparis.com

22 **One Way** [M,NH,B,L,F,V,OC] 33-1/48.87.46.10 ■ 28 rue Charlot (at rue des 4 Fils, M°République) ■ 5pm-2am, cruisy, darkroom, bears 4th Sat, tapas

23 **L' Unity Bar** [W,NH,YC] 33-1/42.72.70.59 ■ 176-178 rue St-Martin (nr rue Réaumur, M°Rambuteau) ■ 4pm-2am, men welcome as guests ■ unity-bar@compuserve.com

24 **L' Utopia** [W,NH,S,WC] 33-1/42.71.63.43 ■ 15 rue Michelle-Comte (M°Rambuteau) ■ 5pm-2am, clsd Sun, clsd 8/1-8/15, theme nights, dancing/DJ Sat, Internet access, men welcome as guests

NIGHTCLUBS

25 **Les Bains** [★GF,D,F,$] 33-1/48.87.01.80 ■ 7 rue du Bourg-l'Abbé (at bd de Sébastopol, M°Etienne-Marcel) ■ midnight-close, gay Sun & Mon

26 **Le Tango** [MW,D,S,$] 33-1/42.72.17.78 ■ 13 rue au Maire (M°Arts-et-Métiers) ■ 8pm-2am Th, 10:30pm-5am Fri-Sat, clsd Aug, waltz, tango, T-dance 6pm-2am Sun ■ frissons@club-internet.fr

RESTAURANTS

Au Marais Gourmand 33-1/48.87.63.08 ■ 26 rue Charlot (M°République) ■ lunch & dinner, clsd Sun, French

Les Epicuriens du Marais 33-1/40.27.00.83 ■ 19 rue Commines (M°Filles-du-Calvaire) ■ noon-3pm & 7pm-midnight, till 1:30am wknds, traditional French

La Fontaine Gourmande 33-1/42.78.42.30 ■ 11 rue Charlot (M°Filles-du-Calvaire) ■ lunch Tue-Fri & dinner Tue-Sun, clsd Mon, French

La Madame sans gène [M,S] 33-1/42.71.31.71 ■ 19 rue de Picardie (M°Filles-du-Calvaire) ■ lunch daily, dinner Mon-Fri, clsd Aug, inexpensive traditional French, theme nights ■ sansgene@club-internet.fr

Les Saveurs de Temps 33-1/48.87.78.68 ■ 3 rue Bernard de Clairvaux (M°Rambuteau) ■ lunch Mon-Fri, dinner nightly, Mediterranean, theme parties

Les Trois Axes 33-1/42.74.68.34 ■ 157 rue St-Martin (M°Rambuteau) ■ lunch Mon-Fri, dinner Mon-Sat, clsd Sun, homestyle French

Le Valet de Carreau 33-1/42.72.72.60 ■ 2 rue du Petit Thouars (M°République) ■ lunch Mon-Fri, dinner Mon-Sat, clsd Sun, creative cuisine, terrace

ENTERTAINMENT & RECREATION

Musée Picasso [WC] 33-1/42.71.25.21 ■ 5 rue de Thorigny (in the Hôtel Salé, M°St-Paul) ■ 9:30am-6pm, clsd Tue

SEX CLUBS

The Glove 33-1/48.87.31.36 ■ 34 rue Charlot (M°Sebastien-Froissard) ■ open late, clsd Mon-Tue, strict dress code, leather/ rubber/ uniform, theme nights, also bar

EROTICA

Rexx 33-1/42.77.58.57, 33-1/42.77.36.22 ■ 42 rue de Poitou (at rue Charlot, M°St-Sébastien-Froissard) ■ clsd Sun, new, custom & secondhand leather & S/M accessories

Paris—04

ACCOMMODATIONS

27 **Hôtel Beaubourg** [GS] 33-1/42.74.34.24 ■ 11 rue Simon le Franc (btwn rue Beaubourg & rue du Temple, M°Hôtel-de-Ville) ■ htlbeaubourg@hotellerie.net

28 **Hôtel Central Marais** 33-1/48.87.56.08 ■ 33 rue Vieille du Temple, upstairs (at rue Ste-Croix-de-la-Bretonnerie, M°Hôtel-de-Ville) ■ central location, some shared baths ■ www.hotelcentralmarais.com

29 **Hôtel de la Bretonnerie** [GF] 33-1/48.87.77.63 ■ 22 rue Ste-Croix-de-la-Bretonnerie (M°Hôtel-de-Ville) ■ clsd Aug, 17th-c hotel w/ Louis XIII decor ■ www.labretonnerie.com

30 **Hôtel du Vieux Marais** [GF] 33-1/42.78.47.22 ■ 8 rue du Plâtre (M°Hôtel-de-Ville) ■ centrally located

31 **Libertel Grand Turenne** [GF] 33-1/42.78.43.25, 800/637-2873 (US#) ■ 6 rue de Turenne (at rue St-Antoine, M°St-Paul) ■ www.libertel-hotels.com

BARS

32 **AccesSoir Café** [M,F,S] 33-1/42.72.12.89 ■ 41 rue des Blancs-Manteaux (M°Rambuteau) ■ 6pm-2am, theme nights

33 **Akhenaton Café** [MW,NH] 33-1/48.87.51.04 ■ 12 rue de Plâtre (btwn rue du Temple & rue des Archives, M°Hôtel-de-Ville) ■ 5pm-2am, cafe-bar

34 **L' Alcantara** [W,NH,F] 33-1/42.74.45.00 ■ 18 rue du Roi de Sicile (M°Hôtel-de-Ville) ■ 5pm-2am, friendly cafe-bar

35 **Amnésia Café** [★MW,F] 33-1/42.72.16.94, 33-1/42.72.02.59 ■ 42 rue Vieille du Temple (at rue des Blancs-Manteaux, M°Hôtel-de-Ville) ■ 10:30am-2am, brunch daily

73 **L'Arène** [MO,S,V,PC] 33-1/42.21.03.53 ■ 80 quai de l'Hôtel-de-Ville (at rue Vieille-du-Temple) ■ 2pm-6am, till 7am wknds, sex shows, blackout parties, strippers wknds

36 **Le Bar du Palmier** [MW,F] 33-1/42.78.53.53 ■ 16 rue des Lombards (at bd de Sébastopol, M°Châtelet) ■ 5pm-5am, terrace

28 **Bar Hôtel Central** [★M] 33-1/48.87.99.33 ■ 33 rue Vieille du Temple (below 'Hôtel Central Marais') ■ 4pm-2am, from 2pm wknds, international crowd, a Marais landmark ■ www.hotelcentralmarais.com

37 **Bears' Den** [M,D,B,V] 33-1/42.71.08.20 ■ 6 rue des Lombards (at rue St-Martin, M°Hôtel-de-Ville) ■ 4pm-2am, theme nights, darkroom ■ www.bearsden.fr

38 **Cox Café Bar** [★M] 33-1/42.72.08.00 ■ 15 rue des Archives (at rue Ste-Croix-de-la-Bretonnerie, M°Hôtel-de-Ville) ■ 1pm-2am, cruisy, terrace

39 **Full-Métal** [M,L] 40 rue des Blancs-Manteaux (M°Rambuteau) ■ 5pm-4am, till 6am Fri-Sat, well-stocked 'hard backroom bar', theme parties, dress code ■ full.metal.online.fr

40 **Le Mic-Man** [M,NH,V] 33-1/42.74.39.80 ■ 24 rue Geoffroy-l'Angevin (at rue du Renard, M°Rambuteau) ■ noon-2am, open later wknds, friendly bar w/ cruisy cave downstairs ■ www.micman.fr

41 **Le Mixer Bar** [★MW,D,YC] 33-1/48.87.55.44 ■ 23 rue Ste-Croix-de-la-Bretonnerie (at rue des Archives, M°Hôtel-de-Ville) ■ 5pm-2am, 3-flr techno/ house bar, theme nights

42 **Monkey's Café** [MW,F] 33-1/42.74.45.00 ■ 30 rue de Roi-de-Sicile (M°Hôtel-de-Ville) ■ noon-2am, Italian

43 **Okawa** [★GS,F,S,YC] 33-1/48.04.30.69 ■ 40 Vieille du Temple (at rue Ste-Croix-de-la-Bretonnerie, M°Hôtel-de-Ville) ■ 9am-2am, cafe-bar in 12th/ 13th century caves, theme nights, cabaret, piano bar Tue-Wed, also restaurant

44 **L' Onix** [M,TG,S] 33-1/42.72.37.72 ■ 15 rue des Lombards (nr rue St-Martin, M°Châtelet) ■ noon-2am, piano bar Wed, Th & Sun, terrace

45 **L' Open** [★MW,F] 33-1/42.72.26.18 ■ 17 rue des Archives (at rue Ste-Croix-de-la-Bretonnerie, M°Hôtel-de-Ville) ■ 10am-2am, Sun brunch, sidewalk cafe-bar; also L'Open Coffee Shop, 15 rue des Archives (33-1/48.87.80.25), salads & sandwiches ■ opencafe@caramail.com

46 **Pub Le Feeling** [MW,NH] 33-1/48.04.70.03 ■ 43 rue Ste-Croix-de-la-Bretonnerie (M°Hôtel-de-Ville) ■ 2pm-2am

47 **QG Bar** [MO,L,V] 33-1/48.87.74.18 ■ 12 rue Simon le Franc (at rue du Renard, M°Rambuteau) ■ 4pm-8am, theme parties Fri, dress code, sex bar ■ www.qgbar.com

48 **Quetzal** [★M,NH,S] 33-1/48.87.99.07 ■ 10 rue de la Verrerie (at rue des Archives, M°Hôtel-de-Ville) ■ noon-5am, cruise bar, Internet access, go-go boys/ shows Mon, Th & Sun, darkroom, terrace ■ quetzalbar.com

52 **Rainbow Cafe** [M,TG,NH,F] 33-1/40.29.05.55 ■ 16 rue de la Verrerie (M°Hôtel-de-Ville) ■ 5pm-2am, clsd Mon, dancing/DJ downstairs wknds

49 **Les Scandaleuses** [W,S,V] 33-1/48.87.39.26 ■ 8 rue des Ecouffes (btwn rue de Rivoli & rue des Rosiers, M°St-Paul) ■ 6pm-2am

50 **Le Sun Café** [M,F] 33-1/40.29.44.40 ■ 35 rue Ste-Croix-de-la-Bretonnerie (at rue du Temple, M°Hôtel-de-Ville) ■ 8am-2am, bar upstairs, tanning salon downstairs, theme nights, DJs

51 **Swetty's Cafe** [M,V] 33-1/40.27.97.42 ■ 49 rue des Blancs-Manteaux (at rue du Temple, M°Hôtel-de-Ville) ■ cruise bar, live music wknds

48 **Le Thermik Bar** [M,V] 33-1/44.78.08.18 ■ 7 rue de la Verrerie (at rue des Archives, M°Hôtel-de-Ville) ■ 4pm-2am, theme nights

CAFES

Café Beaubourg 33-1/48.87.63.96 ■ 100 rue St-Martin (M°Rambuteau) ■ next to Centre Pompidou, chic cafe-bar w/ large terrace

Le Coffe-Shop [MW] 33-1/42.74.24.21 ■ 3 rue Ste-Croix-de-la-Bretonnerie (at rue Vieille du Temple, M°Hôtel-de-Ville) ■ 9am-2am, full bar

RESTAURANTS

A 2 Pas du Dos [★MW] 33-1/42.77.10.52 ■ 101 rue Vieille-du-Temple (at rue des Quatre Fils, M°Hôtel-de-Ville) ■ lunch Tue-Fri & dinner Tue-Sat

L' Alivi 33-1/48.87.90.20 ■ 27 rue du Roi-de-Sicile (M°Hôtel-de-Ville) ■ lunch & dinner, Corsican

Amadéo 33-1/48.87.01.02 ■ 19 rue François-Miron (M°St-Paul) ■ lunch Tue-Fri, dinner Mon-Sat, clsd Sun, creative gourmet

Au Tibourg 33-1/42.74.45.25 ■ 29 rue du Bourg-Tibourg (M°Hôtel-de-Ville) ■ lunch & dinner, French, quiet & romantic setting ■ www.autibourg.com

L' Auberge de la Reine Blanche 33-1/46.33.07.87 ■ 30 rue St-Louis-en-l'Ile (nr Rue des 2 Ponts, M°Pont-Marie) ■ lunch Fri-Tue, dinner Th-Tue, clsd Wed, homestyle French

Le Bucheron 33-1/48.87.71.31 ■ 9 rue du Roi-de-Sicile (M°St-Paul) ■ lunch Mon-Sat & dinner nightly, Italian, also bar

La Canaille [MW] 33-1/42.78.09.71 ■ 4 rue Crillon (M°Quai-de-la-Rapée) ■ lunch Mon-Fri, dinner Mon-Sat, clsd Sun, bistro fare, full bar

Cat'Man 33-1/42.74.43.32 ■ 12 rue du Temple (M°Hôtel-de-Ville) ■ 11am-11pm, clsd Mon, salads & crepes, terrace

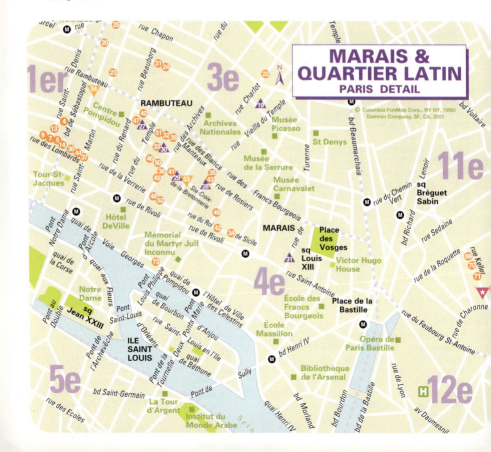

Le Chant des Voyelles [MW] 33-1/42.77.77.07 ■ 4 rue des Lombards (M°Châtelet) ■ lunch & dinner, traditional French, terrace

Le Croc' Man [M] 33-1/42.77.60.02 ■ 6 rue Geoffroy l'Angevin (M°Rambuteau) ■ 7pm-close, clsd Tue ■ www.micman.fr

Le Divin [WC] 33-1/42.77.10.20 ■ 41 rue Ste-Croix-de-la-Bretonnerie (at rue du Temple, M°Hôtel-de-Ville) ■ lunch Tue-Sat & dinner Tue-Sun, clsd Mon

Le Dos de la Baleine 33-1/42.72.38.98 ■ 40 rue des Blancs-Manteaux (M°Rambuteau) ■ lunch Tue-Fri, dinner Tue-Sun, clsd Mon, clsd Aug, gourmet seafood

Eclache & Cie 33-1/42.74.62.62 ■ 10 rue St-Merri (M°Hôtel-de-Ville) ■ lunch & dinner, brunch wknds, bistro fare, terrace ■ aeclache@club-internet.fr

Equinox [S] 33-1/42.71.92.41 ■ 33-35 rue des Rosiers (M°St-Paul) ■ 11:30am-3:30pm & 7pm-midnight, clsd Mon, Québeçois/ French, full bar, piano bar, shows Th-Fri

Le Flyer 33-1/48.04.78.75 ■ 94 rue St-Martin (M°Hôtel-de-Ville) ■ lunch & dinner, clsd Mon, in 14th-c caves w/ 50s decor

Le Fond de Cour [WC] 33-1/42.74.71.52 ■ 3 rue Ste-Croix-de-la-Bretonnerie (in back courtyard, M°Hôtel-de-Ville) ■ lunch & dinner, Sun brunch, gourmet French, terrace

Le Gai Moulin [MW] 33-1/48.87.47.59 ■ 4 rue St-Merri (at rue du Temple, M°Hôtel-de-Ville) ■ noon-midnight, French/ int'l ■ le.gai.moulin@wanadoo.fr

Le Krokodil [★M,S] 33-1/48.87.55.67 ■ 20 rue de la Reynie (at bd Sébastopol, in Les Halles, M°Châtelet) ■ noon-2am, Sun brunch, traditional French, also bar, live DJ, shows Mon-Wed, male strippers Fri-Sat, terrace ■ www.krokodil.fr

Les Mauvais Garçons 33-1/42.72.74.97 ■ 4 rue des Mauvais Garçons (M°Hôtel-de-Ville)

O'2F [GS,S] 33-1/42.72.75.75 ■ 4 rue du Roi-de-Sicile (M°St-Paul) ■ dinner only, French, homestyle French

Le Petit Picard [MW] 33-1/42.78.54.03 ■ 42 rue Ste-Croix-de-la-Bretonnerie (M°Hôtel-de-Ville) ■ lunch Tue-Fri & dinner Tue-Sun, clsd Mon

La Petite Chaumière 33-1/42.72.13.90 ■ 41 rue des Blancs-Manteaux (M°Rambuteau) ■ dinner only, French, menu changes daily

Un Piano dans la Cuisine [S] 33-1/42.72.23.81 ■ 20 rue de la Verrerie (M°Hôtel-de-Ville) ■ 8:30pm-midnight, drag shows Tue-Sun

Piccolo Teatro 33-1/42.72.17.79 ■ 6 rue des Ecouffes ■ lunch & dinner, clsd Mon, vegetarian

Les Piétons [GS] 33-1/48.87.82.87 ■ 8 rue des Lombards (M°Châtelet) ■ 11am-9pm, brunch noon-6pm Sun, Spanish/ tapas, also bar, open till 2am (dancing/DJ Wed)

Plateau 26 [E,K] 33-1/48.87.10.75 ■ 26 rue des Lombards (M°Châtelet) ■ 7pm-2am, till 3:30am wknds, theater-cafe, piano bar, karaoke from 11:30pm Sat

Le Rude [M,WC] 33-1/42.74.05.15 ■ 23 rue du Temple (at rue Ste-Croix-de-la-Bretonnerie, M°Hôtel-de-Ville) ■ noon-2am, French/ American, also bar

ENTERTAINMENT & RECREATION
Gay Beach eastern end of Ile St-Louis ■ sunbathing

BOOKSTORES
53 Les Mots à la Bouche 33-1/42.78.88.30 ■ 6 rue Ste-Croix-de-la-Bretonnerie (nr rue du Vieille du Temple, M°Hôtel-de-Ville) ■ 11am-11pm, 2pm-8pm Sun, lgbt, English titles ■ www.motalabouche.com

54 Pause Lecture 33-1/44.61.95.05 ■ 61 rue de Quincampoix (at rue Rambuteau) ■ 11am-midnight, from 1pm Sun, lgbt ■ www.pauselecture.com

RETAIL SHOPS
7H10 [GO] 33-1/42.71.77.10 ■ 22 rue des Ecouffes (nr rue des Rosiers) ■ jewelry, gifts, antiques

Abraxas 33-1/48.04.33.55 ■ 9 rue St-Merri ■ tattoos, piercing, large selection of body jewelry ■ www.abraxas.fr

Boy'z Bazaar 33-1/42.71.94.00 ■ 5 rue Ste-Croix-de-la-Bretonnerie (at rue Vieille du Temple, M°Hôtel-de-Ville) ■ noon-midnight, 2pm-9pm Sun, gay play clothes, from clubwear to drag to leather; also Boy'z Basics (42.71.67.00), noon-9pm, till midnight Sat, from 2pm Sun

Factory's 33-1/48.87.29.10 ■ 3 rue Ste-Croix-de-la-Bretonnerie (M°Hôtel-de-Ville) ■ 10am-8pm, 2pm-7pm Sun, clothing & accessories

MEN'S CLUBS
Athletic World [V] 33-1/42.77.19.78 ■ 20 rue du Bourg-Tibourg (M°Hôtel-de-Ville) ■ noon-2am, from 4am wknds, gym equipment, bar

EROTICA
Phylea 33-1/42.76.01.80 ■ 61 rue Quincampoix (M°Rambuteau) ■ clsd Sun, vinyl, leather, rubber, corsets, S/M accessories

TTBM 33-1/48.04.80.88 ■ 16 rue Ste-Croix-de-la-Bretonnerie (M°Hôtel-de-Ville) ■ leather, latex, uniforms & fetish gear ■ www.ttbm.com

Paris—05

ACCOMMODATIONS
55 Hotel des Nations [GF] 33-1/43.26.45.24 ■ 54 rue Monge (nr rue des Écoles, M°Pl-Monge) ■ small hotel in the Latin Quarter ■ www.regetel.com/hnations.htm

La Vie en Rose [GF,NS] 33-1/43.54.03.46, 888/866-4730 (US#) ■ Quai de la Tournelle ■ enjoy panoramic views of Paris on the Seine aboard this luxury vessel, 3-night minimum stay ■ www.la-vie-en-rose.com

CAFES
Clickside 33-1/56.81.03.00 ■ 14 rue Domat (off rue Dante, M°St-Michel) ■ 10am-midnight, 1pm-11pm wknds, cybercafe (some qwerty keyboards) ■ www.clickside.com

RESTAURANTS
Restaurant le Petit Prince de Paris [★] 33-1/43.54.77.26 ■ 12 rue de Lanneau (M°Maubert-Mutualité) ■ 7:30pm-midnight, French

ENTERTAINMENT & RECREATION
Open-Air Sculpture Museum 33-1/42.71.25.21 ■ along the Seine btwn the Jardin des Plantes & the Institut du Monde Arabe

Paris—06

ACCOMMODATIONS
56 L' Hôtel [GF] 33-1/44.41.99.00 ■ 13 rue des Beaux-Arts (btwn rue Bonaparte & rue de Seine, M°St-Germain-des-Près) ■ eccentric hotel where Oscar Wilde died

BARS
57 Le Trap [M,S,V,PC] 33-1/43.54.53.53 ■ 10 rue Jacob (at rue des Saints-Pères, M°St-Germain-des-Près) ■ 11pm-close, cruise bar, large backroom, go-go boys Mon & Wed, cover charge Fri-Sat

NIGHTCLUBS
58 La Rive-Gauche [W,D,$] 33-1/42.22.51.70 ■ 1 rue du Sabot (M°St-Sulpice) ■ 11pm-dawn Fri-Sat only

France • Europe

Bookstores

Les Amazones 33-1/40.46.08.37 ■ 68 rue Bonaparte ■ specializes in antique, lesbian & feminist books ■ www.galaxidion.fr/amazones/

La Librairie des Femmes 33-1/42.22.60.74 ■ 74 rue de Seine ■ 11am-7pm, clsd Sun, women's

The Village Voice 33-1/46.33.36.47 ■ 6 rue Princesse (M°Mabillon) ■ 10am-8pm, from 2pm Sun-Mon, till 7pm Sun, English-language bookshop

Paris—07

Accommodations
59 **Hôtel Muguet** [GF] 33-1/47.05.05.93 ■ 11 rue Chevert (nr av de Tourville, nr the Eiffel Tower) ■ recently renovated ■ www.hotelmuguet.com

Paris—08

Accommodations
60 **Crillon** [GF,F] 33-1/44.71.15.01, 800/888-4747 (US#) ■ 10 place de la Concorde ■ ultra-luxe hotel ■ www.crillon-paris.com

Bars
61 **Le Day-Off** [GS,NH,F] 33-1/45.22.87.90 ■ 10 rue de l'Isly (M°Gare-St-Lazare) ■ noon-3am Mon-Fri only, cocktail bar

Nightclubs
62 **Le Queen** [★M,D,TG,S,YC,$] 33-1/42.89.31.32 ■ 102 av des Champs-Élysées (btwn rue Washington & rue de Berri, M°Georges-V) ■ 11:30pm-dawn, very trendy, selective door, theme nights, drag shows, go-go boys ■ www.queen.fr

Restaurants
Le Petit Yvan 33-1/42.89.49.65 ■ 1 bis, rue Jean-Mermoz (M°F-D-Roosevelt) ■ lunch Mon-Fri & dinner Mon-Sat, clsd Sun, traditional French

Sex Clubs
La Banque Club [V] 33-1/42.56.49.26 ■ 23 rue de Penthièvre (off Champs d'Élysées, M°Miromesnil) ■ 4pm-2am, from 2pm Sun, 3 levels, maze, theme nights, also bar ■ banqueclub@aol.com

Erotica
IEM Liège 33-1/45.22.69.01 ■ 33 rue de Liège (M°Liège) ■ clsd Sun ■ www.iem.fr

Vidéovision 33-1/42.93.66.04 ■ 62 rue de Rome (M°Europe) ■ clsd Sun

Paris—09

Accommodations
63 **The Grand** [GF] 33-1/40.07.32.32, 800/327-0200 (US#) ■ 2 rue Scribe ■ ultra-luxe Art Deco hotel

Bars
64 **Mec Zone** [M,L,V] 33-1/40.82.94.18 ■ 27 rue Turgot (M°Anvers) ■ 9pm-6am, from 2pm wknds for underwear parties, cruisy, theme nights, darkroom

Nightclubs
65 **Folies Pigalle** [GS,D,MR,$] 33-1/48.78.55.25, 33-1/42.80.12.03 (BBB info line) ■ 11 place Pigalle (M°Pigalle) ■ midnight-dawn Tue-Sat, more gay at very popular 'Black, Blanc, Beur' T-dance 6pm-midnight Sun & at 'Escualita' (MR-L,TG) from midnight Sun ■ www.disco54.com/foliespigalle

Restaurants
Le 48 Condorcet 33-1/45.26.98.13 ■ 48 rue Condorcet (M°Anvers) ■ lunch Mon-Fri, dinner Mon-Sat, clsd Sun, clsd Aug

Les Colonnes de Madeleine 33-1/47.42.60.55 ■ 6 rue de Sèze (M°Madeleine) ■ lunch & dinner, clsd Sun, French bistro, also bar, open 7pm-4am

Gilles et Gabriel 33-1/45.26.86.26 ■ 24 rue Rodier (M°Cadet) ■ lunch Mon-Fri & dinner Mon-Sat, clsd Sun, clsd Aug

Men's Clubs
IDM [★V] 33-1/45.23.10.03 ■ 4 rue du Faubourg-Montmartre (at bd St-Martin, M°Grand-Blvds) ■ 3 levels, full gym, jacuzzi, bar

Le Mandala [V,SW] 33-1/42.46.60.14 ■ 2 rue Drouot (at rue Montmartre, M°Richelieu-Drouot) ■ noon-1am, till 6am Th-Sat, gym equipment, bar

Erotica
Yanko 33-1/45.26.71.19 ■ 10 pl de Clichy ■ videos & cinema

Paris—10

Accommodations
Hôtel Moderne du Temple [GS,GO] 33-1/42.08.09.04 ■ 3 rue d'Aix ■ economy-class hotel, some shared baths ■ perso.libertysurf.fr/hmt

Bars
66 **Café Moustache** [M,NH,V] 33-1/46.07.72.70 ■ 138 rue du Faubourg St-Martin (at bd de Magenta, M°Gare-de-l'Est) ■ 5pm-2am, patio

67 **Le Coming-Out** [MW,NH,F] 33-1/42.01.01.77 ■ 20 rue Beaurepaire (M°République) ■ 5pm-2am, terrace

68 **Les Rangers** [M,O,L,S,V,$] 33-1/42.39.83.30 ■ 6 bd St-Denis (M°Strasbourg) ■ 1pm-midnight, till 2am Fri, from 2pm wknds, cruise bar & sex club

Restaurants
Le Châlet Maya [MW] 33-1/47.70.52.78 ■ 5 rue des Petits Hôtels (M°Gare de l'Est) ■ lunch Mon-Fri, dinner Mon-Sat, clsd Sun, French

L' Insensé [E] 33-1/42.01.25.26 ■ 10 rue Marie-et-Louise (M°Goncourt) ■ noon-2:30pm & 8pm-11pm, till midnight Fri-Sat, clsd Sun

Men's Clubs
Key West Sauna [★V,SW] 33-1/45.26.31.74 ■ 141 rue Lafayette (M°Gare-du-Nord) ■ noon-1am, till 2am Fri-Sat, gym equipment, jacuzzi

Erotica
IEM St-Maur 33-1/40.18.51.51 ■ 208 rue St-Maur (M°Goncourt) ■ clsd Sun, huge sex shop, whole flr of leather/ latex items ■ www.iem.fr

Paris—11

Accommodations
Hôtel Beaumarchais [GS] 33-1/53.36.86.86 ■ 3 rue Oberkampf (btwn bd Beaumarchais & bd Voltaire, M°Filles-du-Calvaire)

Hôtel Mondia [GF] 33-1/47.00.93.44 ■ 22 rue du Grand-Prieuré (M°République) ■ www.hotel-mondia.com

Libertel Croix-de-Malté [GF] 33-1/48.05.09.36, 800/949-7562 (US#) ■ 5 rue de Malté (M°Oberkampf) ■ www.libertel-hotels.com

Bars
L' Arambar [MW,NH] 33-1/48.05.57.79 ■ 7 rue de la Folie-Méricourt (M°St-Ambroise) ■ noon-2am, theme nights

69 **Interface** [MW,S] 33-1/47.00.67.15 ■ 34 rue Keller (M°Bastille) ■ 3pm-2am ■ kellerfa@club-internet.fr

70 **Le K** [MW,F] 33-1/53.36.03.96 ■ 20 rue Keller (M°Bastille) ■ 5pm-2am, clsd Mon, also restaurant, 8pm-11:30pm, Provençal

71 **Keller's** [MO,L,$] 33-1/47.00.05.39 ■ 14 rue Keller (M°Bastille) ■ 10:30pm-2am, till 4am Th-Sat, raunchy cruise bar, theme parties, strict dress code, darkroom ■ www.Kellers.fr

Paris, Texas [M,NH] 33-1/43.79.90.11 ■ 40 rue Godefroy-Cavaignac (M°Voltaire) ■ 4pm-2am, from 2pm wknds, piano bar downstairs

NIGHTCLUBS

72 **Le Gibus Club** [GF,D,E,$] 33-1/47.00.78.88 ■ 18 rue du Faubourg-du-Temple (M°République) ■ midnight-close, clsd Mon-Tue, gay Th & Sat, also piano bar, live music Sat

RESTAURANTS

Le Temps Au Temps [MW] 33-1/43.79.63.40 ■ 13 rue Paul Bert (M°Faidherbe-Chaligny) ■ 8pm-11pm, clsd Sun, French bistro ■ www.geocities.com/Paris/Salon/4163

Le Sofa 33-1/43.14.07.46 ■ 21 rue St-Sabin (M°Bastille) ■ 6pm-midnight, till 2am Th-Sat, clsd Sun-Mon, also bar ■ lesofa.free.fr

Terranova 33-1/43.67.82.83 ■ 45 rue de Montreuil (M°Faidherbe-Chaligny) ■ noon-2:30pm Mon-Fri & 7pm-11pm nightly, clsd Sun & Aug, Italian

BOOKSTORES

Le Funambule 33-1/48.06.74.94 ■ 48 rue Jean-Pierre Timbaud (M°Parmentier) ■ 2pm-7pm Tue-Sat & by appt, fine art/ photography books, lgbt section

Livralire 33-1/43.73.33.22 ■ 145 rue de Charonne ■ 11am-8pm, clsd Sun-Mon, lgbt section

MEN'S CLUBS

Bastille Sauna [MR,V] 33-1/43.38.07.02 ■ 4 passage St-Antoine (nr rue Keller, M°Ledru-Rollin) ■ gym equipment, bar

SEX CLUBS

Les Docks [V] 33-1/43.57.33.82 ■ 150 rue St-Maur (M°Goncourt) ■ bar, theme nights

EROTICA

Démonia 33-1/43.14.82.70 ■ 10 Cité Joly (M°Pere-Lachaise) ■ clsd Sun, huge BDSM shop ■ www.demonia.com

Kingdom [V] 33-1/48.07.07.08 ■ 19 rue Keller (M°Bastille) ■ clsd Sun, leather, latex, military gear ■ kingdom@citegay.com

Paris—12

RESTAURANTS

Bella Tavola 33-1/44.74.07.06 ■ 161 av Daumesnil (M°Daumesnil) ■ 11:30am-11:30pm

Caviar & Co [MW] 33-1/43.56.13.98 ■ 5 rue de Reuilly (M°Faidherbe-Chaligny) ■ noon-2pm Tue-Fri & 7:30pm-midnight nightly, clsd Sun-Mon, clsd Aug, foies gras & caviar

Paris—13

RESTAURANTS

L' ArtiShow [S] 33-1/45.88.30.98 ■ 27 rue de la Colonie (M°Corvisart) ■ lunch Mon-Fri & dinner Tue-Sat, clsd Sun, French/ Thai, cabaret Sat ■ www.artishowlive.com

Au Pet de Lapin 33-1/45.86.58.21 ■ 2 rue Dunois (M°Massena) ■ lunch & dinner, clsd Sun-Mon, clsd Aug, foies gras & seafood

ENTERTAINMENT & RECREATION

Bibliotheque Marguerite Durand 33-1/45.70.80.30 ■ 79 rue Nationale ■ 2pm-6pm, clsd Sun-Mon, unique collection of written works by & about women

Paris—14

RESTAURANTS

Au Feu Follet [W] 33-1/43.22.65.72 ■ 5 rue Raymond Losserand (M°Gaîté) ■ 7:30pm-close, clsd Sun, Southeast French

Le Petit Léo 33-1/43.20.76.55 ■ 7 rue Léopold-Robert (M°Raspail) ■ lunch Mon-Fri & dinner nightly, hearty French

La Route du Château [MW] 33-1/43.20.09.59 ■ 36 rue Raymond Losserand (M°Gaîté) ■ lunch Tue-Sat & dinner Mon-Sat, clsd Sun, clsd Aug, French

ENTERTAINMENT & RECREATION

Catacombes 33-1/43.22.47.63 ■ 1 place Denfert Rochereau ■ a ghoulish yet intriguing tourist destination, these burial tunnels were the headquarters of the Résistance during World War II

Paris—15

RESTAURANTS

L' Accent [W] 33-1/45.79.20.26 ■ 93 rue de Javel (M°Charles-Michel) ■ 8pm-12:30am, clsd Sun, pizzeria

Le Boudoir [W] 33-1/40.59.82.28 ■ 22 rue Frémicourt (M°La-Motte-Picquet) ■ lunch Tue-Fri, dinner Tue-Sun, clsd Mon, French, also bar, open 5:30pm-1am

L' Hémis [W,S] 33-1/48.56.80.32 ■ 21 rue Mademoiselle (M°Commerce) ■ lunch Mon-Fri & dinner Tue-Sat, clsd Sun-Mon, also bar

L' Imprevu [W] 33-1/40.45.09.81 ■ 7 rue de Cadix ■ lunch & dinner, good fondue & raclette, also bar

Paris—16

MEN'S CLUBS

Eden Forme Sauna [V] 33-1/47.04.41.24 ■ 109 av Victor-Hugo (M°Victor-Hugo) ■ clsd Aug, bar

Paris—17

RESTAURANTS

L' Insolence 33-1/42.29.57.96 ■ 66 rue Legendre (M°Rome) ■ lunch & dinner, clsd Sun, clsd Aug, terrace

Macis et Muscade 33-1/42.26.62.26 ■ 110 rue Legendre (M°Rome) ■ lunch & dinner, cuisine infused w/ essential oils ■ www.saveurs.com/mucis/

MEN'S CLUBS

King Sauna [V] 33-1/42.94.19.10 ■ 21 rue Bridaine (nr place de Clichy, M°Rome) ■ 1pm-7am, bar ■ synergie@hotmail.com

Paris—20

ENTERTAINMENT & RECREATION

Père Lachaise Cemetery bd de Ménilmontant (M°Père-Lachaise) ■ perhaps the world's most famous resting place, where lie such notables as Chopin, Gertrude Stein, Oscar Wilde, Sarah Bernhardt, Isadora Duncan & Jim Morrison

MEN'S CLUBS

Le Riad [SW,V] 33-1/47.97.25.52 ■ 184 rue des Pyrénées (M°Gambetta) ■ Oriental-theme sauna, bar

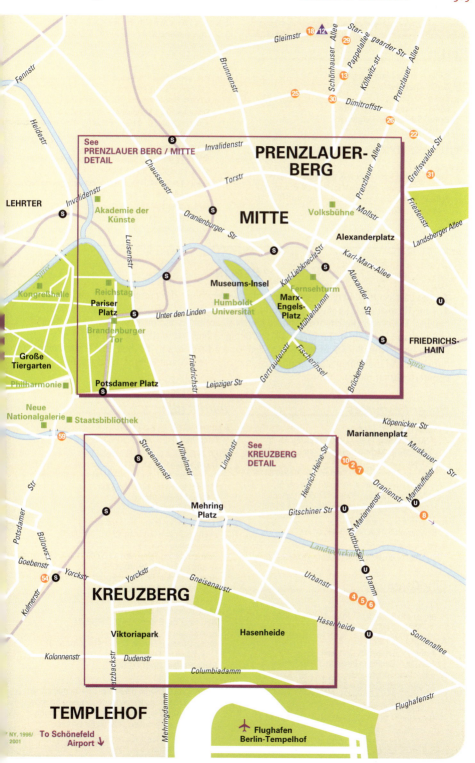

GERMANY

Berlin

Berlin is divided into 5 regions:
Berlin—Overview
Berlin—Kreuzberg
Berlin—Prenzlauer Berg-Mitte
Berlin—Schöneberg-Tiergarten
Berlin—Outer

Berlin—Overview

NIGHTCLUBS

MegaDyke Productions [★W,D] ■ popular parties & events for lesbians, including 'Subterra' & 'Gravity' at SchwuZ & biannual mega 'Lesben Planet' parties
■ www.snafu-de/~megadyke.rainbow

ENTERTAINMENT & RECREATION

English Movie Night 49-30/883.53.25 (theater #) ■ at Kurbel Theater, Giesebrechstr 4 (in Charlottenberg, U-Adenauer Platz) ■ that's (mainstream) movies in English, not British cinema...meet 7pm 1st Tue at the 'Irish Harp Pub' across from the theater; films begin around 8pm; gay travelers very welcome
■ home.t-online.de/home/0307827298-0001/

Schwules (Gay) Museum 49-30/693.11.72
■ Mehringdamm 61 (at Gneisenaustr, U-Mehringdamm) ■ 2pm-6pm, till 7pm Sat ■ www.schwulesmuseum.de

PUBLICATIONS

BlattGold 49-30/215.66.28 ■ monthly entertainment guide for women (in German)
Sergej 49-30/44.31.98.0 ■ free monthly gay magazine
■ www.sergej.de
Siegessäule 49-30/23.55.39-0, 49-30/23.55.39-32 ■ free monthly lgbt city magazine (in German)
■ www.siegessaeule.de

BERLIN

In the past century, Berlin has seen just about everything: the outrageous art and cabaret of the Weimar era; the ravages of world war; ideological standoffs that physically divided families, lovers and the city itself; and a largely peaceful revolution that brought Germany and the world together. Through it all, the Berliners have retained their own brand of cheeky humor—Berliner Schnauze, it's called—and a fierce loyalty to their city. While Berlin's museums and monuments are world-class, the city's real charm is in its art cafes and counter-cultural milieu.

Queer Resources

COMMUNITY INFO

▼ AHA (Lesbian & Gay Center & Cafe), 49-30/692.36.48. Mehringdamm 61, Kreuzberg. 3pm-11pm Sun.
▼ Mann-O-Meter (Gay Center), 49-30/216.80.08, web: www.mann-o-meter.de. Motzstr 5, Schöneberg. 5pm-10pm, from 4pm wknds.
Lesbenberatung (lesbian line) 49-30/215.20.00.

AIDS RESOURCES

Berliner AIDS-Hilfe 49-30/885.64.00.

RECOVERY

49-30/216.80.08. Meets at Mann-O-Meter 5pm Tue.

City Calendar

LGBT PRIDE

3rd or 4th Saturday in June. 49-30/21.68.08 (M-O-M #).

ANNUAL EVENTS

January - Tuntenball. Drag ball.
February - Berlinale: Berlin Int'l Film Festival.
July - Love Parade, web: www.prehm.com/kudamm/LoveParade.
October - Jazz Fest Berlin.
Lesbian Film Festival.
November - Queer Film Festival 49-30/861.45.32.

Tourist Info

AIRPORT DIRECTIONS

Tempelhof, Tegel, and Schönefeld.

PUBLIC TRANSIT & TAXIS

Taxi 49-30/44.33.22.
Express-Bus X9 from Tegel Airport to central Berlin.
U-Bahn (subway) 49-30/194.49.
S-Bahn (elevated train).
Bus 49-30/301.80.28.

TOURIST SPOTS & INFO

Bauhaus Design Museum 49-30/254.00.20.
Brandenburg Gate.
Charlottenburg Palace 49-30/32.09.11.
Egyptian Museum 49-30/20.90.55.55.
Homo Memorial (at Nollendorfplatz station).
Kaiser Wilhelm Memorial Church.
Käthe-Kollwitz Museum 49-30/882.52.10.
Museuminsel (Museum Island).
New National Gallery 49-30/266.26.51.
Reichstag.
Visitor's Center: Europa Center 49-30/62.60.31. Budapester Str 2.
Berlin Hotline 49-30/25.00.25.

WEATHER

Berlin is on the same parallel as Newfoundland, so if you're visiting in the winter, prepare for snow and bitter cold. Summer is balmy while spring and fall are beautiful, if sometimes rainy.

Berlin • Germany

Berlin—Kreuzberg

Accommodations
1. **Transit** [GF] 49-30/789.04.70 ■ Hagelberger Str 53-54 (U-Mehringdamm) ■ also bar ■ www.hotel-transit.de

Bars
2. **Bierhimmel** [GS,YC] 49-30/615.31.22 ■ Oranienstr 183 (U-Kottbusser Tor) ■ 3pm-3am
3. **BKA Cabaret** [GS,D,S,WC,$] 49-30/251.01.12 ■ Mehringdamm 32-34 (at Gneisenaustr, U-Mehringdamm) ■ shows 8pm Wed-Sun, DJ from 11pm Fri-Sat
4. **Dandy Club** [M,L,V,WC] 49-30/691.90.13 ■ Urbanstr 64 (at Leinestr) ■ 10pm-close, cruise bar w/ darkroom
5. **Ficken 3000** [M,D,L,V,YC] 49-30/69.50.73.35 ■ Urbanstr 70 (at Hermannplatz) ■ 10pm-close, cruisy, large darkroom
6. **Mondschein** [M,NH,F] 49-30/693.23.55 ■ Urbanstr 101 (at Hermannplatz) ■ 8pm-3am, till 5am Fri-Sat, darkroom
7. **Roses** [★MW,TG,YC] 49-30/615.65.70 ■ Oranienstr 187 (at Kottbusser Tor) ■ 10pm-close

Nightclubs
8. **Club XS** [M,D,S,$] 49-179/491.18.49 ■ Glogauer Str 2 (at Wiener Str, U-Görlitzer Bahnhof) ■ 10pm-close Th only, erotic techno-parties ■ www.clubxs.de
9. **SchwuZ (SchwulenZentrum)** [★M,D,S,$] 49-30/69.50.78.92 ■ Mehringdamm 61 (at Fuggerstr, beneath the 'Schwules Museum', U-Mehringdamm) ■ 11pm Sat, also 'Club 69' (retro) 1st Fri, 'Subterra' (MW) 2nd Fri, 'Rock Nacht' 4th Fri, 'Gravity' 5th Fri (MW, standards, Latin & soul), 'GaymeBoy' (for youth 16-26) 2nd Th ■ www.schwuz.de
10. **SO 36** [★MW,D,TG,S,V,YC,WC] 49-30/61.40.13.06, 49-30/61.40.13.07 ■ Oranienstr 190 (at Kottbusser Tor) ■ theme nights, also live music venue ■ www.so36.de

Cafes
Melitta Sundström [MW,WC] 49-30/692.44.14 ■ Mehringdamm 61 (at Gneisenaustr) ■ 10am-8pm, till 4pm Sat, clsd Sun, terrace, also lgbt bookstore

Schoko-Café [WO,D,E] 49-30/615.15.61, 49-30/694.10.77 ■ Mariannenstr 6 (at Kottbusser Tor) ■ 5pm-close, cafe, bar & community center, also steam bath

Restaurants
Abendmahl [WC] 49-30/612.51.70 ■ Muskauer Str 9 (U-Görlitzer Bahnhof) ■ 6pm-11:30pm, vegetarian & seafood, also bar (open till 1am), terrace

Locus [★MW] 49-30/691.56.37 ■ Marheinekeplatz 4 ■ 10am-2am, Mexican, full bar, lesbian-owned/ run

Bookstores
Chronika Buchhandlung Kreuzberg 49-30/693.42.69 ■ Bergmannstr 26 (at Marheinekeplatz) ■ 10am-7pm, till 3pm Sat, many lesbian titles

Erotica
Playstixx 49-30/61.65.95.00 ■ Waldemarstr 24 ■ toys, also sex counseling ■ www.playstixx.de

Sexclusivitäten 49-30/693.66.66 ■ Fürbringer Str 2 ■ lesbian sex shop, toys, leather, videos, also escort service ■ www.sexclusivitaeten.de

Berlin—Prenzlauer Berg-Mitte

ACCOMMODATIONS
11 **Le Moustache** [M] 49-30/281.72.77 ■ Gartenstr 4 (at Rosenthaler Platz, U-Oranienburger Tor) ■ also 'Moustache Bar' (M,L,F), open 8pm-close, clsd Mon-Tue ■ www.lemoustache.de

12 **Schall & Rauch Pension** [MW] 49-30/443.39.70, 49-30/448.07.70 ■ Gleimstr 23 (at Schönhauser Allee) ■ also bar & restaurant

BARS
13 **Adonis** [MO,PC] 49-30/447.38.88 ■ Pappelallee 32a (at Schönhauser Allee) ■ 24hrs, darkroom

14 **Altberliner Bierstuben** [M,L,F] 49-30/442.61.30 ■ Saarbrücker Str 16 (U-Senefelder Platz) ■ noon-2am, terrace

15 **Bar 808** [MW,F] 49-30/28.04.67.28 ■ Oranienburger Str 42-43 (at Auguststr) ■ 5pm-3am, from noon wknds, cocktail lounge, DJ Th & Sat, Sun brunch ■ www.barlounge808.de

16 **Bärenhöhle** [M,B,BW] 49-30/44.73.65.53 ■ Schönhauser Allee 90 ■ 5pm-3am, beer bar

17 **Besenkammer Bar** [M] 49-30/242.40.83 ■ Rathausstr 1 (at Alexanderplatz, under the S-Bahn bridge) ■ 24hrs, tiny 'beer bar'

18 **Cafe Amsterdam** [GS,TG,F,YC,WC] 49-30/44.00.94.54, 49-30/231.67.96 ■ Gleimstr 24 (at Schönhauser Allee) ■ 9am-3am, till 5am Fri-Sat, cafe-bar, terrace ■ www.cafe-amsterdam.de

19 **Café Senefelder** [MW,D,F,GO] 49-30/449.66.05 ■ Schönhauser Allee 173 (at Senefelder Platz) ■ 6pm-3am, DJ Fri-Sat, lesbian-owned/run

20 **Dark Star** [MO,L,V] 49-30/442.42.13 ■ Schönhauser Allee 39a (at Eberwalder Str) ■ 10pm-6am, darkroom

DarkRoom [MO,L] 49-30/444.93.21 ■ Rodenbergstr 23 (at Schönhauser Allee) ■ 10pm-6am, uniform bar, darkroom, theme parties wknds ■ www.darkroom-berlin.de

22 **Flax** [MW,F] 49-30/44.04.69.88, 49-30/441.98.56 ■ Chodowieckistr 41 (off Greifswalder Str) ■ 3pm-3am, till 4am Sat, brunch 10am-5pm Sun

Greifbar [MO,L,V] 49-30/444.08.28 ■ Wichertstr 10 (at Greifenhagener Str, S/U-Schönhauser Allee) ■ 10pm-6am, darkroom

24 **Image** [MW,F,WC] 49-30/20.45.25.80 ■ Jägerstr 67 (U-Französische Str) ■ 9am-close, from 2pm Sat, from 11am Sun (all-you-can-eat brunch buffet), cafe-bar, terrace

25 **Jim's** [MW,NH,B,F] 49-30/440.63.79 ■ Eberswalder Str 37 (at Fr-Ludwig-Jahn-Sportpark) ■ 8am-close, from noon Sun, bar & restaurant, bears 2nd Sat

26 **Na und** [GS,NH,F] 49-30/442.89.78 ■ Prenzlauer Allee 193 (at Dimitroffstr, S-Prenzlauer Allee) ■ 24hrs, terrace

Offenbar [GF] 49-30/426.09.30 ■ Schreinerstr 5 (U-Samariterstr) ■ 10am-4am, gay Tue-Wed only, brunch buffet wknds

27 **Oh-Ase** [M,F] 49-30/242.30.30 ■ Rathausstr 5 (at Alexanderplatz, in Rathaus passage) ■ noon-2am, from 3pm wknds, cafe-bar, terrace, tropical decor

28 **Peanuts** [M,F] 49-30/247.70.37 ■ Münzstr 8 (S/U-Alexanderplatz) ■ 6pm-4am, till 5am Fri-Sat

Berlin • GERMANY

29 **Pick ab!** [★M,V] 49-30/445.85.23 ■ Greifenhagener Str 16 (S/U-Schönhauser Allee) ■ 10pm-close, cruise bar w/ darkroom ■ www.pickab.de

29 **Romeo** [M,F] 49-30/447.67.89 ■ Greifenhagener Str 16 (S/U-Schönhauser Allee) ■ 11pm-8am, cafe-bar

30 **Schoppenstube** [M,D] 49-30/442.82.04 ■ Schönhauser Allee 44 (at Eberswalder Str) ■ 10pm-7am, theme nights, terrace, cruisy

29 **Shambala** [GS,NH,F] 49-30/447.62.26 ■ Greifenhagener Str 12 (S/U-Schönhauser Allee) ■ 6pm-3am, cafe-bar, women only from 9pm Mon, jungle decor

31 **Sonderbar** [MW,F,YC] 49-30/425.84.94 ■ Käthe-Niederkirchner-Str 34 (nr 'Märchenbrunnen') ■ 8pm-8am, terrace

Stiller Don [★MW,NH,L,F] 49-30/445.59.57 ■ Erich-Weinert-Str 67 (at Schönhauser Allee) ■ 7pm-close, terrace

NIGHTCLUBS

33 **Ackerkeller** [★M,D,YC] 49-30/280.72.36 ■ Ackerstr 12 (Hinterhaus, enter at Ackerstr 13, U-Rosenthaler Platz) ■ 9pm-close Tue & 10pm-close Fri-Sat

34 **GMF at WMF** [★M,D,TG,S,YC,GO,$] 49-30/215.23.83, 49-30/21.47.41.00 ■ Ziegelstr 22 (S-Oranienburger Str) ■ T-dance 9pm-3am Sun ■ www.bobyoung.de/GMF1.htm

CAFES

Cafe Seidenfaden [WO] 49-30/283.27.83 ■ Dircksenstr 47 (U-Alexanderplatz) ■ 11am-9pm, from 1pm Sun, clsd Sat, drug- & alcohol-free women's cafe, info board

Kapelle [GS,YC] 49-30/449.22.62 ■ Zionskirchplatz 22-24 (U-Rosenthaler Platz) ■ 10am-3am, food served till midnight, also cocktail bar from 8pm

November [MW] 49-30/442.84.25 ■ Husemannstr 15 (at Sredzkistr) ■ 10am-2am, cafe-bar, terrace, brkfst buffet wknds

oxon magenta 49-30/44.73.64.82 ■ Greifenhagener Str 48 (S/U-Schönhauser Allee) ■ 10am-close, vegetarian & seafood, terrace

RESTAURANTS

Schall & Rauch Wirtshaus [MW] 49-30/443.39.70, 49-30/448.07.70 ■ Gleimstr 23 (at Schönhauser Allee) ■ 10am-close

Thüringer Stuben 49-30/44.63.33.91 ■ Stargarder Str 28 (at Dunckerstr, S/U-Schönhauser Allee) ■ 4pm-1am, from noon wknds, full bar

BOOKSTORES

35 **Adam-Buchladen** 49-30/448.07.67 ■ Gleimstr 23 (S/U-Schönhauser Allee) ■ 10am-8pm, till 4pm Sat, clsd Sun, lgbt

MEN'S CLUBS

Gate Sauna [F,V] 49-30/229.94.30 ■ Wilhelmstr 81 (nr Brandenburger Tor, U-Mohrenstr) ■ 24hrs wknds, also bar, theme nights ■ www.gate-sauna.de

Treibhaus Sauna [F,V,YC] 49-30/448.45.03 ■ Schönhauser Allee 132 (U-Eberswalder Str) ■ 24hrs wknds, also bar, student discount

EROTICA

Black Style 49-30/44.68.85.95 ■ Seelower Str 5 (S/U-Schönhauser Allee) ■ clsd Sun, latex & rubber wear, also mail order ■ www.blackstyle.de

Berlin—Schöneberg-Tiergarten

ACCOMMODATIONS

36 **Arco Hotel** [GS,WC,GO] 49-30/235.14.80 ■ Geisbergstr 30 (at Ansbacherstr, U-Wittenbergplatz) ■ centrally located ■ www.arco-hotel.de

37 **Art-Hotel Connection** [M,L,WC] 49-30/217.70.28, 49-30/217.70.29 ■ Fuggerstr 33 (nr Welser Str, U-Wittenbergplatz) ■ also special 'fantasy' apt for kink/SM types, some shared baths ■ www.arthotel-connection.de

38 **Berlin Gay B&B** [MW,NS,GO] 49-30/81.85.19.88 ■ Perleberger Str 7 (at Stephan Str) ■ seasonal, hot tub, shared bath ■ www.gaybed.de

39 **Eulenspiegel Pension** [M] 49-30/782.38.89 ■ Ebersstr 58 (at Innsbrucker Platz) ■ bar on premises

40 **Hotel California** [GF] 49-30/88.01.20 ■ Kurfürstendamm 35 (at Knesebeckstr, U-Uhlandstr) ■ www.hotel-california.de

41 **Hotel Hansablick** [GF] 49-30/390.48.00 ■ Flotowstr 6 (at Bachstr, off Str des 17 Juni) ■ full brkfst ■ www.hotel-hansablick.de

42 **Hotel Sachsenhof** [GS] 49-30/216.20.74 ■ Motzstr 7 (at Nollendorfplatz)

43 **Pension Niebuhr** [GS] 49-30/324.95.95, 49-30/324.95.96 ■ Niebuhrstr 74 (at Savignyplatz) ■ some shared baths ■ www.pension-niebuhr.de

44 **Tom's House Berlin** [MO,L] 49-30/218.55.44 ■ Eisenacher Str 10 (at Winterfeldstr, above 'Tom's Bar', U-Nollendorfplatz) ■ spacious rooms on the 3rd flr of a turn-of-the-century building (no elevator), shared baths

BARS

45 **Andreas Kneipe** [★M,NH,L] 49-30/218.32.57 ■ Ansbacher Str 29 (at Wittenbergplatz) ■ 11am-3am, till 4am Fri-Sat

46 **Blue Boy Bar** [M,V] 49-30/218.74.98 ■ Eisenacher Str 3a (at Fuggerstr, U-Nollendorfplatz) ■ 24hrs, ring bell, hustlers; also 'Fugger-Eck' (GS,NH), 49-30/218.35.06, 1pm-6am, clsd Sun

47 **CC 96** [MO,TG,S,V,PC,WC] 49-30/883.26.50 ■ Lietzenburger Str 96 (at Sächsische Str, U-Uhlandstr) ■ noon-3am, clsd Wed, strippers & drag shows from 8pm

48 **Chez Nous** [GS,S,$] 49-30/213.18.10 ■ Marburger Str 14 (at Tauentzienstr, U-Wittenbergplatz) ■ famous drag revue, shows 8:30pm & 11pm nightly, pricey 1-drink minimum

49 **Club Amsterdam** [M] 49-30/213.32.32 ■ Barbarossastr 38 (at Güntzelstr) ■ 7pm-3am

50 **Dreizehn** [M] 49-30/218.23.63 ■ Welserstr 27 (at Fuggerstr, U-Wittenbergplatz) ■ 5pm-5am, terrace

51 **E116** [M,L,F] 49-30/217.05.18 ■ Eisenacher Str 116 (at Motzstr, U-Nollendorfplatz) ■ 8pm-2am, till 3am wknds, cafe-bar, terrace

52 **Eldorado** [E] 49-30/21.47.55.50 ■ Motzstr 20 (U-Nollendorfplatz) ■ 24hrs ■ www.eldoradoberlin.de

39 **Eulenspiegel** [M,S,V] 49-30/782.38.89 ■ Ebersstr 58 (at 'Eulenspiegel Pension', U-Innsbrucker Platz) ■ 7pm-3am

53 **Fledermaus** [M,NH] 49-30/292.11.36 ■ Joachimsthaler Str 14-19 (U-Kurfürstendamm) ■ noon-4am, till 6am Fri-Sat

54 **Flipflop** 49-30/216.28.25 ■ Kulmer Str 20a (at Yorckstr) ■ 7pm-close, from 11am Sun (brunch served till 4pm)

52 **Hafen** [★M,TG,S,YC] 49-30/211.41.18 ■ Motzstr 19 (at Eisenacher Str, U-Nollendorfplatz) ■ 8pm-close

55 **Harlekin** [M,NH,F] 49-30/218.25.79 ■ Schaperstr 12-13 (at Lietzenburger Str, U9-Spichernstr, in Wilmersdorf) ■ 4pm-close, from 2pm Sun, terrace

56 **Heile Welt** [MW,F] 49-30/21.91.75.07 ■ Motzstr 5 ■ 6pm-close ■ www.heile-welt-berlin.de

57 **Kleist Casino** [M,D,S] 49-30/23.62.19.76 ■ Kleistr 35 (U-Wittenbergplatz) ■ 9pm-close, disco from 10pm Fri-Sat, clsd Mon-Tue, terrace ■ kleistc@aol.com

GERMANY • EUROPE

58 **Knast** [MO,L,V] 49-30/218.10.26 ■ Fuggerstr 34 (at Welserstr, U-Wittenbergplatz) ■ 9pm-5am, uniform bar w/ prison theme, darkroom

59 **Kumpelnest 3000** [GF,D,TG,YC] 49-30/261.69.18 ■ Lützowstr 23 (at Potsdamer Str, U-Kurfürstenstr) ■ 5pm-5am, till 8am Fri-Sat, cocktail bar

46 **Lenz...die Bar** [★M,WC] 49-30/217.78.00 ■ Eisenacher Str 3 (at Nollendorfplatz) ■ 8pm-close, cocktail bar

58 **Memory's** [GS,F] 49-30/213.52.71 ■ Fuggerstr 37 (U-Wittenbergplatz) ■ 4pm-close, cafe-bar, terrace ■ www.memorys-berlin.de

60 **Movie Bar at Regine** [M,F,WC] 49-30/211.77.02 ■ Kleiststr 7 (at Courbièrestr, U-Nollendorfplatz) ■ 4pm-2am, from 2pm wknds, terrace, brkfst buffet wknds

57 **New Action** [★MO,L,V] 49-30/211.82.56 ■ Kleiststr 35 (at Eisenacherstr, U-Nollendorfplatz) ■ 8pm-close, from 1pm Sun, uniform bar, darkroom, very cruisy

61 **Pour Elle** [WO,D,YC] 49-30/218.75.33 ■ Kalckreuthstr 10 (at Nollendorfplatz) ■ 7pm-2am, from 9pm Fri-Sat, clsd Tue, terrace, Germany's oldest lesbian bar, men welcome as guests Mon & Wed

61 **Pussy-Cat** [MW,D,TG,F,E] 49-30/213.35.86 ■ Kalckreuthstr 7 (at Nollendorfplatz) ■ 6pm-6am, clsd Tue, terrace

52 **Scheune** [★MO,L,V] 49-30/213.85.80 ■ Motzstr 25 (at Nollendorfplatz) ■ 9pm-7am, till 9am Fri-Sat, uniform bar, theme nights, darkroom

62 **Spot** [MW,NH,F] 49-30/213.22.67 ■ Eisenacher Str 2 (at Nollendorfplatz) ■ 4pm-4am, open later wknds, from 6pm in winter, terrace

63 **Tabasco** [M,F,AYOR] 49-30/214.26.36 ■ Fuggerstr 3 (at Schönbauser Allee, U-Nollendorfplatz) ■ 6pm-6am, 24hrs wknds, hustlers ■ www.tabasco.de

52 **Tom's Bar** [★M,L,V] 49-30/213.45.70 ■ Motzstr 19 (at Eisenacherstr, U-Nollendorfplatz) ■ 10pm-6am, open later Fri-Sat, very cruisy, downstairs maze

64 **Vagabund** [M,D,P] 49-30/881.15.06 ■ Knesebeckstr 77 (at Uhlandstr) ■ 5pm-late, terrace

NIGHTCLUBS

37 **Connection** [★MO,D,L,V,$] 49-30/218.14.32 ■ Fuggerstr 33 (at 'Art-Hotel Connection') ■ 11pm-close Fri-Sat only, big cruisy techno club, darkroom; also 'Twilight Zone' (L) from midnight Fri-Sat & from 1am Wed & Sun; also 'Connection Garage' sex shop & cinema, open 10am-1am, from 2pm Sun ■ info@connection-berlin.com

CAFES

Begine [WO] 49-30/215.43.25, 49-30/215.14.14 ■ Potsdamer Str 139 (at Bülowstr) ■ 5pm-1am, noon-midnight, clsd Sun, cafe & cultural center, full bar, dancing/DJ Sat night ■ www.begine.de

The Berlin Connection Cafe & Bistro [★M] 49-30/213.11.66 ■ Martin-Luther Str 19 (at Motzstr, U-Nollendorfplatz) ■ 2pm-2am, also bar, terrace

Berlin • GERMANY

Café Berio [★WC] 49-30/216.19.26 ■ Maaßenstr 7 (at Winterfeldtstr, U-Nollendorfplatz) ■ 8am-11:30pm, int'l, brkfst all day, bar till 1am, seasonal terrace ■ www.berio.de

Café PositHiv 49-30/216.86.54 ■ Alvenslebenstr 26 (at Potsdamer Str, U-Bülowstr) ■ 3pm-close, from 1pm Th, from 6pm Sat, clsd Mon, for HIV+ (and HIV-) men and women ■ berlin.gay-web.de/posithiv

Café Savigny 49-30/312.81.95 ■ Grolmanstr 53-54 (at Savignyplatz) ■ 9am-1am, artsy crowd, full bar, terrace

Windows [MW] 49-30/214.23.94 ■ Martin-Luther-Str 22 (at Motzstr, U-Wittenbergplatz) ■ 2pm-4am, from 11am Sun, full bar, terrace

RESTAURANTS

Arc [MW,WC] 49-30/313.26.25 ■ Fasanenstr 81-A (at Kantstr, in S-Bahn arches, Charlottenburg, S/U-Zoologischer Garten) ■ 8am-2am, from 10am wknds, also bar, terrace

Doi Suthep 49-30/396.50.32 ■ Emdener Str 1 (at Turmstr) ■ noon-midnight, Thai

LukiLuki [MW,TG,S] 49-30/23.62.20.79 ■ Motzstr 28 (U-Nollendorfplatz) ■ 6pm-2am, full bar, hardbody & drag-queen servers, brunch buffet Sun ■ www.lukiluki.de

BOOKSTORES

Bruno's 49-30/21.47.32.93 ■ Nürnberger Str 53 (in Charlottenburg, U-Wittenbergplatz) ■ 10am-10pm, clsd Sun, many art photography books ■ www.brunos.de

65 **Prinz Eisenherz Buchladen** [WC] 49-30/313.99.36 ■ Bleibtreustr 52 (in Charlottenburg, S-Savignyplatz) ■ 10am-7pm, till 4pm Sat, clsd Sun, lgbt books & magazines 'in all languages' ■ www.prinz-eisenherz.de

RETAIL SHOPS

Galerie Janssen 49-30/881.15.90 ■ Pariser Str 45 (at Nollendorfplatz, U1/9-Spichernstr) ■ clsd Sun, books & artwork for men ■ gayart@galerie-janssen.de

MEN'S CLUBS

Apollo City Sauna [F,V] 49-30/213.24.24 ■ Kurfürstenstr 101 (in Charlottenburg, U-Wittenbergplatz) ■ gym equipment, tanning booths, also bar

Steam Sauna Club [L,F,V] 49-30/218.40.60 ■ Kurfürstenstr 113 (U-Wittenbergplatz) ■ 24hrs wknds, jacuzzi, also bar ■ www.steam-sauna.de

EROTICA

Beate Uhse International Joachimstaler Str 4 (at Kantstr) ■ cinema, video cabins & bar

City Men 49-30/218.29.49 ■ Fuggerstr 26 ■ videos, magazines, toys

The Jaxx Club [V] 49-30/213.01.03 ■ Motzstr 19 (U-Nollendorfplatz) ■ movies, mags & toys

Mr B 49-30/21.99.77.04 ■ Nollendorfer Str 23 ■ clsd Sun, leather, rubber, toys ■ www.misterb.com

Playground [V] 49-30/218.21.64 ■ Courbièrestr 9 (U-Wittenbergplatz) ■ clsd Sun, also body piercing

Pool Berlin [V] 49-30/214.19.89 ■ Schaperstr 11 (at Joachimstaler Str, in Wilmersdorf, U-Kurfürstendamm) ■ clsd Sun, gay emporium

Berlin—Outer

ACCOMMODATIONS

66 **Artemisia Women's Hotel** [WO] 49-30/873.89.05, 49-30/869.93.20 ■ Brandenburgischestr 18 (at Konstanzerstr) ■ the only hotel for women in Berlin, sundeck, some shared baths ■ www.frauenhotel-berlin.de

67 **Charlottenburger Hof** [GF,F] 49-30/32.90.70 ■ Stuttgarter Platz 14 (at Wilmersdorfer Str) ■ also bar ■ www.charlottenburger-hof.de

68 **Hotel Kronprinz Berlin** [GF] 49-30/89.60.30 ■ Kronprinzendamm 1 (at Kurfürstendamm, in Halensee) ■ www.kronprinz-hotel.de

BARS

Club Zandvoort [M,NH,D,F] 49-30/752.20.77 ■ Friedrich-Karl-Str 15 (at Werderstr, in Tempelhof, U-Ullsteinstr) ■ 8pm-close, clsd Sun

Datscha [M,NH] 49-30/441.98.56 ■ Kranoldstr 18 (at Hertastr, in Neükolln) ■ 5pm-close

Furiosa [W,F] Habelschwerdter Allee 45 (nr Freie Universität) ■ cafe-bar

Lab.oratory [MO,L] Mühlenstr 26-30 (enter on Rummelsburger Platz, in Friedrichshain, S/U-Warschauer Platz) ■ theme nights, large darkroom, 'Ost Gut' fetish dance party from midnight Sat ■ www.lab-oratory.de

69 **Lützower Lampe** [M,D,S,WC] 49-30/321.20.97 ■ Witzlebenstr 38 (U-Kaiserdamm, in Charlottenburg) ■ 10:30pm-close, cabaret & piano bar, drag shows

Remember [M,NH] 49-30/62.70.51.83 ■ Leykestr 18 (at Hermannstr, nr Tempelhof Airport, U-Leinestr) ■ 2pm-close

NIGHTCLUBS

Die Busche [★MW,D,S,$] 49-30/296.08.00 ■ Mühlenstr 11-12 (at Kurfürstr, in Friedrichshain, S/U-Warschauer Str) ■ 9:30pm-5am Wed & Sun, 10pm-6am Fri-Sat, terrace; also 'Kleine (Little) Busche' at Warschauer Platz 18

CAFES

Virtuality Cafe 49-30/88.67.96.30 ■ Joachimstaler Str 41 (S5-Charlottenberg) ■ 10am-close, cybercafe (not gay) ■ www.vrcafe.de

RESTAURANTS

Cafe Rix 49-30/686.90.20 ■ Karl-Marx-Str 141 (in Neükolln) ■ 10am-5pm, Mediterranean, plenty veggie, also bar, open till 1am

Jung 49-30/32.70.24.46 ■ Stuttgarter Platz 21 (in Charlottenburg) ■ 9am-4pm, seasonal terrace

GYMS & HEALTH CLUBS

Apollo Fitness [M,YC] 49-30/784.82.03 ■ Hauptstr 150 (U-Kleistpark) ■ also Borodinstr 16 location (GF), 49-30/927.42.31

Swiss Training [GF] 49-30/754.15.91 ■ Albinostr 36-42 (nr Tempelhof Airport) ■ also Prenzlauer Berg location: Immanuelkirchstr 14, 44.35.83.44 ■ www.swiss-training.com

MEN'S CLUBS

Aquarius [V,SW,WC] 49-30/691.39.20 (hotline) ■ Hasenheide 13 (nr Volkspark Hasenheide, U-Hermannplatz) ■ 24hrs, huge club, also bar & restaurant, large 'cruising garden'

NETHERLANDS

Amsterdam

Amsterdam is divided into 5 regions:
Amsterdam—Overview
Amsterdam—Centre
Amsterdam—Jordaan
Amsterdam—Rembrandtplein
Amsterdam—Outer

Amsterdam—Overview

ENTERTAINMENT & RECREATION

The Anne Frank House 31–20/556.71.00, 31–20/626.45.33 ■ Prinsengracht 263 (in the Jordaan) ■ the final hiding place of Amsterdam's most famous resident ■ www.annefrank.nl

Homomonument Westermarkt (in the Jordaan) ■ moving sculptural tribute to lesbians & gays killed by Nazis

The van Gogh Museum 31–20/570.52.52 ■ Paulus Potterstr 7 (on the Museumplein) ■ a must-see museum dedicated to this Dutch master painter ■ www.vangoghmuseum.nl

PUBLICATIONS

Gay News Amsterdam 31–20/679.15.56 ■ www.gayamsterdam.com

Gay & Night 31–20/420.42.04 ■ free monthly bilingual entertainment paper w/ club listings ■ www.gay-night.nl

Shark 31–20/420.6775 ■ bi-weekly queer-oriented alternative culture guide & calendar (in English) ■ www.underwateramsterdam.com

Amsterdam—Centre

ACCOMMODATIONS

1. **Amsterdam Guest Apartments** [MW,GO] 31–20/320-0849, 877/716-2591 ■ Kolk 16 (at Voorburgwal) ■ landmark building nr Warmoestraat ■ www.thebolt.net/amsapt

2. **Anco** [MO,L,N,GO] 31–20/624.11.26 ■ OZ Voorburgwal 55 (across from the Oude Kerk) ■ 1640 canal house, some shared baths, also bar, open 9am-10pm ■ www.ancohotel.nl

3. **The Black Tulip Guesthouse** [★MO,L,GO] 31–20/427.09.33 ■ Geldersekade 16 ■ Europe's classiest hotel for leather guys, fantasy suite available, also lounge & terrace ■ www.blacktulip.nl

4. **Centre Apartments** [GF] 31–20/627.25.03 ■ Heintje Hoekssteeg 17 ■ www.gay-apartments-amsterdam.nl

5. **Drake's Guesthouse** [M,GO] 31–20/638.23.67 ■ Damrak 61 (above cinema) ■ www.drakes.nl

6. **E&D City Apartments** [M,L] 31–20/624.73.35 ■ Singel 34 ■ 'for the leatherboy & his friend'

7. **Golden Tulip Grand Hotel Krasnapolsky** [GF] 31–20/554.91.11 ■ Dam 9 ■ full-service hotel located in the city center opposite Royal Palace, includes business center & 5 restaurants ■ www.krasnapolsky.nl

8. **The Grand Sofitel Demeure Amsterdam** [GF] 31–20/555.31.11 ■ OZ Voorburgwal 197 ■ 5-star deluxe hotel located in the former City Hall—all rooms w/ canal or courtyard views ■ www.thegrand.nl

9. **Holiday Inn Crowne Plaza Amsterdam City Centre** [GF,SW] 31–20/620.05.00, 800/465-4329 (US#) ■ NZ Voorburgwal 5 ■ www.crowneplaza.nl

NETHERLANDS • EUROPE

10 **Hotel New York** [MW] 31-20/624.30.66 ■ Herengracht 13 (at Brouwersgracht) ■ well-known in the community, bar & coffeeshop
11 **Maes B&B** [MW,NS] 31-20/427.51.65 ■ Herenstr 26 ■ www.xs4all.nl/~maesbb94
12 **Stablemaster Hotel** [MO,L] 31-20/625.01.48 ■ Warmoesstr 23 ■ shared baths, also bar
13 **Tulip Inn** [GF] 31-20/420.45.45, 800/344-1212 (US#) ■ Spuistr 288-292 ■ www.goldentulip.nl/hotels/tiamsterdam

BARS

14 **Argos** [★MO,L] 31-20/622.65.95 ■ Warmoesstr 95 ■ 10pm-3am, till 4am Fri-Sat, the oldest leather bar in Europe, popular darkroom ■ leather@argosbar.demon.nl
15 **Bar Why Not/ Blue Boy Club** [M,S,V,GO] 31-20/627.43.74 ■ NZ Voorburgwal 28 (nr Centraal Station) ■ noon-2am, casual bar, strip shows, cinema & escort services ■ www.whynot.nl
16 **Casa Maria** [M,L] 31-20/627.68.48 ■ Warmoesstr 60 ■ noon-1am, till 3am Fri-Sat, from 2pm Sun
17 **Club Jacques** [MO,L,WC] 31-20/622.03.23 ■ Warmoesstr 93 ■ 8pm-2am, till 3am Fri-Sat, darkroom, theme nights
1 **The Cuckoo's Nest** [MO,L,V] 31-20/627.17.52 ■ NZ Kolk 6 ■ 1pm-1am, till 2am Fri-Sat, cruisy, large play cellar
18 **Dirty Dicks** [MO,L] 31-20/627.86.34 ■ Warmoesstr 86 ■ midnight-4am Fri-Sat, very cruisy, darkroom
19 **The Eagle Amsterdam** [MO,L] 31-20/627.86.34 ■ Warmoesstr 90 ■ 10pm-4am, till 5am Fri-Sat, darkroom
20 **Getto** [★MW,F] 31-20/421.51.51 ■ Warmoesstr 51 ■ 4pm-1am, from 7pm Tue, 1pm-midnight Sun, also restaurant, live DJs, drag-queen bingo Th, Sun brunch
21 **Queen's Head** [M,S] 31-20/420.24.75 ■ Zeedijk 20 (off Nieuwmarkt) ■ 5pm-1am, till 3am Fri-Sat, from 4pm wknds, 'Bingo Paradise' Tue ■ www.queenshead.nl
12 **Stablemaster Bar** [MO,L] 31-20/625.01.48 ■ Warmoesstr 23 ■ 8pm-1am, 2pm-2am Fri-Sat, clsd Tue-Wed, very cruisy, nightly jack-off parties
22 **Vrankrijk** [GS,A] Spuistr 216 ■ rowdy, friendly squat bar, more gay Mon

AMSTERDAM

If you believe that your private life is nobody's business but your own, you'll find a lot of like-minded souls in Amsterdam. Known as the gay capital of Europe, this quaint, compact city is synonymous with liberal thinking. Whether 'window-shopping' in the infamous Red Light District or relaxing in a 'smoking cafe', visitors rave about Amsterdam's open-minded social policies and easy-going atmosphere.

Queer Resources

COMMUNITY INFO
▼ COC 31-20/626.30.87, web: www.cocamsterdam.nl. Rozenstraat 14 (see Jordaan map). Queer info coffeeshop by day w/many group meetings. Popular lesbian disco Sat. Mixed disco Fri & Sun.
Gay & Lesbian Switchboard 31-20/623.65.65. 10am-10pm.

AIDS RESOURCES
AIDS Hotline 0800/022.22.20.

City Calendar

LGBT PRIDE
August. 31-20/623.65.65, web: www.amsterdampride.nl.

ENTERTAINMENT
MacBike (31-20/620.09.85) rents bikes & has created a self-guided tour-by-map of Amsterdam's gay points of interest.

ANNUAL EVENTS
April 30 - Queen's Birthday.
May 4-5 - Memorial Day & Liberation Day.
June - Holland Festival.
July - Zomerfestijn. International performing arts festival.
August - Heart's Day. Drag festival.
October - Leather Pride 31-20/422.37.37, web: www.leatherpride.nl.

Tourist Info

AIRPORT DIRECTIONS
Direct rail connection to Centraal Station (about a 20-minute ride). Driving & parking in Amsterdam are hellish and pricy; take advantage of the excellent transit system instead, or rent a bicycle.

PUBLIC TRANSIT & TAXIS
31-20/677.77.77. Can also be found at taxi stands on the main squares.
KLM Bus.
GVB 33-6/92.92 or visit their office across from the Centraal Station. Trams, buses, and subway.

TOURIST SPOTS & INFO
Anne Frank House 31-20/556.71.00.
Homomonument.
Jewish Historical Museum 31-20/626.99.45.
Rembrandt House 31-20/520.04.00.
Rijksmuseum 31-20/674.70.47.
Royal Palace 31-20/620.40.60.
Stedelijk Museum of Modern Art 31-20/573.27.37.
Vincent van Gogh Museum 31-20/570.52.00.
Visitor's Center: VVV 900/400.40.40, web: www.visitholland.com. Visit their office directly opposite Centraal Station.

WEATHER
Temperatures hover around freezing in the winter and rise to the mid-60°s in the summer. Rain is possible year-round.

Amsterdam • NETHERLANDS

23 **The Web** [MO,B,L,V] 31-20/623.67.58 ■ St Jacobsstr 4-6 (btwn Nieuwendijk & NZ Voorburgwal) ■ 2pm-1am, till 2am Fri-Sat, darkroom, bears Sat

NIGHTCLUBS

Club Trash [★MO,D,L,$] 31-20/679.15.56 ■ monthly leather sex party, 3rd Sat, strict dress code, get info at 'Cockring', 'Mr B', 'RoB', 'Black Body' or in the 'Gay News Amsterdam' ■ www.gayamsterdam.net/trash/

24 **Cockring** [★MO,D,S,V] 31-20/623.96.04 ■ Warmoesstr 96 ■ 11pm-4am, till 5am Fri-Sat, cruisy darkroom, strippers/ sex shows Sun ■ www.clubcockring.com

RESTAURANTS

Camp Cafe [★MW,GO] 31-20/622.15.06 ■ Kerkstr 45 (at Leidsestr) ■ 3pm-1am, till 3am Fri-Sat, cont'l, kitchen open till 11:30pm, also bar, terrace

Gerard 31-20/638.43.38 ■ Geldersekade 23 ■ 5:30pm-11pm, clsd Tue, French

Hemelse Modder [WC] 31-20/624.32.03 ■ Oude Waal 9 ■ 6pm-10pm, clsd Mon, French/ int'l

La Strada [★] 31-20/625.02.76 ■ NZ Voorburgwal 93 ■ 4pm-10pm, Mediterranean, plenty veggie, also bar, open till 1am, till 2am Fri-Sat, terrace, lesbian-owned/ run

No 7 & 9 [GO] 31-20/624.51.73 ■ Warmoesstr 7 ■ 8am-11pm, full bar

Oibibio [WC] 31-20/553.93.28 ■ Prins Hendrikkade 20-21 ■ 10:30am-10pm, vegetarian

Pygma-lion [GO] 31-20/420.70.22 ■ Nieuwe Spiegelstr 5a (in Spiegelhof Arcade) ■ 11am-10pm, till 3pm Mon, clsd Sun, South African

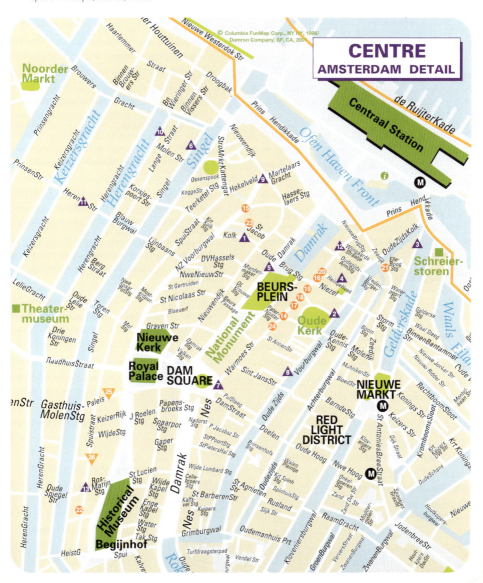

CENTRE AMSTERDAM DETAIL

't Sluisje [★MW,TG,S] 31-20/624.08.13 ■ Torensteeg 1 ■ 6pm-close, clsd Mon-Tue, steakhouse, full bar (open later), drag shows nightly ■ www.sluisje.nl

Song Kwae 31-20/624.25.68 ■ Kloveniersburgwal 14a (nr Nieuwmarkt & Chinatown) ■ 1pm-10:30pm, Thai, full bar, terrace

Tom Yam [WC,GO] 31-20/622.95.33 ■ Staalstr 22 ■ 6pm-10:30pm, clsd Sun-Mon, eclectic/ Thai, terrace ■ www.tomyam.nl

Walem [WC,GO] 31-20/625.35.44 ■ Keizersgracht 449 ■ lunch & dinner, int'l, local crowd, patio

BOOKSTORES

The American Book Center [WC] 31-20/625.55.37 ■ Kalverstr 185 (at Heiligeweg) ■ 10am-8pm, till 10pm Th, 11am-6pm Sun, books & magazines in English imported from US & UK, large lgbt section ■ www.abc.nl

25 **Boekhandel Vrolijk Gay & Lesbian Bookshop** 31-20/623.51.42 ■ Paleisstr 135 (nr Dam Sq) ■ 10am-6pm, from 1pm Mon, till 9pm Th, till 5pm Sat, clsd Sun, lgbt books, videos & gadgets, also mail order ■ www.xs4all.nl/~vrolijk

26 **Intermale Gay Bookstore** 31-20/625.00.09 ■ Spuistr 251-253 ■ 10am-6pm, till 9pm Th, clsd Sun, wide selection of gay men's titles in English & Dutch ■ www.intermale.nl

RETAIL SHOPS

Conscious Dreams Kokopelli 31-20/421.70.00 ■ Warmoesstr 12 ■ 11am-10pm, 'smart warehouse' ■ www.consciousdreams.nl

Magic Mushroom 31-20/427.57.65 ■ Spuistr 249 ■ 11am-7pm, till 8pm Fri-Sat, 'smartshop': magic mushrooms & more ■ www.pulse.nl/mushroom

EROTICA

Adonis [V] 31-20/627.29.59 ■ Warmoesstr 92 ■ cinema, private rooms, darkroom

B1 Cinema 31-20/623.95.46 ■ Reguliersbreestr 4

DeMask 31-20/620.56.03 ■ Zeedijk 64 ■ noon-6pm, clsd Sun, fetish fashion ■ www.demask.com

Drake's 31-20/627.95.44 ■ Damrak 61 ■ videos & magazines, cinema, cruisy ■ www.drakes.nl

Female & Partners 31-20/620.91.52 ■ Spuistr 100 ■ fashions & toys for women, also mail order ■ www.femaleandpartners.nl

Het Gulden Vlies 31-20/627.41.74 ■ Warmoesstr 141 ■ 'condomerie' ■ www.condomerie.com

Le Salon 31-20/622.65.65 ■ Nieuwendijk 20-22 (nr the Spui) ■ sex supermarket, cinema

Man to Man 31-20/625.87.97 ■ Spuistr 21 ■ all-day cinema tickets

Master Leather 31-20/624.55.73 ■ Warmoesstr 32 ■ clsd Sun

Mr B [WC] 31-20/422.00.03 ■ Warmoesstr 89 ■ leather & rubber, also tattoos & piercing ■ www.mrb.nl

Robin & Rik 31-20/627.89.24 ■ Runstr 30 ■ custom leatherwear

Amsterdam—Jordaan

ACCOMMODATIONS

1 **Barangay B&B** [MW,GO] 31-0-62/504-5432 ■ 1777 townhouse nr tourist attractions, full brkfst ■ www.barangay.nl

11 **Freeland Hotel** [GF] 31-20/622.75.11, 31-20/627.75.78 ■ Marnixstr 386 ■ full brkfst

2 **Hotel Pulitzer** [GF] 31-20/523.52.35, 800/325-3535 (US#) ■ Prinsengracht 315-331 ■ occupies 24 17th-century buildings facing the Prinsengracht & Keizersgracht—2 of Amsterdam's most picturesque canals ■ www.sheraton.com

3 **The Jordaan Canal House** [MO] 31-20/620.15.45 ■ Egelantiersgracht 23 ■ full brkfst ■ ourworld.compuserve.com/homepages/hanspluygers

4 **Rainbow Palace Hotel** [M,GO] 31-20/625.43.17, 31-20/626.70.86 ■ Raadhuisstr 33 ■ centrally located nr the Homomonument, some shared baths

5 **Rembrandt Residence Hotel** [GS] 31-20/622.17.27 ■ Herengracht 255 ■ nr Dam Square ■ www.bookings.nl/hotels/rembrandt

BARS

6 **Saarein** [MW,F] 31-20/623.49.01 ■ Elandsstr 119 ■ 8pm-1am, till 2am Fri-Sat, clsd Mon, cafe-bar

7 **Vandenberg** [GS,NH,F] 31-20/622.27.16 ■ Lindengracht 95 ■ 5pm-1am, till 3am Fri, 10am-3am Sat, food served till 10pm, plenty veggie, lesbian owned/ run

NIGHTCLUBS

COC [MW,D,$] 31-20/623.40.79, 31-20/626.30.87 ■ Rozenstr 14 ■ 10pm-5am Fri, women only 10pm-4am Sat, multiculti disco 8pm-2am Sun, HIV+ 8pm-12:30am Th, call for many other parties/ events ■ www.coc.nl

8 **Mazzo** [GF,D,YC,$] 31-20/626.75.00 ■ Rozengracht 114 (nr Westersmarkt) ■ 11pm-4am, till 5am Fri-Sat, clsd Mon-Tue ■ www.mazzo.nl

de Trut [MW,D,A,YC] 31-20/612.35.24 ■ 11pm-4am Sun only, hip underground party, call for location

CAFES

Backstage 31-20/622.36.38 ■ Utrechtsedwarsstr 67 ■ 10am-6pm, clsd Sun, very kitschy lunchroom

Café 't Smalle 31-20/623.96.17 ■ Egelantiersgracht 12 ■ 10am-1pm, brown cafe, full bar, outdoor seating

Reibach [GO] 31-20/626.77.08 ■ Brouwersgracht 139 ■ 10am-6pm, from 11am Sun, lunchroom, artsy crowd

Tops Prinsengracht 480 ■ smoking Internet cafe

't Wonder 31-20/639.10.32 ■ Huidenstr 13 (at Bijbelsmuseum) ■ 2pm-midnight, clsd Mon, smoking coffeeshop

RESTAURANTS

Bojo [★] 31-20/622.74.34 ■ Lange Leidsedwarsstr 49-51 (nr Leidseplein) ■ noon-close Th-Sun, Indonesian

De Bolhoed 31-20/626.18.03 ■ Prinsengracht 60 (at Tuinstr) ■ noon-10pm, vegetarian/ vegan

Burger's Patio 31-20/623.68.54 ■ 2e Tuindwarsstr 12 ■ Italian, plenty veggie

Granada [E] 31-20/625.10.73 ■ Leidsekruisstr 13 ■ 5pm-close, clsd Tue, Spanish, tapas, also bar, live music wknds ■ www.dinnersite.nl/amsterdam/granada

't Swarte Schaep 31-20/622.30.21 ■ Korte Leidsedwarsstr 24 (nr Leidseplein) ■ noon-11pm, French

De Vliegende Schotel 31-20/625.20.41 ■ Nieuwe Leliestr 162 ■ 5pm-11pm, vegetarian

ENTERTAINMENT & RECREATION

De Looier Antiques Market 31-20/624.90.38 ■ Elandsgracht 109 ■ www.looier.nl

BOOKSTORES

9 **Vrouwenindruk** 31-20/624.50.03 ■ Westermarkt 5 ■ antiquarian & secondhand books by & about women, also lgbt ■ www.xs4all.nl/~vind

Amsterdam • NETHERLANDS

10 **Xantippe Unlimited** [GO] 31-20/623.58.54, 31-20/679.96.09 ■ Prinsengracht 290 ■ women's, lesbian section, English titles, lesbian-owned ■ www.dds.nl/~xantippe/

RETAIL SHOPS
Clubwear House 31-20/622.87.66 ■ Herengracht 265 (nr Dam Sq) ■ noon-6pm, till 8pm Th, clsd Sun-Mon, clothing, club tickets & flyers ■ www.clubwearhouse.nl

MEN'S CLUBS
Boomerang 31-20/639.18.25 ■ Heintje Hoeksteeg 8 ■ gay sauna & suntanning studio

Mandate [PC] 31-20/625.41.00 ■ Prinsengracht 715 ■ gay gym, sauna, coffeebar

Modern [OC] 31-20/612.17.12 ■ Jacop van Lennepstr 311 ■ noon-6pm, clsd Sun, sauna

EROTICA
Black Body [WC] 31-20/626.25.53 ■ Lijnbaansgracht 292 (across from Rijksmuseum) ■ rubber clothing specialists, also leather, toys & more ■ www.blackbody.nl

Amsterdam—Rembrandtplein

ACCOMMODATIONS
1 **Aero Hotel** [M] 31-20/662.77.28 ■ Kerkstr 49 (off Leidsestr) ■ some shared baths

2 **Doelen Hotel** [GF] 31-20/554.06.00, 31-20/554.07.77 ■ Nieuwe Doelenstr 24 ■ grand hotel on the River Amstel ■ www.goldentulip.nl/hotels/gtdoelen

3 **The Golden Bear** [M,GO] 31-20/624.47.85 ■ Kerkstr 37 (at Leidsestr) ■ formerly the Hotel Unique, the oldest gay hotel in Amsterdam, since 1948, w/ friendly multilingual staff & clean, spacious rooms, some shared baths ■ www.goldenbear.nl

4 **Golden Tulip Schiller** [GF] 31-20/554.07.00 ■ Rembrandtplein 26-36 ■ art deco style, recently renovated ■ www.goldentulip.nl/hotels/gtschiller

5 **Greenwich Village** [M] 31-20/626.97.46 ■ Kerkstr 25

6 **Hotel Monopole** [GF] 31-20/624.62.71 ■ Amstel 60 ■ centrally located; also 'Cafe Rouge' (M), 31-20/624.64.51, open 4pm-1am, till 3am Fri-Sat ■ www.monopole.demon.nl

7 **Hotel Orfeo** [M] 31-20/623.13.47 ■ Leidsekruisstr 14 (at Prinsengracht) ■ some shared baths, also bar & 24hr sauna

8 **Hotel Orlando** [GF] 31-20/638.69.15 ■ Prinsengracht 1099 (at Amstel River) ■ beautifully restored 17th-c canalhouse

9 **ITC Hotel** [M] 31-20/623.02.30 ■ Prinsengracht 1051 (at Utrechtsestr) ■ 18th-c canal house, great location, also bar & lounge ■ www.itc-hotel.com

10 **Jolly Hotel Carlton** [GF] 31-20/622.22.66 ■ Vijzelstr 4 ■ overlooking the famous flower market & Munt Tower ■ www.jollycarlton.nl

11 **Waterfront Hotel** [GF] 31-20/421.66.21, 31-20/623.97.75 ■ Singel 458 ■ www.waterfront.demon.nl

12 **Westend Hotel** [M,GO] 31-20/624.80.74 ■ Kerkstr 42 ■ friendly staff, some shared baths ■ westendhotel@yahoo.com

BARS
13 **Amstel Taveerne** [M,NH] 31-20/623.42.54 ■ Amstel 54 (at Rembrandtplein) ■ 4pm-1am, till 2am Fri-Sat

14 **April** [★M,V] 31-20/625.95.72 ■ Reguliersdwarsstr 37 (at Rembrandtplein) ■ 2pm-1am, till 3am Fri-Sat, popular happy hour, also cruisy back bar

15 **Cafe de Steeg** [M,S] 31-20/626.45.10 ■ Halvemaansteeg 10 ■ 4pm-2am, till 3am Fri-Sat, from noon wknds

15 **Entre-Nous** [MW,NH] 31-20/623.17.00 ■ Halvemaansteeg 14 (at Rembrandtplein) ■ 8pm-3am, till 4am Fri-Sat

16 **Gaiety** [★M,YC] 31-20/624.42.71 ■ Amstel 14 ■ 4pm-1am, till 3am Fri-Sat, clsd Mon, cafe-bar, terrace ■ www.euronet.nl/users/gaiety

17 **Havana** [M,D,F] 31-20/620.67.88 ■ Reguliersdwarsstr 17-19 ■ 4pm-1am, till 3am Fri-Sat, from 2pm wknds, more women Fri, cafe-bar, (D) wknds

18 **de Krokodil** [M,NH,OC] 31-20/626.22.43 ■ Amstelstr 34 ■ 4pm-1am, till 2am Fri-Sat

AMSTERDAM DETAIL
JORDAAN

NETHERLANDS • EUROPE

19 **Lellebel** [M,NH,TG,F,S] 31-20/427.51.39 ■ Utrechtsestr 4 ■ 8pm-3am, till 4am Fri-Sat, drag bar

20 **Macho Macho** [M,NH] 31-20/622.83.35 ■ Amstel 102 ■ 8pm-1am, till 3am Fri-Sat, brown cafe

21 **Meia Meia** [M,NH] 31-20/623.41.29 ■ Kerkstr 63 ■ noon-1am, till 3am Fri-Sat, cocktail bar, terrace

22 **Mix Cafe** [★MW] 31-20/622.52.02 ■ Amstel 50 ■ 8pm-3am, till 4am Fri-Sat ■ www.mixcafe.nl

23 **Le Montmartre** [★M,NH,YC] 31-20/620.76.22, 31-20/624.92.16 ■ Halvemaansteeg 17 ■ 4pm-1am, till 3am Fri-Sat, very Dutch

24 **Music Box** [M] 31-20/620.41.10 ■ Paardenstr 9 (nr Rembrandtplein) ■ 8pm-2am, till 3am Fri-Sat, clsd Mon, hustlers

24 **Night Life** [GS,AYOR] 31-20/622.17.89 ■ Paardenstr 7 ■ 9pm-2am, till 3am Fri-Sat, hustlers

25 **Reality** [M,NH,MR-AF] 31-20/639.30.12 ■ Reguliersdwarsstr 129 ■ 8pm-3am

26 **Shako** [M,NH,B] 31-20/624.02.09 ■ Gravelandseveer 2 ■ 10pm-3am, till 4am Fri-Sat, terrace

28 **Soho** [★M] 31-20/625.95.72 ■ Reguliersdwarsstr 36 ■ 10pm-3am

29 **Spijker** [MO,NH,L,V] 31-20/620.59.19 ■ Kerkstr 4 ■ 1pm-1am, till 2am Fri-Sat, clsd Sun, darkroom, TVs showing hardcore porno & cartoons

30 **Vive la Vie** [W] 31-20/624.01.14 ■ Amstelstr 7 (at Rembrandtplein) ■ 3pm-1am, till 3am Fri-Sat ■ www.vivelavie.net

NIGHTCLUBS

31 **The Back Door** [M,D,$] 31-6/214.318.61 ■ Amstelstr 32 ■ Fri & Sun only, T-dance 6pm-close Sun ■ www.backdoor.nl

32 **Club BPM** [M,D] Rembrandtplein 17 (at Amstel) ■ 11pm-4am Wed only ■ www.clubbpm.com

33 **Exit** [★M,D,$] 31-20/625.87.88 ■ Reguliersdwarsstr 42 ■ 11pm-4am, till 5am Fri-Sat, 3 bars on 4 flrs, darkroom

34 **iT** [★GS,D,PC,$] 31-20/625.01.11 ■ Amstelstr 24 ■ 11pm-4am Th-Sun, open later Fri-Sat, more gay Th & at 'Gay Gang Bang Night' Sat ■ www.it.nl

35 **You II** [W,D] 31-20/420.43.71 ■ Amstel 178 (at Wagenstraat) ■ 10pm-4am, till 5am Fri-Sat, 4pm-1am Sun, clsd Mon-Wed

CAFES

Downtown [★M] 31-20/622.99.58 ■ Reguliersdwarsstr 31 ■ 10am-8pm, terrace open in summer

Global Chillage 31-20/777.97.77 ■ Kerkstr 51 ■ 11am-midnight, till 1am Fri-Sat, smoking coffee shop, publisher's choice, across from wasserette

The Other Side [M,GO] 31-20/421.10.14 ■ Reguliersdwarsstr 6 ■ 10am-1am, gay smoking coffeeshop

RESTAURANTS

Dia de Sol 31-20/623.42.59 ■ Reguliersdwarsstr 23 ■ open till midnight, tapas/ Mediterranean

Garlic Queen 31-20/422.64.26 ■ Reguliersdwarsstr 27 ■ 6pm-close, clsd Tue, even the desserts are made w/ garlic! ■ www.garlicqueen.nl

Golden Temple [NS] 31-20/626.85.60 ■ Utrechtsestr 126 ■ 5pm-10pm, noon-3pm Tue & Sat, Indian-influenced vegetarian & vegan

Kort 31-20/626.11.99 ■ Amstelveld 12 ■ 10am-10pm, till 11pm Fri-Sat, clsd Tue, French/ Mediterranean, terrace

Malvesijn [MW] 31-20/638.08.99 ■ Prinsengracht 598 ■ 10am-midnight, food served till 10pm, Dutch, also bar, terrace overlooking the canal

Le Monde [MW,GO] 31-20/626.99.22 ■ Rembrandtplein 6 ■ 8am-11pm, brkfst till 4pm (open 4pm-10pm Mon-Fri in winter), plenty veggie, terrace dining

Rose's Cantina [★] 31-20/625.97.97 ■ Reguliersdwarsstr 38-40 (nr Rembrandtplein) ■ 5pm-11pm, Mexican, full bar ■ www.rosescantina.com

Amsterdam • Netherlands

Sarah's Grannies [W] 31-20/624.01.45 ■ Kerkstr 176 ■ 10am-5pm, clsd Sun-Mon, terrace

Saturnino 31-20/639.01.02 ■ Reguliersdwarsstr 5 ■ noon-midnight, Italian, full bar

't Schooiertje 31-20/638.40.35 ■ Lijnbaansgracht 190 (at Looier Antiques Market) ■ 9am-9pm, clsd Fri, full bar

Shizen 31-20/622.86.27 ■ Kerkstr 108 ■ lunch & dinner, clsd Mon, macrobiotic Japanese

Entertainment & Recreation

Bridge-Sociëteit de Looier 31-20/627.93.80 ■ Lijnbaansgracht 185 ■ gay prize bridge 7:30pm Wed

Retail Shops

Conscious Dreams 31-20/626.69.07 ■ Kerkstr 93 ■ 11am-7pm, till 8pm Th-Sat, 2pm-6pm Sun, 'psychedelicatessen'; also 'The Dream Lounge' at Kerkstr 93, Internet access noon-8pm daily (31-20/427.28.29) ■ www.consciousdreams.nl

Men's Clubs

Thermos Day [SW,F] 31-20/623.91.58 ■ Raamstr 33 ■ noon-11pm, till 10pm wknds, cruisy sauna on 5 flrs, also bar & cafe, bears 3rd Sat ■ www.thermos.nl

Thermos Night 31-20/623.49.36 ■ Kerkstr 58-60 (nr Leidseplein) ■ 11pm-7am, till 10am Sun, sauna on 3 flrs, also bar ■ www.thermos.nl

Erotica

The Bronx 31-20/623.15.48 ■ Kerkstr 53-55 (nr Leidseplein) ■ huge gay shop for sex supplies, videos, magazines & toys, also cinema

Amsterdam—Outer

Accommodations

Aadam Wilhelmina Hotel [GF] 31-20/662.54.67 ■ Koninginneweg 169 ■ charming, recently renovated ■ www.euronet.nl/users/wilhlhtl

Chico's Guesthouse [GF] 31-20/675.42.41 ■ St Willibrordusstr 77

Hotel Sander [GF] 31-20/662.75.74 ■ Jacob Obrechtstr 69 ■ also 24hr bar & coffee lounge ■ www.xs4all.nl/~htlsandr

Johanna's B&B [WO,NS] 31-20/684.85.96 ■ Van Hogendorpplein 62 ■ www.johannasbnb.com

Liliane's Home [WO,NS] 31-20/627.40.06 ■ Sarphatistr 119 ■ full brkfst, shared bath, also apt

Prinsen Hotel [GF] 31-20/616.23.23 ■ Vondelstr 36-38 (nr Leidseplein) ■ www.prinsenhotel.demon.nl

Quentin Hotel [GF] 31-20/626.21.87 ■ Leidsekade 89 (at Lijnbaansgracht) ■ some shared baths

Rubens B&B [GF,NS] 31-20/662.91.87 ■ Rubensstr 38 ■ smokefree ■ www.rubensbb.com

Rujo's B&B [MO,GO] 31-20/463-5024 ■ Benno Stokvistr 26 (nr Amstel Station) ■ quiet setting near city centre, hot tub ■ communities.msn.nl/RUJOSBedBreakfast

Toro Hotel [GF] 31-20/673.72.23 ■ Koningslaan 64 (next to Vondelpark) ■ refurbished mansion

Bars

Mankind [M,S,F] 31-20/638.47.55 ■ Weteringstr 60 ■ 11am-1am, till 2am Fri-Sat, cafe-bar, terrace

Nightclubs

De Brug [WO,D] NZ Kolk 25 (at 'Akhnaton') ■ 9pm-2am 1st Sat, for lesbians & bisexual women 35 & older, ballroom dancing till 11pm, disco from 11pm

Melkweg [GS] 31-20/624.84.92 ■ Lijnbaansgracht 234 ■ more women 3rd Sun for 'Planet Pussy', popular music venue, smoking cafe

Restaurants

De Vrolijke Abrikoos 31-20/624.46.72 ■ Weteringschans 76 ■ 5pm-11:30pm, eclectic organic cuisine, plenty veggie, patio

De Waaghals 31-20/679.96.09 ■ Frans Halsstr 29 ■ 5pm-11pm, vegetarian ■ www.waaghals.nl

Gyms & Health Clubs

Eastern Bath House 31-20/681.48.18 ■ Zaanstr 88 ■ women-only Turkish sauna

Fenomeen [F] 31-20/671.67.80 ■ Eerste Schinkelstraat 14 (nr Vondelpark) ■ women-only Mon, Turkish bath, sauna

Erotica

RoB 31-20/625.46.86 ■ Weteringschans 253 (at Reguliersgracht) ■ clsd Sun, Amsterdam's first leather shop ■ www.rob.nl

---

Visit Damron Online!

- search our online database
- get the latest updates
- direct web/ email links
- more categories (including websites)
- shop for discounted guides
- calendar of events
- tour operator listings
- gay travel links & more!

www.damron.com

SPAIN

Madrid

ACCOMMODATIONS

1 **Gay Hostal Puerta del Sol** [M,GO] 34/91.522.51.26 ■ Plaza Puerta del Sol 14, 4° (at Calle de Alcalá, Metro Sol) ■ centrally located ■ *puertadelsol@retemail.es*

2 **Hostal Hispano** [M] 34/91.531.48.71 ■ Hortaleza 38, 3° izq (at Perez Galdos, Metro Chueca)

2 **Hostal Odesa** [★M] 34/91.521.03.38, 34/91.532.08.28 ■ Hortaleza 38, 3° izq (at Perez Galdos) ■ *personal.redestb.es/m.g.d/odesa.htm*

3 **Hostal Oporto** [GF] 34/91.429.78.56 ■ Calle Zorilla 9, 1st flr (Metro Sol) ■ 10-min walk to gay scene, some shared baths ■ *www.hostaloporto.com*

4 **Hostal Sonsoles** [M] 34/91.532.75.23, 34/91.532.75.22 ■ Fuencarral 18, 2° dcha (Metro Chueca) ■ *personal.redestb.es/m.g.d/sonsoles.htm*

5 **Hotel A Gaudí** 34/91.531.22.22 ■ Gran Vía 9 (at Alcala) ■ 4-star hotel in the heart of the city ■ *www.hoteles-catalonia.es*

6 **Hotel Villa Real** [M] 34/91.420.37.67 ■ Plaza de Las Cortes, 10 ■ located in the cultural, political & financial center of Madrid, full brkfst ■ *www.derbyhotels.es*

7 **Mónaco Hotel Residencia** [GF] 34/91.522.46.30 ■ Barbieri 5

8 **Suecia Hotel** [GF] 34/91.531.69.00, 800/448-8355 ■ Marqués de Casa Riera 4 ■ jacuzzis

6 **The Westin Palace** [GF] 34/91.360.77.77, 800/325-3589 ■ Plaza de Las Cortes, 7 ■ grand hotel ■ *www.palacemadrid.com*

BARS

9 **El 17** [M,NH] 34/91.577.75.12 ■ Recoletos 17 (Metro Banco) ■ 9:30pm-3am, till 4am Wed, clsd Aug

10 **A Diario** [MW] 34/91.530.27.80 ■ Zurita 39 (Metro Lavapies) ■ 7:30pm-close, DJ wknds

11 **Adonis** [M,V] 34/91.522.82.65 ■ Tres Cruces 8 (at Gran Vía) ■ 4am-noon, clsd Mon, darkroom

12 **Ambient** [W,NH,F] San Mateo 21 (Metro Tribunal) ■ 8pm-5am, from 9pm Fri-Sat, clsd Mon, pizza, info board

13 **Baticano** [M,NH] Plaza de Colon 8 (Metro Tribunal) ■ 10pm-5am

14 **Black & White (Blanco y Negro)** [★M,D,S,YC] 34/91.531.11.41 ■ Libertad 34 (at Gravina, Metro Chueca) ■ 8pm-5am, till 6am Fri-Sat, strippers, drag shows, disco downstairs ■ *www.black-white.com*

15 **La Bohemia** [W,NH,D,F] Plaza de Chueca 10 (Metro Chueca) ■ 8pm-close, from 9pm wknds ■ *www.interocio.es/labohemia*

16 **El Candil** [GS,TG,S,V] 34/91.522.71.48 ■ Hernán Cortés 21 (Metro Chueca) ■ 8pm-2am, drag shows Fri-Sat

15 **Chueca's Friends** [W] Plaza de Chueca 9

17 **Clip** [M] 34/91.521.51.43 ■ Gravina 8 (Metro Chueca) ■ 8pm-2am

18 **Cruising** [★M,D,V,L] 34/91.521.51.43 ■ Pérez Galdós 5 (Metro Chueca) ■ 7pm-3am, till 3:30am Fri-Sat, cruise bar, darkroom

19 **Dumbarton** [M,NH,P] 34/91.429.81.91 ■ Zorrilla 7 (behind Congress bldg, Metro Sevilla, ring to enter) ■ 7pm-2am

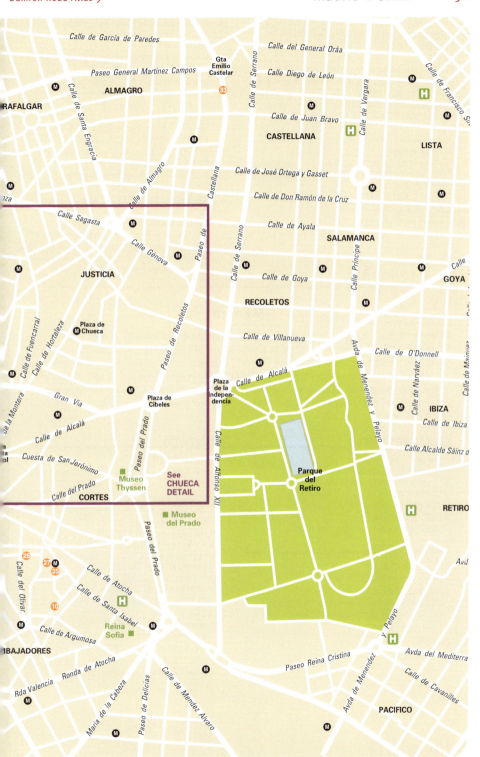

20 **Hot** [M,B,L,V] Infantas 9 (Metro Chueca, ring to enter) ■ 6pm-3am, till 4am Fri-Sat, darkroom, bears 1st Sat
21 **Liquid** [M,D,F,V] 34/91.532.74.28 ■ Barquillo 8 ■ 9pm-3am, till 4am Fri-Sat, clsd Mon
22 **LL Bar** [★M,F,S,V] 34/91.523.31.21 ■ Pelayo 11 (Metro Chueca) ■ 6pm-close, drag shows wknds, strippers Wed-Sun, cruisy, darkroom
9 **Lord Byron** [M,F,OC] 34/91.575.00.00 ■ Recoletos 18 (Metro Banco) ■ 10pm-4am, till 5am Wed, restaurant by day
23 **Lucas** [MW,NH,D,S,YC] San Lucas 11 (Metro Chueca) ■ 8:30pm-3:30am
24 **La Lupe** [★MW,NH,F,S] 34/91.527.50.19 ■ Torrecilla del Leal 12 (Metro Antón Martín) ■ 5pm-2am, till 3:30am Fri-Sat, from 1pm Sun, also cafe
19 **Madrid la Nuit** [M,TG,V] 34/91.522.99.78 ■ Pelayo 31 (Metro Chueca) ■ 8pm-close
25 **Medea** [★WO,D,YC,$] Cabeza 33 (Metro Antón Martín) ■ 11pm-7am, till 10am Fri-Sat, clsd Mon, men welcome as guests

26 **El Mojito** [GS,NH] 34/91.539.46.17 ■ Olmo 6 (Metro Antón Martín) ■ 9pm-2:30am, till 3:30am Fri-Sat, more gay Sun afternoon
24 **El Mosquito** [MW,D] Torrecilla del Leal 13 (Metro Antón Martín) ■ 8pm-3am
27 **New Leather Bar** [MO,D,L,S,V] 34/91.308.14.62 ■ Pelayo 42 (at Gravina, Metro Chueca) ■ 8pm-4am, strippers Th-Sat, darkroom
28 **Olivia 51** [W,D,F,S] San Bartolomé 16 (btwn Figueroa & San Marcos) ■ 8:30pm-close Wed-Sat, dance bar ■ www.interocio.es/olivia
29 **PK2** [M,D,V] 34/91.531.86.77 ■ Libertad 28 (next to 'Truck', Metro Chueca) ■ 8pm-close
30 **Priscilla** [GS,D] San Bartolomé 6 (Metro Gran Vía) ■ 7pm-3am, till 5am Fri-Sat, trendy dance bar
31 **Ras** [★M,S,YC] 34/91.522.43.17 ■ Barbieri 7 (btwn San Marcos & Infantas, Metro Chueca) ■ 10pm-4am, clsd Sun
32 **Regine's Terraza** [MW,YC] 34/91.559.28.75 ■ Paseo de la Castellana 56 (nr Plaza Emilio Castelar) ■ terrace bar
33 **Rick's** [★M,D,YC] 34/91.531.91.86 ■ Clavel 8 (at Infantas, Metro Gran Vía, ring to enter) ■ 10pm-5am, open later Fri-Sat, 'see-and-be-scene'

MADRID

The sprawling capital of Spain, Madrid is both grandiose and intimate, more gifted in spirit and bustling street life than in tourist spots. Of course, even if museums aren't your thing, you shouldn't miss the Prado or Picasso's Guernica in the Sophia Reina Museum. The gay quarter of the city centers on the Plaza de Chueca. You'll also find lots of lesbians in the Embajadores neighborhood. Madrileños know how to have a good time. They also eat dinner late and stay up till the wee hours of the morning. A traditional late-afternoon siesta will help you keep up.

Queer Resources

COMMUNITY INFO
▼ COGAM (Coordinora Gay de Madrid) 34/91.522.45.17, web: www.cogam.org. Calle Fuencarral 37.
Gai Inform (helpline) 34/91.523.00.70.

AIDS RESOURCES
Anti-SIDA Foundation 34/91.536.15.00.

City Calendar

LGBT PRIDE
June.

ANNUAL EVENTS
October/November - International Gay & Lesbian Film Festival, web: www.fundaciontriangulo.es.

Tourist Info

AIRPORT DIRECTIONS
Barajas Airport is a short bus ride or cab ride to the city center.

PUBLIC TRANSIT & TAXIS
Metro 34/91.552.59.09.

TOURIST SPOTS & INFO
Museo del Prado 34/91.420.28.36.
Museo Thyssen-Bornemisza 34/91.369.01.51.
Queen Sofía Nat'l Art Center (home of Picasso's 'Guernica') 34/91.467.50.62.
Royal Palace 34/91.542.00.59.
Visitor's Center: 34/91.541.23.25.
Information Turistica 34/91.366.54.77.

WEATHER
Winter temps average in the 40°s (and maybe even a little snow!). Summer days in Madrid are hot, with highs well into the 80°s.

BEST VIEWS
From the funicular in the Parque des Atracciones.

Madrid • Spain

34 **Rimmel** [M,NH,V] Luis de Góngora 2 (Metro Chueca) ■ 7pm-3am, darkroom, hustlers

30 **Smoke** [W,NH] San Bartolomé 7 (at Plaza de Chueca)

35 **El Sueño Eterno** [M,NH,F] Pelayo 37 (Metro Chueca) ■ 8pm-3am, also cafe

36 **Troyans** [MO,L,V] 34/91.521.73.58 ■ Pelayo 4 (Metro Chueca, ring to enter) ■ 9:30pm-3am, 10:30pm-4am Fri-Sat, clsd Mon, darkroom, cruisy

29 **Truck** [M,D,S,$] 34/91.531.18.70 ■ Libertad 28 (Metro Chueca) ■ 11pm-5:30am, clsd Mon, dance bar, shows Wed-Th ■ www.interocio.es/truck

37 **Truco** [★W,D] 34/91.532.89.21 ■ Gravina 10 (at Plaza de Chueca) ■ 8pm-close, from 9pm Fri-Sat, dance bar, seasonal terrace ■ www.interocio.es/truco

38 **Video Show Bar** [M,V,S] 34/91.522.06.08 ■ Barco 32 (Metro Gran Vía) ■ 4pm-midnight, till 3am Sat, strippers, video cabins

30 **Why Not?** [★GS,$] 34/91.523.05.81 ■ San Bartolomé 6 (Metro Gran Vía) ■ 10pm-4am, fun dance bar

39 **XXX Café** [M,F,S] 34/91.532.84.15 ■ at Clavel & Reina (Metro Gran Vía) ■ 9:30am-2am, from 4pm Sun, cabaret wknds

Nightclubs

37 **Escape** [MW,D,S] Gravina 13 (at Plaza de Chueca) ■ 11pm-4:30am Th & 1am-7am Fri-Sat, drag shows

40 **Goa After Club** [GS,D,$] 34/91.531.48.27 ■ Mesoneros Romanos 13 (at 'Flamingo Club', Metro Callao) ■ 6am-close wknds, also 'Cream' midnight Th ■ www.tripfamily.com

41 **Griffin's** [M,D,S] 34/91.576.07.25 ■ Villalar 8 (Metro Banco) ■ midnight-5am, till 5:30am Fri-Sat, theme nights

42 **Heaven** [M,D,TG,S,V,YC] 34/91.548.20.22 ■ Veneras 2 (at Plaza Santo Domingo) ■ 1:30am-8am, 2am-10am Fri-Sat, popular Wed

43 **Ohm** [M,D] Plaza del Callao 4 (at 'Bash', Metro Callao) ■ midnight-close Fri-Sat, also 'Weekend' at Bash midnight-6am Sun ■ www.interocio.es/ohm

44 **Olimpo** [M,D,S,V] 34/91.531.16.95 ■ Aduana 21 (Metro Gran Vía) ■ 10pm-close, clsd Mon, regular parties, darkroom

45 **Pasapoga** [M,D] 34/91.547.57.11 ■ Gran Vía 37 (Metro Callao) ■ Fri-Sat only

46 **Refugio** [★M,D,L,S,V,$] 34/91.369.40.38 ■ Dr Cortezo 1 (below Teatro Calderón, Metro Sol) ■ midnight-6am, till 8am Fri-Sat, clsd Mon-Tue, theme nights, darkroom ■ www.interocio.es/refugio

47 **La Rosa** [WO,D,S,$] 34/91.531.01.85 ■ Tetuán 27 (Metro Sol) ■ 11pm-6am, popular cabaret night Th, men welcome as guests

15 **Sachas** [MW,D,S] Plaza de Chueca 1 (Metro Chueca) ■ 8pm-5am

45 **Shangay Tea Dance** [★M,D,S,YC,$] 34/91.531.48.27 ■ Gran Vía 37 ■ 10pm-3am Sun

Spain • Europe

48 Strong Center [M,D,L,S,V,$] 34/91.541.54.15 ■ Trujillos 7 (Metro Santo Domingo) ■ 12:30am-7am, till 9am Fri-Sat, strippers, huge darkroom

49 Tábata [MW,D,YC,$] 34/91.547.97.35 ■ Vergara 12 (next to Teatro Royal, Metro Opera) ■ 10:30pm-late Wed-Sat ■ www.interocio.es/tabata

Cafes

Argensola 34/91.319.75.84 ■ Argensola 17 ■ 10am-3am, 9pm-close Sat, also cocktail bar, art exhibits

Cafe Acuarela [MW] 34/91.532.87.35, 34/91.570.69.07 ■ Gravina 10 (Metro Chueca) ■ 3pm-3am, from 11am wknds, funky cafe-bar

Cafe Figueroa [★MW] 34/91.521.16.73 ■ Augusto Figueroa 17 (at Hortaleza, Metro Chueca) ■ noon-1:30am, till 2:30am Fri-Sat, also bar

Cafe la Troje [MW] Pelayo 26 (at Figueroa, Metro Chueca) ■ 4pm-2am, till 3am Wed, full bar

Ciber Espacio Cafe 34/91.308.14.62 ■ Pelayo 42 (Metro Chueca) ■ noon-2am, Internet cafe, also bar

Color [M] 34/91.522.48.20 ■ Augusto Figueroa 11 (Metro Chueca) ■ cafe-bar, tapas & desserts

Mad [★GS,D,S] 34/91.532.62.28 ■ Virgen de los Peligros 4 ■ 10am-2am, open later wknds, 1pm-midnight Sun, cafe-bar

Mama Inés 34/91.523.23.23 ■ Hortaleza 22 (Metro Chueca) ■ 9am-2am, 10am-3am Fri-Sat, sandwiches, pies

La Sastrería [★MW] 34/91.532.07.71 ■ Hortaleza 74 (at Gravina, Metro Chueca) ■ 8pm-2am, till 3am wknds, cafe-bar

Star's [M,D] 34/91.522.27.12 ■ Marqués de Valdeiglesias 5 (at Infantas, Metro Banco) ■ 3am-2am, till 4am Th-Fri, 8pm-4am Sat, clsd Sun, cafe-bar, DJ Th-Sat

Underwood [M,YC] 34/91.532.82.67 ■ Infantas 32 (Metro Banco) ■ 3pm-1:30am, till 2:30am Fri-Sat, cafe-bar

Urania's Cafe [MW] 34/91.522.45.17 ■ Fuencarral 37 (at COGAM ctr, Metro Tribunal) ■ 5pm-midnight, till 1am Fri-Sat, cafe-bar

Restaurants

El 26 de Libertad 34/91.522.25.22 ■ Libertad 26 ■ lunch & dinner, clsd Sun, also bar

A Brasileira 34/91.308.36.25 ■ Pelayo 49 (Metro Chueca) ■ dinner only, Brazilian

Al Natural 34/91.369.47.09 ■ Zorrilla 11 (Metro Sevilla) ■ lunch & dinner, vegetarian

El Armario [MW,S] 34/91.532.83.77 ■ San Bartolomé 7 (btwn Figueroa & San Marcos, Metro Chueca) ■ lunch & dinner, Mediterranean ■ www.elarmariorestaurante.com

Artemisa [MW] 34/91.429.50.92 ■ Ventura de la Vega 4 (at Zorrilla) ■ vegetarian; also Tres Cruces 4 location, 34/91.521.87.21

Café Miranda [MW,S] 34/91.521.29.46 ■ Barquillo 29 ■ 9pm-close, drag shows, kitschy decor

Cañeiro [MW] 34/91.575.51.87 ■ Fernán González 4 ■ Galician

Casa Santa Cruz 34/91.521.86.23 ■ Bolsa 12 ■ Spanish, elegant

Casa Vallejo 34/91.308.61.58 ■ San Lorenzo 9 ■ creative homestyle

El Castro de San Francisco [MW] 34/91.531.27.40, 34/63.628.52.32 ■ Hernán Cortés 19 ■ noon-2am, clsd Sun, upscale cafe-bar & restaurant

Chez Pomme 34/91.532.16.46 ■ Pelayo 4 (Metro Chueca) ■ lunch & dinner, int'l/ vegetarian

Cornucopia [MW] 34/91.547.64.65 ■ Flora 1 (at Plaza Descalzas Reales, Metro Opera) ■ lunch Tue-Fri & dinner Tue-Sun, European/ American

La Dame Noire 34/91.531.04.76 ■ Pérez Galdós 3 (Metro Gran Vía) ■ dinner only, clsd Mon, French

Divina La Cocina [MW] 34/91.531.37.65 ■ Colmenares 13 (at San Marcos, Metro Chueca) ■ lunch daily & dinner Tue-Sat, elegant & trendy ■ divina@retemail.es

La Dolce Vita 34/91.445.04.36 ■ Cardenal Cisneros 58 (Metro Quevedo) ■ lunch & dinner, Italian, full bar

Los Girasoles 34/91.308.44.94 ■ Hortaleza 106 ■ clsd Sun, creative Spanish, tapas

Gula Gula [★MW,S] 34/91.420.29.19 ■ Infante 5 ■ lunch & dinner, clsd Mon, buffet/ salad bar, full bar; also Gran Vía 1 location (34-91/522.87.54)

Hudson [M,S] 34/91.532.33.46 ■ Hortaleza 37 (Metro Gran Vía) ■ 7pm-3am, American food, pizza, also bar

Lombok 34/91.531.35.66 ■ Augusto Figueroa 32 ■ cafe-restaurant, int'l

Momo [NS] 34/91.532.71.62 ■ Augusto Figueroa 41 (Metro Chueca) ■ lunch & dinner, creative vegetarian

Restaurante Rochí 34/91.521.83.10 ■ Pelayo 19 ■ lunch & dinner, Spanish

El Restaurante Vegetariano 34/91.532.09.27 ■ Marqués de Santa Ana 34 (Metro Noviciado) ■ lunch & dinner, clsd Mon, vegetarian, full bar

El Rincón de Pelayo [MW] 34/91.521.84.07 ■ Pelayo 19 (Metro Chueca) ■ lunch & dinner

Sarrasín 34/91.532.73.48 ■ Libertad 8 (Metro Chueca) ■ lunch & dinner, clsd Sun

Yerbabuena 34/91.521.00.23 ■ Barbieri 15 (Metro Chueca) ■ lunch & dinner, Basque, tapas & pinchos

Bookstores

50 A Different Life 34/91.532.96.52 ■ Pelayo 30 (Metro Chueca) ■ 11am-2pm & 5pm-10pm, till midnight Sat, clsd Sun, lgbt, books, magazines, music, videos, sex shop downstairs ■ www.lifegay.com

51 Berkana Bookstore [WC] 34/91.532.13.93 ■ Gravina 11 (Metro Chueca) ■ clsd Sun, lgbt, Spanish & English titles, ask for free gay map of Madrid ■ www.ctv.es/berkana

Retail Shops

Alegria 34/91.532.58.54 ■ Hortaleza 54 ■ men's clothing & underwear; also Augusto Figueroa 15 location (34/91.532.58.54)

Ovlas 34/91.522.73.27 ■ Augusto Figueroa 1 (Metro Chueca) ■ men's clothing

Publications

Entiendes? Apdo 18165, 28080 Madrid ■ bimonthly gay info & culture magazine ■ www.ctv.es/USERS/cogam

MENsual 34/93.412.53.80 ■ slick monthly w/ complete listings for Spain, in Spanish ■ www.mensual.com

Shangay Express 34/91.308.11.03, 34/91.308.66.23 ■ free biweekly gay paper ■ shangay@ctv.es

Zero 34-91/701.00.89 ■ stylish glossy lgbt monthly (en español) ■ www.zeropress.com

Gyms & Health Clubs

Hercules Gym 34/91.522.86.14 ■ Perez Galdos 7 ■ herculesgym@jet.es

Men's Clubs

Adán [V,SW] 34/91.532.91.38 ■ San Bernardo 38 (Metro Noviciado) ■ 24hrs, 3 flrs, also bar

Caldea [F,V] 34/91.522.99.56 ■ Valverde 32 (at Gran Vía, Metro Chueca) ■ 24hrs, gym equipment, bar

Comendadoras [V] 34/91.532.88.92 ■ Plaza Comendadoras 9 (Metro Noviciado) ■ 24hrs, also bar

Cristal [V] 34/91.531.44.89 ■ Augusto Figueroa 17 (Metro Chueca) ■ 24hrs, also bar

Internacional [V,OC] 34/91.541.81.98, 34/91.541.16.17 ■ Altamirano 37 (Metro Moncloa) ■ also bar

Men [V] 34/91.531.25.83 ■ Pelayo 25 (Metro Chueca) ■ bar

Sauna Paraíso [★V,S] 34/91.522.42.32 ■ Norte 15 (Metro Noviciado) ■ gym equipment, also bar ■ www.interocio.es/paraiso

Sauna Plaza [V] 34/91.429.39.49 ■ Gran Vía 88 (in Edificio España, Metro Sevilla) ■ gym equipment, bar

Sauna Príncipe [F,S,V] 34/91.429.39.49 ■ Príncipe 15 (Metro Sevilla) ■ also bar ■ www.interocio.es/principe

Sex Clubs

Hell Buenavista 14 (Metro Antón Martín) ■ 10pm-2:30am, professional party Th, rubber/ leather/ uniforms welcome, selective door

Erotica

B-43 Sex Shop Gay 34/91.531.49.85 ■ Barco 43 (Metro Gran Vía) ■ books, videos, etc

California Valverde 20 (at Gran Vía)

Condoms & Co Colón 3

Happy Sex 34/91.532.44.00 ■ Hortaleza 2 (Metro Gran Vía)

XXX 34/91.522.17.70 ■ San Marcos 8 ■ clsd Mon

Australia

Sydney

Accommodations

201B [MO,SW,GO] 61/413.597.278 ■ luxurious private home, sundeck ■ grant@killarainn.com.au

1. **Brickfield Hill B&B Inn** [GS,NS,GO] 61-2/9211-4886 ■ 403 Riley Street (at Foveaux), Surry Hills ■ beautifully & carefully restored Victorian terrace-house in the gay Oxford St District, close to beaches & downtown ■ www.zip.com.au/~fields

2. **Chelsea Guest House** [GS,GO] 61-2/9380-5994 ■ 49 Womerah Ave (at Oswald Lane), Darlinghurst ■ Victorian w/ courtyard ■ www.chelsea.citysearch.com.au

Echo Point Holiday Accommodation [GF,NS] 61-2/4782-3275 ■ 36 Echo Point Rd (at Cliff Drive), Katoomba ■ rental villas & cottages ■ www.echopointvillas.com.au

3. **Furama Hotel Central** [GF] 61-2/9213-3820, 800/024-231 ■ 28 Albion St (at Elizabeth), Surry Hills ■ www.furama-hotels.com

4. **Governors on Fitzroy B&B** [GS,GO] 61-2/9331-4652 ■ 64 Fitzroy St, Surry Hills ■ Victorian B&B, 3 blks from Oxford St, full brkfst, hot tub, shared baths, garden ■ www.governors.com.au

Jasark Gum View Hideaway [GS,NS,WC,GO] 61-2/4782-9804 ■ 10 Miles Ave (off Lovell St, via Lynne), Katoomba ■ www.jasark.com.au

5. **Manor House Boutique Hotel** [GS,F,SW] 61-2/9380-6633 ■ 86 Flinders St, Darlinghurst ■ terrace mansion, also 'Lush' restaurant & cocktail bar ■ www.manorhouse.com.au

6. **Park Lodge Hotel** [MW,GO] 61-2/9318-2393 ■ 747 S Dowling St (nr Cleveland St), Moore Park ■ 'Sydney's friendliest gay-owned & operated 3-star boutique hotel' ■ www.parklodgesydney.com

7. **Simpsons of Potts Point** [GS] 61-2/9356-2199 ■ 8 Challis Ave, Potts Point ■ Simpsons is a heritage building circa 1892 ■ www.simpsonspottspoint.com.au

Sojourners Sydney [W] 61-2/9516-3221 ■ PO Box 250, Enmore ■ apts

8. **Sydney Apartment** [GF,SW,NS,GO] 61-2/9358-1036 ■ Apt 902, 28 Macleay St (at Rockwall Crescent), Potts Point ■ self-catering studio w/ stunning views, sundeck, nr Oxford St & downtown ■ www.khsnet.com/apart902

9. **Sydney Star Accommodation** [GS] 61-2/9232-4455 ■ 273-275 Darlinghurst Rd (at Liverpool), Darlinghurst ■ stylish & private w/ relaxed personal attention in heart of colorful Darlinghurst ■ www.sydneystar.com.au

10. **Victoria Court Sydney** [GF] 61-2/9357-3200, 1800/630-505 (in Australia) ■ 122 Victoria St (at Orwell), Potts Point ■ historic boutique hotel in elegant Victorian, quiet location w/in mins of Opera House & Harbour, affordable rates ■ www.VictoriaCourt.com.au

11. **Westend Hotel** [GF] 61-2/211-4722 ■ 412 Pitt St (at Goulburn)

Bars

12. **The Albury Hotel** [M,NH,D,TG,S] 61-2/9361-6555 ■ 2-6 Oxford St (at Oatley Rd), Paddington ■ 2pm-2am, till midnight Sun, drag shows nightly

13. **Annie's** [MW,NH,S] 61-2/9360-4714 ■ 563 Bourke St (at Arthur, in the Carrington Hotel), Surry Hills ■ 7pm-close, popular drag shows

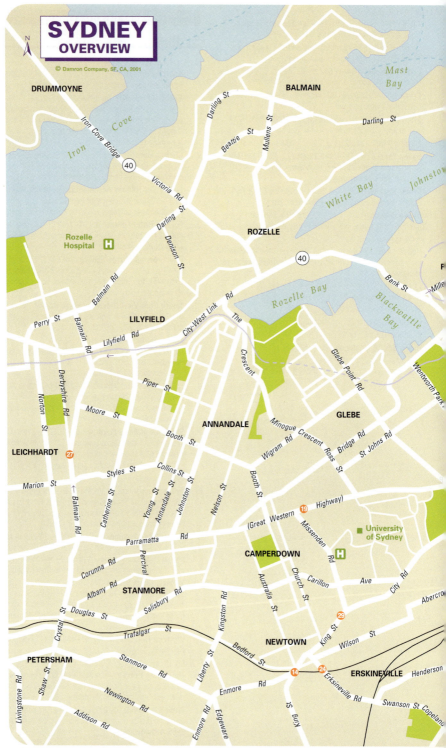

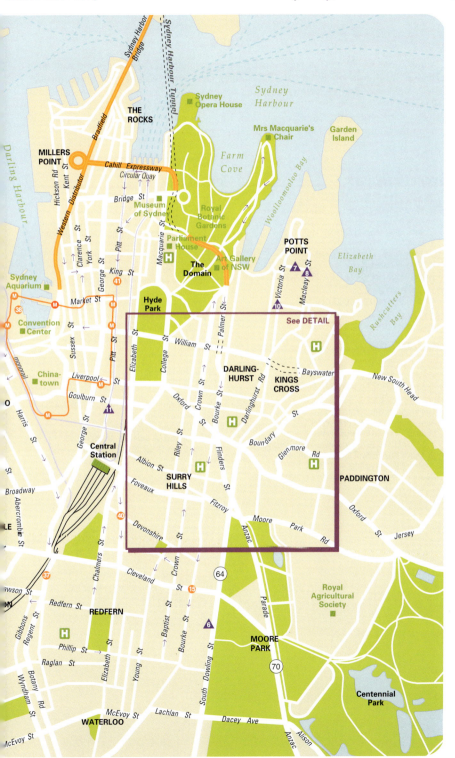

Sydney

Sydney is one of the most popular LGBT travel destinations in the world — and with good reason. Its diversity of cultures and subcultures, great food, tolerant atmosphere, friendly people, and lovely weather draw visitors from far afoot. You'll find most of the lesbians and gay men in Darlinghurst and Kings Cross, especially along the main artery Oxford Street. Sydney will be host to the Gay Games in 2002 and is also home to the biggest annual LGBT party in the Southern Hemisphere — Mardi Gras.

Queer Resources

Community Info
▼ Sydney PRIDE Centre 61-2/9331-1333, web: www.pridecentre.com.au. 26 Hutchinson St, Surry Hills. Drop-in 10:30am-1pm & 2pm-6pm Mon-Sat.
Diversity Bay 61-2/261-893, web: www.diversitybay.com.
Sydney Lesbian & Gay Line 61-2/9207-2800.

AIDS Resources
AIDS Council of NSW 61-2/9206-2000.

Recovery
61-2/9799-1199.

City Calendar

LGBT Pride
March - Sydney Gay & Lesbian Mardi Gras. 61-2/9557-4332, web: www.mardigras.com.au.

Annual Events
January 1 - Sydney Festival.
April - Sydney Leather Pride Week.
October - Go Girl Women's Festival 61-2/9365-5697, web: www.gogirl.com.au.
Manly Jazz Festival 61-2/9977-1088.
Sleaze Ball 61-2/9557-4332.
November 2002 - Gay Games VI 61-2/9380-8202, web: www.sydney2002.org.au.

Tourist Info

Airport Directions
Sydney Airport. Served by Airport Link train, and Airport Express bus. By car, take Rte 64 (South Dowling St.) to Victoria St, Darlinghurst, and Kings Cross.

Public Transit & Taxis
Airport Express 61-2/9669-1118.
State Transit Authority 61-2/131-315 (buses & ferries), 61-2/131-500 (trains).
Monorail 61-2/955-2288.

Tourist Spots & Info
Art Gallery of New South Wales 61-2/9225-1700.
Australian Museum 61-2/9320-6000.
Bondi Beach.
Chinatown.
Darling Harbour.
Featherdale Wildlife Park 61-2/9622-1644.
Manly beaches.
Museum of Contemporary Art 61-2/9252-4033.
The Rocks.
Sydney Harbour Bridge.
Sydney Jewish Museum 61-2/9360-7999.
Sydney Opera House 61-2/9250-7777.
Visitor's Center: Sydney Tourist Information 61-2/669-5111.
Sydney Visitors Centre, 61-2/255-1788. 106 George St.

Weather
Temperate - in the 50°s-70°s year-round. The summer months (January - March) can get hot and humid. Spring (September - December) sees the least rain. It's sunny most of the year. Bring a hat!

Best Views
From the AMP Centrepoint Tower or Mrs Macquarie's Chair.

Sydney • Australia

14 **The Bank Hotel** [MW] 61-2/9557-1692 ■ 324 King St (at Enmore Rd), Newtown ■ noon-close, mostly women Wed, also 'Sleepers' cocktail bar

15 **Bar Cleveland** [GS,A] 61-2/9698-1908 ■ 443 Cleveland St (at Bourke), Surry Hills ■ 11am-2am, till 3am Th, till 5am Fri-Sat, from noon Sun, cocktail lounge, DJ

16 **The Barracks** [M,B,L,PC,S] 61-2/9360-6373 ■ 1-5 Flinders St (at Taylor Square Hotel, enter on Patterson), Darlinghurst ■ 5pm-late, big, cruisy butch bar, strict dress code

17 **The Beauchamp** [★M,NH] 61-2/9331-2575 ■ 267 Oxford St, Darlinghurst ■ noon-close

18 **The Beresford** [M,NH,B] 61-2/9331-1045 ■ 354 Bourke St, Surry Hills ■ after-hrs wknds, beer garden, bears Fri

19 **Caesar's** [MW,NH,D,L,F,S] 61-2/9550-2411 ■ 388 Parramatta Rd (at Barrs, in Petersham Inn), Camperdown ■ 11am-close, drag & strip shows wknds, patio, also restaurant

20 **The Exchange** [M,D] 61-2/9331-1936 ■ 34 Oxford St, Darlinghurst ■ 3 bars: main bar w/ dancing & drag shows; Lizard Lounge upstairs, cocktails, popular w/ women; Phoenix downstairs, dancing, cruisy, cover charge

21 **Flinders** [GS,D,S,YC] 61-2/9360-4929 ■ 63-65 Flinders St, Darlinghurst ■ popular late

22 **Green Park Hotel** [GS] 61-2/9380-5311 ■ 360 Victoria St (at Liverpool), Darlinghurst ■ 10am-1am, noon-midnight Sun, stylish bar

23 **Icebox** [GS,D,A] 61-2/9331-0058 ■ 2 Kellet St, Potts Point ■ dance bar, theme nights, more women Sat, popular 'Milkbar' Fri ■ www.icebox.com.au

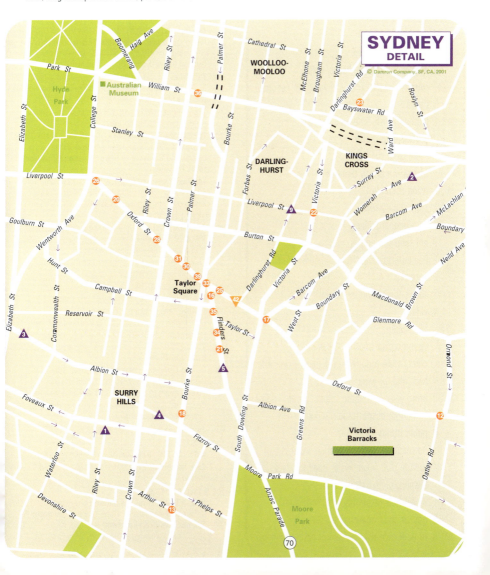

AUSTRALIA

Damron Codes

- ➤ advertiser
- ★ popular
- **MO** men only
- **GF** gay-friendly (mostly straight)
- **GS** gay/straight (evenly mixed)
- **MW** lesbians/gay men
- **M** mostly men
- **W** mostly women (listing names in this color)
- **WO** women only (listing names in this color)
- **NH** neighborhood bar
- **D** live DJ & dancing
- **A** alternative (grunge babes, goths)
- **CW** country western (music, dancing and/or dress)
- **B** bears
- **L** leather, fetish (often a dress code)
- **P** professional crowd
- **MRC** multiracial clientele
- **MR-AF** African-American clientele
- **MR-A** Asian clientele
- **MR-L** Latino/a clientele
- **TG** transgender-friendly
- **F** hot food served
- **E** live entertainment (piano, bands, comedy)
- **K** karaoke
- **S** shows (drag, strip, or cabaret)
- **V** videos
- **18+** 18 & older
- **YC** young crowd (mostly 20-somethings)
- **OC** older/more mature crowd (mostly over 40)
- **BW** beer and/or wine
- **BYOB** bring your own bottle (often "private" clubs)
- **SW** swimming onsite (usually a pool)
- **N** public nudity okay
- **NS** no smoking (anywhere inside business)
- **PC** private club (membership open to out-of-towners; often BYOB)
- **WC** wheelchair access (includes bathrooms)
- **GO** gay-owned/ operated
- **AYOR** at your own risk (beware of bashers or cops)

24 The Imperial [MW,D,S] 61-2/9519-9899 ■ 35 Erskineville Rd, Newtown ■ open late, 3 bars: main bar is mixed, popular w/ women; downstairs is a cruisy dance bar (M); back bar has drag shows and draws in lots of straights & tourists (no surprise there—this is the home of 'Priscilla'; 'Gurlesque' lesbian strip night every other Sun, 'Grrrls Night' Wed

25 Judgement [GS,A] 61-2/9360-4831 ■ 189 Oxford St (at the Courthouse Hotel), Darlinghurst ■ 24hrs

26 Lava Bar [★GS,S] 61-2/9331-3066 ■ 2 Oxford St (top flr of Burdekin Hotel), Darlinghurst ■ many lesbians

27 The Leichhardt Hotel [MW,NH] 126 Balmain Rd (at Short St), Leichhardt ■ friendly pub, popular w/ local dykes

28 Midnight Shift [★M,D,V,YC] 61-2/9360-4319 ■ 85 Oxford St, Darlinghurst ■ video bar downstairs, dance bar upstairs

29 The Newtown Hotel [MW,NH,D,F,S] 61-2/9557-1329 ■ 174 King St (nr Missenden), Newtown ■ 11am-midnight, 10am-10pm Sun, drag shows, piano bar, also restaurant

30 The Oxford [★M,TG] 61-2/9331-3467 ■ 134 Oxford St (at Taylor Sq), Darlinghurst ■ 24hrs, 3 bars: main flr cruise bar & gaming lounge w/DJ; Gilligans, 5pm-late daily, trendy cocktail bar w/DJ; and Ginger's lounge

31 The Palms on Oxford [S] 61-2/9357-4166 ■ 124 Oxford St, Darlinghurst ■ 8pm-late, clsd Mon-Tue, piano lounge & drag shows

32 Spicey Friday [W] Broadway & City Rd (at the Landsdowne Hotel), Chippendale ■ Fri only

33 The Stonewall [★M,D,K] 61-2/9360-1963 ■ 175 Oxford St, Darlinghurst ■ noon-late, pub downstairs, cocktail lounge 2nd flr, dance club 3rd flr, karaoke Tue, women's night Th, patio

34 The Taxi Club [M,D,TG,F,K,PC,$] 61-2/9331-4256 ■ 40 Flinders St (at Grosvenor Club), Darlinghurst ■ 24hrs, karaoke Th, drag shows Fri-Sat

NIGHTCLUBS

35 ARQ [★M,D,S,$] 61-2/9380-8700 ■ 16 Flinders St (at Taylor Sq), Darlinghurst ■ 11pm-6am, 9pm-late Th-Sun, drag shows Th ■ www.arqsydney.com.au

36 Club 77 [M,D,A,S,$] 61-2/9361-4981 ■ 77 William St, Woolloomooloo ■ Th only

20 DCM [GS,D,$] 61-2/9267-7380 ■ 33 Oxford St, Darlinghurst ■ popular late-night, drag shows

37 Hellfire [GS,D,A,L,$] 61-2/9698-8869 ■ 111 Regent St, Chippendale ■ 11pm-4am 1st & 3rd Fri, fetish party

38 Home [★GF,D,$] 61-2/9266-0600 ■ Cockle Bay Wharf (Darling Harbour) ■ open Fri-Sun, gay Sun, also monthly party 'Hey Homo'

39 On the Other Side [★W,D] 61-2/9360-5666 ■ 163 Oxford St (at 'NV'), Darlinghurst ■ 8pm-late Sun

40 Playpen [W,D] 61-2/9698-2997 ■ 451 Elizabeth St (at Devonshire, in Strawberry Hills Hotel), Surry Hills ■ 4pm-midnight Sun, free pool

41 Sublime [GS,D,$] 61-2/9264-8428 ■ 244 Pitt St

CAFES

Café 191 [GS] 191 Oxford St, Darlinghurst

Cafe Salubrious 61-2/9369-2414 ■ 238 Oxford St, Bondi Junction

RESTAURANTS

Balkan Continental Restaurant 61-2/9360-4970 ■ 209 Oxford St, Darlinghurst ■ 11am-11pm, till midnight Fri-Sat, clsd Tue, hearty portions

Sydney • Australia

Betty's Soup Kitchen [MW] 61-2/9360-9698 ■ 84 Oxford St, Darlinghurst ■ noon-11pm, till midnight Fri-Sat, healthy homecooking, plenty veggie

The Boathouse 61-2/9518-9011 ■ Ferry Road ■ lunch & dinner, gourmet seafood, some veggie, great view

Café Brontosaurus 61-2/9550-6652 ■ 110 Erskineville Rd, Newtown ■ 11am-9pm, from 10am wknds, till 8pm Sun, traditional & unusual burgers, cash only

Cafe Comity [GO] 61-2/9331-2424 ■ 139 Oxford St (at Crown) ■ 10am-late, Mediterranean, full bar

chu bay 61-2/9331-3386 ■ 312A Bourke St, Darlinghurst ■ 5:30pm-11pm, Vietnamese, some veggie

Fu Manchu [NS] 61-2/9360-9424 ■ 249 Victoria St, Darlinghurst ■ lunch & dinner, chic noodle bar, plenty veggie, cash only

Green Park Diner 61-2/9361-6171 ■ 219 Oxford St, Darlinghurst ■ burgers, pasta, some veggie, brkfst served all day

Harvest [NS,WC] 61-2/9818-4201 ■ 71 Evans St, Rozelle ■ dinner only, excellent vegetarian, outdoor seating

Iku Wholefood Kitchen [NS] 61-2/9692-8720 ■ 25A Glebe Point Rd, Glebe ■ lunch & dinner, creative vegan/ macrobiotic fare, outdoor seating

Paramount [MW,NS] 61-2/9358-1652 ■ 73 Macleay St, Potts Point ■ gourmet, some veggie, full bar

Ristorante Riva [NS] 61-2/9380-5318 ■ 379 Liverpool St, Darlinghurst ■ dinner only, northern Italian, seafood, some veggie, full bar

Sadé [MW,WC] 61-2/9331-1818 ■ 191 Oxford St (at Taylor Sq), Darlinghurst ■ 7am-3am, chic setting for French-inspired modern Australian cuisine, also bar, outdoor seating, pricey

Thai Kanteen [★BYOB,GO] 61-2/9909-3768 ■ 161-163 Military Rd, Neutral Bay ■ 11am-11pm, provincial Thai ■ www.thaikanteen.com.au

Vinyl Lounge Café [MW] 61-2/9326-9224 ■ 17 Elizabeth Bay Rd, Elizabeth Bay ■ 7am-4pm, from 8am wknds, clsd Mon, light menu, plenty veggie, cash only

Entertainment & Recreation

Coogee Ladies Bath [WO] Beach St, Coogee ■ popular with lesbians, especially evenings

Fallen Angels [GS,WC] 61-2/9557-0011 ■ 70 Enmore Rd, Newtown ■ 24hrs, brothel/ escort service popular w/ lesbians

Gay Skate 61-2/9519-9759 ■ 49 New Canterbury Rd (at Majestic Rollerink), Petersham ■ 7:30pm-10:30pm Tue & Th, $6 ■ www.geocities.com/gay_skate

Bookstores

The Bookshop Darlinghurst 61-2/9331-1103 ■ 207 Oxford St (nr Darlinghurst Rd), Darlinghurst ■ 10am-11pm, till midnight Th-Sun, from 11am Sun, Australia's original lgbt bookstore, int'l magazines & free tourist info ■ www.thebookshop.com.au

Retail Shops

Pop Shop 61-2/9331-7849 ■ 143 Oxford St, Darlinghurst ■ pride gifts & kitsch

Publications

Lesbians on the Loose 61-2/8347-1033 ■ monthly magazine ■ www.lotl.com

Sydney Star Observer 61-2/9380-5577 ■ 94 Oxford St, Suite 21, Level 2, Darlinghurst ■ weekly newspaper w/ club & event listings ■ sso.rainbow.net.au

Gyms & Health Clubs

Bayswater Fitness 61-2/9356-2555 ■ 33 Bayswater Rd, Kings Cross ■ www.bayswaterfitness.com

City Gym 61-2/9360-6247 ■ 107-113 Crown St ■ 24hrs, day passes available ■ www.citygym.com

Men's Clubs

Bodyline Sauna [★V] 61-2/9360-1006 ■ 10 Taylor St (off Flinders), Darlinghurst ■ 24hrs wknds, jacuzzi, sauna, steam, cabins ■ www.bodylinesydney.com

The Den [F,V,PC] 61-2/9332-3402 ■ 97 Oxford St (at Crown), Darlinghurst ■ 24hrs wknds ■ www.deninternational.com

Headquarters [V] 61-2/9331-6217 ■ 273 Crown St (nr Oxford), Darlinghurst ■ 24hrs wknds, theme rms, theme nights ■ www.headquarters.com.au

Ken's at Kensington [SW] 61-2/9662-1359 ■ 83 Anzac Parade, Kensington ■ 24hrs wknds, steam, sauna, spa & gym

Kingsteam 61-2/9360-3431 ■ 38-42 Oxford St, Darlinghurst ■ 24hrs wknds, small sauna, spa, steam & gym

Signal [V] 61-2/9331-8830 ■ at Riley & Arnold Sts (upstairs), Darlinghurst ■ theme nights

Erotica

Adult World [V] 124a Oxford St, Darlinghurst ■ theme rms

Numbers [GO] 61-2/9331-6099 ■ 95 Oxford St (next to 'Midnight Shift') ■ 24hrs, leather, videos, books, toys

Pleasure Chest 61-2/9356-3640 ■ 161 Oxford St, Darlinghurst ■ 24hrs; also 383 Pitt St, 705 George St & 56 Darlinghurst Rd, Kings Cross

The Probe [S] 159 Oxford St, upstairs, Darlinghurst ■ 2-flr sauna, also shop

Ram Lounge 61-2/9264-3249 ■ 380 Pitt St

Toolshed 61-2/9360-1100 ■ 191 Oxford St, downstairs (at Taylor Sq), Darlinghurst ■ clothing, fetish gear, toys, pride items & more; also 81 Oxford St (61-2/9332-2792) & 196-198 King St, Newtown (61-2/9565-1599) ■ www.toolshed.com.au

FEDERATION OF GAY GAMES

Games can change the world.

It's all about…
Inclusion • Participation • Pursuit of Personal Best

Come join us in Sydney for Gay Games VI 2002

Challenge '82
SAN FRANCISCO
USA

Triumph '86
SAN FRANCISCO
USA

Celebration '90
VANCOUVER
CANADA

Unity '94
NEW YORK CITY
USA

Friendship '98
AMSTERDAM
THE NETHERLANDS

Under New Skies '02
SYDNEY, AUSTRALIA
www.gaygamesvi.org.au

For news, Gay Games results, photos, upcoming events and organizational contacts, visit **www.gaygames.org**

ESCAPE the ordinary

We'll change the way you look at the world.

Full Service Online Travel Agency

Travel Articles, News and Reviews

Health Stories

Travel Personals

Celebrity Interviews

Tours and Packages

Story Library

QT magazine

TAKING YOU PLACES.

A GSociety Company

www.QTMagazine.com

QT Magazine, Inc. | 7060 Hollywood Blvd, Hollywood, CA 90028 | 323/512.2920 | info@QTMagazine.com

FRAMELINE

"This is the only place where lesbian and gay work plays entirely on its own terms to audiences with a critical mass sufficient to make things happen"
—B. Ruby Rich

san francisco international lesbian & gay film festival june 20-30, 2002

for hotel reservations during the Festival call Joie de Vivre Hospitality at 1 800 SF TRIPS (1-800-738-7477)

Complete Festival Program available June 1st at: www.frameline.org

Festival Hotline: [415] 703-8663

What do you think?

We listen to our readers — you may have noticed the changes we've made in this edition, in response to your suggestions! We think we've done a darn good job, but there's always room for improvement. How can we make this book more useful for you? Please tell us what you think!

- What's your favorite part of the book? How can we improve it?
  _____
  _____

- How does this guide compare with others you've used? _____
  _____
  _____

- What other cities should we cover in the future? _____
  _____

- Which other Damron guides are you familiar with?
  __ The **Damron Men's Travel Guide** (aka "Address Book")
  __ The **Damron Women's Traveller** (lesbian travel guide)
  __ **Damron Accommodations** (gay B&B guide with photos)
  __ **Damron Amsterdam** (gay tourist's city guide)
  __ **Damron Online** (http://www.damron.com)

- What **new Damron title(s)** would you like to see on the shelves of your local bookstore? _____
  _____

- Please suggest a **gay-oriented activity, attraction, or ongoing event** that you'd like us to list under Entertainment & Recreation in your favorite city (for example, theater, skate/bowl night, or lesser-known tourist attraction):
  _____
  _____

- Do you know of a new business we should list? Or a business whose listing needs to be updated? Or a business that's closed since this book was published? **Please let us know!** _____
  _____
  _____

- May we publish your comments, along with your name and city/state?
  (_) Yes   (_) Initials & City/State only   (_) No

- To be added to our mailing list, please tell us your
  Name: _____
  Address/City/State: _____
  Country/Postal Code: _____

Thank you for your time! Please mail to: **Damron Survey,
PO Box 422458, San Francisco, CA 94142-2458**

Send us an update anytime! You can send email to **update@damron.com.**